Exploring Southeastern Archaeology

Exploring
SOUTHEASTERN ARCHAEOLOGY

Edited by Patricia Galloway and Evan Peacock

University Press of Mississippi / Jackson

www.upress.state.ms.us

The University Press of Mississippi is a member
of the Association of American University Presses.

Copyright © 2015 by University Press of Mississippi
All rights reserved

First printing 2015

∞

Library of Congress Cataloging-in-Publication Data

Exploring southeastern archaeology / edited by Patricia Galloway, Evan
Peacock ; foreword by Jeffrey P. Brain.
    pages cm
Includes index.
ISBN 978-1-62846-240-1 (hardback) — ISBN 978-1-62674-689-3 (ebook)
1. Indians of North America—Southern States—Antiquities. 2. Excavations (Archaeology)—Southern States. 3. Southern States—Antiquities.
    I. Peacock, Evan, 1961– editor. II. Galloway, Patricia Kay, editor.
            E78.S65E93 2015
    975'.01—dc23   2014047540

British Library Cataloging-in-Publication Data available

Essays in Honor of Samuel O. Brookes

To the memory of John W. Baswell

Contents

xi   Foreword
Jeffrey P. Brain

3   Chapter 1. Introductory Remarks
Evan Peacock and Patricia Galloway

PART I: PUBLIC ARCHAEOLOGY AND PROFESSIONAL PRACTICE

9   Chapter 2. Archaeology on the National Forests of North Mississippi: A Brief Retrospective
Evan Peacock

23   Chapter 3. Pimento Cheese and Bacon? Revisiting Mounds in the Lower Mississippi Delta
Cliff Jenkins

PART II: THE ARCHAIC PERIOD

43   Chapter 4. Early Holocene Climate in the Eastern United States: A View from Mississippi
Samuel O. Brookes and Melissa H. Twaroski

55   Chapter 5. Sam Brookes and Prehistoric Effigy Beads of the Southeast
Jessica Crawford

71   Chapter 6. Archaic Chert Beads and Craft Specialization: Application of an Organization of Technology Model
Alison M. Hadley and Philip J. Carr

99   Chapter 7. From Missouri to Mississippi to Florida: Some Research on the Distribution of Poverty Point Objects
Christopher T. Hays, James B. Stoltman, and Richard A. Weinstein

Contents

PART III: THE WOODLAND AND MISSISSIPPIAN PERIODS

119 Chapter 8. Artifact Assemblages from Two Early Woodland Tchula-Period Sites on the Holly Springs National Forest, North Mississippi
Evan Peacock

146 Chapter 9. The Slate Springs Mound, a Woodland-Period Platform Mound in the North Central Hills of Mississippi
Keith A. Baca

166 Chapter 10. Mississippian-Period Occupations in the Ackerman Unit of the Tombigbee National Forest
Andrew M. Triplett

189 Chapter 11. Owl Creek, Thelma, and Bessemer Mounds: Large Peripheral Mississippian Mound Groups and Bet-Hedging
Janet Rafferty

216 Chapter 12. Plaquemine Culture Pottery from the Great Ravine at the Anna Site (22AD500), Adams County, Mississippi
Ian W. Brown

PART IV: THE CONTACT AND HISTORIC PERIODS

243 Chapter 13. Excavations at the South Thomas Street Site (22LE1002): An Early Eighteenth-Century Hamlet Located on the Periphery of the Major Chickasaw Settlement in Northeastern Mississippi
Jay K. Johnson and Edward R. Henry

266 Chapter 14. The Symbiotic Relationship between the National Forests of Mississippi and the Civilian Conservation Corps: The Early History of the Chickasawhay Ranger District
Maria Schleidt

282 Chapter 15. Logging Out the Delta: From Mosquitoville to the Sardis & Delta Railroad
Mary Evelyn Starr

PART V: REFLECTIONS

319 Chapter 16. Brookes@Forest: Building an Epistemic Community for Archaeological Research-in-Action
Patricia Galloway

337 Appendix. Citation for USDA Forest Service National Heritage Award

341 Bibliography

387 Contributors

389 Index

Foreword

Jeffrey P. Brain

I do not recall exactly when I first met Sam Brookes, but it was sometime in the early 1970s when we were both puttering around the Yazoo Basin and Sam began to be involved with the Lower Mississippi Survey (see Figure F.1). He has always been a congenial colleague and a good source of archaeological information, as well as other interesting tidbits. Often in the mail over the years there would be a welcome surprise from him: a clipping, picture, or doggerel of the sort not acceptable in polite company but always illuminating. One of the tamer items was a poem in which the narrator surmised that archaeologists "sifting the sands / of faraway lands," are known to "learnedly quarrel and bicker," but though "rife with degrees / their hypotheses / Still improve when enlightened by liquor."[1]

Then, in November 1985, a more serious document arrived: I received Form 49 prescribed by the US Civil Service Commission (FPM Chapter 736-5049-106, approved OMB Number 50-RO576). It informed me that BROOKES, Samuel Owen, was an applicant for the position of archaeologist with the USDA Forest Service and I was requested to "help determine whether this person is loyal, trustworthy, and of good character." I was instructed to respond to three simple questions:

1. "Has this person ever been fired from any job for any reason?" Well, that was an easy "No" as far as I knew.

2. "Do you have any reason to question this person's loyalty to the United States?" Certainly a "No," for Sam is as red-white-and-blue as any redneck I know.

3. "Is this person reliable, honest, trustworthy, and of good character?" This was a bit harder, but after wrestling with my conscience—for those were mighty hefty attributes akin to sainthood—I of course hit the "Yes" box.

And then I sent it off to the feds.

But I could not resist. I had xeroxed the form before filling it out and on this copy I altered my response to question 3: I checked "No," added an explanation involving some (fabricated) personal tendencies of questionable nature, and sent this copy to Sam without any further comment. Well, I noticed the next time I saw him at SEAC that Sam seemed to be avoiding me. But eventually the truth was revealed and he forgave the prank (at least I hope he has!).

Jeffrey P. Brain

Figure F.1. Sam Brookes (*back row, leaning against right post*) representing Mississippi at the Lower Mississippi Valley Conference on Avery Island in 1978. Other participants (*from top row, left to right*) included Ian Brown, Bruce Smith, Stu Neitzel, Jon Muller, John Belmont; (*front row, left to right*) Steve Williams, Jimmy Griffin, Cynthia Price, Jim Price, Phil Phillips, Alan Toth, Bob Neuman, Jeff Brain, Dan Morse, and Bill Haag. Photo courtesy of Ian Brown.

Of course he got the job, for which we may all be thankful since it has been a platform from which Sam has gone on to make many contributions to the archaeology of Mississippi and beyond. His work has always been solid and informative, and the papers in this volume attest to the breadth of his research. Witness the range of topics that touch upon his organizational ability, pioneering efforts in the field, consideration of climatic as well as climactic events, preference for the earlier eras of prehistory, and focus on stone artifacts.

As a pottery man, I never quite understood Sam's devotion to lithics, but I was always grateful that we had such a deft hand to deal with those matters. On those rare occasions when I ventured into his realm, he very graciously tolerated my efforts and even shared my infamy on occasion. For example, in a 1977 letter he wrote: "One noted archaeologist sent me several pages which disputed every statement I made concerning Dalton and ended up by saying that you and I are very similar—both troublemakers who get our kicks upsetting folks. I was very proud of that."

You *should* be proud, Sam. You've done a great job of "sifting the sands."

Note

1. William J. Frey, "Ye Hearty Archaeologists." 1997. https://www.jiscmail.ac.uk/ (accessed August 20, 2014).

Exploring Southeastern Archaeology

CHAPTER 1

Introductory Remarks

Evan Peacock and Patricia Galloway

Public archaeology is many things: research, outreach, communication, negotiation, resource management, partnerships, stewardship, and service. A career spent working within these challenging arenas is a career that matters. Samuel O. Brookes's career as a public archaeologist demonstrates why.

Sam received his B.A. in Anthropology at the University of Mississippi (Ole Miss) in 1970, where he twice served as assistant for archaeological field schools, followed by a stint doing salvage excavations related to land leveling for the University of Missouri in the summer of 1971. He obtained his Master of Arts from Ole Miss in 1980 with his thesis "The Peabody Phase: Coles Creek in the Upper Sunflower Region" (Brookes 1980a). In 1972, Sam went to work as an archaeologist for the Mississippi Department of Archives and History, a post he held for 12 years. Over this time, he conducted numerous field investigations ranging from salvage excavation at the Grand Gulf Mound (Brookes 1976a) to excavations at the Late Paleo-Indian/Early Archaic Hester site in Monroe County (Brookes 1978, 1979; Brookes and McGahey 1974) to site surveys in Claiborne, Clay, Lowndes, Monroe, and Wilkinson counties (Brookes and Inmon 1973). One result of such wide-ranging work was that Sam became a "go-to" person for anyone interested in the archaeology of the Magnolia State. Following a brief spell with the US Army Corps of Engineers in Vicksburg, Sam became Forest Archaeologist (later Heritage Program Manager) for the USDA Forest Service, National Forests in Mississippi. In this post he acted as mentor to a cadre of young archaeologists and helped fill many a blank space on the archaeological map of the state.

Festschrifts most often are compiled to honor retiring academicians for their scholarly achievements, for their role as educators, and for their service to the discipline. What is sometimes overlooked in our business is that most archaeology, a great deal of educating, and an incredible amount of service goes on outside the halls of academe. Practitioners of cultural resource management are the front line of the discipline when it comes to preserving the world's cultural heritage, seeking balance among numerous parties with vastly different agendas, and educating a varied public while at the same time furthering our knowledge of the human condition over time. The best practitioners manage, somehow, to do all these things well.

Sam is just such a practitioner. His scholarly contributions include detailed descriptions of a number of important sites in Mississippi (Brookes 1969, 1974a, 1975a, 1975b, 1976a, 1979, 1980b, 1981; Brookes and Potts 1981; Connaway and Brookes 1983; Toth and Brookes 1977), illustration and description of notable artifacts and discussions of artifact typology (Brookes 1974b, 1974c, 1974d, 1975c, 1976a, 1976b, 1976c, 1985, 2007; Brookes and Connaway 1975; Brookes et al. 1974), and histories of archaeological projects (Brookes 1977, 2000, 2001). His topical research papers range from work on late prehistoric phases in the Mississippi Delta (Brookes 1980c; Brookes and Taylor 1986) to Archaic-period settlement patterns, raw material exchange, artifact production, and social complexity (Brookes 1997, 1999a, 1999b, 2004; Johnson and Brookes 1988, 1989). We are pleased to include another of his original contributions in this volume.

Sam's service contributions are extraordinary, ranging from duties on behalf of the Mississippi Archaeological Association and the Mississippi Association of Professional Archaeologists (e.g., Briuer and Brookes 1991) to organizing annual meetings for the Mississippi Archaeological Association, the Mid-South Archaeological Conference (Peacock and Brookes 1999), and the Southeastern Archaeological Conference, to being a consultant for museums across the state. His series "Everyman's Guide to Projectile Points" remains one of the most popular features ever to be run in *Mississippi Archaeology* (Brookes 1981, 1982a, 1982b, 1983a, 1983b, 1984). A look at how the "Everyman's Guide" series developed from 1981–1984 demonstrates how he was able to bring avocational readers into the archaeological conversation: what Brookes provided in this popular series was not only the basics like projectile point features and temporal spans—he also showed how he was forming his own thinking and asked avocationals to join in by contacting him with examples and indeed arguments. Those who have attended the presentations he has given to hundreds of groups of all ages and backgrounds over a period of decades will know that this inclusiveness has been a key to his engagement of the public. His Delta mound tours are one of the most important public education events in Mississippi, and he has deservedly been honored by the Mississippi Archaeological Association, the Mississippi Humanities Council, and the USDA Forest Service for his outstanding contributions to heritage concerns in Mississippi and beyond. As for teaching, there are few Midsouth archaeologists who haven't learned something valuable from Sam over the years, and he continues to share his knowledge with professionals, avocational archaeologists, and the public at large in a way that is, in itself, educational for us all.

The chapters in this volume reflect, directly or indirectly, the positive outcomes that can occur as the result of one individual's dedication to his calling. Research reported here demonstrates the influence of Sam's scholarship and the importance of his support for the scholarship of others by facilitating the gathering of data, the evaluation of different methods, and the practicing of archaeology in areas that had been little explored before. Far less visible are the battles that had to be waged to bring those positive outcomes about, battles fought while Sam worked as a professional archaeologist under three different state and federal bureaucracies. As a group, archaeologists are well versed at moving dirt. To shift bureaucracies, one must move mountains. To do so requires patience and persistence, tireless constituency building, and thoughtful value creation. Especially in his role as Heritage Program Manager for the National Forests in Mississippi, Sam made those mountains move, at least a little. Doing so required challenging the status quo, which never has been, is not, and never will be "good enough." Doing so required courage, patience, and diplomatic skill. It also required a willingness to reach out to many communities that admired but did not directly participate in archaeology—at least not before they met him. Not all the battles were won, of course; they never are. But Sam's perseverance in "fighting the good fight" won him the respect and admiration of far more of us than he probably even realizes. We hope that this volume serves as at least a small repayment for his ongoing service to the discipline of archaeology and to the many publics to whom we are beholden.

As a researcher, Sam has an intimate familiarity with Mississippi's prehistoric material record, an accomplishment that allows him to "see" where many of us are in the dark. His connection to the historical past is equally intimate; it is a connection of the spirit as much as the mind. His scholarly work is eclectic, imaginative, and occasionally speculative. This, too, takes courage, and this, too, can be inspirational. Although one might disagree with any particular interpretation that Sam has offered us over the years, such disagreements are the stuff of science; without them we are simply cheerleaders for the latest fad. And more than one example in this volume shows how his ideas have ignited new questions in the testing of the questions he has raised. On offer here is everything from basic description of materials necessary for culture history (Brown), to fundamental investigations of poorly known spatial, temporal, and functional aspects of the material record (Jenkins; Crawford; Peacock Chapter 8; Baca; Johnson and Henry), to explanatory frameworks ranging from social organization at a landscape scale (Hadley and Carr; Hays,

Stoltman, and Weinstein), to environmental (Brookes and Twaroski) and evolutionary (Triplett; Rafferty) approaches. With some history of Southeastern archaeology (Brain; Peacock Chapter 2) and cultural lifeways of different places and times in the Magnolia State (Schleidt; Starr), and with considerations of professional practice (Galloway, Peacock Chapter 2) thrown in for good measure, we have a fair representation of what Sam's career has been all about: concern for all aspects of the archaeological and historical records of Mississippi and places beyond.

Sam's many achievements are a testament to what can be accomplished if we do not give up the never-ending fight to make archaeology better. As a result of his vision, the archaeology of the public lands of interior Mississippi is now taken seriously and is of interest beyond the USDA Forest Service. As a result of his efforts, there are now more well-qualified archaeologists to work on the problems his teams opened up. And as a result of his work, members of the broad range of social worlds he assembled around forest archaeology are aware as they weren't before of the possibilities of focusing on a common goal. For readers of this book, including current and future archaeologists, it may be sufficient just to know that such accomplishments are possible, but we hope that this volume also will demonstrate something of how.

We close this volume by including the nomination for the USDA Forest Service's National Award for Excellence in the Heritage Program that was submitted by his USDA Forest Service colleagues on Sam's behalf. Sam received this well-deserved award in 2011, the year of his retirement from the USDA Forest Service. The day when he "retires" from archaeology hopefully lies many, many years in the future.

Acknowledgments

Our thanks to all the participants in the Southeastern Archaeological Conference symposium that led to this volume, and many thanks to the external reviewers whose substantive and insightful comments led to considerable revision and a much-improved final product. We thank the USDA Forest Service for allowing us to reprint the Heritage Award citation as an Appendix, and our thanks go to Melissa Twaroski and Doug Stephens for their assistance in that regard. We also appreciate the assistance provided by Greg Johnson on the transcription of song lyrics in Starr's chapter.

PART I

Public Archaeology and Professional Practice

CHAPTER 2

Archaeology on the National Forests of North Mississippi: A Brief Retrospective

Evan Peacock

Introduction

Cultural Resource Management (CRM) archaeologists in the United States face a major problem when projects involve narrow, linear corridors (e.g., highways) or relatively small impact areas (e.g., a housing complex, an industrial park, or a borrow pit) (Aldenderfer and Hale-Pierce 1984). Such projects usually entail the mitigation of significant but unavoidable archaeological sites through excavation. While mitigation is better than the alternative (site destruction with no information yield), it is typically affected by a number of biases that negatively impact what is left for future generations of archaeologists to study. Even the best contemporary research designs are just that—contemporary—so that what we recover, how we recover it, and how remains are analyzed and reported may be biased in ways that are not even recognized at present (Dancey 1988; Dunnell 1984; Lynott 1980; McGimsey and Davis 1977; Smith 1983; see Plog 1984:94 and Raab 1981 for rejoinders to this argument). More distressingly, operational biases in CRM, such as a favoring of large, artifact-rich sites and the noncritical use of essentialist site "types," continue despite explicit recognition of the problems created by such practices (e.g., Anderson and Smith 2003; Dunnell 2008a:36–37; Camilli 1988; Fisher 1980; Tainter 1979; Peacock, Feathers, Alvey, and Baca 2008; Ebert 1988) and an impressive body of literature on how they might be addressed (e.g., Aldenderfer and Schieppati 1984; Anderson and Smith 2003; Austin et al. 2002; Barber 2001; Cain 2012; Creasman et al. 2000; Dunnell and Dancey 1978, 1983; Fisher 1980; Gates 2004; McManamon 1984; Means 1999; Mueller 1975; O'Brien et al. 1982; Osborn and Hassler 1987; Rieth 2008; Saatkamp et al. 2000; Schiffer et al. 1978; Sullivan 1998; Wait 1993; Wobst 1983). The fact that such biases continue to exist is clear from even a cursory review of reports on file at state historic preservation offices around the country (Peacock and Burnworth 2010).

As noted four decades ago by Lipe (1974; see also Tainter 1987), federal lands present a special opportunity for preservation, as sites can be avoided with relative ease; a relaxing of pressure that also allows room for more thoughtful consideration of sites not customarily deemed to be significant (Peacock 1996a). National Forests are just the type of federal lands where innovative "out of the box" archaeology can be practiced. For this pressingly important promise to be met, the most basic fieldwork—archaeological site survey—must be carried out at a high level of quality. Meeting this demand requires an adequate number of well-trained personnel and the commensurate dedication of other resources (vehicles, office and lab space, curation funds, etc.). While some agencies remain out of compliance with the core requirements of the National Historic Preservation Act and other legislation (Peacock and Rafferty 2007; see also Meiszner 1981), in relative terms the USDA Forest Service has done well in such regards (Dunnell 2008a:36; see also Meiszner 1981). This has not always been the case; the agency was, in fact, slow to rise to the challenges posed by the passage of historic preservation laws (DeBloois and Schneider 1989; Proper 1988:8), and regional differences were quite pronounced as the agency came into compliance (DeBlooies and Schneider 1989). With some exceptions (e.g., Barber 1981; Geier 1981:26), the Southeast lagged far behind western regions (e.g., the papers in Tainter and Hamre 1988) in broad-scale considerations of heritage management responsibilities, despite having a relatively high timber output (DeBlooies and Schneider 1989:230) and consequent responsibilities under federal law. This certainly was the case for Mississippi (Peacock 1994).

In 1987, Samuel O. Brookes became Forest Archaeologist (later Heritage Program Manager) for the state. Not content with the status quo, Brookes built a strong CRM program, spearheading the hiring of several District Archaeologists and initiating productive partnerships with state universities (Galloway, this volume). Brookes's efforts at program building, his institution of new methods, and his leadership by example helped dispel a damaging myth that the archaeological record of Mississippi's public lands was "impoverished" (Peacock 1994, 1996b). To the contrary, more intensive surveys and a small number of excavations have revealed a wealth of prehistoric and historic remains in the state's National Forests. Because of this work, synthetic treatments of prehistoric settlement patterns and other archaeological phenomena have been made possible at a broad scale. In addition, a number of studies related to historical archaeology on the forests have been conducted, and a body of work related to the management of cultural resources has been developed that complements similar work on public lands in other states (e.g.,

Anderson and Smith 2003; Anzalone 1987; Barber 1981; Geier 1981:26; Plog et al. 1978; Tainter and Hamre 1988).

In this chapter, I briefly discuss what has been learned as a result of such work, focusing on the National Forests of north Mississippi where I worked for several years under Brookes's guidance. Following the overall structure of this volume, I discuss findings under the categories of resource management and archaeological methods, Paleo-Indian and Archaic occupations, Woodland occupations, Mississippian occupations, and Historic-period archaeology. A brief discussion of public archaeology is also included.

Resource Management and Archaeological Methods

While it is all too easy to criticize past practitioners of any profession from a modern standpoint, the fact remains that archaeological survey methods practiced on the National Forests of Mississippi before the Brookes era could scarcely have been better designed to miss sites. To give an example, one common practice of the time was "kick tests," via which a surveyor would place the tip of his or her shovel on the ground and kick the back of the blade to clear leaf litter from a small spot. If no artifacts were seen on the exposed ground surface, it was assumed that none was present, and the surveyor moved on. Given that artifact-free biomantles and layers of organic detritus form over sites after cultivation ceases (see Peacock and Fant 2002 and references therein), it is not surprising that this method rarely produced any positive results. Many sites could have been found simply by walking and visually surveying the partially denuded logging roads common in the forests, but apparently this practice was not being employed in any systematic fashion. At the time I became Zone Archaeologist for the Tombigbee and Holly Springs National Forests (Figure 2.1) in 1992, fewer than 40 prehistoric sites had been recorded on the former (mostly by John Blitz), and only 2 had been recorded on the latter. As was standard practice in the state, Historic-period sites on the National Forests of Mississippi weren't being reported at the time.

Blitz's (1984) work on the Ackerman Unit of the Tombigbee National Forest was of particular import because, even though he was not screening his shovel tests (also following standard practice of the time), he found many sites where very few had been found before (Peacock 1994, 1996b). Also, his work was systematic in that he surveyed a number of quarter sections in their entirety (see also Lovis 1976). This provided an opportunity for a later study assessing the impact of the screening of shovel-test dirt on survey results. A resurvey of the same quarter sections, with screening employed (and with a crew of student hires), yielded a nearly 300 percent increase in site numbers,

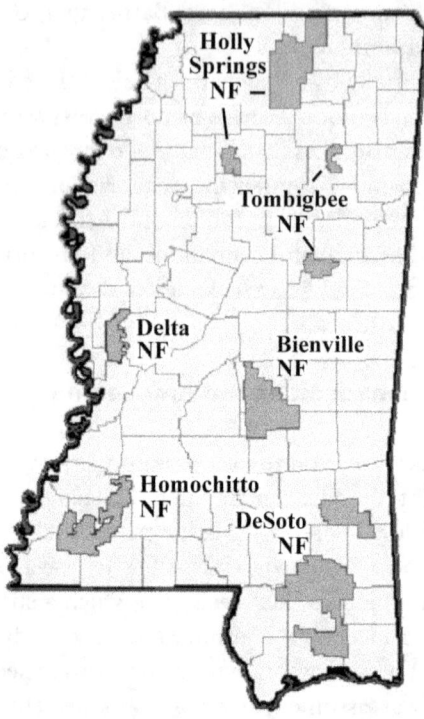

Figure 2.1. National Forests in Mississippi.

including in particular a larger number of small sites with relatively light artifact density (Peacock 1996b; see also Lynch 1980, 1981). Delineation of site sizes and number of occupations present also improved dramatically (see also Aldenderfer and Schieppati 1984; Ammerman 1981; Kintigh 1988; Kraker and Welch 1983; Lightfoot 1986, 1989; Nance and Ball 1986, 1989; Scheitlin et al. 1979; Shott 1985, 1989; Stone 1981). One extremely positive result of this study was that the Mississippi Department of Archives and History (MDAH) began requiring the screening of shovel tests in CRM surveys, a move that doubtless contributed significantly to the explosion in site numbers reported to the state over the last two decades.

Work on the National Forests in Mississippi has also contributed to ongoing efforts to change how the archaeological record is conceptualized. One example involves critical review of how archaeologists use the term "component" which, following the classic Willey and Phillips (1958) approach, refers to the manifestation of a phase (or a cultural period) at a particular site. Many archaeologists informally employ an expanded usage of the term to include artifact patterning and other spatial dimensions of the material record. As a means of characterizing archaeological phenomena, this practice is problematic for a number of reasons. As noted by Rafferty (2008:103), "component boundaries are determined by the definition of the phase. If phases are classes at the scale of occupation, components are occupations that have been classified. Components do not provide a way to recognize bounded phenomena, but merely to classify those (i.e., occupations or parts of occupations) that already have been identified."

Occupations, as used by Rafferty (2002, 2008, following Dunnell 1971; see also Camilli 1988), are artifacts at the scale of assemblage; that is, they are bodies of material displaying continuity in space, time, and form that can be assumed to be the product of a period of continuous residence at a particular locale. Some elaboration is needed to distinguish between archaeological and behavioral meaning. "Continuous" refers to temporal continuity as assessed within the resolution of the archaeological record, using absolute dating, artifact seriation, and/or the known temporal spans of diagnostic artifact types: any site could have been abandoned for a period of time with such an event not being visible archaeologically. Similarly, "occupation" is not a noun in the sense of "the act of occupying," an act which likewise cannot be observed (Camilli 1988:58–59; Larralde 1988:8–9). An occupation is an artifact consisting of one to any number of constituent parts, which can be measured in multiple dimensions just as one measures a projectile point, a potsherd, a hearth feature, a posthole pattern, or any other kind of artifact.

The use of "occupations" is preferable to "components" in settlement pattern analysis (Rafferty 2008; Triplett, this volume) because components represent arbitrary (phase-based) subdivisions of the time-space continuum, so that more than one kind of "thing" can seem to be present when in fact only one phenomenon is represented. For example, in the Tombigbee National Forest, a single occupation spanning from A.D. 400 to A.D. 900 would traditionally be characterized as representing two components, one belonging to the Middle Woodland-period Miller II phase and one to the Late Woodland-period Miller III phase. Such arbitrary subdivisions, or time/space boxes, compress variability in artifact forms, distributions, and patterning within the boxes and contribute to the view that cultural change is always abrupt rather than gradual. The distinction between components and occupations is critical in CRM, where single occupations, even if badly disturbed, may still be considered significant, as all of the artifacts together constitute a "feature" with site-level resolution (Fisher 1980; Kennedy 2011; Parrish and Peacock 2006; Peacock, Feathers, Alvey, and Baca 2008; Peacock and Rafferty 2007), irrespective of how many components are represented.

From both a management and a theoretical perspective, how "sites" are recorded is affected by one's approach in this regard. A study on the Tombigbee National Forest by Parrish and Peacock (2006) demonstrated that what could have been recorded as a single site (a more-or-less continuous occurrence of prehistoric artifacts along the edge of a stream terrace) in fact consisted of three occupations of roughly comparable duration that could be formally delineated in space and time. This finding was ascertained through a combination of fine-scale topographic mapping, artifact spatial distributions, soil chemical analysis, and frequency seriation of ceramics (Parrish 2006; Parrish and Peacock 2006). An earlier study on the Holly Springs National Forest (Peacock and Fant 2002) revealed deep vertical displacement by bioturbation of Woodland-period artifacts from individual, short-term occupations at sites with sandy soils. In the absence of such explicit geoarchaeological research, more than one occupation or longer-term site use might be suspected, and the fact that typical survey methods are inadequate for discovering sites in such settings might not be realized (Peacock and Fant 2002).

Another way of delineating occupations, of measuring occupational duration in relative terms, and of identifying different functional areas within occupations is to employ microartifact analysis in a fashion complementary to more traditional macroartifact analysis (Hull 1987; Metcalf and Heath 1990; Rainville 2000; Rosen 1989, 1993; Sherwood et al. 1995; Vance 1986). Microartifacts (the definition of which varies—see Baumler and Downum 1989; Dunnell and Stein 1989; Fladmark 1982; Madsen 1992; Nicholson 1983; Peacock 1989; Sherwood 2001; Stein and Teltser 1989) may be distributed differently than macroartifacts, e.g., by remaining in place when macroartifacts are removed for use elsewhere or via cleaning of an area. In other words, microartifacts may be more likely to represent primary deposits. This allows inferences relating to occupational duration and site use to be made; for example, a close juxtaposition of micro- and macroartifacts can be used to argue for very short occupational duration (Peacock, Davis, and Ryan 2008; Sherwood et al. 1995). A pilot study of microartifact distributions at 22CS828, a Middle Woodland-period site on the Trace Unit of the Tombigbee National Forest, provided tentative identification of a knapping area and a more accurate measurement of occupation size than was possible from macroartifacts alone (Peacock 2004). Lessons learned from that project informed later archaeological investigations on public lands in Mississippi (Peacock, Davis, and Ryan 2008).

Another management lesson came from field investigation of ridge ends exposed by the lowering of Choctaw Lake, a small impoundment on the Ackerman Unit of the Tombigbee National Forest. Competing arguments over the effects of inundation on archaeological sites had led to a major study by Lenihan et al. (1981), the results of which clearly indicated that submersion beneath large reservoirs constituted a significant negative impact. Companion studies on small, shallow water bodies were lacking, however. Survey, test excavations, and targeted stripping on landforms exposed via the Choctaw Lake drawdown showed that the impacts were the same as in large reservoirs, i.e., that sediments were drawn off the ridge ends, leaving some intact features but essentially destroying the intrasite context for most artifacts (Peacock 1995a).

In sum, National Forests can be considered laboratories for methodological research, the results of which will have broad applications for archaeological practice. Research on paleoenvironments also has implications for modern resource management on National Forests; e.g., the use of early nineteenth-century General Land Office (GLO) survey notes to provide a historical baseline for forest conditions and consequent targets for forest restoration (Peacock, Rodgers, Bruce, and Gray 2008; see also McAnally 2002).

Paleo-Indian and Archaic Occupations

Even in the pre-Brookes era, there were tantalizing hints that the National Forests of north Mississippi might yield important information related to the earliest occupants of the state. In 1984, Richard Marshall published a description of the "Ackerman Cumberland Fluted Point," found "about three miles southeast of Ackerman, Mississippi" by an artifact collector, John Guyton III (Marshall 1984:63). The find locale was the "roadside of a water-washed ditch" where a gravel road traversed a private land parcel within the Ackerman Unit of the Tombigbee National Forest. Marshall (1984:65) believed that the point had been unearthed by heavy equipment during maintenance of the road ditch; however, he did not find any other artifacts at the location. Both John Blitz (personal communication 1996) and I inspected the find spot at later dates, with no other artifacts being noted.

Further finds came with the intensive fieldwork of the Brookes era. A Paleo-Indian Dalton or Quad point fragment was recovered from site 22CH536, one of the sites underneath Choctaw Lake, along with broad-stemmed Middle Archaic and contracting-stemmed Late Archaic points (Peacock 1995a). The Godwin site (22WI613) is a large site found on a high ridgetop in the Ackerman Unit; controlled surface collection across plowed animal food plots produced a Paleo-Indian side scraper, a likely Paleo-Indian biface preform fragment of unidentified material, and a late-stage Dalton preform of unheated gravel chert (Peacock 1998), all on a very small knoll on one end of the site. A few Early Archaic bifaces (e.g., a Big Sandy point) were more widespread along the ridgetop (Peacock 1998). Open-field survey in the Bagley Creek Bottom, on the Holly Springs National Forest in Lafayette County (Peacock 1992a), also produced a number of sites with Archaic-period occupations. A large, bifacial blade of Fort Payne chert from site 22LA692 has one end modified into a "beak" (Peacock 1992a:10), a phenomenon noted at the

Middle Archaic-period Denton site in Quitman County (Connaway 1977). A Middle Archaic-period Benton point was recovered from site 22LA694, while a number of likely Late Archaic-period points were recovered from other sites in the bottom (Peacock 1992a).

More recent work by later generations of archaeologists working on the National Forests of Mississippi has contributed to the record of Paleo-Indian and Archaic-period occupations. For example, a notable find from site 22CH515 on the Ackerman Unit in Choctaw County is a beautiful Paleo-Indian end scraper with two graver spurs (Triplett 2008a). The same site produced a shuttle-type bannerstone broken into two pieces (Triplett 2008a) that likely dates to the Middle Archaic period.

It is clear that there is important information to be had from the National Forests of north Mississippi regarding the Paleo-Indian and Archaic periods. Even with the intensive survey work of the Brookes era, both periods likely remain underrepresented in our knowledge base due to the paucity of diagnostic artifacts relative to later periods when ceramics were being produced. For example, while the Godwin site was discovered during a shovel-test survey, the Paleo-Indian and Archaic-period occupations present were not recognized until surface inspection took place following land clearance and plowing of food plots. Similarly, the Paleo-Indian and Middle Archaic occupations at 22CH515 were unrecognized until test excavations took place at the site. These are useful cautionary tales. Even systematic shovel testing on a grid might not be intensive or extensive enough to reveal the presence of earlier occupations in forested areas (Triplett 2008a), while the more standard "cruciform" shovel-testing method applied when recording sites found via shovel testing may well yield an incomplete picture of what occupations are present at any given site (Peacock 1997:252). Under such circumstances, adopting a conservative attitude toward writing sites off as "not significant" on the basis of shovel-test surveys (Peacock 1996a) is certainly warranted.

Woodland Occupations

Our most substantive increases in archaeological knowledge generated from USDA Forest Service work in Mississippi relate to Woodland-period occupations. This is mostly due to the fact that such occupations have been recorded in large numbers since the Brookes era began (Peacock 1996b, 1997; Peacock, Rodgers, Bruce, and Gray 2008), with hundreds now being known on the Tombigbee and Holly Springs National Forests.

One advantage of having lots of assemblages with which to work is that basic culture historical sequences can be established or refined. For example, prior to the Brookes era, the Woodland-period ceramic sequence for the hill country of north Mississippi was uncertainly known (Ford 1980, 1981, 1988a, 1989; Johnson 1984). Seriation of assemblages from the Holly Springs National Forest clearly demonstrated a temporal shift from grog- to sand-tempered wares (Peacock 1997); a sequence subsequently verified by stratigraphic excavations at the Batesville Mounds site in Panola County (Johnson et al. 2002). A reverse sequence, from sand to grog temper, was found to hold on the Tombigbee National Forest (Peacock 1997).

A notable increase in the number of prehistoric occupations in the uplands during the Woodland period is likely related to the advent of sedentariness, a phenomenon coincident with the appearance of large quantities of ceramics during the preceding Gulf Formational period in the region (Rafferty 1980, 1994, 2002). Under this scenario, human population growth related to sedentariness led to infilling of upland areas over time. Short-term sedentary occupations were present in the hill country of Mississippi by ca. 800 B.C. and became common by the Middle Woodland period (Bacon-Schulte 2008; Peacock, Rodgers, Bruce, and Gray 2008; Rafferty 2002), somewhere between the second and fifth centuries A.D. (Blitz 1984; Peacock 1997:252). Excavations in the uplands remain few in number, but Woodland-period sites on the Ackerman and Trace Units of the Tombigbee National Forest typically display the high artifact diversity (ceramics, flaked stone tools, debitage, ground stone tools, etc.) expected for habitation sites (Parrish 2006; Peacock 2003, 2004; Triplett 2008a). Differences in artifact density at these sites are likely related to differences in occupational duration and/or to landform constraints on community boundaries (put simply, there is more room for a settlement to spread along a stream terrace than on a narrow ridgetop) (Parrish 2006). The hypothesis that sedentary settlement patterns existed during the Woodland period is further supported by the development of midden and/or waste-filled features at some sites (Parrish 2006; Peacock 2003; Triplett 2008a). Evidence for the processing of bone for grease extraction (a sign of the intensive use of local resources when mobility is not an option) has been found at one site (22WI536) on the Ackerman Unit (Parrish 2006).

The most extensive excavations yet undertaken on the Tombigbee National Forest were at Stinking Water (22WI515/516), a large, primarily Woodland-period habitation site located on a first terrace overlooking the Noxubee River bottom (Peacock 2003). The site produced large ceramic and lithic assemblages, and numerous features were recorded, one of which was a plow-truncated pit containing a concentration of Middle Woodland-period sherds. This pottery included grog-tempered broad-line incised and zoned rocker-stamped Marksville types. This was the first recorded instance of such "exotic" Lower Mississippi Valley types on the Tombigbee National Forest (Peacock

2003). Despite the unusual styles, elemental analysis suggests that this pottery is of local manufacture (Baca 2008).

Woodland-period settlement patterns are not as clear on the Holly Springs district. There, large numbers of small, Early Woodland Tchula-period sites that likely date to between the first and third centuries B.C. (Peacock 1996c, 1997) have been found in the high ridge systems. Occupations display very low artifact diversity (mostly ceramics, with limited lithic assemblages of mostly local ferruginous sandstone debitage); midden development has not been noted, and features are limited to sherd concentrations representing broken, discarded vessels, or "pot drops" (Fant 1996a; Peacock 1997, this volume, Chapter 8). An interesting feature of these Tchula sites is that they do not occur south of the Little Tallahatchie River, where ridgetop Woodland sites are few in number (Fant 1996a) and where a different (and possibly somewhat later) Woodland-period ceramic tradition is found (Peacock 1996c:19–20). This remarkable spatial pattern in ceramic distributions may indicate a cultural boundary (Peacock and Rafferty 2001) that extends westward into the Mississippi Alluvial Valley, given that ceramic assemblages from the northern and southern Yazoo Basin will not seriate together (Phillips et al. 1951; Rafferty 2008).

Even less explored are later Woodland-period sites on stream terraces on the Holly Springs district; these have the high artifact density and diversity usually associated with habitation sites, and sometimes include Tchula-period artifacts, suggesting continuous occupation over much longer terms than ridgetop sites. Some terrace sites also contain single conical mounds (Fant 1996b; Peacock 1997). Middle Woodland-period conical mounds are fairly common in the hill country of north Mississippi and central Tennessee (e.g., Ford 1977, 1980, 1988b; Holland-Lilly 1996; Johnson 1969; Johnson et al. 2002; Koehler 1966; Mainfort 1986a, 1988, 2013a), but the idea that mound building began earlier, during the Early Woodland Tchula period (Ford 1988b, 1990), cannot yet be dismissed.

Mississippian Occupations

A dramatic settlement pattern shift occurred at the beginning of the Mississippian period, when occupation of the North Central Hills declined precipitously (Blitz 1984; Johnson 1988; Morgan 1997; Peacock 1997; Peacock, Rodgers, Bruce, and Gray 2008). On the Ackerman Unit, in the few instances where artifacts characteristic of the Mississippian period (shell-tempered pottery) have been found, they are consistently coincident with Woodland materials on stream terraces. This suggests that these artifacts are part of the same, relatively long-term, occupations in prime environmental settings (Triplett 2008a, this volume). A general settlement pattern shift out of the province, rather than nucleation on terraces within the province, is thus indicated by the precipitous drop in site numbers at the end of the Late Woodland period. The limited data available suggest that this shift took place early in the Mississippian period, probably by around A.D. 1000–1100 or so (Peacock 2003; Peacock and Rafferty 2008). The reasons for the shift are currently unknown; the extremely limited archaeobotanical data available suggest that prehistoric maize agriculture was being practiced in the Ackerman Unit area at the time (Peacock 2003), so gaining access to agriculturally suitable soils may not have been a factor. These matters are further discussed by Triplett (2008a, this volume). Following the early Mississippian-period abandonment of the North Central Hills, the province remained essentially unoccupied until the early nineteenth century (Peacock, Rodgers, Bruce, and Gray 2008).

A major breakthrough in Mississippian research in the interior of the state came from Janet Rafferty's (1995) test excavations at the Owl Creek site (22CS502), an early Mississippian mound group on the Trace Unit in Chickasaw County partly owned by the USDA Forest Service. Her work, which followed up on earlier research by Brookes (1977), was made possible by his efforts to get the site interpreted for the public. The project produced a large corpus of data on a major site that was previously poorly understood, including a suite of absolute dates, information on mound-top structures, and interesting comparisons with other Early Mississippian mound sites in the region (Rafferty 1995, this volume).

Historic-Period Archaeology

Relative to the amount of work done on prehistoric materials, archaeological investigation of Historic-period remains is still undeveloped on the National Forests of north Mississippi. However, the recording of hundreds of homesteads, mills, cemeteries, and other sites that were previously either being ignored or not reported to MDAH at least amounts to a measure of respect for Historic-period remains that had been lacking (see Lees and Noble [1990] for a brief discussion of such matters at the national level). As noted by Stewart-Abernathy (1999:238), "U.S. Forest Service archaeologists, such as Sam Brookes, have actively supported consideration of historic sites in the late 1800s and into the 1900s on National Forest lands in Mississippi."

A very few occupations on the Ackerman Unit have been recorded that display a mix of aboriginal (combed) and European ceramics, and these likely date to the early nineteenth century. Old field or other improvements are all but absent on the original land survey maps for the unit, echoing the sparse archaeological record for this time. More in-depth documentary research to establish the identities and ethnicity of the individuals who occupied those sites is only now beginning to be undertaken (Gisler 2014).

McClung (2001) reported on excavations at two twentieth-century sites on the Ackerman Unit. His report, which includes detailed oral history, makes some interesting comparisons between the locations, layout, and structure of African American and Euroamerican farmsteads. The report on mitigation of the mid-nineteenth- to mid-twentieth-century Colclough Farmstead, on the Noxubee Wildlife Refuge in Oktibbeha County adjacent to the Ackerman Unit (Pietak et al. 1999; see also Pietak and Holland 2002), included contextual reference to data from Historic-period sites reported from the Tombigbee National Forest.

A methodological study by Peacock and Patrick (1997) compared the results of field survey on the Ackerman Unit with historical records (original GLO maps, federal land acquisition records, and early USDA soil maps) in terms of site numbers, chronology, and function. Several biases were identified in the historical records, emphasizing the fact that archaeological and documentary data sources are complementary, not redundant. On the Holly Springs district, McAnally (2002) found that Historic-period sites generally occur in the same locations as prehistoric sites, with a high probability of being located on Lexington silt loam soils of 2 to 8 percent slopes.

Public Archaeology

As discussed by Galloway (this volume), USDA Forest Service archaeologists in Mississippi have been in the vanguard of public archaeology efforts since the Brookes era began. There have been, and continue to be, a number of events related to the USDA Forest Service's immensely popular Passport In Time (PIT) program (e.g., Holloway 2004). The one PIT project I oversaw was conducted at the Stinking Water site. As is typical of PIT projects, there were a large number of participants in the dig, representing a wide range of ages, backgrounds, and parts of the country. A point of honor is that Stinking Water remains the only PIT project conducted in the state—and one of the few in the country—for which the results have been published in a peer-reviewed journal (Peacock 2003). Accompanying the scholarly article was a CD designed to present the results of the excavations to the public (Peacock et al. 2003) and which was distributed to the members of the Mississippi Archaeological Association as an accompaniment to the state journal, *Mississippi Archaeology*. I use this CD in my Introduction to Archaeology class at Mississippi State University to inform an artifact classification project. Another public dig, at a stoneware pottery kiln site (22WI692) in the community of Betheden, in Winston County (Peacock 1999), was conducted on the Ackerman Unit in 2002 to celebrate Mississippi Archaeology Month. This project, which remains largely unreported (but see Starr 2013), was led by Terry McClung and Mary Evelyn Starr.

One product of Rafferty's (1995) work at the Owl Creek site was a series of excellent interpretive signs installed at the site, along with a walking trail and other facilities (Peacock and Rafferty 2005). Interpretation has also been emplaced at the Hamill Springs site, a historic mill complex on the Ackerman Unit (Peacock 1992b).

A particular kind of public archaeology involves the professional training of archaeology students, a great deal of which has taken place on the National Forests of Mississippi (Galloway, this volume). Partnerships between the agency and state universities have been extremely useful in this regard; at Mississippi State University, in particular, we have for years participated in challenge-cost share agreements that provide research assistantships for graduate students, a program strongly promoted by Sam Brookes. We have also run field schools on the district as a way of instructing undergraduates in basic field survey methods.

Finally, I and other archaeologists sharing the USDA Forest Service pedigree continue to be contacted by artifact collectors we got to know during our time with the agency. The value of such connections is inestimable, and the increase in public outreach stemming from the Brookes era by itself represents an outstanding legacy for the discipline.

Discussion and Conclusions

Space does not allow discussion of the many other notable advances in archaeology on the National Forests of north Mississippi that occurred during the Brookes era. A running list of the kinds of sites discovered would include the only formally recorded prehistoric quarry for Kosciusko quartzite (22YA822), found on the Yalobusha Unit (Peacock 1995b; see also McGahey 1999); saw and grist mills and other local-scale nineteenth-twentieth-century industrial facilities on the Ackerman Unit (e.g., Peacock 1998); an isolated Middle Woodland-period hearth feature (site 22LA702) on the Holly Springs Unit that yielded a large portion of a quartz-tempered cordmarked vessel and a radiocarbon date of A.D. 400 (Peacock 1992a, 1996a; see Sims and Connaway 2000:Table 20 for calibration); numerous historic cemeteries (Peacock and Patrick 1997); an early twentieth-century experimental government farm

(Peacock 1998); and much more. Several archaeologists have worked on the northern districts, generating technical reports, building databases, working on curation, and interacting with the public. These individuals include David Fant, Michelle McAnally, Horace Mitchell, Parry Ryerse, John Phillips, Gerald Kelso, Terry McClung, Kevin Bruce, Andrew Triplett, and Jessica Gisler. In addition, four Master's theses on northern USDA Forest Service sites (Fant 1996; McAnally 2002; Parrish 2006; Triplett 2008a) have been completed, others are underway, and still others have made use of USDA Forest Service artifacts and/or data (Baca 2008; Bacon-Schulte 2008). While this chapter focuses on the National Forests of north Mississippi, similar progress has been made on the central and southern districts (e.g., Fields 2002; Jackson et al. 2002; Jackson et al. 2006; Keith 1998; see also Galloway, this volume).

The National Forests in Mississippi have recently seen reductions in archaeological staff related to the Great Recession. While the agency may never again see the likes of the 1990s heyday of archaeology, what endures, and what will carry through the crisis, is a legacy of intensive resource management that simply did not exist prior to Sam Brookes's tenure as Forest Archaeologist. Under Sam's guidance, a quantum leap forward was made in USDA Forest Service CRM in the Magnolia State. I am very proud to have been a part of that effort.

Acknowledgments

I thank Janet Rafferty, Jay Johnson, Ed Jackson, and Keith Baca for their assistance in running down information for this chapter, and Sam Brookes for showing a (then) young archaeologist how much could be accomplished by standing firm on one's principles and for being patient with my mistakes along the way.

CHAPTER 3

Pimento Cheese and Bacon? Revisiting Mounds in the Lower Mississippi Delta

Cliff Jenkins

In 2005, a group was formed to explore the development of a self-guided driving tour of Indian mounds in the Lower Mississippi Delta. The tour was envisioned to be similar to the Ancient Mounds Heritage Area in Louisiana and was proposed as a project for the Lower Delta Partnership—a non-profit group that promotes economic opportunities and conservation of environmental and cultural resources in the south Delta. This effort at developing the Lower Delta tour was, of course, inspired by the very popular mound tours led by Sam Brookes. Sam tells me that he got the idea for the tours after the 1991 Southeastern Archaeological Conference in Jackson, Mississippi, when Steven Williams of Harvard University led a similar mound tour. Since that time, Sam estimates that he has led at least 50 mound tours for archaeology groups, the Sierra Club, and the Audubon Society, and since 2002 he has been an integral part of the Great Delta Bear Affair festival, for which he conducts mound tours for the public. Sam also mentioned that one particular tour from Jackson to Natchez prior to a Mississippi Archaeological Association meeting resulted in Marvin Jeter writing up the Mangum Mound report. The tours not only provide the opportunity to see some incredible archaeological sites, but as only Sam can, he also includes entertaining tales along the way, and as the chapter title implies—what is any road trip without some good road food?—the Delta offers some true delicacies.

The Lower Delta Mound Trail development group included individuals from the Lower Delta Partnership, the Archaeological Conservancy, the Mississippi Department of Archives and History (MDAH), the Mississippi Department of Transportation, the US Fish and Wildlife Service, the USDA Forest Service, and the Natural Resources Conservation Service (NRCS). The focus of the group was to identify mound sites that are easily viewable from roadways and that have some interpretive potential. In preparation for making site visits to

Table 3.1. Mound sites visited by the Lower Delta Mound Trail development group.

Site Name	Site Number	County	LMS Number	NRHP Status	Date Visited	Extant Mounds	Mound/Earthwork Cover
Grace	22IS500	Issaquena	21-M-7	NRHP 2002	12/5/2005	Yes	Trees-Lawn
Mayersville	22IS501	Issaquena	21-L-1	NRHP 1980	12/5/2005	Yes	Trees-House-Lawn-Cemetery
Spanish Fort	22SH500	Sharkey	21-N-3	NRHP 1988	12/5/2005	Yes	Trees-Cultivation-Cemetery
Magee	22SH501	Sharkey	20-M-2	Eligible	12/5/2005	Yes	Trees
Mont Helena	22SH505	Sharkey	21-M-2	Eligible	12/5/2005	Yes	House-Lawn
Rolling Fork	22SH506	Sharkey	21-M-1	NRHP 1974	12/5/2005	Yes	Trees-Grass
Cary	22SH507	Sharkey	21-M-5	NRHP 1988	12/5/2005	Yes	Trees
Anguilla	22SH510	Sharkey	21-M-3	Unevaluated	12/5/2005	Yes	Trees
Screws	22SH514	Sharkey	21-N-6	Eligible	12/5/2005	Yes	House-Lawn
Savory (Crippen Point)	22SH518	Sharkey	21-N-10	NRHP 1988	12/5/2005	Yes	Trees
Carter (Chipman?)	22SH532	Sharkey	21-M-11	Eligible	12/5/2005	Yes	Grass-Secondary Growth
Leland	22WS501	Washington	19-M-1	Eligible	12/5/2005	Yes	Trees
Dunleith	22WS502	Washington	19-M-4	Eligible	12/5/2005	Yes	Trees
Sherwood, Stoneville	22WS511	Washington	19-M-3	Eligible	12/5/2005	Yes	Vines
Hollyknowe	22WS512	Washington	19-M-5	Eligible	12/5/2005	Yes	Trees-Cemetery
Arcola	22WS516	Washington	20-M-1	NRHP 1991	12/5/2005	Yes	Trees
Swan Lake	22WS518	Washington	20-M-5	Eligible	12/5/2005	Yes	Grass-Secondary Growth
Trivett	22WS544	Washington	19-M-11	Unevaluated	12/5/2005	Yes	Grass-Secondary Growth
Law	22WS549	Washington	20-L-1	Eligible	12/5/2005	Yes	Trees
Linden (Oak Tree)	22WS551	Washington	20-L-4	Unevaluated	12/5/2005	Yes	Tree-Grass
Lake George	22YZ557	Yazoo	21-N-1	NHL 1964	12/5/2005	Yes	Trees-House-Lawn-Cemetery-Cultivation
Hearn Place	22YZ560	Yazoo	22-N-32	Eligible	12/5/2005	Yes	Grass
Fairview Landing	22YZ561	Yazoo	22-N-9	NRHP 1988	12/5/2005	Yes	Grass
Philips	22YZ865	Yazoo	N/A	Eligible	12/5/2005	Yes	Trees-Grass
Satartia	22YZ608	Yazoo	22-N-7	Unevaluated	12/5/2005	Yes	House-Lawn
Belzoni	22HU500	Humphreys	20-O-2	NRHP 1988	1/25/2006	Yes	Lawn
Reaver Brown	22HU501	Humphreys	21-O-6	Eligible	1/25/2006	Yes	Grass-Secondary Growth

Site Name	Site Number	County	LMS Number	NRHP Status	Date Visited	Extant Mounds	Mound/ Earthwork Cover
Fort Place, Lamkin	22HU504	Humphreys	20-O-3	Eligible	1/25/2006	Yes	Trees-House-Lawn
Laketown	22HU505	Humphreys	20-O-1	NHL 1990	1/25/2006	Yes	Trees
Holly, Atcha-falaya Bayou	22HU506	Humphreys	20-O-4	Eligible	1/25/2006	Yes	House-Lawn-Secondary Growth
Silver City	22HU507	Humphreys	20-O-5	Eligible	1/25/2006	Yes	Lawn-Golf Course
Midnight	22HU509	Humphreys	20-N-1	NRHP 1986	1/25/2006	Yes	Trees
Parker-Sum-merfield	22HU510	Humphreys	20-N-2	NRHP 1997	1/25/2006	Yes	Trees-Cultivation
Wilzone	22HU512	Humphreys	21-N-19	Eligible	1/25/2006	Yes	Cultivation
Sleepy Hollow	22HU515	Humphreys	21-N-11	Eligible	1/25/2006	Yes	Grass
Sky Lake	22HU521	Humphreys	19-N-11	Eligible	1/25/2006	Yes	Cultivation
Gooden Lake	22HU525	Humphreys	20-N-6	Eligible	1/25/2006	Yes	Trees-Grass-Secondary Growth
Little Callao	22HU526	Humphreys	20-N-12	Eligible	1/25/2006	Yes	Grass
Slate	22HU655	Humphreys	N/A	NRHP 1982	1/25/2006	Yes	Trees
Unnamed	22HU676	Humphreys	N/A	Unknown	1/25/2006	Yes	Trees
Gooden Lake South	22HU722	Humphreys	N/A	Eligible	1/25/2006	Yes	Trees
Straight Bayou	22SH503	Sharkey	20-N-3	Eligible	1/25/2006	Yes	Trees
Kinlock	22SU526	Sunflower	19-N-11	Eligible	1/25/2006	Yes	Cultivation
Lake Dawson	22SU531	Sunflower	19-N-6	Eligible	1/25/2006	Yes	Grass
Hardee	22IS502	Issaquena	22-M-8	Eligible	3/13/2006	Yes	Trees
Manny	22IS506	Issaquena	22-M-6	Eligible	3/13/2006	Yes	Trees
Aden	22IS509	Issaquena	22-M-3	NRHP 1988	3/13/2006	Yes	Trees
Stone Mounds	22WR---	Warren	N/A	Unevaluated	3/13/2006	Yes	Lawn
Haynes Bluff	22WR501	Warren	22-M-5	Eligible	3/13/2006	Yes	Trees-Lawn
Glass	22WR502	Warren	24-M-2	Eligible	3/13/2006	Yes	Trees
Dornbusch	22WR510	Warren	22-N-6	Eligible	3/13/2006	Yes	Trees
Fort St. Pierre	22WR514	Warren	23-M-5	NHL 2000	3/13/2006	Yes	Trees
Kings Crossing	22WR537	Warren	23-M-1	Unevaluated	3/13/2006	Yes	Structures-Lawn-Trees
Blakely	22WR543	Warren	23-M-2	Unevaluated	3/13/2006	Yes	Grass
Josephine	22WR610	Warren	24-M-4	Eligible	3/13/2006	Yes	Trees
Hyland	22WR679	Warren	N/A	NRHP 2001	3/13/2006	Yes	Lawn
Lamidoux	22IS512	Issaquena	21-M-8	Unevaluated	12/5/2005	No	Cultivation
Bethlehem Church	22IS514	Issaquena	21-M-12	Unevaluated	12/5/2005	No	Cultivation
Panther Burn	22SH502	Sharkey	20-M-3	Eligible	12/5/2005	No	Cultivation
Blanton	22SH504	Sharkey	22-M-4	Eligible	12/5/2005	No	Cultivation
Delta City	22SH509	Sharkey	20-M-15	Eligible	12/5/2005	No	Cultivation

Site Name	Site Number	County	LMS Number	NRHP Status	Date Visited	Extant Mounds	Mound/ Earthwork Cover
Stalonia	22SH515	Sharkey	21-N-7	Unknown	12/5/2005	No	Cultivation
Arcola High School	22WS513	Washington	19-M-6	Eligible	12/5/2005	No	School Yard
Wayside	22WS541	Washington	19-L-10	Eligible	12/5/2005	No	Cultivation
Deer Lake Village #2	22WS579	Washington	N/A	Eligible	12/5/2005	No	Trees-Secondary Growth
Barry, Stella Plantation	22YZ510	Yazoo	22-N-4	Unevaluated	12/5/2005	No	Cultivation
Melrose Plantation	22YZ550	Yazoo	22-N-29	Unevaluated	12/5/2005	No	Cultivation
Enola Landing	22YZ555	Yazoo	22-N-5	Unevaluated	12/5/2005	No	Cultivation
Panther Valley Plantation	22YZ556	Yazoo	21-N-23	Unevaluated	12/5/2005	No	Cultivation
Waller	22YZ585	Yazoo	21-N-9	Unknown	12/5/2005	No	Cultivation
Mabin, Mabon Landing	22YZ587	Yazoo	21-N-4	Unevaluated	12/5/2005	No	Cultivation
Perry	22YZ589	Yazoo	21-N-2	Unevaluated	12/5/2005	No	Cultivation
Wolf Lake	22HU524	Humphreys	N/A	Unevaluated	1/25/2006	No	Cultivation
Rhodewald Landing	22HU545	Humphreys	N/A	Ineligible	1/25/2006	No	Cultivation
Wasp Lake	22HU554	Humphreys	N/A	Eligible	1/25/2006	No	Cultivation
Evening Star Church	22HU567	Humphreys	N/A	Unevaluated	1/25/2006	No	Cultivation
Small Mound	22HU578	Humphreys	N/A	Eligible	1/25/2006	No	Cultivation
Royal	22HU610	Humphreys	N/A	Eligible	1/25/2006	No*	Trees
Horton	22WS563	Washington	20-N-10	Eligible	1/25/2006	No*	Trees
Potter	22WS564	Washington	19-N-18	Unevaluated	1/25/2006	No	Cultivation
Lakeview Plantation	22YZ566	Yazoo	21-N-13	Unevaluated	1/25/2006	No	Trees-Lawn
King David #1	22IS504	Issaquena	N/A	Eligible	3/13/2006	No	Lawn-Cultivation
King David #2	22IS505	Issaquena	N/A	Unevaluated	3/13/2006	No	Lawn-Cultivation
Jeff Davis	22IS508	Issaquena	22-M-2	Unevaluated	3/13/2006	No	Cultivation
Oak Bend	22WR611	Warren	24-M-7	Ineligible	3/13/2006	No	Industrial

the mounds, the Mississippi Archaeological Site Files were reviewed to identify potential mound sites in the Lower Delta, other than those included on Sam's tours, that might be appropriate for a self-guided driving tour. Some rough maps were made, and we set out to explore the south Delta.

On December 5, 2005, January 25, 2006, and March 13, 2006, site visits were made by the group to evaluate the proposed mounds. The site visits not only

Figure 3.1. Sam Brookes leading a mound tour, with Mont Helena (22SH505) in the background. Photo by Cliff Jenkins.

provided the opportunity to inspect the mounds for their visibility from the road but also to observe the current conditions of the mound sites, many of which had possibly not been revisited by professional archaeologists since they were originally recorded—or at least no updated information had been reported in the site files for many of the sites. As a result of these site visits, a total of 84 mound sites in seven counties were visited (Table 3.1). Of these 84 mound sites, 29 had no visible earthworks remaining. The remaining 55 sites include three National Historic Landmarks, 14 National Register listed properties, 28 National Register of Historic Places (NRHP) eligible properties, and 8 that have not been evaluated for NRHP listing. Over half of the mounds visited are in tree cover with varying states of understory, such as Mound A at the Lake George site, 22YZ557. Most of those covered by trees are surrounded by cultivated fields, as is the case for the Magee Mounds, 22SH501, in northern Sharkey County, and the Leland Mounds, 22WS501, or Avondale Mounds as Cyrus Thomas referred to them in the BAE Mound Explorations report (Thomas 1985). Fortunately, Phillips's prediction (1970:455) that by 1970 this site would be engulfed by the rapidly expanding community of Leland has not come true. Nevertheless, the Leland Mounds are within sight of a restaurant with an excellent pimento cheese and bacon panini, but few *other* "vegetarian" options.

Mounds as islands of trees in cultivated fields is probably the most common condition in which they appear in the Delta, at least for larger earthworks. However, the good news is that very few of the mounds visited were in cultivation themselves. Only six of the mounds were cultivated at the time, including the Sky Lake mound, 22HU521, which has now been removed from cultivation and the tract enrolled in the NRCS's Wetlands Reserve Program. Unfortunately, nearly all of the destroyed mound locations are in cultivated fields, including such locations at multi-mound sites. The trees have been removed from nine visited mounds, and they are now in native or planted grass cover, as is the case at Mounds A and B at the Fairview Landing site, 22YZ561, or in secondary growth, such as Mound A at the Swan Lake site, 22WS518. Structures are present on at least one mound at eight of the visited sites, with Mont Helena, 22SH505, being perhaps the most recognized due to the grandeur of the house and its visibility from Highway 61 (Figure 3.1). Some mound summit structures are not so grand, as in the case of the Quonset hut on top of Mound A and the encampment on Mound B at the Kings Crossing site, 22WR537, just north of Vicksburg.

A few examples are in well-maintained lawns, such as the Failing site, 22SU530, on Mound Bayou in Indianola. A number of mounds we visited have cemeteries on the mound summit, including Mound N, or Location N, at the Lake George site that is actually a portion of the earthen embankment surrounding the site. In many cases, the presence of a modern cemetery on a mound is probably the reason that the mound has survived, especially in the case of smaller earthworks. The Belzoni Mound, 22HU500, now overlooks the city cemetery and has a concrete picnic table on the modified summit. Maybe the most unusual current use of a mound is at the Silver City site, 22HU507, just south of Belzoni. At this site, Mound A is currently being used as a tee box at the Humphreys County Country Club. In addition to revisiting previously recorded sites, we also documented two previously unrecorded mounds, 22HU722 and 22YZ865.

Since the time of the initial Lower Delta mound tour visits, the Mississippi Mound Trail has expanded to include the entire Highway 61 corridor, with potential plans to expand statewide. Examining site records and then verifying them through the site visits conducted by the Lower Delta Mound Trail group pointed out the need to update site information for many archaeological sites. It should come as no surprise that most of these sites are located on private land, and the main threat to them is continued cultivation and changing agricultural practices. Because the NRCS provides technical and financial assistance to private landowners for land leveling, one of the most historically damaging practices to archaeological sites in the Delta, I have continued to examine site records in an effort to improve the information on archaeological sites in the Yazoo Basin.

The remainder of this paper will discuss research conducted since the time of the original mound tour site visits. Since the period from 2000–2004 when I worked for MDAH and first began working with the site file database, I have been interested in the precision of site file database queries. I believe one example of a basic question we should be able to ask of the site file database is, "How many mound sites are recorded in Mississippi?" This, I discovered, became a more complicated question than I originally thought it would be. For one, the somewhat catch-all database field of "Site Description" did not constrain the recording of information to a consistent nomenclature, and a nightmare of abbreviations was carried over from the original Visual Dbase file to the current Access database. After replacing abbreviations with complete words, a query for "Mound" still returned some obvious omissions. For example, the Lake George site was not returned in the mound query. The reason for this was because the "Site Description" field simply stated "See Report." Since that time I have continued to try to improve the information on mounds in the state so as to gain maximum efficiency from the automated database and modern data collection methods.

The National Park Service's Ancient Indian Architecture (AIA) project, funded through the Delta Initiatives, inventoried mound sites in the Lower Mississippi Delta Region, covering all or portions of four states including Mississippi (Prentice 2000). This complex project recognized quality of archaeological data as a major concern. Data quality issues related to mound locations may include such problems as the reported mound may not actually be cultural in origin; the site may have been recorded by a person unable to locate its position accurately on a map; the site may have been reported with general or vague information; the Universal Transverse Mercator coordinates may have been inaccurately entered into the database; or the relatively recent issue of coordinates collected with Global Positioning System (GPS) units using an unspecified datum. All of these issues, and others, are certainly present in the Mississippi records (and doubtless in many other equally crowd-sourced state site files), and each issue was addressed by this mound inventory.

Because location information is so basic to archaeological analysis, for this project I have only attempted to correct mound site and individual earthwork locations in the Lower Delta. No attempt at correcting other data contained within the site file records has been attempted. While the AIA project personnel did an excellent job of inventorying mounds from archival sources, there were no attempts to correct inaccuracies in location information, although coarse evaluations of data accuracy were offered.

Study Area

The study area used for this mound inventory is the area historically considered the Lower Yazoo Basin. The current study area is slightly modified from the area of the original mound site visits and includes all or part of 10 counties generally south of US Highway 82 (although all of Washington County was included) and north of Interstate 20 between the Mississippi River and the Loess Bluffs. During the site visits, a few sites south of Interstate 20 and a couple of sites at the edge of the bluffs were included, but are excluded here. The counties included in this study are all of Washington, Humphreys, Sharkey, and Issaquena; the Delta portions of Holmes, Yazoo, and Warren; and the portion of Leflore and Sunflower south of Highway 82. The small Delta portion of Carroll County south of Highway 82 was also reviewed, but no mounds have been recorded in this area.

Methods

To compile the inventory of mounds a number of archival sources were consulted. The primary sources of information were the Mississippi Archaeological Site Files and the Ancient Indian Architects database. The online Lower Mississippi Survey (LMS) Archives (Steponaitis et al. 2002) also proved to be invaluable for identifying mound locations. Numerous archaeological survey reports and published articles were also examined. In addition, mound sites were visited opportunistically, and GPS waypoints were collected on mound summits whenever possible.

With this primary information gathered on known mounds within the study area, I attempted to establish a more precise recording method by creating two Geographical Information System (GIS) shapefiles. One is a polygon shapefile that outlined the overall site boundary as best it could be determined. The second GIS file created is a point shapefile that records the location of individual earthworks. The point files follow the format of the AIA study by assigning subsite numbers to individual earthworks. For example, Mound A at Winterville is designated 22WS500.001. The creation of subsites is useful because it allows for the documentation of information about each earthwork rather than only overall site information. To distinguish between these two shapefiles, the data recorded by the polygons are referred to as mound sites, and the points are referred to as earthworks.

Attempts were made to locate all recorded earthworks, extant or not. However, some mound sites are poorly documented in the archaeological literature, and mounds that could not be located at least to the quarter section were

Figure 3.2. Bird's Eye image of the Aden Mounds (22IS509) showing the former location of Mound C compared to the site plan map from Phillips (1970: Figure 142). Courtesy of the Peabody Museum Press.

not included in the inventory. US Geological Survey (USGS) topographic quadrangle maps and Soil Surveys, which sometimes show "Indian Mound" symbols, were cross-referenced with reported earthwork locations, and site sketch maps and topographic maps were used when available. USGS orthoimagery was also used to pinpoint locations, and limited use of the Bird's Eye imagery on Bing Maps (captured by low-level aerial photography) was employed to locate some earthworks, such as the former location of Mound C at the Aden site, 22IS509 (Figure 3.2).

The recently acquired Light Detection and Ranging (LiDAR) data for the Yazoo Basin also proved invaluable for accessing current site condition and recording baseline elevation data for the mounds. The LiDAR data was accessed through a GIS server hosted by Delta State University (http://yazoo.deltastate.edu/arcgis/services). One example of the amazing use of LiDAR data is at the Duck Lake site, 22IS522, in southern Issaquena County. The Duck Lake site was documented by the LMS as a perfect orientation of mounds just opposite the mouth of the Yazoo River on an old Mississippi channel (Steponaitis et al. 2002: 23_M_pg_14). To my knowledge, the site has never been topographically mapped, although a sketch map was drawn during an LMS site visit in

2010 NAIP orthophoto, 1-m resolution.   1962 USGS 7.5' Long Lake topographic quad.

Figure 3.3. Duck Lake Mounds (22IS522) comparison of data from aerial image, topographic map, and LiDAR DEM.

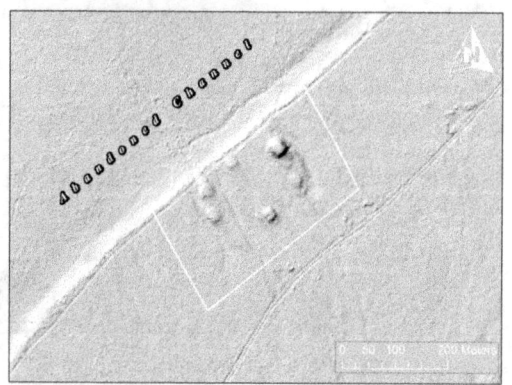

LiDAR DEM with hillshade effect.

Figure 3.4. Duck Lake Mounds (22IS522) LiDAR Digital Elevation Model (DEM) with hillshade effect overlaid with one-foot contours. Elevations in feet AMSL. Elevations in black are maximum individual mound elevations to the nearest foot.

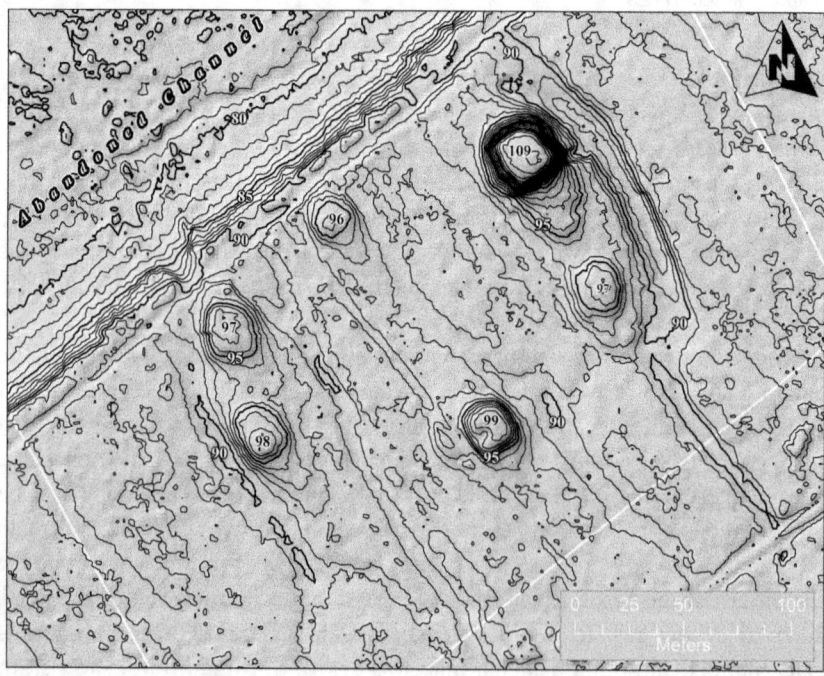

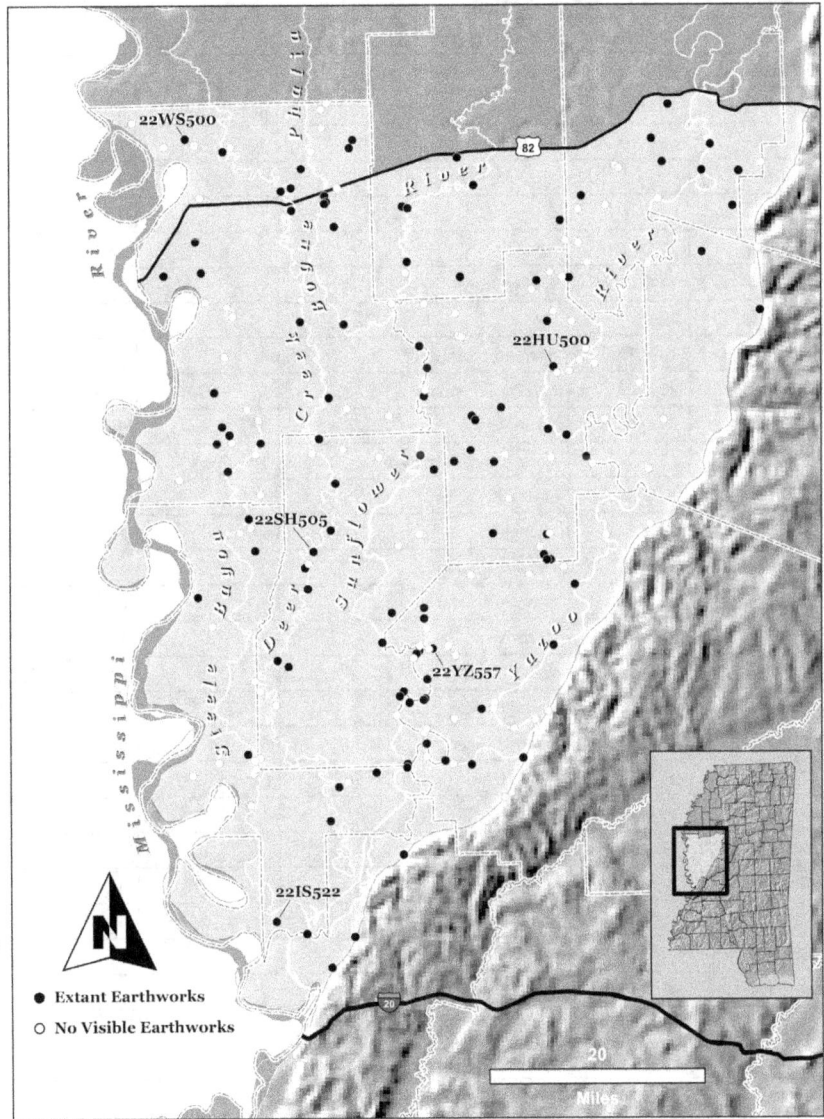

Figure 3.5. Mound sites in the Lower Mississippi Delta.

1973, and the site was recently visited by MDAH archaeologists in 2009 due to a state Antiquities Law violation. USGS quads do not show contours for mounds in this area, and tree cover obscures viewing the site on orthophotos. LiDAR, however, clearly shows this interesting arrangement of mounds—Figure 3.3 is a hillshade image created from the digital elevation model showing six mounds. Figure 3.4 is a zoomed-in view of the same hillshade with one-foot contours

Table 3.2. Mound sites within the study area showing number of reported earthworks and number of extant earthworks.

Trinomial	LMS #	Site Name	Report EW	Extant EW
22HO501	20-O-13	Horseshoe Brake	2	0
22HO512	20-O-14	Bee Lake Plantation	1	0
22HO533	19-O-14	Montgomery Landing	1	0
22HO565	19-P-10	French	1	0
22HO609		Providence, Cox	1	1
22HO1220		Cruger	1	1
22HU500	20-O-02	Belzoni	2	1
22HU501	21-O-06	Reaver-Brown	1	1
22HU502	20-O-07	Payne	1	0
22HU503	19-N-12	Bearden, Mosley	1	0
22HU504	20-O-03	Fort Place, Lamkin	5	2
22HU505	20-O-01	Jaketown	13	2
22HU506	20-O-04	Holly, Atchafalaya Bayou	2	2
22HU507	20-O-05	Silver City	3	1
22HU509	20-N-01	Midnight	2	1
22HU510	20-N-02	Parker-Summerfield	3	1
22HU511	21-O-07	James Wm. Love Farms	2	0
22HU512	21-N-19	Wilzone	1	1
22HU514	20-O-20	Welsh Camp	1	0
22HU515	21-N-11	Sleepy Hollow	2	1
22HU518		Roland Walker	1	0
22HU519		Childs, Martin Lake	3	0
22HU520	20-N-07	McCoy	1	1
22HU521	19-N-11	Sky Lake	2	1
22HU523	20-N-05	Cold Lake	2	0
22HU524	21-N-28	Wolf Lake, Ramaa, West Wolf Lake	1	0
22HU525	20-N-06	Gooden Lake	4	2
22HU526	20-N-12	Little Callao	1	1
22HU528	20-O-08	McClintock	1	0
22HU532	20-O-23	Lundy	1	0
22HU533	20-O-18	Peaster	4	0
22HU534	20-O-19	Peaster B	1	0
22HU536	19-N-10	Jackson Bayou	1	0
22HU539	19-O-12	Simmons	1	0
22HU540	19-O-13	Paxton	2	0
22HU545		Rhodewald Landing	1	1
22HU546		Lewis	1	1
22HU554		Wasp Lake	1	0
22HU567		Evening Star Church	1	0
22HU575		Unnamed	1	0
22HU578		Small Mound?	1	0
22HU579		Unnamed	1	0
22HU581		Unnamed	1	0

Trinomial	LMS #	Site Name	Report EW	Extant EW
22HU595		Sendo I	1	0
22HU610		Royal	1	1
22HU655		Slate	1	1
22HU676		Unnamed	1	0
22HU722		Gooden Lake South	1	1
22IS500	21-M-07	Grace	4	2
22IS501	21-L-01	Mayersville	11	4
22IS502	22-M-08	Hardee	3	1
22IS503	22-M-07	Johnson	1	0
22IS504		King David #1	1	0
22IS505		King David #2	1	0
22IS506	22-M-06	Manny	4	4
22IS507	22-M-01	Thornton	1	1
22IS508	22-M-02	Jeff Davis	4	0
22IS509	22-M-03	Aden	3	2
22IS511	21-M-10	Flannigan	1	0
22IS512	21-M-08	Lamidoux	1	0
22IS513	21-M-09	Alsworth	1	1
22IS514	21-M-12	Bethlehem Church	1	0
22IS515	22-N-02	Leist	3	2
22IS520	22-L-01	Magna Vista	2	0
22IS522	23-M-06	Duck Lake	6	6
22IS523		Unnamed	3	0
22IS529		Unnamed	1	0
22IS558		Whiting Bayou	1	0
22LF505	19-O-02	Shell Bluff	3	0
22LF513	19-O-01	McLean	2	1
22LF514	19-O-05	Old Dominion	1	0
22LF515	19-O-06	Robinson Deadening	2	2
22LF517	19-P-02	Roebuck	2	2
22LF519	19-O-11	Nichols	1	0
22LF528	19-O-10	Hunt	1	0
22LF531	19-O-22	Pleasant Grove	3	0
22LF534	19-O-25	Mosquito Lake	1	1
22LF535	19-O-26	Barry #2	1	0
22LF536	19-O-27	Cockrell	1	0
22LF539	19-P-07	Black	1	1
22LF585		Ft. Loring	1	1
22LF598		Hooper	2	1
22LF606		Unnamed	1	1
22LF617		Unnamed	1	0
22LF622		Unnamed	1	1
22SH500	21-N-03	Spanish Fort	1	1
22SH501	20-M-02	Magee (Deer Creek)	6	2
22SH502	20-M-03	Panther Burn	2	0

Trinomial	LMS #	Site Name	Report EW	Extant EW
22SH503	20-N-03	Straight Bayou	1	1
22SH504	22-M-04	Blanton	3	0
22SH505	21-M-02	Mont Helena	3	1
22SH506	21-M-01	Rolling Fork	3	2
22SH507	21-M-05	Cary	4	1
22SH508	20-M-14	Nitta Yuma	2	1
22SH509	20-M-15	Delta City	2	0
22SH510	21-M-03	Anguilla	1	1
22SH511	21-M-04	Lowery	2	1
22SH512	21-M-06	Moore	1	0
22SH514	21-N-06	Screws	1	1
22SH515	21-N-07	Stalonia	3	0
22SH516	21-N-08	Shannon	1	1
22SH518	21-N-10	Savory (Crippen Point)	8	1
22SH520	22-N-01	Leist	2	1
22SH522	22-N-14	Little Spanish Fort	2	2
22SH523	22-N-16	Hollis (Anderson Landing)	1	0
22SH524	22-N-35	Bachelor's Retreat	1	0
22SH525		Anguilla 2	1	0
22SH530		Updike	1	0
22SH531		Unnamed	1	1
22SH532		Carter/Chipman [LMS # 21-M-11]	2	2
22SH536		Unnamed	1	0
22SH549		Riley	1	0
22SH552	21-M-13	Guiding Star	1	1
22SH648		Ralph Pearce	1	1
22SU526	19-N-01	Kinlock	6	2
22SU527	19-N-02	Shields	3	1
22SU528	19-N-03	Bay Lake	3	1
22SU529	19-N-04	Danzler	1	0
22SU530	19-N-05	Failing	2	2
22SU531	19-N-06	Lake Dawson	4	2
22SU545	19-N-14	Baird	1	1
22SU546	19-N-15	Woodburn	1	0
22SU578	19-O-07	Pritchard	2	2
22SU579	19-O-08	Polk	1	0
22WR---	23-M-04	Johnson	1	1
22WR510	22-N-06	Dornbusch	1	1
22WR537	23-M-01	Kings Crossing	4	3
22WR543	23-M-02	Blakely	1	1
22WS500	19-L-01	Winterville	23	10
22WS501	19-M-01	Leland, Avondale	5	2
22WS502	19-M-04	Dunleith	6	2
22WS503	18-L-03	Shadyside Landing	3	0
22WS504	19-L-02	Bachelor Bend	2	0

Trinomial	LMS #	Site Name	Report EW	Extant EW
22WS505	19-L-03	Ely	1	0
22WS506	19-L-04	Metcalfe	2	1
22WS508	19-L-06	Refuge	4	1
22WS509	19-L-07	Ash Bayou	1	1
22WS510	19-M-02	Sheldon	1	0
22WS511	19-M-03	Sherwood, Stoneville	2	2
22WS512	19-M-05	Hollyknowe	1	1
22WS513	19-M-06	Arcola High School	2	0
22WS514	19-M-07	Polk	1	0
22WS515	20-L-02	Silver Lake	1	0
22WS516	20-M-01	Arcola	6	3
22WS517	20-M-04	Lessiedell	4	2
22WS518	20-M-05	Swan Lake	4	2
22WS519	20-M-06	Clower	1	1
22WS520	20-N-04	Kongo	2	0
22WS521	19-M-10	Hebe	5	5
22WS522	19-M-23	Church	0	1
22WS525	19-M-14	Helm	1	0
22WS528		Dennis, 12 Heads	1	0
22WS529	18-M-17	Kellum	1	0
22WS530	18-M-18	McDearman	1	0
22WS539	19-L-08	Gloster Street	1	0
22WS540	19-L-09	Lake Lee	2	2
22WS541	19-L-10	Wayside	3	0
22WS542	19-M-08	Kirk	2	0
22WS543	19-M-09	King	2	0
22WS544	19-M-11	Trivett	1	1
22WS546	19-M-13	Mount Olive	1	1
22WS549	20-L-01	Law	3	1
22WS550	20-L-03	Griffin	4	1
22WS551	20-L-04	Linden	1	1
22WS552	20-L-05	Granicus	1	0
22WS554	20-M-07	Percy Jones	3	0
22WS555	20-M-08	Woods	1	0
22WS556	20-M-09	Bear Garden	1	0
22WS557	20-M-10	Mathews	2	0
22WS563	20-N-10	Horton	1	1
22WS564	19-N-18	Potter	1	0
22WS566		Gower	1	1
22WS579		Deer Lake Village #2	1	0
22WS581		Indian Mound on Leland Quad	1	1
22WS634		Hoover	1	1
22WS773		Unnamed	1	1
22WS967		Howard New	1	0
22WS1022		Indian Mound on Hollandale Quad	1	0

Trinomial	LMS #	Site Name	Report EW	Extant EW
22YZ---	22-N-36	Mound near Miller Landing	1	0
22YZ508	22-N-27	King, Dave King Place	2	0
22YZ509	22-N-28	Hancock, Jack Laseter	1	0
22YZ510	22-N-04	Barry, Stella Plantation	1	0
22YZ515	22-N-34	Milner Place	2	0
22YZ531	22-N-08	Potato Hill Bayou, Crippen Place	2	1
22YZ550	22-N-29	Melrose Plantation	1	0
22YZ552	22-N-13	Trammell	2	0
22YZ554	22-N-11	Friedlander Place	1	1
22YZ555	22-N-05	Enola Landing	2	0
22YZ556	21-N-23	Panther Valley Plantation	1	0
22YZ557	21-N-01	Lake George, Holly Bluff	25	18
22YZ559	21-N-20	Lindsey Place, Jerusalem	1	0
22YZ560	22-N-32	Hearn Place	1	1
22YZ561	22-N-09	Fairview Landing	3	3
22YZ562	22-N-10	Landrum, Rosenbaum	1	1
22YZ563	21-N-15	Tanglewood Plantation	3	1
22YZ564	21-N-14	Loch Lomond Plantation	1	1
22YZ565	21-N-22	Greenhill Plantation	1	0
22YZ566	21-N-13	Lakeview Plantation, Erickson	2	0
22YZ571	21-O-12	Pete Clark Place	1	1
22YZ574	21-O-19	Zelleria Plantation	1	0
22YZ581	22-N-20	Mengel	1	0
22YZ584	22-N-03	Frank Smith, No Mistake	2	0
22YZ585	21-N-09	Waller	2	0
22YZ587	21-N-04	Mabin, Mabon Landing	2	1
22YZ589	21-N-02	Perry	1	0
22YZ600	21-O-09	Shellwood, Coker	2	0
22YZ603	21-O-13	Caruthers	1	0
22YZ608	22-N-07	Satartia	1	1
22YZ610	22-N-21	Gammel	3	3
22YZ650		MDAH #68	1	0
22YZ865		Phillips	1	1
Total			**444**	**178**

overlaid. With the Yazoo Basin LiDAR data, we now have high-quality elevation data for *every* archaeological site in the Delta.

As a result of the Lower Delta Mound Inventory, a total of 211 mound sites were identified within the study area (Figure 3.5). Of these 211 sites, only 105 (almost exactly half) have extant earthworks, with a total of 444 individual earthworks having been recorded originally (Table 3.2). Of these 444

Table 3.3. Summary of mound data by county.

County	Study Area Sq. mi.	Sq. mi./ Mound	Total Mound Sites	# Mound Sites with Extant EW	% Mound Sites with Extant EW	# Extant EW	# Reported EW	% Extant EW
Carroll	29	0	0	0	0	0	0	0
Holmes	219	37	6	2	0.33	2	7	0.29
Humphreys	431	10	42	19	0.45	23	78	0.29
Issaquena	424	21	20	9	0.45	23	53	0.43
Leflore	240	14	17	9	0.53	11	25	0.44
Sharkey	435	15	29	18	0.62	22	59	0.37
Sunflower	205	21	10	7	0.70	11	24	0.46
Warren	155	39	4	4	1.00	6	7	0.86
Washington	752	15	50	25	0.50	46	118	0.39
Yazoo	348	11	33	13	0.39	34	73	0.47
Total	3238	15	210	105	0.50	178	444	0.40

previously identified earthworks, only 178, or about 40 percent, are extant. Humphreys and Holmes counties have the greatest percentage loss of earthworks, with only 29 percent remaining of those identified. Most of the other counties hover around the average, with the exception of Warren County, where 6 of the 7 reported earthworks in the study area are extant (Table 3.3). Mound density within the study area averages one mound per 15 square miles. Humphreys and Yazoo counties have the highest density of recorded mound sites with one mound per 10 and 11 square miles respectively, while Holmes and Warren counties have the lowest density at one mound per 37 and 39 square miles respectively (Table 3.3).

Conclusions

This project demonstrates how the accumulation of management data can serve research that reveals patterns of activities subsequent to abandonment of ancient sites. The data presented here clearly show a dramatic loss of earthworks in the Lower Delta, and highlight the need for proactive measures to protect the remaining earthworks in the region, in a way that the public can easily understand. In an attempt to raise awareness of the value of archaeological sites in the Yazoo Basin, I am in the early stages of working with county Soil and Water Conservation Districts to contact landowners of significant archaeological sites. Through this endeavor, landowners will be provided with information about the importance of the archaeological sites located on their property and offered recommendations for responsible site management. Another step will be to expand the survey project to inventory mounds in the north Delta, and to continue to examine LiDAR data in an attempt to locate previously undocumented mounds, especially in forested areas of the Delta where archaeological surveys are infrequent. In addition, the effectiveness of LiDAR to identify other kinds of archaeological features should also be explored. Hopefully through these efforts, important cultural resources will be considered along with other resources in future land-management decisions.

PART II

The Archaic Period

CHAPTER 4

Early Holocene Climate in the Eastern United States: A View from Mississippi

Samuel O. Brookes and Melissa H. Twaroski

Background

The Hypsithermal is frequently referred to in archaeological works, but little hard data are usually offered in these reports. Pielou, in her excellent volume *After the Ice Age* (1991:269), has stated that the Hypsithermal has no absolute beginning and end, but rather was time-transgressive. For the purposes of this paper we have selected the period between 6500 and 3000 B.C. to define the Hypsithermal and provide us with a starting and ending point. These dates encompass the latter portion of the Early Archaic period through the latter portion of the Middle Archaic.

Many writers refer to the Hypsithermal as a period of great warmth and dryness. Droughty conditions caused the extension of prairies into the oak-hickory forests of the Central Mississippi Valley (Smith 1986:5). To the south, the weather patterns changed, inducing thunderstorms and lightning-started forest fires that replaced the predominantly hardwood forests of the Coastal plain with fire-tolerant pines (Delcourt and Delcourt 1979; Smith 1986:6). Unfortunately, for a major portion of the Southeast there are relatively few pollen core samples to provide evidence for this dramatic change. Yet these few samples are generally used to paint a picture of the Southeast as a whole. This paper will present a few of the more recently observed and, in our opinion, more compelling facts that suggest a major climatic shift during this time in the Southeast, especially when viewed from Mississippi. In addition to palynological studies, the Quaternary geologic history, floodplain evolution of surrounding areas, and archaeological data will be examined to discern if such a drastic climatic shift is reflected in the material culture of the appropriate time periods. We contend that the evidence suggests two things: (1) western and northern peoples migrated into the Southeast during the early part of the Hypsithermal; and (2) the shift away from the use of local gravels to tabular cherts, limonites, sandstones, and quartzites for tool manufacture can be directly correlated with the environmental effects of this period.

Environmental Evidence

Pielou (1991:269–290) suggests that the Hypsithermal climatic shift varied greatly from one location to another. Furthermore, she asserts (Pielou 1991:270) that all biogeographical zones were shifted hundreds of kilometers northward. Annual rainfall is believed to have decreased, and Pielou describes barren areas with tremendous dust storms caused by high winds (Pielou 1991:271–287). Oak-hickory forests were gradually replaced by pine forests, and they in turn by prairie grasslands. The grasslands were replaced by ragweed, sagebrush, pigweed, and similar species (Pielou 1991:275). Aggravating the situation, the western prairies were devastated by huge wildfires and plagues of grasshoppers, driving out the herbivores (Pielou 1991:289) and therefore, we contend, the humans.

The bulk of Pielou's volume discusses the northern United States and Canada, upwards into the Arctic regions. However, if the Hypsithermal had such an effect on the northern portion of the United States, it stands to reason that its effects must have been even greater in the Sunbelt. Some dramatic evidence of a climatic shift in the southern states (by now starting to sound biblical in its proportions and severity) is to be found in Saucier's (1994) opus. In addressing the "pimple mounds" of Texas, Oklahoma, southern Missouri, Arkansas, and western and southern Louisiana, he presented an interesting explanation for these unusual features (Saucier 1994:162–165). Pimple mounds are typically 50 feet in diameter and 2 to 3 feet high. They occur in clusters and vary in number from 100 to 300 per square mile. They are found upon a variety of soils and landforms but not in low-lying, flood-prone areas. They approach the Mississippi River but are not found on the eastern shore. Finally, they do not touch each other, but occur as single, discrete mounds. Saucier believed this ruled out a geomorphological explanation and suggested territorial animal behavior as being responsible. Ants and/or termites were the suspected culprits. Furthermore, evidence suggests that these features were constructed during the Hypsithermal. However, recent research by Seifert and associates (2009:1–11) suggest that aeolian deposition in the middle to late Holocene was responsible for the pimple mounds, and that new data reinforce the concept of greatly decreased moisture and a shift to prairie vegetation during the middle Holocene (Seifert et al. 2009).

Additional confirmation of the Hypsithermal climatic shift comes from southeastern Missouri, where pollen core samples suggest a period of changing plant communities during this period (King 1981, as reported in Morse and Morse 1983:100–101). The lowest levels indicate the presence of a bottomland hardwood forest with open-water swamps. Beginning around 6700 B.C., the forest began to decline, being replaced by grasses. As time passed, grassland species began to dominate the assemblage, comprising approximately 85 percent of the species present by 5000 B.C. After this (by approximately 4500 B.C.) the grasses declined, and percentages of swamp species increased, although relatively dry conditions persisted until 3000 B.C.

Palynological studies in Florida and the coastal plain of Georgia and South Carolina indicate that the replacement of predominantly hardwood forests with pine occurred relatively slowly from north to south. "The expansion of pine to a new stability was achieved first in South Carolina by about 8000 B.P., last in southern Florida by about 4500 B.P." (Watts et al. 1996:37). Furthermore, Watts et al. (1996:32) note that Florida (in fact, many parts of the Southeast) "today contains species representative of widespread prairie genera ... which are isolated from the great prairies of the central United States, but suggest a biogeographic relationship at some remote time." They suggest that these prairie areas are remnants of the oak/herb plant communities that were replaced by pine. If this were the case, it would have provided human and herbivore immigrants with an environment somewhat similar to the one being devastated behind them, lasting until 3000 B.C. or so in southern Florida. Brown (2003:15) notes that during the Hypsithermal, a prairie corridor extended from the Great Plains to the upper Atlantic coast as evidenced by disjunct species of insects, bison, and prairie chickens in eastern "prairies" in historic times. There is evidence for lowered water tables and the drying out of lakes and swamps during this time (Peacock 2008:71–73). For example, Peacock and Seltzer (2008) examined mollusks (freshwater mussel shells) from the accretional, Middle Archaic-period Vaughn Mound (22LO538) on the central Tombigbee River using a combination of taxonomic, morphometric, trace element, and light isotope data. Contrary to an earlier suggestion (Peacock 2008:95), they found that, on balance, these data suggest the Tombigbee River was "smaller during the Middle Holocene" (Peacock and Seltzer 2008:2562), indicating a hot, dry climate during this time (see also Delcourt and Delcourt 2004; Stein 2005).

The drier climate and sparser vegetation would have had another effect upon the environment. When rain did come, the desiccated and relatively denuded surface would have been subjected to tremendous erosion. This is supported by research on the evolution of the lower Illinois River floodplain at the Koster and Napoleon Hollow sites (Hajic 1981; T. Styles 1984; B. Styles 1986:148–151) and Joseph Schuldenrein's (1996) geoarchaeological research on Mid-Holocene landscape history. These researchers agree that "the Hypsithermal was heralded by increasing sedimentation rates as erosional conditions were accelerated and the climate assumed a warming-drying aspect" (Schuldenrein 1996:24).

Such stream siltation would have buried gravel sources in the streambeds (Bense 1987:397). Not only would the gravel bars be covered with soil, but this soil would have become hard-packed and eventually covered with shrubs and grasses (David Dockery, personal communication 1996). An exception to this would be the pre-loess gravel in areas near steep runoffs, such as along the loess bluffs on the eastern margin of the Lower Mississippi Valley. We contend that the material culture of this time period supports the occurrence of such an erosional episode.

Artifactual Evidence

The first evidence we have of a movement of peoples from the West into the Southeast occurs around 7000–6500 B.C. with the appearance of the Cody complex. Scottsbluff points and Cody knives appear in Louisiana and Arkansas, and several are known from Mississippi (Brookes 2007:4–7; Jeter et al. 1989:89; McGahey 2000:80–84; Morse and Morse 1983:107). Most of the Scottsbluff points are made of non-local cherts believed to derive from Oklahoma and Texas (Schambach and Early 1982; Webb 1981:7). As these styles move from west to east, the Scottsbluff point is modified into a Hardin point, a common form in the Mississippi Valley. Also, the stemmed Cody knife loses the stem and becomes what is known as a Cobbs triangular knife (Overstreet and Peake 1981:182–186; Perino 1985:79). Almost all Hardin points and Cody/Cobbs knives are manufactured from local Citronelle Gravel. The modification of the form of Hardin and Cody artifacts is probably due to the smaller size and generally inferior quality of this raw material. The movement of a Plains bison-hunting culture into the Southeast at a time when the prairies were supposed to be expanding suggests that the Hypsithermal was having an effect. Further supporting this idea is the fact that few other artifactual remains are present, especially diagnostic projectile point/knives, that can be assigned to this period, giving one the impression that local populations have moved. The use of local Citronelle Gravels for 95 percent of the tools of this period suggests that gravel bars were still accessible and that trade or travel to western sources, as suggested by Schambach and Early (1982), was not occurring, at least not in the Mississippi Valley and eastern valley margins.

At approximately the same time, another point form appears in Mississippi. Pine Tree points are plentiful in northeast Mississippi and are the dominant point form of the terminal Early Archaic period (McGahey 2000:80–84). Pine Tree points are unusual in several respects. They are the only Early Archaic corner-notched point/knife form in the region that is not typically resharpened by alternate beveling. Alternate beveling is the predominant resharpening technique in the Southeast, but it is almost nonexistent in the Atlantic Coast region. Distributional and technological evidence suggests that the Pine Tree may be a late variety of Kirk corner notched. Another very unusual feature of the Pine Tree point type is that Kosciusko Quartzite was a preferred material. Kosciusko Quartzite is found in a narrow band in the north-central portion of Mississippi. This material has to be quarried, and it is the opinion of most researchers that thermal alteration is a must for this extremely tough rock to be worked at all. Kosciusko Quartzite is a distinctive greenish-gray, fine-grained material. It was avoided by all Archaic groups except the makers of Pine Tree points. In Mississippi, 51 percent of Pine Tree points are made of something other than local gravels (McGahey 1999:1–11). Kosciusko Quartzite makes up 39 percent of this total, with other exotic material comprising the remaining 12 percent. Kosciusko Quartzite was traded or exchanged up to 80 km from its source. At the Hester site in north Mississippi, Pine Tree points were found in a layer just above Hardin/Lost Lake points and are believed to date from 6500–5000 B.C. (Brookes 1979:109).

At present, few Pine Tree components have been excavated, but the idea of a southward movement of people at the onset of the Hypsithermal is certainly supportive of the argument that the Hypsithermal was a disruptive event in the lives of prehistoric people. Furthermore, the fact that an upland raw material, assiduously avoided by all other groups because of the difficulty in obtaining and working it, was not only being quarried, but actively sought, suggests that the Citronelle gravel beds were being silted over. Supporting this idea is the fact that of all point/knife forms in Mississippi, the Pine Tree is the most curated form, with many examples resharpened until most of the blade has been worn away (Samuel O. McGahey, personal communication 1996). Similarly on the Gulf Coast, Bolen points are the dominant Early Archaic form. There are several varieties of Bolen, and some appear to be earlier than others. Bolens are made from Tallahatta Quartzite 43 percent of the time, and from other quartzite 4 percent of the time, with the remainder, 53 percent, being fabricated from Citronelle Gravel (McGahey 1999:78–80). When the later Bolens are sorted out (the ones that appear to be Hardin/Lost Lake), the percentage of local gravel used drops to 33 percent.

Further evidence comes from the succeeding Middle Archaic period of 5000–3000 B.C. Numerous projectile point forms are present that are radically different from those of the preceding eras. Unlike earlier points, Middle Archaic forms are thick and broad. The fine pressure flaking of earlier times disappears. In the earlier part of the Middle Archaic, corner-notched forms are most common, while in the latter part, broad-stemmed forms predominate. A broad stem as defined here is usually in excess of 20 mm wide.

This period of time, especially ca. 4000 B.C., is when the Hypsithermal was at its maximum. At just this time there is a shift in raw material selection from local gravel to several other sources. In the north, Fort Payne chert is the preferred material, while in central Mississippi, Tallahatta Quartzite is the dominant stone. In south Mississippi, Middle Archaic points are sometimes made from a purplish sandstone quartzite and from limonite. This is a high-quality material composed of iron oxide cements with some polycrystalline quartz and small amounts of chert (Heinrich 1988:A-5). Although quarries of this material have been found in Alabama, it is believed that there are potentially many sources of this material throughout southeastern Mississippi and southwestern Alabama (Rebecca Lumpkin, personal communication 1995). Outcrops of this material have now been documented on Camp Shelby in south Mississippi (McCarty 2011). This material is not a purely occurring quartzite substance, forcing would-be users of this quartzite to search through a lot of poor-quality, friable sandstone to find this higher quality material (Rebecca Lumpkin, personal communication 1995).

As part of the research design for the Midden Mound Project on the Tombigbee Waterway (Bense 1987), several hypotheses were put forward to explain events in the Middle Archaic. One of these hypotheses dealt with the Archaic-period shift to Fort Payne chert for biface manufacture. Prior to the Benton phase in northeast Mississippi, less than 5 percent of tools were made from Fort Payne chert, even though this fine-grained, blue-gray tabular chert is the finest raw material available within 150 km. During the Benton phase, 50–80 percent of all tools were made from Fort Payne chert (Johnson and Brookes 1988:60; Meeks 1999:35). This phenomenon, the almost exclusive use of Fort Payne chert to manufacture a specific point type (Benton), was first noted by Gerald P. Smith (1972) and was formally recognized shortly thereafter by Rafferty et al. (1980). Bense (1987:393) suggested hypothetically that the shift to the use of Fort Payne chert may have resulted from gravel bars being silted over during the Hypsithermal. Vaughn points (Atkinson 1974:132) are another type of broad, thick point from this time period. McGahey (1999:106–107) states that almost 100 percent of Vaughn points are made from Tallahatta Quartzite. Although there is evidence for floodplain gravel bars being buried in the Tombigbee River at that time, Bense (1987:397) rejected her own hypothesis because she thought that gravel would have been available in the tributary stream valleys. However, David Dockery, geologist with the State of

Mississippi Geological Survey, has stated that the same factors at work in the Tombigbee would have been at work in the uplands (David Dockery, personal communication 1996). Thus, the shift to Fort Payne chert and other raw materials can be explained by the effects of the Hypsithermal.

Most researchers agree that both Tuscaloosa and Citronelle Gravel were procured from streambeds where all the sorting had already taken place. There are no known prehistoric quarry sites in Mississippi where gravels were being dug. Most quarry sites are upland sites where tabular material was being procured in Middle Archaic times (Johnson 1981; McGahey et al. 1992). The shift to what has been considered second-line material sources can be documented within the Middle Archaic.

The Benton phase of ca. 4500–3000 B.C. marks the period in the northern part of Mississippi where this shift takes place. In the southern portion of the state, Giliberti (1995) has studied the Beaumont site in the Leaf River floodplain with similar results. The Middle Archaic forms at Beaumont are made of local gravel only 46 percent of the time. The data suggest that the shift from local gravel to tabular chert began in the latter part of the Early Archaic and increased in the Middle Archaic. A serendipitous aspect of this shift to alternate lithics is that people were able to manufacture larger bifaces, because this tabular material is so much larger than the gravel cobbles. These large bifaces occur across most of Mississippi, and oversized blades cross-cut several types (Benton, Castroville, Turkey Tail, and Pickwick). At the Eva site in Tennessee, an oversized Benton blade was found at the pelvic area with a female burial (Lewis and Lewis 1961:115). Many of these Middle Archaic forms were knives, used by both males and females, and do not necessarily represent a male activity.

In addition to the shift to previously unacceptable (or unobtainable) lithic materials, something else unusual happened in the Middle Archaic. Exchange networks appeared over a wide area of the Southeast (Brookes 2004; Crawford 2003; Jefferies 1996; Johnson and Brookes 1987, 1988). Most of the artifacts from sites involved with the networks date to the Middle Archaic period with Cypress Creek, Pickwick, and Benton point types predominating. The former two point types are made from Tallahatta Quartzite, while the latter is made from Fort Payne chert (although a few specimens made of Tallahatta Quartzite have been found in south Mississippi). In the northern part of the state, Pickwick points made from Tallahatta Quartzite have been found in association with caches of Benton points, thus firmly dating Pickwicks to the 3700–3000 B.C. period in this area. Investigations by the Mississippi Department of Archives and History have yielded several large Middle Archaic sites in the Yazoo Basin with Middle Archaic points and classic Bentons made from Arkansas novaculite (Samuel O. McGahey, personal communication 1996). A more recently described cache from Mississippi consists of points and bannerstones, a classic Benton point made from novaculite, and a hypertrophic Johnson point made from Burlington chert (Brookes 2002b). The fact that these lithic exchange networks appear over a large area of the region at the same time suggests that a need for suitable raw material was present. The dust storms and erosion of the Hypsithermal, coupled with reduced stream discharge and velocity, took their toll upon the lithic resources of the region, causing people to modify their behavior accordingly.

As we mentioned earlier, many of these oversized blades appear to be large hafted knives rather than spears. In the course of examining collections of Middle Archaic points, we have noted a peculiar breakage pattern. Many of these points exhibit deep, conchoidal fractures on the edges of the blade. This type of breakage has seldom been noted on earlier points. Middle Archaic bifaces also have a much lower rate of impact fractures than do the earlier forms (McGahey 1999:88–138). This blade damage appears to be the result of the biface being inserted into an unyielding object and twisted. It is entirely possible that most or all of these so-called projectile points of the Middle Archaic period are indeed not points at all but knives, and that projectile points of this period were made from wood, antler, or bone.

Another change in the archaeological record manifests itself in the Middle Archaic period. Throughout the earlier periods, one of the most common artifacts was the unifacial end scraper. Unifacial end scrapers on Middle Archaic sites are nonexistent. At the Middle Archaic Denton site in the Yazoo Basin, none are reported in an analysis of several hundred tools (Connaway 1977:20–21). In fact, the only Middle Archaic sites that yield end scrapers are those containing earlier components. End scrapers were a major part of the toolkit of Eskimo peoples up until very recent times. The Eskimo used these tools primarily to process hides used in their clothing. When people came into America at the end of the last Ice Age, their clothing most probably resembled Eskimo-style clothing. With the retreat of the glaciers and the warming of the Hypsithermal, this type of clothing was not a necessity. Therefore, the disappearance of unifacial end scrapers is suggested to be yet another sign of the Hypsithermal.

If the environment underwent such radical changes during this time, we could also expect to see a shift in settlement patterns. Evidence from northeast Mississippi (Sparks 1987:50) indicates that during the Middle Archaic there is an increase in the use of prairie bottoms and a decrease in use of terraces and uplands. Similarly, Reams (1995:77) found that Middle Archaic sites in south-central Mississippi were seven times more likely to be located within one kilometer of water than were sites of other time periods. The Midden

Mound Project of the Tombigbee found that the large base camps of this period were either in the floodplain or on the edge of the first terrace (Bense 1987:3). Peacock (1988) also found this to be true of Middle Archaic Benton sites. Similar site placement has been noted by other authors (Claassen 1996; Dye 1996). All evidence suggests that flooding was not a concern at this time period, although recent work by Kidder (2006) suggests the same cannot be said for the terminal Late Archaic period in the Lower Mississippi Valley.

The Middle Archaic is also the time period of the Shellmound Archaic (Claassen 1996; Ford and Willey 1941; Jennings 1952; Phillips et al. 1951). Although most shell mounds are found north of Mississippi, one has to wonder how much preservation has to do with this phenomenon. The Denton site is apparently located on an old channel. The deep, conchoidal edge fractures mentioned earlier were first noticed by Brookes on biface blades recovered from Denton, and we suggest that the breakage was caused by using the bifaces to open mussels. Dean Snow (1980:177–181) has been a critic of the idea of people subsisting primarily on shellfish, but numerous researchers have noted an increase in the exploitation of freshwater mussels during the Middle Archaic (Claassen 1996; Neusius 1986; B. Styles 1986:156). The evidence indicates that mussels became very important during this period over much of the eastern United States. Coupled with a shift in settlement patterns to the edge of streams, this fact suggests that people wanted to be as close to the water as possible. Several authors (e.g., Brown 1986; Brown and Vierra 1983) have suggested that aquatic enhancement of riverine environments pulled people to the bottoms rather than people being forced out of the uplands because of harsh conditions there. It appears to us that both factors were at play. As recently noted (Peacock and Jenkins 2010), there are thus far only two sites in Mississippi that have produced unequivocally Middle Archaic-period shell: the Vaughn Mound and the Trice site, both in the Tombigbee drainage. This suggests that something other than preservation bias is at work. Actually, this fact may feed into the idea that gravel bars—i.e., mussel habitat—were silted over.

A totally new type of site also appears during this time period (4500–3000 B.C.), mound sites (Russo 1994). These sites can be both single mounds, as at Banana Bayou (Gagliano 1967), or mound groups such as Watson Brake (Jones 1983). Most occur in Louisiana, but some were constructed in Mississippi. These sites represent the earliest mounds not only in the New World, but they predate any such constructions in the Old World as well. Archaeologists are currently in the process of attempting to determine the function of these mounds. Whatever the function, two things are immediately apparent when one considers these early mounds. These first mounds appear ca. 4500

B.C. and mound building ends around 3000 B.C. This time period brackets the most severe portion of the Hypsithermal (4500–4000 B.C.). The Hypsithermal appears to end rather abruptly around 3000 B.C., and so too does this early mound building. It is also of interest that mound building does appear again in the same region with the Late Archaic Poverty Point culture, but there appears to be a hiatus of some 13 centuries between these two periods. Thus the Middle Archaic mounds are not antecedent to the Late Archaic mounds of the Poverty Point culture, but rather a disparate event occurring some 1,300 years earlier. It can now be stated that there are at least four Middle Archaic mounds in Mississippi. We have already mentioned the Vaughn mound on the Tombigbee River, but this mound is likely more akin to the accretional "midden mounds" on that waterway rather than being an intentionally constructed earthwork. There is, however, a single mound (22LI504) in Lincoln County (Peacock et al. 2010) and a group of three mounds, the Grant Mounds (now destroyed), in what is now downtown Pascagoula (Brookes 2004:111). Botanical materials from the former mound produced a number of radiocarbon dates verifying that it "is an Archaic period construction well over 5,000 years old" (Peacock et al. 2010:364). The latter group of mounds yielded a cache of stone beads, including a classic Middle Archaic zoomorphic effigy form (Blitz 1993b:26; Crawford 2003:153).

In a paper delivered at the William G. Haag Honorary Symposium, Schambach (2005) suggested that Gulf Coast shell was moving north. This is certainly true for the Middle Archaic period as well as for Late Archaic Poverty Point groups. Schambach (2005) makes the point that the toolkit for manufacturing shell beads and gorgets is found at the three primary Poverty Point sites (Poverty Point, Jaketown, and Claiborne). A similar toolkit, along with prepared cores and microdrills, is found at several Middle Archaic sites, and while many of these sites exhibit stone bead making complexes (Hadley and Carr, this volume), shell bead manufacture could have been occurring as well. The exchange networks that move rocks have been discussed in an earlier paper (Brookes 2004). It was noted in that paper that what was often moving in the networks was not needed raw material but special objects: effigy pendants, beads, and bifaces as well as oversize bifaces. Effigy beads, probably all made in Mississippi, are one of the most widely dispersed of the objects moving in the exchange networks (Crawford 2003). These effigy beads are interpreted to be fetishes (Connaway 1977:118–129). Fetishes are powerful objects and are connected with ritual and magic. This ties in with the mounds and mound groups, which are most likely constructed for ritual purposes. I have noted the importance of effigy bifaces in dance ritual in Middle Archaic, Mississippian, and contemporary Creek groups (Brookes 1997:55–70).

Discussion and Conclusions

In conclusion, if our vision of the Hypsithermal as an episode of climatic disruption is valid, we would expect to see an amelioration of these effects beginning in the Late Archaic period. While Fort Payne chert is the finest raw material available in the state of Mississippi, it was used extensively only during the Middle Archaic. After 3000 B.C., this material is almost never used. The same phenomenon holds true for the sandstones and quartzites of coastal Mississippi. While they are very poor as pertains to flaking quality, they were extensively used during the Middle Archaic. After this period, utilization of both these materials drops to less than 5 percent. There is continued use of Tallahatta Quartzite, but in a greatly reduced quantity.

According to Pielou (1991:269–290), after 3000 B.C. the climate began to cool and rainfall increased. This would have served to increase stream velocity and discharge, once again exposing the gravel bars. Johnson and Brookes (1988:53–63) noted a drop-off in the use of Fort Payne chert in the Late Archaic but were unable to explain it. The drop-off is not so much a factor of leaving an available source of quality chert, but of returning to a preferred (and more convenient, if lesser quality) source, the stream gravel. The exchange networks disappeared, and almost no raw material was exchanged for a period of 1,500 years. In addition, settlement patterns shift back to pre-Hypsithermal disruption locales (Reams 1995:83; Sparks 1987:50). Unifacial end scrapers, however, are still lacking in Late Archaic assemblages. Although the climate was cooler, the conditions were nowhere near those of the Late Pleistocene. In fact, in Mississippi end scrapers do not reappear until the Little Ice Age, post A.D. 1400, when they were likely related to the deerskin trade with Europeans.

So, in summation, one sees a number of interesting phenomena coincident with the Hypsithermal event in Mississippi and the Midsouth. Exchange networks moving ideotechnic artifacts, an otherwise inexplicable shift to heretofore unexploited lithic resources, site settlement shifts to areas previously avoided, mound and earthwork construction, and the suggestion of craft specialists all appear at this time. During the thermal maximum of 5000–4000 B.C. this behavior reaches its maximum intensity. With the end of the Hypsithermal at 3000 B.C., all these behaviors either disappear or revert to their previous states. After an absence of 1,300 years some begin to appear again. It is entirely possible that all of this is fortuitous. We think not, however. It is our opinion that the rise of cultural complexity in the Southeast was a long process that began with the "great warmth" and intensified as the Hypsithermal intensified. Cultural complexity arose as a response to a world that was rapidly changing and to ensure their survival, people changed with it. As is most always true when dealing with the unknown, ritual and religion move to the forefront. We feel there is a certain grain of truth in the old maxim, "There are no atheists in foxholes." Faced with a changing environment and ecosystem, the likes of which are totally foreign to us, people did what they felt they had to do to survive, and this involved much more than changing hunting techniques and strategies.

We suggest that the Late Pleistocene was a time of successful expansion of prehistoric people into the Land of Plenty. However, the great warmth of the Hypsithermal period that followed was a time of intense stress. The people who had prospered during the Ice Age found themselves in a changing world that required profound changes in the structure of their societies.

CHAPTER 5

Sam Brookes and Prehistoric Effigy Beads of the Southeast

Jessica Crawford

Introduction

In 1875, William T. Hutchins was plowing a field in what is now Jefferson Davis County, Mississippi, when he uncovered a cache of 469 stone bead blanks and preforms. One of these preforms appears to be that of an effigy bead, and a few look like they eventually would have become some kind of effigy, while the majority are tubular bead preforms and drilled pebbles or pendants. The cache (Figure 5.1) was obtained by J. T. R. Keenan and was donated to the Smithsonian Institution in 1876. It is now known as the Keenan Cache (Connaway 1977:116, 1981:57–58; Rau 1878:293–298). Archaeologist Charles Rau (1878) described the cache in the *Smithsonian Institution Annual Report for 1877*. The Keenan Cache is notable for various reasons: (1) it is the earliest known discovery of stone zoomorphic effigy beads; (2) it is the subject of the first article to address such beads and to suggest that they indicated a degree of prehistoric craft specialization; and (3) the cache contains one of the two known effigy bead preforms and scores of tubular beads in various stages of manufacture.

The Keenan Cache was again mentioned by R. B. Fulton (1898) in a paper about jasper ornaments. In this paper he also described the Fulton Cache (22LI500) (Figure 5.2), which contains 17 finished beads, 8 of which are effigy beads, 7 of which are tubular beads of varying lengths, and 2 of which are "doughnut" shaped. Fulton subsequently donated the cache to the Smithsonian.

In 1885 in Lafayette County, Arkansas, Oscar Lee was digging in a mound on Bodcau Creek when he found a large, yellowish-red effigy bead (Webb 1971a:39). This bead is now in the Gilcrease Museum in Tulsa, Oklahoma, in the Harry J. Lemley Collection (notation R21 on file, Gilcrease Museum).

Jessica Crawford

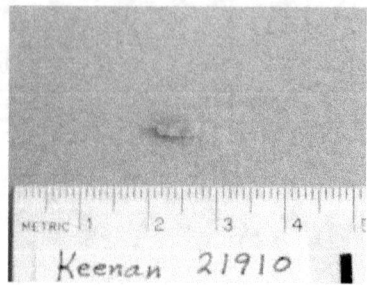
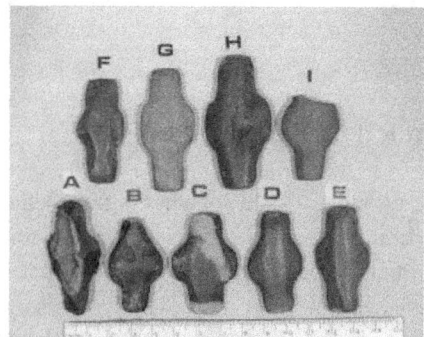

Figure 5.1. Portions of the Keenan Cache. Top (*left to right*): effigy preform, stone drill bit found lodged inside a tubular preform. Bottom (*left to right*): polished, undrilled preforms, a flaked preform. Photo by John Connaway, Mississippi Department of Archives and History.

Figure 5.2. Fulton Cache. Photo by John Connaway, Mississippi Department of Archives and History.

Since the discoveries of the Keenan Cache, the Fulton Cache, and the Lemley Bead, over 100 additional beads with many of the same stylistic characteristics have been found, selected examples of which are discussed below.

By the 1960s, the Late Archaic-period Poverty Point site (16WC5) near Epps, Louisiana, had yielded two zoomorphic beads: the Bertha Hale Bead and another bead now at the Gilcrease Museum in Tulsa, Oklahoma. Both are made of jasper, and though the Gilcrease specimen was broken, each bead was longitudinally drilled and had a "disc" in raised relief on each side. Clarence Webb (1968:315) noted the existence of similar beads in Mississippi, Alabama, and Arkansas, and in an article discussing the extent of the Poverty Point culture he illustrated six zoomorphic beads from Louisiana, Mississippi, and Arkansas. The beads appeared to fit perfectly within the extraordinary lapidary industry for which Poverty Point was then becoming so well known. Haag and Ford concurred when, in 1967, they found a zoomorphic bead while conducting salvage excavations at the Monte Sano Mound (16EBR17) in East Baton Rouge Parish, Louisiana (R. Saunders 1994:121) (see further discussion below).

When Webb (1971b) published another article dealing more specifically with zoomorphic beads and their apparent resemblance to locusts, grasshoppers, and cicadas, he unintentionally sealed their fate to become a generally accepted Poverty Point diagnostic. Subsequent articles describing or reporting discoveries of zoomorphic effigy beads have often referred to them as Poverty Point Locust Beads (see McCrocklin 1992; Moore 1999; Schambach and Newell 1990; Smith and McNutt 1990).

Not long after Webb published his 1968 *American Antiquity* article, amateur archaeologists informed Samuel O. McGahey and John M. Connaway, with the Mississippi Department of Archives and History, that a site in the northern Yazoo Basin was being land leveled (Connaway 1977:1). This site, the Denton Site (22QU522), was originally recorded by Phillips et al. (1951:54), who described it as a site with two mounds and a village area but who made no mention of any beads.

It was at Denton, in the early 1970s, that a young and enthusiastic Sam Brookes encountered his first effigy bead. By the time Connaway and McGahey began their excavations at Denton, the three archaeologists and surface collectors had found several zoomorphic effigy beads there. Connaway, McGahey, and Brookes's work at Denton resulted in the discovery of an extensive lapidary industry. The publication of Connaway's site report, with contributions from McGahey, established Denton as the site that has yielded more zoomorphic effigy beads (e.g., Figure 5.3) than any other, a distinction that remains to this date. At least 19 complete effigy beads (including 2 that were broken and reground) and many portions of broken effigy beads have been found at Denton.

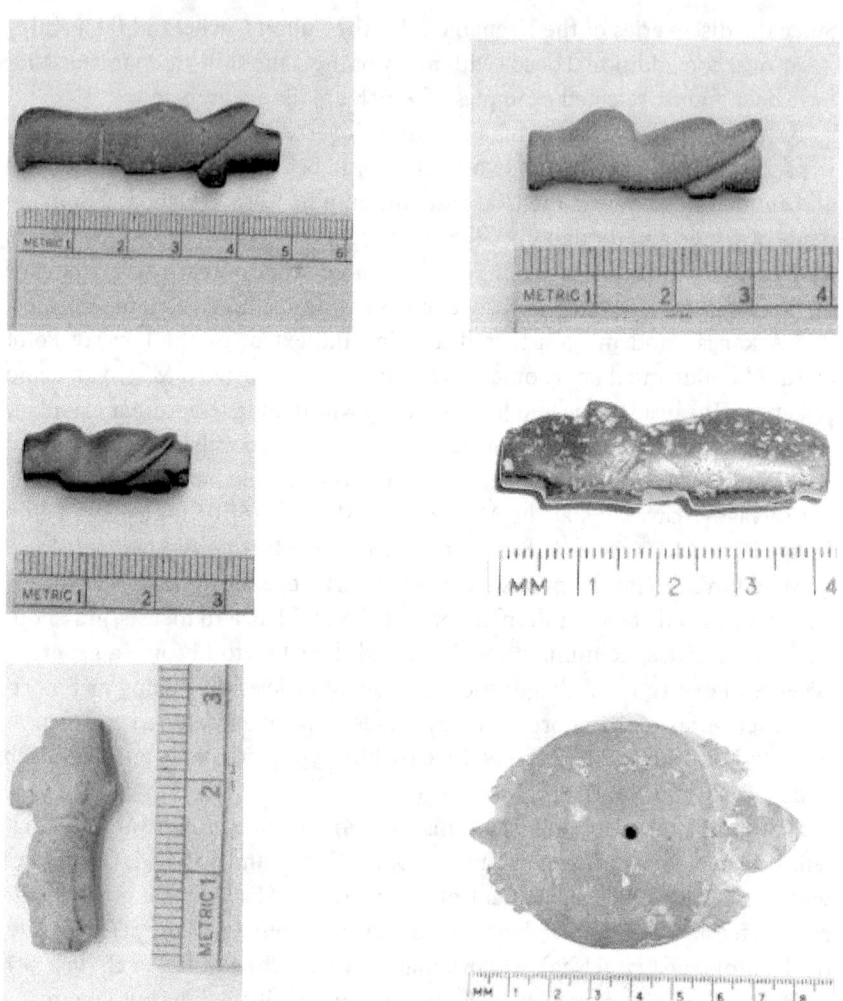

Figure 5.3. Zoomorphic beads and stone turtle from the Denton site (22QU522). Photo courtesy Jessica Crawford.

With assistance from Brookes, John Connaway (1977, 1981) borrowed and analyzed the aforementioned Keenan and Fulton Caches. He also recorded the Captain John Grant effigy bead and tubular beads that were found on the Mississippi Gulf Coast and donated to the Peabody Museum in the late 1800s. Data collected by Connaway in the years since his work at Denton, in the form of recorded formal and stylistic characteristics, photographs, and drawings, are archived at the Mississippi Department of Archives and History Archaeological Survey office in Clarksdale. Connaway's *The Denton Site* (1977) is the most extensive work to date on effigy beads.

Bead Descriptions and Temporal Placement

Since his first visit to the Denton site, Sam Brookes has spent his career contemplating the temporal placement, manufacture, distribution, and meaning of these enigmatic artifacts (e.g., 1997, 1999b, 2004; Brookes and Twaroski, this volume). With only approximately 150 effigy beads known, they are fairly rare artifacts, and their distribution appears to be limited to five southeastern states: Arkansas, Louisiana, Mississippi, Tennessee, and Alabama. The distribution area may expand, however, as two additional beads, one from Oklahoma and one from Texas, have been reported (Crawford 2003:77).

According to measurements taken of 113 effigy beads, the mean length is 37.2 mm and the mean lateral thickness is 16.9 mm. One of the most extraordinary aspects of these beads is the laterally drilled holes. Of 113 beads, the mean diameter of the perforations was 2.25 mm, with a standard deviation of .5 mm (Crawford 2003:72).

In his report on the Denton specimens, Connaway (1977:100–109) described several stylistic elements that occurred on the dorsal, ventral, posterior, anterior, and lateral sides of the beads. The common motifs serve as "stylistic diagnostics" that, as Webb (1971b:106) put it, "integrate the entire group into one concept." The motifs consist of different elements that appear to represent beaks, ears, wings, eyes, legs, feet, and other, unidentifiable, characteristics, such as what is descriptively referred to as a "hump" or "raised tab" (Connaway 1977:100; Crawford 2003:22–33).

As Connaway (1977:100) noted, some beads do bear a morphological likeness to locusts, grasshoppers, or cicadas; but other beads suggest mammals or birds. Visual clues that might reveal what kind of mammal or bird is depicted are often lacking. A number of beads are not recognizable as either mammal or bird. These beads may represent "composite elements of multiple animals" (Power 1999:55) and could represent some type of supernatural being. They are referred to as "composite" creatures—those possessing characteristics of more than one animal and inhabiting other worlds—similar to the winged or plumed serpents, water panthers, or cat monsters featured on ceramics, shell, copper, and stone artifacts of much later periods. Perhaps these effigies were meant to bring together powers of two different animals, the powers of a mammal and the powers of a bird of prey. We may not recognize them, but those who held them certainly would have, and they would have known their powers, too. Brookes (personal communication 2002) uses the example of a dragon: we may not have seen one, but we know what they look like and we know their powers.

Undoubtedly, several of the beads that Webb (1971b) illustrated resemble locusts or grasshoppers, just as several specimens from the Denton site resemble birds, with two appearing to be owls. Brookes has suggested that the owl forms have small "humps" on the back of the head that represent an eye or the owl's ability to turn its head almost completely around (see Brookes 2004).

Brookes recently described two beads he believes represent an Archaic moth or butterfly motif. One of them, the Swindle bead, was a surface find in a field in Monroe County, Mississippi. Twenty-seven tubular beads were also found nearby. Eight of the 27 beads are made of heat-treated chert, 18 are made of a greenish-colored stone called trachyte, and one is made of green-banded slate. The Swindle effigy bead is made of trachyte and is roughly rectangular, with six lateral grooves and one longitudinal groove that cuts across the first three lateral grooves, giving it the appearance of a caterpillar (Brookes 2010; McClung 2003). The other bead is the Heitzman bead, which was found at the Claiborne site in Hancock County, Mississippi. It resembles an insect in its larval form, resting upon a base or platform through which the hole is drilled. Although they are hard to see, it has two defined legs and engraved lines suggesting a segmented abdomen. It also is made of trachyte (Brookes 2010; McClung 2003).

Brookes asserts that trachyte was purposely chosen because the light green color closely resembles the color of the larval forms of many insects, especially the tobacco and tomato hornworms. Just as they recognized the ability of some creatures to inhabit land and water, or sky and land, or all three, prehistoric Native Americans presumably would have noticed the metamorphosis of insects. The transformation from caterpillar to moth or butterfly is a source of wonder to us today, and it stands to reason that this was true in the Middle Archaic period as well. An unattractive creature transforming into a beautiful brightly colored creature with the ability to fly is indeed miraculous (Brookes 2010).

Brookes has argued that the Scales effigy pendant from Oktibbeha County in Mississippi represents a kingfisher and hypothesizes continuity between Middle Archaic-period and Historic Indians. His argument is that the Scales pendant hangs upside down because it was used as a fetish to remove evil spirits. Cherokee priests used Kingfisher effigies hung round their neck to swoop down and pluck out evil spirits. Hanging it around the neck was a convenient way to keep the fetish handy until it was needed. It was not adornment in the usual sense, so how it hung was not important. Kingfishers fly, dive in water to catch fish, and burrow into cutbanks of streams to make nests; hence they are creatures of upper, middle and lower worlds (Brookes, personal communication 2002).

Brookes (personal communication 2002) recognized the common motifs on effigy beads, as well as the fact that there appear to be two distinct styles, or macroforms, depending on the overall shape of the bead and the motifs used to represent elements like eyes, beaks, heads, wings, etc. The two styles are referred to as the Fulton and Denton styles, so named for the sites on which they were first found. The Denton beads are more rounded, with the horizontal axis exhibiting a rounded, almost tubular cross section (Brookes, personal communication 2002; Crawford 2003:44–49). The Fulton and Carpenter beads are more flat and block-like, with a rectangular cross section. For instance, Denton-style beads generally have "pinched heads," and eyes, if represented, are depicted with engraved spirals or circles as opposed to a raised disc as occurs on the Fulton-style beads. Thus far, no pattern has emerged in the distribution of the two styles, as both Fulton and Denton style beads occur on the same sites, as well as throughout the effigy bead distribution area (Crawford 2003).

Clarence Webb's "Poverty Point Locust Bead" designation for effigy beads has enjoyed tremendous staying power. This is in spite of the fact that, in the same article in which he explained his "Locust" theory, Webb (1971b:113) noted that he was unaware of any "cultural unity" among the sites that produced the effigy beads. Instead, he argued that the best indication of the cultural affiliation of the beads would be found in associated artifacts in surface collections from those sites. In his discussion of the beads' possible temporal placement, he described the cultural components present at sites where effigy beads were found. As noted above, two beads are from the Late Archaic-period Poverty Point site, at which he understandably considered Poverty Point to be the principal component. The remaining five sites he described as having strong Archaic components (Webb 1971b:113). These are the Monte Sano site (Louisiana-16EBR17), the Johnny Ford site (Arkansas-3LA5), the Denton site, the Sinner site (Louisiana-16BO1), and Seven Mile Island (Alabama-1LU11). According to Webb (1971b:113), what all five sites have in common is a major Late Archaic occupation. While Late Archaic occupations are indeed present, the major component represented at each of these sites, with the exception of the Johnny Ford site, is in fact Middle Archaic. The bead Webb associated with the Late Archaic/Early Fourche Maline Johnny Ford site actually came from a hill "several hundred meters away" overlooking the site (Frank Schambach, personal communication 2002). According to Schambach, "lots of early points" have been found on this hill.

Little is known about the Seven Mile Island site (not to be confused with the Seven Mile Island that was excavated by Webb and DeJarnette in the 1930s) in Alabama's Pickwick Basin. The two beads from that site were picked up by collectors who found them eroding from a burial containing 30 other stone beads of various tubular shapes. Jolly (1971:134) states that the burial was near a Late Archaic/Early Woodland shell midden. However, it is common for shell middens in the Tennessee River to possess heavy Middle Archaic occupations, so until the nearby shell midden has undergone extensive investigation, a Middle Archaic component cannot be ruled out (Sam Brookes, personal communication 2002).

The Sinner site is a predominantly Middle Caddoan site in the upland ridges west of Lake Bistineau in Bossier Parish, Louisiana (Ford 1936), that has earlier components as well. It is the type site for the Sinner Point, which Webb (2000:10) says occurred frequently there. He goes on to state, "This is an Archaic point, probably of the same period as Evans, with which type they overlap in technology" (Webb 2000:10). Although once believed to be a point type associated with the Poverty Point Culture, the Evans Point is now thought to be Middle Archaic in age, dating somewhere from 6000 to 4000 B.P. (4000 to 2000 B.C.) (J. Saunders et al. 1994; Schambach 1998; Schambach and Early 1982). The remaining two sites mentioned by Webb are Denton and Monte Sano, both of which have major Middle Archaic components.

Prior to their destruction in 1967, the Monte Sano Mounds in Baton Rouge, Louisiana, were investigated by Haag and Ford. Excavations of Mound A, which was approximately 5 m high, revealed a rectangular pattern of postmolds beneath the mound. The initial stage of mound construction was a small, truncated mound about a half a meter high. According to Haag's notes, on top of the truncated mound were two small domes containing the remains of two cremations (R. Saunders 1994:121). Radiocarbon samples of the two features returned calibrated median ages of 6985 and 7450 B.P. (2 sigma) (McGimsey and van der Koogh 2001:23). Mound construction appeared to be completed in one fill episode. Excavations of Mound A also revealed an effigy bead, two tubular beads, and one large biface said to have come from near the top of the mound (R. Saunders 1994:121).

The concept expressed in the oversized biface may be related to that expressed in the caches of oversized bifaces often found on Middle Archaic-period Benton sites (Brookes 1997; Johnson and Brookes 1989). Haag's notes just say the beads were found during excavation of the mound, as was a large, well-made flint blade (R. Saunders 1994:121). It is unclear if the beads were found near the top of the mound with the biface. Therefore we cannot firmly link the zoomorphic bead with the radiocarbon date from the cremations, since the bead appears to have been in the final fill episode and not with the cremation. The effigy bead was likely placed in the mound sometime after 6985 B.P. The surface collection from around the mound also yielded Middle Archaic points (John Connaway and Sam Brookes, personal communication 2002). Although not definitive, it seems likely that the effigy bead has a Middle Archaic affiliation; exactly when during the Middle Archaic is unknown.

Another professionally excavated effigy bead is the Walnut site bead. Excavated in 1980, Walnut (22IT539), in Itawamba County, Mississippi, was a multicomponent site containing deposits ranging from Early Archaic to the present. The major component was represented by a stratified early to late-Middle Archaic midden (Bense 1983). Middle Archaic cultural markers included Eva-Morrow Mountain, Sykes-White Springs, and Benton points (Bense 1983:11). Several burials were uncovered in the midden, most of which Bense (1983:8) believed originated in the Middle Archaic Eva-Morrow Mountain zone. However, she also states that their cultural affiliation was not firmly established, and that the cemetery areas also could be affiliated with the Sykes-White Springs/Benton occupation (Bense 1983:13). An effigy bead, a tubular bead, and a discoidal bead were found with a cremation.

According to radiocarbon dates, what Bense (1983:14) terms the Sykes-White Springs occupation at Walnut occurred between 6500 and 5000 B.P. and evolved into the Benton occupation which occurred between 5800 and 5000 B.P.; the date for the burial with which the effigy bead is associated is somewhere between 6500 and 5000 B.P. (Bense 1983:14). Stylistically, this specimen is not the best example of an effigy bead. It shares some characteristics with other examples: the rounded tab with notches, or grooves, somewhat resembles a couple of other specimens, including one from Mississippi known as the Irby bead, which was found at a site (22PA592) that also had Cypress Creek points in the surface collection (Connaway 1987). However, the fact that it is obviously an effigy is significant. Perhaps this bead is associated with the earlier Middle Archaic occupation and is an early example of an effigy bead, or perhaps it is one that, in light of the current database, is simply not quite like other examples. Not enough is known about effigy beads to say how long they were made. They could have been made over a long period of time, like a thousand years, or they may have been produced in a brief period of time. Effigy beads seem to be so rare that it seems most likely that they were produced and used during a limited time by a limited number of people.

The aforementioned Denton site in Mississippi also offers some of the strongest indication that effigy beads were made and used by Middle Archaic people. The artifacts from Denton make up an extraordinary assemblage with no counterpart anywhere in the Southeast. In addition to the plethora of effigy beads, a stone turtle made of trachyte, bannerstones, stone tubes, and oversized bifaces have also been found at Denton (Connaway 1981). Denton is also the type site for Denton and Opossum Bayou points, which occur in abundance at the site (Connaway 1977; McGahey 2000).

Most of the beads from Denton were found on the surface of the southernmost mound or "rise." Coring of the rise indicated that it may be the remnant of a Middle Archaic mound (John Connaway, personal communication 2002), although as Peacock and Rafferty (2013) note, this possibility should not be treated as a certainty, as many researchers have done. The Denton midden yielded median calibrated radiocarbon dates of 5815 and 5975 B.P. (McGahey 2000). A Denton point was excavated from the midden and a radiocarbon date was obtained from an organic sample slightly above the point. A disc bead and a drilled pendant were also found in the dated midden (Connaway 1977:28; McGahey 2000:132). An Opossum Bayou point was excavated from the Longstreet Site (22QU523) a few miles south of Denton. Longstreet had tubular beads and projectile points like those from Denton. The excavated Opossum Bayou point was near a charcoal sample that produced two calibrated radiocarbon dates of 5602 B.P. and 5732 cal. B.P. (2 sigma) (McGahey 2000). Thus, the Denton and Opossum Bayou point types are securely linked to the Middle Archaic, most likely having been in use from approximately 5970 to 5600 B.P.

Although the Denton effigy beads were surface finds, Connaway (1977) believes them to be associated with the same substantial late Middle Archaic component responsible for the Denton and Opossum Bayou points. There really is no other component that could be responsible for the beads and other unusual artifacts, and Clarence Webb (1971b) agreed (see also Sassaman 2010:120–123). In the Denton site report, Connaway (1977:118) cites four reasons for Webb's belief that the effigy beads were the result of the late Middle Archaic occupation. First, in spite of the fact that effigy beads were surface finds, there is excavated evidence of bead and pendant manufacture at the site, as pebble pendants and disc-style beads were stratigraphically associated with the dated midden. Second, the odds favor a major industry, with one or more classes of artifacts found all over the site, being associated with one major period of occupation. Third, there is no distinct Poverty Point occupation, which would represent the second period of intensive polished stone ornament manufacture at Denton. Fourth, zoomorphic beads are now known to occur elsewhere on pre-Poverty Point Middle Archaic and non-Poverty Point Late Archaic sites. Even without producing an effigy bead in situ, the Denton site thus makes a convincing argument for a Middle Archaic origin for effigy beads. As Webb (1971b) intimated, if any site holds the key to some of the mysteries surrounding effigy beads, Denton is probably it.

Surface collections from the Lower Jackson Mound (16WC10), near the Poverty Point site in Louisiana and once believed to date to the Poverty Point period, contain many Middle Archaic Evans points as well as a red jasper effigy bead. That mound has now been shown to predate the Poverty Point site. Charcoal samples taken from beneath Lower Jackson Mound have been dated to 3955 B.C. to 3655 B.C. (two-sigma calibrated range) (J. Saunders et al.:2001).

Ultimately, the only way to determine a precise chronological placement for effigy beads is to excavate them from undisturbed context. Monte Sano and Walnut are the only examples we have to date in this regard, and there are problems with both beads. Based on the evidence we have and his years of experience, Sam Brookes firmly believes these beads are middle to late Middle Archaic, contemporaneous with the Benton and Denton groups (see also discussion by Hadley and Carr, this volume). The dates from the midden at Denton, 5815 and 5975 cal. B.P. (McGahey 2000:132), and the Benton occupation at the Walnut site, which Bense (1983:14) estimated to date between 5800 and 5000 B.P., may indicate that the Benton and Denton cultures were contemporaneous with the effigy beads. Evidence at Denton certainly suggests contact between the two areas, and the distribution of effigy beads themselves indicates interregional contact. However, the Sykes-White Springs occupation at the Walnut site, which may be the one associated with the Walnut effigy bead, was estimated to date between approximately 6500 to 5000 B.P. (Bense 1983:14). Although this time frame overlaps with the Benton occupation at Walnut, it is somewhat close to the early Middle Archaic dates from the two features from the earliest stages of the Monte Sano Mound. Again, these dates were 6985 and 7450 B.P. (McGimsey and van der Koogh 2001:23). So, were the beads early Middle Archaic or late Middle Archaic? Of course, these are only our arbitrary terms. Early and late Middle Archaic would have meant nothing to prehistoric Native Americans.

Spatial Distributions

Effigy beads are fairly concentrated in several clusters (Figure 5.4) that resemble the distribution of known Middle Archaic sites in the Midsouth. Only beads with known site provenience were used for the distribution map and the site locations were obtained from the state site files. The largest number of Middle Archaic sites occur in major river drainages, with fewer Middle Archaic sites in the counties and parishes along the Mississippi River. Denton is one of the few Middle Archaic sites in the Yazoo Basin. This may reflect "low populations or, alternatively, a masking of the original mid-Holocene archaeological record by erosional and depositional factors associated with the movements of the Mississippi" (Anderson 1996:164). Anderson suggests that the Middle Archaic site clusters were "maintained territorial centers of individual groups," with the voids between them having been "buffer zones" (1996:164). The areas with greater resources are the areas where site density is greatest, and therefore display "the highest levels of sociopolitical complexity" (Anderson 1996:176) in Middle Archaic times. "Evidence for group participation in long-distance exchange, indications for at least occasional if not endemic warfare, and mortuary data suggesting the emergence of appreciable differences

Figure 5.4. Distribution of sites with stone effigy beads.

in individual achieved status are all apparent" (Anderson 1996:164). Archaic people obviously were interacting with and influencing each other. It is here, in what Anderson (1996:176) calls a "varied cultural landscape, characterized by a range of adaptations," that the previously described zoomorphic elements were first represented in stone beads.

Function

Connaway (1977) discussed three possibilities for the use of effigy beads: fetishes, totems, or simple artistic adornments that were "worn for personal pleasure." He saw the fetish theory as the most likely explanation, citing Hodge's (1907) description of the fetish among the American Indian: "in any specific case the distinctive function and sphere of action of the fetish depends largely on the nature of the object which is supposed to contain it" (Hodge 1907:456, in Connaway 1977:123). "The Pueblo tribes have numerous war and hunting fetishes of stone, small figurines cut to resemble various predatory animals .... The protective amulet sometimes took the form of a small figurine of a bird or other animal swift in flight, as the hawk; silent in movement, as the owl; or expert in dodging, as the dragonfly" (Hodge 1907:458, quoted in Connaway 1977:124). As Connaway (1977:125) points out, the animals apparently represented in effigy beads "could easily impart the idea of hunting prowess, which was undoubtedly of great importance to the individual in Middle and Late Archaic times." Another potential insight into effigy bead use is the fact that fetishes were often used by shamans (Connaway 1977:125).

Were shamans or individuals believed to possess spiritual powers as the makers and/or bearers of effigy beads? Spielmann (2002:200) states:

> A number of anthropologists have discussed the ways in which the capacity to transform mundane raw materials into aesthetically pleasing objects is an expression of supernaturally endowed abilities. Because skilled crafting expresses the capacity of the craftsperson to materialize the cosmologically distant, some degree of ritual knowledge may be an important prerequisite to becoming a craft specialist.

Spielmann (2002:200) also notes Gell's (1992) argument that "the technical skills that radically transform mundane elements can create enchanted forms."

It is unlikely the effigy beads represented a set of shared beliefs or religion. However, Morphy (1989) suggests that shininess or brilliance "manifests spiritual power cross-culturally" (Spielmann 2002:200). Effigy beads were probably valued as both sacred and secular objects, as well as objects of power and prestige. The beads may have meant different things depending on who possessed them. Those who made and distributed them might have attached a specific meaning to them, but once the bead traveled hundreds of miles from the maker, it may have changed meaning, although it probably retained its sacredness or power. Gibson's (2001:150) theory concerning the Poverty Point owls seems plausible:

> Owl pendants were not identical but were technically and stylistically similar enough to suggest that the few people who made them all knew the stories behind them. Did that mean they all came from Poverty Point or the Poverty Point area? Probably. Did it mean that they all carried the same message, that they worked the same magic on peoples from Louisiana to Florida? Possibly, if they remained in the same hands that carried them that far; possibly not if they changed hands. I simply cannot imagine a generalized, multicultural owl

symbolism producing such similar items across so large an area, even if it did come down from one ancient mother tongue and a singular worldview.

Of possible significance here is the fact that owls have retained their importance to Native Americans throughout history. Obviously, they inspired the makers of Middle Archaic effigy beads and the Poverty Point people (Sassaman 2010). They are depicted in pottery of much later cultures and are a creature both revered and feared by many historic Southeastern tribes (Brookes 2004).

Power (1999:56) suggests that what is omitted from the representation of an animal is as significant as what is included. "As such, the Archaic effigy beads are stylized; purposefully presented with only essential characteristics or signature elements as defining features" (Power 1999:56). The Fulton B bead may be a deer; if so, the wings and eyes may be emphasizing the deer's speed and the exaggerated eye represents its vision. Or, if it is a combination of animals, it is simply a creature with great speed and excellent vision. Even if the bead was used in different ways as it traveled across the distribution area, all those in possession of such artifacts likely appreciated the fact that it symbolized an animal with great speed and eyesight.

Another mystery is whether the beads changed hands, or whether their distributions were simply the result of the effigy bead producer's/owner's distribution network. Perhaps the most feasible explanation is the former. Effigy beads presumably had sacredness attached to them, but they may have had a secular, functional aspect as well (see also Hadley and Carr, this volume). The distribution of effigy beads may represent the archaeological manifestation of a social network and probably an exchange network as well. If effigy beads were not transported by their original holders, then they were probably exchanged by them for something we have not yet identified or that no longer exists in the archaeological record. Several Middle Archaic interaction/exchange networks are well documented (e.g., Jefferies 1996; Johnson and Brookes 1989; Sassaman 1996). Jefferies (1996:224) suggests that these networks functioned as more than just opportunities to acquire nonlocal resources. They were "risk-averting mechanisms that could be operationalized in times of economic or social stress" (Jefferies 1996:223). These mechanisms, such as feasting and exchange, ensured friendly contact between groups in different areas with different resources (Jefferies 1996:223). Jefferies (1996:225) lists four expectations regarding the establishment of Archaic hunter-gatherer exchange networks:

> First, evidence of social integration and exchange will increase as the risks associated with environmental unpredictability and stress rise. Second, greater social

integration will be reflected by increased evidence for exchange and more stylistic similarity of certain items among interacting groups. Third, groups participating in a risk-reducing network will be distributed over sufficiently diverse habitats to avoid the same shortfall impacting all network participants. Fourth, the geographical extent of the network will be reflected by the distribution of stylistically similar artifacts.

An effigy bead exchange network could fulfill each prediction. The environmental changes brought about by the Hypsithermal, coupled with population increases and decreased mobility, may have resulted in the establishment of "group territories," which would certainly have resulted in environmental and social stress. The stylistic similarity of effigy beads, especially among the beads within the Fulton and Denton styles, could indicate an increase in integration and exchange between or among groups. The effigy bead distribution area certainly covers a variety of habitats, yet each cluster is in a major riverine environment, which conforms to the previously described Middle Archaic settlement patterns. Finally, although it is geographically larger than other Archaic exchange/interaction networks, the extent of effigy bead distribution does not exceed the area one would expect seasonally mobile hunter-gatherers who are interacting with other groups to cover (presuming that the groups in question were not sedentary—see Peacock and Rafferty 2013 and selected references therein for an alternative viewpoint regarding areas where Archaic mounds are found).

Though they are somewhat rare, effigy beads are found at all types of sites. They are found at Louisiana Archaic mound sites such as Stelly (16SL1) and Monte Sano and at campsites with very little depth. They occur at sites that have considerable midden accumulation and at small sites with little evidence of occupation; sites that are hardly "sites" at all. Some of the sites where effigy beads are found, such as Monte Sano and Stelly, may have had a sacred or "ceremonial" significance that could explain the presence of effigy beads. Others may have been places of meeting and exchange, such as Denton. Still others, such as Loosa Yokena (22WR691), near Vicksburg, Mississippi, with its large assemblage of micro-drills, tubular preforms, and two finished effigies (McGahey 2005), could be places of manufacture (see also Hadley and Carr, this volume). However, the majority of effigy bead sites do not show evidence of long-term occupation. Perhaps beads are found on these sites because someone important enough to have them died while there. We know from the two effigy beads and 30 tubular beads that were found with the burial on Seven Mile Island and the Walnut site that they were sometimes, at least, buried with people.

Conclusions

Stone effigy beads are a relatively rare but impressive artifact type likely dating primarily to the Middle Archaic period. Many questions remain to be answered about these intriguing artifacts. What is indisputable is the impressive skill and time required to manufacture effigy beads, from the drilling of the center perforation to the shaping and intricate carving and engraving exhibited on several examples. As is often the case in archaeology, their existence raises more questions than it answers. Perhaps Sam Brookes himself put it best when he said to me, "We can never know for sure. We've been wrong before. But isn't it great fun to speculate?"

CHAPTER 6

Archaic Chert Beads and Craft Specialization: Application of an Organization of Technology Model

Alison M. Hadley and Philip J. Carr

Introduction

Lithic (stone artifacts and waste products) analysis in the southeastern United States tends to focus on descriptions of form, distribution, and raw material. These limited observations lead to considerations of simple patterns related to raw material procurement, manufacture techniques/stages, and mobility. Issues rarely addressed include bias in recovery methods, maintainability or reliability of tool design, and craft specialization. In this chapter, we take ideas and inferences proposed by Sam Brookes as inspiration when considering the lithic assemblage from the John Forrest site (22CB623) in Claiborne County, Mississippi. Brookes (1997, 1999b, 2004; Johnson and Brookes 1989) has conducted extensive research into Middle Archaic-period materials of the western Southeast and has made a case for craft specialization during this time based in part on the production of beads (see also Brookes, this volume; Crawford, this volume). Other researchers differ in interpretations of evidence regarding, for example, the presence/absence of craft specialists and/or characterization of specialists. For the John Forrest assemblage, we use an organization of technology model to investigate the production of lapidary items. Expansion of this model from previous applications is accomplished through a consideration of craft specialization as a socioeconomic strategy with the addition of ideology. Finally, conclusions are drawn regarding whether specialists crafted chert beads and other stone artifacts during the Middle Archaic period.

The John Forrest site dates to the Middle Archaic period based on diagnostic hafted bifaces. Interest in this time period has dramatically increased over the last few decades, especially as evidenced by coverage in edited volumes (e.g., Anderson and Sassaman 1996; Emerson et al. 2009; Gibson and

Carr 2004). In the Lower Mississippi Valley, or LMV, this interest was sparked by the discovery that many of the earthen mounds predate the Late Archaic period Poverty Point site (16WC5), once believed to represent the earliest intentional mound construction in North America (Russo 1994; J. Saunders et al. 1994, 2005; R. Saunders 1994). Additionally, studies of rare artifact types, including stone beads at both mound and non-mound Middle Archaic sites (Crawford 2003, this volume; Hadley 2003; Johnson 2000; McGahey 2005), oversize bifaces (Brookes 2004; Johnson and Brookes 1989), fired earthen objects (J. Saunders et al. 1998; see also Hays et al., this volume), and well-made ground stone objects (Johnson 2000) persist. These investigations have generated an increasing number of hypotheses regarding the lifeways of Middle Archaic peoples. For example, while Joe Saunders (2004) sees no evidence for social inequality at three Middle Archaic mound sites other than the mounds themselves, others interpret the data to indicate the formation of unilineal kin groups (Widmer 2004) and tribes (Anderson 2004). Clearly, economic, social, and/or religious changes were occurring in the LMV during this time relative to what is known about the archaeology of the Early Archaic period. Craft specialization has long been considered by some researchers (e.g., Clark and Parry 1990; Price and Brown 1985) to have a close correlation with increasing cultural complexity, and we suggest that chert bead manufacture has economic, social, and religious implications.

Research in Mississippi and Louisiana has revealed Middle Archaic sites with assemblages generally similar to John Forrest with respect to beads, and these assemblages are influential in shaping the current debate regarding craft specialists. Loosa Yokena (22WR691), Watson Brake (16OU175), and the Keenan Cache are three such examples (Figure 6.1). In fact, McGahey (2005:16) describes the John Forrest lithic assemblage "as virtually identical to Loosa Yokena as far as the lapidary industry is concerned and [it] in fact may represent the activities of a single group of lapidarians who moved from one of the sites to the other, perhaps because of a river channel change." Loosa Yokena is a non-mound site in Warren County, Mississippi. Watson Brake, in Louisiana, is a mound site where analysis of the chipped chert beads resulted in defined production stages (Johnson 2000) used for the analysis of the John Forrest assemblage. The Keenan Cache is a collection of 469 stone objects found by a farmer in Jefferson Davis County, Mississippi, in 1876 (Connaway 1981; Crawford, this volume). The collection contains an array of bead preforms and tubular and zoomorphic beads comparable to those from Middle Archaic contexts. Previous considerations of chert bead assemblages (Connaway 1981; Crawford 2003; Johnson 2000; McGahey 2005), while insightful, have not followed an organization of technology model to examine systematically how this technology was organized.

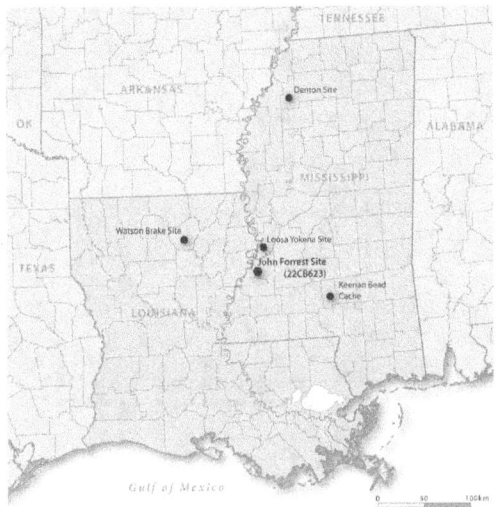

Figure 6.1. Middle Archaic sites discussed in the text.

Theoretical Considerations

Our approach has its roots in the ethnoarchaeological work of Lewis Binford. Viewing material culture within a living cultural system afforded Binford a unique perspective (e.g., Binford 1962), which eventually led to the development of an organization of technology framework. Binford and Binford (1968:2) observed that, "Since artifacts are cultural data and since they once functioned as elements of a cultural system, many of the explanations we might offer for observations made on the archaeological record will refer to organizational features of past cultural systems."

Michael Schiffer (1972:157) expanded on this, stating that to use "archaeological data to infer past activities or organization," archaeologists need a testable framework. Schiffer's proposed framework was a behavioral system in which the entire "life cycle" of an artifact was considered within its living, systemic context before entering the archaeological context. The multiple processes that make up the systemic context were defined as storage, transport, procurement, manufacture, use, maintenance, recycling, and discard (Schiffer 1972:158). An organization of technology approach incorporates the systemic context or life history framework (Bradley 1975; Collins 1975; Sheets 1975; see discussion by Carr and Bradbury 2011) in an attempt to infer social and economic strategies (Binford 1979; Carr 1994; Nelson 1991).

Margaret Nelson (1991:59) created a diagram depicting levels of analysis that Carr and Bradbury (2011) recently modified as an organization of technology model (Figure 6.2). This new model emerged from application of the

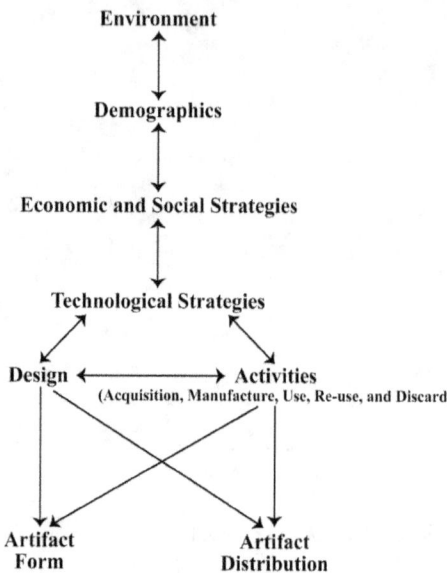

Figure 6.2. Organization of technology model developed by Carr and Bradbury (2011) originally adapted from Nelson (1991).

approach, consideration of entire lithic assemblages, and efforts to display the interaction between one level and another. As with the original diagram, the head of the model is the environment, followed by demographics, and the base is comprised of artifact form and artifact distribution. As cogently discussed by Nelson (1991), the bottom is situated in the archaeological record and the top is the most distant from that record with regard to making inferences from lithic assemblages. That is, an analyst would proceed through a number of successive inferences from artifact form and artifact distribution before making inferences concerning the environment. Past environments are reconstructed more directly through other specialties with their accompanying datasets, such as geoarchaeology, paleoethnobotany, and zooarchaeology (Carr et al. 2012). Thus, at a minimum a lithic analyst should have knowledge of environmental factors affecting raw material availability. Nonetheless, the impact of the environment on artifact form and distribution is mediated through a number of factors accounted for in the model (see counter argument by Andrefsky [1994] concerning the importance of raw material availability). That is, these are conditions managed through technological strategies when implementing social and economic strategies.

Until now, the impact of demographic factors on lithic assemblages has received little attention. While we see advantages to determining population size and other parameters through archaeological data other than lithics, demographics also impact the form and distribution of artifacts; hence these factors have a role to play in the organization of technology.

A major advantage of an organization of technology approach is the importance placed on social and economic strategies, and how technological strategy is shown as being responsive to these in a given environment. Such strategies can be highly variable, necessitating flexibility in the model. In previous organization of technology studies, assumed social and economic strategies have been derived from ethnographically documented hunter-gatherer lifeways, especially the reliance on mobility. However, "there is no evident theoretical conflict" preventing applying this approach to modeling a broad range of economic and social strategies (Carr 1994:2). For example, Cobb (2000) combines a political-economic framework and organization of technology to examine social asymmetry, interregional exchange with regard to influence by elites, and gendered labor divisions. Here, our focus is craft specialization and its specific place in the organization of technology model, as explored through an examination of chert bead manufacture in terms of whether Middle Archaic lapidarians were craft specialists. Sam Brookes (2004) and others (Connaway 1981; Hadley and Carr 2010; McGahey 2005) have suggested that craft specialists produced Middle Archaic chert beads. Other researchers disagree that specialization was necessary or is evident during this time (Johnson 2000; J. Saunders 2004). Craft specialization is one strategy with implications for the design of material culture and associated activities; these in turn influence artifact form and artifact distribution. However, defining specialization, identifying craft specialists using archaeological evidence, and incorporating craft specialization into a model of the organization of technology are not simple and straightforward tasks. The John Forrest lithic assemblage and related assemblages provide data relevant to these problems.

The John Forrest Site and Lithic Assemblage

The John Forrest site in Claiborne County, southwestern Mississippi, lies between the Mississippi River and the Natchez Trace Parkway. Bordered on the west by a steep slope to the lowlands and to the north by James Creek, the site (an area approximately 420 m north-south by 245 m east-west) is located above the floodplain on Pleistocene uplands; the present Mississippi river channel is approximately three and a half kilometers to the west. The floodplain encompasses abandoned meander belts and active and abandoned river channels; the location of the site above the floodplain has ensured its preservation. We are uncertain of the exact Middle Archaic-period location of the river, but it would have been no more than 19 km to the west of the site, based on the current size of the river valley (Aslan and Autin 1999). The soil at the John Forrest site is a Memphis silt loam (0–2 percent slope) (Lane and Cole 1963) developed on a Pleistocene-aged loess (Aslan and Autin 1999:Figure 2, p. 803). The site location allows access to a diverse range of upland and lowland resources, which we assume to have been the situation in prehistory as well. A more detailed understanding of the paleoenvironment in the vicinity of the site would aid in making and testing cultural inferences.

A significant amount of surface collection, but only minimal subsurface testing, has been conducted at the site. Historically, the land was used as a hunting camp for many years, being periodically plowed and planted with deer feed, allowing the landowner to amass a large collection of lithic artifacts (n = 3,411) and identify concentration areas within the site. Sam McGahey, of the Mississippi Department of Archives and History, introduced us to the site, leading to the only formal investigations there in a joint field school between the University of Southern Mississippi and the University of South Alabama. Shovel tests were excavated on a five-meter grid at the southern end of the site where the landowner observed concentrations of beads and bifaces. A total of 534 shovel tests and seven 1-×-1-m units were excavated with the matrix being screened through one-eighth-inch mesh hardware cloth. Artifact recovery was restricted to the plowzone, as no intact deposits were identified at the site.

The large collection of artifacts from the site has allowed us to investigate the general nature of the site assemblage despite the lack of features and datable deposits. Following the field school, the landowner provided us with access to the surface collection for a detailed analysis. The chipped stone assemblage includes 1,283 bifaces, 368 hafted bifaces, 422 cores, 99 chipped beads, and 1,169 pieces of debitage. The hafted bifaces provide the best evidence for the date of the site, with the majority identifiable to culture-historical types associated with the Middle Archaic period. The majority of the identifiable hafted bifaces are Sykes-White Springs (n = 82). Interestingly, 81 percent of the non-hafted bifaces exhibit a highly polished surface visible without the aid of a microscope. Experimentation and microwear analysis, still relatively rare in the Southeast (Franklin et al. 2012), are needed to determine the exact source for the polish. Additionally, the collection has a variety of ground stone artifacts, including 90 modified greenstone pebbles, 4 greenstone pebble beads, 21 abraders, 5 axe fragments, 1 plummet preform, 15 atlatl-weight preforms, 3 hammerstones, 1 nutting stone, and 39 other ground stone objects of unknown function. Shovel test and unit excavations recovered a large chipped stone assemblage (n = 10,971), which, unlike the landowner's collection, is unbiased by what is visible on the surface.

Table. 6.1. Middle Archaic bead manufacture assemblages.

	John Forrest Surface Collection	Loosa Yokena	Watson Brake
Blade Cores	322	0	16
Blades	397	4,173	70
Microdrills	0	159	247
Chert Beads and Bead Blanks	99	7	120

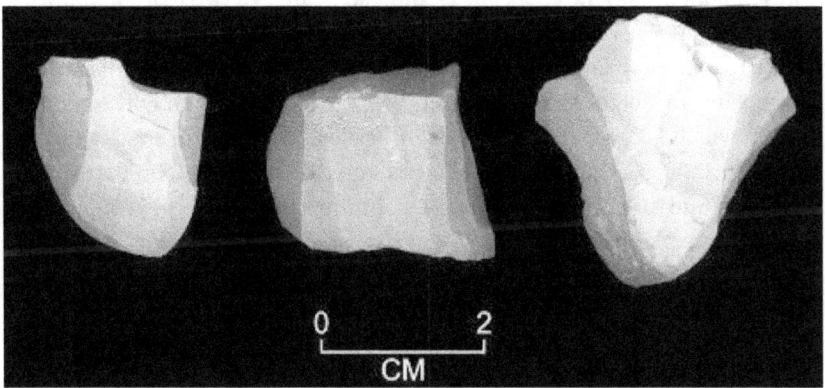

Figure 6.3. Typical blade cores in the John Forrest surface assemblage. Photo by Sarah Mattics.

These collections have been analyzed using standard methods. Artifacts were initially grouped by techno-functional categories as defined by Andrefsky (1998). A detailed analysis of each artifact was conducted, with specific attributes being defined using a combination of features noted by other researchers (e.g., Andrefsky 1998; Johnson 1979, 2000; McGahey 2000). While the John Forrest assemblage contains an interesting array of lithic artifacts (see Hadley 2003), we focus here on those associated with bead manufacture for comparison with Watson Brake, Loosa Yokena, and the Keenan Cache (Table 6.1).

Debitage totals 1,169 pieces from the surface collection and 10,867 flakes from shovel-test and unit excavations. The surface-collected debitage was not studied in depth due to collector bias; analysis of the surface collection only involved separating blades (n = 397) from nonblades (n = 772). By comparison, 4,173 blades were found at Loosa Yokena (McGahey 2005:Tables 1–11) and 70 at Watson Brake (Johnson 2000:99).

In the surface collection, 322 blade cores were identified (Figure 6.3). Attributes recorded included number of platforms, platform flake scars, complete blade scars, blade remnants, and other flake removals. Platforms were defined as prepared flaked surfaces creating an edge from which blades could be removed. The average number of platform facets was 1.8. Over half of the cores (n = 181) had one platform from which blades were removed in a single direction. Blade cores with removals from opposite directions, forming a bifacial edge, were less common (n = 85). These were not typed as bifaces because the two sides did not form flat, parallel faces and because the overall artifact morphology was roughly cubical or spherical. Conversely, Johnson (2000:96) types bifacial cores as bifaces for the Watson Brake assemblage. Two blade cores at John Forrest had no platform preparation. The remaining 54 blade cores did not fit into these categories and had a range of two to four platforms.

The blade cores from John Forrest are generally similar to those from Loosa Yokena (n = 442) and Watson Brake (n = 16), differences with the latter likely being a result of sample size. The average length of John Forrest cores is 3.8 cm, which is comparable to Watson Brake and Loosa Yokena blade cores (Johnson 2000; McGahey 2005). Those at Loosa Yokena and John Forrest have a range of one to four platforms while all but two blade cores at Watson Brake have a single platform (Johnson 2000; McGahey 2005). At John Forrest, true blade removals were counted separately from possible blade removal remnants and non-blade removals. Because remnant blade scars did not retain the original length, it was impossible to determine if they were technically the dimensions of a blade (i.e., twice as long as wide). However, based on the surrounding scars, it is plausible that these remnants were blade removals. The average number of blades taken from each blade core from the site (based on complete and remnant scars) is 3.8 removals, and the average of non-blade flake removals is 8.6. Johnson (2000:98) notes that the blade cores at Watson Brake were not intensively used based on the low blade scar average (3.6); blade cores apparently were more intensively used at John Forrest. The most probable use for the blades removed from the cores was in the manufacture of microdrills.

Although the excavated materials have only had a preliminary sort, a number of microdrills (n = 40) have been noted, and these are similar in morphology to those reported from Watson Brake and Loosa Yokena. There are 154 microdrills and 93 microdrill preforms from Watson Brake and 159 microdrills from Loosa Yokena (Johnson 2000:99; McGahey 2005:9). McGahey (2005:9) notes that most of the microdrills at the latter site "exhibit parallel blade scars on the dorsal surface indicating that they were struck from the platform." Johnson (2000:99) was able to demonstrate that 30 percent of the preforms and 5 percent of the used microdrills from Loosa Yokena were certainly struck from blade cores.

Chipped stone beads recovered from the John Forrest Site represent one of the material culture classes that make the collection of particular interest. The 99 artifacts representing the bead production sequence make up less than 5 percent of the surface collection, but this is a significant amount compared

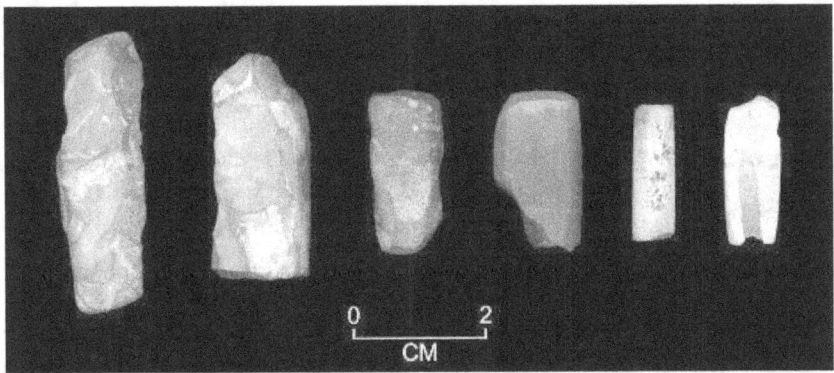

Figure 6.4. Stages of chert bead manufacture as seen in the John Forrest surface assemblage. Photo by Sarah Mattics. Originally published in Peacock (2005).

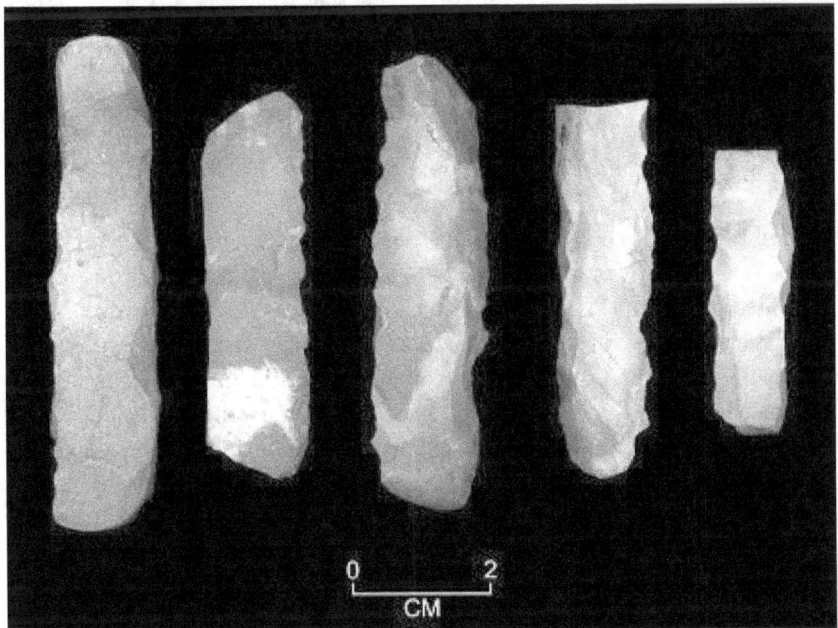

Figure 6.5. Chert bead preforms from the John Forrest surface assemblage. Photo by Sarah Mattics.

to the seven such artifacts recovered from Watson Brake (Johnson 2000:100) and comparable to the 120 listed in tables from Loosa Yokena (McGahey 2005:Tables 1–11). The raw material used in the production of chipped stone beads is Citronelle Gravel, with heat-treating making the majority of the pertinent artifacts a red color. Local chert gravels were also the main source for chipped-stone bead material at both Loosa Yokena (McGahey 2005) and Watson Brake (Johnson 2000). Based on the Watson Brake artifacts, Johnson

(2000:100) developed a bead production trajectory, essentially confirmed by McGahey for Loosa Yokena (Figure 6.4), which was employed to classify the John Forrest materials. The first step in bead manufacture was selection of appropriately sized gravels and knapping these into trifaces or quadfaces so that each face is roughly equal in size (Figure 6.5). Over half of the beads at John Forrest (66 percent) were classified as representing this first stage of production. The second stage involved grinding the chipped edges to transform the cross section from triangular/square to round and to smooth the ends. Evidence for grinding was found on 26 stage-two beads, and one specimen was completely ground. The final stage of manufacture was drilling, evidence of which was found on five artifacts. Only one complete chert bead was found during excavations at John Forrest.

Ground (as opposed to knapped and ground) beads are another part of the lapidary industry at the John Forrest site that resembles artifacts at Loosa Yokena (McGahey 2005) and the Keenan Cache (Connaway 1981). Ground beads are generally made from greenstone, a softer material than the chert used for chipped stone beads. Employing the Mohs Hardness Scale, greenstone is softer at a five or six as compared with chert, which has a hardness of seven. For this reason, a different manufacturing strategy is represented, so ground beads were analyzed separately from the chipped stone beads. All four of the ground beads at John Forrest are made from greenstone pebbles, which may be trachyte. In her work with Archaic effigy beads, Jessica Crawford (2003:12) identified greenstone as trachyte from the Ouachita Mountains, but it is also likely found in the gravel bars of the Mississippi River and its tributaries.

The presumed first stage for greenstone bead production was grinding and cutting the pebbles into the desired shape. Ninety greenstone pebbles from John Forrest were ground flat on an edge or had small, incised grooves. These pebbles may represent the first stage of manufacture, but are not clearly recognizable as bead blanks. McGahey (2005:13) described a total of 121 similarly faceted pebbles at Loosa Yokena, which he believed represented the first step in testing the workability and color of the pebbles for bead manufacture. Drilling was the second and final stage of the ground bead manufacture. Three of the greenstone beads at John Forrest are ground into cylinders and one has been completely drilled. A fourth bead is teardrop-shaped with an incompletely drilled, conical-shaped hole at the apex. While greenstone is still a hard material, we assume that the use of chert microdrills would enable relatively quick work. Greenstone bead technology is represented at many sites throughout Mississippi, including Loosa Yokena (McGahey 2005), Denton (Connaway 1977; Crawford 2003), and the Keenan Cache (Connaway 1981).

In sum, although the John Forrest site lacks intact deposits, the assemblage is useful in discussing stone bead manufacture during the Middle

Archaic period. The site contains a Middle Archaic component based on the diagnostic hafted bifaces. While in need of additional supporting evidence, McGahey (2005:18) has suggested that the exact same occupants were at the John Forrest and Loosa Yokena sites. Loosa Yokena has a radiocarbon date of 5730 ± 110 B.P. (cal. two-sigma) from a feature containing a chert bead preform (McGahey 2005:6–7). This date is significant because, as McGahey (2005:7) notes, it is the first radiocarbon date from a feature containing a chert bead from this region. The feature and artifacts within the lower buried A horizon at Loosa Yokena date comfortably within the Middle Archaic period, bolstering this temporal assignment for the John Forrest bead assemblage.

Middle Archaic Lapidary Specialists?

Stone beads are one of the more interesting classes of Archaic material culture found in the Southeast (see Crawford, this volume; Sassaman 2010). Beyond the intriguing diversity in raw materials, sizes, and forms, consideration of the manufacturing process of chert beads elicits an appreciation for the efforts of prehistoric people rising to a feeling of awe. That chert microdrills were used to perforate Stage 2 chert beads is well demonstrated by the Keenan Cache, which included a broken microdrill in a partially drilled bead (Connaway 1981:63–67). We liken this process to drilling a hole through a pine tree with a pine 2 x 4 board, but on a scale that only adds to the difficulty.

While chert beads have been illustrated in the American archaeological literature for decades (see Crawford, this volume, and references therein; Sassaman 2010:Figure 4.5), certain factors have worked to limit broad recognition of the presence of this artifact class, such that colleagues are often surprised to hear of Archaic stone beads. One of these factors is the limited range of distribution: Louisiana, Mississippi, and adjacent parts of Alabama and Arkansas (Crawford, this volume). Additionally, stone beads are only one of many interesting items in the material culture inventory of famous sites such as Poverty Point (e.g., Webb 1968). Another issue is that complete beads are relatively rare, and bead preforms and associated stone tools were not always recognized as such in the past. Bead preforms may have been identified in other collections as large drills, drill preforms, or bifacial tools. Due to the small size of microdrills, some form of fine screening is necessary for their recovery, but any form of fine screening is rare on lithic sites in the Southeast (Price 2012). With increased interest in Middle Archaic-period bead manufacture, we hope that more sites with associated evidence are identified via appropriate recovery and analytical techniques.

Although the Archaic period was once thought to be a time when prehistoric people simply became better at food extraction and produced the anomalous Poverty Point site, archaeologists in the Southeast have recently recognized the high degree of cultural complexity that existed at the time (Gibson and Carr 2004). Craft specialization has not always received the same level of discussion as other aspects of cultural complexity, such as mound building, sedentariness, and trade (e.g., Kidder and Sassaman 2009), but ethnographic data have long been used to demonstrate a relationship between cultural complexity and craft specialization (Clark and Parry 1990).

If Middle Archaic lapidary assemblages were an elephant, then researchers, while not blind, have hold of different parts of the animal and are wearing variously tinted glasses when examining their particular part. There are at least three different camps: those who believe there were no specialists; those who believe in specialists; and those who suggest that there were what might be termed "semi-specialists." Evaluation of the evidence presented by each of these camps is difficult because definitions of craft specialization are rarely provided.

Based on the Watson Brake assemblage, Johnson (2000) provides an excellent description of the stages of chert bead manufacture. He asserts that bifacial reduction of bead preforms and production of microblades is "relatively unsophisticated" and "would require more patience than skill" (Johnson 2000:103). Interestingly, this is despite Johnson's observation that Stage 2 beads from Watson Brake have encircling striations perpendicular to their long axes, reminiscent of turning on a lathe, and that "bow drills must certainly have been used to drill the beads" (Johnson 2000:100). This is significantly earlier than the initial presence of the bow and arrow in the LMV (Blitz 1988). Yet Johnson (2000:103) states, "There is no indication of craft specialization at Watson Brake, either in the technology of production or in the end products themselves."

The no-specialization camp is also occupied by Joe Saunders (2004:154), who echoes Johnson's argument that "the blade/drill technology at Watson Brake did not require a level of specialization" and who is concerned that craft specialization is indicative of "economic support for a specialist by his/her society." He does describe one phase of occupation at Watson Brake Mound D as a "bead workshop" (J. Saunders 2004), but the intensity of production is viewed as being at such a low level that it could not have provided economic support for the makers. Of course, this assumes that craft specialization means full-time specialists. Joe Saunders (2004:153–154) goes on to reconcile the large count of microdrills with the low count of beads and lack of finished beads by suggesting that microdrills were used in the production of bone or shell beads, or, alternatively, that finished chert beads were being removed from the site. In considering the Frenchman's Bend Mounds (16OU259) and

Plum Creek Archaic sites along with Watson Brake, Saunders (2004:157) sees economic redundancy but variation in the lapidary industry, attributable in part to sample size and recovery methods. He not only concludes that there was an absence of craft specialization, but also that these Middle Archaic people were "affluent hunter-gatherers" with egalitarian social relations, who built mounds (J. Saunders 2004:160).

In contrast, Connaway (1981) and Brookes (2004) argue for lapidary specialists, especially if the Keenan Cache and zoomorphic beads are considered as ideotechnic artifacts. In particular, Connaway (1981:70) views the Keenan Cache as the work of "an individual artisan whose job it was to manufacture them for some specific reason." He speculates that zoomorphic beads had a socioreligious purpose, perhaps as fetishes (Connaway 1977, 1981). The more recent argument by Brookes (2004) for lapidary specialists is based on a variety of observations and inferences, including ones concerning technology. Using the Keenan Cache as evidence, Brookes (2004:106) suggests:

> the cache demonstrates aspects of Middle Archaic technology never before demonstrated. The bead blanks, after being flaked to desired shape, were hafted and turned on a lathe. It is probable that this was a simple lathe, but the technology was there. Also the beads were drilled, often from one end, with a small chert bit from a microblade. Some beads are in excess of 9 cm in length. This suggests that drilling was not done by twirling a bit that was loosely held in the hand. A drill press of sorts, well braced and solid, would be needed for such an operation. It is possible that the bow was used in this process, though it could be that a pump drill, perhaps used with a spindle whorl, was employed in the manufacturing process. At any rate, the manufacture of stone beads in the Middle Archaic was far more complex than previously suspected.

Brookes goes on to suggest that the size of the cache, the time involved in manufacturing and equipment maintenance, and how the technology differs from that used at the Denton site are all indicators that some people were specialists. Additionally, the 80-plus "strikingly similar" zoomorphic beads are taken as evidence that only a few individuals were involved in their manufacture (Brookes 2004:107). This is counter to observations by Webb (1971b:113) specifically regarding "locust beads," for which he sees variability in size, raw material, and appearance not as representing manufacture at a single site, but as representing the "spread of a basic concept." Similarly, due to their rarity Blitz (1993:33) does not view locust beads as fetishes, arguing instead that "locust beads may have been emblematic of a corporate group and its descent-sanctioned rights, perhaps functioning as a totemic symbol." Despite some disagreement over the specifics of manufacture, all four of these researchers would agree that zoomorphic beads fit the description of ideotechnic artifacts. Brookes (2004:108) goes on to say, "Specialists are necessary not only for their skill in flaking or carving but also for their power or magic, which becomes part of the artifact."

Following from consideration of Loosa Yokena, Denton, and the Keenan Cache, McGahey (2005) argues for some form of specialization, with some individuals having been better at, and more engaged in, the production of beads. Interestingly, he suggests that perforated discoidals found at Loosa Yokena were "flywheels for pump drills" used in chert bead manufacture and that "personal experience indicates that the pump drill is more effective than a bow drill" (McGahey 2005:16). He notes that sites with significant bead-manufacturing evidence are rare, and suggests that zoomorphic beads at Denton were not made on-site based on a lack of manufacturing debris, which further suggests "a certain degree of specialization." While this is a vague statement, to his credit McGahey (2005:18) provides a definition and more specific characterization of specialization:

> Specialist, in considering lapidary work of the Late and Middle Archaic groups of the area under consideration, has been implicitly understood to mean one who works at least almost exclusively at one task and is predominately supported by others while he goes about his work.... the individual responsible for the Keenan Cache was relatively specialized in that he had spent much more time in learning and practicing his craft than most of the members of his group. His lapidary work was probably somewhere on the continuum of development from an arrangement where everyone produced his own beads to that of full-time specialist subsidized by the rest of the group.

While this characterization reflects some other scholars' views regarding economic support of specialists (e.g., J. Saunders 2004), the substantial literature on craft specialization shows that researchers are moving beyond simple attempts to document specialization. Efforts to unpack the complexity often subsumed under the term "specialist," and to investigate gender roles in relation to specialization rather than assuming the specialists were men, are underway (e.g., Cobb 2000). Therefore, this compromise scenario "between no specialists and specialists" needs as much critical examination as the others.

An intriguing definition of craft specialization was offered by Clark and Parry (1990) that has labor, rather than time, as its focus, leading to consideration of who benefits from that labor. In their view, if one's production of durable goods is for oneself or one's dependents, it is not craft specialization, no matter the scale of production, consistency of product, knowledge required, and so on. They succinctly define craft specialization as "*production of alienable, durable goods for nondependent consumption,"* allowing for more than one type of craft specialization (Clark and Parry 1990:297). Distinctions are made as to whether craft specialization is independent or attached, and production scales are characterized as ad hoc, part-time, or full-time. They use these distinctions in examining relationships between specialization and cultural complexity, through statistical testing of data derived from ethnographic cases (Clark and Parry 1990:Tables 1 and 2). Their definition has the advantage for archaeologists of identifying craft specialization through the distribution of end products relative to the location of manufacture, as Brookes (2004) and McGahey (2005) did in the case of zoomorphic beads at Denton. Qualifying the economic focus of Saunders (2004) and McGahey (2005), Clark and Parry (1990:298) state, "craft specialization can be voluntary or compulsory and does not necessarily entail compensation in subsistence products or their equivalent."

Some may question the utility of this definition because of a lack of focus on technology. Also, craft specialization defined in this manner is likely present in all societies, in the least complex form of independent craft specialization at an ad hoc scale of production (e.g., Costin 1991; see reaction by Clark 1995). In terms of an organization of technology model, one could argue that craft specialization is a technological strategy because it involves the keepers of knowledge and tools that form a technical system. This point is made by Brookes (2004) with regard to the knowledge and equipment used in drilling long, tubular chert beads. However, craft specialization as defined by Clark and Parry is best considered as an aspect of social and economic strategies, with implications for technological strategies.

With regard to the ubiquity of craft specialization, McGahey (2005:18) notes that the definition of craft specialization traditionally used in studies of Archaic-period lapidary finds implies that specialists would occur "only at or above the chiefdom level of sociopolitical organization." However, Clark and Parry's definition of craft specialization, with its focus on labor, allows for variation in craft specialization in different types of social structures to be explored. This is pointed out by Cobb (2000:36), who states:

> Because specialization is a form of production, it must be examined within the wider arena of social relations that constitute the labor process ... one must closely examine the underlying relations that structure production as it may be manifested by specialization. These deeper relations involve a complex articulation of production, distribution, exchange, and consumption at an economic level, as well as mediation of these processes through social and symbolic means.

Ultimately, variability in the production of chert beads can be explored by applying the organization of technology model. As currently developed, application of the model allows us to consider systematically: (1) data regarding lapidary assemblages, and where gaps in the data corpus exist; (2) the model itself and how it can be expanded to include ideotechnic artifacts; and (3) whether craft specialists were responsible for Middle Archaic-period lapidary assemblages.

Chert Beads and Model Application

The chert beads and related stone tools at the John Forrest site provide a way to explore the organization of this lithic technology and the question of craft specialization. While we follow others regarding the use of additional equipment, such as a pump or bow drill, in the manufacture of stone beads, specific discussions of such equipment in the organization of technology model are beyond the scope of this paper. We include data from related sites, including Loosa Yokena and Watson Brake, to explore this bead production technology. Chert beads do not seem to be part of what Hayden (1998:2) dubs a "practical technology . . . to solve practical problems of survival and basic comfort." Hence it is necessary to broaden the scope of the model, not simply to allow its application to "prestige technologies" (Hayden 1998:11) or ideotechnic artifacts such as beads (Brookes 2004:101), but also to consider the greater cultural milieu. Based on the work of others (Johnson 2000; McGahey 2005), blade cores, blades, and microdrills are key components in the production of beads and are considered here. The organization of technology model is best applied by starting with the top two levels for context, then moving to the bottom and working up to social and economic strategies.

Environment and Demographics

Social and economic strategies shape and are implemented by technological strategies, and these strategies are conducted in and are shaped by the environment and demographics. Because our focus is on chert beads and related lithic assemblages, the overall environmental description for the Middle Archaic is broad while the raw material environment receives attention at a local level. Due to data constraints, discussion of demographics is quite general. Certainly, examining both the environment and demographics in more detail at multiple scales would enhance our understanding of social and economic strategies during the Middle Archaic period.

The Middle Archaic (8900–5700 cal. B.P.) corresponds to the Mid-Holocene Altithermal, Hypsithermal, or Climatic Optimum (Anderson 2001; Brookes and Twaroski, this volume). Early characterizations of Mid-Holocene paleoenvironments focused on the climatic stability of this period, noting that in the Southeast the climate was generally warmer and dryer (Schuldenrein 1996). More recent paleoclimatological reconstructions taking account of the synergistic effect of multiple factors, including the atmosphere, ocean, and vegetation (Ganopolski et al. 1998) demonstrate that this period was marked by global climatic variability relative to earlier and subsequent periods (Sandweiss et al. 1999). Climate during the Mid-Holocene was different from today, but these differences were highly variable across space and time. For example, the Southeast was likely wetter, with more extreme seasons (Anderson 2001:158; Watts et al. 1996:36). While this variable environment did not determine the strategies used by Middle Archaic peoples, environmental conditions would have had an impact on strategy choice and the success of a particular strategy (see Brookes and Twaroski, this volume). A final point to consider here is that our current paleoclimatic reconstructions are incomplete (Peacock 2008), and with future work these reconstructions may very well change.

Raw material availability is an important environmental factor to be considered in the organization of Archaic-period stone bead technology. The overwhelming focus at the John Forrest site was on locally available materials. The majority of the chipped stone assemblage consists of Citronelle Gravels, with minor amounts of Fort Payne chert from the Tennessee River Valley (e.g., Futato 1999) and Tallahatta Sandstone (a.k.a. Tallahatta Quartzite, found in east-central Mississippi and west-central Alabama—Curren 1982; Lloyd et al. 1983; Maudsley 1998). The Citronelle Formation is a "band of secondarily deposited gravels" that extends along the entire eastern rim of the Mississippi Alluvial Valley (Stallings 1989:38). This material is dominated by tan-colored cobbles, but colors range from reds to grays. A water-rolled cortex was commonly observed on early stage beads at the site. These gravels are abundant in James Creek, which is located approximately 250 m to the north of the site. Interestingly, the raw materials predominantly used for bifaces, cores, and beads at Watson Brake (Johnson 2000:95) and Loosa Yokena (McGahey 2005:7) were also tan gravels. In fact, Johnson (2000:102) describes the Watson Brake assemblage as resembling a "generalized Archaic source-area technology" to which drill and bead production was added. The raw material used for the ground beads was likely available in the gravels (Crawford 2003; Hadley 2003).

You cannot eat rocks, so settling next to a lithic source in an area devoid of subsistence resources is not a strategy well suited to hunter-gatherers. Given that the occupants of John Forrest, Loosa Yokena, and Watson Brake had choices about where to settle, how much of a consideration was it to be near a raw material source? That is, were there sacrifices made in access to subsistence resources or social networks in order to be near lithic material because of the importance of stone in implementing social and economic strategies? If so, then this observation provides interesting insight into the energetics and workings of Middle Archaic peoples in the region.

Brookes (2004:107) points out the lack of exotic raw materials used in bead production. Although Fort Payne chert was being moved long distances and appears in the John Forrest assemblage in a very minor amount in the bifaces (n = 60, 4.6 percent) and hafted bifaces (n = 17, 4.6 percent), it is noteworthy that people in the LMV did not acquire large amounts of Fort Payne chert nor use this material in the production of beads, either due to choice or lack of access.

With regard to demographics, specific discussions are rare for the Middle Archaic period in the Southeast, and data are even rarer. In a recent overview, Kidder and Sassaman (2009:677) state for the Middle Archaic, "Human groups, their mobility already restricted by rising population pressure resulting from natural demographic increase, would have encountered greater competition for restricted or scarce resources."

This is as specific as the available information is for this period. Certainly more detailed demographic data would provide additional insights. For example, McGahey (2005) has pointed out that the scale of production is much greater at Loosa Yokena and the John Forrest sites compared to others in Mississippi. Is this because more people at these sites engaged in bead production? Or, were many beads being produced by a few people? Answering such questions will lead to a better understanding of the complex world of Middle Archaic peoples.

Artifact Form and Artifact Distribution

The lowest levels in the organization of technology model are artifact form and artifact distribution. Artifact form is the aspect of Middle Archaic bead technology for which we have the greatest amount of information. Descriptions of the various forms of stone beads date to the original analysis of the Keenan Cache by Charles Rau back in 1877 (Connaway 1981; Crawford, this volume). In terms of artifact form, the chert beads at John Forrest are restricted in size and color because they are made from the local gravels. Bead blanks vary in length from 20 to 77 mm, with the one complete bead measuring 21.2 mm. Other tubular beads from sites discussed here measure from 10 to 24 mm, with some variability outside of this range, and zoomorphic beads are on average longer at 37.2 mm (Crawford 2003:9). Chipped stone beads tend to be tubular, while ground stone beads are more variable, including tubes, discoidals, and teardrop shaped. The majority of the chert beads at John Forrest were heat-treated, resulting in a waxy sheen and reddening of the material. Chert beads at Watson Brake and Loosa Yokena are also commonly red, although they display more variation in raw materials. Also, for the zoomorphic beads the most common raw material is red jasper (Connaway 1981; Crawford 2003:10). McGahey (2005:11) notes that color was an important factor in choosing materials for beads, but does not elaborate. The selection of red for both the chipped and zoomorphic beads suggests a pattern in its selection. However, heat-treatment is also used to improve the quality of the material before knapping, and the red color may be an unintentional result of the manufacturing process. Additional research is needed to determine what significance red beads had during the Middle Archaic.

Chipped beads have fewer shapes and colors compared to ground beads. However, while we characterize these types of beads differently based on material and manufacturing process, there may or may not have been a difference to Middle Archaic peoples. The questions remain: did the chert beads and ground beads function differently? Were the chert beads harder to make and thus represent a more valuable object, or identify a person of a different status or clan? One way to explore these questions would be to look at the distribution of beads at sites and look at their association with other artifacts and features.

The details of artifact distributions can be observed at two scales: regional and site-level. The regional distribution of stone beads still needs refinement within the boundaries, but the general limits have been established (see Crawford, this volume). As Brookes (2004:107) states, "Zoomorphic beads are found in five states, Louisiana, Arkansas, Tennessee, Alabama, and Mississippi, [and] the beads were being made and put into the Middle Archaic exchange network. Since so many have been found in Mississippi, and the remainder are all from adjacent states, it is suggested that zoomorphic beads were made in Mississippi." There is a very limited amount of data available on the site-level distribution of chert beads and manufacturing material, due to limited excavations and much locational data being limited to site-level provenience. However, the identification of a workshop at Watson Brake Mound D and the fact that two units at Loosa Yokena produced the majority of beads in various stages points to a need for more intrasite data.

At this point in Middle Archaic bead research, the only lithic artifacts that are confidently linked to bead manufacture are blade cores, blades, and microdrills. Blade cores are characterized by their size and shape, which are likely influenced by the exclusive use of Citronelle Gravels. The blade cores at Watson Brake, Loosa Yokena, and the John Forrest site share similar shapes, lengths, and number of platforms (Johnson 2000:98; McGahey 2005:10). Blades were not studied in depth at the John Forrest site because, as noted earlier, the landowner had indicated a lack of interest in collecting debitage and it was assumed that his collection was biased. The debitage from the John Forrest site surface collection is composed of larger flakes, which probably do not represent those that were used to make the microdrills. However, the blades from excavated contexts at Loosa Yokena and Watson Brake were small enough to be products of the blade cores. The microdrills at Loosa Yokena and Watson Brake both demonstrate retouch from the ventral side of the blades, as well as narrow or tapered ends that were hafted (Johnson 2000:99; McGahey 2005:11).

Blade cores, blades, and microdrills are viewed as a continuum of tool manufacture. Blade cores were used to make blades, which were then worked into microdrills. Many of the details about this manufacturing process are not well understood. Johnson (2000) demonstrates that many of the microdrills were not removed from blade cores, and the variability of this production step in other assemblages has never been explored. Was it easier to make microdrills from blade or flake cores? Blade cores generally require more skill to produce, but were there advantages to blades over other flakes in making microdrills? Blade cores allow for a more standardized flake, which may have been important in the production of microdrills. As Joe Saunders (2004:153–154) demonstrates in his discussion of microdrills, there is still uncertainty as to how microdrills were used, and on what material. The type of drill used, hafting element, and material drilled could be identifiable with careful experimentation and micro-wear analysis.

In terms of the distribution of blade cores, blades, and microdrills at a regional level there is limited information. However, it is significant that these three sites with chert beads also have numerous blades, blade cores, and microdrills. It is also interesting that these tools were not found in the Keenan Cache, which has unfinished beads. Blades, blade cores, and microdrills appear to be evenly distributed in the unit excavations at Loosa Yokena, with large numbers of blades throughout (McGahey 2005). Conversely, blades and blade cores are highly concentrated in Mound D at Watson Brake (Johnson 2000; J. Saunders 2004). These artifacts are best identified together to determine if beads were manufactured at a site. Microdrills pose a problem because they can easily be missed without fine screening, and blade cores and blades have other uses beyond bead manufacture. Thus it would be easy to overlook a bead-manufacturing site if the beads, bead preforms, and microdrills were not found or identified properly. To understand the regional distribution of blades, blade cores, and microdrills, more excavation that specifically takes note of this technology is needed. Additionally, excavated collections could be reanalyzed specifically to identify these artifacts.

Design and Activities

Moving through the organization of technology model, design and activities are the next considerations. Traditionally, tool design is considered as *reliable* or *maintainable*. Activities can be thought of as everything that people do, but for practical purposes with regard to technology, activities minimally include raw material procurement, artifact manufacture, use/reuse, and discard.

Not serving the same practical purpose as projectile points and other stone tools, beads were not designed with either reliability or maintainability as primary considerations. Interestingly, reliable designs involve high-quality materials and overdesigned parts to ensure that a tool will work when needed. Chert beads could be said to be overdesigned in that other materials, especially bone, would serve to make a tubular bead and, with chert, small rounded chert pebbles occurring in abundance in James Creek could simply be drilled through the center with less chance of failure than that of the thin-walled tubular beads. Clearly, design choices were dictated by something other than attempts to minimize time and energy expenditure. Expanding the concept of design beyond considerations of reliability and maintainability is necessary to investigate adequately the organization of chert bead technology and that of other prestige artifacts, or what Clark and Parry (1990) call "hypertrophic artifacts."

Hypertrophic goods are the polar opposite of the products made by craft specialists in a factory, which are "cheap, common, utilitarian goods made for an impersonal market" (Clark and Parry 1990:293). Hypertrophic goods are special products designed to communicate social messages, and Clark and Parry (1990:296) argue that "exaggerated energy costs endow an item with more information." Interestingly, they make the point that because hypertrophic goods are designed with a different purpose than simple utility, their production is not inefficient. This is because the increased effort has the added benefit of conveying information. From a Darwinian evolutionary perspective, such apparent wasteful activities could be explained as *costly signaling* (see Peacock and Rafferty 2013 and references therein). Beads are manufactured based on design choices, and the choice of using chert as a raw material, given the level of technology, provides important information about social and economic strategies however it may be viewed theoretically. We consider the tubular chert beads manufactured at the John Forrest site as hypertrophic goods and will return to this point when discussing subsequent levels of the model.

Activities lie at the same level in the model as design. For our purposes, the activities minimally necessary for discussion are those involving the use history of tubular chert beads. This history played out in the context of many other activities and included everything from subsistence practices to leisure time. Greater consideration of activities in the broadest sense would add clarity and accuracy to inferences regarding social and economic strategies, but is beyond the scope of this work. Here, we discuss tubular chert bead raw material procurement, manufacture, use, and discard.

Raw material procurement was simplified for Watson Brake, Loosa Yokena, and John Forrest because all three sites are situated near sources of gravel chert. The Keenan Cache is located in Jefferson Davis County, Mississippi, which has sources of Citronelle Gravel chert. This suggests that site location near a raw material source for chert bead manufacture and other chipped-stone tool-using activities was a consideration in the context of the other activities that were necessary for survival.

Based on current evidence, similar manufacturing techniques were employed at all three sites. McGahey (2005) essentially describes the same manufacturing process as outlined by Johnson (2000) for Watson Brake. The John Forrest bead materials fit comfortably in the Watson Brake stages, while McGahey (2005) notes the similarity of Loosa Yokena with John Forrest and goes so far as to suggest that these assemblages were produced by the same people. All stages of manufacture are present in the John Forrest assemblage. The manufacture of a chert bead during the Middle Archaic period apparently required new technologies and tools, such as a means to secure the bead during the drilling process and perhaps a pump drill. The number of people who had access to these technologies and tools and provided labor for the manufacturing process is considered at higher levels in the model. We assume that chert bead manufacture was a labor-intensive process. Experimentation is necessary to test this assumption and reveal specifics of the manufacturing process.

The use of beads, especially tubular beads, has not been given much consideration. Presumably this is because beads were obviously used for personal adornment. Zoomorphic beads have been called fetishes (Connaway 1981; Sassaman 2010) and totemic symbols (Blitz 1993b), and Brookes (2004) sees them as having been made by specialists who imbued them with magic (see also Crawford, this volume). Long tubular beads could have served as shaman "sucking tubes," used to suck and blow away diseases, accounts of which can be found in both ethnographic and ethnohistorical accounts (Frison and Norman 1993; Mandelbaum 1940; Venegas 1759). Stone tubes that possibly functioned in this way are found at archaeological sites dating to Paleoindian times (Sellet et al. 2010; Wheat 1979). As prestige items or hypertrophic goods, chert beads served as "texts" that "become the objectification or instantiation of meaning or ideology" (Clark and Parry 1990:296). It is also possible that beads were simply valued as objects of adornment and had no other function or meaning. Unfortunately, the context of the archaeological beads has not been helpful in resolving their exact use.

Finally, there is discard. A consideration of discard is hampered by the lack of undisturbed contexts at John Forrest. The landowner did suggest that beads were more concentrated in one area of the site, but preliminary analysis of shovel-test data does not indicate any particular concentration of beads and/or microdrills. At Watson Brake a bead workshop was identified, but microdrills were widely distributed in the excavation units. For Loosa Yokena, spatial analysis was not conducted, but data tables indicate that chert bead preforms are evenly distributed for test units, while three of the 20-meter square surface collection units had concentrations of 10 to 13 bead preforms (McGahey 2005). The Keenan Cache provides an interesting case and generates many questions. Were these materials buried with the intention of retrieval or were they part of a ritual (Brookes 2004:107)? Was it the result of the work of a single individual, as some have assumed (Connaway 1981; McGahey 2005; Rau 1878), or did multiple people contribute to the cache? Due to a lack of preservation and disturbance, it is unknown whether the complete bead from the John Forrest site was in a burial or represented a small cache that had been dispersed.

One of the more intriguing aspects of the Keenan Cache, as well as the assemblages recovered from John Forrest and Loosa Yokena, is the number of "discarded" artifacts in various stages of production that do not *appear* to be failures. Yet identifying these artifacts as viable in the chert bead-manufacturing process could be a result of our lack of understanding of the constraints of bead manufacture. However, the fact that certain pieces appear to be taken well into the production process, such as a Stage 3 bead that is ground but not yet drilled, raises questions concerning the production process. For example, did this artifact remain at this stage of production because the maker lacked access to equipment to drill the bead? Certainly, other potential explanations are plausible. Greater consideration of artifact form and distribution, coupled with experimentation, will allow us to sort through these explanations and choose the one that best fits the evidence.

Technological, Social, and Economic Strategies

Together, design and activities provide information concerning the technological strategy. Traditionally, technological strategies are characterized simply as *expedient* or *curated* (Nelson 1991). Clearly, several aspects of curation apply to stone beads in that they were produced in advance of use and transported from location to location (Odell 1996), as evidenced by some sites emphasizing production and others with only finished products. Our conception of technological strategy is that it includes the knowledge, tools, and skills to accomplish a task, as well as a plan to expend time and energy efficiently within social and economic situations. Given the potential nuances of technological strategy, it is difficult to imagine where any technology fits into the expedient-to-curated continuum, and this is perhaps especially true for prestige or hypertrophic items such as chert beads. One aspect of the technological strategy evident for the three major bead sites under consideration here is their location at a source of raw material. Affording knappers easy access to raw material by site location is part of the technological strategy. A relatively sophisticated knowledge base and set of tools for the manufacture of chert beads was also necessary, which ranges from the production of microdrills to a pump drill, and includes a vise or means to secure beads during the drilling process. Whether everyone in the group had access to these tools, possessed the knowledge and skills for their operation, and had the time and energy to expend in the production of chert beads is under debate.

Craft specialization as defined by Clark and Parry (1990) concerns labor and who ultimately possesses the fruits of that labor. Clearly, this is a social/economic strategy that has implications for the technological strategy. Typical studies investigating the organization of technology restrict considerations of social and economic strategies to mobility and the forager-collector dichotomy. If chert beads were made by people with high rates of residential mobility, then we would expect the distribution of activities and artifacts to be greatly different than what would be expected in a sedentary settlement pattern, which is proposed by Peacock and Rafferty (2013) for the Middle Archaic period in the LMV. While we do not explore these implications further here, it also clear that social and economic strategies must go beyond a singular focus on mobility.

On the one hand, one could hypothesize a social/economic strategy that includes egalitarianism, in which the occupants of the John Forrest site had equal access to prestige items because everyone possessed the knowledge, tools, and skills to manufacture these items. The fact that a local raw material was chosen for the manufacture of the chert beads supports such a hypothesis of equal access. On the other hand, one could hypothesize that not everyone in the group was of equal skill with regard to chert bead technology. These skills would include knapping the preform, manufacturing and maintaining a pump drill, and so on. An efficient expenditure of time and energy would be to allow those with the highest skill levels to specialize in the production of chert beads at the cost of being supported to some extent by others. This support would come from the makers' ability to trade these items or by being attached to elites who controlled the items.

Interestingly, Bar-Yosef and Kuhn (1999) see the production of composite tools during the Upper Paleolithic of the Old World as evidence of changes in social and economic strategies related to the support of skilled individuals. Bar-Yosef and Kuhn (1999:332) argue:

> The creation of elaborate technological aids to foraging or other work carries with it a significant amount of "frontloading," expenditure of time and energy well in advance of any possible return. On one hand, this requires a certain degree of foresight on the part of toolmakers. Perhaps more importantly, it requires a significant amount of cooperation and coordination of activities among members of a social group. The investment of significant amounts of time and labor in the production of elaborate technology, the potential benefits of which might not be realized for days, weeks, or even years, means that individuals were free to divert this time and labor from more immediately pressing concerns such as getting food or shelter. If an individual is able to devote many hours or even days to the manufacture of an artifact, someone else must be carrying at least part of the load with respect to gathering and processing other resources. This "division of labor" might have been transitory and minor compared to the types of occupational differentiation seen in later and larger-scale societies, and we are not arguing for rigid permanent occupational specialization during the Upper Paleolithic. Nonetheless, the ability to shift the burden of daily subsistence labor to another individual at least temporarily would be vital to the evolution of some complex technologies that began to appear in the Upper Paleolithic. Conversely, the absence of such options for cooperation would inhibit the amount of time and energy any single individual could afford to put into tool manufacture, regardless of the potential payoffs of having more elaborate implements.

Presumably, this temporary shift of labor resulted in the manufacture of composite tools that were shared within the group, thus conforming to the definition of craft specialization followed here. This highlights the fact that craft specialization, broadly defined, is potentially part of a common human adaptation and not restricted to ranked and state societies.

In our opinion, Brookes (2004) has made a strong argument for craft specialization for Middle Archaic-period lapidary makers in Mississippi, using a wide variety of sites and range of artifacts, including zoomorphic beads (see discussion by Crawford, this volume). No zoomorphic beads or preforms were recovered from Watson Brake, Loosa Yokena, or the John Forrest site. We infer from the John Forrest assemblage that craft specialists manufactured the tubular beads there, based on the lack of finished products in comparison to unfinished items in various stages of production. Alternatively, individuals could have made these items for themselves and their dependents and, upon leaving the site for some reason, took the completed beads with them. Of equal importance to examining craft specialization is investigating chert bead manufacture as wasteful behavior and exploring alternate hypotheses (see Peacock and Rafferty 2013).

That alternate explanations exist does not indicate that this intractable problem must remain unresolved. Experimentation to replicate the bead-manufacturing process would provide important insights. The type of drill used, how it was used, and the material upon which it was used can be determined through use wear and experimentation. More extensive excavations are needed to produce adequate samples for intersite and intrasite comparisons. Additionally, analyses specifically focused on artifact standardization would be useful. Logically, with craft specialization there are fewer producers, resulting in relatively little variability within the artifact category (Costin 1991). Measuring the amount of artifact standardization is the most common approach to looking for craft specialization in the archaeological record.

A final important point is that ideology should be added as having an overarching impact on the entire organization of technology model. While new to the model, archaeologists have had a long and recurring interest in ideology. Additionally, Brookes (2004) labeled chert beads as ideotechnic items and suggested that the key element in the manufacture of chert beads was not the knapping or drilling, but rather a supernatural component. While some may say it is impossible to get into the minds of prehistoric peoples, ideology ultimately has an impact on artifact form and distribution. Failure to recognize this point and include ideology in the model would mean that some variation in artifact form and distribution would always remain unexplained or misunderstood.

Summary and Conclusions

Following Brookes (2004), we have employed data from a number of sites that have produced chert beads to investigate the question of Middle Archaic-period craft specialization in the Southeast. We focused on a relatively new piece of the "elephant" by incorporating the John Forrest site assemblage, and we also differed from previous researchers by using an organization of technology model. It is clear that there is variation in the final form of chert beads and in their distribution within and between sites. That being said, the organization of technology model was not particularly well suited to considering chert beads. These prestige/hypertrophic artifacts caused a rethinking of certain aspects of the model, especially the levels of technological strategy and social and economic strategy. The addition of ideology as an overarching consideration is significant. Certainly, some variation in artifact form and artifact distribution is explicable only with a consideration of ideology. Thus, the model is incomplete without the addition of ideology.

Our employment of an accepted and broad definition of craft specialization could be viewed as a means to support the case made by Brookes (2004:106) that the makers of Middle Archaic-period chert beads at the John Forrest and other sites were craft specialists. In actuality, this definition allows for a shift in focus, from the simple question of the presence or absence of craft specialization in a situation where craft specialization is undefined to questions concerning whether specialists were full- or part-time and attached or unattached. New studies are required to answer these questions, such as experimental replication of chert beads; use-wear analysis of microdrills; more specific study of artifact form to address standardization; and, more fieldwork to better understand intersite and intrasite distribution. We would recommend that a single individual conduct the standardization analysis to minimize bias, and note that such a study would likely have the fewest obstacles to completion.

There is a growing interest in Archaic-period research in the Southeast, especially the Middle Archaic. Due to the work of Sam Brookes and others, the dominant mode of thinking about hunter-gatherers, dating back to the nineteenth century and reified in the 1950s, is no longer tenable. Such thinking is captured in the following quote describing Archaic-period cultures in the Eastern Woodlands:

> Individuals in this society among the men would be outstanding or important according to their ability as individual hunters or according to their talent as shamans or medicine men. We have little or no indication of any degree of specialization in particular crafts, or of the development of specific role in the community [Griffin 1952:354].

While we would dispute the lack of craft specialists based on current data, the role of "shamans or medicine men" is something that has largely been ignored in Archaic-period archaeology in the Southeast outside of discussions of chert beads. The work of Sam Brookes and others in this regard will continue to inspire new research into this fascinating artifact class, place, and time.

Acknowledgments

We are grateful for Samuel Brookes's career in Mississippi archaeology and for his excellent insight into the Middle Archaic. Without his enthusiasm and assertion that important cultural innovations and movements begin in Mississippi, we might never have explored the social implications of this collection. We would also like to thank Evan Peacock for inviting us to participate in the SEAC symposium, which developed into this volume. Thanks are due to Andy Hilburn for the nice map and Sarah Mattics for the artifact photos. We appreciate the many conversations that we have had with colleagues since we first started working with the John Forrest site and collection. We especially thank Andrew Bradbury for his comments on a draft of this paper. Finally, we would like to thank the landowner, John Forrest, for donating the surface collection and allowing us to excavate on his property, which inspired us to look into Middle Archaic cultural complexity.

CHAPTER 7

From Missouri to Mississippi to Florida: Some Research on the Distribution of Poverty Point Objects

Christopher T. Hays, James B. Stoltman, and Richard A. Weinstein

The Poverty Point site (16WC5) in northeast Louisiana is justly famous for its massive earthworks, a unique lapidary industry, and an exchange system that brought in copper, lead, soapstone, and numerous varieties of chert from all over the Eastern Woodlands (Figure 7.1). However, the artifact that is most truly diagnostic of both the Poverty Point site and Poverty Point culture, the plentiful and enigmatic Poverty Point object (also known simply as "PPO"), has received comparatively little research attention. Its importance to Poverty Point culture is highlighted by the fact that when Clarence Webb (1968, 1982) delineated the extent of the culture, he used sites containing PPOs or related baked-clay objects ("BCOs") as his boundary markers.

PPOs are one of the most widely distributed artifact types in the Southeast. They are found primarily in the Lower Mississippi Valley (LMV), but they have also been found at sites extending from coastal Louisiana eastward along the Gulf Coast to northeast Florida (a distance of approximately 960 km), northward from the coast approximately 960 km to the Cairo, Illinois, area, and even up into the lower Ohio Valley to near Louisville, Kentucky. This huge area can be subdivided into about 10 distinct regions of PPO concentrations (Figure 7.2). These include eastern Florida (particularly at the Harris Creek site [8VO24] on Tick Island), the northwest coast of Florida, the Mississippi/Louisiana Gulf Coast, south Louisiana, south Texas, the Poverty Point area, the Yazoo Basin, eastern Arkansas, the Central Mississippi Valley, and the Falls of the Ohio.

Because PPOs can be sorted easily into a standard set of types, archaeologists have typically classified and quantified their numbers at sites, but rarely do they analyze the PPOs any further. Typically they have assumed that PPOs were used primarily as a type of "cooking stone" to hold and release heat when

Christopher T. Hays, James B. Stoltman, Richard A. Weinstein

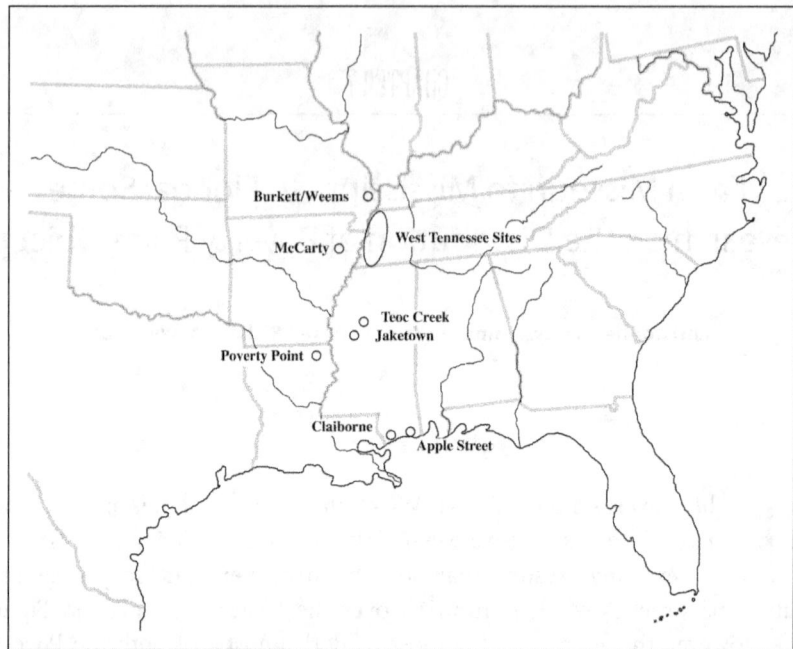

Figure 7.1. Map of sites from which Poverty Point Objects (PPOs) were thin-sectioned during 2010–2011.

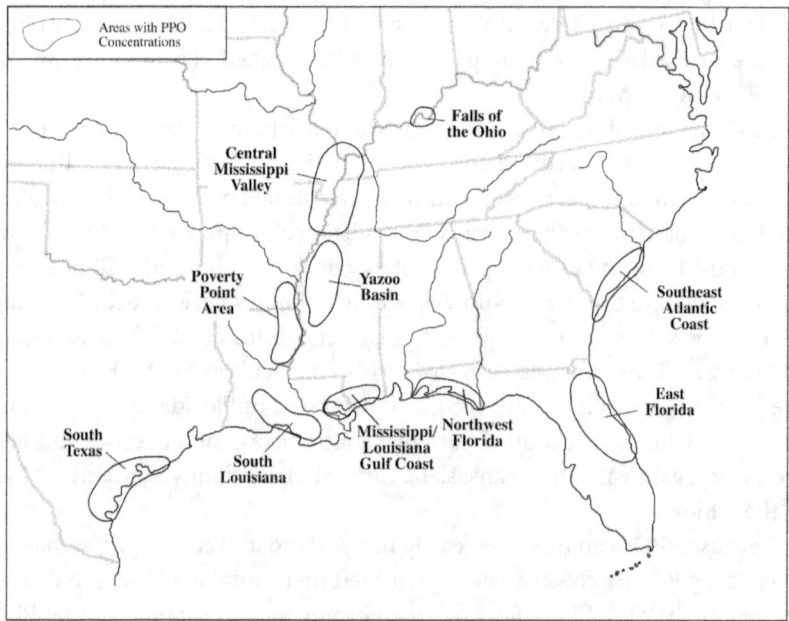

Figure 7.2. Ten general areas of PPO concentrations.

roasting food. In 2009 we began a multiyear research project on the function, distribution, and meaning of PPOs in order to explore their greater research potential and the complexity of their use. We have, for example, discovered that PPOs have sometimes been traded or transported between sites that are several hundred miles apart, such as from Poverty Point to Tick Island in eastern Florida or from the Mississippi Gulf Coast site of Claiborne (22HA501) at the mouth of the Pearl River to Poverty Point (Hays, Stoltman, Tykot, and Weinstein 2010). We have identified distinct regional patterns in the distribution of types (e.g., mulberried spheroids were almost exclusively made on the Gulf Coast but were transported to Poverty Point: Hays, Weinstein, and Stoltman 2010). And we are convinced that the function and meanings that Poverty Point peoples associated with some of the PPOs must have extended beyond their use as quotidian baking stones (Hays, Weinstein, and Stoltman 2010; Hays et al. 2011).

We are currently working toward publication of a comprehensive analysis and interpretation of the results of our multiyear research project. In this chapter we report on a portion of that work, primarily the results of our thin-section analyses of baked-clay objects conducted during 2010–2011. In addition, we discuss relevant thin-section analyses from previous years. The thin sections were analyzed by Stoltman using a point-counting procedure to record the bulk composition of each PPO (Stoltman 1989, 1991). Bulk composition is expressed quantitatively as the percentages of the following three natural ingredients: matrix (i.e., clay), silt, and sand. A sand-size index is also recorded for each thin section. The basic underlying assumption of this analysis is that local manufacture of fired-clay products is the more probable alternative to importation when their physical properties match those of local sediments and/or demonstrably local artifacts.

We thin-sectioned 27 PPOs from a wide range of locales including the Burkett (23MI20) and Weems (23MI25) sites in southeast Missouri, six sites in western Tennessee, the McCarty site (3PO467) in northeast Arkansas, the Teoc Creek site (22CR504) in the Yazoo Basin, and the Claiborne and Apple Street (22JA530) sites on the Mississippi Gulf Coast. We selected samples from these areas to answer questions raised by our previous work, and also to ensure that we had examined samples from most of the important regions with PPO concentrations.

In all of our thin-section analyses of PPOs, we attempted to answer three basic questions: (1) What is the primary sedimentary composition of PPOs within a region? (2) What types of PPOs are present in a region and are there any PPOs unique to that region? and (3) Is there any evidence that some of the PPOs in a region are nonindigenous and, in fact, may have been brought into that area from someplace else? Most of this chapter is devoted to addressing these questions for PPO samples from three areas: southeast Missouri, west Tennessee, and the Mississippi Gulf Coast.

Missouri Samples

Poverty Point objects or baked-clay objects have been recorded at sites in southeastern Missouri since as early as the late 1800s (Williams 1991:96). Excavations at the adjacent sites of Burkett and Weems and at the Hearns (23MI7) site have produced some of the largest samples of these objects in the region (Klippel 1969; Thomas et al. 2005; Williams 1968). While most of the PPOs in southeast Missouri date to the O'Bryan Ridge phase of the Late Archaic period, they continued to be used and produced in the region in declining but appreciable numbers into the Mississippi period (ca. 10 to 20 at sites in each post-Archaic time period: Williams 1991). The range of types is limited, but includes distinct biconical shapes, poorly defined spheroid and biscuit shapes, a few melon-shaped forms, and some tabular and potato-shaped forms (Thomas et al. 2005; Williams 1968).

To address our questions about PPOs in this region, we received a loan from the University of Missouri of approximately 200 PPOs from the Burkett and Weems sites. Based on a visual inspection of the objects, we noted the following trends. The majority are round/spheroidal or amorphous in shape (Figure 7.3). There is a sizable number of biconical objects, although many of them were barely distinguishable from the rounded objects since the ends were not very pointed (Figure 7.4). There are also a few ellipsoidal objects.

The vast majority of the Missouri PPOs have a sandy composition, which is to be expected since the soil samples curated with the PPOs were texturally very sandy, probably a sandy loam. It should be noted that Thomas et al. (2005:93–101) report that soil texture can vary considerably at the Burkett site from sandy to clayey to silty. Seven PPOs, two from Burkett and five from Weems, were selected for thin sectioning in order to sample a range of styles (biconicals, spheroids, and ellipsoids) and composition (very sandy, moderately sandy, clayey).

The thin-section analysis demonstrated that, in fact, there are two distinct compositional groups (Figure 7.5 and Table 7.1). Most of the PPOs are sandy (i.e., have > 20 percent sand) with very little silt (i.e., less than 10 percent silt). Interestingly one of the objects in this group (23-3) is composed of two very distinct clays (Figure 7.6). On the left part of the thin section is fine clay with almost no inclusions and on the right is extremely sandy clay, which is the predominant soil type in the object. In contrast to the five sandy PPOs, two (one each from Burkett and Weems) are composed almost entirely of clay (or matrix) with very little silt or sand.

Some Research on the Distribution of Poverty Point Objects

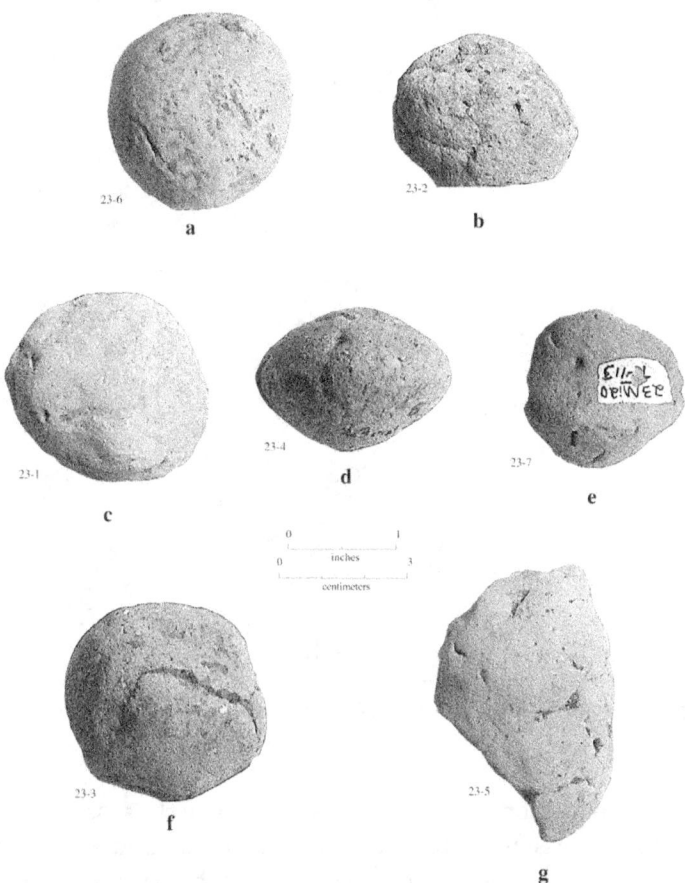

Figure 7.3. PPOs thin sectioned from the Burkett/Weems sites. (a. spheroidal; b. biconical; c. biconical; d. biconical; e. biconical; f. biconical/spheroidal; g. potato-shaped). Photo courtesy Christopher T. Hays, James B. Stoltman, and Richard A. Weinstein.

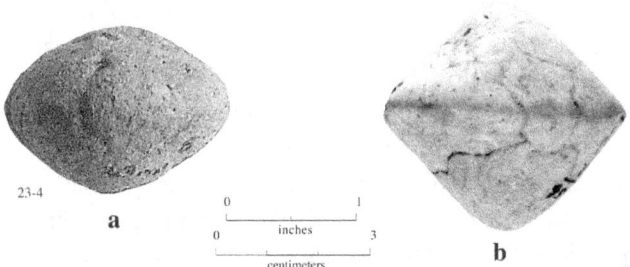

Figure 7.4. Comparison of Weems (a) and West Tennessee biconicals (b). Photo courtesy Christopher T. Hays, James B. Stoltman, and Richard A. Weinstein.

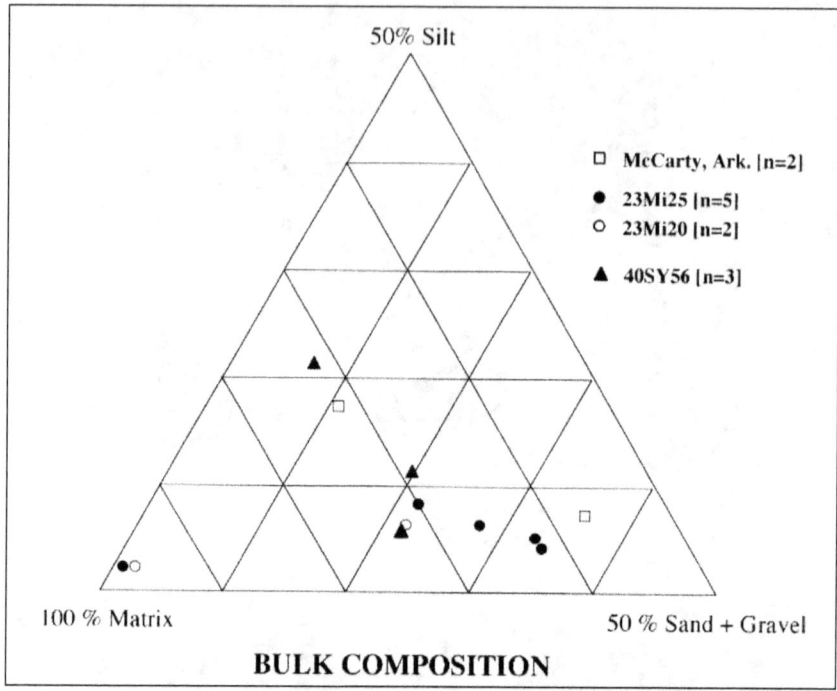

Figure 7.5. Ternary graph of PPOs from Burkett/Weems, McCarty and 40SY56 (biconicals from West Tennessee).

One clear conclusion concerning the Missouri objects is that *none* of them appear to be imports from either Poverty Point or the Yazoo Basin, since they do not fit the compositional characteristics of either area. Particularly, the Missouri objects have low silt content, which is distinctively different from the high silt content of LMV PPOs. Therefore we find no evidence of the movement of baked-clay objects between Poverty Point and southeast Missouri. This is not surprising since the main components containing PPOs at the Burkett and Weems sites appear to predate Poverty Point and Jaketown by several hundred years. Radiocarbon dates from Burkett indicate baked-clay objects were in use there as early as 2300 B.C., which is quite a few hundred years before PPOs appear at the Poverty Point site (Thomas et al. 2004:120).

There is, however, an intriguing similarity in composition between three of the biconicals from Tennessee (two from 40SY56 and one from 40DY42) and the five sandy PPOs from Missouri (Figures 7.5 and 7.9). Since the soils at 40SY56 are primarily silt loams (loessal soils cover much of western Tennessee adjacent to the Mississippi River), this suggests the possibility that these two biconicals were made somewhere in the Burkett/Weems vicinity. However, in form and style the Burkett/Weems biconicals are quite different from those

Some Research on the Distribution of Poverty Point Objects

Table 7.1. Bulk composition for Arkansas and Missouri PPOs.

Site	Type	Thin Section #	% Matrix	% Silt	% Sand	Sand Size Index
Arkansas						
McCarty (3PO467)	?	3-6	57	7	36	1.51
McCarty (3PO467)	?	3-7	72	17	11	1.00
Missouri						
Weems (23Ml25)	Biconical	23-1	70	8	22	1.21
Weems (23Ml25)	Biconical	23-2	62	4	34	1.17
Weems (23Ml25)	Biconical/Spheroidal	23-3	66	6	28	1.06
Weems (23Ml25)	Biconical	23-4	62	5	33	1.53
Weems (23Ml25)	Potato-shaped	23-5	97	2	1	1.00
	Mean ± 1 std dev	[n = 5]	71.4 ± 14.7	5.0 ± 2.2	23.6 ± 13.5	1.19 ± .21
Burkett (23Ml20)	Spheroidal	23-6	96	2	2	1.40
Burkett (23Ml20)	Biconical	23-7	72	6	22	1.06

Figure 7.6. Thin section of PPO from Weems site composed of two distinct clays (fine clay on the left and extremely sandy clay on the right). Photo courtesy Christopher T. Hays, James B. Stoltman, and Richard A. Weinstein.

found in southwest Tennessee. Specifically, as noted earlier, the Missouri biconicals are poorly formed, whereas the biconicals found at 40SY56 are well made.

There are some notable compositional similarities that can be observed between Missouri PPOs and those of the neighboring states of Arkansas and Tennessee. In contrast to the LMV sites in Mississippi and Louisiana, which have generally high-silt/low-sand compositions, the preponderance of those from Missouri and Arkansas plus four from Tennessee have generally low-silt/high-sand compositions (i.e., no more than 11 percent silt and no less than 20 percent sand). It seems most parsimonious to view this as a regional pattern that can be associated with the central Mississippi Valley region.

Tennessee Samples

In several papers Smith (e.g., 1996, 1998) has documented the presence and extent of PPOs at sites throughout western Tennessee, and he has set up a series of associated Poverty Point phases in the region. The dates and cultural affiliations of these objects are not entirely clear, however, since the collections are associated with mostly small-scale investigations and few definitive radiocarbon dates. Most of the PPOs probably date to the terminal Archaic or Poverty Point periods, but it seems likely that they were used in limited numbers in the Woodland period, since some have been found in association with Early to Middle Woodland pottery (Mainfort 1997; Smith 1998).

To address our questions about the Tennessee samples, we obtained a loan from the Chucalissa Museum in Memphis of all the PPOs from western Tennessee that were large enough to be identifiable to type (Figure 7.7). In total, this included approximately 30 objects. We selected 13 of them for thin sectioning from six sites, three from southwest Tennessee (40SY56, 40FY36, and 40TP37) and three from northwest Tennessee (40DY42, 40GB42, and 40OB54). These samples were selected based on the following criteria: first, we wanted a wide representation from sites throughout west Tennessee; second, we selected samples made of a highly unusual and intriguing white clay that we wanted to know more about; and third, we included some samples that we believed might be imports into the region (Figure 7.8).

Thin-section analysis revealed that the PPOs from west Tennessee are diverse in composition: seven have sand counts of 2 percent or less; four, by contrast, have high sand percentages, ranging from 20 to 26 percent; and two have relatively high amounts of silt (i.e., 15–21 percent) with relatively low sand percentages of 1–7 percent (Figure 7.9 and Table 7.2). This diversity in composition is apparent even within sites. For example, both site 40GB42 in northwestern Tennessee and site 40SY56 in southwest Tennessee have PPOs of three distinct compositions: some are very clayey, some are siltier, and others are somewhat sandy. Thus, on the whole there does not appear to be a particular mineralogical composition characteristic of the region. The styles of PPOs found in west Tennessee are a bit more diverse than those in southeast Missouri. They include well-formed biconicals, biscuits, cylinders, round/spheroids, and ellipsoids; yet they are not nearly as diverse nor as consistent

Some Research on the Distribution of Poverty Point Objects

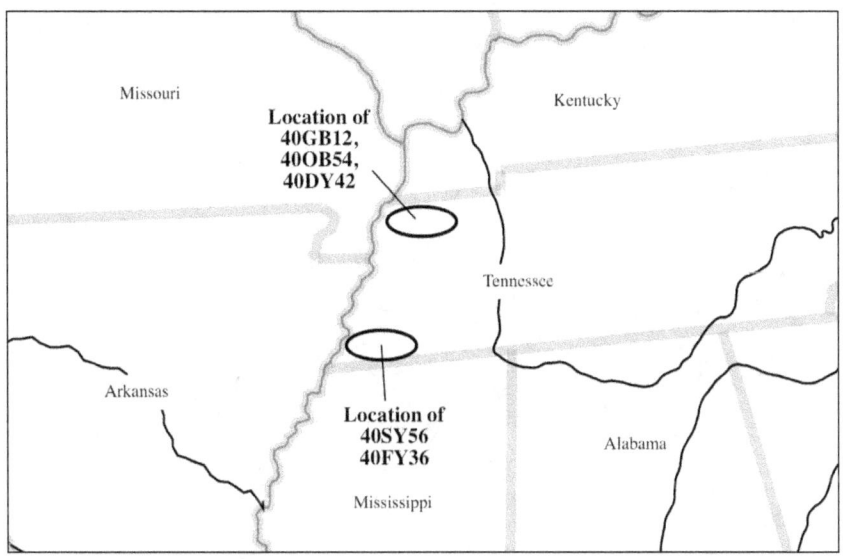

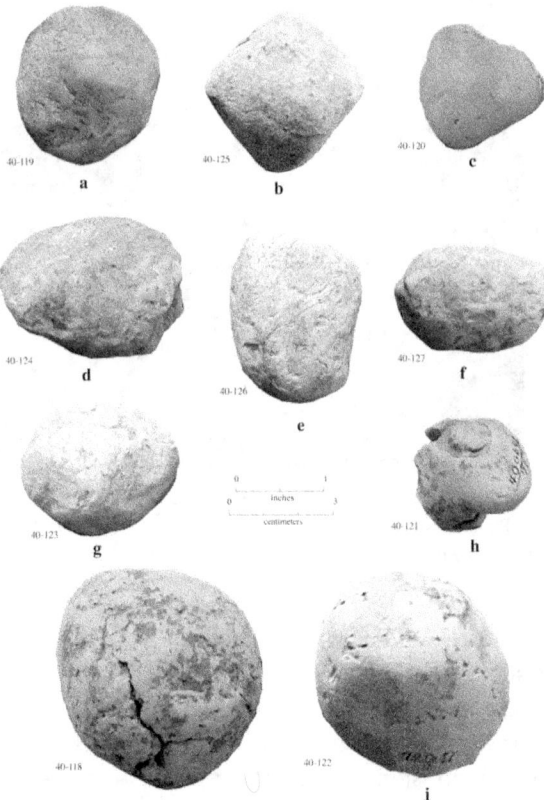

Figure 7.7. Location of sites with samples from West Tennessee.

Figure 7.8. PPOs thin sectioned from West Tennessee sites (a. biconical; b. biconical; c. biconical; d. ellipsoid; e. cylinder; f. cylinder; g. spheroidal; h. spheroid with cane impression; i. spheroid; j. ellipsoid). Photo courtesy Christopher T. Hays, James B. Stoltman, and Richard A. Weinstein.

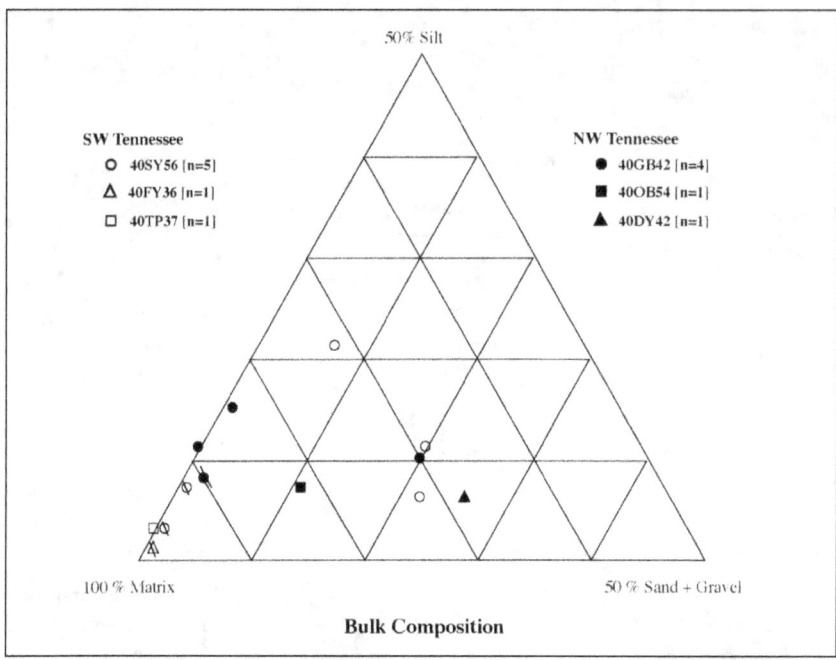

Figure 7.9. Ternary graph of PPOs from West Tennessee sites.

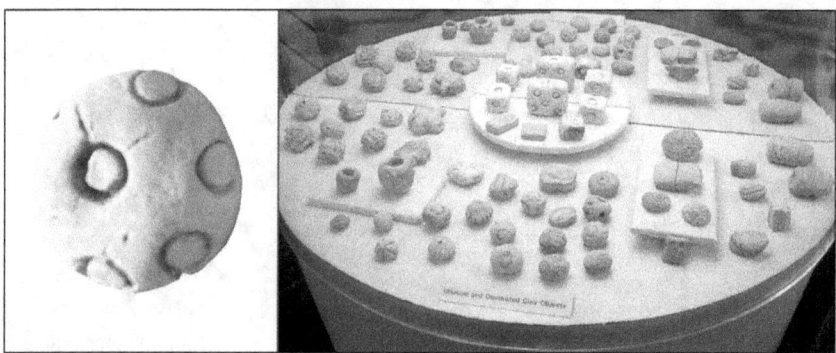

Figure 7.10. Biscuit-shaped object with cane impressions from West Tennessee (*left*) and unusual and decorated PPOs on display at Poverty Point (*right*). Photo of Poverty Point artifacts by Hieronymous Rowe at en.wikipedia (http://en.wikipedia.org).

in their stylistic forms as those found at Poverty Point or within the Yazoo Basin's Poverty Point-era sites.

The west Tennessee objects include several types with distinctive regional characteristics. First, a small number of them are ellipsoidal or spheroidal objects with cord or fabric impressions. As far as we know, only one other site has objects with fabric impressions: Poverty Point (with approximately 17 specimens). The Tennessee fabric- and cord-marked objects may be associated

Table 7.2. Bulk composition for Tennessee PPOs.

Site	Type	Thin Section #	% Matrix	% Silt	% Sand	Sand Size Index
Southwest Tennessee						
40SY56	Biconical	40-115	72	21	7	1.38
40SY56	Biconical	40-116	72	6	22	1.04
40SY56	Biconical	40-117	69	11	20	1.04
40SY56	Cylindrical	40-126	96	3	1	1.00
40SY56	Cylindrical	40-127	92	7	1	1.00
40TP37	Ellipsoid	40-122	97	3	0	—
40FY36	Spheroidal	40-123	98	1	1	1.50
Northwest Tennessee						
40GB42	Spheroidal	40-118	89	11	0	3.00
40GB42	Biconical	40-119	90	8	2	2.60
40GB42	Biconical	40-120	84	15	1	2.50
40GB42	Spheroidal	40-121	70	10	20	1.02
40OB54	Ellipsoid	40-124	82	7	11	1.00
40DY42	Biconical	40-125	68	6	26	1.08

with Early and Middle Woodland occupations, since these decorations commonly show up on early pottery in the region. Another distinctive PPO type in west Tennessee is the biscuit-shaped object with cane impressions (Figure 7.10). The only other site with PPOs with similar cane impressions is Poverty Point, which has some cube-shaped and biscuit-shaped objects exhibiting such decoration.

Finally, one very distinctive quality of some of the west Tennessee PPOs is that they are made of dense, kaolinitic white clay (e.g. 40-123 in Figure 7.8). We thin-sectioned four of these PPOs (40-119, 40-123, 40-126, and 40-127) from three different sites (40SY56, 40FY36, and 40GB42). All four had highly birefringent bodies with very little silt or sand and, importantly, were white (10YR8/1) in color. Webb et al. (1969:61) refer to very similar PPOs in private collections in northwest Tennessee that are made of "firm white clay." We believe that the most likely source of this clay is the borderline region of northwest Tennessee and southwest Kentucky, which contains deposits of Eocene-age kaolinitic clays known as "ball clay" (Olive and Finch 1969 and Figure 7.10). These deposits are being actively mined today for a variety of purposes, including the production of dinnerware and electrical porcelain.

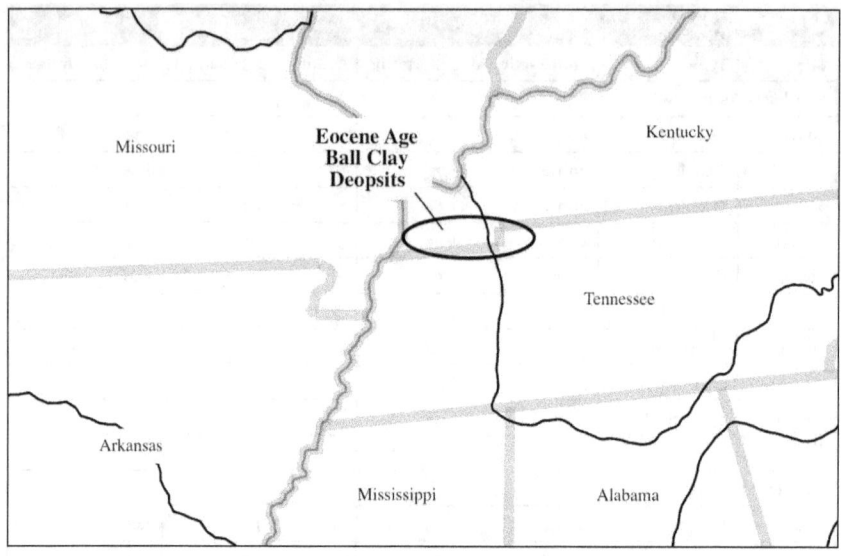

Figure 7.11. Location of ball clay deposits in northwest Tennessee area.

The only other site with PPOs with this combination of color and texture is Poverty Point (Figure 7.10; see PPOs in the center of the unusual and decorated collection). These PPOs, which are in the "unusual" collection at Poverty Point, are distinctive also because they have cane impressions, which, as noted above, are distinctly characteristic of west Tennessee PPOs. Taken together, these data strongly suggest that the white cane-impressed PPOs at Poverty Point were imported from west Tennessee.

The evidence for imported PPOs in west Tennessee is mixed. One of the PPOs (40-120) has a high percentage of silt (i.e., 15 percent) and only 1 percent sand. Although this is typical of objects originating at Poverty Point, because much of western Tennessee has silty loams, the origin of this PPO must be regarded as uncertain. PPO 40-115, however, has a high silt content (21 percent) and moderate sand content (7 percent) that is characteristic of Yazoo Basin PPOs, and is unlike the composition of the major soil type at the site (40SY56) where it was found (Fayala silt loam [Sease et al. 1970]). Therefore, it seems plausible that 40-115 was imported. Finally, as noted before, two of the biconicals found at 40SY56 have relatively sandy compositions and may have been imports from the southeast Missouri area.

Mississippi Sites: Teoc Creek and Gulf Coast

During the year 2010–2011, we thin-sectioned a sample of PPOs from both the Yazoo Basin and the Mississippi Gulf Coast. For the Yazoo Basin, we selected

Figure 7.12. Biconical PPO fragments thin sectioned from Teoc Creek. Photo courtesy Christopher T. Hays, James B. Stoltman, and Richard A. Weinstein.

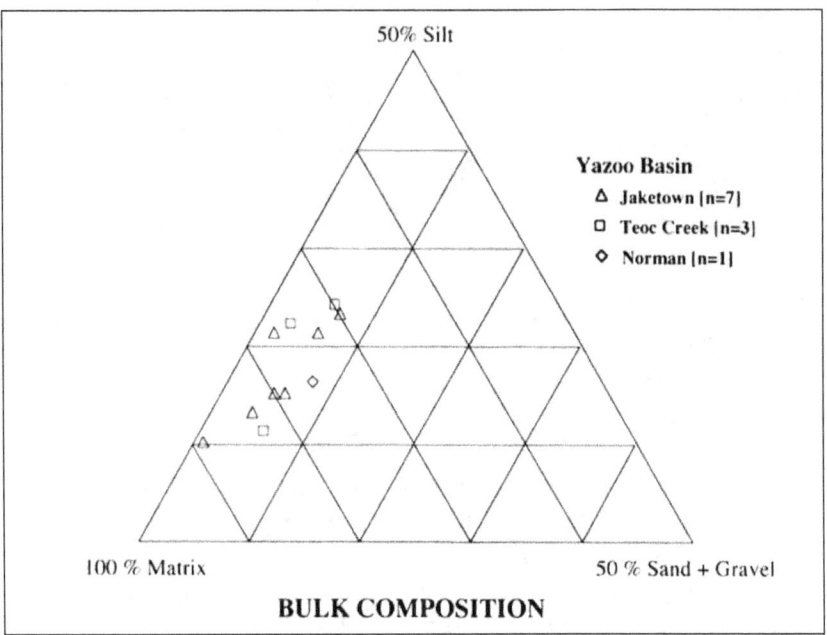

Figure 7.13. Ternary graph with all Yazoo Basin PPOs.

three biconicals from the Teoc Creek site (Connaway et al. 1977; Figure 7.12 and Figure 7.13). The three are similar in composition, consisting of variable but relatively high amounts of silt (i.e., 11–24 percent), and small amounts of fine sand (i.e., 6 percent or less). This compositional mixture is similar to the PPOs that we had previously thin-sectioned from the other major Poverty Point-era Yazoo Basin sites of Jaketown (22HU505) and Norman (22QU518) (Hays, Stoltman, Tykot, and Weinstein 2010). Indeed, one of the most striking patterns among the PPOs we have observed across the Southeast is the

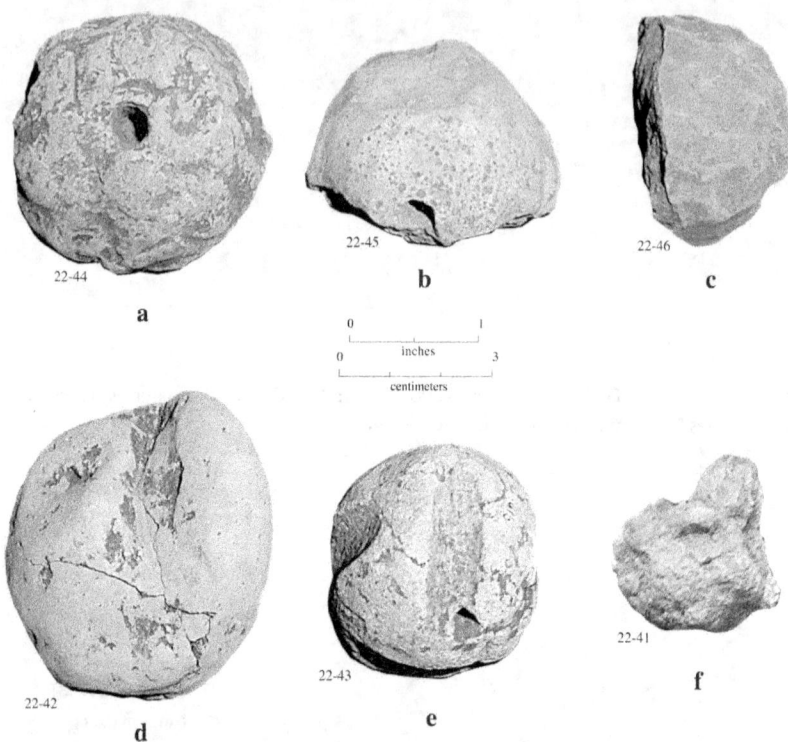

Figure 7.14. PPOs/BCOs thin sectioned from coastal Mississippi sites (a. perforated mulberry; b. dimpled PPO; c. dimpled PPO; d. melon, longitudinal grooved; e. melon, lateral grooved; f. mulberry fragment). Photo courtesy Christopher T. Hays, James B. Stoltman, and Richard A. Weinstein.

remarkably consistent composition of PPOs from the Yazoo Basin, with their relatively high silt content (ranging from 10 to 24 percent) and moderate values of fine sand (i.e., 1–8 percent). This pattern stands in stark contrast to the PPOs from other regions, such as Poverty Point or Claiborne, where there is a great diversity of both styles and composition, and the Missouri and west Tennessee sites that, as mentioned above, have diverse compositions.

To address our research questions about the relationship between Mississippi Gulf Coast sites and Poverty Point, we obtained loans of PPOs from Claiborne from both public and private sources and the loan of a single PPO from the Apple Street site (Figure 7.14). From the Claiborne site we selected five PPOs, including one (22-44) with a distinctive roughened surface treatment that Webb (1982:39) referred to as mulberried (hereafter such PPOs are referred to as mulberries). Two of the other PPOs that we selected from Claiborne are what Webb et al. (1969:16) referred to as spheroidal dimpled, having

Some Research on the Distribution of Poverty Point Objects

Table 7.3. Bulk composition for Claiborne and Apple Street PPOs.					
Type	Thin Section #	% Matrix	% Silt	% Sand	Sand Size Index
Claiborne					
Melon, Longitudinal Grooved	22-30	50	8	42	1.59
Biconical	22-31	42	3	55	1.69
Cylindrical Grooved	22-32	55	6	39	1.58
Cross Grooved	22-33	61	7	32	1.50
Melon, Longitudinal Grooved	22-34	52	5	43	1.80
Melon, Longitudinal Grooved	22-42	81	19	0	—
Melon, Lateral Grooved	22-43	72	5	23	1.64
Perforated Mulberry	22-44	74	6	20	1.27
Dimpled PPO	22-45	75	16	9	1.00
Dimpled PPO	22-46	68	18	14	1.06
Mean ± 1 std dev	[n = 10]	63.0 ± 12.9	9.3 ± 6.0	27.7 ± 17.4	1.46 ± .28
Apple Street					
Mulberry Fragment	22-41	77	6	17	1.78

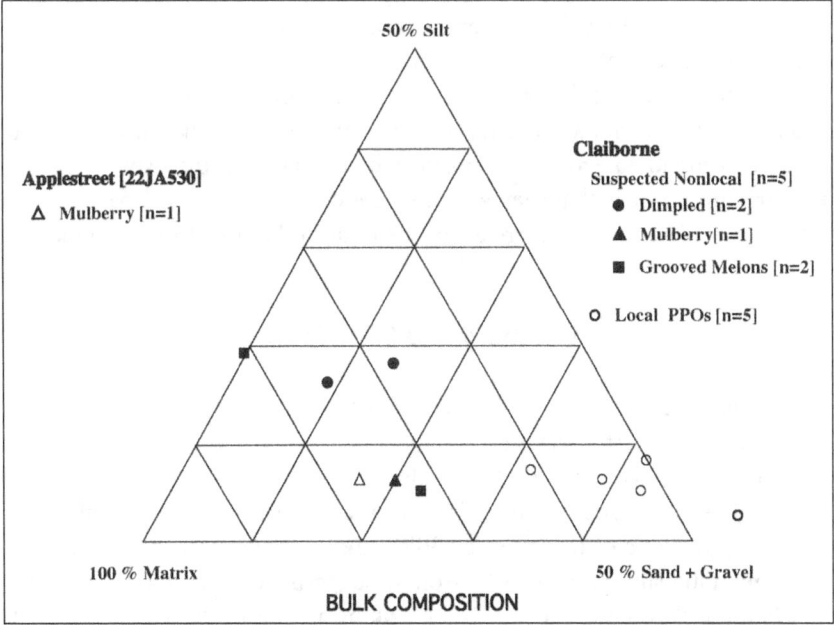

Figure 7.15. Ternary graph of relevant PPOs thin sectioned from Caliborne and Apple Street sites.

a faceted or dimpled surface treatment to produce a golfball-like appearance (22-45 and 22-46). The other two PPOs selected included one with unusual lateral grooves (22-43) and a melon-shaped PPO with a silty composition (22-42). The Apple Street PPO is a mulberry (see Figure 7.14). Previously, we had analyzed thin sections of five PPOs from Claiborne (Hays, Stoltman, Tykot, and Weinstein 2010), and in our discussion below we compare them to the results of our 2010–2011 samples from Claiborne.

Accepting the five sandy PPOs as local Claiborne products, it is noteworthy that none of the six new PPO samples from Claiborne and Apple Street fall within the compositional range of variation of the local Claiborne PPOs (Table 7.3). At least one of the new samples (22-42), a melon-shaped PPO, has a compositional profile that places it fully within the range of variation of PPOs and sediments from the Poverty Point site. We regard it as an actual import from Poverty Point. The two dimpled PPOs (22-45 and 22-46) stand out as outliers, with compositions that are intermediate between the sandy local PPOs of Claiborne and the silty PPOs of Poverty Point (Figure 7.15). Their derivation must currently be regarded as unknown, but it is noteworthy that Poverty Point has 51 dimpled PPOs and they are not present at any of the Yazoo Basin sites (Webb et al. 1969).

As for the mulberried PPOs (one each from Claiborne and Apple Street and three from Poverty Point), there appears to be a notably uniform compositional pattern that is consistent with the view of a common origin. Generally, these five mulberries have moderate sand percentages (i.e., between 10 and 20 percent) and low silt values (i.e., 11 percent or less) (Figure 7.15). Since this compositional pattern is matched at no site or region in our current sample, we are unable to make a positive identification of their source. A view we currently favor is that they were made locally on the Gulf Coast, using a distinctive recipe that is a correlate of their cultural or functional uniqueness.

Summary and Conclusions

Our visual and thin-section analyses of PPOs conducted during 2010–2011 revealed distinct patterns in each region that we studied. Our thin-section analysis of the Missouri objects revealed that they break distinctly into two groups: those with sandy composition (the vast majority) and those with clayey composition. None of the over 200 PPOs that were visually inspected had a predominantly silty paste, which strongly suggests none came from the Poverty Point or Yazoo Basin areas. Other striking aspects of the Missouri objects include their limited range in types, mostly biconical and spheroidal, and their overall crude appearance, particularly when compared to the comparatively well-formed and diverse types in the LMV. As noted above, since the main occupations of the O'Bryan Ridge phase in southeast Missouri predate Poverty Point culture sites by at least several hundred years, it is not surprising that there is no clear evidence of any interrelationship. However, the fact that both cultures have numerous biconical objects and their sites are located on or very near the Mississippi River suggests that they may have some connection. This is an issue we will be considering in our continuing research.

Our analysis of the west Tennessee artifacts indicates that there is considerable diversity in the composition of the objects, ranging from very silty to very clayey to somewhat sandy, even within one site. Stylistically the PPOs in west Tennessee are, for the most part, better made than the Missouri ones, and they have a range of types that include biconicals, ellipsoids, biscuit shapes, and rounds. The west Tennessee objects, however, are not as diverse as those from Poverty Point or the Yazoo Basin sites, lacking many of the classic Poverty Point types such as cylindrical and cross grooved, biconical grooved, and melons. We noted some distinctive surface treatments on a few of the west Tennessee PPOs that are not common in classic Poverty Point sites. These include cordmarked and fabric marked and objects with round cane impressions. Moreover, we note that PPOs at three different sites are made of distinctive white, kaolinitic clay, the most likely source for which is clay deposits in northwest Tennessee. The only other site with PPOs of this type is Poverty Point, and we think it likely that the ones found at that locale came from west Tennessee.

The results of our analysis of the Teoc Creek biconicals demonstrated, once again, that the Yazoo Basin PPOs are homogeneous in composition. The three Yazoo Basin sites from which we have samples are separated by over 160 km, but their PPOs are made of basically the same proportions of sand, silt, and clay. Finally, our analysis of the Claiborne and Apple Street PPOs revealed, as we had suspected, that PPOs were moving back and forth between the Gulf Coast and Poverty Point. We got further support for our argument that the sandy mulberries found at Poverty Point were coming from the Gulf Coast, and this year we demonstrated that Poverty Point objects were being moved to Claiborne. We suspect that our sample only represents a small portion of the PPOs that were moving between the sites, and indeed Webb et al. (1969:3, 28) hint at this when they mention that 2.8 percent (n = 357) of the PPOs at Claiborne were silty or clayey, while at Poverty Point they estimated .66 percent were coarse sandy (i.e., they found 39 coarse sandy PPOs out of the 5,908 checked for this attribute). A more detailed discourse on the implications of these results will be forthcoming, along with a full discussion and analysis of all of the results of our ongoing study into the distribution and movement of PPOs within the Poverty Point exchange system.

Acknowledgments

The authors would like to thank and acknowledge several institutions and their representatives who generously loaned us artifact samples for the thin-section study. These include the Museum of Anthropology, University of Missouri; the C. H. Nash Museum at Chucalissa; the Hancock County Historical Society; the University of Southern Mississippi; the Louisiana Division of Archaeology and the Louisiana Division of State Parks; and the Mississippi Department of Archives and History. Catherine and Phillip Burgess loaned us samples from Claiborne from their private collection. Research grants from the University of Wisconsin-Washington County Foundation and the Department of Anthropology and Sociology, University of Wisconsin, provided money for various laboratory analyses and trips to professional meetings and conferences. Lastly, colleagues at the authors' institutions provided invaluable advice and support. We would particularly like to thank Donald Hunter of CEI for his work on the map figures and artifact photos.

PART III

The Woodland and Mississippian Periods

PART II

CHAPTER 8

Artifact Assemblages from Two Early Woodland Tchula-Period Sites on the Holly Springs National Forest, North Mississippi

Evan Peacock

Introduction

In 1992, only two prehistoric archaeological sites had been recorded on the Holly Springs National Forest (which at that time included only the Holly Springs Ranger District; it now includes the Yalobusha Unit, formerly part of the Tombigbee National Forest). Today, there are approximately 200 prehistoric sites known on the Holly Springs District, most of which date to the Woodland period. At least 150 of these sites can be further attributed to the Early Woodland Tchula period (see Phillips 1970) based on ceramic markers such as Withers Fabric Marked, Cormorant Cord Impressed, and Twin Lakes Punctated (Brandon and McNutt 1995; Ford 1990; Peacock 1996c; Phillips et al. 1951:73). Given that most of these Tchula-period sites are small, with relatively light artifact density, it is likely that many have been missed, even with the intensive shovel testing and screening inaugurated on the National Forests in Mississippi by Sam Brookes (see Peacock 1994, this volume, Chapter 2). Couple this caveat with the fact that much land remains to be surveyed on the Holly Springs District (not to mention private land inholdings within and outside of the USDA Forest Service proclamation boundaries), and it is not exaggerating to suggest that thousands of small, Tchula-period sites exist within the high ridge systems of Benton, Marshall, and Tippah counties, Mississippi.

To date, information on these sites derives mostly from shovel-test surveys and is available primarily in technical reports submitted to the Mississippi Department of Archives and History by USDA Forest Service archaeologists. Excavations have been carried out at a number of sites, but only a few of these (Fant 1996a; Peacock and Fant 2002) have been reported in any form. In this paper, I briefly recap what is known about Tchula-period sites on the Holly

Springs National Forest. I then report on two Tchula-period occupations, 22BE588 and 22BE554, tested by the late David Fant in 1996 and 1998, respectively. I compare assemblages and site structure between these two occupations, others reported from the Holly Springs National Forest, and one at the approximately contemporary Fulmer site (40SY527) in Shelby County, Tennessee (Weaver et al. 1999), focusing primarily upon site function and occupational duration. Finally, I offer some suggestions for future research involving these intriguing upland, Early Woodland-period sites.

Background

The Tchula period in general remains poorly understood, both as a cultural period and a chronological period. The widest possible span indicated by a literature review is 800 B.C.–A.D. 410 (Peacock 1996c:17; Wilkins 2004), although Childress et al. (1999) argue for a 400–100 B.C. time span. Excavations of Tchula occupations have taken place mostly in the Lower Mississippi Alluvial Valley, or LMV (Brookes and Taylor 1986; Connaway and McGahey 1971; Griffin 1986; Morse 1986; Phillips 1970; Rolingson and Jeter 1986; Weinstein 1991; see also Wilkins 2004). In north-central and northwest Mississippi, Tchula-period materials have been discussed under the general name "Lake Cormorant Culture" (Phillips 1970; see Ford 1990; Weinstein 1991:161). Problems with the myriad terms employed for grouping archaeological phenomena have been discussed elsewhere (e.g., Dunnell 2008b; Peacock 2003; Rafferty 1986), and further critique is outside the purpose of this paper. Suffice to say that Tchula-period sites on the Holly Springs National Forest were identified based on ceramic markers that presumably make them roughly coeval with similar phenomena in the northern part of the Yazoo Basin (Phillips 1970) and the lower Central Mississippi Valley (e.g., Morse 1986:79–81).

Excavations of Tchula-period sites in the hill country east of the Yazoo Basin have focused primarily upon mounds (Ford 1990), and the likelihood that mound building first appeared in the area during the Tchula period has grown increasingly strong over time (Brookes 1988; Ford 1988a, 1990; Mainfort 1986b; Weinstein 1991). A broader context for understanding phenomena like mound building has been slower in coming, however, as surveys in the area prior to the USDA Forest Service surveys of the Brookes era were relatively small-scale affairs (e.g., Johnson 1984). The many Tchula-period sites in the Holly Springs District therefore came as a surprise resulting from (1) the low level of prior work on the Forest (see Peacock, this volume, Chapter 2); and (2) the traditional fixation of archaeologists on square holes in the ground, especially at mound sites, rather than appreciation for the power of survey data. It was survey data obtained from sites on the Holly Springs District that allowed basic questions of local ceramic chronology, such as change through time in temper modes, to be answered (Peacock 1996c). However, shovel-test survey data may be of limited utility when questions related to occupational duration and site function are asked. The picture obtained from surveys on the Holly Springs District was one of small occupations of short duration, with very limited artifact inventories (mostly pottery, with a small amount of sandstone/siltstone debitage and even less chert debitage) and a low likelihood of features such as pits, postholes, or hearths (Fant 1996a; Peacock 1996c). Based primarily on survey data, I suggested (Peacock 1996c:19) that these Tchula sites represented "special-purpose, short-term occupations," and both Fant (1996a:58) and I noted the need for more excavation to address such questions. Interestingly, Tchula-period diagnostics do not appear to occur south of the Little Tallahatchie River (Fant 1996a; Peacock 1996c).

Previous Excavations

Some Tchula-period occupations on the Holly Springs District have seen excavation. The Chewalla Lake Mound (22MR502), in Marshall County, was recorded by Stuart Neitzel in 1966 (site card on file, MDAH). This badly damaged conical mound was apparently associated with a nearby habitation site that yielded grog-tempered plain and fabric-marked pottery as well as "quartz/grit"-tempered plain sherds, chert debitage, and a "perforator." The mound was rebuilt by the USDA Forest Service using a sketch map provided by Neitzel, but some question remained about whether any original mound remained intact beneath the modern reconstruction. Fant tested this site in the late 1990s and informed me that he did encounter undisturbed mound fill, but this work has not been formally reported. Limited test excavations at a few Woodland-period sites were conducted in the late 1990s by Johanna Bettis, a graduate student at Eastern New Mexico University, but these have not been formally reported either. Limited excavations at a Tchula site by a University of Mississippi field school led by Janet Ford at around that same time also remain unreported.

Excavations at two sites, 22MR539 and 22BE585, have been reported. Site 22MR539 was tested to investigate artifact movement in the almost pure sand deposits found occasionally on upland ridges in the Holly Springs Ranger District (Peacock and Fant 2002). Four 1-×-1-meter units produced 91 artifacts, all Tchula-period ceramics except for five sandstone flakes (Fant 1996a; Peacock and Fant 2002). Site 22BE585 was tested with volunteers from the Mississippi Archaeological Association in 1995. Four 2-×-2-meter units produced Tchula-period ceramics, fired clay, and very low numbers of lithics (described as fire-cracked rock or flakes, but not otherwise analyzed) (Fant 1996a). Some possible features were recorded, but these were delineated based on texture, not color or artifact content, and it is likely that they were natural disturbances. Limited though they are, these excavations support the assessment of short occupational duration and low artifact diversity derived from shovel-test surveys (Fant 1996a; Peacock 1996c).

Study Sites

The two assemblages described in this chapter (Figure 8.1) have not been previously reported, although I have a copy of a partial draft manuscript by Fant (1996c) on excavations at 22BE588, which is discussed further below.

Site 22BE544 was found during a timber sale survey (Peacock 1993). This small site (ca. 700 square meters) was very well preserved based on the soil profile. Artifact density was heavy,[1] with 17 sherds and one piece of fired clay being recovered. The sherds included two grog-tempered plain, nine grog-tempered fabric-impressed (Withers Fabric Impressed), and six grog-tempered eroded.[2] Site 22BE588 was recorded in a land exchange survey conducted by Fant (1994). Ceramic density at this small site (ca. 900 square meters) was heavy, with seven grog-tempered plain sherds, four grog-tempered fabric-impressed sherds, one grog-tempered punctate ("small triangular impressions" just

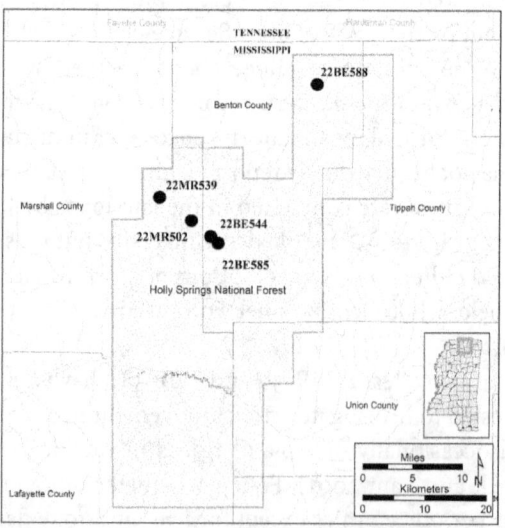

Figure 8.1. Holly Springs National Forest with location of selected Tchula-period sites. Map by Ryan Shears.

beneath a folded-lip rim, "probably related to the Cormorant or Crowder rim treatments" [Fant 1994:5]) sherd, and one grog-tempered, interior red-slipped sherd being recovered (Fant 1994). The assemblages of Tchula-period ceramics and almost nothing else at these two sites are typical of shovel-test survey collections from the Holly Springs District.

Fant tested site 22BE544 in September 1998. While the artifacts were available for analysis, no field notes, photos, or other documents have been found, other than some limited transit data produced when he was laying out base lines for excavation. Accordingly, what can be said about the occupation is limited to what can be deduced from information on the artifact bags and via analysis of the artifacts. The same caveats hold for 22BE588, except that some limited information is provided in the partial draft manuscript (Fant 1996c) mentioned above. Almost everything in the report is general background on local culture history and natural setting, and as no artifact separation had been made within the bags, there is no indication that the materials were ever analyzed. The only concrete information related to the excavations is as follows (Fant 1996c:3):

> Site 22BE588 is a small Early Woodland site located in the Holly Springs National Forest ... within the uplands of the North Central Hills Physiographic Zone. The site was first discovered in December of 1993 by the author and by Jim Walden, a heritage resource technician (Fant 1994). The site is located in Benton County, Mississippi about two and a half miles from the Tennessee State Line ... The site occupies a small east west trending ridge-toe overlooking a seep of swampy creek bottom to the west. The area is drained by tributaries of the Wolf River.
>
> Shovel testing during the survey phase indicated good subsurface integrity, but artifact density was relative unimpressive co[n]sisting of seven Plain sherds, four Fabric Impressed sherds, one Punctated Rim sherd, and one Plain sherd with a red slipped interior. Out of the nine shovel tests dug on the site, five produced artifacts. It must be noted, however, that previous work in the area suggest[s] that shovel tests are not representative of subsurface deposits when dealing with these small upland, woodland sites. Examples can be seen in test excavations at 22BE585 ... and 22SY527, the Fulmer site (Weaver et al. [1999]). Both of these sites produced few artifacts from initial survey shovel testing, but relatively large concentrations during testing and or excavation phases. Due to subsurface integrity and the propensity of the small Early Woodland site to produce relatively large ceramic assemblages, site 22BE588 was considered to be a candidate for further testing.
>
> The phase II testing of site 22BE588 began on 7/15/1996 and ended on 7/20/1996. Testing was done by a three person crew consisting of the author and three heritage resource technicians Steve Jones, John Stanton, and Newnoon

Table 8.1. Bag list and provenience information, 22BE588.

Bag #	Unit	Level	Notes
11	0E0N	ST, Lev. 1	
17	0E2S	ST, Lev. 1	
90	8E4N	ST, Lev. 2	
55	2W2N	ST, Lev. 1	
19	2W2S	ST, Lev. 1	
20	2W2S	ST, Lev. 2	
34	2W4S	ST, Lev. 2	
93	3W1S	Lev. 1	excavation unit
94	3W1S	Lev. 2	excavation unit
95	3W1S	Lev. 3	excavation unit
96	3W1S	Lev. 4	excavation unit
no number	3W1S	Mixed	clean up of walls
26	4W2S	ST, Lev. 2	
5	6W0N	ST, Lev. 1	
16	6W0N	ST, Lev. 2	
15	6W2N	ST, Lev. 1	
16	6W2N	ST, Lev. 2	
23	6W4N	ST, Lev. 1	
24	6W4N	ST, Lev. 2	dug on July 17
70	6W4N	ST, Lev. 2	dug on July 19
82	6W4N	Lev. 2	excavation unit
83	6W4N	Lev. 3	excavation unit
81	6W4N	Uncertain	excavation unit
30	6W2S	ST, Lev. 2	
42	6W4S	ST, Lev. 2	
31	8W2N	ST, Lev. 1	
32	8W2N	ST, Lev. 2	
39A	8W4N	ST, Lev. 1	
40	8W4N	ST, Lev. 2	
89	8W4N	Lev. 1	excavation unit
90	8W4N	Lev. 2	excavation unit
91	8W4N	Lev. 2	"pottery concentration, 11 -1 4 cm"
92	8W4N	Lev. 3	excavation unit; "20 cm to subsoil"
39B	8W2S	ST, Lev. 1	
10	10W2N	ST, Lev. 2	
49	10W2N	ST, Lev. 1	
51	10W4N	ST, Lev. 1	
52	10W4N	ST, Lev. 2	
43	10W2S	ST, Lev. 1	
44	10W2S	ST, Lev. 2	
48	10W4S	ST, Lev. 2	
62	12W2N	ST, Lev. 2	
65	12W4N	ST	level unknown
79	14W0N	ST, Lev. 1	

Bag #	Unit	Level	Notes
78	14W2N	ST, Lev. 2	
75	14W4N	ST, Lev. 1	
U1 and U2	unknown	unknown	two bags, probably surface collections
no number	various?	various?	ceramics pulled for photos; original provenience unknown

Phifer. During testing a two meter grid was placed over the area, and a topographic map was constructed for the site [note: this has not been located]. Shovel tests were dug at each two meter interval for the production of an artifact distribution map [note: this has not been located]. Finally three 1×1 meter test units were excavated within the site.

In this chapter, I include here the information taken from the bags (Tables 8.1 and 8.2) as this chapter will serve as the primary report for the work. As indicated for 22BE588 (Fant 1996c), both sites apparently were investigated using a combination of shovel tests (bags labeled "ST") dug on a grid and excavation of standard-sized units. It is likely that the shovel tests represent simple holes rather than more formal units (e.g., 50 × 50-cm shovel-test pits), and based on standard practice of the time these holes probably averaged around 30 cm in diameter. At site 22BE588, the shovel tests appear to have been dug in levels, presumably of arbitrary 10 cm thickness; this does not appear to have been the case at 22BE544, where shovel testing to subsoil is assumed. Unless otherwise noted on the bags, and as indicated for 22BE588 (Fant 1996c), I assumed that excavation units were 1 × 1 meter in size, and many bags specifically verified this. I also assumed that the northeast corner of units served as datum points unless otherwise noted, as was the case with several units at 22BE544. It is clear from the bags that Fant was excavating almost exclusively in arbitrary 10-cm levels; the few exceptions are noted in tables below. I am assuming that excavation ceased in the units when sterile soils were reached, a supposition supported by the fact that most excavation units were dug to the same approximate depths. I found nothing on the bags to indicate that any subsurface features had been encountered at either site, although one bag contained sherds from a "pottery concentration," found from 11–14 cm below surface in Unit 8W4N at 22BE588 (Table 8.1).

At site 22BE588, Fant established a benchmark arbitrarily marked 0E0N.[3] Twenty-five shovel tests and three 1-×-1-meter units were dug (Figure 8.2). Artifacts were found to a depth of 30–40 cm. Two unnumbered bags contained large numbers of artifacts, including a relatively large proportion of eroded sherds. These bags presumably represent general surface collections, suggesting that at least part of the site was denuded at the time of excavation. A further unnumbered bag containing many sherds was marked "pulled for photos." I was unable to link these artifacts with specific proveniences.

Table 8.2. Bag list and provenience information, 22BE544.

Bag #	Unit	Level	Notes
146		Surface	lithics
73A	unknown (NE)	Lev. 2	10–20 cm
123	0N10W	ST	
71	0N2W	ST	
70	0N4W	ST	
69	0N6W	?	no artifacts
122A	0N6W	Prob. Lev. 1	
122B	0N6W	Lev. 2	"Unit 10"; 10–20 cm
132	0N6W	Lev. 3	20–30 cm; "1 x 2 m"; "Unit 10"
67	2N2W	ST	
133	2N4W (SW)	Lev. 3?	20–25 cm; "Unit 9"; unsure why other levels not represented
61	4N0E	ST	
62	4N2W	ST	
88	4N4E	Lev. 1	0–10 cm; "1 x 1"; "Unit 6"
89	4N4E	Lev. 2	10–20 cm
93	4N4E (NW)	Lev. 3	20–30 cm; "Unit 6"
63	4N4W	ST	
64	4N6W	ST	
59	6N0E	ST	
58	6N2W	ST	
44	8N0E	ST	
43	8N2E	ST	
110	8N4E	ST	
46	8N4W	ST	
41	10N0E	ST	
86	10N0E (SE corner)	Lev. 1	0–10 cm; "Unit 5"
87	10N0E (SE)	Lev. 2	10–20 cm; "Unit 5"
90	10N0E	Lev. 3	20–30 cm
106	10N10W	ST	
42	10N2E	ST	
40	10N2W	ST	
109	10N4E	ST	
39	10N4W	ST	
38	10N6W	ST	
37	10N8W	ST	
92	10N8W (SW)	Lev. 1	0–10 cm; "Unit 7"
94	10N8W	Lev. 2	10–20 cm; "Unit 7"
100	10N8W	Lev. 3	20–30 cm; "Unit 7"
16	12N2E	ST	Unsure why 2 bag numbers for 12N2E
30	12N2E	ST	Unsure why 2 bag numbers for 12N2E
33	12N2W	ST	
105	12N4E	ST	
119	12N4W	Lev. 1	0–10 cm; "Unit 9"

Bag #	Unit	Level	Notes
131	12N4W	Lev. 2	10–20 cm; "Unit 9"
111	12N8E	Lev. 1	"Unit 8"
118	12N8E	Lev. 2	10–20 cm; "Unit 8"
36	12N8W	ST	
121	12N8W (NE)	Lev. 3	20–30 cm; probably 12N8E
130	14N10W	ST	
7	14N2E	ST	
145	14N3E	Surface	Unsure why bag number is later than those from excavated levels
140	14N3E	Lev. 1	0–10 cm; "Unit 13"
141	14N3E	Lev. 2	10–20 cm; "Unit 13"
142	14N3E	Lev. 3	20–30 cm; "Unit 13"
104	14N4E	ST	
4	14N4W	ST	
6	14N8W	ST	
137	15N3E (NE)	Lev. 1	0–10 cm; "Unit 2"; presumably should be "Unit 12"
138	15N3E	Lev. 2	10–20 cm
139	15N3E	Lev. 3	20–30 cm; "Unit 12"
134	15N4E	Lev. 1	0–10 cm
135	15N4E	Lev. 2	
136	15N4E	Lev. 3	20–30 cm; "Unit 11"
143	15N5E	Lev. 1	0–10 cm; "Unit 14"
144	15N5E	Lev. 2	10–20 cm
19	16N0E	ST	
18	16N2E	ST	
83	16N2E (SW)	Lev. 1	0–10 cm; "Unit 4"
84	16N2E (SW)	Lev. 2	10–20 cm; "1 x 1 m"; "Unit 4"
20	16N2W	ST	
8	16N4E	ST	
21	16N4W	ST	
95	16N6E	ST	
22	16N6W	ST	
17	18N0E	ST	
31	18N2W	ST	
15	18N4E	ST	
14	18N6E	ST	
97	18N8E	ST	
74	19N4E	Lev. 1	0–10 cm; "Unit 2"
75	19N4E	Lev. 2	10–20 cm; "Unit 2"
76	19N4E	Lev. 3	"Unit 2"
77	19N4E	Lev. 4	
27	19N4E	Lev. 4	30–35 cm; "Unit 2"; unsure why two Level 4 bags, why one with earlier bag #
10	20N0E	ST	
23	20N0E	Lev. 1	0–5 cm; "1 x 2 m"

Bag #	Unit	Level	Notes
49	20N0E	Lev. 2	10–20 cm; "1 x 2 m"; "Unit 1"
73	20N0E	Lev. 3	20–30 cm; "1 x 2 m"; "Unit 1"
2	20N2E	ST	
11	20N2W	ST	
79	20N2W	Lev. 2	10–20 cm; "Unit 3"
81	20N2W	Lev. 3	20–30 cm; "Unit 3"
82	20N2W	Lev. 4	30–40 cm; "Unit 3"
3	20N4E	ST	
9	20N6E	ST	Unsure why 2 bag numbers for 20N6E
13	20N6E	ST	Unsure why 2 bag numbers for 20N6E
99	20N8E	ST	
28	22N2W	ST	
114	2S4W	ST	
115	4S4W	ST	

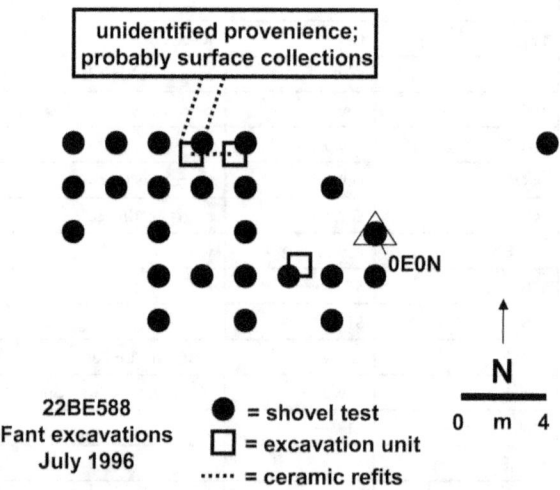

Figure 8.2. Plan of excavations, 22BE588. Dashed lines between boxes indicate ceramic refits. Triangle-with-dot symbol indicates 0E0N benchmark as well as Shovel Test 0E0N.

A concerted attempt was made to make ceramic refits across excavation units, with the hope of revealing something about occupational duration and site structure. Unfortunately, while several refits were made, only two units were so linked (Figure 8.2).

Excavations at 22BE544 were far more extensive, with 51 shovel tests, 14 1-×-1-meter units, and two 1-×-2-meter units having been dug (Figure 8.3). Artifacts were found to a maximum depth of 20–30 cm.

Artifact Assemblages from Early Woodland Tchula-Period Sites

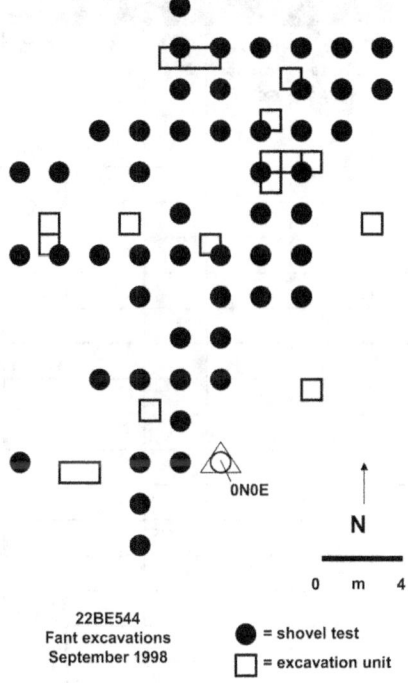

Figure 8.3. Plan of excavations, 22BE544. Triangle-with-dot symbol indicates oNoE benchmark.

Artifact Assemblages

Because I have not had the opportunity to reanalyze Fant's original survey collection from 22BE588, for the sake of consistency data from the original survey collections are not included in the artifact tabulations reported herein. Also, based on knowledge of local soil formation processes, there is no apparent reason to make vertical distinctions in artifact occurrence at such shallow sites (Peacock and Fant 2002), so data are reported by excavation unit/shovel test only. Where shovel tests and excavation units coincide, the data are combined.

Ceramics

There exists in the literature a lot of anguish over distinguishing between grog-tempered ceramics with sandy versus "chalky" pastes, presumably reflecting a hope that such differences, if properly denoted, will carry chronological or functional meaning (e.g., Ford 1981, 1988a, 1989; Holland-Lilly 1996; Mainfort

Table 8.3. Ceramics from Fant's excavations at 22BE588.

Provenience	grog plain	grog plain interior RS	grog plain interior GS	grog FI	grog FI interior RS	grog FI interior GS	Grog CI	grog CI interior RS	grog punc	grog eroded interior GS	grog eroded	quartz plain	fired clay
0E2S				1									1
2W2N	1												
2W2S	2			5			2					1	
2W4S				1									1
3W1S	1			7							4		4
4W2S				3									
6W0N				4							4		
6W2N	1										2		1
6W4N	12			20							25		7
6W2S	2										1		
6W4S				2									
8W2N	5			5	3						5		5
8W4N	8		1	23	1		3				20		
8W2S											2		
10W0N				1							1		
10W2N	1			1									
10W4N	1										3		
10W2S				1							1		
10W4S				2									
12W2N				2							1		
12W4N				1									
14W0N											1		
14W2N													1
14W4N				1									
Surface?	18	1	7	55	2	2				2	118		9
Pulled for photos	2			5			2	1	2*				
Total:	54	1	8	140	2	6	7	1	2	2	188	1	29
Percent total:**	13.11	0.24	1.94	33.98	0.49	1.46	1.70	0.24	0.49	0.49	45.63	0.24	

* Includes 1 with small, round punctations (Vessel 3) and 1 with nicked rim.
** Excludes fired clay.

1986b, 1994; Mainfort and Chapman 2004; Morse 1986:79–81; Phillips 1970; Smith 1979; Weaver 1963). This inductive approach to classification has proved to be of little value (Peacock 1997; Walling et al. 1995; Weaver, Buchner, and Starr 1999). Variability along this (or any other) dimension should be explored using problem-oriented classes designed for specific purposes; e.g., if sandy pastes are suspected of affecting the performance of a pot, then reasonably one would suspect a correspondence with particular vessel forms or sizes. No such correspondences have been noted at this point, but simple temper/surface finish types have been shown to have chronological meaning in the study area (Peacock 1996c) and are used here. In this scheme, grog is simply noted as present or absent; sandy sherds with no grog are considered to be sand-tempered, while quartz temper stands out from sandy pastes quite distinctly and is also noted via simple presence/absence. For what it is worth, sandy pastes are quite rare in the ceramic assemblages from both sites reported here, a distinction that did at least aid in the recognition of a few individual vessels at 22BE588 (no attempt was made to distinguish different vessels in the larger assemblage from 22BE544).

Ceramics from 22BE588 are shown in Table 8.3. A total of 412 sherds was recovered, all but two of which are grog-tempered. The other two are quartz-tempered, i.e., they contain "easily visible angular and subangular pieces of clear quartz" (Peacock 1996c:18). This temper type is widespread if not especially common at Tchula sites on the Holly Springs District (Fant 1996a; Peacock 1996c) and apparently lasted until at least A.D. 400 in north-central Mississippi (Peacock 1996c).

An attempt was made to derive a vessel count from the 22BE588 assemblage, based on rim forms and sizes, slips, and temper characteristics; descriptions are given below, with sample photos shown in Figure 8.4. A minimum of 27 vessels is represented; the actual number is likely much higher. A brief description of the vessels is as follows:

Vessel 1. Grog-tempered fabric-impressed; straight, thickened rim, inwardly tapered lip. Orifice circumference calculated from rim to be 105.6 cm (Figure 8.4A).
Vessel 2. Grog-tempered fabric-impressed; everted, folded rim.
Vessel 3. Grog-tempered plain (exterior); straight, thickened rim, slightly rounded lip; interior row of small, closely spaced punctations just below lip; punctations narrow, taller than wide, ca. 2.6 mm in height, 1.8 mm wide (Figure 8.4B).
Vessel 4. Grog-tempered cord-impressed; everted rim; exterior row of individual cord impressions ca. 6.8 mm below lip; impressions run from near-vertical to diagonal (leaning to the left); some impressions show three cord twists of the same size, some show two, suggesting two different episodes of punctating (Figure 8.4G).

Vessel 5. Grog-tempered fabric-impressed; slightly everted, slightly thickened folded-lip rim (Figure 8.4D).

Vessel 6. Grog-tempered fabric-impressed; slightly everted, folded-lip rim (Figure 8.4C).

Vessel 7. Grog-tempered cord-impressed; slightly inverted rim, rounded lip; exterior row of individual vertical cord impressions, just below lip; interior red-slipped. Flat lip marked with row of individual cord impressions perpendicular to lip.

Vessel 8. Grog-tempered eroded; straight, slightly thickened folded-lip rim.

Vessel 9. Grog-tempered eroded; straight rim, rounded lip.

Vessel 10. Grog-tempered fabric-impressed; straight rim, flat lip.

Vessel 11. Grog-tempered fabric-impressed; thickened rim, inwardly tapered lip.

Vessel 12. Grog-tempered plain; thickened rim, flat lip.

Vessel 13. Grog-tempered eroded; straight rim, rounded lip.

Vessel 14. Grog-tempered, thickened, exterior-nicked rim, rounded lip.

Vessel 15. Grog-tempered, thickened rim; rounded lip; exterior row of closely spaced, individual vertical cord impressions on rim.

Vessel 16. Grog-tempered fabric-impressed; markedly sandy paste.

Vessel 17. Grog-tempered fabric-impressed; markedly sandy paste.

Vessel 18. Grog-tempered fabric-impressed; interior red-slipped.

Vessel 19. Grog-tempered fabric-impressed; interior gray-slipped.

Vessel 20. Grog-tempered fabric-impressed.

Vessel 21. Grog-tempered fabric-impressed; slightly everted rim; flat lip; interior row of individual vertical cord impressions from interior wall to approximate center of lip (Figure 8.4E).

Vessel 22. Grog-tempered plain; slightly everted, slightly thickened rim; rounded lip. Exterior, horizontal groove beneath lip may be broad-line incision.

Vessel 23. Grog-tempered fabric-impressed; folded-lip rim; fold unusually narrow.

Vessel 24. Grog-tempered fabric-impressed; slightly everted rim, rounded lip.

Vessel 25. Quartz-tempered plain.

Vessel 26. Grog-tempered plain; interior gray-slipped.

Vessel 27. Grog-tempered plain; interior red-slipped.

Ceramics from 22BE544 are listed in Table 8.4. The assemblage is similar to that from 22BE588, with a few rare surface treatments (e.g., red slipping on quartz-tempered vessels) likely being represented due to a larger sample size. Again, a range of vessel sizes and forms is represented, with folded-lip rims, straight rims, narrowly to extremely everted rims, flat and rounded lips, etc. (Figure 8.5). One cord-impressed rim sherd has closely spaced, vertical cord impressions within a zone created by an individual, horizontal cord impression. Another interesting sherd has a thin, flat lip extending horizontally from the rim of a shallow bowl, similar to Vessel Form 2 at the Fulmer site (Weaver, Buchner, and Starr 1999:Figure 7.10).

Artifact Assemblages from Early Woodland Tchula-Period Sites

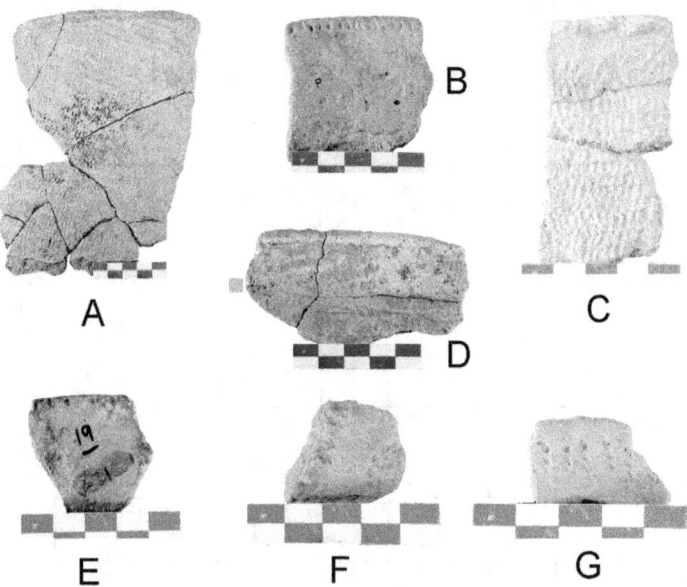

Figure 8.4. Representative sherds from 22BE588. A–Vessel 1; B–Vessel 3; C–Vessel 6; D–Vessel 5; E–Vessel 21; F–an unusual body sherd with curvilinear, individual cord impressions, found with artifacts "pulled for photos"; G–Part of Vessel 4 showing individual, three-twist cord impressions. Scales are in cm. Photos by Paul Jacobs.

While no systematic analysis of vessel forms was undertaken, a wide range of forms is represented in both assemblages. Weaver, Buchner, and Starr (1999) describe several "hypothesized" vessel forms from the Fulmer site. Sherds from 22BE588 and 22BE544 conform minimally to their Forms 2 (large flaring rim bowl), 6 (carinated bowl), 8 (small hemispherical bowl), 10 (large globular jar), 11 (medium globular jar), and 12 (conoidal bowl/beaker). Two flat basal sherds were recovered at 22BE588, while rounded bases were recovered from both sites. Slips were found on plain, fabric-impressed, and cord-impressed sherds. Red slips were easily discernable; what are labeled "gray" and "buff" slips appear to be intentional slips rather than floated surfaces, and sherds so designated stood out easily from the rest of the assemblages. The grog-tempered, black-slipped sherd from 22BE544 is, to my knowledge, the only one of its kind to be reported from a Tchula-period occupation.

Lithics

Lithics from 22BE588 are limited to sandstone/siltstone flakes and angular chunks of various sizes, and five flakes of homogenous, gray chert (Table 8.5)

Table 8.4. Ceramics from Fant's excavations at 22BE544.

Provenience	grog plain	grog plain interior RS	grog plain interior GS	grog plain exterior BS	grog FI	grog FI interior RS	grog FI interior GS	grog FI interior buff S	grog Cl	grog punc	grog eroded	grog eroded interior RS	grog eroded interior buff S	quartz eroded	quartz eroded interior RS	fired clay
0N2W					1						3					
0N4W	1															
0N6W	1	1			4						11					
2N2W							1									
2S4W	1															
4N4E	2				1											
4N2W											1					1
4N4W					1						3					
4N6W					1											
4S4W																2
6N0E											2					
6N2W							1									
8N0E					3						1					1
8N2E	1				1											
8N4E		1			3						8					1
8N4W											1					
10N0E	5	1			16						20					
10N2E					3						3					1
10N4E					2						1					
10N2W								1			4					
10N4W											7					
10N6W				1												
10N8W	6				18						86					24
12N2E					1						15					9
12N4E	1				1									3		
12N8E	5				11	1					97				1	2
12N2W		1			1	1					1					1
12N4W																

Provenience	C1	C2	C3	C4	C5	C6	C7	C8	C9	C10	C11	C12	C13	C14	C15	Total
14N2E																
14N3E	16				3						112					27
14N4E	1				1											
14N4W											1					3
14N8W					1						1					9
15N3E	9				24	1					64	1	1			2
15N4E	20	1			67		2				112	1				30
15N5E	10		1		48		1				111	1				
16N0E					7						2					1
16N2E	3				13	1					33					
16N4E					5						4					1
16N6E	1										2	1				
16N2W																
16N6W	1															5
18N0E					1											
18N4E	1										4					12
18N6E											6					1
18N8E	1				3											
18N2W					6						9	2				6
19N4E	4				7			1			53	1				
20N0E	3				4				2		29					
20N2E	1				9	1			1		9					
20N2W	4				1						51					
20N4E					1						1					
20N6E					1						11					
22N0E					1						16					
22N2W									1	2	1					
unknown provenience																
Total:	98	5	1	2	315	8	2	1	7	2	925	6	1	3	1	146
Percent total:	7.12	0.36	0.07	0.15	22.88	0.58	0.15	0.07	0.51	0.15	67.18	0.44	0.07	0.22	0.07	

Table 8.5. Lithics from Fant's excavations at 22BE588.

Provenience	sandstone/siltstone debitage	chert debitage	other
0E0N	1		
0E2S	2		
3W1S	7	1	
6W2N	3	1	
6W4N	7	1	1
6W4S	1	1	
8W2N	1	1	
8W4N	1		
10W2N	2		
10W2S	1		
14W2N	2		
Surface?	6	1	1
Total:	33	5	4

of uncertain origin. The chert flakes all are late-stage, with no cortex, multiple platform facets, and multiple dorsal scars: three whole flakes, a proximal and a medial fragment were recovered. A whole flake from Unit 6W2N shows a distinct polish along one edge that likely is use wear. No attempt was made to look for use wear on the sandstone/siltstone debitage, which was identified on the basis of "an edge formed by two converging planes" (Parrish 2006:130). These flakes often display other features related to conchoidal fracturing, including striking platforms and bulbs of percussion. Materials in this category range from fine-grained brown siltstones to relatively fine-grained ferruginous sandstones, all presumably acquired locally, and flakes range from very small to several centimeters in length. Other lithics recovered from 22BE588 are pieces of ferruginous sandstone and small quartz pebbles, none of which are obviously modified but which are likely artifactual (see Peacock and Manning 2008). No bifaces, ground stone, or any formal lithic tools were recovered from the site.

The lithic assemblage from 22BE544 is similar in overall terms to that from 22BE588 in that there are relatively few lithics compared to ceramics and the majority of the flaked stone consists of sandstone/siltstone debitage (Table 8.6). There are some interesting differences, however, one being the presence of bifaces at 22BE544. These few bifaces are all "indeterminate" in form; i.e., they are not easily recognizable projectile points or drills. They appear to represent efforts to form bifaces from small pieces of parent material, or fragments of bifaces that have been used to the point of exhaustion, including pieces showing heavy tip/edge wear indicative of secondary use. Overall, lithic artifact

Figure 8.5. Siltstone biface from 22BE544; long edge (middle image) shows use wear (battering). Photo by Paul Jacobs.

diversity is higher at 22BE544, including a siltstone biface with a few flakes removed from one edge that presumably was a rough "chopping tool" (Figure 8.5). While sandstone/siltstone debitage has been recorded at many Tchula sites on the Holly Springs District (Fant 1996a; Peacock 1996c), actual tools of this locally available rock have not been previously reported. Tool production, rather than or in addition to maintenance/rejuvenation, is suggested by the wide range of sizes and shapes represented in the sandstone/siltstone debitage at both sites, which includes easily recognizable flakes and angular chunks of various sizes. A very few pieces of ground siltstone were also recovered at 22BE544, including one large flake with a ground exterior surface. One small, white quartzite hammerstone was recovered from 22BE544. Original length cannot be measured as the artifact is broken on both ends along the long axis, but it is only 3.17 cm wide at its widest point. The breaks are likely from use, as hammerstone wear is visible extending from one edge up to a broken surface. It is highly probable that this stone is of local origin, and that it was being used to work small pieces of locally available raw materials.

The apparent difference in artifact diversity between the two lithic assemblages may be functional, or it may be attributable to the difference in sample sizes. One interesting difference that is unlikely to be due to sample size is that, while debitage from 22BE588 suggests a high degree of curation (i.e., finished chert tools were being rejuvenated rather than manufactured on site), debitage from 22BE544 is more indicative of local procurement of raw materials and on-site production of stone tools. One indication of local procurement is

Table 8.6. Lithics from Fant's excavations at 22BE544.

Provenience	sandstone/siltstone debitage	quartzitic claystone debitage	quartzitic claystone biface	chert debitage	quartz debitage	petrified wood debitage	chert biface	quartz hammerstone	siltstone biface	ground sandstone	other
0N4W	1										
0N6W		1					1				10
0N10W											1
2S4W											2
4N0E											2
4N4E											4
4N4W	2										
4S4W											1
8N0E		1									
8N4E			1								1
8N4W		1									
10N0E	3	2									8
10N2E		1									1
10N2W											1
10N4W											1
10N8W	1	2									11
10N10W											1
12N4E		1		1							
12N8E		1		2				1			3
12N2W	1			1							
12N4W	2	2									3
14N2E	1										

Provenience											Total
14N3E	5	2		1		2	1				10
14N8W											1
15N3E	12	8									12
15N4E	9*	1	1			1				2	5
15N5E	6	2		1	1	1				1	7
16N2E	5					1					4
16N4E		1					1				
16N6E		1									
16N4W								1			1
18N4E											1
18N6E		1									
19N4E	3	2									12
20N0E	2	2									2
20N2E	3										
20N2W	1	1		2	1		1				3
20N6E	1										
20N8E											1
22N0E	2										1
surface	4	2	1								1
unknown provenience		1									
Total:	64	36	4	9	6	2	3	1	3	3	111

* Includes the two ground sandstone from same provenience.

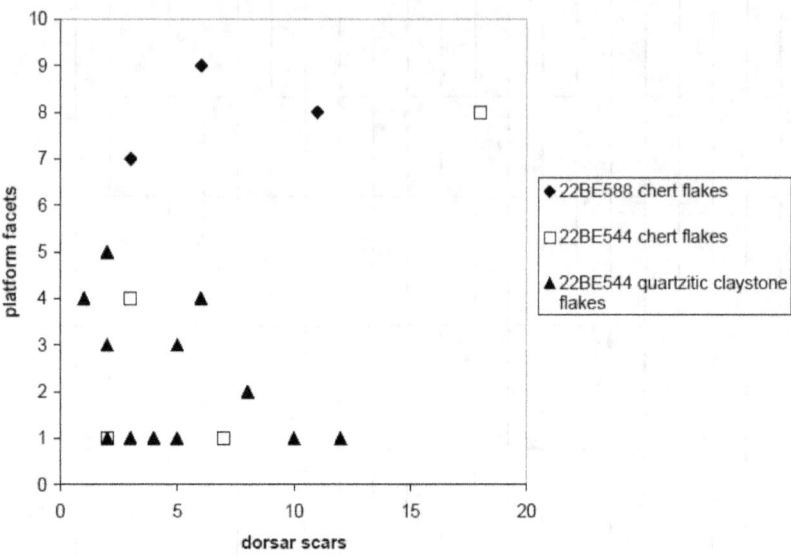

Figure 8.6. Dorsal scar and platform facet counts on whole flakes from 22BE588 and 22BE544.

the relatively large quantity of what is labeled "quartzitic claystone" recovered from 22BE544. I do not believe that this unusual material has been described in the archaeological literature before. It consists of small (pebble to small gravel-size), blocky pieces with a weathered, whitish cortex. The interior ranges from a speckled, grayish-white that looks very much like Tallahatta Quartzite to a slightly grainy but otherwise homogenous grayish-green color: short, laminar inclusions appear to be plant fossils. Several specimens of this material were sent to David Dockery and James Starnes, Office of Geology, Mississippi Department of Environmental Quality, who suggested that it "probably represent[s] a locally quarried quartzite" (David Dockery, personal communication 2012). They referred me to a description in the Benton County geology bulletin by Lusk (1956:30), who states:

> Probably the most interesting lithologic feature of the Ackerman formation [now mapped as the Nanafalia formation] is the quartzitic claystone that is found at or near the top of the formation ... It is light gray, contains an abundance of root and plant impressions, and ranges in thickness from a few inches to a little more than a foot.

While this "claystone" has not yet been verified as the source of the raw material in question, much of the debitage consists of blocky, weathered pieces almost certainly of local derivation. A local source for lithic materials is also supported by an analysis of whole flakes: using platform facets and dorsal scars as gross indicators of stage of tool production/rejuvenation, the few whole flakes available from 22BE588 appear to be late-stage, while those from 22BE544 (including those of quartzitic claystone) appear to be earlier-stage (Figure 8.6). A local origin for the few pieces of petrified wood debitage (Table 8.6) also is assumed.

Chronology

No charcoal was in the collection from 22BE588, but two pieces from 22BE544 were available for radiocarbon dating. These were identified by Jennifer Seltzer, Department of Entomology, Mississippi State University prior to submission to Beta Analytic, Inc., for AMS standard dating. One was a piece of chestnut (*Castanea* sp.) wood from Unit 0N6W, while the other was a piece of relatively thin-walled nutshell from Level 3 of Unit 20N0E. The latter specimen was highly carbonized and identification to species was not possible. Although the context for these specimens is only loosely known, accepted absolute dates for Tchula occupations are quite rare (see discussion in Childress et al. 1999), so the decision was made to date both specimens from 22BE544.

The results were disappointing. Both samples returned multiple intercepts at the 2-sigma span, none of which fell within reasonable expectations for a Tchula-period occupation. The specimen from Unit 0N6W (BETA-316359) returned a conventional radiocarbon age of 420 ± 30 B.P., or a 2-sigma calibrated date range of A.D. 1440–1460 (relative area under probability distribution = 0.93 [Reimer et al. 2004]), while the specimen from Unit 20N0E (BETA-317797) returned a conventional radiocarbon date range of 110 ± 30 B.P., or a 2-sigma calibrated date range of A.D. 1800–1940 (relative area under probability distribution = 0.69 [Reimer et al. 2004]). Ironically, these late dates are reminiscent of similarly incongruous radiocarbon results obtained from the Fulmer site (Childress et al. 1999). Based on the limited chronological information available, there is little doubt that the Tchula occupations on the Holly Springs District fall within the 400 B.C.–100 B.C. span suggested by Childress et al. (1999).

Comparison with Fulmer

The Fulmer site is similar to the Tchula sites recorded on the Holly Springs District in that it is a small, single, relatively short-term Tchula-period occupation located on an upland landform. Some concentrations of fire-cracked

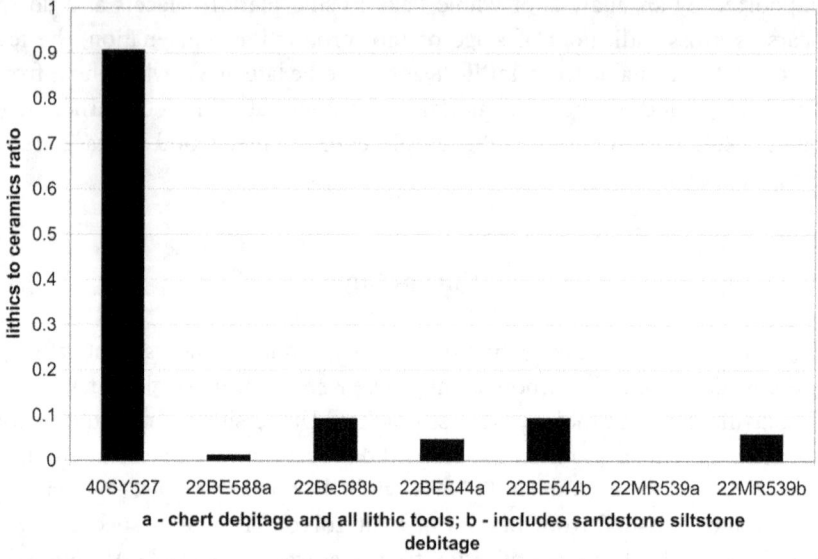

Figure 8.7. Lithic:ceramic ratios from the Fulmer site (40SY527) and Holly Springs District Tchula-period sites.

rock, ceramics, ferruginous sandstone, and fired clay likely representing hearths were noted at Fulmer, but more formal features (pits, postholes, discrete hearths, burials, etc.) were lacking.

These similarities aside, there are some notable differences between Fulmer and the Holly Springs sites, primarily in the lithic assemblages recovered. While not especially common, a number of flaked tools (adzes, projectile point/knives, drill fragments), chert cores (amorphous and bipolar), unifacial tools (scrapers/spokeshaves), blades, and "pebble tools" were recovered at Fulmer (Weaver, Buchner, and Starr 1999), along with a greenstone celt fragment, a siltstone gorget fragment, ground sandstone, a single hammerstone, and a large number of flake tools. One Early Archaic-period Decatur point was recovered at Fulmer, so not all of the flaked stone artifacts can be assigned with certainty to the Tchula occupation, but it is reasonable to suggest that most can, a suggestion borne out by the fact that all the other bifaces and formal tools recovered conform to Woodland-period types (Weaver and Childress 1999).

As noted above, the lithic assemblage from 22BE544 is more diverse than that from 22BE588, but at both sites lithics are a relatively minor component of the entire artifact assemblage when compared to Fulmer. To illustrate this point, the lithic to ceramic ratios were calculated for Fulmer, 22BE588, 22BE544, and 22MR539. Because no sandstone/siltstone debitage is specifically noted as being present at Fulmer, I calculated the ratios for the Holly Springs District sites both with and without this class being included. Despite the small samples, the results from the three Tchula occupations on the Holly Springs District look quite similar, and all look remarkably different from Fulmer, which has proportionately a much higher number of lithic artifacts (Figure 8.7). Given this difference, it is reasonable to suggest that different site uses are represented. Although located on an upland landform, Fulmer is much closer to a sizable waterway (the Loosahatchie River) than are the Holly Springs sites. Although interpreted as a short-term occupation, Fulmer also contained what was interpreted as a thin sheet midden, indicating longer occupation than that evidenced at the Holly Springs sites. Given the midden, the range of artifacts recovered, and the likely presence of hearths indicated by fired clay and sandstone concentrations, Fulmer certainly was a habitation site. Weaver and Childress (1999) are equivocal about whether Fulmer represents a sedentary or a seasonal occupation, but I suggest, based on the bulk of the evidence, that it was a short-term sedentary occupation, following Rafferty (1980, 1985a, 1994, 2002).

Discussion and Conclusions

In their conclusion to the Fulmer site report, Weaver and Childress (1999:182) ask, "Does Fulmer represent the remains of a small, sedentary (year-round) household site occupied by 'Lake Cormorant' culture-bearers? Perhaps, but as with so many archaeological queries, firm answers cannot be derived from the excavation of a single site." This chapter on Fant's previously unreported excavations on the Holly Springs National Forest, while providing a welcome body of additional data, has not supplied answers to broad-scale questions related to settlement and subsistence. If Fulmer is accepted as a habitation site, my original assessment of the Holly Springs Tchula-period sites as special-purpose sites seems defensible, given their differences with Fulmer. However, there are still interesting differences among the Holly Springs sites' artifact assemblages that, while possibly being due to sampling error, may reflect real variability worth exploring, so the occupations should not at this point be considered members of a uniform "class" of site.

A simple model of expectations regarding three different site types—special-purpose, seasonal habitation, and sedentary occupation—is given in Figure 8.8. Two dimensions are used: artifact diversity and restriction of tool forms. Artifact diversity is expected to be higher at sites occupied year-round, where a wider range of activities would have been carried out. Conversely, task-specific sites (e.g., a rock quarry) should have less diverse assemblages,

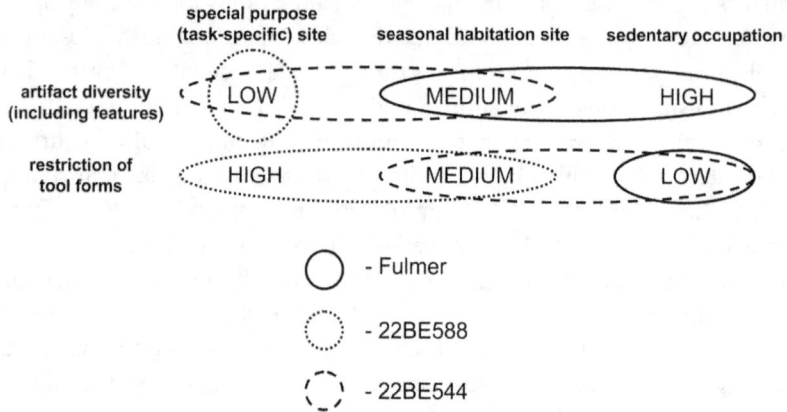

Figure 8.8. A simple model for site use based on artifact diversity and restriction of tool forms.

while seasonal habitation sites should be intermediate in artifact diversity. As regards restriction of tool forms, from an evolutionary perspective there should be stronger selection for particular forms (those that are most efficient) at task-specific sites, some such selection at seasonal habitation sites where the range of resources being exploited was limited, and weaker selection at sedentary occupations to which resources might be transported in partially or fully processed form. In relative terms, Fulmer falls on the "medium to high" end of the range: "medium" because of the lack of discrete features found at the site. Site 22BE588 falls at the low end of the range, primarily due to the late-stage nature of the debitage. Site 22BE544 falls between the other two sites.

Exploring the extent to which such perceived differences are real or are an artifact of sampling error is worthy of much further study. Other goals for future research include obtaining absolute dates from a number of occupations, specifically identifying the sources of the raw materials represented at upland Tchula-period sites, investigating the role of the Tallahatchie River as a cultural boundary, and exploring duration in both relative (e.g., via seriation or refitting of sherds and/or debitage) and absolute terms. The latter goal may be met by employing absolute dating methods such as luminescence or rehydroxylation (Wilson et al. 2009) on sizable samples of ceramics until redundancy in results is reached.

While there is clearly a long way to go in obtaining even a basic understanding of the archaeology of the Tchula period, a context for developing research questions is emerging from the survey work carried out on the Holly Springs National Forest. The as-yet poorly understood phenomenon of large numbers of Tchula-period occupations in the North Central Hills north of the Tallahatchie River is but one of many surprises that emerged as a result of work carried out during Sam Brookes's tenure as Forest Archaeologist for the National Forests in Mississippi. His hiring of archaeologists such as David Fant contributed significantly to opening up the interior of the state to scientific archaeological exploration.

Acknowledgments

I thank Joe Seger, director of the Cobb Institute of Archaeology at Mississippi State University, for support for radiocarbon dates. Thanks also to Jennifer Seltzer for the charcoal identifications, David Dockery and Jim Starnes for looking at some strange rocks, Kim Harrison and Caitlin Stewart for checking out rocks in a road cut for me, and Paul Jacobs for the artifact photos. Keith Baca ran down some old reports, which were very useful. Thanks, of course, to Sam Brookes for all the great USDA Forest Service years. Finally, I dedicate this chapter to the late David Fant. David was a beautiful human being and a dedicated professional who passed away far before his time, and I am not alone in missing him a great deal.

Notes

1. As noted in Peacock (1993:4), I used a consistent method for recording artifact density in my many USDA Forest Service survey reports. If the number of artifacts recovered was less than the number of shovel tests dug, density was described as light; if it was equal to or up to twice the number of shovel tests dug, density was moderate; if it was higher than twice the number of shovel tests dug, density was heavy. Unmodified sandstone and artifacts collected from exposed ground surfaces were not used in the calculation of artifact density.

2. This tabulation is from a reanalysis of Holly Springs site collections by Peacock (1996c:Table 2.1) and should take precedence over the data presented in the original report.

3. The benchmark at 22BE588 was actually labeled oNoE, but the order of direction signifiers on the artifact bags was not consistent, so I changed all provenience labels to EW/NS designations for consistency with the majority of the bags from the site.

CHAPTER 9

The Slate Springs Mound, a Woodland-Period Platform Mound in the North Central Hills of Mississippi

Keith A. Baca

Introduction

Platform mounds, once thought to have been constructed exclusively in the late prehistoric Mississippi period (A.D. 1100–1500) in much of the interior southeastern United States, are now known to have also been built during the preceding Middle to Late Woodland periods (ca. 200 B.C.–A.D. 1100) in regions previously believed to lack them (Anderson and Mainfort 2002:13, 16; Boudreaux and Johnson 2000; Brose 1988; Brown 1994; Jeffries 1994; Johnson et al. 2001; Knight 1990, 2001; Kwas and Mainfort 1986; Lindauer and Blitz 1997; Mainfort 1986a, 1988, 2013b; Mainfort and Walling 1992, 1996; Pluckhahn 1996, 2003; Rafferty 1983, 1987, 1990, 2002; Welch 1998). The Slate Springs Mound (22CA502, also known as the West Mound) in Calhoun County, Mississippi, is now recognized as such a Woodland site. In 1992, test excavation of the mound revealed fill stages and yielded charcoal samples that produced radiocarbon dates ranging from the early to middle first millennium A.D., within the Middle to early Late Woodland periods; in addition, chronologically diagnostic Middle to Late Woodland potsherds (sand-tempered fabric-impressed and cordmarked, grog-tempered cordmarked) were recovered from mound fill and from surrounding fields.

The Slate Springs Mound is unique in that it is currently the only confirmed Woodland-period platform mound in the extensive North Central Hills physiographic zone of Mississippi. The site is also anomalous in that only a solitary mound is present, whereas other Woodland platform mounds tend to occur in groups with other flat-topped mounds and/or with conical burial mounds;

and, unlike at a number of such sites, no extraregional ceramics have been recovered. Overall, the Slate Springs site is enigmatic not so much for what is present, but for what is absent.

The intent of this report is to place this significant but little-known site in its context in regional prehistory by presenting the results of limited test excavation of the mound conducted in 1992, and of general surface collecting and shovel testing of the field surrounding the mound in 1991 and 1992. Prior to this report, information about the site was largely unpublished, consisting of the initial survey report (Haag 1952), a National Register of Historic Places nomination document (Baca 1992), and a Mid-South Archaeological Conference paper (Baca 1993). Brief mentions of the site appear in a few previous publications (Carleton 1999:152; Galaty 2008:267; Rafferty 2002:205, 222; Sims and Connaway 2000:221).

Location and Physiographic Setting

The Slate Springs Mound is a relatively small, flat-topped earthen structure (Figures 9.1 and 9.2) located approximately 3 km north of the village of Slate Springs, in southern Calhoun County, Mississippi, within the North Central Hills physiographic province (Figure 9.3). The mound is situated on a first terrace about 100 m east of the right bank of Shutispear Creek, a northwesterly flowing tributary of the Yalobusha River. The site is indicated as an "indian [sic] mound" on map sheet 87 of *Soil Survey of Calhoun County, Mississippi*

Figure 9.1. Slate Springs Mound (22CA502), February 27, 1992, looking north. Dewitt Spencer stands at the foot of the mound's south corner. Photograph by Keith A. Baca.

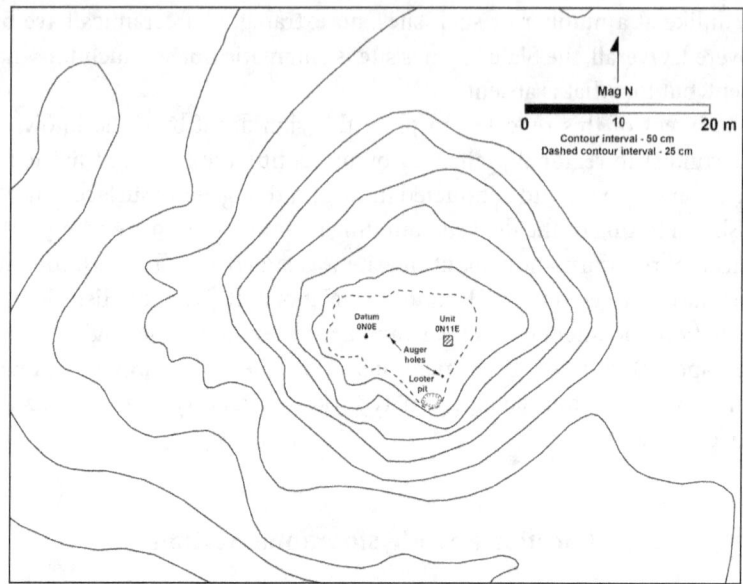

Figure 9.2. Topographic map of Slate Springs Mound (22CA502).

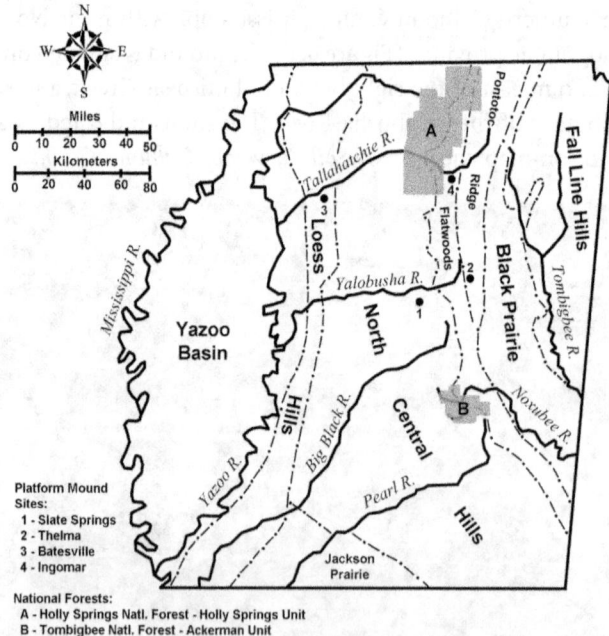

Figure 9.3. Map of northern Mississippi showing locations of Woodland period platform mound sites, physiographic zones, and National Forest units discussed in text.

(McMullen et al. 1965), in an area mapped as Freeland silt loam, 2 to 5 percent slopes, severely eroded (FrC3).

History of Investigations

The site was initially recorded in the early 1950s by archaeologist William G. Haag, then of the University of Mississippi, during his pre-inundation survey of the Grenada Reservoir in the Yalobusha River valley and some of its tributaries. The results of Haag's survey are presented in the unpublished report "Archaeological Survey of the Grenada Reservoir in Mississippi" (Haag 1952). Haag named the site the West Mound after Ruble West, the leaseholder of the property, but it has been renamed the Slate Springs Mound (see also Rafferty 2002:205, 222; Sims and Connaway 2000:221) to prevent its confusion with the previously recorded and published West Mounds (22TU520), a Late Mississippian site in the northern Yazoo Basin of Mississippi (Buchner 1996; Dye and Buchner 1988; Phillips et al. 1951:51, 321). Haag's report briefly describes the site as follows:

> Ca 1. The West Mound. A large, truncated-pyramidal mound with associated village. Located about two miles north of Slate Springs ... U.S. [Army Corps of] Engineers Grenada Reservoir map F8. Although the site lies within the Skuna [actually Yalobusha] drainage on Shutispear Creek, its elevation is 262 feet ... well above the flood pool. It is of some significance, though, to an understanding of the entire Reservoir and warrants inclusion in the survey. The mound is quite square, ninety feet on a side and rather uniform in height, twelve feet. For an area of perhaps 1000 feet radius about the mound sporadic artifacts are seen. At the time of the survey all the surrounding area was in pasture, so that but few potsherds and flints were revealed. Six sherds of Tishomingo Cord-marked and three sherds of Tishomingo Plain were found, and one side-notched, bevel-edged, projectile point [Haag 1952:1–2].

In his summary analysis of the sites recorded during his survey, Haag (1952:27) comments that "[t]he truncated pyramidal mound is typical of those in the Mississippi Embayment except that it is not very large and occurs alon[e] rather than in a group." Subsequently, he notes that "only in the extreme eastern end of the reservoir [area] does a truncated pyramidal mound appear (Ca 1). Because of its relatively small size and occurrence alone, this mound probably represents an early invasion of Temple Mound concepts" (Haag 1952:29). In his concluding recommendations for further archaeological work, Haag states that "[t]he pyramidal mound, Ca 1, need not be considered here for it is far outside the flood pool limits and will serve as a reserve site for future excavation by some interested agency. It may be said here, though, that this site would probably be most revealing as to the time and condition of the introduction of Temple Mound I ideas and practices" (Haag 1952:30).

Following Haag's survey, the Slate Springs Mound was subjected to no further archaeological investigation for almost 40 years. Then in 1991, the Mississippi Department of Archives and History (MDAH) selected the site for fieldwork to obtain data for its nomination to the National Register of Historic Places. Accordingly, the author, then a staff archaeologist with MDAH, made two reconnaissance visits to the site in June 1991, and subsequently directed a test excavation and a topographic mapping survey of the mound in January 1992. The mound was listed on the National Register in December 1992. During the course of the fieldwork, artifacts were also collected from two newly discovered nearby sites (22CA552 and 22CA553). The artifacts and field records, plus reserved unanalyzed charcoal and sediment samples, are curated at MDAH's Historic Preservation Division in Jackson, Mississippi.

Mound Condition, Topography, and Dimensions

At the time of the 1990s fieldwork, the Slate Springs Mound was covered with deciduous trees (Figure 9.1). At this writing, the mound's tree cover remains undisturbed. In the early 1990s the area surrounding the mound was in pasture (Figure 9.1), but has since been planted with pine trees. The four corners of the nearly square mound point to the cardinal directions (Figure 9.2), a trait shared in common with several other regional Woodland-period platform mounds (Carleton 1999; Rafferty 2002:223). No earthen summit-access ramp, a common feature of platform mounds, was apparent during the author's visits to the site. Possible vestiges of a ramp are suggested by the topographic map's irregular, slightly projecting contour lines on the southwest side of the mound (Figure 9.2), but this is inconclusive and contrasts with the ramp locations on the northeast side of some other Woodland platform mounds (e.g., Rafferty 2002:223). A relic hunter's pit measuring about 2 m in diameter and 1.2 m deep is located near the south corner of the mound's platform summit (Figure 9.2).

Some discrepancy exists between the mound's dimensions reported by Haag (1952:2) and those obtained during the 1990s fieldwork. Whereas the mound's 1952 horizontal dimensions were stated as "ninety feet [30.5m] on a side," the 1990s measurements for each side of the mound are considerably greater, averaging 125 ft/42 m per side at the base. Also, the 1990s maximum height measurement of 3 m (10 ft) is less than the height reported in 1952, "twelve feet" (3.7 m). It is not stated in the 1952 report whether the mound's dimensions were measured or only estimated, but the reported height of 12 ft may be a result of "the common tendency to over-estimate the height of mounds," as an early investigator of Mississippi's Indian mounds noted (Brown 1926:26). However, that the 1990s mound measurements are wider and lower than the figures given in Haag's report suggests possible vertical deflation and horizontal spreading of the mound, perhaps due to some disturbance and resulting erosion subsequent to Haag's visit. As was observable during the 1990s fieldwork, and as evident in the topographic map (Figure 9.2), the northern half of the mound summit is not uniformly level, but slopes down toward the north, unlike the southern half of the summit, which is nearly flat. This unevenness of the summit is not mentioned in Haag's 1952 report. An inconclusive suggestion of possible past disturbance of the mound's original contours was provided by leaseholder Mickey West, who told the author in 1991 of his vague childhood memory (apparently dating to the mid-1950s) that the mound had been cleared and partially plowed by his father, Ruble West, in an attempt to put it into cultivation. This recollection is reinforced in that no trees are visible at the mound's location indicated on the 1958 aerial photograph used for map sheet 87 of the Calhoun County soil survey book (McMullen et al. 1965). The reported cultivation activity, which evidently was soon abandoned, may explain the somewhat deflated appearance of the north half of the mound. However, since the south half of the mound retains a nearly level platform summit and the southwest and southeast sides of the mound are relatively steep, the essentially square, flat-topped form of the mound is still quite evident (Figure 9.2).

Subsurface Testing of Mound

Mound Stratigraphy

During the author's first visit to the site in June 1991, two bore samples were taken from the mound with a 7-cm-diameter bucket auger in an initial attempt to gain an indication of its internal composition. Both sample columns were extended down to premound subsoil. The first auger column was placed at the top center of the mound and the second about 4.5 m north of the south summit corner (Figure 9.2). In general the auger testing revealed that the mound fill color and texture varies little between the top of the mound and the original premound subsoil. A conspicuous exception to the generally homogeneous character of the mound fill was first encountered in the form of a 2 cm-thick horizontal band of white (2.5Y 8/2) silty clay loam, which was

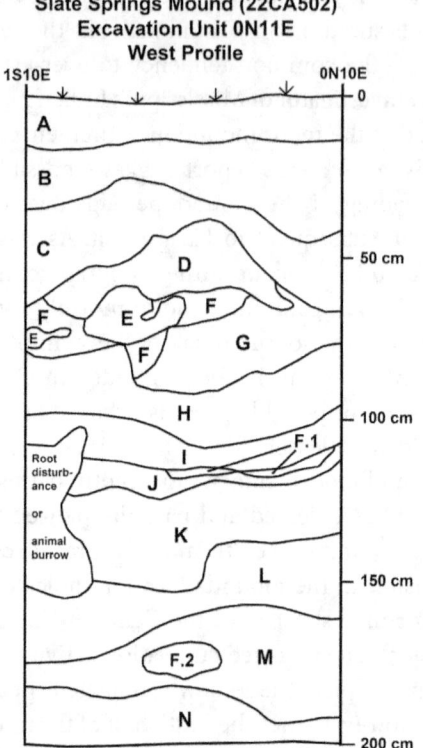

Figure 9.4. Stratigraphic profile of test excavation (west wall), Slate Springs Mound (22CA502).

revealed in the second auger column about 90 cm beneath the summit. This light-colored layer was subsequently found to extend to a point 2.5 m southwest of the second auger column, where it appeared as a 3- to 4-cm stratum in the cleaned-off north wall of the relic hunter's pit, also at a depth of around 90 cm. This white stratum of fill contrasted sharply with the otherwise dark brown to yellowish brown silt loam and clay loam seen in the remainder of the relic hunter's pit walls and in the auger samples.

In January 1992, a 1-×-1-meter test pit was excavated to a depth of 2 meters beneath the mound summit (Figures 9.2 and 9.4). The excavation could not be widened or extended to the base of the mound due to time limitations. The excavated mound fill was screened through quarter-inch (.64 cm) mesh. Following excavation, the pit was backfilled. The unit was designated by its northeast corner, 0N11E, as measured by tape 11 m east of a large aluminum stake which was driven into the approximate top center of the mound as a datum for the topographic mapping survey. (Upon completion of the fieldwork, the stake was driven completely into the ground as a permanent reference marker for future work at the site.) The pit was excavated by strata (fill-loading zones and features discernible by variability in color and texture of the soils), and within zones by arbitrary levels (10 cm or less). Stratigraphic zones (labeled A through N in Figure 9.4) were generally faint; the west wall of the test unit exhibited the most variability (Figure 9.4).

It is notable that high-contrast, white silty clay loam identical in color and texture to the deposits observed in the second auger column and in the relic hunter's pit appeared at roughly the same depth in the 1-×-1-m test unit. In profile, however, the deposits of white fill as observed in the west wall of the 1 × 1 (labeled E in Figure 9.4) did not occur in a thin, even layer as was seen in the auger column and relic hunter's pit, but instead resembled individual basket loads that were dumped and left unspread. However, the fact that this light-colored fill appeared at approximately the same depth in several subsurface exposures suggests that this conspicuously contrasting zone represents a horizontally extensive capping layer laid down between mantles of fill. The occurrence of strata with contrasting colors has been noted in other pre-Mississippian flat-topped mounds, an effect described by Knight (1990:171) as "a sandwiching of layers."

Above and underneath the white-colored deposits, the mound fill throughout the test pit was of relatively uniform but subtly varying texture and coloration indicative of fill loading, consisting of irregularly alternating layers of loam, silty loam, and clay loam of slightly different shades of brown. Beginning in Zone I at approximately 100-cm depth and continuing down to 120 cm in the west half of the test unit, increasingly abundant charcoal, including chunks as large as 2 cm in diameter, was encountered in the fill matrix.

Features

The base of the charcoal-containing fill of Zone I was underlain by Feature 1, a double lens-shaped layer (labeled F.1 in Figure 9.4) of silt loam with a hardened, brittle texture and a yellowish-brown color (10YR 5/4) resulting from in situ burning of wood, evidenced by charcoal fragments within the lenses of Feature 1 as well as in the directly overlying fill matrix of Zone I. Due to the restricted horizontal extent of the excavation, whether the charcoal and the underlying fire-hardened and -discolored soil represents the remains of a possible building which stood on the summit of an earlier mound stage is unknown, although no obvious preserved structural elements such as postmolds, charred thatch, charred wooden posts, wall trenches, or fired daub were found. The intact state of Feature 1 suggests that it may be a burned surface or hearth on a previous platform summit (e.g., Knight 1990:170–171;

Lindauer and Blitz 1997:173) upon which a fire was burned shortly preceding the addition of more fill of a new construction stage to create a higher mound summit.

Feature 2 consisted of a discrete deposit of charcoal (labeled F.2 in Figure 9.4) within Zone M, located at a depth of ca. 170–180 cm. Unlike Feature 1, no fire-discolored or -hardened fill was associated.

Artifacts

Few artifacts were encountered during testing of the mound. All of the prehistoric items are interpreted as incidental inclusions in fill presumably brought in from a nearby occupation area.

Six Woodland-period potsherds (see below) were recovered from the 1-×-1-m test unit: one sand-tempered fabric impressed from the 10–20-cm level below the surface in Zone B, one sand-tempered cordmarked from the 110–120-cm level in Zone I, one sand-tempered plain and one grog-tempered plain from the 160–170-cm level in Zone N, and one grog-tempered plain from the 190–200-cm level in Zone O. One additional grog-tempered plain sherd was recovered from a depth of 125 cm in the bore hole placed about 3 m south of the 1 × 1.

Radiocarbon Dates

Four samples of wood charcoal obtained from the test excavation were submitted to Beta Analytic, Inc., for radiocarbon dating (Table 9.1). The previously published results (Sims and Connaway 2000:221) have been recalibrated using CALIB 5.0.2 (Reimer et al. 2004) for presentation here.

Except for the date from the context closest to the top of the mound, the dates conform to the order of stratigraphic superposition. However, the implied temporal span of more than 500 years seems anomalous as the dates are derived from samples vertically distributed in only about a meter of fill. Moreover, no indicators for the passage of a lengthy period of time (mottling due to weathering, development of an A horizon) were observed in the zones of fill separating the four charcoal deposits. That the three samples yielding the earliest dates (Beta-63788, -64735, and -62801) were derived from small, discrete concentrations of charcoal gives rise to the suspicion that these three charcoal samples may represent secondary deposits, inadvertently included in loads of mound fill taken from earlier, off-mound occupation areas. The fact that the excavation also recovered habitation debris (potsherds) from the fill reinforces this scenario. Possible evidence of mixing of off-mound materials of different ages in mound fill can be adduced from the fact that the deepest level

Table 9.1. Radiocarbon dates, 1 x 1 m test unit 0N11E, Slate Springs Mound.

Lab no.	Depth below surface	Age (B.P.)	2 sigma cal range intercepts	Relative area under distribution
Beta-63788	60–70 cm	1720 ± 50	A.D. 144=147	.002
Beta-63788	60–70 cm	1720 ± 50	A.D. 171–193	.015
Beta-63788	60–70 cm	1720 ± 50	A.D. 211–427	.983
Beta-51398	100–110 cm	1310 ± 50	A.D. 641–783	.935
Beta-51398	100–110 cm	1310 ± 50	A.D. 787–824	.044
Beta-51398	100–110 cm	1310 ± 50	A.D. 841–861	.021
Beta-64735	160–170 cm	1520 ± 50	A.D. 428–633	1.0
Beta-62801	175–180 cm (Fea. 2)	1800 ± 70	A.D. 72–392	1.0

of the excavation, although it yielded the sample producing the oldest Middle Woodland date (1800 ± 70 B.P.; cal. 2-sigma range A.D. 70–390, rounding to the nearest decade), also yielded a grog-tempered plain sherd, in this area a likely Late Woodland artifact (see below). In contrast, the bedded deposit of abundant charcoal yielding the age of 1310 ± 50 B.P. (cal. 2-sigma range A.D. 640–780, rounding to the nearest decade), together with the underlying lens of fire-hardened and discolored soil, is an unambiguous product of in situ burning, marking an actual event associated with the mound's construction and/or use. This later date, when considered alone, would seem to place the Slate Springs Mound in the Late Woodland period. However, the three earlier dates, although their depositional context may seem questionable, nevertheless cannot be dismissed out of hand and must be taken into account when considering the age of the mound. Taken together, then, the absolute dates appear to bracket the construction/use span of the mound within the Middle Woodland to early Late Woodland periods.

Off-Mound Occupation Areas

According to Haag's 1952 survey report, only a few artifacts were collected from the field surrounding the mound, consisting of grog-tempered potsherds of likely Late Woodland affiliation ("[s]ix sherds of Tishomingo Cordmarked and three sherds of Tishomingo Plain") and a probable Early Archaic diagnostic, a "side-notched, bevel-edged projectile point" (Haag 1952:2). The low recovery of material was attributed to the fact that the surface of the field was obscured by pasture vegetation at the time of Haag's site visit. Although the 1952 report implies that surface artifacts were found in proximity to the mound, the 1990s investigations revealed that the nearest concentrations of cultural debris are located at least 150 m away; the only artifacts found near the mound were two potsherds (one sand-tempered plain and the other sand-tempered eroded or possibly fabric-impressed) from the bare surface of the field about 10 m west of the western corner of the mound.

At the time of the 1991 and 1992 site visits, the field around the mound remained in pasture, with grass cover ranging from sparse to absent in some areas and dense in others. As had been the case during Haag's visit, artifact occurrence was quite scant, and no darkened soil indicative of midden was observed anywhere. As described below, nearly all off-mound artifacts found in the 1990s investigations were found on two low terrace knolls; these two discrete artifact scatter loci, designated sites 22CA552 and 22CA553, were respectively located several hundred meters southeast and south of the mound.

Site 22CA552

In 1991, 18 shovel tests were dug in various areas where the grass cover was relatively dense, in the northeast, southeast, and southwest quadrants of the field surrounding the mound. The shovel-test holes were about 35 cm wide and 35 cm deep; the soil removed from each hole was screened through quarter-inch mesh. These tests yielded only five artifacts (1 grog-tempered plain and 2 sand-tempered plain sherds, a biface thinning flake of pink chert, and the distal portion of a Madison triangular point of red chert), found in a cluster of four positive tests located around 270 m southeast of the mound. A couple of additional artifacts were collected from the surface of this area during a visit in 1992 (a battered hammerstone of yellow quartzite and a pitted ferruginous sandstone cobble). The area from which this shovel-test and surface material was obtained, designated site 22CA552, measures about 140 m north-south by 50 m east-west.

Site 22CA553

Reinspection of the field around the mound in 1992 found the grass cover on the southwestern quadrant of the field much diminished from what had been present during the 1991 visit. As a result, a general surface collection was made there from an area measuring some 150 m north-south by 50 m east-west. This area, the northern limit of which is about 150 m south of the mound, has been designated archaeological site 22CA553 by MDAH. A Late Archaic or Early Woodland Flint Creek point of Citronelle or Tuscaloosa Gravel chert was found, while Woodland-period diagnostics include two sand-tempered plain and two grog-tempered plain sherds, along with two unfinished, narrow bifaces with straight stems (possibly Middle Woodland) of gravel chert. Also recovered were a few dozen pieces of local chert debitage, as well as a hammerstone of pink quartzite, three smoothed tabular (metate?) fragments of ferruginous sandstone, and three broken pitted ferruginous sandstone cobbles.

Ceramic Affiliations

As discussed by Ford (1977, 1980, 1981, 1989), Johnson (1984, 1988), and Peacock (1997, 2003, this volume, Chapter 8), archaeological investigation of the interior uplands of Mississippi has lagged behind that of better known adjacent regions to the west (the Yazoo Basin/Lower Mississippi Valley) and to the east (northeast Mississippi and Tombigbee River valley). In addition, because of the perceived presence in the North Central Hills of a "mixture of ceramic types which have been recognized and defined separately in the two regions" (Ford 1980:26), researchers in the North Central Hills have tended to borrow existing ceramic typologies from those surrounding areas. This approach was first taken in the analysis of North Central Hills ceramics by Haag, who stated that the Grenada Reservoir area "lies in a zone that is transitional between clay-grit [grog] tempering to the west in the Mississippi Delta and sand-tempering to the north and east in North Mississippi and Alabama" (Haag 1952:18). As a result, Haag (1952) classified his Grenada Reservoir survey ceramics using types that had been defined by Phillips et al. (1951) for the Lower Mississippi Valley and by Jennings (1941, 1944), Cotter (1950), and Cotter and Corbett (1951) for northeast Mississippi.

The latter four works established the Middle and Late Woodland Miller ceramic sequence for northeastern Mississippi. Jenkins (1981) modified and refined the Miller sequence for the central Tombigbee River valley, dividing the Miller sequence into the Middle Woodland-period Miller I (ca.100 B.C.–A.D. 300) and Miller II (ca. A.D. 300–600) phases, followed by the Late Woodland Miller III phase (ca. A.D. 600–1100). The date ranges for Miller-style ceramics are a couple of centuries earlier north of the central Tombigbee Valley (Ford 1989, Rafferty 1987, 1990; Walling et al. 1991). The Miller ceramic sequence is characterized by gradual shifts in tempering agents and surface finishes through time: Miller I is dominated by sand-tempered fabric impressed (Saltillo Fabric Marked), Miller II by sand-tempered cordmarked (Furrs Cord Marked), and the Miller III phase by grog-tempered wares, both cordmarked and plain (Tishomingo Cord Marked and Tishomingo Plain, respectively). Peacock (1997) performed a seriation of ceramic assemblages from the Ackerman Unit of the Tombigbee National Forest, well within the eastern section of the North Central Hills (Figure 9.3), which revealed that the Miller sequence is applicable there. This finding necessitates a modification of Johnson's (1988) model positing that the Miller ceramic tradition does not extend into the North Central Hills from the east.

In striking contrast is the pattern revealed by seriation of assemblages from the Holly Springs unit of the Holly Springs National Forest in the extreme northern portion of the North Central Hills (Peacock 1997; Figure 9.3): although the temporal shift in surface finishes from fabric impressed to cord-marked is the same as in the Miller region to the east and southeast, the change in temper through time is reversed, from grog to sand. Moreover, because surface-finished sherds in the Holly Springs assemblages are dominated by grog-tempered fabric impressed, with some grog-tempered sherds bearing individual cord impressions, Peacock (1997:245–246, this volume, Chapter 8) assigns this material to the Early Woodland (or early Middle Woodland) Tchula period (ca. 400 B.C.–100 B.C.), originally defined for northwest Mississippi by Phillips et al. (1951:432) and Phillips (1970:878–880). Similar Tchula assemblages have been identified from sites in the North Central Hills south of the Holly Springs National Forest (Ford 1989, 1990), to the west in the Loess Hills at the Batesville Mounds (Johnson et al. 2002), and in western Tennessee (Mainfort and Chapman 1994). Assemblages containing grog-tempered fabric-impressed materials representative of Tchula occupations in northern and northwestern Mississippi may somewhat predate northeastern and eastern Mississippi Miller I occupations with their assemblages dominated by sand-tempered fabric-impressed, although this is uncertain due to the shortage of radiocarbon dates from Tchula contexts (Ford 1996; Peacock 1996c, 1997, this volume, Chapter 8).

The Slate Springs Mound and nearby sites 22CA552 and 22CA553 are located in the heart of the North Central Hills, about equidistant between the Holly Springs Unit of the Holly Springs National Forest and the Ackerman Unit of the Tombigbee National Forest (Figure 10.3). How do these three sites fit, chronologically and spatially, in view of Woodland-period ceramic traits documented in other areas of the North Central Hills? Haag (1952: 2) classified his small collection of sherds from the field around the mound as "Tishomingo Cord-marked" and "Tishomingo Plain." These types were named and defined by Jennings (1941:200–201) to denote pottery containing clay or grog temper in a sandy-textured paste. This is in contrast to clay/grog-tempered sherds from other sites in the Grenada Lake survey which are described by Haag (1952:20) as having a "smooth" and "chalky" textured paste, and classified by him as "Mulberry Creek Cord-marked" and "Baytown Plain," following the Phillips et al. (1951) Lower Mississippi Valley typology. As previously discussed, the 1990s fieldwork recovered an additional six grog-tempered sherds, all plain: three from the mound and three from the nearby occupation areas (one from 22CA552, two from 22CA553). In this report, no paste texture distinctions are attempted for these sherds, as no known chronological, cultural, or functional inferences can be drawn from such an exercise (Peacock 1997:241–242, this volume, Chapter 8).

In addition to the grog-tempered sherds, 12 sand-tempered specimens recovered in the 1990s fieldwork include 1 sand-tempered fabric impressed from mound fill; 1 sand-tempered eroded (possibly fabric impressed) from the field just west of the mound; 1 sand-tempered cord marked from mound fill; and 9 sand-tempered plain (1 from mound fill and the rest from off-mound contexts). Sand-tempered fabric-impressed and cord-marked pottery in northeast Mississippi is commonly identified by the type names Saltillo Fabric Marked and Furrs Cord Marked, respectively (e.g., Jenkins 1981), after Jennings's original designations (Jennings 1941:199–201, 1944:411–412).

Although few in number, the sherds with textured surface finishes are not inconsistent with the Miller ceramic tradition of the Middle and Late Woodland periods. This impression is reinforced by the absence of any pottery that might suggest affinity with the Early or Middle Woodland Tchula tradition documented farther north in the North Central Hills and in the Yazoo Basin, i.e., grog-tempered fabric-impressed or grog-tempered individual cord impressed (Peacock 1997, this volume, Chapter 8). Although Haag (1952) found clay/grog-tempered fabric-impressed sherds at 5 of the 48 sites he recorded in the Grenada Lake area (classified in his report as "Withers Fabric-impressed" following the Phillips et al. [1951:73] Lower Mississippi Valley typology), those sites are located in the western portion of his survey area, in Grenada County. No such material has been found at the Slate Springs Mound, or, according to the MDAH state archaeological site inventory, at any of the 32 additional recorded prehistoric sites within a 10-mile (15-km) radius of the mound.

The presence of a partial Madison triangular point along with grog-tempered pottery in the assemblage from off-mound site 22CA552 reinforces the probable presence of a Late Woodland occupation, as the Madison point was introduced to Mississippi during Late Woodland times (McGahey 2000:200–201). The recovery of three grog-tempered sherds from the mound excavation, including one found in the deepest level (190–200 cm), implies that the mound was built in the Late Woodland period, an impression reinforced by the radiocarbon date most likely representative of an in situ context: cal. A.D. 640–780, rounding to the nearest decade (see Table 9.1).

A particularly revealing category of negative evidence is signified by the absence of Mississippi-period (post-A.D. 1100) shell-tempered ceramics in any of the collections from the mound, from nearby sites 22CA552 and 22CA553, and from all but one of the additional 30 recorded prehistoric sites within a 10 mile (15 km) radius of the mound. (The sole exception is site 22CA514, located some 5 miles [8 km] north of the mound, from which 2 shell-tempered sherds are recorded.) The extremely scant presence of Mississippian occupations in the region in general is evident in the results of Haag's (1952) Grenada Lake survey: only one shell-tempered sherd (Barton Incised) was found out of a total of 1,287 sherds collected from 48 sites. A later survey of several reservoir areas in the North Central Hills likewise recovered very few shell-tempered ceramics (Broyles et al. 1982:149). Further confirming the scarcity of Mississippian occupation of the region are the results of a more recent survey that included wide-ranging areas of the North Central Hills and adjacent Loess Hills (Johnson 2001:137–138): of a total of 919 sites recorded in a 157,214-acre survey universe, only 22 sites yielded shell-tempered sherds. Rafferty (2002:222) notes that "[m]any ... Woodland flat-topped mounds ... had been recorded or discussed in earlier literature under the assumption that they were constructed during Mississippian times." In the case of the Slate Springs Mound and its environs, the lack of shell-tempered ceramics in any context strongly suggests that the mound is not the product of a Mississippian occupation. This is conclusively confirmed by the mound's suite of exclusively Woodland-period radiocarbon dates discussed above.

Peacock (1997:238, 244, 253) has noted that most of the Tchula and Miller sites recorded in the National Forests of the North Central Hills tend to be located in two separate major drainage basins. The streams in the Tchula area (the Holly Springs Unit of the Holly Springs National Forest and adjacent areas of Lafayette County) (Figure 9.3) flow westward to the Yazoo Basin in the Mississippi River drainage, where Tchula stylistic traits are most common. In contrast, the Miller-affiliated Woodland-period sites of the Ackerman Unit of the Tombigbee National Forest (Figure 9.3) are located on land drained by the Noxubee River, a tributary of the Tombigbee River. Peacock (1997:244) has posited that "the Miller ceramic tradition [may be] bounded [on the west] by ... the drainage divide between the Tombigbee and Yazoo River basins," although he cautions that "there is no simple, overreaching correlation between drainage basins and ceramic styles" (Peacock 1997:253). Indeed, the Slate Springs Mound and other Middle to Late Woodland-period sites in the area with Miller-like ceramics do not conform to this dichotomous geographic pattern, as these sites are located not in the Tombigbee drainage, where the Miller tradition is centered, but on tributaries of the Yalobusha River, which flows west into the Yazoo Basin where the Tchula and later Marksville, Baytown, and Coles Creek traditions are dominant (Kidder 2002). It should be noted, however, that these sites, while west of the Tombigbee-Yazoo Basin drainage divide, are not far from it: the Slate Springs Mound is in the upper reaches of the Yalobusha River drainage, only about 15 miles (24 km) west of the divide (Figure 9.3). In this respect, the Slate Springs site shares something in common with the much larger, multimound sites of Ingomar (22UN500) (Rafferty 1987, 1990) and Pinson (40MD1)

(Mainfort 1986a, 1988, 1996, 2013b). As noted by Rafferty (1987:148) and Johnson (1988), Ingomar and Pinson are also Woodland-period sites with platform mounds located near the divides of major drainage systems. In view of the Miller-like ceramic assemblages of the Slate Springs locality, the Tombigbee-Yazoo divide in the North Central Hills might be regarded not as a discrete borderline between the Miller tradition on the east and the Tchula, Marksville, Baytown, and Coles Creek traditions to the west, but as a fairly broad transitional zone. (See also Rafferty's [1994] seriation of assemblages containing Miller tradition ceramics from sites on both sides of the Yazoo Basin-Tombigbee Basin divide in Union, Lee, and Pontotoc counties, Mississippi.)

Regional Comparisons and Contrasts

Platform mounds, whatever their age or cultural affiliation, are rare in the North Central Hills of Mississippi. Other than the Slate Springs Mound, the only known examples are Nanih Waiya (22WI500) in Winston County (Carleton 1999), Hurricane Landing (22LA516) in Lafayette County (Thorne 1981), and the Old Hoover Place (22HO502) in Holmes County (Lorenz 1990, 1996). Of these three mounds, Hurricane and Old Hoover are known to date to the post-A.D. 1000 Mississippi period. The mound at the multi-occupation Nanih Waiya site in Winston County has been proposed as a Middle Woodland-period structure by Carleton (1999:125), but this is uncertain, as it has not been excavated and directly dated by absolute means. Consequently, the Slate Springs Mound is currently the sole confirmed Woodland-period platform mound in the entirety of the North Central Hills (Figure 9.3).

To cite other known Woodland-period mounds of flat-topped configuration in northern Mississippi, it is necessary to widen the geographic scope beyond the North Central Hills to encompass adjacent physiographic regions (Figure 9.3). To the west in the Loess Hills, the construction of the Batesville Mounds (22PA500) was initiated the Early Woodland period and may have extended into the Middle Woodland; both Early to Middle Woodland Tchula tradition ceramics and Middle Woodland Marksville pottery were recovered (Johnson et al. 2002). On the Pontotoc Ridge to the east, a radiocarbon date obtained from the one remaining mound at the Thelma site (22CS501) suggests that it was built in the Late Woodland period, but the ceramics from the site include shell-tempered sherds as well as grog-tempered material, interpreted by Johnson and Atkinson (1987:69) as indicative of a later, transitional Late Woodland-Mississippian occupation (see also Rafferty, this volume). In the Flatwoods, the platform mound at Ingomar has been dated definitively to the Middle Woodland period (Rafferty 1987, 1990).

Looking beyond northern Mississippi to adjacent regions, the Pinson Mounds site in western Tennessee (Mainfort 1986a, 1988, 1996, 2013b) exhibits a number of similarities to Ingomar, and the two sites are apparently roughly contemporaneous (Mainfort and McNutt 2004). Also in western Tennessee are Middle Woodland platform mounds at the Johnston site (40MD3) (Kwas and Mainfort 1986) and the Savannah site (40HR29) (Welch 1998). Along the Tennessee River in northern Alabama, the Walling Mound (see Knight 1990:1–4 for the various site numbers employed) and the Florence Mound (1LU10) (Boudreaux and Johnson 2000) have been identified as Middle Woodland-period platform mounds of the Copena tradition. A few Baytown- (early Late Woodland-) period platform mounds may be present in the Yazoo Basin of western Mississippi (Kidder 2002:82).

Aside from the fairly superficial parallel of the mere presence of a platform mound, it is strikingly apparent that the Slate Springs site shares little else in common with any of the other sites mentioned above in terms of size and complexity. In contrast to most (if not all) of the other platform mounds mentioned above, the Slate Springs Mound is rather small. As mentioned above, it is also notable that the Slate Springs site consists of a solitary mound, whereas most other Woodland-period platform mounds occur in groups with other flat-topped mounds and/or with conical burial mounds. There is no evidence for additional mounds anywhere in the vicinity of the Slate Springs site; Haag's (1952) report does not mention any mounds nearby, and no topographical features suggestive of mound remnants were observed during the 1990s investigations. On some Woodland platform mounds, midden deposits containing food remains (animal bone, charred plant material, etc.) have been found on the summits or dumped down the sides; this has been interpreted as evidence of ritual feasting (e.g., Blitz and Mann 2000:38; Knight 1990:158–164, 2001:323–325; Lindauer and Blitz 1997; Milanich et al. 1984:102). However, no bone or non-wood floral material of any kind has been found at or around the Slate Springs Mound.

Discussion and Conclusions

Haag (1952:29) interpreted the Slate Springs Mound's relatively small size and solitary occurrence as evidence of an undeveloped, early phase of a platform mound-building tradition in the region. Accordingly, Haag (1952:29–30) assigned the mound to Ford and Willey's (1941:328–330, 344) Temple Mound I stage, which was equated with an "early Middle Mississippian period" in western Mississippi (Ford and Willey 1941:348). In Ford and Willey's pan-regional culture-historical scheme, a relatively continuous and brief developmental trajectory from Temple Mound I to Temple Mound II or fully developed Mississippian was postulated. Phillips (1970:7) realigned Temple Mound I with Coles Creek, a Late Woodland culture of the Lower Mississippi Valley spanning ca. A.D. 700–1200 (Kidder 2002:69). However, it is likely not the Coles Creek period but the preceding early Late Woodland Baytown period (A.D. 500–700) and/or Middle Woodland Marksville period (200 B.C.–A.D. 500) of the LMV (Kidder 2002) that coincide with the age range of the Slate Springs Mound.

As outlined above, other than the exceptions of the Hurricane Landing Mound in Lafayette County and the Old Hoover Mound in Holmes County, no Mississippi-period mounds, and few Mississippian sites of any kind, have been discovered in the North Central Hills. The preponderance of evidence accumulated from throughout the North Central Hills supports the view that, for presently unknown reasons, most of the region was largely abandoned by the beginning of the Mississippi period (Peacock 1997:252, 2003:50–51; Peacock et al. 2008). Because the Slate Springs Mound is now known to date to the Middle or early Late Woodland period, the site does not represent an Emergent Mississippian platform mound-building trend in the region, as believed by Haag. On the contrary, it seems to be a temporally and spatially isolated anomaly.

Rafferty (2002:224) has stated that "[c]rucial to understanding the relationships among [platform] mounds and to Woodland habitation sites is information about occupation duration, continuity of mound building, kinds of features and artifacts found in mounds, and contemporaneity." The chronological and functional relationships, if any, between the Slate Springs Mound and the two nearby sites 22CA552 and 22CA553 are uncertain, but both the ceramic and chronometric data suggest that they are partially contemporaneous in the Middle and/or early Late Woodland periods. The occupation debris at both 22CA552 and 553 is not plentiful, conforming to the pattern noted by Rafferty (2002:224): "Habitation evidence is either unknown or seems to be relatively light at most of the large Middle Woodland mound sites in the north-south strip from Tennessee to Mississippi. . . . Most Middle Woodland habitation sites in the central region are hamlet-sized."

Knight (1990:162–163) has postulated that the widespread but scant occurrence of Woodland-period platform mounds across the southeastern United States suggests sporadic, relatively short-term, non-hereditary concentrations of political power held by a few individuals in otherwise non-stratified societies (see also Milanich et al. 1984). The isolation and small size of the Slate Springs Mound conforms to this hypothesized pattern. How this mound was integrated into a settlement system context is unknown due to the lack of intensive and extensive survey in the locality. Assuming that the mound represents some sort of public sociopolitical center, it does appear that no site hierarchy exists in the surrounding region, given the small size of the mound and the lack of superordinate (i.e., multimound) sites anywhere in the area. As a result, the influence exerted by the site most probably was limited to a relatively small territory. This impression is reinforced by the lack in the (admittedly small) artifact samples from the mound and from nearby sites of extraregional ceramics or other exotic trade materials, which have been found at larger Woodland mound centers like Ingomar (Rafferty 1990:100–101) and Pinson (Mainfort 1986a:35–46).

Although modest in scope, the investigations accomplished at the Slate Springs Mound so far have been fairly productive, but more detailed insights into this site's functional role in the regional Woodland-period settlement system must await further excavation of the mound and intensive survey of the surrounding area. Fortunately, the mound's long-term protection is secure due to its formal designation as a Mississippi Landmark. Under provisions of the Mississippi Antiquities Law, destruction or alteration of Mississippi Landmarks is prohibited, ensuring that this ancient monument will be preserved as a valuable repository of archaeological data.

Acknowledgments

I wish to express my appreciation of the late David Fant, Cliff Jenkins, Evan Peacock, Janet Rafferty, and Julie Baca, all of whom generously volunteered their assistance in the fieldwork. Evan also deserves much credit for finally prevailing upon me to revise and update my two-decades-old conference paper for publication—*praestat sero quam nunquam*. Mrs. Ruble West and Mickey West, leaseholders of the land on which the mound is located, provided gracious hospitality during the fieldwork. Because the Slate Springs Mound is on sixteenth-section public school land, thanks are due to Dewitt Spencer, the Calhoun County superintendent of education at the time of the 1990s site investigations, for his enthusiastic support during the process of designating the mound a Mississippi Landmark. Jeffrey Alvey, my colleague at the Cobb Institute of Archaeology, efficiently prepared the digital figures from my smudged old field drawings.

Finally, although he was not directly involved in this project, Sam Brookes nonetheless certainly deserves recognition for doing so much in his leadership role with the National Forests in Mississippi to bring to light the prehistory of Mississippi's North Central Hills (in addition to many other regions of the state). Specifically, Sam saw to it that Zone Archaeologists were assigned to National Forest units in that region, and these individuals included the above-named David Fant and Evan Peacock for the Holly Springs National

Forest and the Tombigbee National Forest, respectively. Without the copious amounts of Woodland-period data that Sam's dedicated archaeologists recovered from these two forests, the Slate Springs Mound would have been much harder to place in perspective. It is through such networks of colleagues and friends that archaeological knowledge of this once little-known region has advanced.

CHAPTER 10

Mississippian-Period Occupations in the Ackerman Unit of the Tombigbee National Forest

Andrew M. Triplett

Introduction

The culture-historical dichotomy drawn between the Woodland and Mississippian cultural traditions in the Southeast is quite distinct. Woodland peoples have been viewed as egalitarian groups who lived in scattered, nucleated villages along the main rivers or in small hamlets located in the uplands, making sand- and/or grog-tempered pottery and primarily hunting, with some cultivation of native crops for food (Anderson and Mainfort 2002:1–19). In contrast, the Mississippian period (following Rafferty and Peacock 2008a:6) is most often characterized by inferred hierarchies of mound complexes with surrounding villages whose inhabitants subsisted primarily upon maize agriculture and made mussel shell-tempered pottery. As drawn, this change in cultural patterns is so pronounced that it is often taken to indicate an influx of foreign "Mississippian" peoples from other regions of the continent into a given area (e.g., the Tombigbee and Black Warrior River valleys [Jenkins and Krause 1986:90]).

A body of research has begun to refute the stark contrasts drawn between these two periods (Anderson and Mainfort 2002; Bozeman 1982; Hogue and Peacock 1995; Mistovich 1988, 1995; Peacock 1997, 2003; Peacock and Rafferty 1996; Rafferty 1996, 2001, 2002, 2003). As Rafferty has pointed out (1996, 2001; Rafferty and Peacock 2008b), in the Black Prairie region of eastern Mississippi, just to the west of the Tombigbee River valley (Figure 10.1), there are indications of continuity in settlement patterns between the two periods. Quite often the same landform or area was either continuously settled or repeatedly resettled over extended periods of time that encompassed both the Woodland and Mississippian cultural traditions.

Mississippian-Period Occupations in the Ackerman Unit

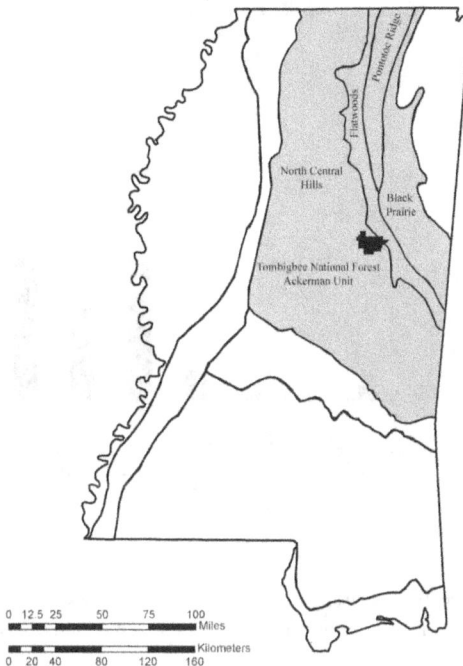

Figure 10.1. The Ackerman Unit of the Tombigbee National Forest and surrounding physiographic provinces of Mississippi.

To the west of the Black Prairie is the North Central Hills physiographic province (Figure 10.1), within which lies most of the 44,000 acres of the Ackerman Unit of the Tombigbee National Forest. The Noxubee River and its principal tributaries, the Little Noxubee River and Mill Creek, drain the area within the boundaries of the Ackerman Unit before eventually emptying via the Noxubee River into the Tombigbee River farther south.

Numerous archaeological surveys conducted on the Ackerman Unit indicate a long history of occupation. A dramatic increase in the number of occupations concurrent with the Woodland period (Figure 10.2; see also Parrish 2006 and Peacock 1997) may indicate a switch from a mobile existence during the Paleo-Indian and Archaic periods to a sedentary settlement pattern coincident with the adoption of ceramics (Bacon-Schulte 2008; Rafferty 1994) and brought about by range compression caused by increases in population density in the region (Rafferty 1994:420). Sites containing Woodland-period occupations are found on all landforms on the Ackerman Unit, something also likely a product of increased population density as earlier sites are found

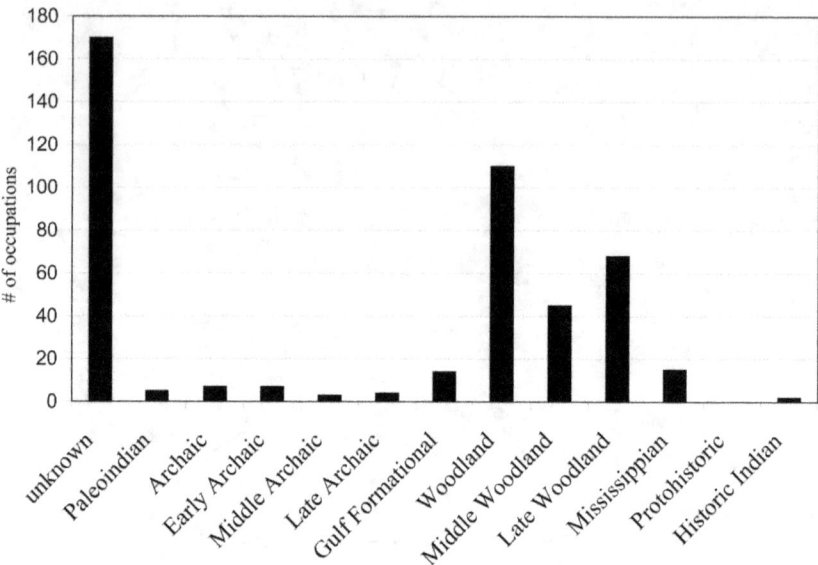

Figure 10.2. Number of prehistoric occupations at sites within the Ackerman Unit of the Tombigbee National Forest. "Woodland" = undifferentiated component dating from ca. 200 B.C.–A.D. 900.

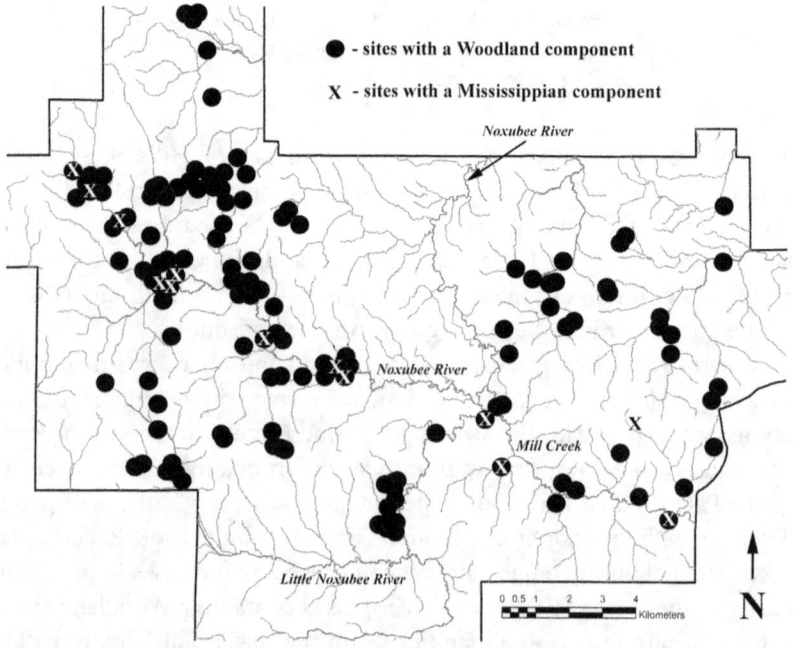

Figure 10.3. Sites containing Mississippian-period occupations within the Tombigbee National Forest, Ackerman Unit.

primarily along the larger waterways. Twelve of the 13 Mississippian components (represented by the presence of shell-tempered pottery; see Feathers 2006) recorded on the Ackerman Unit as of 2007 (Triplett 2008a) are located at sites with much larger Late Woodland-period occupations, and all but one are concentrated along the Noxubee River or one of its main tributaries (Figure 10.3).

The dramatic decrease in the number of Mississippian-period components within the Ackerman Unit, and the concentration of sites with such components along major streams, could indicate population consolidation (i.e., nucleation) or the movement of some part of the population out of the area late in prehistoric times. Research in the western portion of the Black Prairie has revealed numerous small sites containing mussel shell-tempered pottery. While some have suggested that these occupations represent expansion away from the Tombigbee River and into the uplands during the Protohistoric period (Futato 1989; Johnson 1996; Johnson and Sparks 1986; Johnson et al. 1994), others believe them to represent continuity in upland settlement patterns from the Woodland through the Mississippian periods (Hogue and Peacock 1995; Peacock and Rafferty 1996; Rafferty 1996, 2001, 2003; Rafferty and Peacock 2008b). This issue is complicated because of the equivocal evidence (plain mussel shell-tempered pottery) being used to place these occupations chronologically (Johnson 1996:244; Peacock and Rafferty 1996:249).

Recent work using a combination of absolute dates and frequency seriations suggests that there was an expansion of settlements marked by shell-tempered pottery in the Black Prairie beginning ca. A.D. 1200 (Rafferty and Peacock 2008b). This apparent increase in site numbers is attributed by Rafferty and Peacock (2008b:258) to "selective pressures related to the onset of climate change, possibly coupled with adoption of maize-based subsistence." It has also been hypothesized that by about A.D. 1100 the North Central Hills were abruptly abandoned (Blitz 1984; Peacock 2003; Peacock et al. 2008), suggesting a place of origin for the movement of early agricultural groups into the Black Prairie (Rafferty and Peacock 2008b). This hypothesis is bolstered by data from Stinking Water (22WI515/516), a large, multicomponent site located beside the Noxubee River in the Ackerman Unit. Diagnostic artifacts indicate that this locale was occupied from the Archaic into the Mississippian period, but was abandoned around A.D. 1000 (Peacock 2003:47).

Two hypotheses can explain the co-occurrence of Woodland- and Mississippian-period diagnostics in the Ackerman Unit area. The first hypothesis is that the Woodland and Mississippian materials represent continuous occupation, with the sites being abandoned early in the Mississippian period. The second hypothesis is that the components do not represent continuous occupations but that the shell-tempered pottery indicates resettlement in the

Mississippian period. These hypotheses were tested via a program of systematic shovel testing at eight sites to determine the location and size of the occupations with shell-tempered pottery, followed by test excavations at three sites designed to measure the degree of co-occurrence between earlier and later pottery types.

Delineating Occupations

An occupation is a "spatial cluster of discrete objects which can reasonably be assumed to be the product of a single group of people at that particular locality deposited over a period of continuous residence comparable to other such units in the same study" (Dunnell 1971:151). As such, an occupation can be considered an artifact at the scale of assemblage (Parrish and Peacock 2006; Rafferty 2008). A class of artifact at this scale is needed to examine culture change and artifact distributions because it "allows artifacts at smaller scales to be associated in meaningful assemblages" (Rafferty 2008:102).

Determining the spatial boundary of an occupation is dependent upon field and proveniencing methods, because spatial associations are based upon propinquity (Rafferty 2008). Demonstrating that individual artifacts, including features, are associated is of utmost importance. Horizontal boundaries can be detected via spatially extensive methods such as controlled surface collection or shovel testing at even intervals (e.g., Parrish and Peacock 2006). Stratigraphic excavation can be used in determining the vertical (temporal) boundaries of an occupation, as artifacts from the same occupation would be expected to be associated in a depositional layer (Rafferty 2008).

Systematic Shovel-Testing Methods and Results

Eight sites were chosen for investigation based upon the documented presence of Mississippian-period artifacts (see Triplett 2008a). Because disparate methods of artifact collection had been used previously, systematic shovel testing (Roskams 2001:49) was employed to delineate concentrations of shell-tempered pottery within the larger site (see also Bozeman 1982; Lorenz 1996). Sites were shovel tested on 10-meter grids following the orientation and shape of the landforms (see Triplett 2008a for details).

Shovel testing confirmed that shell-tempered ceramics are present at the eight sites investigated, albeit in relatively small proportions (Table 10.1). Mixed grog- and shell-tempered sherds may represent the transition from grog to mussel shell pottery tempers in this area. There is some debate as to

Mississippian-Period Occupations in the Ackerman Unit

Table 10.1. Pottery totals from sites systematically shovel tested, listed by temper and surface finish.

	22CH514	22CH515	22CH516	22CH719	22CH814	22WI508	22WI666	22WI865
Fiber								
plain		2						10
punctate								3
eroded								9
Sand								
plain	5	20	3	2	1	9	3	24
broad line incised			1	1				
punctate								1
slipped		1	1			2		2
eroded	6	5	4	1	1	8	8	33
Grog								
plain	17	84	33	11	19	33	26	29
burnished				1	1			
broad line incised		1	1					1
thin line incised		1	2		1			
cord marked	8	30	16		3	23	8	2
fabric marked		1				1		1
punctate				1				1
check-stamped		1						
slipped	3		1	1		2	3	
eroded	13	35	16	11	11	16	71	30
Grog/Bone								
plain							1	3
eroded							2	
Bone								
plain		1						
Grog/Shell								
plain				1				1
eroded		4		2			1	2
Shell								
plain	2	1	2			1	1	6
slipped		2						2
eroded		1	2	1	1		3	8
Total Per Site	54	190	82	33	38	95	127	168

the chronological position of grog/shell-tempered pottery. Jenkins (Jenkins and Krause 1986:93) places this pottery early in the Mississippian period, during the Summerville I phase. Steponaitis (1983:158), though, believes that it is present throughout the Mississippian period. On the Ackerman Unit, it is usually found at sites with Late Woodland and Mississippian components, suggesting continuity of settlement.

As will be discussed further below, these ceramic data were employed in frequency seriations. To further investigate intrasite spatial relationships, three sites were chosen for test excavations, the results of which are discussed first.

Excavation Methods and Sites

A paradigmatic classification (Table 10.2) was developed for determining which of the shovel-tested sites to excavate. The paradigm was based on several mutually exclusive dimensions: total area containing Mississippian materials, type of landform on which the site was located, and the number of components (identified by diagnostic pottery tempers and surface decorations) present. This classification was constructed to incorporate the greatest amount of variability among sites based upon the information gathered through systematic shovel testing. Testing sites on different landforms, with varying degrees of Mississippian occupation and with varying lengths of habitation, was considered the best way of determining the timing of the Mississippian-period habitation of the area (see Triplett 2008a for more detailed discussion of dimensions).

As can be seen in Table 10.2, sites 22CH515 and 22WI666 are both included in the class defined as being located on a terrace, having three or more components present, with an estimated area producing Mississippian materials of between 101 and 500 square meters. Of the two, site 22WI666 was chosen for excavation because it was judged to be less disturbed and therefore had a higher possibility of containing features.

In spite of only a single shell-tempered eroded sherd being recovered at 22CH814 (Table 10.1), the site was chosen for further investigation based upon several factors. First, it was the only terrace location with just two components represented. Also, the Mississippian occupation, according to the initial survey in 2006, was very small (approx. 25 square meters), a finding that was not contradicted by systematic shovel testing. This was the only site with a Mississippian occupation under 100 square meters in size in which the location of the shell-tempered pottery was known, providing an interesting contrast to the larger sites being considered.

Site 22WI865 is the only site found to date on the Ackerman Unit that has two spatially separate Mississippian occupations, i.e., two distinct concentra-

Mississippian-Period Occupations in the Ackerman Unit

Table 10.2. Paradigmatic site classification for Ackerman-Unit occupations.

			Estimated total area containing Mississippian materials											
			0–100 m²				101–500 m²				501 m² and larger			
			Type of Landform											
			F	T	R	O	F	T	R	O	F	T	R	O
22CH514	Number of Identifiable Components Present	1–2												
		3+		X										
22CH515		1–2												
		3+						X						
22CH516		1–2												
		3+		X										
22CH719		1–2			X									
		3+												
22CH814		1–2		X										
		3+												
22WI508		1–2												
		3+		X										
22WI562		1–2			X									
		3+												
22WI666		1–2												
		3+						X						
22WI865		1–2												
		3+												X

F = Flood plain   T = Terrace   R = Ridgetop   O = Other

tions of shell-tempered ceramics as revealed by systematic shovel testing. It is also distinct in its paradigmatic classification: the estimated total size of the Mississippian occupation is over 500 square meters; it is the only site under consideration located on a bluff; and it contains four identifiable components.

Excavations were conducted by the 2007 Mississippi State University field school under the direction of Evan Peacock. Fieldwork consisted of topographic mapping and the excavation of 1-×-1-m test units using natural levels subdivided into maximum 10-cm increments as necessary. Unless otherwise noted, soils were dry-screened through quarter-inch (.64 cm) hardware cloth.

22CH515

During systematic survey of the site, shell-tempered pottery was recovered from a shovel test (Figure 10.4) on a slight downhill slope in the southeastern area of the site. It was thought that any artifacts found in this area had most likely eroded down the slope, and also that the most probable area to

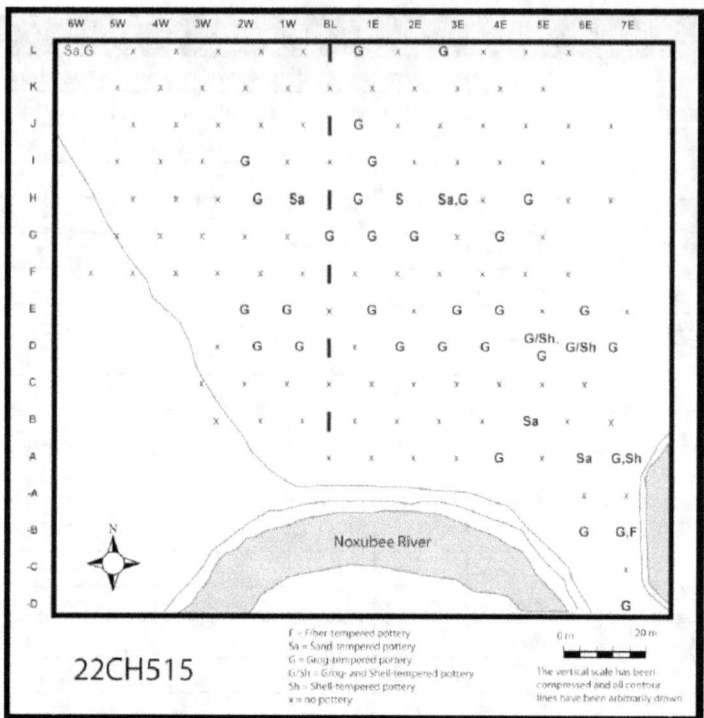

Figure 10.4. 22CH515, shovel-test placement and pottery distribution.

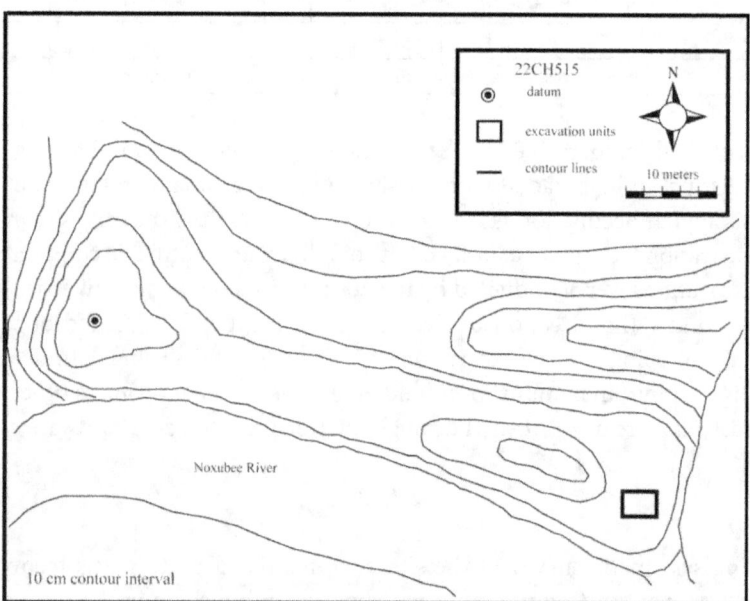

Figure 10.5. 22CH515, topographic map showing excavation unit placement.

Table 10.3. 22CH515, pottery counts by excavated unit.

Unit	fiber plain	fiber eroded	sand plain	sand fine-line incised	sand eroded	grog plain	grog broad-line incised	grog fine-line incised	grog fabric-marked	grog slipped	grog eroded	grog/shell plain	shell plain	shell slipped	shell eroded
20S60E	1		1		3	7			1	2					
20S61E			2		3	4					2		1		2
20S62E	1		3		1	4	3	1	1		3		1		
20S63E	1	1	9	2	2	5	1			1			3	1	
21S60E	1		3		6	1					2				1
21S61E					4	1					7		1		
21S62E			3			5					3		1	1	
21S63E					3	6	1				6		1		
22S60E			5		1	5					1				
22S61E			9		2	8	1					1	4		
22S62E	2		3		5	7	2				4				1
22S63E	1		6			8	2			1			1		

Table 10.4. 22CH814, pottery counts by excavation unit.

Unit	grog plain	grog cord-marked	grog fine-line incised	grog broad-line incised	grog slipped	grog/shell plain
44S9W	3					
45S9W	1					1
45S2W		1				
45S1W	1		1			
45S0E	1			1		
46S9W	2	2				1
46S2W					1	
46S1W	1					
46S0E	3					
53S2W	6					
53S1W	1					
53S0E	3					

encounter features would be on the level area above. Consequently, a block of 12 test units was placed on the level area approximately 5 m south of this particular shovel test (Figure 10.5). The soils in the unit were rather disturbed, and no features or postholes were encountered in any of the excavated units.

The systematic shovel testing conducted prior to excavation indicated a previously unknown Gulf Formational component present, as evidenced by fiber-tempered pottery (Table 10.1). This finding was further substantiated by the recovery of eight additional fiber-tempered sherds from the excavation units. (Analyses do not include any pottery pieces smaller than ca. 20 mm.) Several sand-tempered plain and eroded sherds were also present (Table 10.3). Due to the lack of diagnostic surface decorations (e.g., cord marking or fabric marking), it could not be determined if the sand-tempered pottery represented a Middle Woodland component. Most of the sherds recovered are grog-tempered, including two fabric-marked sherds, and are assignable to the Late Woodland period. A Mississippian component was marked by the recovery of 19 shell-tempered sherds.

22CH814

The original shovel-test survey of this site (Figure 10.6), conducted in the summer of 2006, recovered a single shell-tempered sherd. It was decided to open a block unit approximately 2 m south of the shovel test that produced this sherd (Figure 10.7), in the hope that additional shell-tempered sherds would be recovered and features would be encountered. Nine adjacent units

Mississippian-Period Occupations in the Ackerman Unit

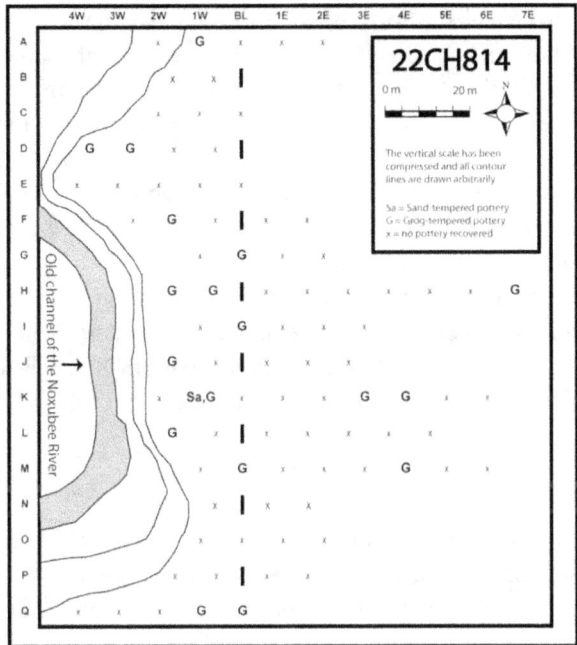

Figure 10.6. 22CH814, shovel-test placement and pottery distribution.

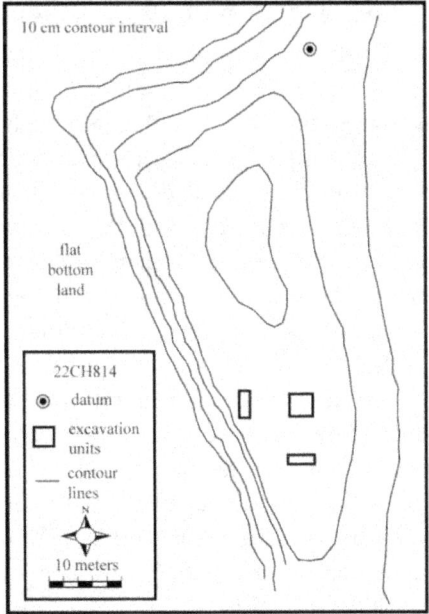

Figure 10.7. 22CH814, topographic map showing excavation unit placement.

were excavated to subsoil, forming a 3-×-3-m block. It became evident, in light of the very thin soil horizons (Triplett 2008a), that this site had been impacted by previous activities. No features or postholes were encountered.

Due to the lack of features and the paucity of pottery in the initial block unit, it was decided to excavate two other 1-×-3-m blocks in close proximity, one 6 m to the west and the other 6 m south (Figure 10.7). Unfortunately, as with the original test units, these units produced very few ceramic artifacts and no features were encountered.

A total of 34 grog-tempered and three grog/shell-tempered sherds was recovered (Table 10.4). The grog-tempered sherds, particularly the cord-marked ones, indicate a Late Woodland occupation. No shell-tempered pottery was recovered from any of the excavation units at this site.

22WI865

Excavated soil at this site was water-screened through quarter-inch and sixteenth-inch stacked screens in order to recover small artifacts. The latter material has not been processed or analyzed, but has been retained for future research.

Systematic shovel testing suggested two spatially separate areas of occupation (Figure 10.8). One was in a midden in the northernmost area, closest to the bluff above the Little Noxubee River, which contained diagnostic pottery tempers and surface finishes representing all of the known pottery-producing cultural periods of the region. Two separate 1-×-1-m test units were placed in this area, as well as an irregular block unit that eventually consisted of six 1-×-1- and one 1-×-.50-m test units (Figure 10.9). The other pottery concentration, on the southern end of the site, indicated Late Woodland and Mississippian components. Soils in this area were much shallower and had been heavily disturbed. A large block unit was laid out in approximately the middle of the several shovel tests that contained shell-tempered pottery. Initially, this block consisted of 20 contiguous 1-×-1-m units; four additional 1-×-1-m units were opened up when no features were encountered in the initial units.

Unit 15S11E was located in the deepest part of the midden and is the only unit at this site reported by zone/level. The pottery recovered there includes three fiber-tempered, three sand-tempered, and 19 grog-tempered sherds (Table 10.5). It appears that, even though this is a relatively deep midden, it has been somewhat disturbed either by bioturbation or human activities. The majority of the sherds were approximately the size of a US 25-cent piece (ca. 24 mm), and the distribution of artifacts within the unit shows signs of disturbance, with a grog-tempered sherd being recovered from level B4 along with fiber-tempered sherds. The block unit near the midden contained the greatest

Mississippian-Period Occupations in the Ackerman Unit

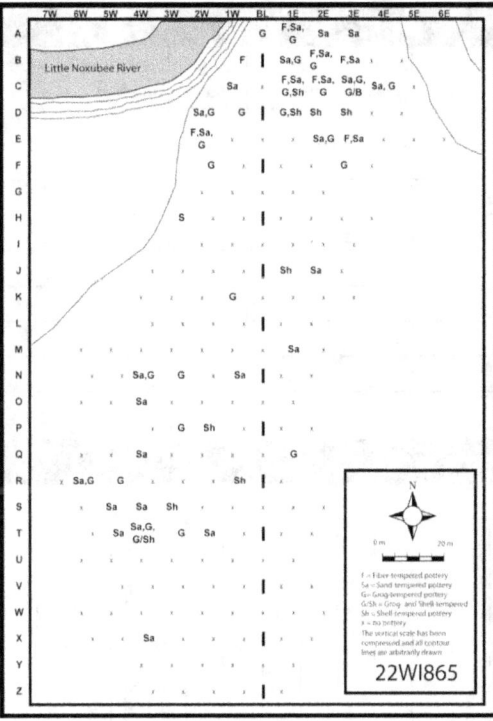

Figure 10.8. 22WI865, shovel-test placement and pottery distribution.

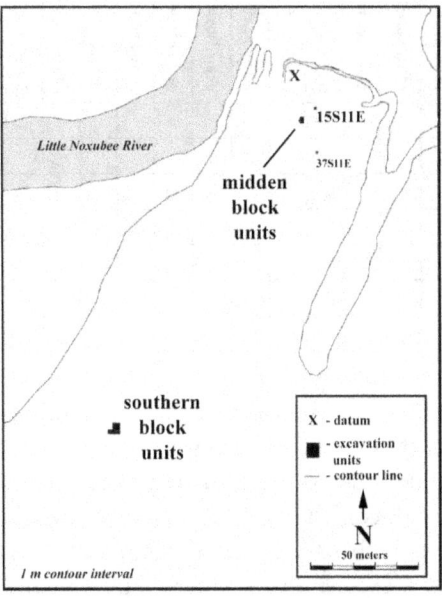

Figure 10.9. 22WI865, topographic map showing excavation unit placement.

Table 10.5. 22WI865, Unit 15S11E, pottery by zone/level.

Temper/Surface Finish:	fiber plain	sand plain	sand eroded	grog plain	grog cord-marked	grog fine-line incised	grog eroded
Zone/Level							
A				3			
B1				2	1		
B2	1		3	8			3
B3							
B4		2				1	
B5			1				
C1							

Table 10.6. 22WI865, midden block, pottery by excavated unit.

Unit	midden block wall scrapings	fiber plain	fiber dentate stamped	fiber eroded	sand plain	sand fabric-marked	sand cord-marked	sand broad-line incised	sand punctate	sand dentate stamped	sand slipped	sand eroded	bone plain	grog/bone plain	grog plain	grog broad-line incised	grog broad-line incised/zoned punctate	grog rocker stamped	grog punctate	grog cord-marked	grog slipped	grog eroded	grog/shell plain	shell plain	shell fine-line incised	shell broad-line incised
21S4E	3			6	1	1	1	1	1	1		3			16					1		17		3		
21S5E	1	2	2	3			1								4			1		1	1	5	1	6		2
22S3E	1			3			1								7		1		1	1			1	2		
22S4E			1	1								1		1	6					1		5				1
22S5E			1									1			8	1			1			4	1	6		
22.5S4E			1	2											1				1			1				
23S5E	1		1	9								2	1		8					2		6			1	1

diversity of pottery tempers and surface finishes at this site. Diagnostic pottery tempers and surface decorations/finishes from all of the known pottery-producing cultural periods for this area are present (Table 10.6). The pottery recovered from 37S11E consisted of three sand-tempered, 14 grog-tempered, and one shell-tempered sherd. The pottery recovered from the southern block unit consisted almost exclusively of either grog-tempered or shell-tempered pottery (Table 10.7).

Table 10.7. Ceramics from southern excavation block, 22WI865.

Unit	sand plain	sand eroded	grog plain	grog burnished	grog fine-line incised	grog broad-line incised	grog slipped	grog eroded	grog/shell plain	shell plain	shell cordmarked	shell eroded
166S89W			1					1	1	3		
166S88W			1	1				1		1		1
166S87W			3							2		1
166S86W			4		1			3				
167S89W			4					2		1		1
167S88W			5				1	7				2
167S87W			3	1	1			3		2	1	
167S86W			1					5		1		2
168S89W			3				1	3		1		1
168S88W			4				1	3		1		
168S87W			2	2			1			2		2
168S86W			2					2				1
169S91W			7									
169S90W			1		1			1				1
169S89W			1							1		
169S88W			2					1	1	1		
169S87W			2				1	1		3		1
169S86W			2			1		2		1		
170S90W			6		1							4
170S89W	1	1	2				1	5				
170S88W			1	1			1	1		2		
170S87W			7				1	5		2		1
170S86W			2			1	2	2				

Statistical Analyses

Spatial information on the distribution of pottery tempers recovered during excavation was used in measuring the tendency of pottery classes to agglomerate about a central location within each excavated site, using the arithmetic mean (Thomas 1986:65). If the mean location of each pottery class is significantly different, it is an indication that they are from separate occupations. If

22CH515 Grog Mean			
3W 2N	2W 2N	1W 2N	0W 2N
3W 1N	2W 1N	1W 1N	0W 1N
3W 0N	2W 0N	1W 0N	0W 0N
9 + 3	6 + 3	3 + 3	0 + 3
12	9	6	3

30/12 = 2.5

22CH515 Shell Mean			
	2W 2N	1W 2N	0W 2N
3W 1N	2W 1N	1W 1N	0W 1N
3W 0N	2W 0N	1W 0N	0W 0N
6 + 1	6 + 3	3 + 3	0 + 3
7	9	6	3

25/11 = 2.27

22CH515 Sand Mean			
3W 2N	2W 2N	1W 2N	0W 2N
3W 1N	2W 1N	1W 1N	0W 1N
3W 0N	2W 0N	1W 0N	0W 0N
9 + 3	6 + 3	3 + 3	0 + 3
12	9	6	3

30/12 = 2.5

22CH515 Fiber Mean			
3W 2N		1W 2N	0W 2N
3W 1N			
		1W 0N	0W 0N
6 + 3		2 + 2	0 + 2
9		4	2

15/6 = 2.5

Figure 10.10. 22CH515, arithmetic mean of pottery classes.

22WI865 (Midden) Grog Mean		
	1W 2N	0W 2N
2W 1N	1W 1N	0W 1N
	1W 0N	0W 0N
2 + 1	3 + 3	0 + 3
3	6	3

12/7 = 1.71

22WI865 (Midden) Shell Mean		
	1W 2N	0W 2N
2W 1N	1W 1N	0W 1N
		0W 0N
2 + 1	2 + 3	0 + 3
3	5	3

11/6 = 1.83

22WI865 (Midden) Sand Mean		
	1W 2N	0W 2N
2W 1N	1W 1N	0W 1N
	1W 0N	0W 0N
2 + 1	3 + 3	0 + 3
3	6	3

12/7 = 1.71

22WI865 (Midden) Fiber Mean		
	1W 2N	0W 2N
2W 1N	1W 1N	0W 1N
	1W 0N	0W 0N
2 + 1	3 + 3	0 + 3
3	6	3

12/7 = 1.71

Figure 10.11. 22WI865, midden units, arithmetic mean of pottery classes.

22WI865 (Southern Block) Grog Mean					
		3W 4N	2W 4N	1W 4N	0W 4N
		3W 3N	2W 3N	1W 3N	0W 3N
		3W 2N	2W 2N	1W 2N	0W 2N
5W 1N	4W 1N	3W 1N	2W 1N	1W 1N	0W 1N
	4W 0N	3W 0N	2W 0N	1W 0N	0W 0N
5 + 1	8 + 1	15 + 10	10 + 10	5 + 10	0 + 10
6	9	25	20	15	10

85/23 = 3.70

22WI865 (Southern Block) Shell Mean					
		3W 4N	2W 4N	1W 4N	0W 4N
		3W 3N	2W 3N	1W 3N	0W 3N
		3W 2N	2W 2N	1W 2N	0W 2N
	4W 1N	3W 1N	2W 1N	1W 1N	0W 1N
	4W 0N		2W 0N	1W 0N	0W 0N
	8 + 1	12 + 10	10 + 10	5 + 10	0 + 10
	9	25	20	15	10

79/21 = 3.76

Figure 10.12. 22WI865, southern block, arithmetic mean of pottery classes.

the mean locations are similar, this suggests that the pottery classes are from a single occupation. Also, the number of grog- and shell-tempered sherds recovered from the excavation units are displayed in line graphs. Co-occurrence of both types of pottery, with similar proportions in each unit, would indicate a single occupation. Alternatively, a mutually exclusive pattern of occurrence, in which the pottery tempers are not present within the same units, is an indication that two separate occupations are present. Due to small sample sizes, 22CH814 is not included in these analyses.

Results from 22CH515 (Figure 10.10) show the arithmetic mean for three of the four pottery classes to be 2.5. The mean for the shell-tempered pottery is 2.27, which shows that the central tendency for all four pottery classes is very similar, suggesting that a single occupation is present. Results similar to those from 22CH515 were encountered when computing the arithmetic mean for the midden block and southern block units at 22WI865 (Figures 10.11 and 10.12). In both blocks, the shell-tempered pottery has a slightly different arithmetic mean from the rest of the pottery classes represented, but there is still a high coincidence of occurrence between the grog-tempered and shell-tempered pottery. In the midden block, shell-tempered pottery occurred in six of the seven units (85.7 percent) that contained grog-tempered pottery. Shell-tempered pottery was present in 21 of the 23 units (91.3 percent) that contained grog-tempered pottery in the southern block unit as well.

The results from the midden block unit seem to indicate that this area of the site, much like the excavated portion of 22CH515, was continuously occupied over an extended period of time. The southern block unit appears to have been a spatially separate occupation, as suggested by the shovel-test data. The pottery recovered from this area was almost exclusively grog- or shell-tempered, with only two sherds of sand-tempered pottery having been recovered, suggesting occupation during the Late Woodland and into the Mississippian period.

As can be seen in Figure 13, there is co-occurrence of grog- and shell-tempered pottery from 22CH515 (Figure 10.13), with a general pattern in which, once shell-tempered pottery is established, it increases in numbers along with grog-tempered pottery. This accords well with expectations that the proportions of the two tempers would not vary much if the Late Woodland and Early Mississippian materials are part of one occupation.

The line graphs for the two block units at 22WI865 (Figures 10.14 and 10.15) also indicate a general pattern of shell-tempered pottery increasing in numbers along with the grog-tempered pottery. The units that have very few shell-tempered sherds in relation to the number of grog-tempered sherds may be exceptions to this and may represent the earliest part of the occupation. The data gathered through shovel testing and excavations, as well as the statistical

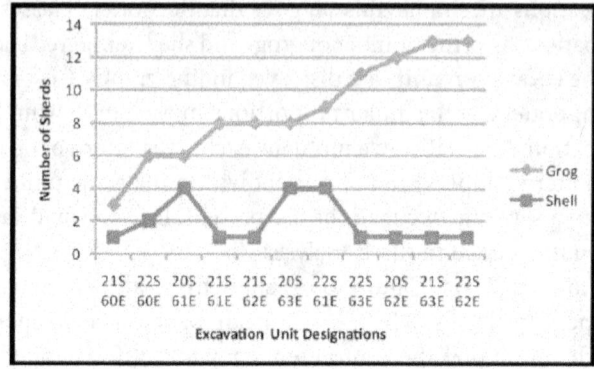

Figure 10.13. 22CH515, co-occurrence of grog-tempered and shell-tempered pottery.

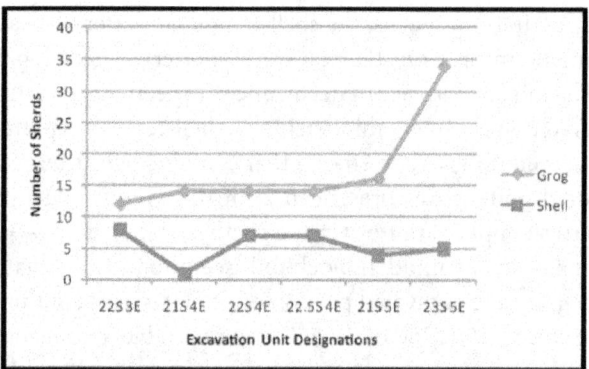

Figure 10.14. 22WI865, midden block, co-occurrence of grog-tempered and shell-tempered pottery.

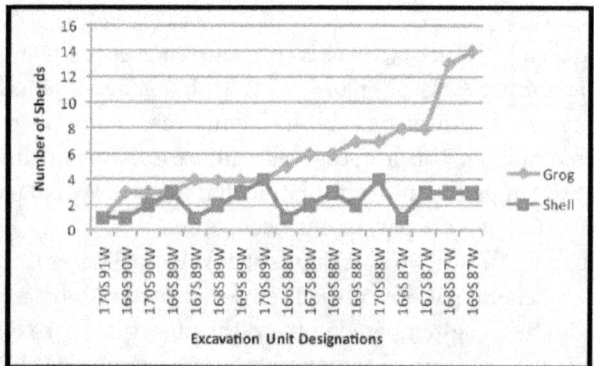

Figure 10.15. 22WI865 south block unit, co-occurrence of grog-tempered and shell-tempered pottery.

analyses, suggest that two spatially separate occupations are present at this site. The area closest to the Little Noxubee River exhibits a well-developed midden, an abundance of artifacts, and in some areas, deep cultural deposits; all of these have been shown to be indicators of long-duration sites (Rafferty 1994). The distribution of pottery as seen in both shovel testing and excavations shows that this area was occupied frequently—and possibly continuously—over a long duration of time. Conversely, the southern area of the site appears to contain a distinct, single occupation with both grog- and shell-tempered pottery present.

Frequency Seriation

Each of the sites under consideration contains occupations that potentially span hundreds to thousands of years. Another way to test for continuity of occupations is through the use of frequency or occurrence seriations (Dunnell 1970; Lipo et al. 1997). Artifact classes, the members of which are the result of homologous transmission, will display a unimodal frequency distribution through time. If artifact classes do not produce a unimodal frequency distribution, homologous transmission has not occurred (Lyman and O'Brien 2003:270). There are three requirements of artifact groups for seriations to work (Dunnell 1970). The first is that the groups must be of comparable duration; if they are noncomparable, they will not seriate together. The second is that all of the assemblages come from the same area. This is because heritable continuity deals with both the spatial and temporal aspects of the artifact groups (Lipo et al. 1997). The final requirement is that all of the assemblages must come from the same cultural tradition or lineage. If these three requirements are met, then heritable continuity is demonstrated by display of a deterministic seriation (Lyman and O'Brien 2003:270; see also Parrish and Peacock 2006; Rafferty 2008). Assemblages from sites with multiple, non-sequent occupations should not seriate with those from single-occupation sites.

Pottery was classified using temper and surface finish types, allowing for other local assemblages classified in the same manner (e.g., Parrish 2006; Peacock 2003) to be included in the seriation. Only assemblages with 35 or more identifiable (non-eroded) sherds were included in the seriations; eroded sherds were not used in frequency calculations. For ease of display, some classes (e.g., sand-tempered punctate, grog-tempered rocker stamped, bone-tempered plain) were not used, as they had so few occurrences that their omission had no impact on the frequency percentages used in the ordering of the seriation. The frequencies for each class of pottery were calculated, and the assemblages were then ordered using the Seriationmaker macro (Lipo 2001).

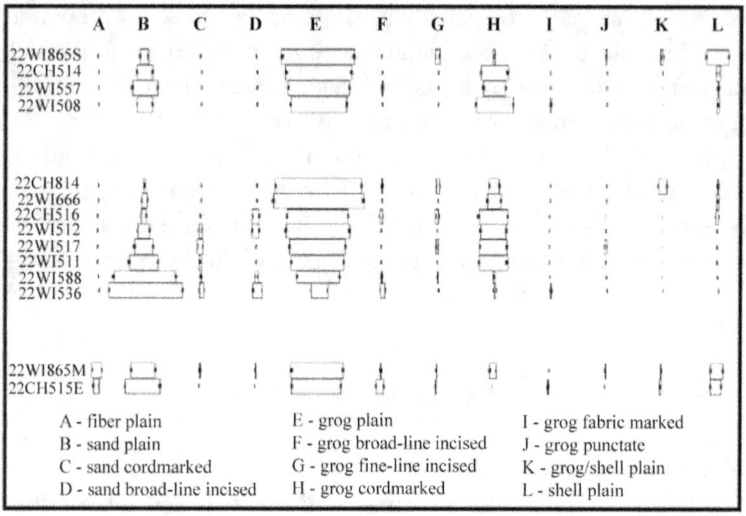

Figure 10.16. Frequency seriations I, II, and III (*from top*) of ceramic assemblages from the Ackerman Unit of the Tombigbee National Forest.

An error factor of 5 percent was chosen because sample size varies greatly between assemblages.

Figure 10.16 shows that not all of the assemblages are of comparable duration. Three separate seriations are constructed, indicating that some sites were occupied for much different periods of time than others. Seriation I is populated by short-duration assemblages, as indicated by the relatively small number of pottery classes represented and the minimal changes in frequencies over time. It appears that the sites in this seriation were generally occupied later than those represented in the other seriations, with mostly Late Woodland and Mississippian occupations indicated. The assemblage recovered from the southern block unit at 22WI865 (22WI865S) is included in this seriation.

Seriation II consists of assemblages with a greater number of pottery classes, probably indicating that these sites were occupied for longer durations. The sites represented seem to follow the general pattern of settlement in the North Central Hills, with primarily Middle and Late Woodland period occupations. The few Mississippian components present in this seriation are all associated with much larger Late Woodland components; none are found at sites with only a Middle Woodland component. These patterns strengthen the assertion that the Late Woodland and Mississippian-period components share a cultural lineage and are likely part of the same occupations.

Seriation III includes the excavated portions of the two longest-duration sites. It was decided to use the excavated units instead of the entire sites because, as noted earlier, systematic shovel testing at 22WI865 indicated that it contained two spatially separate occupations. Accordingly, this site was divided, for the purpose of seriation, into assemblages consisting of the ceramics found in the northern, or "midden," occupation (22WI865M) and the southern occupation (22WI865S). The excavated units at 22CH515 (22CH515E) and the midden at 22WI865 contain diagnostic pottery tempers for all of the known ceramic periods in this region. While these sites could represent many smaller, short-duration occupations spanning several cultural periods (Rafferty 2003:172), they more likely represent continuous occupation over a long time span at locations closest to the water (presumably the most favorable area of the sites).

Even though three separate seriations were created from these assemblages, the implications of all are the same. All of the seriations indicate that their respective assemblages belong to the same cultural tradition, thus, "heritable continuity is assured and phylogenetic affinities between the seriated assemblages are guaranteed" (O'Brien and Lyman 2000:287). The short-duration sites appear to have been occupied later than the others, primarily during the Late Woodland period, possibly because of settlement shifts away from uplands to terraces along the major waterways. The seemingly abrupt end to the grog-tempered plain curve in all three seriations accords well with the hypothesis that this area was rapidly abandoned at the very beginning of the Mississippian period.

Conclusions

The purpose of this research was to ascertain if cultural lineage continuity could be shown between the Late Woodland and Mississippian occupations at selected sites on the Ackerman Unit of the Tombigbee National Forest. Two hypotheses were tested for this purpose. The first was that the Late Woodland and Mississippian components found together at these sites indicate continuous occupation, with the sites being abandoned early in the Mississippian period. The second hypothesis was that these components did not represent continuous occupations but resettlement of Woodland-period site locales later in the Mississippian period. The best way to determine this was through delineating the occupations present at the sites. The spatial aspect of the occupations was addressed through systematic shovel testing, while the temporal aspect was met through stratigraphic excavations, and frequency seriations were used to determine if there was cultural lineage continuity present.

Statistical analysis of sherd distributions shows clear evidence of spatial and temporal continuity, indicating that one Late Woodland/Mississippian occupation was present at 22CH515, 22WI865M, and 22WI865S. At each site, the coincidence of shell-tempered pottery and grog-tempered pottery was strong. At sites 22CH515 and 22WI865, shell-tempered pottery occurred with grog-tempered pottery in 38 of the 42 test units (90.47 percent).

The data gathered through systematic shovel testing and excavation were used to construct three separate seriations, with differences between them relating to the duration over which the sites were occupied. In each seriation, regardless of duration, the sites showed clear continuity, and thus cultural inheritance, between the assemblages. From these results, a strong case can be made for lineage continuity between the Late Woodland and Mississippian components at these sites; i.e., the components are simply arbitrary divisions of single occupations.

It appears that this area was relatively heavily inhabited during the Woodland period in general. During the Late Woodland period, the population seems to have begun nucleating along the terraces of the major waterways (Triplett 2008a:Figure 1.2). At some point between A.D. 1000 and 1100 the area was abandoned, but not before shell-tempered pottery started being made. The length of occupation during the period in which shell-tempered pottery was made seems to vary. At several sites, the Mississippian end of the occupation was so ephemeral that no additional shell-tempered pottery could be located during the systematic shovel testing (e.g., 22CH514, 22CH516, 22CH814, and 22WI508). Other sites, though, such as 22CH515 and 22WI865, seem to have had more substantial occupations at this relatively late date. It may be that these were some of the last sites in the area to have been abandoned.

While more absolute dates from excavation contexts would be helpful in further testing these hypotheses, the case for settlement continuity across traditional culture-historical boundaries and abandonment of the area early in the Mississippian period cannot be falsified based on the results of this research.

CHAPTER 11

Owl Creek, Thelma, and Bessemer Mounds: Large Peripheral Mississippian Mound Groups and Bet-Hedging

Janet Rafferty

Introduction

The Owl Creek Mounds site has the largest number of mounds (5) of any Mississippian[1] mound group in eastern Mississippi. About 15 km southwest is another five-mound group, Thelma Mounds, which has a Late Woodland radiocarbon date but which likely overlaps in age with Owl Creek. These two mound complexes share many traits in common with the Bessemer Mounds site in north Alabama, which had three mounds and has produced one early Mississippian-period date. The three sites can be usefully compared to attempt to characterize and explain changes in settlement patterning that occurred in the time from A.D. 800–1200 and after in the region.

These three are among the earliest sites displaying mounds that were built following an apparent post-Middle Woodland hiatus in mound building in the region. The hiatus lasted from ca. A.D. 450, the latest date from the late Middle Woodland Miller mound site in Lee County, Mississippi (Walling et. al 1991:61), until ca. A.D. 800, the age yielded by the remaining mound at Thelma. All three multimound sites are located on the northern periphery of the Tombigbee-Black Warrior valley. In contrast, Moundville, the only post-A.D. 1200 large mound group (Knight and Steponaitis 1998), is located near the center of the valley. In addition to Moundville, several other single-mound but very long duration occupations (including those at Lyon's Bluff, Lubbub Creek, and the Curry site, 22OK578) are situated in the central valley (Figure 11.1). They all saw primary use in the period after A.D. 1200. At about this time, Owl Creek, Bessemer, and, presumably, Thelma were abandoned. It is this shift over time, from periphery to center and including not just mounds but the accompanying hamlets, farmsteads, and villages, that is the focus of this

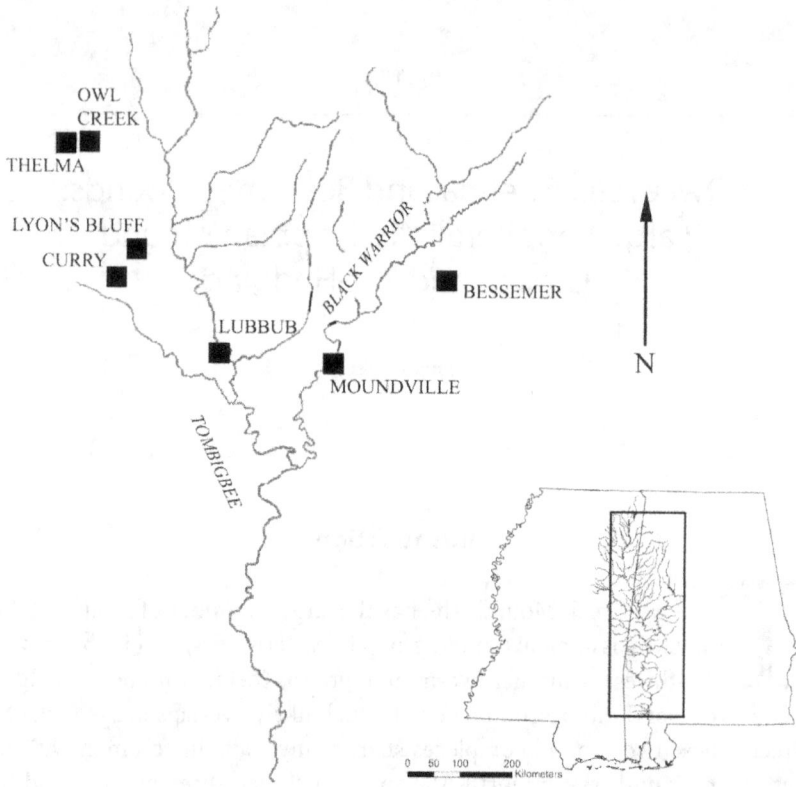

Figure 11.1. Location of Mississippian mound sites discussed in this chapter.

chapter. Particular attention is given to research done in 1991–1992 at the Owl Creek Mounds group in northeast Mississippi, funded by the USDA Forest Service, National Forests in Mississippi, which owns two of the five mounds as part of the Trace Unit of the Tombigbee National Forest. The research was encouraged by Sam Brookes, Forest Archaeologist, who recognized the site's importance (Brookes 1977) and its potential for public interpretation.

Owl Creek Mounds (22CS502) is located on Goodfood Creek, a perennial stream about 1 km from Chuquatonchee Creek, which flows into Tibbee Creek, a tributary of the Tombigbee River. The site is about 100 km from the Tombigbee along the streams and about 45 km due west of the river. Thelma Mounds (22CS501) is on an intermittent tributary of Little Houlka Creek, which in turn flows into Houlka Creek, a tributary of Chuquatonchee Creek. The site lies 90 km from the Tombigbee along the streams and 70 km due west of the river. Bessemer (1JE12-14) is similarly situated near the edge of the drainage basin, but on the east side. It is on Valley Creek, which is a tributary of the Tombigbee, via the Black Warrior River, which lies about 30 km west of the site in a direct line. Via Valley Creek, the distance to the Black Warrior is 40 km; the junction with the Tombigbee at Demopolis, Alabama, is an additional 240 km distant. This illustrates how far these large mound groups in upland settings were removed from the main rivers.

History of Investigations

The five mounds at Owl Creek, which encircle a central open area, were first noted and described in 1805 by Dr. Rush Nutt, who kept a diary of his travels through the area (Jennings 1947). More detailed descriptions were made by Moreau B. C. Chambers in connection with excavations he carried out at the site in 1935 for the Mississippi Department of Archives and History (MDAH) (Brookes 1977; Rafferty 1995:6–9).

Although Chambers's 1935 work included excavation of trenches into Mounds II, IV, and V (Brookes 1977; Rafferty 1995), the results were never written up. The artifacts were sent to Louisiana State University in Baton Rouge at the request of James Ford, but they were not included in any of his published work and remained in curation at LSU until moved to MDAH. A number of small surface collections made by Chambers and other archaeologists (Stu Neitzel, Richard Marshall, James Atkinson) from 1935 to 1986 are extant (Rafferty 1995). The main information on the site comes from test excavations carried out in 1991–1992 (Rafferty 1995) as part of a cost-share agreement between Mississippi State University and the USDA Forest Service, which owns the northern part of the site, including Mounds I and II. Limited testing was also done on the eastern edge of the site in 1999 by Peacock (Peacock and Rafferty 2005).

Thelma Mounds was reported by Moreau Chambers in 1935 (MDAH site files). It was composed of five mounds and an apparently associated village site. The site was visited in 1942 by Natchez Trace Parkway archaeologists (Natchez Trace Parkway Archaeological Survey site card 1942, amended 1948). Only four mounds were recorded in 1942,[2] but Mound 5 was quite small, as well as being distant from the other mounds, and might have been overlooked. This is particularly the case since it appears the Parkway archaeologists did not have Chambers's site record, the result being that the mounds were renumbered by them. Three of the mounds (Chambers's Mounds 2, 3, and 4) were destroyed by bulldozing before 1970, as noted by McGahey (1971:14) and on the MDAH site card (which calls them Mounds 1, 2, and 3, using the Parkway numbering system). Atkinson (1986) notes that they were removed during landleveling. Only one mound, Chambers's Mound 1 (Parkway Mound 4) remains easily visible today.

A number of surface collections have been made at Thelma, and several are reported by Johnson and Atkinson (1987). Their work in 1984–1985 involved excavation of a 1-×-1-m unit to a depth of 116 cm in the remaining mound, with a posthole digger hole dug from there to an old humus layer at a depth of 169 cm below surface (Johnson and Atkinson 1987:63, 66). A topographic map was also made of the mound (Johnson and Atkinson 1987:65).

The three mounds at Bessemer are known as the domiciliary (platform), ceremonial (oval), and burial mounds (DeJarnette and Wimberly 1941; Welch 1994). They are arranged in an arc around an open area. The earliest work at the site was done in the 1880s by the Smithsonian Institution, with some digging on the top of each of the mounds (Thomas 1894:290–292). The main excavations at Bessemer occurred in 1934–1935 and 1939–1940 (DeJarnette and Wimberly 1941). This included complete excavation of all three mounds as well as extensive work to find and excavate sub-mound and associated features and midden (DeJarnette and Wimberly 1941; Welch 1994). Welch (1994) examined unpublished field documents and reanalyzed all the extant pottery in the collections, which added a considerable amount of information on mound stratigraphy and chronological ordering of features to that presented by DeJarnette and Wimberly (1941).

Chronology

It is important to establish the temporal frames for occupation and mound building at each of the three sites as part of understanding why they are similar. The available information relating to this includes the radiocarbon dates mentioned briefly above, which can now be reviewed in more detail, and pottery traits that changed in frequency through time and thus provide some temporal diagnostics.

There are six C-14 dates from Owl Creek, all from locations within three of the platform mounds (Table 11.1, Figure 11.2). The samples from Mound I were from three contexts within the top two meters. Zone YY/AAA, representing an episode of mound construction, lay at a depth of ca. 120–140 cm below the mound surface; the sample was taken from a charcoal concentration in the zone. The date has a central calibrated intercept of A.D. 815 (Table 11.1). Based on the cultural chronology established in the Tombigbee valley (Jenkins and Krause 1986), the age is Late Woodland. It is likely, given the later ages of the remaining five dates and the ceramic data discussed below, that the charcoal on which this date was based was included in mound fill taken from a Late Woodland habitation area at the site.

Another radiocarbon sample from Mound I came from Feature 9, a 50–55-cm deep wall trench running east-west and parallel to the south side of the

Table 11.1. Radiocarbon dates from Owl Creek, Thelma, and Bessemer.

Site	Context	Lab No.	RYBP	-2 sigma cal A.D.*	+2 sigma cal A.D.	Intercept probability	Source
Thelma	Thelma Mound 1	Beta-11833	1270 ± 135	540	1020	1	Johnson and Atkinson 1987
Owl Creek	Owl Creek Md I, Zn AA/YYY	Beta 47735	1180 ± 120	640	1050	0.98	Rafferty 1995
	Owl Creek Md I, F9	Beta 63121	820 ± 100	1020	1310	0.97	
	Owl Creek Md I, PH79	Beta 64288	860 ± 70	1030	1270	1	
	Owl Creek Md II, Zone G	Beta 63122	850 ± 50	1040	1270	0.82	
	Owl Creek Md II, F41	Beta 64289	900 ± 80	1010	1270	0.99	
	Owl Creek Md V, Zone G	Beta 63123	880 ± 60	1030	1260	1	
Bessemer	Bessemer Structure 13	UGa 1663	880 ± 55	1030	1250	1	Walthall and Wimberly 1978

* Calibrations done using CALIB 6.0 (Stuiver and Reimer 1993).

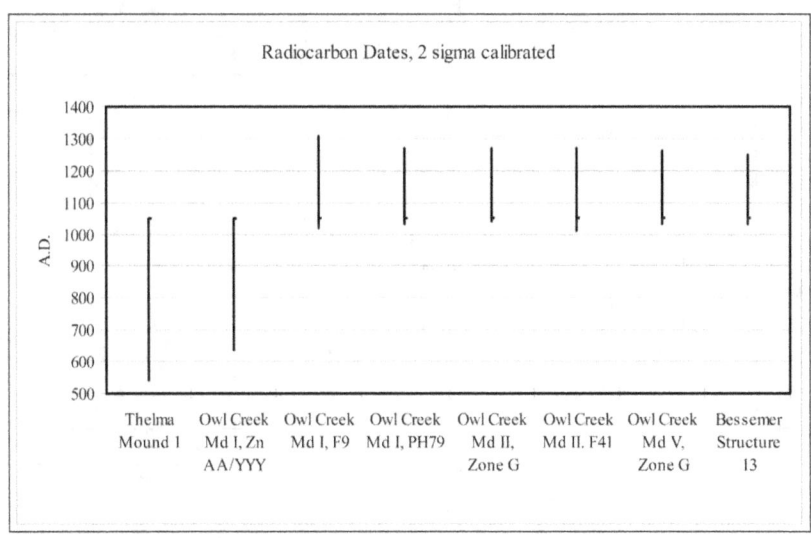

Figure 11.2. Radiocarbon dates from Owl Creek, Thelma, and Bessemer.

mound. The excavated feature fill, from a two-meter long segment of the wall trench, produced only one plain shell-tempered sherd; the calibrated date of A.D. 1220 is Early Mississippian. A posthole (PH 79) from an overlying wall trench produced the third sample, which gave a calibrated date of A.D. 1190 (Table 11.1). The uppermost one meter of mound construction included several rebuilt wall trenches, as noted below, as well as various postholes and a small pit filled with charred corn cobs.

The two dates obtained from Mound II indicate that it was constructed in the same time frame as Mound I (Table 11.1, Figure 11.2). One dated a charcoal

Table 11.2. Artifacts from areas at Thelma Mounds collected by Atkinson in 1973 and Chambers in 1935.

	Atkinson surface collections										Chambers collection
	Area 1	Area 2	Areas 2 and 3	Area 3	Areas 4 and 6	Area 4	Area 6	Area 5	Spring	Total	
Pottery											
sand-tempered plain	2							8		11	10
sand-tempered eroded											1
sand-tempered red-slipped		2								2	
sand-tempered combed	1									1	
grog-tempered plain	31	7	14	2	12	4		63	1	134	98
grog-tempered cord-marked					1	1				2	2
grog-tempered eroded	3		4					6		13	2
bone- and grog-tempered plain	5							1		6	
grog- and shell-tempered plain	1							2		3	
shell-tempered plain	3		1		3			2		9	6
shell-tempered eroded	1									1	
Lithics											
contracting stemmed projectile point								1			
triangular point preform	1									1	
biface fragments								2		2	1
ground sandstone			1					2		3	1
pitted sandstone								3		3	
ground siltstone celt fragment			1							1	
chert hammerstone							1			1	
chert chunks and flakes	5		3		1			22		31	7
siltstone flakes								2		2	
sandstone chunks	1		3							4	2
Historic artifacts										0	
turquoise glass	1									1	
flat metal								1		1	
Bone											
pig tooth	1									1	
unidentified bone								1		1	1
Total	56	9	27	2	17	5	1	116	1	235	131

sample taken from about 1.5 m below the modern mound surface in Zone G and the other was from a large posthole, Feature 41, that was dug before mound construction began. The dates overlap at one standard deviation and are in correct stratigraphic order, with calibrated ages of A.D. 1195 and A.D. 1135, respectively. The sixth C-14 date was obtained from Zone E4 of Mound V, from scattered charcoal at a depth of ca. 90 cm below the surface or 20–30 cm above the mound base. This date (Figure 11.2) is similar to four of those obtained from Mounds I and II. No charcoal samples large enough for submission were obtained from limited excavation in Mounds III and IV. The calibrated radiocarbon date intercepts suggest the mounds were built between A.D. 800–1175; if the one early date is disregarded, construction occurred within 100 years each way of A.D. 1175 (Figure 11.2).

Thelma has produced only one radiocarbon date, from Mound 1 (Johnson and Atkinson 1987); it falls in line with the earliest date from Owl Creek (Table 11.1, Figure 11.2). The one pertinent date from Bessemer (Walthall and Wimberly 1978:118–120) is from a wall trench building, Structure 13, that was at one end of an area encircled by a small palisade. As argued by Welch (1994), orientation and overlap of buildings with one another and with the edges of mound fill zones can be used to establish fairly securely a sequence of public structure and mound construction events at the site. He argues that Structure 13 predated the nearby rectangular mound. The calibrated 2-sigma C-14 date of A.D 1030–1250 (Table 11.1, Figure 11.2) is similar in age to five of the dates from Owl Creek.

The relatively small frequencies of decorated and burnished shell-tempered pottery in the mounds at Owl Creek accord with the radiocarbon dates to indicate an Early Mississippian occupation, as derived from ceramic studies at Moundville. Incised, punctate, slipped, and engraved sherds make up from 0–18 percent of mound-context pottery at Owl Creek. One of the defining criteria of the Moundville I period is the high percentage, about 92 percent, of undecorated pottery (Steponaitis 1983:99). The low quantity of burnished sherds from Owl Creek Mounds (6 out of 316 from Mound I and even lower representation in other mounds) is in accord with the small amounts characteristic of Moundville I, dated from A.D. 1050–1250 (Knight and Steponaitis 1998:8). The surface collections made at Thelma confirm that the occupation occurred primarily in the period when grog-tempered pottery predominated (the Late Woodland Miller III period) but with a consistent minority of shell-tempered sherds indicating that shell tempering had begun to be adopted. When this occurred is unknown, but it was probably between A.D. 1000–1100. The incised, black-filmed, and engraved shell-tempered sherds from Bessemer span the earliest to latest part of the Moundville I period (Welch 1994:14–15). These pottery cross-dates accord well with the available radiocarbon dates from the three sites.

Janet Rafferty

Mound Layout and Use

All three sites have multiple flat-topped mounds, with no conical mounds recorded at any of them, although the configuration of Mound 5 at Thelma is ambiguous, as discussed below. Aside from Moundville, they are the only three sites with these traits in the upper-central Tombigbee valley. The presence of both oval and rectangular mounds at Owl Creek and Bessemer (and possibly at Thelma) is also distinctive.

Nutt's and Chambers's descriptions of Owl Creek agree that all five mounds were flat topped. A detailed topographic map made in 1991–1992 (Figure 11.3) indicates that Mounds I, IV, and V were constructed in rectangular shape, with Mounds I and IV appearing to have ramps on the sides facing the central open area. It seems certain from Chambers's work that Mound II was oval, its modern crescent shape being due to damage incurred since 1935 (Rafferty 1995). Chambers depicted Mound III as round rather than rectangular in a sketch map (Rafferty 1995:6); the mound has been largely destroyed by cultivation since. The open area in the midst of the mounds at Owl Creek is about 1 ha in size, while the entire site covers 4 ha.

Nutt in 1805 described a ditch running around the site's perimeter, outside the mounds, but no sign of this was found in twentieth-century work at the site (Brookes 1977). Chambers did not mention the ditch in his notes, nor does it appear on his sketch map (Rafferty 1995). It is also absent from the topographic map made in 1991–1992 (Figure 11.3). Five ground-penetrating radar transects that were placed south and west of Mound IV in 1992 did not detect any sign of a filled ditch in the posited area. Given the very sparse evidence of habitation found at the site (discussed below), it is doubtful that it was fortified. Other visible features at the site include a possible borrow pit north of Mound I and historic and recent features, including a nineteenth-century roadbed.

The locations of the mounds at Thelma are reconstructed in Figure 4, using sizes, distances, and directions given on Chambers's 1935 site card. The mounds were not explicitly described by him as rectangular or flat topped, but the remaining mound is clearly so (Johnson and Atkinson 1987). Chambers gives figures for the length and width of Mounds 2, 3, and 4. This, along with his notation of their orientation to the cardinal directions, implies that they were rectangular, not circular. For Mound 5 he gives only a diameter and no orientation, indicating that it was circular.[3] The 1987 topographic map shows a well-defined ramp on the north side of Mound 1 (Johnson and Atkinson 1987:65). It is unknown if ramps were present on the other mounds. Figure 11.4 follows Chambers, as well as a magnetic gradiometer (Geoscan FM-256) image made during fieldwork in 2013 (Figure 11.5), in depicting Mound 1 as oriented WSW to ENE.

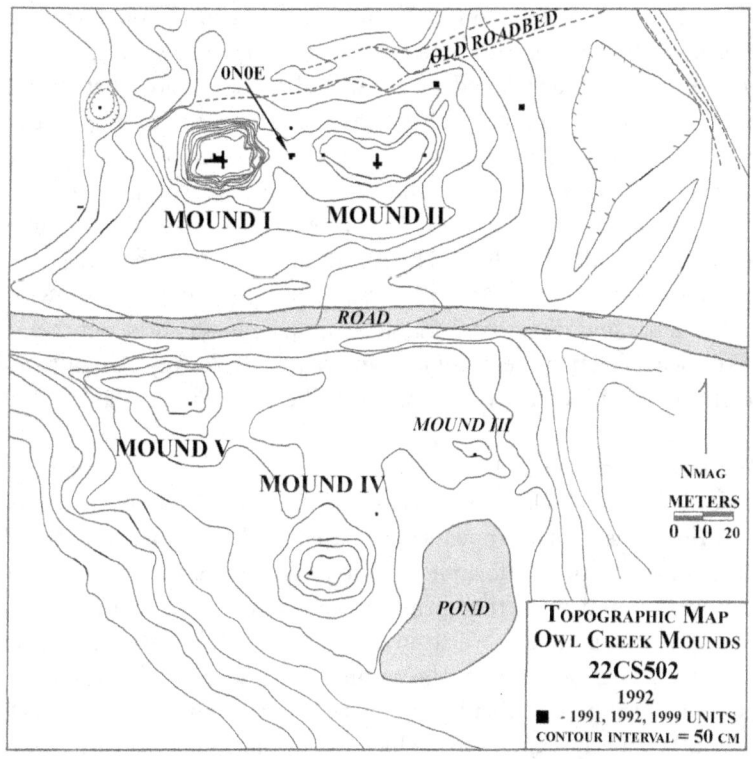

Figure 11.3. Topographic map of Owl Creek Mounds. Adapted from Rafferty (1995:Figure 4).

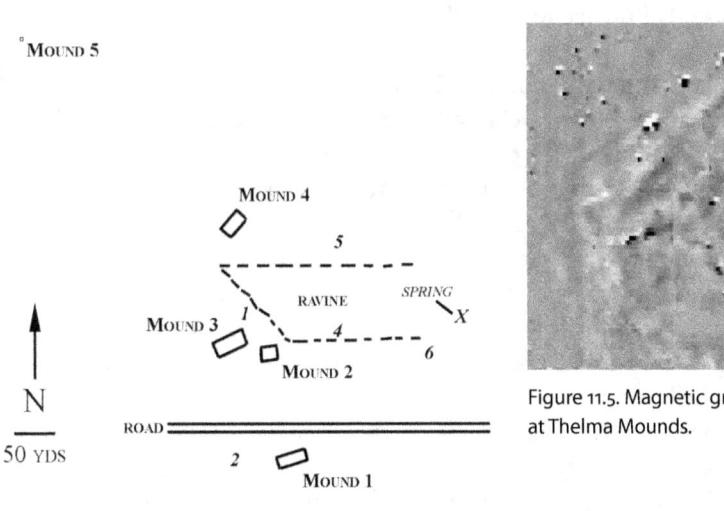

Figure 11.5. Magnetic gradiometer image of Mound 1 at Thelma Mounds.

Figure 11.4. Plan map of Thelma Mounds.

The mounds at Thelma do not delineate a clear plaza or open area. Nonetheless, it can be inferred from the reconstructed map that the area bordered on the west by Mounds 1, 3, and 4 was ca. 1.85 ha. It is possible that Mound 5 is Middle Woodland in age, given that it may have been conical in shape. If it is treated as part of the same occupation as the other mounds, the overall size of the site is 150–200 × 650 m or 8–13 ha. Without inclusion of Mound 5, the area is 5 ha, more similar to Owl Creek. The presence of a village site was noted by Chambers. The artifacts collected by Atkinson (Table 11.2) show that all parts of the site produced artifacts, with Areas 1 and 5 (Figure 11.4) showing the largest number and diversity. Ceramics dominate in all areas, but the size of each surface collection area is unknown, so artifact density cannot be calculated; it can be said to have been low everywhere, with the possible exception of Areas 1 and 5.

The area among the mounds at Bessemer is ca. 1.2 ha. The overall site size is unclear, although Welch (1994:25) asserts that a sheet midden extended for 260 m. This measurement appears to be based on the distance from the structures southwest of the platform mound to the structure that was found north of the oval mound, even though no other features were found in the area between the two mounds (Welch 1994:Figure 1). If this distance is used, the site area would be about 2.6 ha. The mounds at Bessemer include 1JE14, a rectangular platform mound that had a stairway on the southeast corner (DeJarnette and Wimberly 1941:28–29), which led to the open area surrounded by the mounds. A second mound, 1JE12, was oval with a small oval flat-topped addition on one end of the flat top. The third mound, 1JE13, was oblong with a flat top.

Table 3 gives calculations of mound volumes for each site, based on mound sizes reported in Rafferty (1995), DeJarnette and Wimberly (1941), Johnson and Atkinson (1987), and Chambers's record for Thelma (MDAH site file). These represent the best data on the mid-twentieth-century sizes of the mounds. Erosion, cultivation, and other factors had damaged many of them by then, so the computed volumes must be regarded as minimums. The volumes were calculated using formulae for truncated pyramid shapes for the rectangular mounds and truncated cones for the circular and oval mounds. For oval shapes, the length and width were averaged to obtain a diameter before the formula was applied. For Mounds 2 and 3 at Thelma, for which Chambers did not give top dimensions, the volume was computed using length × width × height. Fortunately, the mounds were not tall, so this probably does not add much error. If Mound 5 at Thelma had a conical shape rather than being flat topped, its volume would increase. Thelma had the largest volume of dirt in mounds, with Owl Creek having the smallest and Bessemer's mounds being intermediate in volume (Table 11.3).

Table 11.3. Mound volumes at Bessemer, Owl Creek, and Thelma.

Site	Mound	Base radius or length	Base width	Top radius or length	Top width	Height	Volume ft³	Volume m³
Owl Creek	I	29.5 m	21.5 m	20 m	10.5 m	5 m		2015
	II	16.9 m		15 m		2 m		1600
	III	5 m		4 m		0.76 m		48.5
	IV	20 m	20 m	13.2 m	10 m	2.4 m		610
	V	24 m	24 m	20 m	16 m	1.6 m		707
Total								4981
Thelma	1	126 ft (39 m), 25 m*	20 m*	12 m*	5 m*	10 ft (3 m), 1.7 m*		1056
	2	72 ft	63 ft			6 ft	27,216	
	3	135 ft	66 ft			5.5 ft	49,005	
	4	95 ft	55 ft	75 ft		5.5 ft	25,713	
	5	12.5 ft		est 6 ft		7 ft	1960	
Total							103,894	6525.5
Bessemer	Oval platform	58 ft		36.25 ft		10 ft	71,006	
	Knob on oval	21 ft		14 ft		8 ft	7800	
	Platform	120 ft	120 ft	60 ft	60 ft	11 ft	92,400	
	Burial	37.75 ft		22.5 ft		7.5 ft	21,839	
Total							193,045	5405

* Measurements in feet are from Chambers's 1935 site card, converted in parentheses to meters; other measurements in meters are from the topographic map in Johnson and Atkinson (1987).

In terms of mound use, there is evidence from wall trenches and postholes that Mounds I, II, and IV at Owl Creek served as platforms for structures. The top of Mound I was best preserved and most extensively excavated. On it, the south walls of two successive wall trench buildings, Features 9 and 29, were uncovered. Both walls were 6 m long, with their locations indicating that the buildings were centered east-west on the top of the mound (Figure 11.6). Wall trenches ran north from each end of this wall in both buildings. On the east end, two wall trenches 2.85 m apart extended to the south, forming a possible porch or screen (Figure 11.6). Postholes indicating two other building phases were also found, reflecting at least four episodes of building construction in the top meter of mound fill.

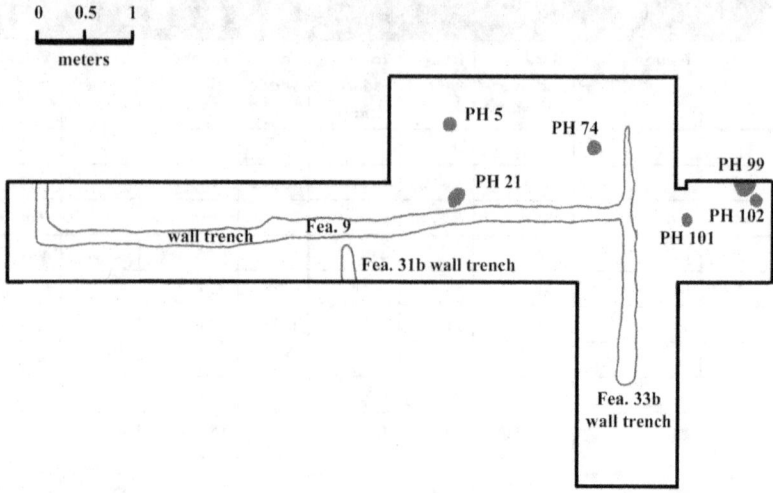

Figure 11.6. Features on Mound I at Owl Creek. From Rafferty (1995:Figure 14).

Few artifacts were recovered from the mound fill or from features on Mound I. Zones B, E, and G, from which the various mound-top structures originated, produced a total of 51 lithic artifacts (3 chert bifaces, 1 piece of ground sandstone, 4 sandstone flakes, and 43 chert flakes). The pottery density was also low, 254 sherds. The total of 305 artifacts in 10 m³ of excavation yields 30 artifacts per m³. This includes counts of grog- and sand-tempered pottery that may already have been in the mound fill before it was placed on the mound, as discussed below. A 1-×-1-m unit on the east side of the mound showed higher artifact density, with 9 flakes and 101 sherds recovered in 1 m³ of fill.

Microartifact samples were taken from strata inside the Mound I structures in the hope of obtaining information on building use. Analysis of 57 samples from the Feature 9 wall trench, thin strata inside the Feature 9 building, and zones representing mound fill produced virtually no microartifacts, with the exception of tiny charcoal fragments. Two chert microflakes were recovered in the sample that came from the top of Feature 9 (Rafferty 1995:123). Whatever activities were carried out in the structures on top of Mound I, they did not generate many artifacts. No evidence of sustained habitation, feasting, or storage of surplus in the form of large pits, was found in the excavated areas on Mound I.

Mound II was also used repeatedly as a substructure. It has been heavily impacted by Chambers's excavation, borrowing of dirt from the south side, and bulldozing, which removed 25–50 cm of dirt from the top of the mound in the 1960s before the remainder was protected by purchase (Rafferty 1995). Chambers's L-shaped trench in the mound was partly cleaned out in 1992 and the profiles recorded again. Several 1-×-1-m units were also excavated, three of them to the base of the mound. This work documented wall trench fragments originating in at least three levels, indicating that the mound had a complex history of structure building and use, interspersed with additions of dirt to the mound (Rafferty 1995:64–84).

The excavated portion of Mound IV was not deep enough to reveal much detail about rebuilding. The 1-×-1-m unit excavated in the mound in 1992 intersected a wall trench at a depth of ca. 60 cm below surface and postholes originated in three zones. Chambers's work in the mound uncovered a large pit, 0.9 × 1.5 × 1 m in size, which originated in the middle portion of the mound fill, about 1 m below the surface (Rafferty 1995:32). This may represent an empty storage pit, as artifacts were not noted by Chambers nor do any survive in the collections. The pit may be associated with one of the building episodes in evidence in the 1992 work. One feature, a fired area, was found in the limited 1991–1992 work in Mound III. No features were detected in Mound V, nor did Chambers uncover any features in Mound V trenching.

No evidence of postholes or other features was found at Thelma in the 1-×-1-m unit excavated in Mound 1. Only 35 sherds were recovered in the 1.16 m^3 (30 sherds/m^3) of dirt removed (Johnson and Atkinson 1987:64). The magnetometry done in 2013 at the site revealed that Mound 1 has a rectangular building on or under it (Figure 11.5); its use as a substructure mound, similar to Mound I at Owl Creek, seems likely.

The rectangular and oval mounds at Bessemer also both contained evidence that structures had been built and rebuilt on the sequential platforms that existed between episodes of mound building (DeJarnette and Wimberly 1941; Welch 1994). Artifact density was relatively low here too. While the dirt from the Bessemer mounds presumably was not screened, all three mounds were excavated completely (DeJarnette and Wimberly 1941). This resulted in the recovery of 1,159 sherds (DeJarnette and Wimberly 1941:80) from the 5400 m^3 fill of the mounds (0.2 sherds per m^3). The burial mound at Bessemer did contain a number of burials, including some intruded from the surface rather than included in the mound proper.

The uses of the mounds not already discussed (Mounds III and V at Owl Creek; Mounds 2, 3, 4, and 5 at Thelma) are unknown. No prehistoric burials have been found at Owl Creek or Thelma, either on or off the mounds. That Mound 5 at Thelma is circular and set far from the other mounds suggests the possibility that it may be a Woodland conical mound, but this has not been investigated.

Occupation Delineation

The regional co-occurrence of grog- and shell-tempered sherds (and the presence of mixed grog- and shell-tempered pottery) has occasioned various explanations. These are reviewed for the Black Warrior valley in Alabama by Welch (1994). The basis of disagreement lies in whether variability and change are treated as being continuous through time and space, as advocated early and explicitly by James Ford (1954; Phillips et al. 1951), or whether phenomena are seen to occur as essentialist entities with clear temporal-spatial boundaries (Jenkins and Krause 1986). The co-occurrence of grog and shell tempers in assemblages can be seen as representing a change occurring in the same population from predominant use of grog as temper to predominant use of shell. The change has been characterized as relatively abrupt once shell temper came under selection (Feathers 2006, 2009). Conversely, there has been a strong tendency among regional archaeologists to treat the two temper modes as essentialist categories, representing two non-contemporary groups of people, Late Woodland (grog temper) and Mississippian (shell temper) (Jenkins and Krause 1986:92).

Welch (1994) grappled with bringing the pottery from Bessemer to bear on this controversy; as it turned out, he felt he had been unsuccessful in solving it, partly given recovery methods and lost provenience information for the Bessemer collections. The problem remains, however, and its pertinence to understanding not only Bessemer but also Owl Creek and Thelma is plain, as all the assemblages contain mixtures of grog- and shell-tempered sherds (Table 11.4).

The first task is to examine whether the presence of sherds tempered with grog, mixed grog and shell, and shell represent two separate or one continuous occupation at each site. Occupations can be conceived as artifacts at the scale of assemblage (Dunnell 1971; Rafferty 2008) and as the largest depositional unit recognizable in archaeology. The data are complicated by mixture of the two temper types in mound deposits. Mound construction episodes may have translocated into the mounds pottery from previous occupations or from an earlier part of the occupation during which the mounds were built. There are several ways to examine whether sherds displaying grog- and shell-temper modes, even those found in mounds, were deposited contemporaneously or whether some are the result of inclusion of secondary debris in mound fill. If grog-tempered sherds were redeposited, they would be expected to be on average smaller and more likely to be eroded than shell-tempered sherds, if the latter were deposited during mound use. This can help establish whether the mounds were built when the temper modes were both in use, as opposed to being built after grog tempering had declined or ceased. Artifacts deposited

Table 11.4. Pottery assemblages from Bessemer, Owl Creek, and Thelma.

	mussel shell	grog & shell	grog	bone & grog	sand	lime-stone	untempered	Total	Source
Owl Creek									
All mounds	493	38	56		158			745	Rafferty 1995
	66.17%	5.10%	7.52%		21.21%				
Surface, non-mound units, shovel tests	148	23	36	1	83		1	292	
	50.68%	7.88%	12.33%	0.34%	28.42%		0.34%		
Bessemer									
All mounds	704		433		22			1159	DeJarnette and Wimberly 1941
	60.74%		37.36%		1.90%				
Old humus	602		800		20	6		1428	
	42.16%		56.02%		1.40%	0.42%			
Thelma									
Mound 1 unit	1		30		3	1		35	Johnson and Atkinson 1985
	2.86%		85.71%		8.57%	2.86%			
Chambers surface collection	6		102		11			119	Analysis by Keith Baca 1983
	5.04%		85.71%		9.24%				
Atkinson surface collection	10	3	149	13	19			194	Analysis by Atkinson, reanalysis by Rafferty, 2012
	5.15%	1.55%	76.80%	6.70%	9.79%				

as part of the same occupation should also show similar spatial patterns in non-mound parts of a site (e.g., Triplett, this volume). Welch's (1994) examination of various modes of rim shape, handle shape, and decoration are also pertinent, as they may reveal continuity, if not contemporaneity, between the two temper modes.

In Mound I at Owl Creek, shell-tempered (including mixed shell/grog-tempered) sherds were found along with both grog-tempered and sand-tempered pottery. Use of sand tempering had largely ceased before A.D. 750–800 (Jenkins and Krause 1986:62–63, 73), so the coincidence of sand-tempered and shell-tempered sherds in the mound cannot easily be explained by their temporal overlap. Both the sand-tempered and the grog-tempered sherds are on average smaller and more likely to display eroded surfaces than the associated shell-tempered pottery, so most of them were probably incorporated in the dirt prior to its use in mound construction (Rafferty 1995:25). Production of grog-tempered and shell-tempered pottery overlapped in time (Rafferty 2001; Rafferty and Peacock 2008) and that may also be represented by some of the grog-tempered sherds in Mound I. Shell tempering was not employed regularly in the region until A.D. 950 or later (Rafferty and Peacock 2008:260–261; Welch 1990), increasing rapidly to become the dominant temper mode by A.D. 1050.

The mix of pottery tempers in sherds recovered from Mound II is also interpreted as representing Woodland sherds that were mostly in the fill before it was deposited and shell-tempered sherds that were associated with mound use, by the same reasoning and kinds of evidence presented for Mound I. Pottery from Mound V was sparse (56 sherds in 1.2 m^3 of excavation). About 79 percent was shell-tempered, the remainder being grog-tempered or sand-tempered (Rafferty 1995:23). Fifty-four of the sherds were from Zone E, a 25-cm-thick fill zone; they include one sand-tempered fabric-marked sherd, which can be assigned confidently to the Middle Woodland period and therefore cannot have been made at the same time as the shell-tempered pottery. Again, this evidence tends to indicate that the sand-tempered sherds, at least, were present in the fill used to build the mound. Only three grog-tempered sherds were recovered, all from Zone E.

Shell-tempered and mixed shell/grog-tempered sherds were found in the deepest pottery-bearing zones in all five mounds at Owl Creek and in 15 of 17 mound features that produced pottery. Units that reached mound bases, on the east edge of Mound I, in the center of Mound II, and in Mound III, all yielded such pottery. This finding, along with Chambers's recovery of shell-tempered sherds at the base of Mound II and deep in Mound IV, provides evidence that all five mounds were constructed, used, and abandoned during the period when shell temper was in use.

Sherds collected at Thelma by Chambers in 1935, Atkinson in 1973, and the Mound 1 testing, mentioned above, include sand, grog, and shell tempers (Table 11.4). More precise Woodland diagnostics are present also, in the form of both sand-tempered and grog-tempered cordmarked sherds from the surface collections and grog-tempered cordmarked sherds from the mound excavation (Johnson and Atkinson 1987:64). A complicating factor is that there is a Historic Indian occupation at the site, as attested by Atkinson's recognition of Chickachae Combed, Plain, and Red-Slipped sherds in two of the surface collections (Atkinson 1986; Johnson and Atkinson 1987:64). Chickachae types are tempered with fine sand (Quimby 1942) or grog (Blitz 1985), making it difficult to separate plain Chickachae sherds from Woodland sand-tempered and grog-tempered pottery. The observation that sherds of the three main temper modes (sand, grog, and shell) are associated in all collections made at Thelma suggests continuity of occupation at the site from late Middle Woodland through Early Mississippian times, with the Historic Indian sherds resulting from a separate, later, occupation.

Table 11.5. Bessemer pottery type seriation. Data from Welch 1994.

Rim Type	Unflared Folded		Unflared Not Folded		Angular Flare Folded		Angular Flare Not Folded		Smooth Flare Folded		Smooth Flare Not Folded		Total
Rim Assemblages	n	%	n	%	n	%	n	%	n	%	n	%	
Shell-tempered Decorated	14	26.92	1	1.92	19	36.54	14	26.92	3	5.77	1	1.92	52
Shell-tempered Plain	30	34.48	4	4.60	29	33.33	13	14.94	7	8.05	4	4.60	87
Grog-tempered Plain	20	54.05	13	35.14							4	10.81	37
Grog-tempered Decorated									1	50.00	1	50.00	2
Sand-tempered Plain											2	100.00	2

The pottery assemblage from Bessemer has been reviewed thoroughly by Welch (1994). There is a large quantity of grog-tempered pottery, indicating that the occupation began prior to Moundville I, during which period grog tempering ceased to be used, at least in the central Black Warrior valley (Knight and Steponaitis 1998:9). Compared to Owl Creek, Bessemer produced proportionately more grog-tempered and less shell-tempered pottery (Table 11.4). A series of luminescence dates run on potsherds from West Jefferson contexts at three sites near Bessemer shows that shell-tempered and grog-tempered pottery production overlapped in that area, with no precedence of one over the other (Feathers 2009:129–131). The dates for both temper modes were distributed between ca. A.D. 900–1200, with a few shell-tempered sherds dating considerably earlier. The presence of both tempers at Bessemer could thus be explained at least partly by coincident manufacture.

Welch proposes a temporal sequence of types, defined by jar rim shape and decoration, that connects grog-tempered and shell-tempered pottery. He was unable to confirm or disconfirm this sequence using pottery from features and middens at Bessemer (Welch 1994:22–24). The posited sequence does allow the pottery types to be successfully seriated using the six rim shape types. This was done by collapsing the types proposed by Welch into five temper/decoration types (Table 11.5) and treating each type as an assemblage over which the rim shape types were distributed. The seriation confirms the order suggested by Welch (1994:22–24), indicating that there is change from sand-tempered smooth flared rims without folds to grog-tempered and then shell-tempered angular flared rims with and without folds. That such a seriation is possible, despite some small samples, shows that there is continuity in rim styles across the ordered temper types. This is the strongest current evidence for there being one continuous occupation at Bessemer, during which temper changed from a predominance of grog to a predominance of shell temper.

Extent of Habitation

It is natural to focus on the mounds at a site containing them, but the extent of non-mound habitation is crucial to understanding these large mound groups' roles in associated settlement patterns. At Owl Creek, several surface collections have been made by archaeologists under varying conditions, beginning with Chambers in 1935, when much of the non-mound portion of the site was in row crops. The collectors uniformly recovered few artifacts: only 155 sherds were contained in six surface collections (Rafferty 1995:18). The best provenienced collections, made by Jim Atkinson in disked areas south of Mounds IV and V (Figure 11.7), produced 34 sherds in areas totaling perhaps 3,900 square meters, which is 0.009 sherds per square meter.

To obtain better information on the density and distribution of artifacts at the site, systematic shovel testing was undertaken in 1992, by which time the site surface was concealed by grass, pine forest, and brush. The entire site, excepting the mounds, was examined using a 30-m grid of shovel tests that extended at least 100 m beyond the mounds in every direction except west of Mound I, where a small drainage bounds the site (Figure 11.7). A major ridge west of the site was also tested. This grid was supplemented by tests dug at 10-m and 20-m intervals in the cardinal directions from each shovel test on the original grid that produced artifacts. The 161 30-cm diameter shovel tests were excavated to subsoil. After a soil sample was obtained from each, the dirt was screened through quarter-inch mesh.

The 21 positive shovel tests (Figure 11.7) produced a total of 26 sherds. As was the case with Atkinson's collections, the shovel testing indicated very low-density artifact scatters. North of Mounds I and II, only sand-tempered sherds and Historic period artifacts were recovered. The shell-tempered sherds mostly came from the vicinity of Mound III, perhaps from mound fill scattered by cultivation, and from between and south of Mounds IV and V (Figure 11.7), near where Atkinson's surface collections had been made in 1973. Taken together, the few artifacts found in both mound and non-mound contexts led to the argument that the site was vacant of significant habitation, at least in the Mississippian period, when the mounds were built and used (Rafferty 1995). About half the sherds recovered in the shovel tests were

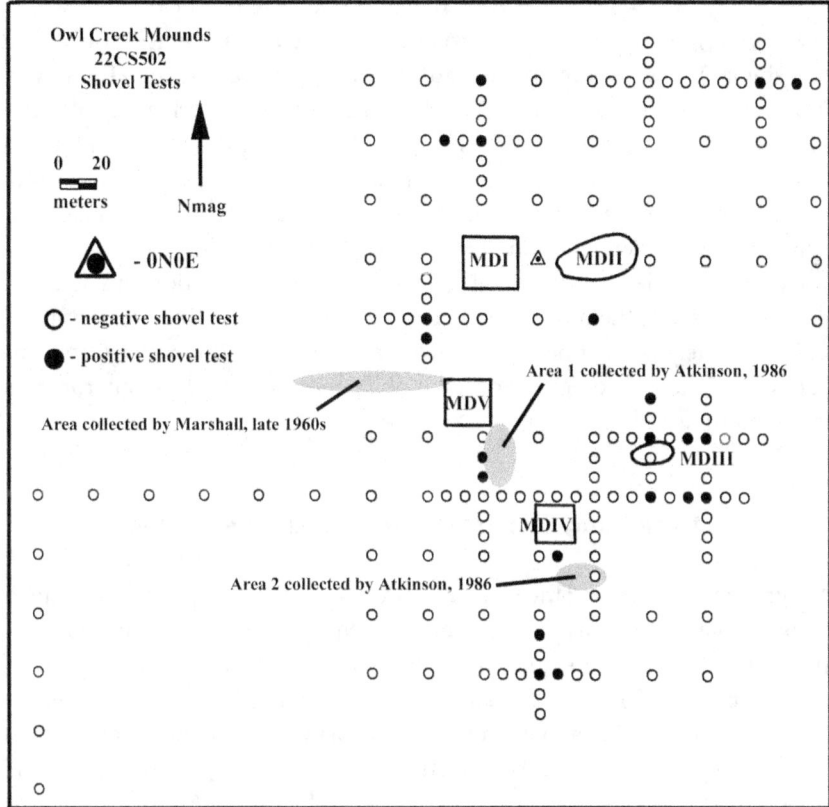

Figure 11.7. Map of Owl Creek Mounds site. Adapted from Rafferty (1995:Figure 38).

sand-tempered or grog-tempered, representing remnants of the Woodland portion of the occupation, the artifacts from which appear largely to have been incorporated in the mounds.

In three surface collections made at Thelma over the course of 40 years, beginning in 1935, a total of 402 sherds was recovered (Table 11.2; Johnson and Atkinson 1987:Table 2). This total excludes the 16 Historic Indian sherds assigned to Chickachae plain, Combed, and red-slipped by Atkinson (Johnson and Atkinson 1987:64). While inconclusive, indications are that there was scattered evidence of habitation at Thelma. Artifact density in any one area is impossible to determine with current information.

Even less information is available from non-mound contexts at Bessemer, excluding the structures noted above in the vicinity of the platform mound, which Welch (1994) argues convincingly were pre-mound public buildings, not residential households. The 1930s work concentrated on the mounds and on finding structures elsewhere at the site. Despite extensive efforts, with many areas stripped of plow zone by hand (DeJarnette and Wimberly 1941; Welch 1994), the only domestic structures were two wall trench houses and one single post structure, found under or near the oval mound. These were "ordinary houses with hearths" (Welch 1994:13), with no overlapping patterns. Many postholes were also uncovered (Welch 1994:8), as well as fragments of other wall trenches. Another wall trench house, Structure 4, was 60 feet north of the mound and was the only one found at the site that was not immediately adjacent to or under a mound. It appears that few habitation areas were present at the site, at least during the period of mound construction and use. That does not preclude the possibility that a more densely occupied area was there in immediately prior times. As at Owl Creek, much of the pottery from the Late Woodland portion of the occupation appears to have been incorporated in the mounds.

Explaining Owl Creek, Thelma, and Bessemer

The comparisons among the three sites are summarized in Table 11.6. It shows many similarities in disparate ceramic, mound, site layout, and artifact density traits. Most of the similarities can be ascribed to functional aspects of the occupations. This implies that their inception may be understood best by invoking processes of parallel evolution to explain many of the shared traits at the three sites, with historical connections being reserved primarily to explain shared ceramic styles.

Mound building and mound centers assume a prominent position in models of Mississippian period settlement patterning. In these models, the main role of platform mounds is as an indicator of hierarchical organization and the existence of chiefs, who are assumed to have had power and authority over other parts of society (Anderson 1994; Blitz 1993a; Peebles and Kus 1977; Welch 1990, 1991). In accord with this formulation, some authors have proposed that the Mississippian period be defined partly by the existence of "a ranked level of sociocultural integration" (Smith 1986:53; see also Smith 1978:486; 1990:1–2), marked by the construction of substructural mounds (Welch 1991; 1994:13, 25). A good example of the use of platform mound construction as a direct and unequivocal correlate of ranked organization is a paper by Schurr and Schoeninger (1995), which compares Ohio valley Mississippian and Fort Ancient traditions on the assumption that the lack of platform mounds in Fort Ancient indicates a tribal society, while their presence in Mississippian settlement patterns is indicative of a chiefdom.

Cultural or progressive evolutionary theory underlies many such accounts. One of the most influential is that of Peebles and Kus (1977). Focusing on the Moundville phase of the Black Warrior River valley, the article demonstrated

Table 11.6. Comparison of attributes of Owl Creek, Thelma, and Bessemer.

Traits	Owl Creek	Thelma	Bessemer
Mound Number	5	5	3
Mound Volume	4981 m^3	6525.5 m^3	5405 m^3
Mound Use	Substructure—Mounds I, II, and III	Mound I possible substructure	Substructure—platform and oval mounds; Burial—burial mound
Mound Shape	Mounds I, IV, V—rectangular, flat-topped; Mound II—oval, flat-topped; Mound III—circular, flat-topped	Mounds 1, 2, 3, 4—rectangular, flat-topped; Mound 5—circular, flat-topped or conical	Platform—rectangular, flat-topped; Oval—oval, flat-topped; Burial—circular, flat-topped
Non-mound Habitation Evidence	Low density, mostly Woodland	Low (?) density, mostly Woodland	Low (?) density, mostly Mississippian (?)
Overall Size	4 ha	5 ha (excluding Mound 5); 8–13 ha (including Mound 5)	2.6 ha
Size of Area Enclosed by Mounds	1 ha	1.85 ha	1.2 ha

how the settlement pattern of the phase as then known could be characterized as displaying a three-tier site hierarchy, with site size and location held to be determined largely by the power relationships among settlements in the three tiers: villages without mounds, single-mound villages, and Moundville itself. An extensive discussion of the mortuary evidence for status ranking at Moundville was also presented (Peebles and Kus 1977).

The use of progressive theory in anthropology and archaeology has been thoroughly analyzed and found wanting (Dunnell 1980, 1988; Harris 1968:653). The theory is essentialist in nature, assuming that phenomena take the form of bounded entities (formulated as stages) such as tribes and chiefdoms, with variability within the phenomena treated as irrelevant noise (Leonard and Jones 1987; Welch 2006). The theory has no mechanisms to explain why change takes the form it does but rather assumes that change is internally driven (orthogenetic) and progressive, with entities becoming larger and more complex through time. The theory tends toward ethnocentrism because of this latter, commonsensical, assumption (Dunnell 1982). It does not provide a satisfactory basis for scientific explanation (Dunnell 1980). To the fairly large extent that Mississippian mounds and settlement patterns have been explained by invoking change from tribe to chiefdom, from egalitarian to ranked sociopolitical organization, or from simple to complex chiefdom, the explanations are vulnerable to the critique that they are grounded in suspect reasoning.

A strand of functionalist theory also runs through treatments of Mississippian settlement patterning. Settlement patterns are viewed as synchronic systems, with the parts having different roles that serve to maintain the functioning of the whole. Functionalism treats change (if at all) as transformation, in which the system flips from one state to another. Again, this is conceived as an internally driven process. Anderson's (1994) model of cycling chiefdoms is a well-explicated example. The idea of progress from one stage to another can be joined relatively easily with a functionalist view of change, as both see change as orthogenetic.

In Darwinian evolutionary theory, one way that building mounds, monumental architecture in general, and other manifestations of "wasted" energy has been explained is by recourse to the concept of costly signaling. This explanation sees wasteful signaling as a way to display fitness, which results in the signaler gaining adherents (Neiman 1997). Bruce Trigger (1990:125) captured the equation of waste with power that underlies much archaeological thinking:

> At the most elementary and general level, political power is universally perceived as the ability of a ruler to consume some of the energy he controls for non-utilitarian purposes. It is because of this that monumental architecture constitutes a universally understood expression of power and also why the basic significance of monumental architecture and luxury goods is so readily apparent to archaeologists.

The progressive evolutionary model for Moundville and its theoretical underpinnings have been revised by Knight and Steponaitis (1998), who claim an adherence to practice theory, which concerns "how elites actively work to win and consolidate power over followers" (1998:25). As explanation, this is not far removed from costly signaling. Knight's (2004) paper on mound-top excavations at Moundville makes this similarity even more clear, as he discusses certain kinds of artifacts as representing display items used to impress onlookers.

Darwinian evolutionary thinking reverses the causation implied by Trigger, Knight, and Steponaitis, which lodges explanation in the actors. Instead, it sees variation, and thus differential fitness, as always present in any population. This variation has no inevitable outcome, such as the formation of a chiefdom. If number of adherents is equated with power, however, then such costly signalers might be said to accrue power to themselves through waste. But, whether called power, prestige, or charisma, this outcome can be seen as the result of selection, not decision making. Thus, explanation is lodged in an evolutionary process, natural selection, that is not an intrinsic trait of the phenomena; rather, it is part of theory. Costly signaling can take forms such as feasting and display of difficult-to-make or difficult-to-obtain items; both feasting and display can be seen as ways to show that the person or group involved has resources to waste, by giving them away or by emphasizing effort and energy expended in obtaining the display items. Such traits will be selected for if they enhance survival or reproductive success, usually at the scale of the individual. Aranyosi (1999) argues that costly signaling is more likely to become fixed in resource-rich environments.

Costly signaling is a potential explanation for aspects of mound use at Owl Creek, Thelma, and Bessemer. Poor animal bone preservation may account for the lack of exotic bird and predator bones (see also Knight 2004). But display artifacts—burnished or highly decorated pottery, objects made of exotic stone, other highly crafted artifacts—are not present in significant amounts at Owl Creek. Two postholes, a feature, and Zone Q in Mound I yielded 19 sherds of a fine buff paste shell-tempered vessel, red-slipped with a red-painted design, identified with the type Hiwassee Island Red on Buff, a likely import from the Tennessee valley (Rafferty 1995:36). Its association with mound-top structures indicates it might have been connected with costly signaling. Near the site, in Goodfood Creek, a polished limonite spud ax was found (Rafferty 1995:152) that likely came from the site.

At Bessemer the main findings that suggest display of costly items are whole and partial shell-tempered pottery vessels. Thirteen were found, 12 in burials and 1 in Fill 2 of the burial mound (DeJarnette and Wimberly 1941:87–91). Eight of the vessels are black-filmed and 6 of these also have incised designs; 1 of the remaining filmed vessels has engraved lines that were filled with hematite. This vessel has terraced sides and a cut-out rim (DeJarnette and Wimberly 1941:90), similar to several from Moundville (Steponaitis 1983:218). Other than this, the filmed pots from burials are bowls and bottles. Only 5.6 percent (73 of 1,306) of the shell-tempered sherds from Bessemer were black-filmed or black-filmed and incised, according to DeJarnette and Wimberly's analysis (1941:81), so such vessels are overrepresented (making up 58 percent of the vessels) in burials. That they were made as grave goods seems unlikely, given their condition (6 of 13 were incomplete and 4 are worn severely), so it is possible that they were originally used in open-air displays, where they became weathered or broken.

Also found in burials at Bessemer were 38 conch columella beads, one copper plate, and a limestone discoidal. These grave goods represent loss of items that had occasioned some cost to manufacture and to obtain raw materials (copper and marine shell) for manufacture. These items also might be interpreted as having once been placed in displays. While important to note, these hints of costly signaling are not a prominent aspect of the Bessemer site assemblage.

Mounds are often seen as the primary location of feasting (Blitz 1993a; Hayden 1998), which can be understood as a form of costly signaling. One mismatch between the expectation of feasting refuse and the data from Owl Creek, Thelma, and Bessemer is the small quantity of artifacts recovered, despite extensive archaeological investigation at Owl Creek and Bessemer. Feasting is recognized partly by the large amount of food residues and discarded ceramics that are held to result from it, especially in the form of mound-side middens (Smith and Williams 1994). No such deposits have been found at any of the three sites.

More salient at the three sites discussed here are phenomena that may be attributed to another evolutionary mechanism, bet-hedging, that also addresses waste. Bet-hedging theory proposes that, in marginal or unpredictably fluctuating environments, waste can be selected for because it dampens population growth over the shorter term and allows groups to survive situations of lessened environmental productivity (Dunnell 1989; Madsen et al. 1999). This survival is at the expense of groups living in the same environment but not practicing bet-hedging, who are more likely to show greater rates of population increase in the short run, followed by crashes that occur as a result of changes in carrying capacity (Dunnell 1989). Environmental carrying capacity is crucial to this argument, as it is population size relative to carrying capacity that determines whether bet-hedging will be selected. Aranyosi's (1999) discussion of Irish megaliths provides an example in which rocky, less productive soils are the location of most of the megaliths. Seen as bet-hedging, the distribution of megaliths is explained by the marginal environments in which they are located, with marginality measured in terms of agricultural carrying capacity (Aranyosi 1999:370). This is a case where bet-hedging was selected due to fluctuations in productivity that are primarily spatial rather than temporal.

The three cases discussed here also represent spatial rather than temporal variability, in the context of the evolution of maize agriculture. Arguably, agricultural productivity was less able to increase in the upper reaches of the Tombigbee/Black Warrior valley than in the central part, which had larger expanses of fertile soils as well as somewhat longer growing seasons.

Construction of costly facilities such as mounds may be regarded as a form of waste. There also is some evidence at Owl Creek and Bessemer for wasteful activities that preceded mound construction and that may mark the beginning of selection for bet-hedging. At Owl Creek, two large and carefully constructed features, a large posthole (F41) found in 1992 and a multilayer fire basin excavated by Chambers, were in place before Mound II was built. These features provide the only evidence for special activities that occurred prior to mound construction; the test excavations in other parts of Mound II and in the other mounds were not extensive enough to reveal more. At Bessemer there is good evidence for a succession of public buildings under and adjacent to the platform mound. These include a series of large wall trench and single post circular buildings, plus a double fence encircling rectangular buildings (Welch 1994:8–12). Additionally, an extensive stone pavement was found under the oval mound; it covered ca. 7600 square feet (850 square meters) (DeJarnette and Wimberly 1941:7–9).

Bet-hedging appears to be a viable explanation for the large scale of mound building at the three sites, especially because mound construction occurred during the Late Woodland/Mississippian transition. During the Late Woodland period in the region, settlement expanded to the maximum extent reached by sedentary populations. Habitation sites marked by grog-tempered plain and cordmarked pottery, assigned to the Late Woodland Miller III period, are found in a variety of lowland and upland environments in the upper Tombigbee valley. These locations include the main valley and its tributaries (Futato 1989:315; Rafferty 1996), Pontotoc Ridge and the North Central Hills (Peacock 1997; Rafferty 2002), the western part of the Black Prairie (Rafferty 1996), and the northern flatwoods (Rafferty 2002; Rafferty and Peacock 2008). In north-central Alabama, a similar pattern holds. In the upper part of the Black Warrior valley, in the Bessemer region, small occupations of the Late Woodland West Jefferson phase were scattered in a variety of physiographic settings (Futato 1989:241–242).

Such spatially extensive habitation is an indication that the hunter-gatherers who occupied the region were near carrying capacity (Peacock 2002). It is in this kind of context that bet-hedging may be selected for, especially in upland areas where resource intensification or further broadening of diet was not easily done. Mussels were not available in great quantity in these tributary valleys and other wild resources were already in use. Cultigens provide one source of food the use of which might have been intensified. Significant evidence for use of native cultigens, such as chenopod, sunflower, and marsh elder, has not been found at Woodland sites in the region (Gremillion 2002; Scarry 1993). Maize was recovered at Owl Creek, with several cob fragments present in a small pit, Feature 50, on Mound I (Trinkley 1994) and a few kernels and cupules found in eight other features in Mounds I, II, and IV (Rafferty 1995:136). No maize has been recovered at Thelma in the very limited excavation there, nor was any reported at Bessemer. Maize has been found at Bessemer-area West Jefferson occupations, and there is evidence that it became more common through time in West Jefferson sites (Scarry 1993). This level of presence likely indicates that a maize-based agroecology had been established, with maize adapted to local conditions in each area (Hart 1999).

Despite the relative ubiquity of maize in Late Woodland/Early Mississippian times in some of these peripheral areas, its greatest importance in the diet appears to have been attained later, in the Middle to Late Mississippian period, and farther south, in the central valley. This is shown by carbon isotope analyses done on skeletal material from Moundville phase sites (Schoeninger and Schurr 1998; Schoeninger et al. 2000) and from Lyon's Bluff and nearby sites in the central Tombigbee valley (Hogue 2007). Isotope values became less negative from Moundville I through Moundville III (Schoeninger and Schurr 1998), indicating that maize was increasingly important in the diet during the period from ca. A.D. 1200–A.D. 1550. It made up 40 percent of the calories consumed in Moundville I and 65 percent in Moundville II and III (Schoeninger and Schurr 1998:128). Data from Oktibbeha County burials in the central Tombigbee valley show the same pattern (Hogue 2007).

The overall sequence of change in settlement and subsistence in the peripheral parts of the Tombigbee-Black Warrior valley, then, is from (1) widely dispersed Late Woodland populations living in hamlet- and village-sized settlements; to (2) building of large vacant mound centers (Owl Creek, Thelma, and Bessemer); to (3) abandonment of these centers and of the surrounding areas. It appears defensible to conclude that construction of large mound centers in the periphery allowed populations to dampen growth and persist there until A.D. 1200–1250. In the central Tombigbee valley, the health of Miller III people was generally poor and conflict was common (Hill 1981; Shuler et al. 2012; Welch 1990) The peripheral areas arguably avoided these difficulties, first via bet-hedging and then by deserting the peripheries to move downstream, where intensified maize agriculture could be practiced more successfully.

Without carbon isotope and demographic data from burials (Madsen et al. 1999), it will be difficult to decisively test the bet-hedging hypothesis to explain the construction of large mound centers in the peripheral parts of the Tombigbee and Black Warrior valleys. Detailed examination of settlement pattern change, with assemblages organized using a fine-scale chronology, could provide evidence of the population size changes that bear on this hypothesis. Some of this is available for the Owl Creek area (Rafferty 1996, 2002), but has not been compiled for the Thelma or Bessemer regions. The bet-hedging hypothesis does account for many of the similarities among the three sites, especially the large amount of earth incorporated in mounds, the peripheral location of the sites, and the dispersed nature of the settlement patterns. It is not denied that other factors, including costly signaling and the role that mound centers might have played in strengthening ties among widely dispersed small settlements, could also be significant aspects of a full explanation.

Bet-hedging might be applied to other large mound groups that were built in upland areas in the Late Woodland to Early Mississippian period in the Midsouth. Examples are Toltec Mounds in Arkansas (Rolingson 1990) and the

Ames (Mickelson and Goddard 2011) and Obion (Garland 1992) mound sites in western Tennessee

Acknowledgments

Thanks are due to Sam Brookes, who first drew my attention to the Owl Creek Mounds site and its importance; to Keith Baca and Jim Atkinson, who helped locate artifacts and information about Thelma Mounds; to students in the 1991 and 1992 MSU field schools at Owl Creek and to the field assistants for those projects, Robert Bryan, Chris Davies, Terry Lolley, and John Underwood.

Notes

1. Use of cultural periods (Mississippian, Late Woodland, Middle Woodland) causes considerable awkwardness to cogent writing when one is examining changes that cut across the usually accepted period boundaries, as is the case here. There is no theoretically grounded reason why cultural traits (even those, like shell or grog tempering, that are used to define such periods) should begin or end their temporal distributions at the period boundaries (e.g., Feathers 2006, 2009). Period names are used here for convenience of reference but are not held to represent congeries of traits that share the same time or space distributions.

2. One of the mounds (Chambers's Mound 5) was said by Johnson and Atkinson (1987:63) to have been removed by terracing between 1935 and 1937, but this terracing occurred south of the east-west road and could not have destroyed Mound 5, which was located well north of the road.

3. Errors were made in transcribing the dimensions of Thelma's mounds from Chambers's site form to the table given by Johnson and Atkinson (1987:64). Mound 1, the one tested by Johnson and Atkinson, is recorded by Chambers as 126 ft long, no width given, 10 ft high; Mound 2 was $72 \times 63 \times 6$ ft; Mound 3 was $135 \times 66 \times 5.5$ ft, with this height measured at the west end; Mound 4 was $95 \times 55 \times 5.5$ ft, with a length of 75 ft given for the top; Mound 5 was 25 ft in diameter and 4 ft high (Chambers's 1935 site card, MDAH site file).

CHAPTER 12

Plaquemine Culture Pottery from the Great Ravine at the Anna Site (22AD500), Adams County, Mississippi

Ian W. Brown

Introduction

I'll never forget the first time I descended into the Anna site Great Ravine. Although I had walked all over Anna in the summer of 1971 as part of Jeff Brain's Lower Mississippi Survey's operations, our efforts were confined to the area on and around the mounds. At one point, in peering over the edge of the terrace into the depths below, I made a mental note to do all that I could to avoid ever venturing into such treacherous terrain. Little did I know that about 10 years later I would be hanging on to a long rope—for dear life, I might add—gingerly making my way down a near vertical slope. Even though the bottom of the Great Ravine was far below what I could actually see when I threw my body over the edge, the trust that I had in my friends convinced me that the trip was worth risking life and limb. I remain convinced that was so.

But first let's take a look at the Anna site (22AD500) itself, which is a notable landmark in the prehistory of Mississippi (Figure 12.1). It is, in fact, a National Historic Landmark, a distinction that is most deserved. The site itself is located in the northern extreme of Adams County and consists of eight mounds, with six of them arranged along the edge of a flat bluff top overlooking the Mississippi alluvial valley (Figure 12.2). At one time in late prehistory the Mississippi River flowed directly beneath the site, and even then the ravines that surround Anna must have been of phenomenal depth. Early visitors to Anna would either have followed a thin ridge that heads due east of the site, or they would have had to come from the river itself, scaling the bluffs that rose to the east. An old historic trail, which is still quite visible in the forest, ran through the site. It may even have been the same artery that was used in prehistoric times. And what a sight the big mound at Anna would have been to any traveler who approached it from the west. Mound 3, the largest

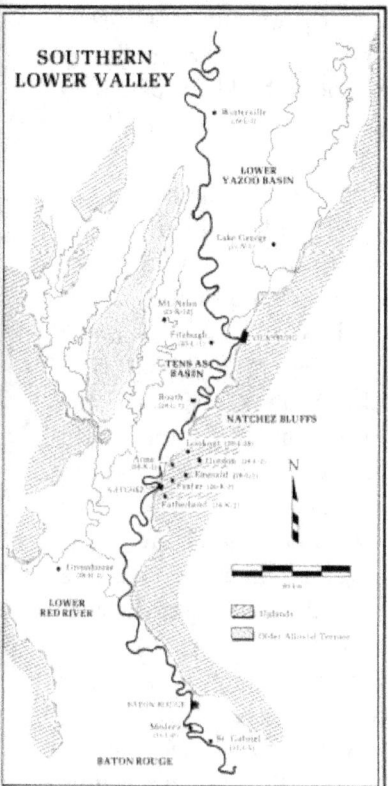

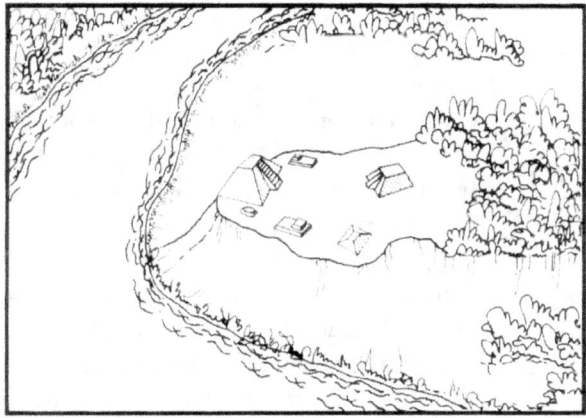

Figure 12.1. Selected Plaquemine sites in the Natchez Buffs and surrounding regions (from Brown 1985:Figure 1). Used with permission of the *Midcontinental Journal of Archaeology*.

Figure 12.2. An artist's rendering of the Anna site from Brain 1978: Figure 12.6. Courtesy Jeffrey P. Brain.

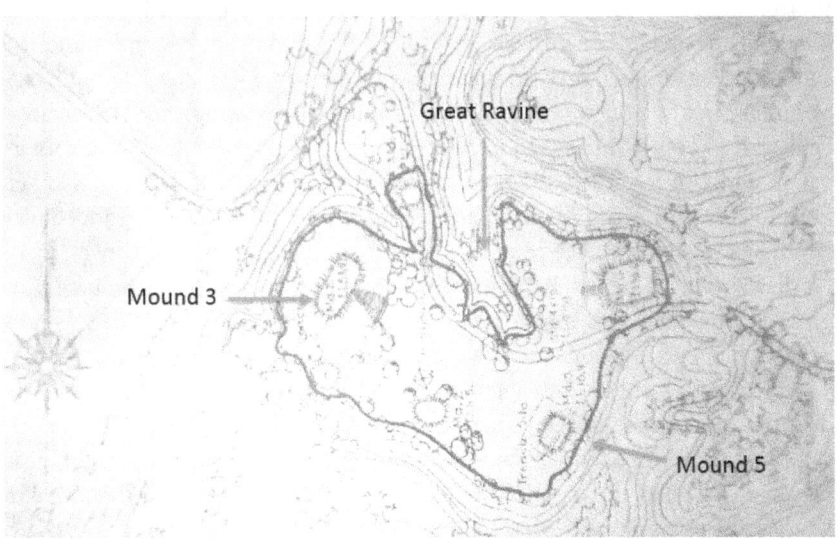

Figure 12.3. Location of Mounds 3 and 5 and the Great Ravine at the Anna site. Adapted from Jennings (1940:Figure 2).

mound (Figure 12.3), currently rises 16.5 m above the plaza, but when viewed from the alluvial valley it would have been impossible to determine where bluff ended and mound began. In short, the residents of buildings placed on the summit of this tumulus would surely have elicited a certain amount of awe and respect from any visiting emissaries.

John L. Cotter (1951) was the first to publish a detailed description of the site and of Colonel Stowers's magnificent collection from Mound 5, but long before that most early recorders of Mississippi's antiquity who passed through the Natchez region made note of this enormous site. Benjamin L. C. Wailes, arguably Mississippi's first professional archaeologist, was well aware of Anna as early as the mid-nineteenth century (Brown 1998:173–174). Warren K. Moorehead (1932:162–163), who followed in Wailes's footsteps in the twentieth century, also recognized the importance of this site, as did Calvin Brown (1926) and James A. Ford (1936:111). The National Park Service was so intrigued by the size and importance of Anna that there were detailed plans to make it into a park, complete with a museum (Jennings 1940:Figure 3). The nearby Emerald site (22AD504) ended up receiving this honor, for at least the park dimension, but that decision had more to do with proximity to the Natchez Trace than to the relative importance of the two sites.

Anna currently remains a landholding of the Stowers family. Mrs. Luther Stowers graciously permitted the Alabama Museum of Natural History to conduct its Summer Expedition at Anna in 1997. For well over three decades now the museum has been taking high school children into the field on scientific projects, and in 1997 I was fortunate to host the Expedition at the Anna site. Our objectives that season were to explore the summit of Mound 3 and the Mound 4 Flats immediately to the east, with the hope of uncovering information relating to Plaquemine culture architecture (Brown 1997, 2007). The crew consisted of approximately 20 expedition participants over a four-week interval. In addition to myself, the professional crew consisted of Richard S. Fuller, Duke Beasley, Tony Boudreaux, Hunter Johnson, and Patrick Livingood. Fuller led the excavations on the Mound 3 summit, while Livingood, a University of North Carolina–Chapel Hill student who was just entering the graduate program at Michigan, was his able assistant. Following a systematic coring program, a block excavation was opened in the northwestern end of the Mound 3 summit. As a result of plowing and other disturbances, the upper levels were disturbed, but a wall trench structure was eventually detected that ran parallel to the western end of the block. This wall relates to a large structure that was placed on Mound 3 during the Emerald phase (A.D. 1500–1650), as described in Lauren A. Downs's (2004) Master's thesis on the Mound 3 Summit excavations.

In 1997 we also investigated the Mound 4 Flats, again with the hope of uncovering architectural remains. Two blocks were opened up in this part of the site. Block 1 was very interesting because it produced the remains of a small, buried mound. There is no visible surface expression to this mound, but excavations revealed a clear dome. Beasley excavated this area and discovered evidence of feasting behavior, which was the focus of his Master's thesis (Beasley 1998, 2007). A wall trench dating to the Anna phase (A.D. 1200–1350) was discovered beneath this small mound. On the southern end of the Mound 4 Flats another block was excavated under the direction of Tony Boudreaux. A series of individually set post features arranged in an oval pattern came to light not far below the surface. This unusual structure was the subject of Jennifer Warhop's Master's thesis (Warhop 2005).

The Anna Great Ravine

Let us now turn our attention to a part of the site that few visitors of the past or present have ever seen—the Great Ravine (Figure 12.3). I can assure the reader that only the hardy prehistoric Indian would ever have approached Anna from the north, but thankfully a couple of modern Natchez residents elected to do so, or an important part of the Anna story would never be known. In 1980, as I was planning some new investigations in the Natchez region, Smokye Joe Frank and Robert Prospere told me of some discoveries that they had recently made in a ravine adjacent to the Anna site. Upon showing me some of the pottery that they had picked up in a wash far below the site, I immediately decided to take the plunge and see the context of these finds. Unfortunately there was only one way to get down to the Anna Great Ravine, and that involved a long rope. I did once take an Alabama Anthropology Club group into the ravine and, to this day, I thank my lucky stars that all of them came out unscathed. I would bet that each of these trusting students retains a vivid memory of this unique excursion into the past. Four of them even decided to pursue archaeology as a career! Over the years there have been reports of panthers and bears in the Great Ravine and I myself can testify to coyotes and water moccasins, so clearly one must be an animal-lover of sorts to make the plunge. As there are many diversions in the flow of the water below, with multiple side ravines, one would be hard-pressed to discover the source of the artifacts without a knowledgeable guide.

I myself have made the journey into the Great Ravine perhaps half a dozen times in the past three decades, and though some discoveries were made each time, none have ever matched the initial finds that were made by Prospere and Frank. That's because the materials that they discovered had had ample time to accumulate. No one knows exactly how this concentration of artifacts came about. The collection definitely has nothing to do with burials, because there are no whole vessels involved and human bones are totally lacking. But then again, the remains do not appear to be simply garbage, because if that were the case large quantities of animal bones would be expected as well. Instead, what exists, or rather existed, as the pickings are now very slim, are large fragments of plain and decorated vessels. I myself believe that there once must have been a large pit, or perhaps several moderate-sized pits, that were once filled with numerous smashed vessels. As the Great Ravine gradually extended into the site, eroding the soil from above, eventually one or more of these pits were penetrated. Then it was only a matter of time before the contents came crashing down into the depths. Through time, and with ample amounts of rain, the sherds were cleansed of their dirt and began to sit on little pillars of earth, somewhat akin to pedestals in an exhibit. Here they sat waiting for another crush of earth from above to hide them forever. It is archaeology's good fortune that Prospere and Frank interrupted this process when they ventured into the Great Ravine in the late 1970s.

The Pottery Collection

This report deals only with the pottery collection amassed by Robert Prospere.[1] Even though the material must necessarily be considered one big surface collection because it lacks provenience information, it is important to note that the Great Ravine pottery is atypical. Although many of the same types and varieties occur in well-controlled excavations from Anna, the pot fragments from the Great Ravine are not simply larger versions of excavated sherds. If, as I suspect, the bulk of these artifacts are smashed pots from a single or multiple pits, they may be saying something about the kinds of vessels that were used in ritual contexts. We will never know for sure, or at least not until an intact pit is actually investigated, but it will perhaps be beneficial to at least get the Great Ravine material on record. The rest of this paper is a descriptive report on the Prospere Collection from this important location. It is based on a more detailed analytical report, which is preserved in manuscript form in the Gulf Coast Survey Archives at the University of Alabama (Brown 2011).

Table 12.1 is a listing of the pottery in Prospere's collection from the Great Ravine. A total of 208 sherds was found from a maximum of 177 vessels. I will present the material in a general chronological order. The earliest pottery in the collection is a sherd of Tammany Punctated, *var. Duckroost*, which dates to the Tchula period (Figure 12.4a) and a Marksville Stamped, *var. Manny* sherd of Marksville period date (Figure 12.4b). The latter is heavily waterworn. There is very little Baytown period material to speak of in the collection, but

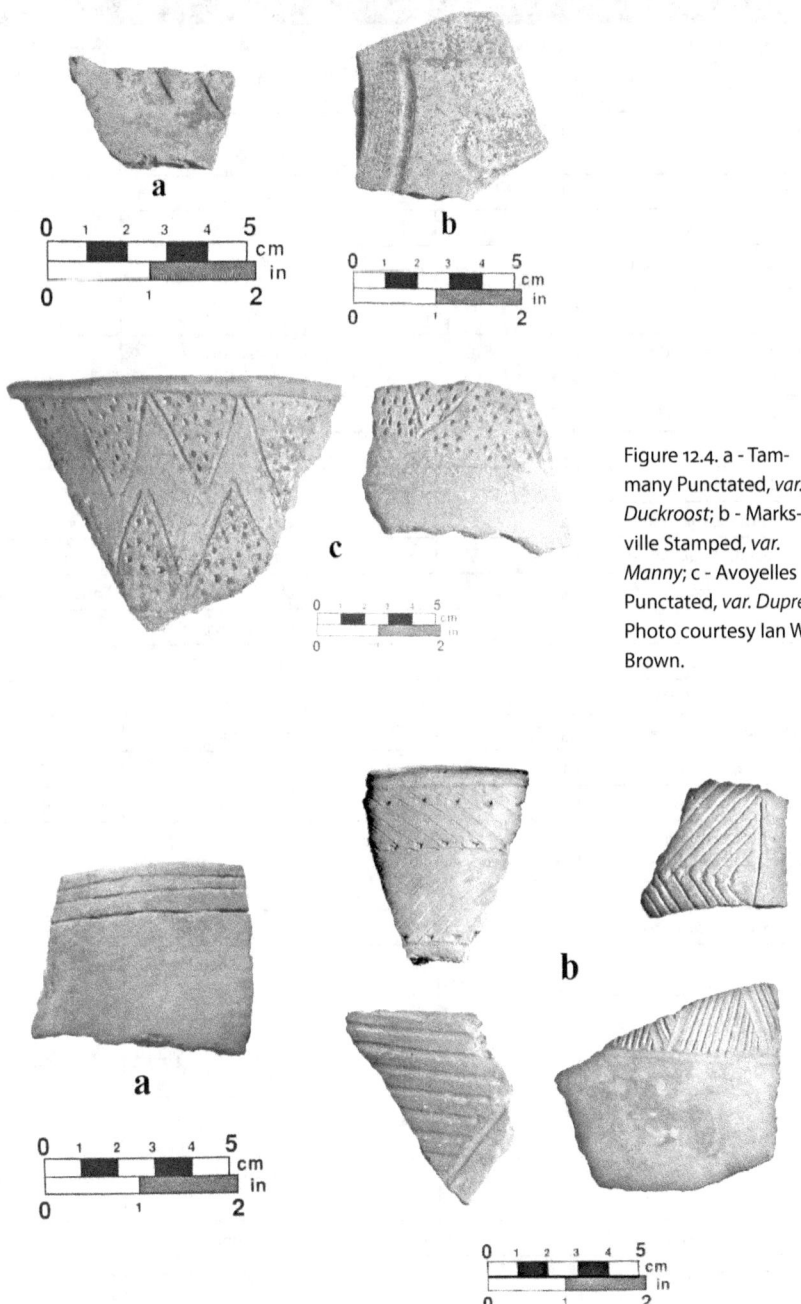

Figure 12.4. a - Tammany Punctated, *var. Duckroost*; b - Marksville Stamped, *var. Manny*; c - Avoyelles Punctated, *var. Dupree*. Photo courtesy Ian W. Brown.

Figure 12.5. a - Coles Creek Incised, *var. unspecified*; b - Mazique Incised, *var. Kings Point*. Photo courtesy Ian W. Brown.

Table 12.1. Pottery from the Great Ravine at the Anna site.

Type/Variety	No. of Sherds	Maximum No. of Vessels Represented	Period	Natchez Region Phases
Addis Plain, *var. Ratcliffe*	1	1	Late Mississippi, Historic	Emerald, Natchez
Addis Plain, *var. Ravine*	8	8	Mississippi	
Addis Plain, *var. unspecified*	24	24	Mississippi	
Unclassified Combed, Incised, and Punctated on Addis Plain *var. unspecified*	1	1	Late Mississippi	
Unclassified Incised on Addis Plain, *var. unspecified*	2	2	Mississippi	
Anna Engraved, *var. unspecified*	1	1	Early Mississippi	
Anna Incised, *var. Anna*	7	7	Early Mississippi	Anna
Anna Incised, *var. unspecified*	1	1	Early Mississippi	
Avenue Polychrome, *var. Avenue*	2	2	Terminal Mississippi	
Avoyelles Punctated, *var. Dupree*	2	2	Coles Creek	Gordon
Barton Incised, *var. Arcola*	5	4	Late Mississippi	Foster, Emerald
Barton Incised, *var. Barton*	2	2	Late Mississippi	
Barton Incised, *var. Portland*	1	1	Historic	
Barton Incised, *var. unspecified*	3	3	Mississippi	
Baytown Plain, *var. unspecified*	3	3	Post-Tchula	
Bell Plain, *var. unspecified*	1	1	Mississippi	
Coleman Incised, *var. Bass*	2	2	Mississippi	Foster, Emerald
Coleman Incised, *var. Coleman* and Plaquemine Brushed, *var. Plaquemine*	1	1	Mississippi	
Coles Creek Incised, *var. unspecified*	1	1	Coles Creek	
Combination Coles Creek Incised, *var. Hardy* and Mazique Incised, *var. Manchac*	1	1	Terminal Coles Creek	Gordon
Cracker Road Incised, *var. Cracker Road*	1	1	Terminal Mississippi, Historic	
Cracker Road Incised, *var. unspecified*	1	1	Terminal Mississippi, Historic	
Fatherland Incised, *var. Fatherland*	8	6	Late Mississippi, Historic	Emerald, Natchez
Fatherland Incised, *var. Pine Ridge*	1	1	Mississippi	Foster
Fatherland Incised, *var. Stanton*	1	1	Mississippi, Historic	Foster, Emerald, Natchez
Fatherland Incised, *var. unspecified*	5	2	Mississippi, Historic	
Grace Brushed, *var. Grace*	1	1	Early Mississippi	Anna
Grace Brushed, *var. Grand Gulf*	1	1	Late Mississippi	

Plaquemine Culture Pottery, the Great Ravine at the Anna Site

Type/Variety	No. of Sherds	Maximum No. of Vessels Represented	Period	Natchez Region Phases
Hollyknowe Pinched, *var. Patmos*	3	1	Terminal Coles Creek, Early Mississippi	Gordon, Anna
L'Eau Noire Incised, *var. L'Eau Noire*	3	3	Early Mississippi	Anna
L'Eau Noire Incised, *var. unspecified*	2	2	Early Mississippi	
Leland Incised, *var. Blanchard*	4	1	Late Mississippi, Historic	Emerald, Natchez
Leland Incised, *var. Bovina*	1	1	Late Mississippi	
Leland Incised, *var. Ferris*	2	2	Mississippi	Foster
Leland Incised, *var. Foster*	11	8	Mississippi	Foster, Emerald
Leland Incised, *var. Leflore*	5	1	Late Mississippi, Historic	Emerald, Natchez
Leland Incised, *var. Leland*	5	3	Mississippi	Foster
Leland Incised, *var. Russell*	3	3	Late Mississippi, Historic	Emerald, Natchez
Maddox Engraved, *var. Emerald*	6	6	Mississippi, Historic	Foster, Emerald, Natchez
Maddox Engraved, *var. Silver City*	11	7	Mississippi	Foster, Emerald
Marksville Stamped, *var. Manny*	1	1	Middle and Late Marksville	
Mazique Incised *var. Kings Point*	5	5	Coles Creek	Balmoral
Mazique Incised, *var. Manchac*	21	20	Coles Creek, Mississippi	Gordon, Foster, Emerald, Natchez
Mazique Incised, *var. unspecified*	3	1	Coles Creek, Mississippi	
Mississippi Plain, *var. unspecified*	6	2	Mississippi	
Mound Place Incised, *var. Chickasawba*	1	1	Late Mississippi	
Mound Place Incised, *var. unspecified*	2	2	Mississippi	
Moundville Incised, *var. unspecified*	3	3	Mississippi	
Mulberry Creek Cord Marked, *var. Smith Creek*	1	1	Late Baytown, Early Coles Creek	Sundown
Nodena Red and White, *var. Nodena*	1	1	Late Mississippi	
Parkin Punctated, *var. Hollandale*	1	1	Mississippi	Anna, Foster
Plaquemine Brushed, *var. Plaquemine*	15	15	Terminal Coles Creek, Mississippi	Gordon, Anna, Foster
Pouncey Pinched, *var. Patosi*	1	1	Early Mississippi	
Pouncey Pinched, *var. unspecified*	1	1	Mississippi	
Tammany Punctated, *var. Duckroost*	1	1	Tchula	Homochitto
Winterville Incised, *var. Winterville*	1	1	Mississippi	Anna, Foster
Total	208	177		

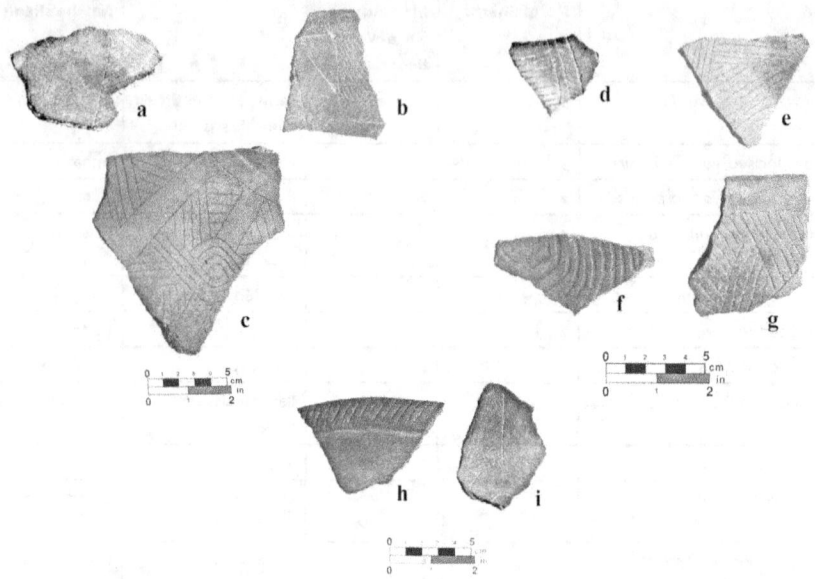

Figure 12.6. a–g - Anna Incised, *var. Anna*; h - Anna Incised, *var. unspecified*; i - Anna Engraved, *var. unspecified*. Photo courtesy Ian W. Brown.

there is some late to terminal Coles Creek pottery in the form of Avoyelles Punctated, *var. Dupree* (Figure 12.4c), Coles Creek Incised, *var. unspecified* (Figure 12.5a), and Mazique Incised, *var. Kings Point* (Figure 12.5b). All the rest of the material relates to the Plaquemine Culture.

In all probability most of the pottery is decorated simply because it was high-graded during collection. The plain pottery consists essentially of rims or very large body sherds of grog-tempered Addis Plain, and there are also some large portions of whole or nearly whole unusual vessels of a new variety named Addis Plain, *var. Great Ravine*. I was tempted to call the variety "Crud," but as that name harkens back to "Cahokia Crud" or Stump Ware (Milner 1998:17–18; Titterington 1938), I certainly do not want to suggest historical connections. Suffice to say that this small sample of plain ware sherds from Anna is not a pretty sight, and yet there is enough uniformity to the material to warrant varietal assignment. The ware itself is the standard "heterogeneous grog-tempered" Addis Plain, with an inclination toward *var. Ratcliffe* in that the vessels are highly oxidized. There is no additional smoothing to the surface, either on the interior or exterior. In fact, there appears to have been a purposeful roughening up of the surfaces. At least five of the vessels are small open bowls of saucer shape and size, which have gently rounded bases.

As might be expected, Anna Incised is also well represented in the Prospere Collection from the Great Ravine. Line-filled triangles appear to be the basic motif, but when the design expands, as it does for sherds b and c in Figure 12.6, it is obvious that far more complexity is involved. Sherds e and g in Figure 12.6 also have line-filled triangles, but for e there appears to be a curvilinear element in one corner. Sherd a has multiple parallel lines as fillers of alternating bands, while f has an unusual tight spiral. The latter looks like a Leland Incised, *var. Ferris* treatment that was simply applied to the interior.

Anna Engraved (Figure 12.6i) is a new type, but obviously it is closely related to Anna Incised. In the Mobile-Tensaw Delta of Alabama we found considerable utility in separating D'Olive Engraved from D'Olive Incised because it clearly has chronological significance, with the engraved type occurring earlier in the Pensacola culture sequence (Fuller and Brown 1998; Fuller 2003:43–44). In the Lower Mississippi Valley Anna started off its professional life as Anna Interior Engraved (Ford and Willey 1940:55) but, as Phillips (1970:102) pointed out, most of the lines were not executed post-firing. Consequently, we're really talking about the narrowness of the lines and the care with which they were executed on a dry paste. Phillips elected to include the *Anna* variety under the L'Eau Noire Incised type, emphasizing decorative treatment over placement on vessel. But when Williams and Brain (1983:118–120) revisited the issue as part of the Lake George site analysis, they found it useful to resurrect the Anna type in order to keep together varieties that had interior designs on grog-tempered bowls and plates. They retained the "Incised" name in its binomial designation for the same reason put forth by Phillips. The only reason why I am reviving Anna Engraved here is to account for interior decorated sherds on an Addis Plain ware in which all lines, both boundary and filler, are very fine and post-fired. The treatment is admittedly rare, but I suspect it might be significant.

It is also rare to find Avenue Polychrome in the Natchez Bluffs region, so when it does occur it really does need to be highlighted (Figure 12.7). Despite extensive digging in three blocks during the 1997 excavations at Anna, not a single Avenue Polychrome sherd was found. Interestingly enough, the two sherds in the Prospere Collection are not from the same vessel. Both are probably portions of bottles. It is worth mentioning that Avenue Polychrome is a terminal prehistoric/protohistoric marker in northwestern Mississippi and eastern Arkansas (Brain et al. 1974:Table 1; Brown 2008:Table 16.2), which is supportive of Anna's occupation having continued as late as the mid-sixteenth century. There are many other good standard Mississippian types in the collection as well, including Nodena Red and White, *var. Nodena*, Parkin Punctated, *var. Hollandale*, Pouncey Pinched, *var. Patosi*, and Winterville Incised,

Ian W. Brown

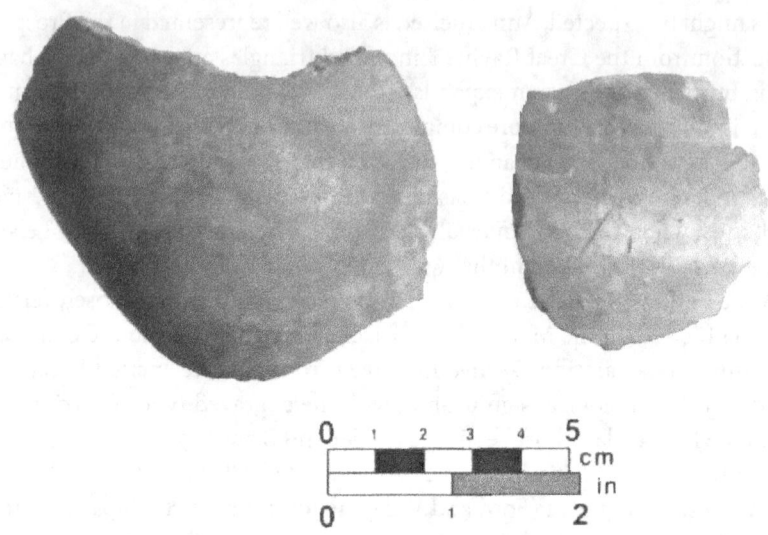

Figure 12.7. Avenue Polychrome, *var. Avenue*. Photo courtesy Ian W. Brown.

Figure 12.8. a - Mulberry Creek Cord Marked, *var. Smith Creek*; b - Nodena Red and White, *var. Nodena*; c - Parkin Punctated, *var. Hollandale*; d - Pouncey Pinched, *var. Patosi*; e - Winterville Incised, *var. Winterville*. Photo courtesy Ian W. Brown.

Plaquemine Culture Pottery, the Great Ravine at the Anna Site

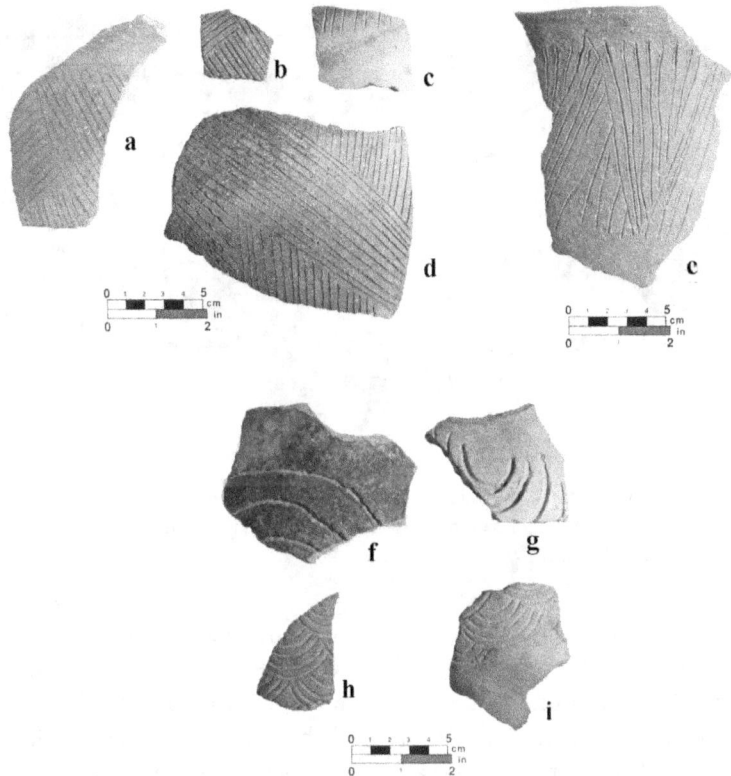

Figure 12.9. a–d - Barton Incised, *var. Arcola*; e - Barton Incised, *var. Barton*; f–g - Coleman Incised, *var. Bass*; h–i - Coleman Incised, *var. Coleman*. Photo courtesy Ian W. Brown.

var. Winterville (Figure 12.8). Either there are a lot of Mississippian influences at Anna in terms of the movement of people or trade, or this is simply part of the Anna repertoire. If the latter, however, those connections do not show up clearly in the excavations we have conducted at the site, which is very curious indeed.

There are five sherds of Barton Incised in the collection that fit the sorting criteria for *Arcola* in that they have well-executed rectilinear lines on the shoulder of shell-tempered vessels (Figure 12.9a–d). Sherds a and d are possibly portions of the same vessel with ware equivalent to Mississippi Plain, while c occurs on Bell Plain ware, and b is somewhere in between the two, all very disturbing to the archaeologist who insists on neat orderly packaging. All of these sherds display line-filled triangles as the recurring pattern. Barton Incised, *var. Barton* also occurs in the collection, as represented by this crudely executed pattern of line-filled triangles on the neck of a coarse shell-tempered jar (Figure 12.9e).

Figure 12.10. Combination of Types-Varieties. a - Coleman Incised, *var. Coleman* and Plaquemine Brushed, *var. Plaquemine*; b - Coles Creek Incised, *var. Hardy* and Mazique Incised, *var. Manchac*. Photo courtesy Ian W. Brown.

Two different vessels of Coleman Incised, *var. Bass* vessels are represented (Figure 12.9f–g). The designs of both are confined to the shoulders and, perhaps, to the bodies of medium-sized jars. The two Coleman Incised, *var. Coleman* sherds (Figure 12.9h–i) are probably from the same vessel, a thin carefully made beaker. It exhibits a fish-scale pattern over the greater portion of its exterior surface, stopping short of where the body curves inward to form the base.

Vessels that combine types are a typological nightmare when one is determined to place sherds in nice, neatly labeled cultural containers. Yet, they are a boon to those interested in establishing contemporaneity between types/varieties, as well as in exploring potters' decisions as to what designs might occasionally be considered complementary. Two sherds in the Great Ravine at Anna reveal interesting combinations. In Figure 12.10a the decorations Coleman Incised, *var. Coleman*, and Plaquemine Brushed, *var. Plaquemine* combine on a flared jar. The brushing is confined to a band on the neck and consists of horizontal strokes within opposing triangles. The incised line that forms the triangles was applied prior to brushing. The shoulder of the vessel, and perhaps the whole body, bears a fish-scale pattern, which can also be seen on the two Coleman Incised, *var. Coleman* sherds in the collection. Figure 12.10b combines on a flared jar Coles Creek Incised, *var. Hardy* and Mazique Incised, *var. Manchac*. The decorative zones are large enough so that had the sherd been broken into smaller pieces they would have been divided into these distinct type-varieties. Types are not "supposed" to do such combining

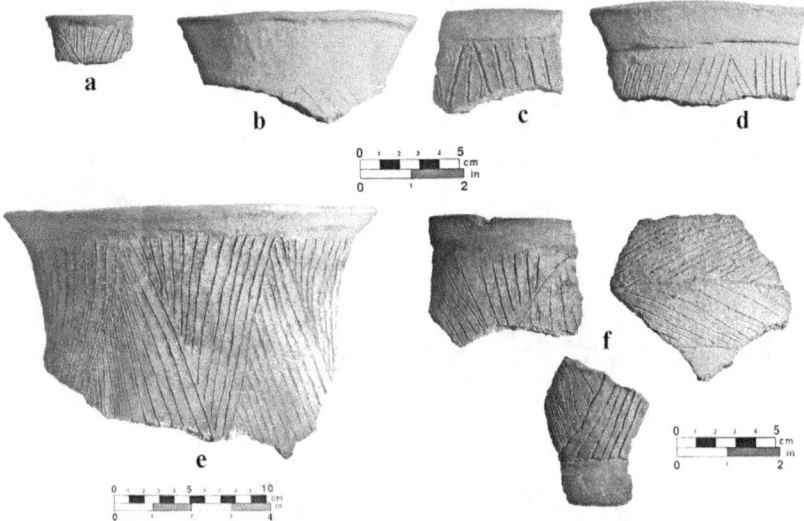

Figure 12.11. a - Barton Incised, *var. Barton*; b–f - Mazique Incised, *var. Manchac*. Photo courtesy Ian W. Brown.

in the Lower Mississippi Valley, but this sorter at least is content with such, because it is possible to learn much from the "rule-breakers."

Twenty-one sherds from 20 distinct Mazique Incised, *var. Manchac* vessels occur in the Prospere Collection (Figure 12.11b–f). *Manchac* is not only the best represented type-variety in the collection, but it also wins the award for the largest sherds (e.g., Figure 12.11e). All of the vessels are flared jars and some exhibit soot marks on the exterior, evidence for a cooking function. Thirteen of the vessels exhibit typical line-filled triangles, one vessel has a herringbone design, and one vessel bears line-filled diamonds (Figure 12.11f).

Plaquemine Brushed, *var. Plaquemine* is well represented in the collection from the Great Ravine, both in terms of numbers and in the size of the sherds (Figure 12.12). As with the *Manchac* sample, despite the quantity of *Plaquemine*, there are no sherds that join. Each one represents a distinct vessel. The most common form is the flared jar, but in one case a deep bowl is represented. There is a wide selection of brush strokes that occur in varying combinations. The principal brush strokes are either parallel to the rim in wide horizontal bands or set at an angle, but what the potters did afterward varied considerably. Sometimes the horizontal brushed zone is decorated with columns of punctations (Figure 12.12g), or sometimes single diagonal incisions run through the zone forming triangles (Figure 12.12h). Brush-filled triangles are also common, sometimes in combination with horizontal brushing (Figure 12.12i). The only difference between this and *Manchac* is that brushing

Figure 12.12. a–j - Plaquemine Brushed, *var. Plaquemine*. Photo courtesy Ian W. Brown.

was used instead of incising. I have no doubt that the same people were making both kinds of pots. Three *Plaquemine* vessels exhibit the "classic mode," a row of circular or rectangular punctations at the base of the decorative zone (Figure 12.12j).

There are two Grace Brushed sherds in the Prospere Collection (Figure 12.13). One I have assigned to *var. Grace* based on the rectilinear brushing and the other to *var. Grand Gulf* because of the curvilinear treatment. What bothers me, though, is that despite appearances, the latter might not actually be Grace Brushed. The various lines, which are neatly executed, could have been made with a comb that had between four and six prongs, but if so there is a typological problem. We unfortunately lack a shell-tempered type for combing!

And here's another problem, an unclassified combed, incised, and punctated sherd on Addis Plain, *var. unspecified* ware that defies classification (Figure 12.14). It is from a flared jar that has a curvilinear combed design on its shoulder that presumably extended over much of its body. The broad band of

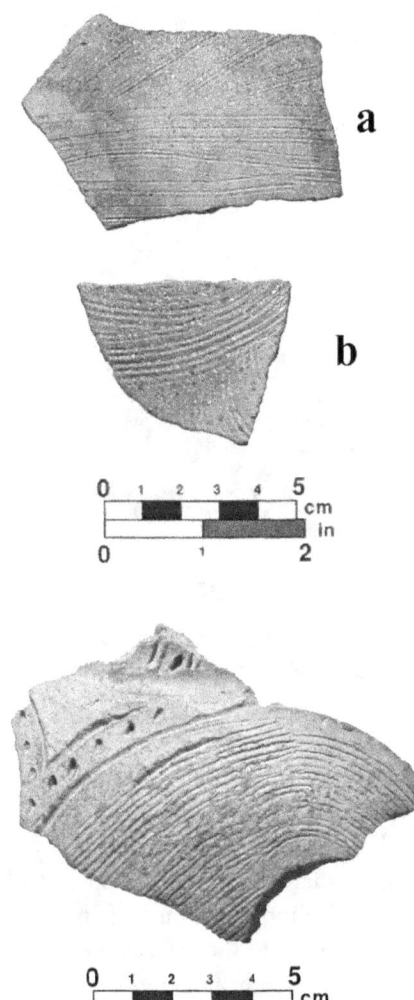

Figure 12.13. a - Grace Brushed, *var. Grace*; b - Grace Brushed, *var. Grand Gulf*. Photo courtesy Ian W. Brown.

Figure 12.14. Unclassified Combed, Incised and Punctated on Addis Plain, *var. unspecified* ware. Photo courtesy Ian W. Brown.

combing, which almost appears to be brushing, was made with an instrument that had four prongs. It was lifted and placed adjacent to previously executed runs so that the overall impression is one of continuity. Two incised lines form an inverted "V" at the shoulder of the vessel and a single row of punctations graces the interior of the resulting band. This is obviously a Matthews Incised (Phillips 1970:127–128) or Moundville Incised (Steponaitis 1983:323–326) idea, but the vessel lacks shell. The body decoration is reminiscent of the Caddoan type Cowhide Stamped (Suhm and Jelks 1962:29, pl. 15), but it sure would be nice to know what the rim decoration was like. All that can be said at this

Figure 12.15. a–c - Moundville Incised, *var. unspecified*; d - Mound Place Incised, *var. Chickasawba*; e - Mazique Incised, *var. unspecified*. Photo courtesy Ian W. Brown.

point is that it is a "ringer," locally made I believe, but with influences from the Caddoan country to the west and perhaps from Mississippians to the north and east.

There is definitely Moundville Incised at the Anna site, as represented in three sherds from the Prospere Collection (Figure 12.15a–c). Moundville Incised is almost unheard of in the Natchez Bluffs region. The type is far more at home to the east, as the name itself implies. It is characterized by a series of incised or punctated arches arranged around the shoulder of coarse shell-tempered jars. What makes these three sherds from Anna so troublesome, however, is that a is on Bell Plain ware and b and c are on Addis Plain. Had coarse shell been involved, a would have been sorted as *var. Moundville*, with the eyelash motif (Steponaitis 1983:Figure 42a–h), and b and c would have been classified as *var. Douglas* (Fuller and Stowe 1982:64–65). I do realize that what I have done here is a major *faux pas* in type-variety terms, in that Moundville Incised is always supposed to be coarse shell temper, but in my defense it could be that the Natchez potters who made these vessels were simply unaware of that rule. They may have just copied the type onto their own typical Addis Plain pottery. I could have (and perhaps should have) sorted the sherds as "Unclassified Incised and Punctated on Bell Plain/Addis Plain," but if I did so the likelihood is that we would lose sight of them. Moundville

Incised was the idea, of that I have no doubt, and so I highlight that connection by using the type. Having done this, though, I am hesitant to apply any cross-dating principles. The *Moundville* variety is early in the Mississippi period while the *Douglas* variety is very late, but whether comparable dating can be used for these three sherds from Anna I cannot say. It should also be pointed out that although b and c seem to be portions of the same vessel, they are not. An incised line forms the border between the neck and shoulder of sherd c, which is just barely visible at the top of the sherd, but that line is absent on sherd b. I suspect that the same potter may have been involved in their construction, however, because they certainly do look a lot alike.

Mound Place Incised, *var. Chickasawba* consists of finely crafted vessels bearing multiple horizontal lines on ware equivalent to Bell Plain. In the Mobile-Tensaw Delta I would have unhesitatingly put this specimen under *var. McMillan* (Fuller and Brown 1998:Table 2, Figure 68e, Figure 74a). Although Fuller and Stowe (1982:66) felt that the Mound Place type "appears to have been halted around the area of Vicksburg by the stubborn Plaquemine Culture," the Anna site is clearly deep within the heart of Plaquemine country. In fact, it is quite possible that this sherd from Anna (Figure 12.15d) is the best example of the *Chickasawba* variety on record, both in terms of quality of manufacture and sheer size. The vessel itself is a simple bowl with a thickened rim. As with the *Waltons Camp* variety of Mound Place Incised in the Pensacola Culture (Fuller and Stowe 1982:66–68), the *Chickasawba* sherd from Anna has a loop, which forms a horizontal "P." Whether or not an effigy adorno or lug also once existed is not evident, but these traits are certainly characteristic of the *Chickasawba* variety elsewhere.

There are more ringers in the collection that make for uneasy sorting using the type-variety system alone. For example, had less of the sherd in Figure 12.15e existed I would have felt reasonably comfortable classifying it as *var. Manchac*. As it is, I am not overly happy even with the Mazique Incised designation, but it is tentatively sorted as such so that it does not get lost, which so often happens with "Unclassified Incised" sherds. The design consists of a continuous pattern of alternating line-filled triangles and diamond zones on the body of a jar. Wide-spaced multiple horizontal lines occur on the neck. The latter tend to be broad and U-shaped in cross-section, whereas the rectilinear lines are narrower, deeper, and more pointed. All in all, the vessel decoration screams Caddoan to me, but thus far I have been unable to place it.

Here are some other conundrums. Three of the sherds in Figure 12.16 (a–c) fit the L'Eau Noire Incised, *var. L'Eau Noire* description to the letter. I have classified the d sherd under the L'Eau Noire Incised type, but I am not pleased with that decision. Its design consists of four parallel lines arranged in a stepped fashion, but what bothers me is that the lines are trailed, which

Figure 12.16. a–c - L'Eau Noire Incised, *var. L'Eau Noire*; d–e - L'Eau Noire Incised, *var. unspecified*. Photo courtesy Ian W. Brown.

is not supposed to happen with the type. Moreover, the ware verges on Bell Plain, which is also not supposed to happen. The trailed treatment, however, is more typical of Leland Incised, but that type of course requires curvilinear lines. Obviously, I opted for rectilinearity as the deciding factor for classifying the sherd as L'Eau Noire Incised, but I could just as easily have flipped a coin. The other sherd that I classified as L'Eau Noire Incised also has a stepped design, which presumably repeats around the entire body of the vessel (Figure 12.16e). However, the ware for this sherd is definitely Bell Plain, which, again, is not supposed to happen.

Here's another typological puzzle. I debated including the vessel represented by the two sherds in Figure 12.17a as Anna Incised, but elected to classify it as Leland Incised, *var. Blanchard* based on its design, which consists of a series of festoons arranged along the interior rim of the bowl. The bowl itself is carinated, and its lip has notching on the exterior. Although the design fits the criteria for *var. Blanchard*, it should be noted that the line treatment is not quite right. Instead of trailed incisions, the lines are pointed and were drawn when the ware was relatively dry. Another problem, perhaps more critical, is that whereas *Blanchard* in the Yazoo Basin occurs on shell-tempered ware, this vessel from Anna is decidedly Addis Plain, *var. Greenville*. In the Pensacola

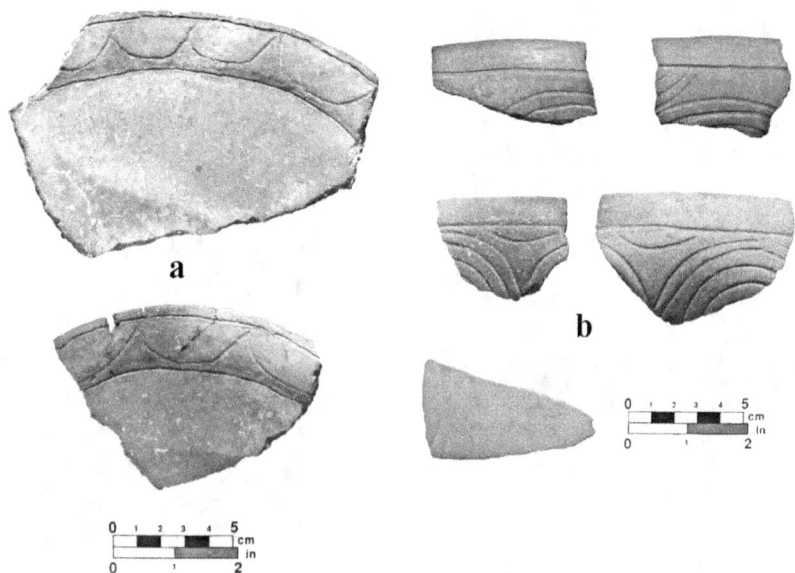

Figure 12.17. a - Leland Incised, *var. Blanchard*; b - Leland Incised, *var. Leland*. Photo courtesy Ian W. Brown.

Culture area along the northern Gulf Coast this decoration fits snugly within the D'Olive Incised type; *var. D'Olive* in fact, but the ware for D'Olive Incised is also shell and the line treatment tends toward trailed (Fuller and Stowe 1982:56). When festoons are used instead of arches the result is a sun pattern, a design that also appears on sandstone disks (alternatively or simultaneously, it could be a scalp pattern). Anna can now be added to the mix with Fatherland (Neitzel 1965:Figure 21b) as sites in the Natchez Bluffs region that have exhibited the sun design on up-facing surfaces such as plates and disks. This practice has been observed along a broad arc in the western portion of the southeastern United States from sites dating from the late Mississippi period (Brown 2004).

As would be expected for a prime Plaquemine mound center like Anna, the type Leland Incised is very commonly represented in the Prospere Collection. Included are the *Leland* variety (Figure 12.17b), the *Foster* variety (Figure 12.18a), and the *Russell* variety (Figure 12.18b). These three varieties differ from each other primarily on the size and amount of shell in the ware, which is not something that gives one a great deal of confidence in sorting. Certain Leland Incised vessels, like *Ferris* (Figure 12.18c) and *Leflore* (Figure 12.18d) can at least be sorted on the basis of design mode, but that offers minimal comfort when the size of the sherd diminishes. That "unspecified" category looms large.

Figure 12.18. a - Leland Incised, *var. Foster*; b - Leland Incised, *var. Russell*; c - Leland Incised, *var. Ferris*; d - Leland Incised, *var. Leflore*. Photo courtesy Ian W. Brown.

I would be remiss not to mention the fine representation of Maddox Engraved, *vars. Emerald* and *Silver City* in the Prospere Collection from the Great Ravine. They are separated essentially in terms of the quality of the technique, with *Emerald* being the sloppy version of crosshatching fillers between trailed lines (Figure 12.19a). *Silver City*, on the other hand, is somewhat more nicely executed (Figure 12.19b–c). I basically separate it using the "Wow factor." If I say "Wow," it more often than not ends up in the *Silver City* box. Having said that, though, I know of no distributional differences that would suggest that the two varieties have spatial, temporal, or social distinctions, so I'm beginning to feel that pure excitement may not be a valid sorting criterion. The sherds are a striking red, but this is not paint. It is a highly oxidized paste.

I would like to make mention of a number of sherds and partial vessels in the Prospere Collection that indicate the site continued to be occupied much later than is often realized. The Avenue Polychrome and Nodena Red and White sherds mentioned earlier (Figures 12.7 and 12.8b) are indicative

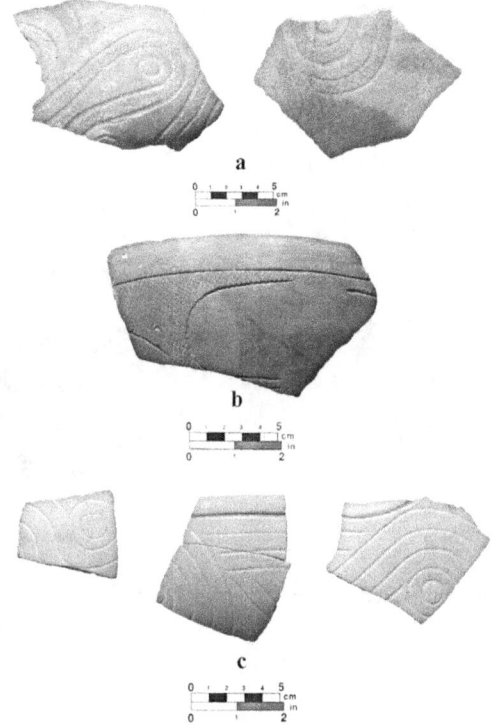

Figure 12.19. a - Maddox Engraved, *var. Emerald*; b–c - Maddox Engraved, *var. Silver City*. Photo courtesy Ian W. Brown.

of a protohistoric component at the site, and the strong presence of Fatherland Incised, *var. Fatherland* (Figure 12.20a) in the collection confirms it. This material probably dates to either the Emerald or historic Natchez phase. Varieties *Pine Ridge* and *Stanton* also occur (Figure 12.20b–c), but sometimes it is only possible to classify as to type, as in one example of a Fatherland Incised, *var. unspecified* partial vessel (Figure 12.20e). This simple bowl has a two-line band that undulates around the body of the vessel, forming a squashed scroll pattern. Nested festoons, presumably four to the pot, drop from a rim line in the intervening spaces. The design reminds me of the haunches for a frog effigy, as I have seen similar end pieces elsewhere in the Lower Mississippi Valley. This might be what the Anna potter was aiming for, but obviously it is quite abstract. The base of the vessel is round and slightly concave.

One type that I can certainly vouch for as protohistoric or historic is Cracker Road Incised. I defined this type in the Yazoo Bluffs region when I was doing my graduate research at Fort St. Pierre and surrounding sites back in the 1970s (Brown 1979:645–654; 1983:3–4, Figs. 5–7). The vessel shown in Figure 12.21a

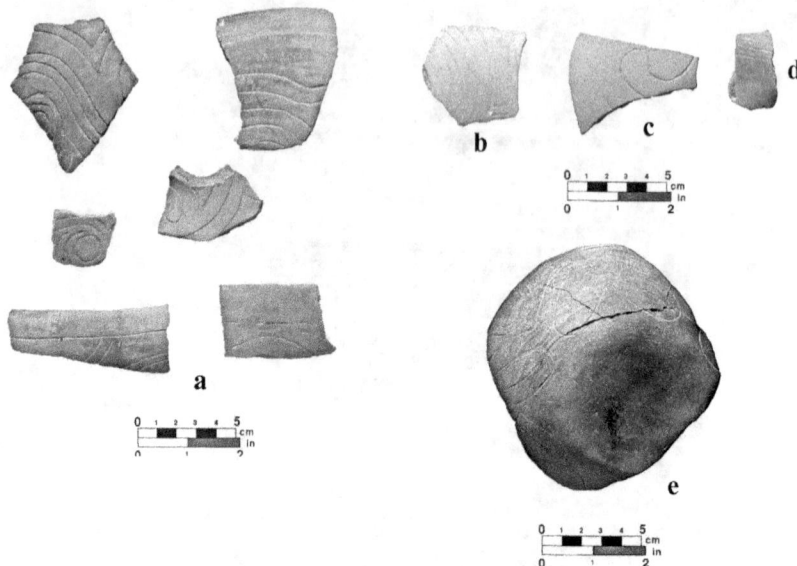

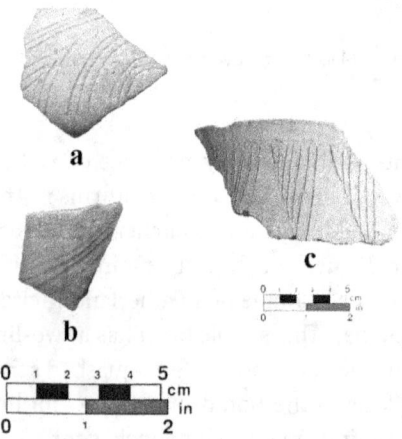

Figure 12.20. a - Fatherland Incised, *var. Fatherland*; b - Fatherland Incised, *var. Pine Ridge*; c - Fatherland Incised, *var. Stanton*; d–e - Fatherland Incised, *var. unspecified*. Photo courtesy Ian W. Brown.

Figure 12.21. a - Cracker Road Incised, *var. Cracker Road*; b - Cracker Road Incised, *var. unspecified*; c - Barton Incised, *var. Portland*. Photo courtesy Ian W. Brown.

is a bowl decorated with a typical three-line sunburst pattern. The idea for such apparently came from the Fatherland Incised type, the prime difference between the types being that Cracker Road Incised is shell tempered. The ware for both of these particular sherds is Bell Plain. Finally, the *Portland* variety of Barton Incised is definitely of late-seventeenth-/early eighteenth-century date in the Yazoo Bluffs region (Brown 1979:613–616; 1983:6, Figure 13.9). It consists of bands of line-filled triangles that alternate with plain triangles and, to my way of thinking, is a solid historic marker (Figure 12.21c).

Concluding Thoughts

Having relayed all this information, I must confess that I am not especially happy with my way of thinking. Hopefully the reader has gained an appreciation of the degree and diversity of ceramic material from the Prospere Collection, but one may also detect a certain amount of frustration in my applying the type-variety approach to its classification. Years ago Smokye Joe Frank told me that when he gave Jon Gibson a tour of Anna and showed him the pottery, Jon said words to the effect, "Well Phillips's classification seems to work well at Anna." I can add to that by saying, "It does and it doesn't." Using the system has certainly helped me sort the material into piles that can be described and presented, but too often there are ringers that send things spinning. Tempers do not hold to the standards, design modes break down, or vessel shapes just don't fit expectations. As I hope I have shown, this is not the end of the world. Had I not used the system to begin with, I would not have recognized all that was strange, and it is often the strangeness that is most interesting with regard to human behavior. If this material came out of a series of pits, which I believe is likely, the one thing that can be said about them is that the events they represent do not fit the pattern of the normal course of life at Anna. The pots are certainly not like those found with burials in Mound 5 at this site (Cotter 1951); and nor are they akin to the standard wares associated with life on and around the mounds that are commonly found in middens. I suspect that these pits, or at least their contents, were associated with festive occasions wherein peoples came from afar bearing vessels that were somewhat different from the Anna site norm. As the pottery in the Great Ravine collection dates from different times, with the bulk of them ranging from the early Mississippi period to protohistoric times, the suggestion is that the events themselves were not all that uncommon. What exactly the festivities entailed can only be imagined at this distant date. Sadly enough, pots can only tell us so much.

Note

1. The stone artifacts in Prospere's collection consisted of two Edwards Stemmed, *var. unspecified* projectile point/knives; two unclassified projectile point/knives; and a broken pebble celt (Brown 2011:94–96, Figure 83).

PART IV

The Contact and Historic Periods

CHAPTER 13

Excavations at the South Thomas Street Site (22LE1002): An Early Eighteenth-Century Hamlet Located on the Periphery of the Major Chickasaw Settlement in Northeastern Mississippi

Jay K. Johnson and Edward R. Henry

Chief Fattalamee, finding that the warriors had the best time of it, that slave Catching was much more profitable than formall haranguing, he then turned Warrior too, and proved as good a man hunter as the best of them. But for this infringing the Constitutions, the people don't regard him as king, for it seems they're of a whiggish opinion that the Duties of the King and people are reciprocall that, if he failes in his they've sufficient cause to neglect their's.
—**Thomas Nairne,** letter to the Charles Town Board of Commissioners reporting on his 1708 visit to the Chickasaw Nation (Moore 1988:38–39)

Introduction

During the course of monitoring a pipeline route, a small archaeological site containing a Woodland and a Chickasaw component was located in the Coonewah Creek drainage of central Lee County, northeastern Mississippi (Johnson 2009). The site (22LE1002) is located on a ridge just to the south of the Mississippi Department of Transportation (MDOT) right-of-way for the relocation of State Route 6. Four small features and several post molds were uncovered in a stripping operation that was designed to locate cultural resources. In accordance with data recovery stipulations specified by Mississippi Department of Archives and History (MDAH) in consultation with the Chickasaw Nation and the Tennessee Valley Authority, these features were excavated and the spoil dirt from the site left over by the stripping operation was screened (Johnson and Henry 2011). Here, we discuss the findings from this work.

Natural and Cultural Background

The physiography and ground cover of the project area are determined primarily by the underlying geology. The survey area falls within the Black Prairie physiographic zone (Lowe 1911), which is characterized by rolling uplands and broad, flat stream bottoms. The primary geological formation underlying this zone is the Selma Chalk (Stephenson and Monroe 1940), on which developed clay and clay loam soils that supported oaks and hickory where the soil was relatively deep and red cedar, sweetgum, post oak, and prairie grasses where the soil was thin (Kuchler 1964; Lowe 1911). These broad upland prairies were a major factor in the early historic settlement of the region and may have been an important factor in a late prehistoric Chickasaw shift to an upland settlement system in northeastern Mississippi (Johnson 1996; see also Peacock and Rafferty 1996).

A substantial amount of archaeological research has been done in and around the city of Tupelo, Mississippi. Jennings (1941) set the stage for all the work to follow in his report of work done in preparation for the construction of the Natchez Trace Parkway. In that report he defined the major ceramic types for the Woodland and Chickasaw occupations of the area, and his sequence has withstood the test of time with minor revisions (Bohannon 1972; Cotter and Corbett 1951; Jenkins 1981). The Chickasaw portion of the ceramic sequence has also been refined (Atkinson 1987; Lieb 2004; Stubbs 1982) but still remains essentially the same. Although the region was obviously used during the Archaic period (see for example Johnson and Brookes's (1989) review of Benton caches in the area immediately to the south) and although Woodland sites are common in Lee County (Jennings 1941), there is relatively little Mississippian occupation in the uplands in the vicinity of the survey area (Johnson 1996; Stubbs 1983), even though there are Mississippian-period sites to the south of Lee County in the upland Prairie (Hogue and Peacock 1995; Rafferty 1996). Most of the archaeological research in Lee County has focused on the intensive colonial period Chickasaw settlement that centered on the city of Tupelo (Atkinson 1987; Johnson 2000; Johnson et al. 2008; Stubbs 1983; Underwood 1998). The majority of the recorded sites that fall near 22LE1002 relate to the Chickasaw occupation of north Mississippi.

Field Methods

The portion of the site exposed in the pipeline stripping lies just to the south of a narrow strip of mowed grass that is situated between the pipeline right-of-way and the recent road cut. The site undoubtedly continues to the north as far as the road cut because Chickasaw and earlier artifacts were found there. The edge of the road cut is located about 15 m from the southern limits of an earlier reported site, 22LE1002. The site card indicates a probable Woodland component on this site and nothing more, although the sample is small. Because the recorded site and the new site area are located on the same ridge, separated by a short distance, and both contain similar Woodland-period material, upon consultation with MDOT archaeologist John Underwood, the decision was made to consider these two locations to be part of the same site rather than assigning another site number.

Four pit features and 14 possible postholes were exposed in the stripped area. Feature 1 is a small, shallow pit that we cross-sectioned in order to determine whether it was a root stain or cultural feature. Feature 2 is a slightly larger pit. Several artifacts were uncovered in the process of troweling the surface to define the pit outlines. The edge of Feature 3 was clipped by the stripped area and shows only in the profile. Feature 4 is, by far, the largest of the features (Johnson and Henry 2011:Figures 1.13, 1.14). Once again, a small collection of artifacts was recovered while the feature was being exposed. In addition, a fairly large surface collection was made on the slope of the road cut. The surface collection and the artifacts recovered while troweling the surface of the features indicated that the site was occupied, at a minimum, during the Middle Woodland period and again during the early eighteenth century by a small group of Chickasaws.

In consultation with the Chickasaw Nation, the Tennessee Valley Authority, MDAH, and the Pontotoc, Union, Lee Development Authority, the following mitigation plan was developed: The remainder of the site would not be stripped. Instead, the pipeline would be run under the site using the same boring technology used in placing the pipeline under existing roads. All exposed features and postholes would be excavated by hand, using trowels. Each feature would first be sectioned by removing the southern half. The profile would be recorded and the remainder of the feature would be removed. A flotation sample would be taken for Features 2 and 4, which were of sufficient size to make this practical. All of the remaining feature fill would be water screened, using nested quarter-inch and window-screen mesh. In addition, the Chickasaw Nation requested that the back dirt be water screened.

During the initial evaluation of the site, what appeared to be human bones were found near the crest of the road cut, just to the north of the heaviest concentration of postholes exposed in the stripping operation. MDOT and the Chickasaw Nation were contacted. John Underwood and a crew of MDOT archaeologists visited the site on August 28, 2009, in order to evaluate the find. During a subsequent visit on September 2, 2009, they dug a north-south line of shovel tests through the east-west center of the site so that the southern boundary could be determined. Three out of four shovel tests were positive. The southernmost positive shovel test was located approximately 53 m south of the road cut and 40 m south of the pipeline right-of-way (Underwood 2009). The bones proved to be the remains of a human burial that extended into the road cut. The burial was later removed and reburied elsewhere.

Data Recovery

Posthole and feature excavation began on November 17, 2009, and concluded on November 20, 2009. Water screening pit and posthole contents as well as the back dirt continued until December 17, 2009. Eddie Henry served as field director, supervising a crew of three graduate students from the University of Mississippi.

As noted above, although the original mitigation design for the site included mapping and excavation of the features and postholes, the Chickasaw Nation requested that the side cast from the trackhoe stripping be water screened in order to recover a larger sample of artifacts. This turns out to have been a very good idea. It involved back dirt from an area 3.7 m wide and 38 m long, which had been stripped to an average depth of 36 cm. This is the equivalent of more than 140 1-×-1-m squares excavated into Level 4. Putting it another way, we water screened approximately 50 cubic m of what was essentially plowzone. More than 95 percent of the artifacts we recovered from the site came from this operation. We would know considerably less about the site without having screened the backfill.

In order to explore spatial patterns in the distribution of artifacts, the continuous pile of back dirt that was deposited by the trackhoe along the southern edge of the stripped area was broken into two-meter segments, numbered from 1 to 19 going from west to east. That is, the screened segment began at the western end of the stripped transect where we had stopped stripping with the discovery of Feature 4. It continued four m beyond the location of Feature 1, the first indicator that we had encountered a site. Recall that Feature 1 appears to have been a small pit dug into the subsoil but which contained no artifacts. What we have, then, is a long, narrow, controlled surface collection.

As a first step in screening the back dirt, the fill from each of the 19 segments was removed from its location on the crest of the ridge to a portion of the pipeline right-of-way to the east of the site, close to the place where the pipeline was to run under a small stream. Each segment was stockpiled in a separate location and the piles were labeled using pin flags. A low dam was made in the stream using rip rap and black plastic in order to impound a reservoir of water to be used in the screening.

Each back dirt pile was transported from the holding area to the screen by wheelbarrow. Coarse- and fine-screen materials were returned to the University of Mississippi, Oxford, where the coarse-screen artifacts were washed and dried. For the fine-screen materials, rootlets were removed by flotation, after which the heavy fraction at the bottom of the bucket was washed to remove the clay. What remained in the bottom of the bucket was sorted by hand to recover the numerous tiny flakes, sherdlets, and trade beads. More than 2,300 artifacts were recovered from the fine screen, most of which were flakes or thermal shatter.

Artifact Analysis

A total of 8,999 prehistoric or early contact period artifacts were recovered during the excavation of the site. The majority, 6,671, were recovered from the quarter-inch screen. Ceramics, including sherdlets, make up more than 65 percent of the artifacts. Trade goods account for only 89 of the total count of artifacts, and glass trade beads make up 81 of the Colonial period European-made artifacts from the site. All but two of these were recovered as a result of water screening the backfill.

The fine-screen portion of the collection was processed, sorted, and tallied by Johnson. The quarter-inch screen sample was sorted and counted by Henry in consultation with Johnson. Diagnostic artifacts were bagged separately for further evaluation by Johnson.

Ceramics

Four ceramic typologies have focused on the material from northeast Mississippi. The first of these was done for the National Park Service by Jesse Jennings (1941) and reports on the artifacts he and Albert Spaulding had recovered from sites in the Tupelo area. John Stubbs (1982) conducted a survey of Chickasaw sites located primarily in Lee County and introduced type-variety nomenclature. Janet Rafferty's (1985b) article reports on the first comprehensive attempt to seriate Protohistoric and Historic period ceramics from the Black Prairie. James Atkinson (1987) reexamined the Spaulding and Jennings collections to define additional types and varieties for Chickasaw ceramics. Finally, Brad Lieb (2004) took part in a comprehensive restudy of the Spaulding and Jennings collections in order to derive a fine-scaled chronology based on pit features. As it turns out, the Lieb seriation is more useful for our purposes than Rafferty's. In the first place, the earlier analysis was based on site assemblages while, because of his access to National Park Service data, Lieb was able to seriate pit assemblages which, for the Chickasaw occupations, presumably represent a much shorter span of time. For that reason, a tighter chronology is possible. Using the Lieb seriation, we have been able to measure change among the early eighteenth-century Chickasaw in 20- to 30-year increments (Johnson et al. 2008). Also, Rafferty's seriation is based primarily on temper modes, while Lieb included a good deal of stylistic information. Given the nature of ceramic studies in the region, he relied on type-variety classifications, and while there are certainly methodological difficulties with that approach, it did allow him to document some extremely informative aspects of the Chickasaw ceramic sequence, especially in terms of external relationships.

All sherds small enough to fall through a half-inch screen were judged too small for meaningful analysis. These 3,041 sherdlets were counted but not further analyzed. The remaining ceramics were first sorted on the basis of temper. Following the pioneering typology published by Jennings (1941), three temper types were identified. Coarse fossil shell temper was designated Wilson Plain. Fine shell temper, in sherds that often have exterior polishing, was classified as Oktibbeha Plain. These are classic Chickasaw ceramic types. The remaining sherds are sand-tempered. This poses a problem in assigning these sherds to types, since Jennings describes two sand-tempered types for the area. One, Ridge Plain, he found on Chickasaw sites. And the other, Baldwin Plain, was made during the Early and Middle Woodland periods in northeast Mississippi. Lieb (2004) describes Ridge Plain as containing relatively little, fine-grained sand. The sand-tempered sherds from our collections are heavily tempered, suggesting a Baldwin paste. Moreover, the paste composition is quite similar to the paste on the fabric-impressed and cord-marked sherds from our collection. These sherds are unquestionably Woodland, supporting the Baldwin designation. Finally, as will be seen, the Chickasaw occupation at this site appears to be relatively early and short, during a period of time when, according to the Lieb seriation of the WPA-era midden pits (Johnson et al. 2008), Ridge Plain is rare.

The ceramic assemblage (Table 13.1) clearly suggests that 22LE1002 was occupied at least two times in the past. The Baldwin Plain and Furrs Cord-marked sherds indicate that the site was occupied during the Middle Woodland, Miller II phase. The preceding Miller I phase is characterized by Baldwin Plain and Saltillo Fabric Impressed sherds. The eight Saltillo Fabric Impressed sherds in the collection suggest that this Woodland occupation began at the onset of the Miller II phase.

The Chickasaw ceramics are a little more difficult to place within the Chickasaw period. Using the pit feature seriation based on the Jennings/Spaulding collections (Johnson et al. 2008), it can be suggested that the assemblage falls at the beginning of the eighteenth century. That is, fossil shell temper

Table 13.1. Sherds from 22LE1002 broken down by type, temper, and period.

Woodland Sherds	Count
Baldwin Plain	1,319
Baldwin paste, punctated	4
Baldwin paste, incised	3
Baldwin paste, brushed	3
Furrs Cordmarked	87
Saltillo Fabric Impressed	8
Total	**1,424**
Chickasaw Sherds	
Oktibbeha Plain	136
Oktibbeha paste, incised	2
Wilson Plain	1,136
Wilson Brushed	6
Wilson paste, incised lines	5
Wilson paste, punctations	3
Total	**1,288**

predominates and there is no Ridge Plain (assuming that we are correct in classifying the sand-tempered sherds as Baldwin Plain). However, the pit assemblages falling at this point in seriation also contain minority amounts of live shell-tempered ceramics. These could either be the tail end of a live shell-tempered Chickasaw ceramic tradition that dates to the sixteenth and seventeenth centuries or they could represent ceramics brought into Chickasaw territory with refugees from the Lower Mississippi Valley. The fact that the assemblages co-occur at this point in the seriation with Lower Valley incised motifs on fossil shell-tempered sherds suggests the latter. It may be that live shell tempering is absent from the 22LE1002 assemblage as a result of the peripheral location and small size of this site. It is an unlikely location for refugee groups.

Excepting a few large sherds from the features and some of the postholes, all of the sherds were from the plowzone and appear to have been subjected to the destructive effects of cultivation. The fact that sherdlets (n = 3,041) outnumber sherds (n = 2,715) is testimony to the fact that the assemblage is badly weathered. As a consequence, the sherds are too small to do much with beyond basic chronological assignment and plotting the density of material on the site.

Lithic Artifacts

Nearly 3,000 lithic artifacts were recovered, including bifaces, scrapers, gun spalls, and debitage. The majority (2,006) of these are tiny flakes and pieces of thermal shatter recovered from the fine screen. These are too small to do anything other than sort by raw material. Of the remainder, 907 are the result of aboriginal tool manufactures. Five are gun spalls, two of which are native-made and three of which are the exhausted remains of European artifacts.

For most of prehistory, the major source of raw material for tool production in northeast Mississippi was the Tuscaloosa Gravels found in gravel bars and terrace deposits in the nearby Tombigbee River valley. This gravel chert is generally yellowish-tan to cream in color and it turns dark red when heated. It is identified primarily on the presence of water-worn cortex and color. At about the beginning of the eighteenth century, the Chickasaws began relying on another resource, a tabular light gray chert. The nearest source for tabular chert is the Fort Payne formation, which outcrops throughout northern Alabama and extreme northeastern Mississippi. Johnson (1997) has argued that a tabular raw material was preferred because the Chickasaw were manufacturing large amounts of small scrapers from specialized flakes that can best be drawn from cores that are larger than the Tuscaloosa Gravels. These scrapers were needed to meet the demands of the expanding trade in skins during the early Colonial period. A third, previously unidentified chert was observed in the collection from 22LE1002. This is a dark gray, opaque chert. This may also be from northern Alabama or southern Tennessee, somewhere within the Fort Payne or adjacent formations.

Flakes

There are three primary tool production technologies evident on Chickasaw sites (Johnson 1997). A bifacial reduction technique was used to manufacture arrow points and large knives. Bifacial cores were likely also used to produce expedient flake tools. Bifacial flakes are defined on the basis of multifaceted platforms that form an acute angle with the dorsal surface. There is also a good deal of regular core reduction directed in part toward producing flakes suitable for either scraper production or expedient flake tools. Core flakes have only one or two facets on their platforms, and the angle of the platform to the dorsal surface is generally broad. Finally, and this technology produces a flake type that is characteristic of Chickasaw assemblages, small, nearly exhausted cores and bifaces were placed on an anvil and smashed, producing many small, bipolar flakes. These flakes have a flat fracture face with exaggerated compression rings, no bulb of force, and crushed platforms.

When these flake types are tabulated by raw material, the anticipated characteristics of a Chickasaw lithic industry are evident (Table 13.2). That is, core flakes and bipolar flakes are twice as common in the Chickasaw gray chert assemblage as they are on Tuscaloosa Gravel. The presence of bipolar flakes drawn from Tuscaloosa Gravel cores is also of interest. In fact, Tuscaloosa

Table 13.2. Flakes from 22LE1002 broken down by type and raw material.

	Tuscaloosa Gravel		Chickasaw Gray Chert		Dark Gray Chert	
	count	proportion	count	proportion	count	proportion
Missing platform	227	0.4112	50	0.3185	16	0.3077
Biface flake	293	0.5308	84	0.5350	32	0.6154
Core flake	19	0.0344	10	0.0637	3	0.0577
Bipolar flake	13	0.0236	13	0.0828	1	0.0192
Total	552		157		52	

Gravel makes up about 60 percent of the Chickasaw lithic assemblages dating between 1700 and 1730 (Johnson 2004). The Tuscaloosa bipolar flakes suggest that at least some of the Tuscaloosa debitage is the result of the Chickasaw occupation at the site. Likewise, the bipolar flakes on the dark gray chert suggest that this material was also used by the Chickasaw. There is additional evidence for these assertions when thumbnail scrapers and gun spalls are considered in terms of raw material.

Cores

The 22LE1002 assemblage contains nine cores, six of which are bipolar (Table 13.3), attesting to the importance of this technology at the site. Since bipolar technology is common on Chickasaw sites dating to the first half of the eighteenth century (Johnson 1997), it is not surprising that three of these cores are made from Chickasaw gray chert. The presence of the technology on both Tuscaloosa Gravel and the dark gray chert supports the suggestion that the materials were used by the Chickasaw as well.

Table 13.3. Cores from 22LE1002 broken down by type and raw material.

	Tuscaloosa Gravel		Chickasaw Gray Chert		Dark Gray Chert	
	count	proportion	count	proportion	count	proportion
Flake Core	1	0.3333	2	0.4000		
Bipolar core	2	0.6667	3	0.6000	1	1.0000
Total	3		5		1	

Bifaces

Twenty mostly fragmented bifaces were recovered. These artifacts were sorted by raw material and stage of manufacture. Those on which a bifacial edge had been established, but the flakes that were drawn from that edge did not completely cover both faces of the biface, were classified as preforms. These artifacts were also thicker, showing more hinge fractures and areas of cortex. Finally, where possible, the bifaces were sorted into chronological types using standard point types developed by earlier workers in the area (Cambron and Hulse 1975; Ensor 1981; Futato 1975). Half of these were small triangular points that can be assigned to either the Mississippian or Chickasaw periods. Since there is no evidence for a Mississippian occupation at this site, they are clearly Chickasaw tools, almost certainly arrowheads. The fact that the only bifaces made on Chickasaw gray chert fall into this category supports this association. Eight of the 10 Chickasaw triangular points were made from Tuscaloosa Gravel, and this is another indication that the Chickasaw occupation of this site dates to around 1700. The seriation of the Jennings/Spaulding midden pits shows a gradual replacement of Tuscaloosa Gravel with Chickasaw gray chert beginning at 19 percent for the Early period (1650 to 1700) followed by 39 percent during the Early Middle period (1700 to 1730). Stone tools become noticeably less common during the Late Middle period (1730 to 1740) and are replaced almost entirely by metal tools during the Late period (1740 to 1750) (Johnson 2004:Table 3.22).

Another trend that is evident in the Spaulding/Jennings restudy is the replacement of small triangular arrowheads, Madison points, by longer, parallel-sided arrowheads, or Dallas points. Only five of the triangular points from 22LE1002 are complete enough to be assigned to one type or another. Two are Madison and three are Dallas points.

Finally, the Chickasaw bifaces are the only ones that include unfinished forms (Table 13.3). It is clear that the Chickasaw were manufacturing arrowheads at the site. However, this does not necessarily mean that biface manufacture was not taking place at 22LE1002 during the Woodland period.

Excepting the two Archaic points, the biface and ceramic assemblages are quite similar. About half of the bifaces (10 of 18) are the result of the Chickasaw occupation. About half of the ceramics (1,224 of 2,712) were used by the Chickasaw.

Thumbnail Scrapers

There are three aboriginal artifact attributes that are unequivocal markers of a late-seventeenth- or early eighteenth-century Chickasaw assemblage: fossil shell-tempered ceramics, Chickasaw gray chert, and thumbnail scrapers. End scrapers also show up during the Middle Woodland but they are considerably larger than the Chickasaw scrapers (Johnson and Hayes 1995). The Chickasaw scrapers are about the size of a man's thumbnail and are relatively uniform in terms of manufacturing technology (Johnson 1997). They are made on core

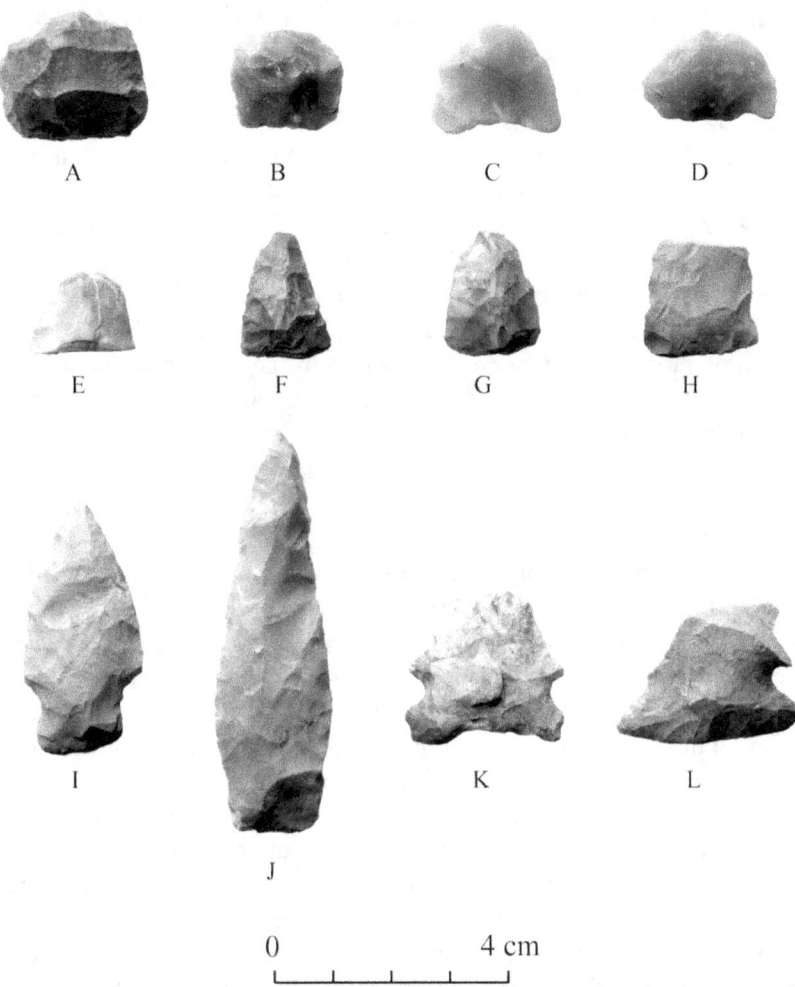

Figure 13.1. Lithic Artifacts from 22LE1002: A - Native-made biface used as gun spall, B - British gun spall, C–D - French gun spalls, E - Native-made biface used as gun spall, F–G - thumbnail scrapers, H - Dallas point, I - Bakers Creek point, J - Bradley Spike, K - Kirk point, L - Pine Tree point. Photo courtesy Jay K. Johnson and Edward R. Henry.

flakes with a plunging termination and a medial dorsal ridge. This provides ideal blanks, with the ridge reinforcing the tool longitudinally and the termination unifacially retouched to form a sharp, but broad, angle bit. As indicated above, these tools are characteristically made from Chickasaw gray chert.

Water screening at 22LE1002 produced two thumbnail scrapers (Figure 13.1 F–G). One is made on a relatively large flake of Tuscaloosa Gravel, but some bifacial flaking was needed to shape the ventral surface. This is common of thumbnail scrapers made on gravel cherts, as it is difficult to produce broad flakes with completely flat ventral surfaces. The second scraper is made from the dark gray, opaque chert that constitutes nearly 7 percent of the flake assemblage at 22LE1002. This artifact is indisputable proof that some, if not all, of this chert was brought to the site by the Chickasaw. The fact that it was made from a flake large enough that the ventral surface required no retouch suggests that this is a tabular chert. None of the flakes show the cortex characteristic of relatively small gravel cherts such as Tuscaloosa.

The relatively small number of thumbnail scrapers in the 22LE1002 assemblage is significant. The ratio of scrapers to Chickasaw period bifaces is 0.20. That same ratio for Early period pit features in the Jennings/Spaulding collection is 0.30, but is very close to 0.50 for all subsequent periods. Remember that the end point for the Early period is A.D. 1700.

Gun Spalls

Students of eighteenth-century firearms reserve the term "gun flint" for those made from blade segments, a distinctive technology that only became common in the last quarter of the century. Prior to that time, Europeans used large, wedge-shaped flakes in manufacturing what are called gun spalls (Hamilton 1979). All of the European-made examples in our collection are gun spalls.

One of the gun spalls is made from a raw material type that is British in origin (Figure 13.1 B). This is a relatively dark gray flint that is translucent at the edges. The 22LE1002 example has been heavily worked bifacially to reestablish the edge. The original surface of the spall is all but obliterated. In addition, it was rotated in the flintlock so that all four edges show the heavy battering that is characteristic of gun spalls. It is clearly exhausted.

Two gun spalls are made from an equally distinctive, honey-colored, translucent French flint. Both are heavily reworked. One shows the use wear characteristic of gun spalls on two edges (Figure 13.1 D). The other shows an attempt at bifacial rejuvenation that was unsuccessful, resulting in edges that were too convex, concave, or too thin (Figure 13.1 C). It was discarded without being reused. Both still show small facets retaining the original surface of the spall. Two relatively thick, roughly rectangular bifaces are examples of native-made gun spalls. One is Chickasaw gray chert (Figure 13.1 E) and the other is the dark gray chert that has been identified as a probable alternative Chickasaw chert source (Figure 13.1 A). Both show diagnostic edge wear.

Given that the ceramics, most of the lithics, and the trade goods (see below) suggest that this site dates to the early 1700s, there are an unusually large number of gun spalls from 22LE1002. Like most Chickasaw gun flints, these are heavily retouched and on two to four sides show the edge-battering characteristic of use in a flintlock. Multiple edge use and heavy retouch are much more common early in the Jennings/Spaulding sequence, as are native-made gun spalls (Johnson 2004). Also, French gun spalls are much more common in the first half of the sequence, prior to the battle of Ackia in 1736, after which trade relationships with the French broke down.

The lithic and ceramic assemblages from 22LE1002 complement each other nicely. Both show about an even mix of Middle Woodland and early eighteenth-century Chickasaw artifacts. The lithic assemblage, in particular, reflects the transformation of aboriginal technology and economy that occurred with European intrusion into the South. The Chickasaw developed an elaborate toolkit focused specifically on processing skins for trade with the Europeans. This included scrapers, large bifacial knives, and stone awls (Johnson 1997). Only the scrapers are present in the 22LE1002 assemblage, but the adaptation of the tabular Chickasaw gray chert in order to accommodate the production of these tools had begun during the period of time when the site was occupied. This is significant because traditional historical accounts of trade into the interior of the South suggest that the primary trade prior to 1715 was in slaves, and that the skin trade did not become important until after that time (Johnson 2000:95). Our findings, however, corroborate the results of the restudy of the Jennings/Spaulding collections. Skins appear to have been a focus of the trade from the beginning of intensive contact, perhaps as early as 1680.

What is unusual in the lithic assemblage is the relatively large number of gun spalls. Ceramic and all other indicators suggest that the site was occupied sometime around A.D. 1700. Gun spalls are not common at the beginning of the eighteenth century in the Jennings/Spaulding collection. However, the sites that produced that material are located within the central focus of Chickasaw settlement. 22LE1002 is a small, peripheral hamlet, one that, perhaps, focused more completely on the skin trade than did the larger, "downtown" settlements.

Trade Goods

The South Thomas Street excavations produced a good sample of European trade goods, including glass trade beads, metal artifacts, and, as described above, gun spalls. There is, as might be expected, considerable chronological and economic information to be derived from the analysis of the trade goods.

Beads

A total of 83 glass trade beads was recovered, mostly from the fine-screen fraction. All were small enough to pass through the quarter-inch screen but

Table 13.4. Glass trade beads from 22LE1002 classified using the Tunica Treasure typology (Brain 1979).

Type	Description	Count
IIA1s	rounded ends, simple construction, opaque white, small	17
IIA1m	rounded ends, simple construction, opaque white, medium	8
IIA5m	rounded ends, simple construction, opaque, dark burgundy, medium	5
IIA6s	rounded ends, simple construction, translucent, dark blue, small	18
IIA6m	rounded ends, simple construction, translucent, dark blue, medium	1
IIA7s	rounded ends, simple construction, opaque, turquoise, small	27
IIA8s	rounded ends, simple construction, opaque, light powder blue, small	1
IIA8m	rounded ends, simple construction, opaque, powder blue, medium	1
IVA2s	rounded ends, compound construction, translucent, light green inner layer, opaque, brick red middle layer, transparent, clear outer layer, (Cornaline d'Aleppo), small	3
IVA2m	rounded ends, compound construction, translucent, light green inner layer, opaque, brick red middle layer, transparent, clear outer layer, (Cornaline d'Aleppo), medium	1

several were recovered from that screen in the field before being washed through to the lower screen. There is a substantial literature on trade beads, but the primary reference for this part of the Southeast has become Brain's analysis of the "Tunica Treasure" (Brain 1979). It is the appropriate basis for the analysis of the Tupelo region beads for several reasons. In the first place, the Trudeau site (16WF25), where the large collection of Tunica artifacts was found, is located in Louisiana, not far from the Mississippi River, and was occupied by the Tunica from 1731 to 1764 (Brain 1988:65). The Tunica were certainly participating in the same trading network as the Chickasaw, perhaps with a greater reliance on French traders, but as both the British and the French were buying their trade beads from the same sources, this does not appear to be a problem. The Tunica Treasure constitutes one of the largest collections of mid-eighteenth-century trade goods to have been analyzed, including more than 186,000 beads. Brain did a masterful job of synthesizing the earlier, not always generally available, literature. Finally, *Tunica Treasure* is well illustrated, with several color plates devoted to beads alone.

One of the standard manufacturing techniques for trade beads was to draw out a long tube of glass and snap it into small, bead-sized segments. The glass tube may have one or more layers of different glass with differences in transparency or color. Brain calls these compound beads. There may also be surface decoration impressed in the molten glass; these are called complex beads. The ends of the broken segments may be either left as they are or rounded by tumbling the beads in hot sand; these are rough ended or rounded in Brain's terminology. All of the 22LE1002 beads are either rounded, simple construction (IIA) or rounded ends, compound construction (IVA). They are further broken down by color and translucence, with each type assigned a number (Table 13.4). Some bead types have traditional names in the trade bead literature. Type IVA2, for example, is called a Cornaline d'Aleppo. Finally, perhaps because we water screened the feature fill and side cast from the stripping, there is an unusual number of small, so-called seed beads in the 22LE1002 assemblage (over 80 percent by count). Following Brain (1979:98), we have subdivided each of the numbered types into small (≤ 4 mm in diameter) and medium (5 to 9 mm in diameter). All measurements were made using calipers, rounding to the nearest mm. None of the beads from 22LE1002 is large according to Brain's scheme.

Glass Pendant

One small, roughly equilateral triangle of glass was recovered from the water screen. It measures approximately 13 mm on a side and is about 2 mm thick. This appears to be an example of the Chickasaw reworking European trade goods. Similar but larger glass triangles with holes for suspension were recovered from one of the burials from the Haynes Bluff site (22WR501) on the bluff line of the Lower Yazoo Basin near Yazoo City (Brain 1988:Fig 167) and are interpreted as "glass pendants made from melted IIA7 beads." That would make them turquoise, the same color as our example.

Following Brain (1979), the combined date range for sites containing beads found in the 22LE1002 assemblage is 1600 to 1820, not too informative. Looking at it another way, the site can date no earlier than 1700, the youngest date for the appearance of any of the beads in the collection. Allowing for the possibility that beads could have been kept as heirlooms, the site could date up to the time of Removal in the late 1830s. However, we can do better than that. There does not seem to have been much heirloom behavior at Chickasaw sites. Beads appear to have made their way into the archaeological record within a few years of having been traded. And while some beads were

Table 13.5. North Mississippi bead assemblages broken down by manufacturing technique.

	22Le1002	22Le907	MLe18	MLe14	MLe90	22Le912	MCs16
Drawn, faceted							0.4713
Drawn, untumbled, compound		0.0081				0.1409	0.2011
Wound, medium-large		0.0041	0.0357	0.0038	0.0968	0.0014	0.2240
Drawn, untumbled		0.0459		0.0001	0.0020	0.7360	
Drawn, tumbled, compound	0.0602	0.0486		0.3251	0.5331	0.0493	0.0278
Drawn, tumbled	0.9398	0.8851	0.6071	0.6470	0.2426	0.0722	0.0458
Wound, very large		0.0014	0.2500	0.0145	0.1254	0.0002	0.0215
Wound, faceted		0.0027	0.0357	0.0011			0.0085
Drawn, inlays		0.0041	0.0714	0.0065			
Total	83	740	28	14862	981	6272	2228

traded for several decades, their popularity appears to have waxed and waned, creating some general trends in the Chickasaw bead assemblages. Drawing on one of the largest collections of Chickasaw beads to have been studied to date, Rausch (2004) described the beads excavated from four sites by Jennings and Spaulding in anticipation of construction of the Natchez Trace (Jennings 1941). What's more, these site assemblages, along with the material from 22LE912, were studied by a group of specialists and a great deal of data relating to the technological, economic, and social changes that occurred during the eighteenth century has been assembled (Johnson et al. 2008). The five sites have been closely dated on the basis of ceramics, lithic, and metal trade goods and assigned to four periods: Early (1650–1700), Early Middle (1700–1730), Late Middle (1730–1740), and Late (1740–1750). Because this dating was based on a seriation of midden pit contents and most of the beads came from burials, the beads played no role in the seriation. The beads can, however, be used to seriate the burials or they can be studied using whole site assemblages. The latter approach is most useful for our purposes.

The five sites, from earliest to latest, are 22LE912 and MLe18 (22LE504) which are located in southern Tupelo and date from about 1700 to 1730, although two of the midden pits from MLe18 fall into the Early period. Site MLe14 (22LE524) is located along Kings Creek in central Tupelo and is the "Chickasaw Village Site" stop along the Natchez Trace. The majority of the midden pits from this site date from about 1730 to 1740, although two pits appear to date to the end of the Early Middle period. Site MLe90 (22LE505),

Big Town, is located on the north edge of the Chickasaw settlement and dates from 1740 to 1750. Two additional bead assemblages are included in Table 13.5. The Meadowbrook site (22LE912) is located in south Tupelo and is one of the few sites dating to the last half of the eighteenth century to have been studied so far. It likely dates to the 1770s. The final site, MCs16 (22CS503), is the Bynum Mounds, a Middle Woodland burial mound with intrusive Chickasaw burials dating to the first quarter of the nineteenth century (Cotter and Corbett 1951).

When the bead assemblages from the sites are grouped by method of manufacture, there are some obvious trends in the data (Table 13.5). Some bead types, drawn, tumbled, and wound very large, are found throughout the sequence but are more common early. Wound medium-large beads are found throughout the sequence but are more common late. There are two basic types of faceted beads. Wound beads can be pressed against flat surfaces while still molten: this is the earlier form. Or, facets can be ground on drawn beads. This is one of the major bead types at Bynum, the early nineteenth-century assemblage. Drawn beads with inlays, almost always longitudinal stripes, are restricted to the earliest three assemblages. Compound drawn beads, those with two or more layers of glass that have been tumbled, are found in the last three bead assemblages but are a majority at MLe90. Compound beads which have not been tumbled are common only in the final two assemblages. Finally, drawn beads that were not tumbled are found in small numbers in the middle two assemblages, anticipating something that was much more common in the third quarter of the eighteenth century, as evidenced by the Meadowbrook assemblage.

Where does the 22LE1002 assemblage fit in this sequence? All of the beads from the site are drawn with tumbled ends. The fact that there are no wound beads or drawn beads with inlays or wound beads with facets suggests that it predates the tabulated assemblages. The one compound bead type, Cornaline d'Aleppo, is generally considered to be a very early eighteenth-century type (Brain 1979:106), and four were found at 22LE907, supporting this assignment. However, 306 were found at the Trudeau site, which dates to the mid-eighteenth century (Brain 1979:106). Recall, also, that the total site assemblage at Trudeau was more than 186,000 beads. They are an apparent rarity at that time and place. They show up again in the late-eighteenth-century 22LE912 assemblage, accounting for less than 1 percent of the total. More bothersome to their early dating are the 94 examples from an assemblage of 1,305 beads from a Chickasaw grave near New Albany, Mississippi. The remainder of the beads from this assemblage more closely resemble the Bynum Mound assemblage, and an early nineteenth-century date for the New Albany burial is assured by the inclusion of a Jefferson Peace Medal, which was minted in 1801 (Johnson 2000:109–113). However, less than 10 percent of the New Albany assemblage is made up of donut-shaped, tumbled, drawn beads, the exclusive form found at 22LE1002. The presence of the Cornaline d'Aleppo beads in association with the Peace Medal appears to be an example of heirloom behavior.

Other than the relative abundance of Cornaline d'Aleppo beads and the absence of any of the decorated wound bead types that are common at MLe18 and MLe14, the only other aspect of the 22LE1002 assemblage that may be distinctive is the abundance of seed beads, most of which are turquoise (IIA7). Turquoise beads make up 67 percent of the assemblage from 22LE907 and nearly 18 percent of the beads from MLe18 while occurring less than 5 percent of the time at MLe14, MLe90, and 22LE912 and not at all at MCs16, suggesting at least that this color of bead is an early eighteenth-century characteristic. Although seed beads made up a portion of the Jennings/Spaulding assemblages, they were in a minority and were not sorted into separate categories. Nor were seed beads counted separately in the Trudeau analysis. In both cases, recovery did not include water screening, and at least some seed beads were likely to have been missed during excavation. The bead assemblage from 22LE1002 appears to predate the 22LE907 and MLe18 assemblages, falling sometime at the very beginning of the eighteenth century. Whether or not seed beads predominate at other sites dating to this period is yet to be determined.

Metal Artifacts

Other than several lead shot and a .22 bullet recovered from the fine screen, all dating to the twentieth century, only three metal artifacts were recovered. All three appear to date to the Chickasaw occupation of the site. An iron knife blade was recovered from the bottom of Post Hole 19 and two copper artifacts were found in the fine screen. The knife blade fragment was 11.6 cm long and 2.1 cm wide when it was recovered. One end was rounded, and the other was broken. There is a tang a short distance from the broken end, apparently meant to attach a wooden handle. This appears to have been a case knife similar to a large paring knife. These were common trade items during the eighteenth century (Brain 1979, 1988). Once it dried out, the knife blade disintegrated.

Two small pieces of copper were recovered from the fine screen. One was rolled to form a small bead 7 mm long and 2 mm in diameter. The other is a narrow strip of copper, 10 mm long and 5 mm wide. It is curled up at one end and, if it had been rolled, it would have been formed into a similar bead. This metal is extremely thin, less than one mm, and thinner than the copper that shows up in tinkler cones, which are a common Chickasaw artifact and are, presumably, reworked from trade kettles.

Summary and Conclusions

Taken together, the artifact assemblage from 22LE1002 forms a coherent picture. The first substantial occupation occurred during the Middle Woodland period. Plain, sand-tempered sherds with a few fabric-impressed surface treatments mixed with mostly cord-marked sherds suggests accumulation at the beginning of the Miller II phase. Features 2 and 4 date to this period. The similarity of small macrobotanical assemblages derived from the flotation of samples from these pits supports the rough contemporaneity of these features (Kistler 2011). Each assemblage indicates a generalized subsistence with no evidence for corn agriculture. Other than the Woodland sherds, there are several bifaces that can be dated to this period. All are made from thermally altered Tuscaloosa Gravel. There is also a good deal of Tuscaloosa debitage. However, at least some of this must be related to the following, Chickasaw occupation of the site.

The late-seventeenth- and eighteenth-century Chickasaw made use of Tuscaloosa chert in tool production, but beginning at about 1700, they also began to use a light gray, tabular chert. So while the light gray chert from the site is certainly related to the Chickasaw occupation, at least some of the Tuscaloosa debitage must also have been produced by the Chickasaw. This is borne out by the fact that one of the thumbnail scrapers, a diagnostic Chickasaw period tool, is made from Tuscaloosa Gravel. Another thumbnail scraper is made from a third, dark gray chert that has not been recognized at other Chickasaw sites but is a consistent minority at this site. Bipolar cores, a second ubiquitous component of Chickasaw lithic assemblages, are present at the site and are also made from Tuscaloosa chert as well as light and dark gray chert.

The glass trade bead assemblage from the South Thomas Street site is composed exclusively of drawn, tumbled forms with a large number of small, seed beads. The majority color is turquoise. The single compound form from 22LE1002 is the Cornaline d'Aleppo type, a predominantly early bead. Altogether, the bead assemblage suggests a date of sometime around 1700.

The Chickasaw ceramic assemblage tells a similar story. That is, plain, fossil shell-tempered sherds predominate. There are no examples of live shell-tempered sherds that are common in mid-seventeenth-century Chickasaw sites. Nor are there any clear examples of Ridge Plain, a sand-tempered Chickasaw type, which is common after about 1740. From about 1700 to 1730, Chickasaw assemblages from sites located a few miles to the north of the South Thomas Street site contain minority Yazoo Basin types, suggesting that refugee groups from that area were taken in by the Chickasaw (Lieb 2004). None of these live shell-tempered types were found at 22LE1002.

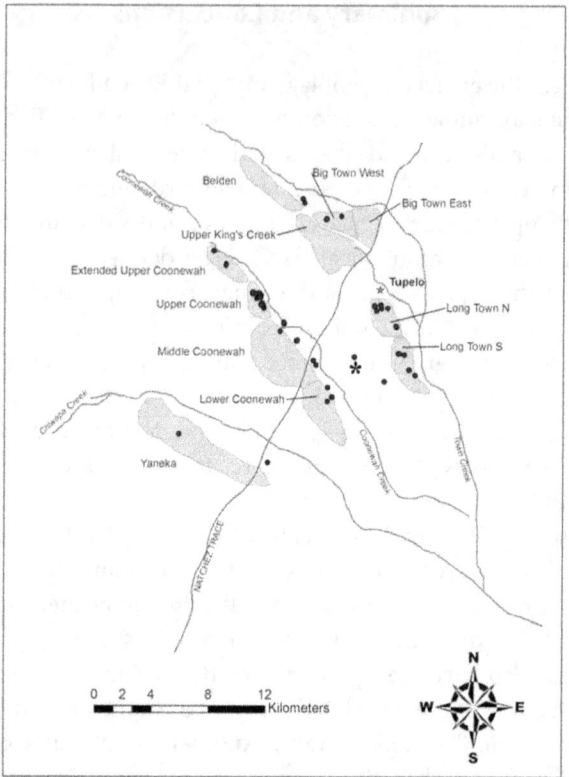

Figure 13.2. Chickasaw features, 1681–1720, midpoint dates, 22LE1002 shown as asterisk (after Cegielski and Lieb 2011:Figure 3).

In fact, there are some aspects of the South Thomas Street assemblage that can best be understood from a regional perspective. Three of the sites dug by Jennings and Spaulding in the mid-century (Jennings 1941) and recently restudied (Johnson et al. 2008) are located in the heartland of the eighteenth-century Chickasaw occupation and provide a background against which to evaluate the South Thomas Street occupation. They are MLe14, MLe18, and MLe90. In addition, 22LE907 was excavated in the 1990s (O'Hear and Ryba 1998; Underwood 1998) and is located within the Chickasaw core area. Finally, 22LE678 was excavated in anticipation of the reroute of Highway 6 (Johnson and Haley 2006) and is located in the upper Chiwapa Creek drainage, to the west of the core area.

Cegielski and Lieb (2011) have plotted the distribution of Chickasaw settlement for the last 200 years of their occupation in Mississippi. The Chickasaw response to the dynamics of European colonization is clearly told in the distribution of their settlement. Beginning in about 1650, their villages

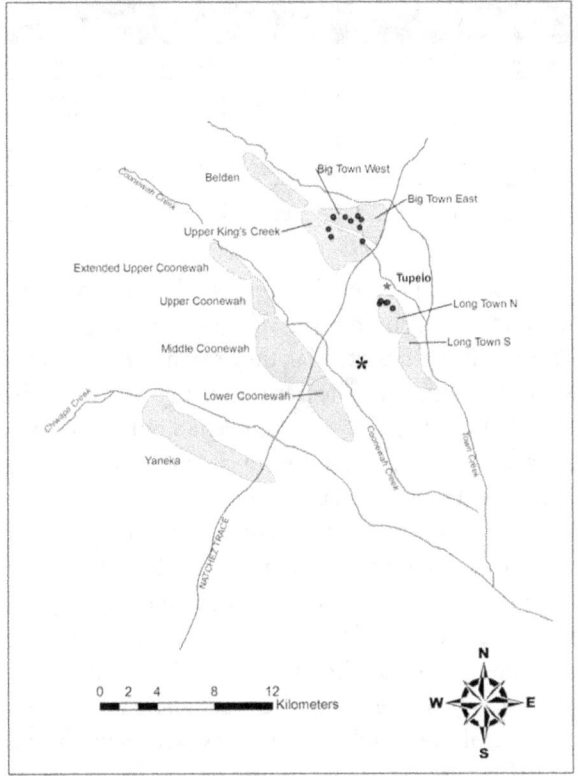

Figure 13.3. Chickasaw features, 1721–1736, midpoint dates, 22LE1002 shown as asterisk (after Cegielski and Lieb 2011:Figure 4).

were dispersed over three major drainages, covering portions of three counties in northeastern Mississippi. By 1680, the settlement distribution had constricted somewhat (Figure 13.2). By 1720, all of the Chickasaw occupation was restricted to a relatively small area along King and Town Creeks (Figure 13.3). This is the core area of the Chickasaw occupation for the rest of the first half of the eighteenth century. The Chiwapa and Coonewah Creek drainages, including the location of the South Thomas Street site, had been abandoned.

So the South Thomas Street site assemblage must be interpreted both in terms of its peripheral location and its relatively early date. These five sites are characterized in terms of four artifact types in Table 13.6. Some of the differences between the sites are clearly the result of the remarkable changes in technology and economics taking place during the early Colonial period. For example, the relative importance of arrow points at 22LE1002 and 22LE678 is likely the result of the fact that the bow and arrow were just then being replaced by flintlock rifles. The relative lack of thumbnail scrapers at these two

Table 13.6. Beads, gun spalls, scrapers, and arrow points from selected Chickasaw sites in the Tupelo region.

	22Le1002	22Le678	22Le907	MLe18	MLe14	MLe90
Beads	83	12	704	28	14,862	981
Gun spalls	5	1	15	10	27	38
Scrapers	2	2	—	17	24	2
Arrow points	10	3	—	31	42	4

earlier sites can also be interpreted in terms of technology and economics. These tools are much more common at MLe18 and MLe14, the two sites dating to between 1700 and 1740. In particular, they reach their peak at MLe14, which dates to between 1730 and 1740, the period during which the deer skin trade was at its peak but at which point metal tools had not yet replaced stone tools among the Chickasaw. The vast amounts of deer skins that were processed for the skin trade required these specialized tools.

Although we are now able to map chronological changes in Chickasaw technology and settlement distribution in a good deal of detail (Cegielski and Lieb 2011; Johnson et al. 2008), we are just now approaching the question of how the sites along Chiwapa and Coonewah Creeks related to the core Chickasaw settlement along King and Town Creeks. The South Thomas Street site offers an opportunity to address this question. There is the presumption that these small, peripheral sites would have had less access to European trade. For example, two artifact types, trade beads and gun spalls, are relatively unusual at 22LE678, the Chiwapa Creek site. They are, however, relatively common at the South Thomas Street site.

The South Thomas Street site assemblage contains five gun spalls, a tool that only became common in the Jennings/Spaulding site assemblages after about 1730. However, the excavations at 22LE907 yielded 15 gun spalls. The midden pits at this site date between 1700 and 1730, mostly 10 to 20 years later than the probable date for the South Thomas Street site. It could be argued that the relative importance of both arrow points and gun spalls at the South Thomas Street site reflects a primary emphasis on hunting at this peripheral site. However, only one native-made gun flint was found in the much smaller excavations at 22LE678, the other peripheral site. The fact that two of the five gun spalls from the South Thomas Street site were native made is likely an expression of its early period of occupation. That two of the European gun spalls were French in origin and the other is British is also an expression of the early date for the site. At the turn of the century, the Chickasaw were actively establishing trade relations with both colonial powers.

The bead count at the South Thomas Street Site is problematic if the assumption that the larger, core area sites had better access to European trade is true. There are a couple of considerations here. In the first place, of the core sites under consideration, only at 22LE907 was water screening employed, and that site produced a large collection of trade beads. Without water screening at the South Thomas Street site, many if not most of the seed beads would have been missed. Only 14 of the beads from South Thomas were larger than seed beads. There is, however, another consideration that must be taken into account when comparing the South Thomas Street bead assemblage and the one from 22LE907. Although we know that there were burials at the South Thomas Street site, the one known burial from that site did not contain beads. All but 27 of the 704 beads from 22LE907 came from burials. A similar situation occurred at MLe18, MLe14, and MLe90.

So, although the peripheral location of the South Thomas Street site fits the known pattern of Chickasaw settlement in terms of chronology in that the Coonewah Creek drainage was completely abandoned by 1721, the assemblage does not show any of the more obvious implications of its peripheral location. It may be that a core-periphery model is irrelevant to the organization of Chickasaw society during the period of dispersed settlement at the beginning of the eighteenth century. Thomas Nairne, a trader and diplomat from Charles Town, visited the Chickasaws at about this time and noted a decided independence of individual Chickasaws in their participation in the trade with the Europeans (Moore 1988:39). Should we expect anything less in terms of individual communities?

CHAPTER 14

The Symbiotic Relationship between the National Forests of Mississippi and the Civilian Conservation Corps: The Early History of the Chickasawhay Ranger District

Maria Schleidt

The history of the National Forest System began with establishment of the first forest reserves in Wyoming (Yellowstone Park Timber Land Reserve) and Colorado (White River Timber Land Reserve) in 1891. Up until 1907 all forest reserves created by the Bureau of Forestry were located on the West Coast. However, between 1907 and 1909 eight National Forests (formerly forest reserves) were established within the eastern half of the country: Arkansas (now Ouachita), Ozark, Choctawhatchee, Ocala, Marquette, Michigan, Superior, and Minnesota National Forests. During the next two decades (1918–1928), 12 new National Forests were proclaimed, mostly in the Southeast. But the greatest increase took place during the 1930s, when 24 additional forests were added to the roster of eastern forests, all during Franklin D. Roosevelt's presidency (USDA Forest Service 1997). All but seven of these National Forests are located within the Southeast.

Three major factors led to the creation of the National Forests in the East: (1) the Weeks Law of 1911; (2) the Clarke-McNary Act of 1924; and (3) President Franklin D. Roosevelt's own interest in the conservation of forested lands on the east coast. The Weeks Act of 1911 allowed for the creation of National Forests by purchase (USDA Forest Service 1976). The law made it possible for the federal government to purchase privately owned land for the protection of watersheds. Prior to the passage of this law, the president had the authority under the Federal Forest Reserve Act of 1891 to set aside or reserve timberlands only from the public domain (West 1992). The enactment of the Weeks Act aided in the expansion of the National Forest System east of the Great Plains, an area which by that time was largely in private hands.

On June 7, 1924, Congress passed the Clarke-McNary Act of 1924, thus giving the USDA Forest Service the authority to purchase "forested, cut-over, or denuded land within the watersheds of navigable streams" (Clarke-McNary Act, 43 Stat.). The act amended the Weeks Act and made it possible for the USDA Forest Service to purchase lands (1) which were once in timber or which could be used to produce timber, and (2) for streamflow protection. Moreover, the act authorized technical and financial aid to the states for forest fire control and for production and distribution of forest tree seedlings.

Shortly after Roosevelt's election in 1932, he proposed the idea of enlarging the National Forest System within the eastern half of the country (Conarro 1977; *Hattiesburg American* 31 August 1933:1). To that end, the USDA Forest Service ordered C. E. Beaumont, a forest examiner, to conduct surveys in Missouri, Texas, Louisiana, Mississippi, Alabama, and North and South Carolina. With congressional approval the president set aside 50 million dollars for land purchases. Although the National Forest Reservation Commission had established a number of purchase units in 1929 and 1930, land was not purchased until the new funding was made available.

New National Forests for Mississippi: An Overview

Within the state of Mississippi, the new funding translated into the acquisition of seven purchase units that eventually would become five of the six National Forests in Mississippi. The Homochitto Purchase Unit, the first to be established, was created in May 1930. Four other units were approved on August 30, 1933: the Holly Springs Purchase Unit, which would eventually become the Holly Springs National Forest, and the Leaf River, Biloxi, Black River, and Chickasawhay Purchase Units, which would be combined to create the De Soto National Forest. In 1934, the Bienville Purchase Unit was approved from lands acquired in Scott, Newton, Smith, and Jasper counties. The final purchase unit created during this era, the Delta Purchase Unit, was approved on March 7, 1935, by the National Forest Reservation Commission so as to create a bottomland hardwood forest (Conarro 1977). President Roosevelt proclaimed the Bienville, De Soto, Holly Springs, and Homochitto Purchase Units National Forests in 1936 (USDA Forest Service 1997). It was not until 1961 that the Delta Purchase Unit would attain the status of a National Forest.

The National Forests in Mississippi, like many of the southeastern National Forests established during Roosevelt's presidency, were as much a product of the USDA Forest Service's eastern expansion as they were of the president's New Deal program. In fact, the early history of these forests is intertwined with that of the Civilian Conservation Corps (CCC). It was this symbiotic relationship that shaped the infrastructure of the National Forests in Mississippi.

As the National Forest Reservation Commission began approving the purchase of land in Mississippi in 1933, the CCC followed with the establishment of three camps (F-1, F-2, and F-3) on the Homochitto Purchase Unit in May and early June 1933.[1] Later that same year, five new camps were constructed on the four purchase units that would eventually be christened the De Soto National Forest (Camps F-4, F-5, F-6, F-7, and F-8).[2] All of the CCC companies sent to the De Soto National Forest were from the Army Second Corps Area (New York and New Jersey), which had spent the spring in the West and were then sent to the Southeast to escape the harsh winters of Wyoming and Utah.[3]

The following year the National Forests in Mississippi acquired 11 new camps. In May 1934, Potts Camp (F-9) was constructed on the Holly Springs Purchase Unit. This company was the only veteran company to serve in the National Forests in Mississippi. Later that same year, Camp Waterford (F-19) and Camp F-17 were added to the Holly Springs Purchase Unit. The Bienville Purchase Unit was granted 3 CCC camps (F-13, F-15, and F-18); Camp F-13 was home to Company 1415, the first African American company to work within the National Forests in Mississippi. The De Soto (F-10, F-12, F-16) and the Homochitto (F-11, F-14) National Forests were further augmented with an additional 5 camps.[4]

Beginning in 1935, things began to change for the CCC camps located on the National Forests in Mississippi.[5] First, camps F-1 through F-4, having completed their program of work for the USDA Forest Service, were evacuated and closed down between 1935 and 1937.[6] Secondly, only four new CCC camps were constructed (F-21 to F-24) on the Bienville, De Soto, and Homochitto Purchase Units in 1935. (For the second time an African American company was organized to assist the USDA Forest Service in the new forests within the state.) Moreover, Camps F-20 and F-25 were approved, but never established in Mississippi.[7] By mid-1935, all Army Second Corps Area companies were shipped out of Mississippi, with the majority of the companies being sent to California.

Work continued on these forests with the addition of Camp F-26 built on the Homochitto National Forest in 1937, Camp F-27 at W. W. Ashe Tree Nursery on the De Soto National Forest in mid-1939, and Camp F-29 at the Bienville National Forest in 1939. (Camp F-28, approved to be built in 1939 on the Holly Springs National Forest, was canceled.)[8]

The construction of both CCC camps and USDA Forest Service buildings was an early task assigned to the young men. In the course of nine years, CCC enrollees under the leadership of USDA Forest Service project superintendents built seven work centers and erected 40 lookout towers throughout the

National Forests in Mississippi.⁹ Of the original work centers and fire towers, only four work centers (Wausau, Airey, Paret, and Forest Work Centers) and 13 towers remain today.

A review of historic photographs of the former work centers, the 1990 architectural survey of historic USDA Forest Service buildings in Mississippi (Hopkins 1990), and an inventory of the current buildings found at the four remaining work centers reveal an architectural design common to all the work centers. The designer(s) of these structures is not known; research into early USDA Forest Service documents has failed to shed any light on the subject. Nonetheless, the overall concept and design of a National Forest work center in Mississippi can be identified. Original work centers consisted of a 100-ft high Aermotor tower with a 7 ft by 7 ft hipped cab, a five-room dwelling for the dispatcher (known colloquially as the ranger's residence), the dispatcher's office, an equipment depot of varying size (three to five bay doors), an oil house, a grease rack, a pump house, and two poured concrete dynamite bunkers located at a distance from the main buildings. In some cases a garage was constructed next to the dispatcher's house to serve as a private garage to house the dispatcher's personal car.

Congress decreed an end to the Civilian Conservation Corps program in mid-1942 (Ermentrout 1982; Salmod 1967). After nine years in service, all 26 USDA Forest Service camps, with the exception of Camp F-8 on the Chickasawhay Ranger District of the De Soto National Forest, were evacuated and dismantled by the US Army Corps of Engineers.

The CCC on the Chickasawhay Ranger District

The example of the establishment and history of the CCC on the Chickasawhay Ranger District of the De Soto National Forest provides a detailed portrait of the contribution of the CCC camps to the emergence of Mississippi's National Forests. The National Forest Reservation Commission created the Chickasawhay Purchase Unit on August 30, 1933, with the approval to buy 192,000 acres within Jones, Wayne, and Greene counties. The land under consideration was located within the Chickasawhay River drainage, hence the name for the district. Two attorneys from the Department of Agriculture arrived in southeast Mississippi in late October 1933 to begin examining reports on titles to land under option of purchase (*Hattiesburg American* 26 October 1933:1). From 1933 to 1936, 150,000 acres of clear-cut land were purchased from many small property owners. However, large tracts of land were also bought from six major landowners: (1) Wausau Southern Lumber Company, (2) Robinson Land and Lumber Company, (3) Kalmia Realty and Insurance Company, (4)

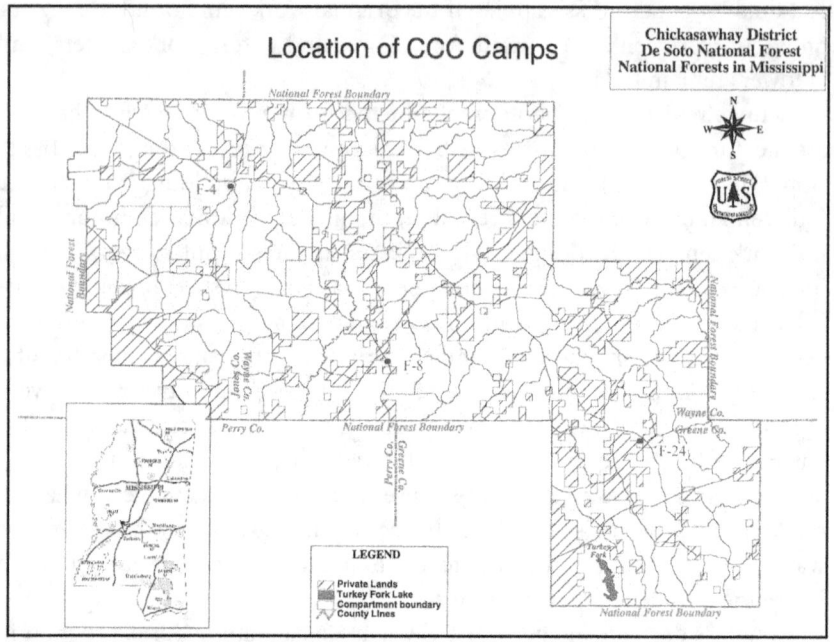

Figure 14.1. Location of CCC camps, Chickasawhay District, De Soto National Forest. Map courtesy of USDA Forest Service.

John W. Blodgett & Sons, (5) Bentley and Pope, and (6) Alabama Land and Development Company, a subsidiary of the Gulf Mobile and Ohio Railroad (Conarro 1977). On June 16, 1936, Franklin D. Roosevelt proclaimed this land as part of the De Soto National Forest (USDA Forest Service 1997).

Preparations for new CCC camps on the Chickasawhay Purchase Unit (Figure 14.1) began in September 1933 when the federal government announced plans to place one camp on each 25,000 acres of new National Forest lands in Mississippi (*Hattiesburg American* 25 October 1933:1). All camps located within the Chickasawhay Ranger District were under the supervision of the US Army's Fourth Corps. Initially, they belonged to District G, headquartered at Fort Barrancas, Pensacola, Florida. In 1937, all southern Mississippi camps were incorporated into District E with its headquarters located at Camp Beauregard, Louisiana, and later in 1940 at Fort McComb, Mississippi.[10]

Local lumber companies such as Eastman, Gardner & Co, Gilchrist-Fordney Lumber Co., J. J. Newman Lumber Co., and the Crosby Lumber Co. were contracted by the federal government in September and October to deliver half a million feet of lumber to various CCC camps in southeast Mississippi (*Laurel Leader Call* 30 September 1933:1, 27 October 1933:1).

Figure 14.2. Entrance to CCC Camp F-4.
Photo courtesy of USDA Forest Service.

Figure 14.3. Water tower, CCC Camp F-4.
Photo courtesy of USDA Forest Service.

Figure 14.4. Steam shovel at work near Ovett, Misssissippi. Photo courtesy of USDA Forest Service.

On October 10, 1933, the *Laurel Leader Call* (10 October 1933:1) announced the creation of a camp 19 miles southeast of Laurel and 5 miles from Ovett. A team consisting of an army officer, a USDA Forest Service engineer, and two local representatives from Jones County visited the forest to select the location for Camp F-4 (Figures 14.2 and 14.3). Also known as the Pat Harrison Camp, it was located on FS Road 205 in Jones County.

Meanwhile, Lieutenant F. W. Waites visited the Richton area in mid-October to review the area selected for the establishment of Camp F-8, a former Crosby and Rowland Lumber Company campsite (*Richton Dispatch* 20 October 1933:2). Located on FS Road 202 and approximately 12.5 miles northeast of Richton in Wayne County, this camp would prove to be the only camp in the National Forests in Mississippi to remain in active use until shortly after World War II.

The Early History of the Chickasawhay Ranger District

On November 2, 1933, two northern CCC companies arrived in southeast Mississippi. Company 1251 (Camp F-8) arrived in Richton at 10:40 a.m. from Fort Dix, New Jersey, while the men from Company 231 (Camp F-4) disembarked at Ovett later that same day from Fort Barrancas, Florida. Both companies had been recruited from New York and New Jersey in May 1933 and sent out to Wyoming and Utah, where they spent the summer involved in erosion control projects. Their work included building mountain roads, buildings, bridges, and the Potato Wash Dam (CCC 1934).

During their two-year stay on the Chickasawhay Purchase Unit, both companies worked on numerous projects. Their work with the USDA Forest Service included building the district's infrastructure: truck trails, bridges, fences, and miles of fire lines. As in many of the other southern National Forests, the enrollees collected pine seed, planted millions of slash and longleaf pines, worked on erosion-control projects, served as lookouts, and fought dozens of fires (Figure 14.4).

Two major projects carried out by most of the CCC enrollees on the Chickasawhay Ranger District were tree planting and fighting fires. Tree planting was a winter activity conducted by the enrollees and from time to time contracted out to local men. Under the supervision of two or more foremen, three to five 20-man crews, an assistant leader, and two leaders per crew carried out the planting. The earliest evidence of a tree-planting class was a three-day workshop for leaders and assistant leaders taught by the district's first ranger, A. K. Dexter, at both Camps F-4 and F-8 on December 3–5, 1934 (*Crystal Camp Chatter* 17 November 1934:5). Other District Rangers followed suit, as in the case of Ranger Carl Benson, who instructed Camp F-8 and F-24 leaders and assistant leaders on how to plant trees with a dibble bar at Wausau Work Center in 1937 (Tally Interview, September 15, 2003). More than 47 million trees were planted across the district between 1934 and 1941 on 36 pine and hardwood plantations and experimental plots by the CCC with an occasional hired crew or a WPA crew.[11]

While not all enrollees planted trees, most were obliged to help fight fires (Figure 14.5). The CCC enrollee was usually involved in both fire presuppression and suppression. As part of the presuppression effort, the USDA Forest Service outfitted each camp with back pumps, flaps, axes, buckets, and rakes for each man to use. Moreover, a fire truck, several drums of water, and portable phones were assigned to all three camps. Standby fire crews were established; usually, two barracks at each camp were given fire duty for a week (*The Herald* 19 December 1936:4). Enrollees on the district were also assigned to serve as lookouts on any one of the six fire towers, a task most of the enrollees did not relish because of the isolation (Landrum Interview, April 12, 2002).

Figure 14.5. CCC firefighter at work. Photo courtesy of USDA Forest Service.

In the event of a fire (suppression), the dispatcher at Wausau Tower contacted the nearest CCC camp for assistance with firefighting, day or night. In some cases, the enrollees were enlisted to help out on fires located on private land, as in the case of Mr. James Morgan's farm, where cattle and crops were saved by members of Company 5417 in 1938 (*Laurel Leader Call* 4 January 1938:5). Effective fire-fighting practices by both the district and the CCC enrollees helped the Chickasawhay Ranger District win the Silver Fire Cup, "awarded quarterly by the Supervisor's Office to the National Forest in Mississippi showing the greatest improvement in fire control over a corresponding period for the preceding year" (*Laurel Leader Call* 7 January 1938:3), at least once (*Pine Tree Newspaper* 30 January 1937:5).

In addition to the aforementioned projects, the men of Companies 231 and 1255 not only assisted hired carpenters in the construction of the structures located within their own camps, but also erected five lookout towers and built the Wausau Work Center. Beginning in the spring of 1934, the task of constructing a work center for the Chickasawhay Ranger District fell to Company 231 and a handful of men from Company 1255. The first two structures to be built were the dynamite bunkers, followed by the lookout tower (Bailey Interview, January 28, 2002). The equipment depot and the oil house were constructed during the summer and early fall, and the dispatcher's residence was completed sometime in late October or early November.

On Saturday nights, two or three trucks, depending on the number of young men who wanted to go to town, would drive the enrollees to the town of Ovett to attend dances and an occasional movie (Bailey Interview, January

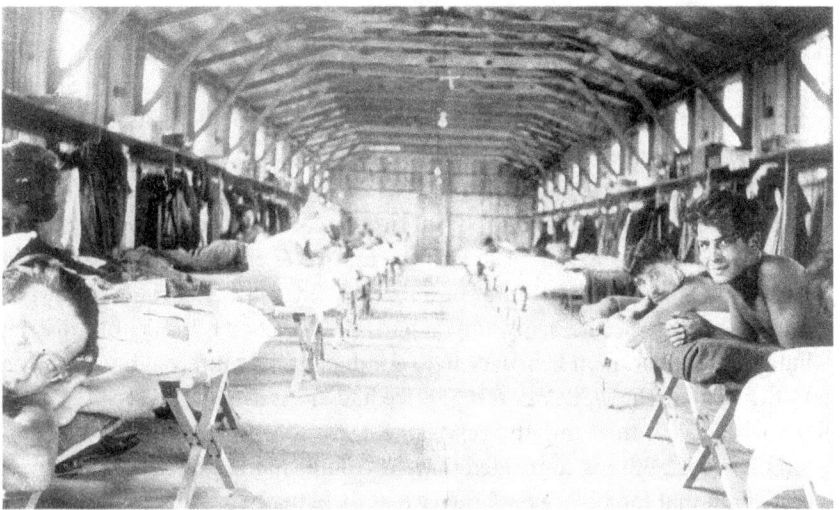

Figure 14.6. Interior of CCC barrack. Photo courtesy of USDA Forest Service.

28, 2002). By 10:30 or 11:00 p.m., the men were transported back to the camp. Those who chose to remain in the camp (Figure 14.6) could spend their free time at the recreation hall and watch movies, have their hair cut at the barbershop, or shop at the commissary.

Enrollees were issued two uniforms: a formal uniform and a work outfit. The dress uniform, worn during the weekly inspections which took place every Saturday morning, consisted of a work outfit, a most uncomfortable uniform for southern summers. In the field, the men wore tan-colored dungarees, a shirt, and a hat; many of the enrollees in the camps made alterations to their field uniform by cutting their dungarees off at the knees (Bailey Interview, January 28, 2002). All these uniforms were laundered by locals for 25 cents once a week; the enrollees would bag their dirty clothes, and a local boy would pick them and take them home to be washed by his mother. Once washed, the laundry was returned to the camp the following week.

On Sunday, October 21, 1934, the National Forests in Mississippi held its first dedication (*Laurel Leader Call* 22 October 1934:1): the Wausau Work Center, with its new 100 ft high lookout tower, equipment depot, and dispatcher's dwelling, was opened to the general public. Forest Supervisor Ray Conarro and District Ranger A. K. Dexter spoke to a crowd of more than 2,000 invitees from Jones and Wayne counties, including members of the US Army and local county representatives. The enrollees from Camps F-4 and F-8 assisted in serving a luncheon consisting of a barbecue and soft drinks.

Although most enrollees were happy to have three square meals a day and a job that provided money for their families back home, not all the members of Camp F-4 were content. It seems that in early 1934 the enrollees of Company 321 claimed that the leaders at the camp showed "a decided preference ... to Southerners, especially those who have but recently enlisted."[12] Sixteen men refused to work any further on February 7, accepted dishonorable discharges, and returned home. Others, like Mr. Rost and the 110 enrollees who signed the letter, asked the director of CCC to investigate the situation at the camp and correct the situation. Within two days, Robert Fechner telegraphed special investigator J. S. Billups to visit the camp and check into the complaint of discriminatory actions.[13] Interviews were held with 54 enrollees between February 15 and 16. The army, for its part, sent Major H. F. Nichols, district adjutant, to the camp on February 16 to conduct its own internal investigation into the matter. The USDA Forest Service had an Assistant Forest Supervisor, R. J. Riebold, visit the camp the very same day.

In his report, Billups concluded that the trouble in the camp stemmed from a knife fight that took place on January 6, 1934, between a "Laurel thug" and an enrollee.[14] The incident bred discontent that grew further when enrollee James Fell, who had been in charge of the powder crew, was replaced by L. D. Strickland, a local who had extensive experience with dynamite. His investigation also indicated that foreman G. A. Toole, "a nervous and high strung individual had on one occasion threatened to draw his knife on a CCC enrollee."[15] He recommended that Mr. Toole be transferred to another camp and that two new foremen be added to the camp's roster. With the aid of a quick investigation, open dialogue between the enrollees and the US Army and the USDA Forest Service, and transfer of one foreman, the camp returned to its peaceful ways.

Change came to the Chickasawhay Ranger District during the summer of 1935 with a new set of CCC companies and the addition of a new camp. All five CCC companies from the Second Corps Area that had been stationed on both districts of the De Soto National Forest were transferred to California. Enrollees from southern states replaced the northern companies. On August 9, 1935, Company 5413, comprised of young men from Louisiana and southern Mississippi, arrived at Camp F-4. Company 5417 was stationed at Camp F-8 four days earlier. They, too, hailed from the southern coastal states: Florida, Alabama, Mississippi, and Louisiana. A third company, Company 4441, also from Mississippi, made itself at home in Camp F-24, situated in Greene County. All in all, 1935 saw an increase in the number of enrollees working within the district and a change from Second Corps companies to those of the Fourth Corps Area.

During the course of the next two years, much was accomplished within the district. Camp F-4 built a rustic fence around the perimeter of the camp and a fishpond 18 ft long as part of its camp beautification project (*Pine Tree News* 7 September 1935:1). The enrollees, with the assistance of their camp educational advisor, won the blue ribbon at the South Mississippi Fair for their educational exhibit (*Pine Tree News* 16 November 1935:2). For the USDA Forest Service, the enrollees strung 20 miles of telephone lines, constructed 35 miles of firebreaks, one lookout tower, and 55 miles of roads and trails, to name a few of their accomplishments.

The men of Camp F-8, along with fighting fires and planting trees, worked on a number of construction projects, including the Thompson Creek Recreation Area. The men were given the task of developing a 30-acre recreation area north of the Wausau Work Center. The centerpiece of the new recreation area was a large swimming hole surrounded by picnic tables, grills, a flowing well, a well house, latrines, and a pavilion.[16] It was there that the CCC held its annual anniversary celebrations.

The "youngest" of the three camps, Camp F-24, was built 22 miles southeast of Richton in Greene County on County Road 273. It was established on June 17, 1935, with a group of 25 men originally from Company 1486 stationed at Camp F-16 on the De Soto National Forest (CCC 1936). Following two weeks of dynamiting tree stumps, construction began on July 6 and was completed on July 27, 1935. The main body of Company 4441 arrived on July 17, 1935, ready to assist in completing the camp construction. In their first year, the enrollees planted over 2.8 million trees, cleared 40 miles of fire lanes, built 13.5 miles of roads and five creosote bridges, and installed 43 concrete and galvanized iron culverts (CCC 1936).

The End of an Era

Beginning in late 1935, President Roosevelt called for a reduction in the number of CCC camps in an attempt to balance the budget during an election year (Salmond 1967). On January 1, 1936, the Corps closed 489 camps; Roosevelt requested that an additional 247 camps be closed by June 1. His request was met with an outcry from many states whose citizens had come to depend on the funds the program administered to the dependents of the enrollees and by local communities for whom a camp proved to be an economic stimulant. However, by March 1938, 291 camps were ordered to shut down so as to meet the 1938–1939 budgetary reductions. Within the state of Mississippi seven camps were given notice to close their gates, including Camp F-4 (LLC, 10 March 1938:3). On October 8, 1937, Company 5413 evacuated Camp F-4 and was transferred to California. Their departure effectively shut down the camp, for no other company was ever sent to replace the outgoing company. The camp was transferred to the USDA Forest Service for administrative use, and at some point after the Company 5413 departure, enrollees from Camp F-8 were sent to salvage the camp. By April 18, 1938, caretaker's services were terminated and most rigid buildings within the former camp were dismantled.[17]

The Civilian Conservation Corps came to end in June 1942. Two factors led to the demise of the program: an improved economy and the call to arms. Enrollment dropped as more men joined the workforce. At the start of 1941, the Corps had 300,000 young men enrolled in the program, but by the end of the year the number had dwindled to a mere 160,000 enrollees (Salmond 1967). Although President Roosevelt favored retaining the CCC and possibly combining it with the National Youth Administration so as to save the government $100 million, Congress withdrew all funding and, one by one, camps across the nation were closed down (Ermentrout 1982).

Company 3497 was pulled out of Camp SP-5 in Tishomingo and combined with Company 4441 on March 3, 1942, in the course of which the newly combined company was renamed Company 3497. (This was a common practice toward the end of the CCC era when enrollments dropped and companies were combined to create a normal-sized company.) Two months later on May 23, Camp F-24 was evacuated and closed (*Wayne County News* 28 May 1942:1). The army transferred custody of the camp to the Army Corps of Engineers (Mobile District) on August 21 and by November 4, 1942, Camp F-24 had been released to Camp Shelby and completely dismantled.[18]

Camp F-8 met another fate. Due to incomplete records, many of the details of the last three years of the camp's existence are unknown. What is recorded is that Company 5417 evacuated sometime before the end of 1941 and was replaced by Company 4425, a Junior Colored company hailing from Mount Olive. The company remained at Camp F-8 until July 18, 1942; their evacuation effectively marked the end of the camp's CCC phase.

Approximately eight months after the camp was evacuated, the Office of the Chief of Engineers (War Department) proposed transferring Camp F-8 to the Defense, Health and Welfare Services.[19] Two days later the Federal Security Agency (FSA) whose job it was to liquidate the hundreds of CCC camps across the nation, approved the transfer. The camp was transferred yet again on September 9, 1943, this time to the State of Mississippi. For a period of approximately six months, the camp served as a medical center. Twenty-six buildings and an assortment of tanks, heaters, stoves, chairs, and other incidentals were used as part of a venereal disease rapid treatment center. In a letter dated March 16, 1944, the Mississippi State Board of Health notified the Liquidating Office of the FSA that it no longer had a need for the camp and that it would be evacuating it within a few days.[20] The state suggested that the federal government might want to use the former CCC camp as a prisoner-of-war camp.

By April 13, the decision to convert the camp into a prisoner-of-war camp was made as evidenced by a telegram sent by the regional liquidating officer to his director at the FSA in Washington, D.C.[21] An inventory of all the buildings and operating accessories within Camp F-8 was submitted by the State to the Liquidating Office on June 8, 1944, and the camp was formally transferred to the USDA Forest Service.

Shortly before the Mississippi State Board of Health closed down the rapid treatment center at Camp F-8, the USDA Forest Service wrote to the FSA inquiring as to whether or not the camp could be converted into a branch camp for prisoners of war.[22] The USDA Forest Service's Timber Production War Project was interested in working with the US Army to supply them with a free source of labor.

During the second half of 1943, the US Government began to ship German and Italian prisoners of war captured in North Africa to prisons in the United States (Skates 2001). The federal government decided that it was less expensive to house and feed prisoners of war on American soil. Moreover, the prisoners could be put to work on a number of non-military jobs. Four major POW base camps were constructed by the US Army in Mississippi: Camp Clinton, Camp McCain, Camp Como, and Camp Shelby. In 1944, the four base camps established 15 branch camps, 10 in the Delta and 5 in southeast Mississippi. The five branch camps in the Piney Woods of Mississippi were situated in Brookhaven, Picayune, Saucier, Gulfport, and Richton (former Camp F-8). Army personnel from Camp Shelby oversaw operations at the Richton camp. For the most part, the prisoners sent to Richton worked on forestry projects. Work included planting seedlings, harvesting timber, and clearing land.

Although World War II ended in May 1945, the POWs imprisoned in Mississippi were not sent back to their homelands until 1946. Proclaiming that the United States had a labor shortage, President Truman recommended that the prisoners of war remain in this country until the labor shortage was over. Many of the prisoners in the Mississippi camps remained working for three years. By mid-1946, the Richton branch camp had been evacuated and dismantled by the army.[23] Thus the third and final chapter in the life of Camp F-8 came to a close after more than 12 years in service.

Overall, more than 2,000 Civilian Conservation Corps enrollees worked in the Chickasawhay Ranger District from 1933 to 1942. They constructed the roads, fire lines, fences, and bridges. These young men erected six lookout towers and constructed two recreation areas and one work center. They planted over 47 million pines and three experimental plots, strung miles of telephone lines, and fought countless forest fires. The men of Camps F-4, F-8, and F-24 built the founding physical infrastructure of the Chickasawhay Ranger District, and along with the mature longleaf pines and the gravel roads, the Wausau Work Center is today a visible reminder of the enrollees' legacy.

Seventy years later, little remains of Camp F-4 (site CK-343-1) and Camp F-24 (site CK-444-5). After the buildings were dismantled and removed, the areas were returned to timber production and most of the cement slabs and foundations were destroyed and carted away. Although like all other camps, Camp F-8 (site 22WA622) had its buildings removed and shipped for reuse by the military at another location, it suffered less damage once it was returned to the USDA Forest Service. Its foundations were not tampered with and became incorporated into pine plantations. Hopefully, one day the site will be able to share its remaining secrets with future archaeologists.[24]

Notes

1. Record of Occupancy, April 1, 1933, to March 31, 1941, Camps F-1–F-3, National Forests in Mississippi; Records of the Southern Regional Office, CCC, 1937–1942; Records of the USDA Forest Service, Record Group 95, National Archives and Records Administration, Southeast Region (East Point, Georgia).

2. (Camps F-4, F-5, F-6, F-7, and F-8) (Record of Occupancy, Camps F-4–F-8, National Forests in MS; RG 95 NARA, Southeast Region [EP]).

3. CCC 1934; *Wayne County News* [WCN], 14 September 1933:1.

4. Record of Occupancy, Camps F-9–F-18, National Forests in MS; RG 95, NARA, Southeast Region.

5. Record of Occupancy, Camps F-1 and F-4, National Forests in MS; RG 95; NARA, Southeast Region (EP).

6. *Laurel Leader Call*, 10 March 1938:3.

7. Record of Occupancy, Camps F-20–F-25, National Forests in MS; RG 95; NARA, Southeast Region (EP]).

8. Record of Occupancy, Camps F-26–F-29, National Forests in MS; RG 95; NARA, Southeast Region (EP).

9. Inventory of Buildings and Structures Which Are to Be Continued Indefinitely, 1948–1961, Engineering, Supervisor's Office, National Forests in Mississippi, Jackson.

10. Camp Inspection Report, Follow-up Report, Camp F-8, Company 5417, Richton, Mississippi, December 7, 1940; Stack 530 65:25:6; Records of the Civilian Conservation Corps, Record Group 35; National Archives at College Park, Maryland.

11. Report on Plantations or Seedings, 1935–1941, Form 134, De Soto National Forest, Chickasawhay Ranger District, Laurel, Mississippi.

12. Charles W. Rost, to Mr. Robert Fechner, Washington, D.C., February 7, 1934; Folder F-8; Records of the Civilian Conservation Corps, Record Group 35, Stack 530 65:25:6; National Archives at College Park, Maryland.

13. Robert Fechner, Director, CCC, Washington, D.C., to J. S. Billups, Fort Worth, TX, February 12, 1934; Folder F-8; Records of the Civilian Conservation Corps, Record Group 35, Stack 530 65:25:6; National Archives at College Park, Maryland.

14. Mr. J. S. Billups, Laurel, MS, to Mr. Robert Fechner, Director, CCC, Washington, D.C., February 16, 1934; Folder F-8; Records of the Civilian Conservation Corps, Record Group 35, Stack 530 65:25:6; National Archives at College Park, Maryland.

15. Mr. J. S. Billups, Special Investigator, ECW, to Mr. R. M. Conarro, Forest Supervisor, Brookhaven, MS, February 16, 1934; Folder F-8; Records of the Civilian Conservation Corps, Record Group 35, Stack 530 65:25:6; National Archives at College Park, Maryland.

16. Camp Inspection Report, Camp F-8, Company 5417, Richton, Mississippi, Special Report, June 16, 1938; Stack 530 65:25:6; Records of the Civilian Conservation Corps, Record Group 35; National Archives at College Park, Maryland.

17. Record of Occupancy, Camp F-8, National Forests in MS; Record Group 95; NARA, Southeast Region (EP).

18. Record of Occupancy, Camp F-24, National Forests in MS; Record Group 95; NARA, Southeast Region (EP).

19. M. L. Parler, Jr., Major, Corps of Engineers, to The Director, Civilian Conservation Corps, Washington, D.C., March 25, 1943; Folder F-8; Records of the Civilian Conservation Corps, Record Group 35, Stack 530 65:25:6; National Archives at College Park, Maryland.

20. William G. Hollister, Assistant Surgeon USPMS, to M. A. Stephens, Liquidating Officer, Washington, D.C., March 16, 1944; Folder F-8; Stack 530 65:25:6; Record Group 35; National Archives at College Park, Maryland.

21. Richard H. Lyle, Regional Director, to M. A. Stephens, Liquidating Officer, Washington, D.C., April 13, 1944; Folder F-8; Records of the Civilian Conservation Corps, Record Group 35, Stack 530 65:25:6; National Archives at College Park, Maryland.

22. W. M. Palmer, Jr., Acting Area Forester, to Richard H. Lyle, Regional Director, Federal Security Agency, Atlanta, March 9, 1944; Folder F-8; Stack 530 65:25:6; Record Group 35; National Archives at College Park, Maryland.

23. Record of Occupancy, Camp F-8, National Forests in MS; Record Group 95; NARA, Southeast Region (EP).

24. Much valuable local evidence related to the CCC was found in local town newspapers and even CCC camp newspapers; specific stories are cited in the bibliography of this volume. Transcripts of oral history interviews, all available at the Chickasawhay Ranger District, are simply cited by date of interview in the bibliography. Original archival documentation is cited in footnotes due to the requirement for citation specificity.

CHAPTER 15

Logging Out the Delta: From Mosquitoville to the Sardis & Delta Railroad

Mary Evelyn Starr

Many people vaguely know that the Yazoo-Mississippi Delta was once forest like a lot of the rest of the state, but few know when and how that changed and even fewer know much about the detailed tiny actions of acquiring forested land, logging it out to make profit on the wood, and eventually building a political economy and a railway infrastructure to make that possible. In this chapter, I demonstrate how documents in land offices and in possession of individuals can still tell significant parts of that story—including the details of the malarial miasmas of backswamp conditions for the labor it required—and thereby define what can be expected archaeologically, establishing a documentary framework for investigating a stupendous case of land alteration (which hasn't stopped yet).

Mosquitoville: Parrott and Chorley Begin Clearance of the Delta

When Sam Brookes came to Quitman County to conduct archaeological work in 1971, the landscape was entirely dominated by cotton, but there were still men alive who had seen it as "big woods," complete with bears and panthers. The county was logged off between 1880 and 1920, and there had been a large number of sawmills throughout the county. In fact, had Sam's excavation on Pecan Lake (reported in Connaway 1982), which was intended to test for Archaic deposits, moved a short distance north, he would have encountered the remains of the 1890s Sledge Brothers and Alexander sawmill instead of a Mississippian wall trench house. Quitman County was a Reconstruction-era creation, a gumbo-dominated backswamp with a sparse population that probably largely duplicated Mississippi-period settlement patterns. The Coldwater River was the means of moving logs and other forest products out of the area, and the siltier soils along the banks of the Coldwater were the first areas to be cleared for farming. The first timbering in the area that became the town of Sledge was done by two English emigrants, John Parrott (1844–1920) and John Chorley (1861–1930). Parrott called his Pecan Bayou camp "Mosquitoville," and from the back porch of the cotton trailer-cum-mobile home at the Starr headquarters on the Alexander place, Sam would have been looking out toward it. John Parrott kept a journal; however, only one volume (December 1886–April 1889) is known to survive as a typescript produced by my great-great-aunt Eloise Winston Taylor, daughter of an early Pontotoc County historian (Winston 1931). I have deposited a copy of this diary with the Mississippi Department of Archives and History. The Parrott diary is probably a unique document for the area and time, and an important resource for the study of pre-railroad logging.

Local folklore has it that John Parrott was a Welshman; on July 12, 1888 he made an unfavorable comparison of Birmingham, Alabama, with "a Welch Iron town." However, his tombstone says "born in England" and the Parrett River and villages of this name are in the west of England, in Somersetshire, across the Severn estuary from Wales. When J. O. Chorley's son George registered for the WWI draft, he gave his father's birthplace as "Wardiscomb." Consultation of atlases fails to reveal any such place, but Chorley was illiterate, his son would have had only a verbal basis for the name, and a large majority of -combe toponyms are found in the southwestern counties. Both Parrott and Chorley were Methodists, a denomination then prevalent in Wales and the industrial west of England. Based on such various pieces of circumstantial evidence, Parrott and Chorley's connection may have been as fellow westcountrymen.

Small-time loggers like Parrott and Chorley used oxen and caralogs to skid timber to bayous, as several passages from Parrott's diary show:[1] The men and teams or yokes hauling the timber were hired on a temporary basis.[2] The caralog was a cart with two wheels of diameter about 2 meters; a boom, winch, and chain was attached to the axle to lift the butt end of the log to make it easier to skid.

On the bayou banks, loggers chained the logs together with toggles (short chains connecting two small steel wedges at either end) and then used ash-helved pikes.[3] Besides skid roads in the woods, driving logs in the bayous required the cutting of float roads.[4] This work was done when the water was low, in preparation for a drive when the rise came.[5] Parrott made dugout canoes for use in driving his rafts of timber.[6] Englishmen were traveling by dugout canoe in Africa, South America, and Asia as well at this time, and dugouts continued in use in the Delta into the 1920s. Driving timber by water was still practiced after the construction of the railroad and dummy lines;

contractors called for their toggles to be returned as soon as the logs were loaded on cars.

Another seemingly anachronistic fact shown by the Parrott diary is that deadening was the method of clearing patches for cultivation; although he does not describe it in detail.[7] It must have consisted of girdling trees and knocking or chipping off the bark to kill the trees, as Neolithic people have done around the world. The practice is mentioned in timber deeds into the 1910s.

Small steamboats penetrated the Coldwater country to take out stavebolts and heading blocks for the vast quantities of foodstuffs and commercial products sold by the barrel.[8] White oak timber was the primary material for barrels. Among the first timber contracts recorded in the same area Parrott had cut over a decade before, after the Yazoo & Mississippi Valley Railroad (YMV) was built 1901–1902, were scattered stands of white oak sold for cooperage.

Although logging was his main business, Parrott spent a great deal of time hunting, fishing, trapping, and "bumming." He describes the extensive wildlife of the bottoms: deer, turkey, coon, opossum, squirrel, muskrat, wolf, bear, catamount, panther, beaver, mink, otter, "trout" (bass), catfish, bees, duck, and goose. His descriptions of what he saw on his deer stand, his fish trap or trap lines, acquisition of new guns, and hunts are often more detailed than the notes on work.[9] However, Parrott felt that those times were passing.[10]

Parrott dug wells and ditches and also helped far-flung neighbors on their farms.[11] His nearest villages were Mastodon, at the foot of the bluff where there was a store, and Pleasant Grove, farther into the hills, where he attended church, funerals, and weddings; voted and attended political events; and went to Christmas parties, dances, and visiting.

Parrott handled all parts of the timber work: measuring timber and making contracts; engaging sawyers and teams; cutting and trailing logs and working in the bayous; making canoes, paddles, wedges, and pike poles; doing his own blacksmith work; hiring, paying, and managing his white and black workers; and fetching and issuing their rations. He struggled to keep hands and teams and sometimes complained of his labor.[12] He did not keep a mule or horse and often walked to Mastodon, Pleasant Grove, and Sardis, occasionally taking a train in to Memphis, to Jackson, or to visit friends in Alabama. His walking ability was legendary and attested in the diary.[13]

He makes many mentions of deaths and illnesses, and doctored himself as well as his young partner Chorley and other men.[14] He often commented on the unhealthy locale.[15] Besides various "digesting apparatus" (May 6, 1888), complaints Parrott suffered from included many unspecified colds and fevers—the primary cause of sickness was of course malaria.[16] As anyone who has visited Sledge can attest, the name "Mosquitoville" was no joke.[17]

Johnnie Parrott's diary demonstrates an extensive use of the landscape, exploiting fish and game as well as timber, coupled with land clearing and small-time farming. He appears to have been cutting primarily cypress brakes, leaving the oak-hickory ridges and ash-gum flats away from the bayous to be cut after the railroad arrived little more than a decade later. Timber sales after dummy lines were being built off the YMV main line would sometimes assign various cuts off the same tract to different companies (oak being the most valuable construction material, then hickory-pecan for tools and vehicles, with ash and gum sometimes sold separately and the cypress worked by specialized crews prepared for water and platforms above the buttresses).

Parrott and Chorley began to acquire farmland in the 1890s and to plant cotton as the land was logged out. In March 1890, the LNO&TRR Co. made a warranty deed to John Chorley.[18] Certificate No. 937 of the LNO&T Land Department was for 40 acres in S25T7R10W. The sale was at 8 percent interest, with notes of $48 due on November 13, 1889, 1890, 1891, 1892, and 1893 (at the end of the crop). The deed excluded any land in a 50-ft right-of-way, if the railroad were to cross the land, including all "cuts, embankments and ditches and other works necessary to secure and protect the main line switches and branches of the railroad." The note was marked canceled January 12, 1892, when Chorley sold the land.[19] Thus Chorley only owned the land for about a year, making a warrantee deed to W. D., O. D., and N. R. Sledge and G. H. Alexander, all of Panola County, in February 1890; the consideration was $91.80 and the four remaining notes of $48 due to the LNO&TRR, and Chorley made his "X" before Panola County justice of the peace R. H. Barham.[20] Chorley is the spelling adopted by Parrott; other Panola County residents would spell it Charley, Chorly, and Chorlie. That the land was sold to Sledge Brothers may indicate that Chorley had tried and failed to make a crop, as they were the main furnishing merchants and land speculators in the area. Chorley continued to buy small tracts through the 1890s. The value of land increased rapidly with the construction of the Yazoo & Mississippi Valley railroad through the Sledge brothers' land.

Despite his intentions mentioned in the diary, Parrott apparently did not formally purchase land until 1898.[21] The land is very near his Mosquitoville camp. Delta Development Co., a large-scale holder of swamplands, sold 80 acres in S2T8R10W to Parrott for $480 in December 1897 ($6.00/acre). The deed was signed by George E. Ross Lewin as president of Delta Development Co. (DDC) in Arapahoe County, Colorado (Denver).[22] Parrott executed a deed of trust to secure the payment of three notes for $150 due in December 1898, 1899, and 1900, with 8 percent interest, and a marginal note indicates that the notes were satisfied.[23] A note on DDC stationery is attached to other mortgages on page M:45. The stationery is headed "Hardwood Timber & Cotton

Lands, W. F. Swan, manager, Biloxi, Miss., 190___." The note is addressed to Messers. Sledge & McGee, Mastodon, Mississippi, and states that three notes are enclosed for collection, including Parrott's ($100). Parrott executed a deed of trust in favor of N. T. Burraughs, for a second 80-acre tract in S2T8R10W, for four notes of $100 each, due on January 1, 1890, 91, 92 and 93, at 8 percent interest from January 8, 1889 ($5/acre, discounting interest). This land is adjacent to the 80 acres he had purchased the year before; the two tracts together were still known as the Parrott Place when it was taken from Starr farms in the Reagan-era farm foreclosures; Parrott's house still stood in the 1970s. The deed of trust was released as satisfied two and a half years early.[24]

Timber companies followed as fast as the YMV was built. In an August 1901 timber contract for $575 Chorley sold to the Chickasaw Cooperage Co. of Memphis all the white oak on an imprecisely located tract in S22T7R9. He also granted free ingress and egress for cutting and removing the timber within five years. Many others, including old friends mentioned in the Parrott diary, sold white oak timber to Chickasaw Cooperage between May 1901 and September 1902. In August 1906, J. O. Chorley sold a half acre to St. Phillip Baptist Church for $25, a still active congregation in Sledge,[25] and in 1924 he sold an acre for $50 to Spring Hill Baptist Church adjacent to the Fair View Colored Methodist Episcopal Church, Mastodon Circuit, Sardis District of North Mississippi Conference, that had been deeded by J. J. Allen in November 1900 for $35.[26] These grants indicate that sharecroppers were pouring into the area and beginning to work the freshly cleared lands around Sledge.

Parrott never married; on March 9, 1889, his diary noted poignantly, "received a letter from Miss Lillian Dunlap that settle me from any further connections with the Dunlap family I always expected to be a member of the family but Peggy say No." Chorley's children became his heirs. John Parrott died away from his home while in Memphis on June 17, 1920, and his will, made 10 days before his death, was brought for probate by John O. Chorley, who had been named in it as executor without bond.[27] Parrott left his land in Quitman County to Chorley's sons George (160 acres, S2T8R10W) and Curtis (70 acres, S22 and S9T7R9W) and his $1,200 in Liberty Bonds at the Bank of Sardis and $200 in cash at the Bank of Sledge to Chorley's three younger daughters to be divided equally, as well as $500 in cash to the oldest daughter Ida B., with any residue after the settlement of his debts to be divided equally among the Chorley daughters.

Although a generation younger, John Chorley outlived his partner by only 10 years. His will was probated in Panola County in October 1930, although at that time he considered himself a resident of Sledge.[28] "Realizing the certainty of death," he first asked that his debts and funeral expenses be paid. He left to his wife, Kate, their residence in Sledge and the houses and lots occupied by DeWitt Hicks, Dr. J. D. House, and Mrs. Mary Freeman, as well as three one-story brick store buildings occupied by Helm & Reid, general merchants, Miss Ocie Jepsen, and Dear Brothers' Café. Kate was to hold these properties for life and afterward they were to be divided among his six children. To his four daughters, Mrs. Mary Freeman, Mrs. Gladys Sorrels, Mrs. Ida Lee Whatley, and Jessie Chorley, he left equal shares in the 640 acre Rice Place in Panola County (S29T7R9W). To his sons George and E. C., he left land in Quitman County (S26T7R10W). To his grandson J. O. Chorley, he left two vacant lots in Sledge. His mercantile stocks, bank stocks, gin stocks, notes, and accounts were to be divided equally among the six children.

The partnership lasted longer than both of them: Parrott and Chorley are buried in the same plot at Pleasant Grove Cemetery.

The Yazoo & Mississippi Valley Railroad and Logging at Sledge

By 1900, the State of Mississippi had granted much of the backswamp portion of the Delta to various railroad companies to entice them to develop the region. Some lands had been offered and lost several times due to the speculative nature of nineteenth-century railroad construction. The Mississippi & Tennessee (M&T) was completed to Batesville in 1855 and met the "Main" or Mississippi Central at Grenada in 1858. The Louisville, New Orleans and Texas (LNO&T) was built through Tunica and Coahoma counties in the 1880s. The M&T passed through old settled country in the loess hills and so did not spur a logging boom. The LNO&T initially served the plantations on the higher, sandier parts of these Delta counties, but would also provide the shipping for numerous spurs and sawmills. There is abundant documentary evidence of the timber era from these counties, particularly in eastern Tunica County and southern Coahoma County, but it will not be included in this essay. The construction of the Yazoo & Mississippi Valley Railroad (YMV) around the turn of the twentieth century through Tunica, Quitman, and Tallahatchie counties did produce a short-lived timber boom, largely over by WWI, as northern timbermen rushed to log out the area and sell the lands on to cotton planters. In the 1880s, the state had made a major effort to attract buyers for swamplands; Indiana, Illinois, and Kentucky provided many investors in hardwood timber, as those states would soon be stripped of their valuable oak and hickory forests. Quitman County in particular had a very large number of timber companies, which had cleared most of the county and turned it over to cotton farmers by 1920. The history of these companies can be traced in part through the records of the chancery clerks.

Table 15.1. YMV spur and tram contracts in Quitman County deed books.

Citation	2nd party	Location	Date	Plat
Y:171	McPherson Bros.	Stalls	Oct 1907	Present
Y:174	Russe & Burgess		Oct 1907	Removed
Y:176	C. S. Gladden	3miles long, S5,6 T26 R1W and S1 T26 R2W near Alfrey		Removed
Y:179	E. W. Taylor	Sledge, S 21,20,19 T7 R10W; S 27, 28, 20 T7 R10W	Oct 1906	Torn out
X:486	Chess & Wymond		Apr 1907	Torn out
X:489	W. B. Crane & Co.	1/2 mile near Falcon	Aug 1907	Present
X:609	Lamb-Fish Lumb. Co.	3 miles, S22, 21,20, 29 T26 R1W near Chancy	May 1908	Torn out
X:324	Bell & Coggeshall	2 miles, S 20, 21, 22 T27N R1W near Lambert	Apr 1905	Torn out
W:288	Bell & Coggeshall	2 miles T27R1W near Lambert		No plat
X:332	B&C to J. E. Bell	Transfer of lease		No plat
W:291	W. B. Crane	5 miles	Dec 1905	Cut out
W:596	Sligh Furn. Co. and E. W. Taylor, from Lilley Lumber Co.	2.5 miles, transfer of lease	May 1906	No plat
W:598	Mahlon Bell & Co.	Under Coldwater trestle at Hinchcliff	July 1906	No plat
X:86	L. Marks	His business	Nov 1906	Plat
X:89	W. W. Dickason, etc.	Sidetrack at Vance	Sept 1906	No plat
V:250	Bacon-Nolan	3.5miles, S 14, 15, 22, 23 T 26N R1W at Chauncey	Mar 1905	Torn out
V:351	Bell & Coggeshall	Per plat	Mar 1905	None
V:410	Chess & Wymond	S 36, 33 T27N R1W, Buford Lake	Apr 1905	Cut out
V:434	Interstate Cooperage	4.5 miles per plat, south of Lambert	May 1905	Drawn in book
V:546	Bell & Coggeshall	2 mi. in T27N R1W near Lambert to extend 3/4 mi.	Aug 1905	None

After the arrival of the YMV, large-scale lumbering could begin in earnest. Between 1902 and 1920, an extensive network of logging trams was laid out to carry timber and lumber away from Quitman County. Almost every named location along the YMV (Yellow Lake, Sledge, Falcon, Rowland, Darling, Essex, Hinchcliff, Burgess, Marks, Van Buren [Lambert], Yarborough, Oliverfried, Denton, Longstreet, Lake Buford, Carr, Vance, Harriet, Chancey, and Pates) had at least one dummy line extending into tracts of timber owned very largely by northern timber companies. A major hindrance to reconstructing and locating these early twentieth-century "trams" or "dummy lines" (logging railroads) is the fact that almost all of the relevant plats have been stolen from the records of the Quitman County chancery clerk. Hopefully, copies remain in Cook County, Illinois (home of the Illinois Central), or in the records of the former Railroad Commission in Jackson, Mississippi. Extensive record search has documented many aspects of these operations, but is not included here for lack of space. These findings in part confirm and in part refute the conclusions of Howe (2003), who has produced a map that purports to show all Mississippi dummy lines. For instance, Charles Estes, Holmes Lumber Co., Mossman Lumber Co., Quitman Lumber Co., Ryan-Stimson Lumber Co., Sligh Furniture Co., E. W. Taylor, and Taylor & Estes all supposedly ran logging railroads out of Sledge (Howe 2003). However, these appear to be various users of the same dummy line. These logging trams are summarized in Table 15.1.

The Sardis & Delta Railroad: The "Carrier Line" and Industrial Logging in the Delta

In the same year that the YMV was being pushed through the Delta, a Pennsylvania timber company moved into Sardis, in Panola County, to build a 25-mile line through the loess bluffs and into the Delta to the Coldwater-Tallahatchie confluence. This logging railroad, officially titled the Sardis & Delta Railroad, but generally known as the "Carrier Line," was immortalized in a song of that title by a blind musician, Sid Hemphill, that Alan Lomax (1993) considered America's great native ballad:

Nobody had a nickel, you couldn't get a dime
If you want to make your money, boys, work on Mr. Carrier's line.

    Refrain. Oh, my honey babe . . . .

Mr. Dave Cowart went on Mr. Carrier's engine; Mr. Carrier he looked and laughed,

Mary Evelyn Starr

"Tell you, Dave Cowart, don't run my train too fast."

Mr. Dave told Mr. Carrier, "Man, don't you know I know your rule?
Tell you, Mr. Carrier, a train ain't no mule."

Mr. Dave Cowart went down to Baptist; Mr. Carrier stood on the railroad track.
"Send back Dave Cowart. Get Mr. Bailey back."

Mr. Dave told Mr. Carrier, "Man, fire me if you will.
Every time it come a shower of rain, he can't run it up Johnson Hill."

Mr. Carrier said, "Dave Cowart, see what you have done.
You left Sardis at twelve o'clock, done made it back at one."

Mr. Dave said, "Well, Mr. Carrier, let me have my way.
Let me run this Seven Spot. I'll make three trips a day."

Mr. Carrier said, "No, Dave Cowart, tell you in time.
Can't let you run the Seven no more." "Well, I'll have to run the Nine."

Everybody around Sardis said, "Mr. Carrier, I know you got your way.
Mr. Bailey's much too old a man to run your train like Dave."

Last one Monday morning, it come a shower of rain.
Nine come to Ballentine, blowing like a fast train.

When the Nine got over to Sardis with a large load of logs,
Mr. Carrier told the people at the plant, "Yonder train off the Yellow Dog."

They said to Mr. Carrier, "Man, ain't you 'shamed,
Looking out the window, don't know your own train?"

Mr. Carrier went to Dave Cowart, "Dave, I done told you so.
Train cost too much. You can't run my train no more."

Mr. Carrier's timber mens quit too. Thought they all was mad.
They didn't like his paydays, cuz he's paying 'em off in brass.

Mr. Carrier's timber mens left, and they thought they was going home.
Stopped down the railroad, farming at Malone's.

Mr. Carrier went down to Malone's. He didn't mean no harm.
He didn't know his timber men knowed how to farm.

Oh, they couldn't pay 'em no greenbacks, couldn't pay 'em no gold.
Couldn't pay 'em no silver. All his banks done closed.

Mr. Carrier's engine left Sardis then. She left there mighty hot.
Got down to Malone's Trestle, where he could wreck that Seven Spot.

Well, they telephoned to Mr. Carrier, "Don't you think it'd be nice?
"Telephone to Sardis and get Dr. Rice."

Mr. Carrier said to Dave Cowart, "Man, ain't you 'shamed?
You done wrecked my Seven Spot, done scalded preacher's hand."

Mr. Carrier said to the conductor, "Doctor, think you can save his life?"
Conductor says, "He's a lazy man. He won't hardly die."

He wore a might fine coat, boys, might fine shirt.
Rid that train every day. He didn't never work.

I played on Mr. Carrier's railroad, Sardis on Main and Beale.
I made dollars down there without working in the field.

Tried to carry him down to Emma's. Aunt Emma hollered and screamed.
"Needn't cry, Miss Emma, but he got scalded by the steam."

Transcription by David H. Evans (1976). Used with permission.

The circumstances of the song appear to place the incident sometime around the 1907 panic, which threw lumber workers all over Mississippi out of work. Hemphill mentions payments in "brass," greenbacks, gold, and silver being suspended by bank closures. In the cash-poor economy of the late nineteenth and early twentieth century, many planters and sawmillers paid in brass tokens redeemable in their stores. This prevented an outlay of cash and at the same time kept the employee dependent on his employer for supply. The tokens are sometimes referred to as "brozene" in reference to the copper alloy most commonly used. Other employers used paper coupons or "hand checks," also for use in their commissaries. In some places and at some times these private coinages circulated in the wider population, in the same way cotton-seed certificates did. Search of a large collection of Mississippi tokens does not reveal the Carrier company having any made in its own name.[29]

The Carrier family, from Buffalo, New York, had already created a timber empire in Jefferson County, Pennsylvania, about 160 miles south, building sawmills and buying out others and involving multiple Carrier men in the business from 1865 to the end of the century. By the time the Jefferson County history was written in 1888, "the pine timber [was] almost a thing of the past ... and it [would] take but a few years to exhaust the hemlock. The grand forests of magnificent trees ... have all fallen before the lumberman's axe" (Scott 1888). Many of the New York, New England, and Pennsylvania timbermen had already moved on to Kentucky and Indiana, whence they would descend on the South to destroy its forests even more rapidly.

Cassius M. Carrier purchased several large tracts in Quitman County in 1899. Delta and Pine Land Co. (DPL) of Jackson, Mississippi, had bought several townships in 1889.[30] These remote transactions of large blocks indicate that the lands were swamp, not desirable to settlers. Therefore, they are likely to have seen little or no actual settlement except for perhaps some hunting/fishing camps and a little stream-side poaching of timber. DPL sold Carrier 11,646 acres in T28R1E for $64,058, of which $40,000 was paid down. In return, Carrier made a deed of trust to DPL for $24,058, the balance, at 6 percent, due in four months.[31] This is the partial township in old Panola County, below the Choctaw-Chickasaw line, along the route of present Highway 6, comprised of land now drained by the Quitman-Panola Canal. Subsequently, DPL deeded Carrier an additional 160 acres in T28R1E for $885.[32] Delta Development Corp. sold C. M. Carrier another 3,116 acres in T9R10W for $17,141.[33] This is another fractional township above the Choctaw-Chickasaw line, immediately west of the large DPL block. The transaction was made by G. E. Ross Lewin, president of Delta Development, in Arapahoe County, Colorado. The lands were adjacent to and immediately north of the T28NR1E tract. In November 1899, C. M. Carrier, of Carrier, Pennsylvania, made a second large purchase from DPL, 3,578 acres in T27R1E, including the confluences of the Coldwater, Tallahatchie, and Yocona rivers, for $19,680.[34] DPL later sold Carrier an additional 320 acres in T27R1E for $1,762 and 42 acres in T28NR1E for $235.[35] In these transactions, DPL president Benton appeared in Chicago and secretary Watson in Jackson.[36]

Carrier would later sell the western 10,000 acres, more than half of this grant roughly west of Ash Log Bayou, to a rival northern lumber company, Taylor & Crate (T&C) of West Virginia, in a transaction disguised as $10 and "other good and valuable consideration."[37] T&C logged it from a spur off the YMV ca. 1907–1919. Carrier would also make exchanges with another northern timber baron, J. R. Darnell, who built the Batesville Southwestern Railroad south of the Tallahatchie, to adjust their boundaries and allow them to cut all along the riverbanks.

Three purchases in Sardis in late 1900 provided the beginning of the Carrier mill site and quarters. In November 1900, C. M. Carrier of Buffalo, New York, bought a residence and lot from W. H. and Victoria Short, of Sardis, for $2,500.[38] Carrier was to take possession January 1, 1901. In December 1900, G. W. Ballentine of Panola County sold C. M. Carrier 45 acres adjoining the Short purchase in the S34T7R7 for $567.12.[39] This was to be the sawmill site. The sale was made with the understanding that M. T. Riles had a lease on a lot in this land on which he had a gin house and machinery, and that Carrier was not to interfere with Riles's occupancy until the expiration of Riles's lease, or when he surrendered it. Ballentine further reserved all the buildings on the land, if he would remove them.

In December 1900, a charter for the Sardis & Delta Railroad was granted by Governor A. H. Longino.[40] The individuals petitioning for this charter were Cassius M. Carrier; Robert M. Carrier of Sardis; Louis M. Parr of Brockwayville, Jefferson County, Pennsylvania; A. W. Shands of Sardis and T. J. Hunter of Sardis. Shands was the corporation's lawyer, who would represent them in many lawsuits. The line was to begin at a point about a mile south of Sardis and to run southwesterly to some point on the Yazoo & Mississippi Valley Railroad in Quitman County (which had not yet been completed; the connection would never materialize, perhaps because it would have entailed bridging the Coldwater). The construction was to begin "at once" and to be completed in two years. The capital stock was fixed at $100,000 divided into $100 shares. The initial officers were C. M. Carrier, president; H. J. Hunter, vice president; and R. M. Carrier, secretary-treasurer. At the initiation of this project, R. M. Carrier was 25 years old.

The legal origin of the Carrier Lumber & Manufacturing Company is documented in the Panola County Chancery Court records.[41] The petition for a corporate charter was approved in February 1903. C. M. and R. M. Carrier and any others who became associated would do business by the sign of "C.M. Carrier & Son." The corporation was to be domiciled in the First Court District of Panola County, near Sardis PO, and the charter was to run 50 years. The capital stock of $60,000 was to be divided into 600 shares of $100 each. When the stock was subscribed up to $20,000 the corporation could commence business. As to its activities, the charter provided for a full range of lumber business tasks: the company would manufacture and sell lumber, with the power to acquire and grant property, real, personal, and mixed, necessary for that business; it would purchase and erect buildings, railroads, trams, and other appurtenances for a sawmill and plane mill to manufacture logs into timber and lumber; it would also purchase and erect store buildings and transact a general merchandise business. The company would also develop a settlement, building water and electric light works to be used by the plant and for sale to the public and building and leasing tenement houses. It would have the power to sell and dispose of the commodities and manufactured articles; to construct and operate booms, dams, and other devices for moving logs and other floatables in a way not in contravention of state law; to acquire and use teams, wagons, and drays for the lumber business; to establish and operate branch lumber yards, offices, and agents in Mississippi and other states; to acquire and operate buildings and machinery for manufacturing lumber into furniture, wagons, buggies, handles, spokes, and other products chiefly of wood; and to buy materials for the completion of such articles. Carrier & Son had the power to borrow money to be used in operations and to secure payment by mortgages or bonds and to enjoy all rights and privileges granted corporations under Chapter 25 of the Code of 1892. Management and control was vested in a board of directors of two to five stockholders to be chosen annually. The delay between the grants of the railroad charter and corporate charter may have something to do with the state's skepticism about the timber barons they had invited down to subdue the Delta; under populist governors the state had passed laws limiting the size of landholdings to control the power of these huge capitalist interests.

Right-of-way leases and construction of the Sardis & Delta Railroad (S&D) began in late 1900 and early 1901, as the line was being built. The leases were made over several years (1900–1903), but were all filed at the same time, in 1906, after the S&D was in full operation.[42] Apparently, Robert Ruffin served as Carrier's agent in obtaining the 28 required leases. Many of the deeds follow a general formula, but many are sketchy and incomplete, and there are many errors in the locations, including incorrect Township and Range calls. The deeds are not detailed enough to precisely locate the right-of-way, but rather refer to the right-of-way "as surveyed," "as laid out," or in some cases even "as built." Due to inaccurate and conflicting property descriptions, the lands were further traced in the Chain of Title to Land Deeds, 1836–1909, First District. These will be cited in the immediately following paragraphs as "chain." The descriptions below are arranged in geographical order, west and then south along the route.

On December 29, 1900, G. W. Ballentine, for $1 and the benefit of a railroad, granted a strip "as surveyed" in S34T7R7 and S4T8R7, with a 50-ft construction easement and then only as much land as needed for operation of the railroad.[43] This would allow the railroad to run west from the old gin site purchased from Ballentine. On the same day, Miss M. P. Ballentine granted, for $1 and the "benefit of a railroad to cross my land within one year," a right-of-way to a strip "as surveyed and located" on S3T8R7. The right-of-way was to be as much as 50-ft wide during construction, and then only as wide as needed for the roadbed and ditches.[44] According to the chain of title, George W. Ballentine was buying land in the area by 1853.[45] Mrs. Angeline Robertson and Mrs. Martha S. Corr granted a right-of-way 25 ft either side of the centerline "as surveyed" along with right to borrow and dump, in exchange for $100 for relinquishing their homestead rights to the land in S4T8R7.[46] On February 6, 1901, N. F. and Josephine Dorr granted a right-of-way of 25 ft either side of the centerline through S5T8R7, in exchange for $250 and benefits.[47] H. H. Hays and wife, E. F. Hays, granted a strip through S5T8R7 for $150.[48] This is the tract at the southeast corner of Davis Chapel and Old Panola roads. About 200 m south of this antebellum Methodist church and cemetery, the old railroad crossing can be seen as hanging cuts along this now deeply entrenched road; other cuts through ridge ends can be seen in adjacent pastures.

On March 5, 1901, W. H. Short granted a right-of-way through S6T7R7.[49] This appears to be an error intending T8SR7W, west of Old Panola Road, since the chain of title for Section 6T8R7 indicates that Short granted the right-of-way in fractional NE and SE quarters. On March 8, 1901, R. H. Taylor granted a right-of-way through S1 and 2 T7R8 (T8R7?).[50] This is the large tract in the McIvor Creek Canal bottom now owned by the Mississippi Department of Wildlife, Parks and Fisheries, where the ranger reports occasional finds of railroad metal. On May 18, 1901, Mrs. L. C. Short granted a right-of-way through S35T7R8.[51] This is along the side of McIvor bottom, where topography would confine the railroad to the southwest corner of this quarter section. These lands had been in several generations of the Short family since Monroe Short bought the land in 1867.[52] C. L. Gordon and wife, Alice S. Gordon, granted a 50-ft strip through S34T7R8 in exchange for $250 for releasing their homestead and dower rights.[53] On February 8, 1901, E. A. Jackson and wife, Jessie F., granted right-of-way through S34T7R8 for $1.[54] This land had been in the Jackson family since at least 1877. In this area a pronounced grade with corrugated iron culverts can still be seen.

W. E. and Etta E. Johnson granted a right-of-way through the S33T7R8. The right-of-way was 25 ft either side of the centerline, with an additional 25-ft construction easement, and sufficient land for a sidetrack and depot building. The grant was made under the condition that the S&D have a sidetrack on Johnson's land by September 25, 1901, and that they establish a shipping point and "house sufficient to store freight that may be shipped to this point."[55] The location of this station is of particular interest, as the Sid Hemphill song mentions the trouble the log trains had getting up "Johnson's Hill." The Johnson land is the high point of the railroad route. In September 1902, for $25, Johnson agreed to allow the S&D to abolish the sidetrack to remove the frog, switch points, switch stand, rail, and ties they had placed there.[56] From Johnson's

Hill, the line descended along the Davis Creek valley. J. M. McClure granted a right-of-way through S33T7R8, with the understanding that he would also have a shipping point, and that if any houses were to be moved, it would be at the expense of the S&D.[57] On February 7, 1901, Isaac C. Carver, for $1 and benefits granted a right-of-way of 25 ft either side of the centerline, in S33T8R7 (well south of the S&D, perhaps meant to be T7SR8W). Carver released his homestead rights and received $25 for damages occasioned by dumping and wasting soil.[58]

W. H. and S. E. Bailey made their right-of-way grant in a partly filled out, partly blank form contract. The terms were $1 and benefits; the width of the strip was left blank, as was the date. The lands were in S32T7R8 (again probably erroneous, perhaps intended as T7R7, at Davis Chapel, or T8R7, at Peach Creek) and S5T8R8 (which would be adjacent land if the Peach Creek location is assumed), comprising 25 ft either side of a centerline "as surveyed" and including the right to borrow and waste earth. For $50, the Baileys released all rights of homestead and dower (Panola DB A12:22). Mrs. S. M. Gillespie, Mrs. L. E. Wilson, F. L. Gillespie, J. A. Gillespie, and Etta Wilson granted 25 ft either side of the centerline through S5T8R8, and rights to dump and borrow, in exchange for $75 to release their homestead rights.[59]

On February 12, 1901, J. W. and N. A. Davis, for $1, granted a right-of-way of 25 ft either side of the centerline and right to dump and borrow, for a strip through S6T8R8 in return for $60 to release their homestead claim.[60] On May 11, 1901, M. M. Davis granted a 50-ft strip through the S6T7R8 (T8R8?) for $130 and the benefit of the railroad to pass through "within one year from date."[61] Martha M. Davis first bought land in this section in 1883, but portions had passed to others, and in the 1890s J. W. Davis sold portions of the land to various buyers, including Mrs. M. M. Davis, T. J. Davis, and J. W. Joudon. J. M. and M. H. Wilson granted a right-of-way through S6T8R8 for $25.[62] J. M. Wilson, A. L. Wilson, R. S. Wilson, Nora O'Rear, T. E. O'Rear, and Oscar O'Rear quitclaimed all title and interest to the right-of-way through S32T7R8W.[63] Mrs. M. E. Wilson granted the rights S32T7R8 in exchange for $60 for herself and $20 for the O'Rear children.[64] On August 8, 1901, G. A. St. John granted a right-of-way through S6T8R8.[65] In the chain, these tracts derive from John Wilson's 1853 state patent. Also, evidently after construction was completed in 1902, J. M. Wilson sold a one-acre lot adjacent to the S&D railroad track.[66] The sale was made under the condition that "no mercantile business is to be carried on" on the land.

On April 11, 1901, J. D. Malone, for $1 and benefit of having a railroad was granted a right-of-way in the S1T8R9, with right to cut and fill, and sufficient land to build a freight house, platform, and siding with the understanding that the S&D would build the facilities and have them ready to receive freight by

October 1, 1901.[67] This is evidently the area that would be known as "Malone's Trestle," the big bend where the S&D turns south onto the Delta, the site of the train wreck in Sid Hemphill's song. The indicated route of the S&D is along the valley of Davis Creek, which would have been bridged at its confluence with Peach Creek, at their common debouchment from the hills. These creeks have now been confined to drainage ditches, but in 1900, they spread their waters over an alluvial fan. On February 9, 1901, E. T. and Beulah I. Bell granted, for $1, a 25-ft right-of-way, "as surveyed" along the range line between S7 and S12.[68] The townships are not indicated, but this is evidently the township line between T8SR8W and T8SR9W, at Ballentine. W. T. and M. L. McCoy also granted a right-of-way to follow the range line.[69] Today, this is a rough tract, highly impacted by erosion and deposition, canalization, and gravel mining, along Sand Bed Road. On February 23, 1903 A. M. and G. W. Ballentine leased a right-of-way to the S&D "where it is now located" in S18T8R8W, along with such land as necessary for bed and ditching, on the condition that a station with a platform and sidetrack for public shipping be maintained "where they are now" (Panola DB A12:20). This is at Ballentine, also known as Hays Brothers & Hall. On March 14, 1901, J. C. Wilson granted a right-of-way through S18T8R8 (Panola DB A12:44). Here the S&D was running along the foot of the bluff below Ballentine.

This right-of-way and the southern extension of the S&D can be traced on modern USGS 7.5-in quadrangle maps (Crowder [1982], Sardis [1982], Asa [1983], Curtis Station [1983], and Pleasant Grove [1983]). From these leases, it appears that the railroad had been completed through Ballentine by 1903, as planned in the original charter. South of Ballentine, at the station or lumber camp known as Baptist, the line entered Carrier's large tract of timber, extending south to the confluence of the Coldwater and the Tallahatchie, so no further rights-of-way were required. This was a huge investment, with 10–15 miles of track laid before timber extraction could begin. No record has been found of purchases of timber in the hills. This land had been in cultivation since ca. 1840, so the upland hardwood woods had already been steadily exploited for fuel and construction (perhaps including tie-hacking in 1856 as the main line was built and in 1865–1866 when it was rebuilt) for 60 years when Carrier arrived. He may have made cash purchases of logs along his right-of-way that were not recorded in the deeds. The depth of the investment can be seen when we consider that the YMV, backed by the massive wealth of the Illinois Central, was building south through the eastern edge of the Delta at the same time Carrier's line was being built; the many northern timber firms that would exploit the rest of Quitman County did so with short trams off the YMV, with rails and other materials leased from the YMV. Although the hauls would have been longer than the 2–5 miles typical of the Quitman

County dummy lines, Carrier could have exploited his timberlands from the YMV as efficiently, if not more efficiently, than through building his own railroad. The major obstacle to this would have been bridging the Coldwater at or near Marks. The S&D therefore appears to have been an overcapitalization. Panola County's other early twentieth-century logging railroad, the Darnell Lumber Company's Batesville Southwestern from Batesville to Crowder, built 10 years later, was also judged overly expensive for what was in essence only a log-hauling road.

On May 8, 1903, C. M. Carrier et al. sold their 23,836 acres of timber and 52 acres of mill and tenement sites to the C. M. Carrier & Son Corporation in return for the issuance of $40,000 (400 shares) of stock to C. M. Carrier and $20,000 (200 shares) to R. M. Carrier. Both father and son appeared before the Panola County clerk. The Panola County warranty deed of May 1903 from C. M. and R. M. Carrier to C. M. Carrier & Son duplicates the Quitman County record.[70] The big block of timbered land in the Delta and the Sardis lots "on which the mills, stores and tenement houses, etc., of C.M. Carrier & Son are now located," and the "residence lot near the town of Sardis now occupied by R.M. Carrier," sold for $40,000 (averaging $41.68/acre). Also in June 1903, the corporation granted a lot and residence near Sardis to Alice B. Carrier, for $2,000.[71] Alice Bridgeforth Carrier was Robert's wife; this was the Short house, which had been Carrier's first purchase in Sardis.

On June 11, 1903, C. M. Carrier & Son gave R. M. Carrier a warranty deed for $100,000 for the timberlands but not the mill site and house;[72] C. M. Carrier, president, appeared in Cook County, Illinois; R. M. Carrier, secretary, appeared in Shelby County, Tennessee.[73] Robert Carrier then gave a deed of trust to James F. Hunter and Tennessee Trust Co. on the 23,836 acres of timberland, for the $100,000 debt to his father. The debt, at 6 percent interest, was to be cleared by semiannual payments of $25,750 through 1907. Hunter quitclaimed the 23,000 acres back to R. M. Carrier early, in 1906.[74] On the same day, R. M. Carrier gave a second, junior, deed of trust to attorney William A. Percy of Memphis on the 23,836 acres for a debt of $230,000 due between 1904 and 1909.[75] The indenture was made with the condition that the timber could be cut for manufacturing purposes so long as Carrier was not in default. The debt schedule, at 6 percent interest, was for $51,650 semiannual payments through 1909. C. M. Carrier released R. M. Carrier's deed of trust of June 11, 1903, in 1904 and 1905.[76] The deed of trust to Percy was also satisfied and canceled well in advance of its due date.[77] Cassius M. Carrier had seen the land purchases and railroad completed before he turned the operation over to his 26-year-old son, Robert M. Carrier, who refinanced the operation, as indicated above. It would be 1909 before the note was paid off and the senior Carrier relinquished all his interests.[78]

The 1903 records are the first mention of the Sardis main store associated with the Carrier operation. This is later described as a two-story brick or "stone" building called the Supply Store (probably the pressed concrete block building on the Martin Brothers Scrap Metal yard). A 1984 MDAH National Register nomination for "The Architecture of Andrew Johnson in North Mississippi" claims that the "C.M. Carrier and Son's building" was built by Andrew Johnson (1844–1921), a Sardis architect and construction contractor. "Swede" Johnson studied at Uppsala University and immigrated to Illinois in 1865 on money received as a prize in a design contest. By 1870, he had moved his shop, family, and crew of Swedish construction workers to Sardis, where he built the Panola County courthouse (1873) and jail (1871) in Sardis. Between 1870 and 1910, Johnson also built or remodeled many houses in and around Sardis, as well as churches and Illinois Central depots. Swede Johnson was 66 in 1910; he appears to have retired about this time (Holland and Gordon 1984). On January 1, 1906, Mrs. Alice B. Carrier mortgaged the Supply Store and lot to Mrs. M. R. Bridgeforth of Louisville, Kentucky (her mother?).[79] The loan was for $5,000 for two years, with $30 payable monthly.

Completing the transfer to R. M. Carrier's control, in October 1905 the Carrier and Son charter was amended to change the name to Carrier Lumber & Manufacturing Co.[80] R. M. Carrier secured funds to operate and develop the Quitman and Panola lands through a mortgage to Fidelity Trust Co. of Buffalo, New York. The funds were provided through 100 bonds of $1,000 ($100,000) "in gold coin of the US of the present standard of weight and fineness," repayable from October 1, 1905, at 6 percent semiannually, "in like gold coin" in April and October yearly. The lands mortgaged were the 23,836 acres of timberland.[81] The note was satisfied November 18, 1910.[82] In 1906 R. M. Carrier gave his father another deed of trust on the 23,836 acres, again with Will Percy as trustee; a debt junior to the $100,000 debt to the Tennessee Trust Co. (Quitman DB V:406).[83] The note, at 6 percent interest, was to be repaid with annual notes of $50,000 or more, with alternating semiannual interest payments. Also in 1906, the Tennessee Trust Co., with James F. Hunter as trustee, released R. M. Carrier's 1903 $100,000 debt as paid in full.[84] C. M. Carrier appeared in Buffalo City, Erie County, New York, to quitclaim the lands he had bought from DPL in 1900 (Y:331) to Carrier Lumber & Manufacturing Co. for $58,804.65. Also in 1910, R. M. Carrier's $100,000 mortgage on the timberlands, with Fidelity Trust Co. of Buffalo, was canceled as satisfied.[85] The rapid repayment of these large debts indicates that cutting was progressing rapidly and profitably, despite factors such as the 1907 business depression. There are numerous timber contracts from Quitman County that provide detailed descriptions of the methods used and prices of various types of lumber, which cannot be provided here for lack of space.

These large loans were at least in part for the construction of the Sardis & Delta Railroad. The line had to traverse 10 miles before reaching the timber stand to be cut, a large outlay. Although no longer present or functional, the documentary evidence for the line can be traced by its lasting toponyms, artifactual traces, and even standing buildings and settlements. While folklore and Silver's (1957) description indicate that the S&D was a lightly built, crooked, and unballasted temporary railroad, it required considerable cut and fill work, particularly in the loess bluffs section. The traces of grades are still quite evident on the ground, and landowners report occasional finds of small spikes, tie plates, and rail braces. Malone's Trestle is a crossing over the Peach Creek-Davis Creek. Malone's lease called for a freight house, platform, and siding. The ruins of this frame building are still standing in the Davis Creek bottom. The S&D was also operated as a common carrier of freight and passengers, although its main purpose was always hauling logs. Around 1920, passengers paid 20¢ to travel from Pleasant Grove to Sardis; this included use of a canvas sheet to protect the traveler from sparks and soot. There were flag stops, platforms, sidings, and freight houses every few miles along the S&D, but no documentary evidence has yet been found indicating the volume of trade. Ballentine is an old farming settlement at the foot of the bluff that was crossed by the Sardis & Delta ca. 1901–1927. Baptist was one of the Carrier logging camps, immediately south of Ballentine. The area was marked by Swango Chapel as late as 1940. Lake Carrier is a large lake in Bobo Bayou. It was the main woods camp of Carrier's operation. A spur from the main line of the Sardis & Delta ran west to the camp. When the first detailed maps were made in the 1930s, there was still dense agricultural settlement along the lake and the old railroad spur. In 1906, Curtis was a station on the Sardis & Delta Railroad of Carrier Lumber Co., with a store run by Curtis M. Swango, manager for the Carrier Co. Curtis Station is now a small farming settlement on Highway 6 between Marks and Batesville. To the south lies Locke Station, another S&D stop, now an isolated farming community. The end of the line, at mile 26, was called Red Gum. Historic maps report other flag stops along the line (Hays, Davis Chaple, McIvor, Lauve, Wood's Hotel, Johnson's Hill, Burke, Dye).

On January 11, 1911, A. M. Ballentine made a 10-year contract with Carrier Lumber & Manufacturing Co. for all timber on Sections 14 and 15 in T8R8.[86] This tract would be at the old Star Place settlement; the proper description is probably T8R9, or immediately west of the Ballentine headquarters, in the Viney Rough. The 700 acres of timber was sold for $7,500, with Ballentine reserving the trees in the house lot in Section 14 and the right to cut firewood for his farm tenants as long as the wood was not merchantable. Ballentine also granted the right to construct and maintain a railroad from the S&D across any of Ballentine's lands to be used to haul anything needed for logging and to remove Ballentine's or anyone else's logs. In building the spur, Carrier agreed not to "throw up any high dumps on the land...except where the railroad will cross a creek or bad wet place." He was also allowed to "do such small amount of ditching as may be needed at any point to keep water off the railroad." Carrier was to pay half the taxes on land with timber on it, excepting any drainage district taxes, and to remove all rails, ties, and other railroad structures except dumps within 60 days of the expiry of right of entry. At the same time, Ballentine's bank, with J. Q. West as trustee, released the timber from its deed of trust.[87] The S&D used a steam skidder with 800-ft cable and a log loader, and may have laid down temporary dummy lines off their main line.

Records of lawsuits are also revelatory of aspects of Carrier's business. In the first of a series of hard-fought legal battles, in 1912, Mrs. S. A. Gordon sued the Sardis & Delta over crossings on her plantation in the Panola County Circuit Court. The appeal *Sardis & Delta Railroad Co v. Gordon* (57 So. 219) was brought over the failure of the S&D to construct and maintain two plantation crossings on their line over her farm. The penalty for this failure was $250 ($4058 Mississippi Code 1906) and actual damages of $200. A jury verdict awarded her $250. On appeal, Shands & Montgomery for the S&D argued unsuccessfully that Gordon did not establish that actual damages had occurred, and further, that the crossings should only be in as good a condition as the plantation road leading to the crossing. The state court found no error and affirmed the original award. There was no requirement in this legislation for actual damages to be shown, the lack of a usable crossing being taken in itself as harm.

In *Board of Supervisors of Quitman County et al. v. Carrier Lumber & Mfg Co. et al.* (60 So. 326, 103 Miss. 324), argued before the Mississippi Supreme Court January 1913, R. M. Carrier successfully disputed the county's construction of a dam or levee across a bayou that fell into the Coldwater, increasing the overflow onto Carrier's timberlands. Quitman County had had a levee built across one bayou and when they planned a second levee, Carrier sought an injunction, as damming these tributaries/distributaries on the west bank of the Coldwater would increase flooding of timber on the east bank. Although slow and sluggish, the Coldwater was considered navigable, and when the flow was high from the hills, it backed up into bayous. Bookter Bayou (no longer on maps) was 300 feet wide and 16 feet deep when Quitman County let a contract to build a levee to prevent this distribution of floods. Carrier claimed that increasing overflow on the other bank continually and perpetually injured and depreciated his timberlands, and an injunction was granted. The county filed a demurrer and a motion to dissolve the injunction, which were overruled, and so an appeal was filed. Quitman County contended that the Board of Supervisors has full jurisdiction over roads and bridges, including the right to build causeways and levees, such as that planned at Bookter Bayou, by §170 of the 1906 constitution. Justice Reed noted that while the county has these powers, they did not extend to construction of levees across water courses "whereby the natural flow of the water will be prevented." By §4449 of the 1906 Code, causeways are distinguished from levees, causeways being a raised roadbed through lowlands, but when a road, on a causeway or not, reaches a bayou, a bridge, not a levee, should be built. The Board of Supervisors was not proceeding under any right to eminent domain, because they did not offer Carrier anything for the damages. For these reasons, Carrier was entitled to the injunction to restrain and abate the obstruction of the bayous. Mississippi at that time followed an ancient common-law theory of riparian landowner's rights that "water runs, and ought to run, as it is wont to run (*aqua currit et debet currere ut currere solebat*)." Quitman County chancellor Denton was upheld in overruling the Board of Supervisors' motion to dissolve the injunction.

In another case brought before the state supreme court in January 1913, *Carrier Lumber & Mfg Co. v. Boxley et al.* (60 So. 645, 103 Miss. 489), Carrier unsuccessfully appealed an award made by the Panola County Circuit Court to the mother of a 19-year-old employee killed in an accident. Mrs. Boxley and the siblings of G. H. Boxley brought a suit for $20,000 for his death. He had been on top of the load engaged in unloading logs from the log train, with other workmen, under a supervisor, when the logs slipped, rolled, and threw him to the ground, where a log fell on his skull, killing him instantly. In the trial, the jury was instructed that they could award only actual and compensatory damages, but no punitive damages. The jury returned an award of $6,800. Carrier's lawyers claimed that this was $6,000 expectancy compensation and $800 impunity damages, but the record did not show any such wording, rather that the jury simply found for the plaintiff $6,800. The supreme court upheld this award. G. H. Boxley, Jr. (1891–1910), is buried at Pleasant Grove Community Cemetery, beside his father G. H. Boxley, Sr. (1845–1905), and mother Amanda P. Boxley (1861–1946). The young man's tombstone reads, "How many hopes lie buried here?" He had evidently been the head male of the family since he was 14 years old.

There is little record of Carrier land transactions in Panola County in the 1910s, but copies of the 1913 Sardis *Southern Reporter* newspaper have been preserved and shed a different sort of light on the Carrier mills in that year. This is the same year that the newspaper serialized a bitterly Redemptionist history of Reconstruction in Panola County (Kyle 1913). Lumber and oil mills are reported to be obeying the new 10-hour-day law, with two 10-hour shifts at plants; workers had not liked having three 8-hour shifts due to decreased pay

(*Southern Reporter* 28:15). In January, George Maddux began work in the Carrier box factory (*Southern Reporter* 28:16), and Will McCutcheon, who had left several months before to work in Arkansas, returned to his old job with Carrier (*Southern Reporter* 28:18). In February, the Honorable G. D. Shands was up from New Orleans, to visit with his wife and son, A. W. Shands, who was a main lawyer for the Carrier firm, and Louis H. Bradley, foreman of the box department, resigned with plans to leave Sardis with his wife to make a home in the Far West (*Southern Reporter* 28:20). The next week G. D. Shands returned to New Orleans, but his wife remained with her son; at the same time, Mrs. R. M. Carrier had as her guests for several weeks Miss Elsie Bridgeforth and Miss Blanc, of Louisville, Kentucky; Elsie was recently back from an "extended tour" of Europe (*Southern Reporter* 28:21). D. B. Cowart, the engineer of Sid Hemphill's song, who had been to Waco, stopped off in Sardis to visit friends (*Southern Reporter* 28:22). At 5 on a Wednesday evening, as a local freight was switching a coal car into the oil mill, a boxcar of red gum lumber fresh from Carrier's mill "straddled the tracks and tried to run crosswise." The car was destroyed and the lumber scattered, resulting in a 2-hour traffic delay on the Illinois Central as wreckers removed the debris and salvaged the boxcar trucks (*Southern Reporter* 28:22, 21 February 1913). In late February, Miss Bridgeforth finished her visit to her sister and returned to Louisville (*Southern Reporter* 28:23) and toward the end of March Shands's mother also returned to New Orleans and "Master Bobbie Carrier" (R. M. Carrier, Jr.) had "a number of little folks go down to his home" for a Monday afternoon Easter-egg hunt (*Southern Reporter* 28:27). By April, Mrs. Carrier had taken her "handsome little son Bobbie" to Louisville for the summer, meaning Mr. Carrier would make frequent trips to Louisville to "avoid the lonesome feeling that comes when loved ones are gone." He made the first of the short trips to Kentucky the Saturday of the same week his wife and son left (*Southern Reporter* 28:29). In April, John B. Chafin, formerly with Carrier but then working in Memphis, was in town "shaking hands with Sardis friends" (*Southern Reporter* 28:30), and in May, Calvin Speers began working at the Supply Store Co. (*Southern Reporter* 28:32).

Besides the legal entanglements over taxes and compensation, some the result of locals seeking redress from "deep pockets" and others the result of Carrier's own attempts to maintain all his advantages, in the mid-1910s he was also engaged in a lawsuit for divorce brought by his wife. The suit (Jefferson Circuit Court Action 98135) was carried out in her home, Louisville, Kentucky, and her petition was granted ca. 1916. That the marriage had not been happy is perhaps indicated by mentions of her extended absences on home visits in the 1913 issues of the *Southern Reporter*; Sardis in 1910 would not have suited a lady from Louisville "society." In December 1916, Alice B. Carrier, unmarried, granted the Sardis home and house lot and the Supply Store and its lot to R. M. Carrier.[88] She signed the deed fulfilling an agreed property settlement.[89] In March 1917, R. M. Carrier granted the same property to the Carrier Lumber & Mfg. Co. for a nominal $1.[90] However, Carrier reserved the right to at "any time" remove from the building "now being constructed and to be used by [Carrier] as a residence" all the woodwork, mantles, windows, doors, panels, etc., placed in the house, "being the same material purchased in England" as well as all electrical light fixtures. Through the 1910s and 1920s also Carrier occasionally bought or sold residential lots in Sardis.

In *Jagoe et al. v. Carrier Lumber & Mfg. Co.* (81 So. 132, 119 Miss. 564), argued before the Mississippi Supreme Court in March 1919, W. R. Jagoe successfully had a decree against his land claim reversed due to the underhanded machinations Carrier employed. The disputed Panola County land (S26T9R9W) was "in a vast territory of wild, timbered and uncultivated lands, most of which is subject to overflow, and all of which at various seasons of the year, if not actually under water, is 'cut off almost from civilization.'" Due to remoteness from highways, towns, and railroads these lands at the Tallahatchie-Coldwater confluence, a mile or two from Cook's Water Hole, "a well-known resort for expert huntsmen and heretofore rather famous as a retreat for bear" and not having been cultivated, it "has been infinitely more profitable and practical for the owner of the land in controversy to have preserved the land as timber." Jagoe's lawyer was Lomax B. Lamb, of Batesville; Carrier's were J. B. Harris of Jackson and Shands & Montgomery of Cleveland. Carrier had been in negotiations to buy the disputed land when a levee tax deed was found outstanding in the Delta & Pine Land Company's holdings and bought by Carrier with the intention of contesting Jagoe's long-established title. When the lands were sold for these levee taxes in 1872, they were owned by Harrison, and since that time, the appellant Jagoe and his predecessors in title, back to Harrison's heirs, had the land assessed to them and had paid all taxes and "constantly exercised such acts of ownership over the lands as an owner would expect to do ... with property of this kind." In fact, the tract was popularly known as the "Jagoe and Martin lands." Justice Stevens found that the chancellor in the county court erred in finding insufficient evidence for Jagoe's claim of adverse possession, and that "without doubt" equity and justice were on the side of Jagoe, particularly as Carrier had already acknowledged Jagoe's claim by negotiating to purchase the land before discovering and adopting the levee tax deed tactic. The lands were awarded to the appellant, Jagoe.

News of the Carrier operation from the *Southern Reporter* weekly newspaper in 1920 sheds further light on the Carrier operation. James F. Carlton returned from a trip to Mexico, hiring labor for the mill, as the "demand for men is greater than the supply." A number of Mexicans had been working satisfactorily for several months (*Southern Reporter* 25:41). In this same period, Carrier Lumber & Mfg. Co. ran a regular ad in the paper, saying, "We have on hand plenty of good slab wood at 75¢ for big two-horse wagon load—get in next winter's supply now" and the Supply Store Company advertised Columbia Gramophones (crank record players) (*Southern Reporter* 25:42). In September there was a small fire at Carrier's; a dust explosion in the cyclone[91] that picked up refuse for feeding the boiler was the cause, but there was no damage beyond burning up the kindling, as the boiler house supporting the cyclone was brick with a metal roof (*Southern Reporter* 25:49).

In November 1923, Carrier Lumber and Manufacturing bought all the merchantable timber on 70 acres in S13T9R9, with right to enter, from Ernest Bensinger for $250.[92] This small tract would be one of Carrier's last timber purchases. The land is east of the big block, and north of where Highway 6 now runs. Despite his original intention to manage the lands for multiple cuts, it appears that Carrier had in fact practiced traditional "cut and run" management, and the time for "running" was fast approaching. In August 1925, Carrier, president, M. B. Cooper, vice president, and C. M. Swango, general superintendent, then entered grants of power of attorney, with each authorized to convey any land owned by the company by deed.[93] This resolution indicates that Carrier Lumber and Manufacturing was about to begin winding up its business.

By 1926, R. M. Carrier was further cutting his ties to Sardis and Panola County. He commissioned a brick-and-stone Jacobean Revival house at 642 South Willett in the Central Gardens neighborhood of Memphis from designer Bryant Fleming. The house, called Carrier Hall, is listed on the National Register of Historic Places. On March 19, 1999, the *Memphis Flyer* reported that the house was for sale for nearly a million dollars and that Carrier had moved his home from New York to Memphis in 1926, after sending his architect Bryant Fleming to England to gather elements for the house. This is not entirely accurate; Carrier had placed the English antiques in his Sardis home in 1916–1917, around the time of his divorce, and retained the right to remove them when he sold the property, as already mentioned. Materials noted by the *Flyer* are early Tudor mantles, paneling, and paintings on glass for lead casement windows. Carrier Hall has a sunken garden with stone balustrades along the street side and a rear main entrance off Central Gardens Court. The entry and downstairs living rooms have checkerboard slate and marble floors. There are antique beams and plasterwork in the informal rooms. The great hall, sitting rooms, and library have hand-carved paneling and 8-in to 10-in oak flooring. How long Carrier held the Memphis property is unknown, as by the time of his death he had a residence in Oxford/University, Mississippi, as well. Perhaps Carrier Hall was his own taste, but perhaps it was an attempt to impress or placate his first wife. If so, she would never have enjoyed these antiques, as the divorce took place about the same time the Sardis house was being built. Carrier also maintained a country house for his bird hunting trips, served by an airstrip in Panola County.

In September 1927, Carrier Lumber and Manufacturing sold to Condon Engineering Co., of Delaware, three acres of the mill lot.[94] Condon Engineering Co. also obtained right to ingress and egress over an alley or lane east from the public road. In a deed filed in December 1928, but made pursuant to a resolution of the board of directors made August 17, 1925, the lumber company sold a three-acre Sardis lot to the Curtis Planting Co.[95] Curtis Planting Co. was probably the land at Baptist and Curtis Station, operated after the logging as a cotton plantation by Curtis Swango, Jr., of Como.

In November 1928, Carrier Lumber and Manufacturing bought "all the merchantable timber" on SW 1/4 Section 18, Township 8 Range 8.[96] This is land at Ballentine that had probably already been cut, with this deed formalizing the payment for interests of other heirs. In the summer of 1929, the lumber company sold lots around the Sardis mill site to O. D. B. Causey for $1,500,[97] to R. W. Thomas for $500,[98] and to M. F. Clayton.[99] The sales were made by Swango.

On December 9, 1929, Carrier Lumber and Manufacturing sold a half interest in the sawmill grounds, for $5,000 to G. W. Ballentine, from whom Carrier had originally purchased the tract.[100] Excepted from the sale were 10 specific items:

  Sawmill building and additions, all machinery therein and all contents
  All machinery and tools in the machine shop building
  Large watertank and all water pipe lines except pipe in 3 wells
  Sawmill, railroad and logging equipment
  All lumber stacked on the land
  Hose huts, hose and reels
  Yard office building near the sawmill
  Oil house building west of the supply room
  Contents of the veneer shed "just south" of the MF Clayton lot
  Contents of the supply room and all other buildings except the Supply Store

Carrier had 60 days to remove the sawmill equipment, railroad and logging equipment, and building contents and to put them all on the space bounded on the north and east by the sawmill building, on the west by a line parallel with the west end of the track "upon which the log Derrick stands," and on the south by the south line of the spur. He was to have a further 24 months to remove all this stockpiled gear. Carrier retained right of egress and ingress for two years and conversely granted Ballentine ingress and egress over the strip between the two-story brick building and the ICRR spur, about 20-ft wide, immediately south of the Supply Store. The agreement was signed by Curtis Swango in his capacity as general superintendent.

On the next day, December 10, 1929, the Sardis & Delta deeded a portion of its right-of-way to Carrier Lumber and Manufacturing.[101] Also on December 10, 1929, the S&DRR granted G. W. Ballentine the roadbed and right-of-way beginning at the west boundary of the Carrier mill lot through the Section 4, "being the strip" deeded to the S&D by M. B. and G. W. Ballentine in 1900.[102] For $1, the S&D also deeded to the N. F. Dorr estate the 50-ft wide strip across S5T8R7, granted by N. F. Dorr in 1901.[103] On the same day, Carrier offered all his fee simple right-of-way (50-ft wide) to the Panola County Board of Supervisors for a nominal $1.[104] The grant was to begin at Davis Chapel/Old Panola Road and to run 9 miles west to the Sardis-Ballentine Road. The Board of Supervisors was offered this opportunity to lay out a public road within five years; if not, the land was to revert to the original estates it derived from. It seems that the county did not take up this offer. However, below Ballentine to the Coldwater-Tallahatchie confluence, most of the grade was converted into county roads (Hayes Road, Pea Farm Road, Bobo Road, and Jamison Road).

The dissolution of Carrier Lumber and Manufacturing took place through the granting of a new corporate charter for the Carrier Lumber Co. of Sardis (May 1930), with officers M. B. Cooper of Sardis and James E. Emigh of Memphis.[105] This successor company, retaining the Carrier name but perhaps without Carrier's actual participation, was authorized for $100,000 capital in $100 shares. The company's powers were similar to those authorized for the original lumber company, including provisions for rental houses, light and gas fees, and a general merchandise store. At least part of the plant (box factory?) was still in operation in 1930, when Carrier Lumber Co. advertised for 8-in diameter and up to 21-in gum bolts,[106] to be bought at $7.50 a cubic cord, cash, delivered to the yard in Sardis (*Southern Reporter* 75:39, 27 July 1930). This would probably have been local second-growth delivered by motor truck or farm wagon.

The final liquidation of the Carrier property in Sardis took place in 1933–1936. While it had been agreed in 1929 that the Carrier company would remove the sawmill equipment, this may not have taken place yet, or at least not been completed. In November 1933, Carrier Lumber and Manufacturing granted G. W. Ballentine the remaining half interest in title to the sawmill building and additions on the 38 acres comprising the sawmill grounds.[107] The property description is the same as that from the 1929 sale. The personal property was enumerated as including machinery and tools, watertanks, water pipe, lines above and below ground, sawmill, railroad and logging equipment, railroad rolling stock and steel, skidders, loaders, boilers, and engines. Both Carrier Lumber and Manufacturing and Ballentine had the right to sell any part of the property within 12 months, provided the other agreed and approved the price. If a buyer was found, and the other party proved disagreeable, the unwilling party had to buy at the offered price from the other. Anything on the lot not sold within 12 months would belong "absolutely" to Ballentine.[108]

In March 1936, Carrier Lumber and Manufacturing deeded to M. B. Cooper 16.5 acres.[109] The price was $7,500 for the mill site and buildings and machinery in and about the flooring mill and box plant used by Carrier Lumber Co., including lumber buggies, a Porter locomotive (#7), switch tracks and sidings, track scales, all equipment used on the switch and siding, two mules and a horse, and all supplies, materials, and equipment used in the box and flooring plants. Carrier retained the right to occupy and jointly use part of the office building near the track without liability or rent. No office equipment, supplies, materials, furniture, or fixtures were included in the conveyance. Carrier also retained right of ingress and egress for use of the office and to remove personal property.

Despite the dissolution of the Carrier Lumber and Manufacturing Co., the logging out of the bottomland tracts, and Carrier's removal to Memphis, he continued to own much land in Quitman and Panola counties. Although the timbering was done, Robert Carrier continued to purchase land around Sardis, mostly small hill farms bought at public auction due to farm foreclosures during the 1930s. These may be the lands he maintained for hunting. Carrier made his last home in Oxford. The Robert M. and Lenore W. Carrier Foundation was organized in 1953 and managed by Union Planters Bank, Memphis, as a scholarship for Quitman and Panola county students at Ole Miss.

In 1954–1955 University of Mississippi professor of history James Wesley Silver interviewed Robert M. Carrier and many other north Delta lumbermen, ranging from the timber barons like Carrier to timber and sawmill workers. His research was intended for a biography of Carrier, but this biography never materialized. In his autobiography, Silver states:

> For years I believed in the academic leadership of Chancellor Williams. Perhaps I should have been forewarned regarding his conduct in crisis situations [desegregation]. In gratitude for the financial contributions to the university of Robert M. Carrier, who had made his fortune in Mississippi timber, Williams decided to have his biography written and asked me to do it. After deciding that Carrier had performed constructively in the organization of the lumber industry, I accepted. For the better part of a year I worked night and day on the project and had achieved a considerable rapport with him. But he was terminally ill, and in his last days became obsessed with the erroneous notion that I intended to "expose" his

rumored complicity in a Sardis murder in his younger days. Without consulting me, he requested Williams to stop the enterprise, assuming as head of the chain of command, the chancellor could give the order which would be obeyed. Williams called off the writing, at that time 90 percent complete. As I had been foolish enough to proceed without a formal contract, I felt I had no recourse except to comply. I published a couple of articles from the material I had assembled, it is true, but the incident undoubtedly diminished my respect for the judgment of academic administration and may have influenced my later behavior [Silver 1984:62].

Silver's articles based on the Carrier material are "Paul Bunyan Comes to Mississippi" (Silver 1957a) and "The Hardwood Producers Come of Age" (Silver 1957b). His card file of notes is included in the University of Mississippi Williams Library Special Collections, as part of a large collection of papers placed there by Silver in the 1980s, long after his retreat from Mississippi as a consequence of race-war politics (see http://www.jstor.org/stable/2954385 for special collections file materials). While in his autobiography Silver says he was "90 percent" through with the Carrier biography, no such typescript or manuscript has been noted in the Silver papers, only the note cards, as reviewed so far. J. W. Silver's other source materials for these articles are *American Lumberman*, Chicago, 1899–; *Hardwood Record*, Chicago, 1895–1939; *Lumber*, St. Louis, 1918–1939; *Lumber Trade Journal*, Chicago, 1882–1931; *St. Louis Lumberman*, 1888–1918; and *Southern Lumberman*, Nashville, 1881–.

Carrier and his wife are buried in Oxford Cemetery. There are only two graves in the Carrier plot, which has a limestone balustrade. The tombstone inscriptions read:

Robert Moorhead Carrier, May 16, 1876–Sept. 12, 1957
Lenore Woollard Carrier, Jan. 23, 1895–May 30, 1963

The contrast between the Carrier saga and the pre-railroad logging described in the Parrott diary is immense. The concentration of landholding and the depth of capital investment are the most obvious contrasts. Workers were specialized, with part-time farmers working as unskilled woods crews and many nonlocals filling skilled and managerial plant and train jobs. Mexicans and northerners joined the native workers; in the sawmill, plant jobs were highly specialized. The cross-cut saw and axe were still essential, but the steam skidder had replaced many mules and oxen. The train allowed men to live around Sardis or Pleasant Grove, avoiding malaria, and ride down to work daily. When crews were kept in the woods camps, they lived in larger crews with more amenities, such as a clubhouse and sports teams. Robert Carrier himself could be absent for longer periods of time without his workers disappearing, since other hired men supervised the workers. His work was office work, and when he did go to the woods it was generally for hunting and fishing expeditions; Hemphill seems to make fun of his lack of knowledge about the actual workings of his empire. The experience must have been a shock to the men he hired locally as well; they went from can-til-can't farming with one payoff when they sold their cotton to fairly steady and regular wages through the year, even if they were drawn in kind at the Supply Store. The S&D logging era lasted only one or two generations, from 1900–1930, and quickly faded as the timber was cut out. Game was exhausted and the first hunting laws were coming into effect; lawsuits against the railroads for livestock killed by trains were leading to fence laws that would prevent poor people from keeping open-range cattle. As the eroded hill farms were fenced, improved cattle began to be bred. The railroad grade quickly faded into pastures and woodlots.

The End of the Big Woods

Mississippi is outranked only by Indiana in leading the nation in extinct towns, based on the total number of named places dropped from the federal census, 1870–1960 (Adkins 1979: Table 1). Adkins (1979:132) shows only five extinct sawmill towns in the Delta and three in the North Central Hills, in contrast to over 50, including Mish (Starr 2002a, b), in the Piney Woods/Coastal Meadows region. Adkins believes that lumbering in the Delta was conducted more from temporary camps (like the flag stops listed for the S&D), while actual towns were more common in the southern part of the state. So, while the lumber era was as typical and as significant in the Delta as it was in the Piney Woods, the extinct sawmill town is a much scarcer resource in the Delta. This is because the Delta land was suited for farming, and so most towns that began as sawmills continue to exist as farming settlements in the Delta, while the steep, dry and barren Piney Woods could not support much agriculture after the timber had been cut, and were allowed to grow back up, or, if returned to federal ownership or to the occasional responsible corporate stewards, were replanted. Most sawmill towns were located along railroads; indeed, railroads were extended into the vast forests of the Delta and Piney Woods only after the marketable timber near streams had been cut and floated to the large mid- and late-nineteenth-century mills on the coast and the Mississippi River. Railroads allowed mills and supplies to be transported to the timberlands, the lumber products to be shipped to market, and the mill and ancillaries to be removed once the stand was cut out. They also provided the source of supplies for the managers and workers, such as groceries, drink, clothing, tools, and household equipment. While the Phase I and II archaeological investigations at Mish in Covington County revealed the low level of historical documentation relating to the sawmill era in the Piney Woods, it appears that the Delta's logging era is even more poorly represented in the historical record. The investigations at the Chancey (Lamb-Fish Lumber Co.) extinct sawmill townsite (Starr 2003) did not allow time for a detailed document study, but this research has since been carried out for Lamb-Fish and the many other logging companies operating in the county ca. 1900–1920. Search of the issues of *The Journal of Mississippi History* revealed very few articles about logging, and only one pertaining to the Delta, Silver's highly anecdotal account of the Carrier operation (Silver 1957a).

The argument has been made that the area would have remained undeveloped if it had not been in essence given away to large corporate interests, almost all from out of state. Railroad land grants began with the Illinois Central in the antebellum period, and much of the land in the Delta was granted multiple times before a railroad (the Yazoo and Mississippi Valley) succeeded in entering the area. Most people saw timber as simply an encumbrance on lands they wished to convert to cotton production. It was to be removed as rapidly as possible, and in solid blocks that could then be put to the plow, as many logging contracts specify. After the merchantable timber was removed, planters would have the remaining trees deadened, reserving smaller trees for fences and firewood for tenants. By 1920, Quitman County was a sea of stumps, briars, and cotton patches; the first cultivation was made among the stumps. Around 1925, my grandfather, F. R. "Ned" Starr, was a young teenager, taking crews into the cutover to prepare it for cultivation, the men using saws and the women hoes and axes to pile and burn tops and grub roots. The population of the county, like most of the Delta, peaked ca. 1940, and declined rapidly thereafter. The heavy, cold wet clay soils were very productive, but hard to work; Ned Starr served on the WWII draft and ration boards and was reprimanded for the quantity of rubber boots he issued to sharecroppers for winter plowing. After the war most farms quickly converted to wage labor and tractors. The 2010 population approximated that of 1910; the peak farming era lasted less than a century. Mosquitoville and Parrott's farm now have 25-year-old trees on them and the Carrier tract has been extensively reshaped for rice and soybean cultivation, where it has not been reforested through the USDA Conservation Reserve Program (CRP). Perhaps much of the county should never have been cleared, but rather, as Carrier had initially intended, managed perpetually for high-quality bottomland hardwood production. It will be a generation before the CRP lands and farms foreclosed in the 1980s and 1990s produce merchantable trees. In the meanwhile, employment and income in Quitman County seem certain to remain very limited.

Acknowledgments

Like my grandfather, Ned Starr, and my father, Raynor Starr, I grew up in a version of the landscape Johnnie Parrott described a century after his time. I consider his diary, associated artifacts (pike and toggles) and the folklore about him an important inheritance. I don't know if Sam Brookes ever read the diary, but I offer this essay to him in memory of the summer he spent with my family and all the entertainment and instruction he gave me throughout my childhood. This research has been subsidized in part by James "Jimbo" Mathus of Oxford, John Pritchard of Memphis, and Steven Skinner of North Carolina. A much more extensive and comprehensive version of this research is available from the author.

Notes

1. Quotes from Parrott's diary will be cited by date in the day/month/year form as in the original: 7 October 1887, "cutting Road I have only one team hauling logs this week Mr Bruckners wagon broke down I am afraid that I will not get in all the timber before it rains again"; 11 October, "hauling logs wagons and carrylogs all fixed in good order looks like they are going to do something this week."

2. 6 August 1887, "Johnny Davis and myself started off for Jonestown I am now on the hunt for ox teams to haul my timber with these men around here think I cannot get any teams only what is around here but I am going to try"; 8 August, "failed to get any teams around here [Jonestown]"; 9 August, "Got on train and went to Memphis went to a circus Left Memphis for Batesville got there about dark walked out to Mr John Towes found his ox teams all broke up a good many of his oxen having died"; 10 August, "walked back to Batesville in search of a Nigger that put logs in Squirrel lake last season found him down at Courtland 6 miles below Batesville said he wanted hauling to do but had no log wagon or carlog promised to come up and see the timber."

3. 12 January 1888, "making pike poles at the mill rain all day I think we will get to float timber tomorrow"; 25 January 1888, "fixing pike poles" to "float" or "drive" the logs down to a sawmill on South Lake, a distance of only a few miles.

4. 28 September 1887, "Started too hauling and tor'd the road all up if the don't quit they will not be able to haul on it no more they ought not to have done anything while it was so wet."

5. 27 April 1888 "cutting tree tops out of float road."

6. 21 January 1887, "Making Dugouts at the mill"; 26 January, "finishing Dugouts and making pike poles"; 10 March 1887, "finished making dugout went down to the mill"; 7 March 1888, "making some canoe paddles"; 21 March 1888, "In afternoon me and Mr JJ Davis began making a small dugout"; 22 March 1888, "made a little canoe"; 11 January 1889, "Went down to Burrels Bayou after dugout could not get it its being on the other side Went back to camp and went around by Flag Lake got dugout out with a long pole."

7. 11 May 1887, "barking Gum trees"; 17 February 1889, "went all over my Island deadening"; 21 February, "Johnny [Davis] and me tackling the old deadening it is sure a tough Job."

8. 15 February 1887, "Mr Greer and Jack Mills out through here hunting stave timber but I don't think they will find much"; 8 April 1888, "floating Logs in Pecan Bayou current swift cannot float after today until it change"; 9 April, "Mr Greer got through Pecan Bayou with his stave boat"; 27 June 1888, "went back to Mosquitoville water rose so that I had to strip off and wade in to get my boat water near deep enough to [float] in the Bayou if it was running the other way I think Mr Greer and Jack Mills will get out with their stave boat now"; 29 June, "Greer and Mills gone off with their stave Boat. But I think they will get swamp'd if ever they try to run it down the Mississippi River."

9. 18 December 1887, "off for a hunt before daylight went around horseshoe Brake could see no deer but lots of squirrels shot 3 times at geese flying empted my Winchester at squirrels killed 9 went about 100 yards with empty gun and there stood a fine old Buck looking at me I showed him my Gun and told him to take a good look at me for the next time I meet him I intended to take his hide off."

10. 23 February 1888, "caught one coon with about 22 traps setting catching fur around here is about play'd out there is no Beaver left and very few Otter"; 24 February, "went around traps caught the big pile of nothing shall take up traps in morning except a few in Otter's slide"; 30 October 1888, "I never expected to see all those brakes completely cleared of Beaver and Otter"; 3 November 1888, "moved back to Mosquitoville I expect it is the last move I shall make at trapping everything is caught out except a few coons."

11. 9 November 1887, "digging Guber peases"; 10 January 1888, "helping kill hogs"; 26 September 1888, "pick cotton in afternoon"; 27 September, "pick cotton in morn'g Stayed all night at Mr Barhams"; 29 November 1888, "Went out to Mr Dunlaps cotton picking did not have much of a picking."

12. 4 July 1887, "went out to Mastodon after rations Mr Chorley I think is trying to boss me and everything else around camp He have graduated the quickest of any greenhorn that I ever saw.... one thing is certain he will have to stop throwing his insults at me and treat me and who ever I choose to bring here with common civility or I shall give him orders to pull out of Mosquitoville He will find that I am yet the boss of this ranch"; Saturday, 23 July 1887, "sawing off in forenoon everybody but me went out to the hills I have to fix up everything ready for work on Monday if I don't stay here my Niggers will not come back Sunday evening If I have to work Niggers I am going to have them earn their Dollar a day."

13. 9 May 1887, "Went up to Askews Bluff cross Coldwater and back again looking at the floats in Cypress Brakes got back to Mr Dunlaps tired out having tramp'd I expect 45 miles"; 11 August 1887, "got on train at Sardis and went up to Coldwater walked from there out 22 miles west to the mouth of Arkabutla Creek to see Mr Bill Bright he is putting raft logs into Strayhorn and Arkabutla Creek."

14. 1 October 1887, "stewing up roots for Mr Chorley I think he will get over his chills this time if he will take care of himself"; 6 November 1887, "Mr Chorley very sick with fever today if he do not take better care of himself he will be carried to the Bone Yard the first thing he knows"; 1 February 1888, "Mr Chorley sick again today he have a rough time of it as soon as he gets well of one thing, something else takes hold of him"; 7 March 1888, "the cold weather is making Mr Chorley sick the best thing he can do is get out of the bottoms I think he dont seem to be able to stand the swamps It take a man with a constitution like a alligator to stand this old Bottom."

15. 15 June 1888, "I think the sights I saw on the trip will satisfy me with the Coldwater country Most of they folks have fine crops. But the looks of the people especially the women

out to settle the question with anyone about living in the Mississippi bottoms if they can in any way make a living out of it They women all look like the were about half dead."

16. 9 June 1887, "went back to camp sick had a heavy fever in night thought I was going to play out for awhile Chorley got scared and went out after a mule for me to ride out"; a week later, 15 June, he was still sick: "little better to day cold will play out after awhile I think"; 16 June, "getting better can walk around some today"; 17 June, "went to Mastodon my head all in a buzze like something was trying to get out"; 18 June, "think I will be alright in a few days."

17. 2 May 1888, "went back to camp mosquitoes awful we can hardly stand them with smoke"; 11 May, "hauling Logs weather hot enough for August and mosquitoes worse then I ever saw them"; 28 May, "went back to Mosquitoville and found the mosquitoes all there."

18. Quitman Deed Book (DB) H:367.

19. Quitman DB H:367.

20. Quitman DB H:370.

21. 13 February 1889, after a visit to Jackson, apparently to file claims, "there is a devil of a lot of work to be done on my 80 acre farm before it will be fit to raise cotton But if I had bought it five years ago I could have had it all in good fit by this time."

22. Quitman DB L:512.

23. Quitman DB M:52.

24. Quitman County Deed Book G:527.

25. Quitman DB W:588.

26. Panola DB A19:374 for the 1924 transaction, Panola DB A8:216 for the one in 1900.

27. Panola County Will Book C:124.

28. Panola Will Book C:351.

29. Private collection, identity withheld.

30. Panola DB A6:18.

31. Quitman DB M:402.

32. Quitman DB M:458.

33. Quitman DB M:589.

34. Quitman DB N:81.

35. Quitman DB N:333.

36. Quitman DB N:332.

37. Quitman DB R:176.

38. Panola DB A9:138.

39. Panola DB A8:228.

40. Panola DB 29:322.

41. Panola Charter Record 1902:8: Incorporation of C. M. Carrier & Son.

42. Recorded in Panola DB A12:20–46 in 1906.

43. Panola DB A12:22; Panola DB J:36.

44. Panola DB A12:20.

45. Panola DB J:122; Panola DB A5:181.

46. Panola DB A12:24.

47. Panola DB A12:26.

48. Panola DB A12:32.

49. Panola DB A12:42.

50. Panola DB A12:42.
51. Panola DB A12:40.
52. Panola DB Q:9.
53. Panola DB A12:30.
54. Panola DB A12:34.
55. Panola DB A12:34.
56. Panola DB A12:34.
57. Panola DB A12:38.
58. Panola DB A12:26.
59. Panola DB A12:32.
60. Panola DB A12:28.
61. Panola DB A12:30.
62. Panola DB A12:44.
63. Panola DB A12:46.
64. Panola DB A12:46.
65. Panola DB A12:40.
66. Panola DB A10:51.
67. Panola DB A12:36.
68. Panola DB A12:24.
69. Panola DB A12:38.
70. Panola DB A8:486.
71. Panola DB A8:501.
72. Described in Quitman DB S:304.
73. Quitman DB S:317.
74. Quitman DB X:70.
75. Quitman DB S:322.
76. Quitman DB V:405; Quitman DB V:404.
77. Quitman DB T:173.
78. Panola DoT 29:397.
79. Panola DoT 64:240.
80. Panola Charter Record 1, p. 31.
81. Quitman DB W:249.
82. Quitman DB AA:44.
83. Quitman DB AA:44.
84. Quitman DB S:319 and Panola DoT 25:510; Quitman DB X:70.
85. Quitman DB AA:44.
86. Panola DB A14:57.
87. Panola DoT 62:237.
88. Panola DB A8:501.
89. Panola DB A14:439.
90. Panola DB A14:448.
91. A "cyclone" is a dust collector or extraction fan used in sawmills.
92. Panola DB A19:282.
93. Panola DB A19:438.

94. Panola DB A19:57.
95. Panola DB A21:72.
96. Panola DB A21:57.
97. Panola DB A20:486.
98. Panola DB A20:487.
99. Panola DB A20:509.
100. Panola DB A21:155.
101. Panola DB A21:156.
102. Panola DB A21:158.
103. Panola DB A21:153.
104. Panola DB A21:160.
105. Panola Charter Record 166.
106. A bolt is an 8-ft length of timber.
107. Panola DB A21:401.
108. Panola DB A21:401.
109. Panola DB A23:53.

Additional Sources Used

Government Documents and Periodicals

US Geological Survey quadrangle maps
1982 Crowder 7.5" topographic quadrangle.
1982 Sardis 7.5" topographic quadrangle.
1983 Asa 7.5" topographic quadrangle.
1983 Curtis Station 7.5" topographic quadrangle.
1983 Pleasant Grove 7.5" topographic quadrangle.
Panola County First Judicial District Deed Books (abbreviated Panola DB)
Panola County First Judicial District Record of Corporate Charters
Panola County First Judicial District Will Books
Quitman County Deed Books (abbreviated Quitman DB)
Quitman County Deeds of Trust

Periodicals

Memphis Flyer, http://www.memphisflyer.com/, 19 March 1999.
Mississippi Reports, Volumes 103, 119.
Sardis *Southern Reporter* weekly newspaper.
Southern Reporter (1st series), Volumes 57, 60, 81.

PART V

Reflections

CHAPTER 16

Brookes@Forest: Building an Epistemic Community for Archaeological Research-in-Action

Patricia Galloway

Introduction

In previous chapters we have seen specific discussion of the archaeological work done by forest archaeologists under Sam Brookes's supervision. What I am going to focus on here is his work as a "meta-archaeologist," an archaeological administrator with the USDA Forest Service who created and maintained an environment in which good and ethical archaeology was done, leading to publications and other kinds of additions to the database of archaeological resources for Mississippi. Secondarily, Brookes has been instrumental in furthering and promoting the careers of the archaeologists under his supervision, as well as those of academic archaeologists and their students, mostly in Mississippi. Finally, Brookes was required to promote archaeology as another public value of forest preservation and management, and he used this work to move forest archaeology into a leadership position for promoting archaeology in Mississippi generally, spearheading many activities that have come to be routine today. I am therefore interested here in the importance to archaeology as a practice and profession of this example of what often remains "invisible work": the creation of institutional infrastructure of which the well-known activities of archaeology are the outward sign. The USDA Forest Service award citation that was read at the 2011 Southeastern Archaeological Conference symposium honoring Sam Brookes's work (see Appendix) addressed a lot of what I will say in the sense of citing *what* he was able to accomplish, as have many comments and acknowledgments in the preceding chapters of this volume, but did not specify *how*.

Theory

From a theoretical point of view, this investigation falls at a nexus between the social study of science and the anthropology of work, directed toward understanding the functioning and maintenance of an extended working environment that includes as human members people of multiple skills and tasks, partnering with others from other working contexts and also with descendant communities, avocational participants, and even children; and in addition a full range of nonhuman actors, including tools and equipment and theoretical constructs as well as the physical and intellectual objects of the archaeological work, in this case mostly (but not entirely) the discoveries yielded by survey and testing in aid of cultural resource management rather than full-scale excavation. I am going to argue, as is increasingly common in studies of work, that in a real sense all successful professional work environments are places where people learn together, and the National Forests in Mississippi's archaeological work is no exception, although the team carrying it out has been distributed over the landscape rather than working together in a single location. As archaeologists, we have not until recently looked reflectively at our own work, but Ian Hodder and others working on the ethnography of archaeology have proved that we can do so with profit (Edgeworth 2006; Hodder 2003). In the case before us, I think we will see that the important advances that have come from the work of the National Forests in Mississippi archaeological team were no accident, but the result of the learning power of a community of practice and the importance of its efforts to share the results of that learning, leading to the active and sustained involvement of others not formally members of that community. I will draw together several anthropological concepts to help to sketch the process by which forest archaeology in Mississippi developed: community of practice, reflective practice, infrastructure, and epistemic culture.

First, I want to think about the forest archaeology that developed under Brookes's leadership as a *community of practice*. The term was originally developed by Jean Lave and Etienne Wenger along with their concept of "situated learning" (Lave and Wenger 1991). They argued that learning is not exclusively an individual phenomenon, but takes place as specific groups of people, engaged in a mutually interesting pursuit, interact and exchange information (Wenger 2006). Therefore to make a study of a community of practice it is necessary, according to Wenger, to define the domain of interest (in this case, archaeology in general and forest archaeology in particular), the specific community pursuing it (in this case the archaeologists pursuing forest archaeology in Mississippi) and the shared practice that develops as distinctive to the community (a forest archaeology developed in a specific geographical context, which I will suggest has itself been a source of discovery).

To enlarge on the process by which the members of a community of practice pursue their own development of understanding through practice, I think it is helpful to think of everyday work using the concept of *reflective practice* as developed by Donald Schön: a way of proceeding through practice as a questioning, experimental process where each task is a small experiment whose observed outcome drives the emergent course of the work (Schön 1983; see also Orlikowski 1996 for a conception of this process as "situated change"). Schön has successfully argued that this process is not just an ideal of scholarly research design, but a sign of professional practice during everyday work. Further, it is a good fit with archaeology, where it is well known that research designs and practice are frequently tweaked on a daily basis during field investigations to take account of unsuspected and often unsuspectable findings.

Practices do not exist in a vacuum, but are situated in and supported by existing conventions, which practices in turn alter by reproducing them with variations. To provide a framework for the emergent practices of forest archaeology I want to use the concept of *infrastructure*, as developed by sociologists Anselm Strauss and Susan Leigh Star (Star and Ruhleder 1996). Infrastructures are the frequently invisible, taken-for-granted structures that frame our everyday lives and practices, structures that we may change but must also work within in a dialogic way. They are characterized by their embeddedness in the situation, their transparency, reach or scope, association with a community of practice, embodiment of standards, dependency on an installed base, and (especially) they are most visible on breakdown (Star and Ruhleder 1996:113). For the issue at hand, the rich set of established infrastructures includes lithic and pottery typologies and time sequences, academic and bureaucratic systems of status and reward, legal frameworks governing cultural heritage preservation, field archaeology survey and excavation methods, routines and practices of forest care, and formal relationships among established institutional entities (for example, federal government represented by the USDA Forest Service, state government represented by the Mississippi Department of Archives and History and state universities, and controllers of land use such as the US Army). All of these interlocking infrastructures (and others) constitute the environment within which the USDA Forest Service archaeological work has to take place, hence all of them had to be deployed or negotiated so that learning work and the production of knowledge could in fact happen (Strauss 1982), and at times the "creative destruction" wrought by new findings could make specific infrastructures visible and an issue for overt study. And here I intend to attempt to frame or map them using Strauss's concept of social worlds and arenas as presented by Adele Clarke (see Clarke 2005). In such a mapping, other "social worlds" or communities are seen as related to the community of interest as participants in various aspects of the arena in question, in this case the archaeology of Mississippi.

Finally, I want to develop the argument that under Brookes's direction the team constituted by the Mississippi forest archaeologists developed beyond that of a community of practice, which carries out work and improves its understanding of the work over time, approaching an *epistemic community*, which in the course of its work produces new knowledge by analyzing the objects of its attentions and actively pushing the boundaries of existing infrastructures. Karin Knorr-Cetina defines epistemic community as tied to a specific knowledge setting and making up one of the structures of a knowledge society. Such a cultural entity is constituted in her study by a field of scientific enquiry together with the institutions, practices, and physical objects that provide and are the context of its material support (Knorr-Cetina 1999:8). Like the communities she discusses, high-energy physics and molecular biology, I suggest that it is entirely appropriate to consider that the Mississippi Forests archaeological team, its external partners, and the infrastructural equipment of archaeological practice, participating in the larger arena of North American archaeology, constrained by a framework of statutory compliance in cultural heritage preservation, and directed at a set of geographical areas where potential evidences of previous human habitation may exist, together constitute an active laboratory where we know—on the evidence of the essays in this book—that new knowledge has been and is being created.

Method

As I started out, I was going to put together an institutional history as seen from the perspective of a single biography. The appropriateness of such an approach emerges from the fact that although individuals working inside especially governmental institutions are working within the confines of a set of laws, regulations, policies, and procedures constituting a particular statutory infrastructure, all such workers—especially if they command a body of knowledge and skills that others need but do not well understand—negotiate their own micro-institution, not likely to be like that of anyone else, by the way they fill in and modify those parts of the infrastructure that remain ill-defined, just to get their work done. In Strauss and Star's work this underspecified area calls forth "articulation work," or the creative improvisation—articulated in the form of reflective practice as mentioned above—that emerges to bridge between defined and undefined regions of infrastructure (see also Strauss et al. 1997; Wiener 1991). If workers are successful in effectively defining formerly informal portions of infrastructure or creating entirely new infrastructural segments, they may leave behind at least some lessons and hopefully a functioning infrastructure that the next person can take advantage of rather than starting from scratch. I thought that would certainly be the case here; I wanted to portray the Brookesian micro-institution and how Brookes and the growing cohort of forest archaeologists constructed it in the give and take of everyday routine work by undertaking new activities that would become established fixtures.

I knew that if I had to track down every word of report about Brookes's activities I would, at my current distance from Mississippi, have a difficult problem on my hands. It would be difficult to access the records of his office because official recordkeeping in government generally eventuates in the retention of at most 1 to 5 percent of records, frequently those of the most uninformative kind with respect to actual governmental activity (Cook 2011:3). Further, because they generally tend to present the agreed story of what happened, leaving out struggles and improvised articulation work, they might even obscure the story I was trying to find. Accordingly, I decided to take advantage of a less formal, already existing temporal transect through those 24 years by using a printed source that reflected the grassroots effects of Brookes's work, a source that was available to me directly: the *Mississippi Archaeological Association Newsletter* from 1987–2011. I had a fairly good idea of how representative this source was through my experience as its editor for about half of that time. It was also clear that for the period of interest, although the *Newsletter* was sponsored ostensibly by the avocational community, nearly all of the communities involved in Mississippi archaeology appeared in its pages and contributed to its content at one time or another, so it represented the multiple heterogeneous voices of the stakeholders in Mississippi archaeology and their views of changes and developments over time.

I then reread these sources from 1987 to the present. I found it possible to put together a list of USDA Forest Service activities in Mississippi on a reasonably accurate timeline. In doing this, I also compiled several other kinds of data that reflected historical context. I noted what issues in current archaeology were being discussed in the *Newsletter*—including looting of archaeological sites, the passing and implications of the Native American Graves Protection and Repatriation Act (NAGPRA), public outreach projects of the USDA Forest Service like the Passport In Time (PIT) program, and the Camp Shelby land swap—and how they were differentially interesting to amateur and professional audiences. It was also obvious that the realities of the actual ecology of the forest had a huge impact on the work of the archaeologists: environmental requirements as articulated in the National Environmental Policy Act (NEPA), the rhythms of timber harvests, and the vicissitudes of violent weather and pest infestations all appeared in the pages of the *Newsletter*, all of them reported by the forest archaeologists. Using the timeline I was also able to construct the growing network of USDA Forest Service staff in Mississippi, to add other active contacts to the network, and to inventory other non-field activities, including Delta tours, Mississippi Archaeological Association (MAA) chapter meetings, meetings of the Mississippi Association of Professional Archaeologists (MAPA), and formal relations with MDAH, the Mississippi Department of Transportation (MDoT), the US Army Corps of Engineers (CoE), and the three Mississippi public universities with archaeology programs, University of Mississippi (UM), Mississippi State University (MSU), and University of Southern Mississippi (USM). The data thus gathered enabled me to construct the narrative of the emergence of the National Forests in Mississippi archaeological team as a community of practice, tracing its activities within the controlling infrastructure created by federal and state laws, the USDA Forest Service as an agency charged with sustainable care of National Forests, and the interaction with other government agencies, non-governmental organizations, and significant individuals.

Prologue: Existing Models in 1987

First it should be observed that Sam Brookes had at least two very relevant examples before him to draw upon for how to construct a community of archaeological practice around the National Forests in Mississippi task space. Legendary by that time was the work of the university-based Lower Mississippi Survey (LMS), with its core scholar-practitioners—Philip Phillips, James A. Ford, and James B. Griffin—and their students and the mobilized local archaeologists and avocationals who were vital to its success and progress in the generation of knowledge from archaeological survey and excavation in the Lower Mississippi Valley (Lee Arco, personal communication 2012; Williams 2002; see also Weinstein 2005). However successful the LMS was, however, the fact that the source of a good deal of its influence was the location of its principals in midwestern and eastern universities of significant prestige also meant that its representatives could not be active and on the spot at all times, hence its dependence on local archaeologists and especially the participation of independent avocational archaeologists as informants for the survey that the LMS could not undertake without their help. Thus the efforts of the LMS were only as sustainable as the loyalties of a founding partnership could make them, extended by the cross-breeding of student careers and the sustained infrastructural work of Steve Williams in maintaining the base of the LMS at Harvard, and all of these factors were potentially inspirational to Brookes and others who were well acquainted with LMS researchers and whose work dialogued with LMS findings. In fact, at the time when Sam Brookes was a graduate student and beginning his professional career, the LMS was beginning a new program of work in Mississippi, with Phil Phillips's (1970) summative work on the Lower Yazoo Basin coming to fruition and that of Jeffrey Brain on the Tunicas and of later students like Ian Brown and Vincas Steponatis just beginning to be planned in the region (Brain and Williams 1971). Yet there was no really thorough account of how the LMS community had been constructed, so it remained a unique accomplishment rather than a detailed roadmap.

Perhaps a more applicable example, designed to be capable of organizing archaeological effort on a local level and of incorporating and thereby coopting avocational efforts more effectively, could be drawn from the creation, just across the river from Mississippi, of the Arkansas Archeological Survey (AAS) system of station archaeologists, under the rubric of "public archeology," by Charles McGimsey and Hester Davis beginning in 1967 (McGimsey 1972; White 1999). The creation of the AAS, drawing on the best features of state archaeological programs all over the United States, was meant to serve as a model for state programs, and it rested on a set of principles and arguments for what services such a program ought to provide and how it might provide them. The Survey depended upon the claims of carefully crafted state law and the permanent and trusted presence of "station archaeologists" situated all over the state. This had already proved to be a sustainable infrastructure that depended on balancing the tensions of the employment of archaeologists as distributed university faculty, their devotion to the intensive study of the specific regions where they were located, and their loyalty to a distributed community of practice. Also important was the ability of the station archaeologists to persuade amateur archaeologists to cooperate in approved activities through the creation of the Arkansas Archeological Society in 1960 and support of its annual excavation and educational program, designed for individuals with an interest in archaeology to learn and qualify as avocational archaeologists.

The program worked in Arkansas and even gained national influence, but there was no similar infrastructure of a unified university system in Mississippi to start the synergy, nor in spite of efforts did the centrally situated MDAH have the funding to create stand-alone offices in all state regions. Brookes had at first worked in the MDAH Clarksdale office along with Sam McGahey, who moved to Jackson to become State Archaeologist, and then with John Connaway, who remained there alone after Brookes left; James Barnett, along with being site manager for the Grand Village of the Natchez Indians and Historic Jefferson College beginning in 1982, was an archaeologist, but his primary task was site management; and historical archaeologist Jack Elliot was eventually placed by MDAH at Mississippi State University, but not until 1987. It is also worth noting that when McGimsey wrote, the USDA Forest Service had only two people on its whole staff to advise on the implications of federal law for archaeology on all the National Forests (McGimsey 1972:111), so National Forest archaeology had been neglected in Arkansas as well as in Mississippi.

The primary difference from both of these models in the Mississippi USDA Forest Service setting, and a significant advantage in the absence of an established research program and an academic niche, was its federal leverage. The LMS was limited in being able to exercise its power through influence in person and through academic publication: it could make use of legal claims but did not do so, preferring to obtain access through private agreements that left it with greater freedom to retain materials for study as long as necessary. The AAS was a state entity but one that had limited power of enforcement, instead bringing persistent presence and surveillance to bear in order to mitigate what McGimsey and Davis had targeted as the greatest threat to archaeological sites in the Mississippi Valley: agricultural disturbance. But by the time that Brookes began working for the USDA Forest Service in 1987, several legal tools, influenced by the public archaeology work in Arkansas and elsewhere, were already in place to govern the treatment of federal government lands in the National Forests. The limitation here was that the tools alone were supposed to dictate the archaeological steps that could be taken. Pursuit of new archaeological knowledge was not the specific goal: instead the official purpose of archaeology for the USDA Forest Service was the performance of routine data gathering as a step in a decision tree for maximizing forest products yields while complying with several kinds of preservation laws (USDA Forest Service 1988).

Brookes and the Construction of the USDA Forest Service in Mississippi Team

When Brookes came to the USDA Forest Service he brought with him formal qualifications and professional connections. He had the Master's-level training typical of professional archaeologists in the United States and gained at a Mississippi university, guaranteeing local experience (Brookes 1989, 2000). He had considerable experience as a government archaeologist, having spent 13 years doing county surveys and excavations for the Mississippi Department of Archives and History as a field archaeologist stationed in Clarksdale. He had also spent 2 years as a federal archaeologist with the Corps of Engineers at Vicksburg. He was therefore well acquainted with the communities of professional and avocational archaeologists in Mississippi and with the archaeology of Mississippi and the region, as well as with the state and federal legal frameworks for historic preservation work as they affected archaeology. What may also be very important, however, is the many years he spent as an avocational collector while a boy in Virginia, repeatedly surveying newly plowed fields, an experience that must have laid a valuable foundation for the recognition of the value of repeated survey as a mode of revealing archaeological features in space and time.

At the USDA Forest Service, Brookes was initially alone in 1987 as Heritage Program Manager, having succeeded Mark DeLeon. When he started his work the USDA Forest Service was mostly concerned with meeting its Cultural Resource Management (CRM) obligations under the National Historic Preservation Act (NHPA) of 1966 and the Archaeological Resources Protection Act (ARPA) of 1979. It would be a mistake, however, to assume that the environment of forest archaeological work was only based on this statutory framework. Instead, and I think very significantly, it had to include the culture of forest work, which entailed care of the forests, support of their harvest and use, and creation of recreational activities. CRM obligations plus timber sales equaled a need for archaeological surveys, which were far beyond the reach of a single archaeologist and were initially carried out by contractors. These surveys had been going on for some time but were poorly specified and left the lone Forest Archaeologist with impossible follow-up work to do to achieve adequate results (Peacock 1994). Clearly more than one archaeologist would be needed to do an adequate job of carrying out official tasks in the National Forests in Mississippi.

Even before the passage of NAGPRA in 1990, the National Forests in Mississippi under Brookes's leadership, in the light of the Mississippi attorney general's ruling in the 1980s extending the protection of the state's grave desecration law to human burials of any time period, had moved proactively to create a memorandum of agreement with Mississippi tribal governments regarding consultation upon discovery of human remains, and after NAGPRA was passed the Mississippi forests were already positioned to comply. Then in 1991 the National Environmental Policy Act began to require environmental impact statements for land disturbance, while the new Passport In Time program of public participation in forest archaeology began to be promoted nationally, offering a program of public involvement that could provide assistance without cost to USDA Forest Service archaeologists in carrying out both required survey and archaeological testing. Mississippi was by that time well on the way to being able to take advantage of that program. In 1992, after five years, Brookes had put together a team of four forest archaeologists from graduate students of state universities who were placed on four of the state's National Forests (Brookes himself was in charge of the Delta forest

Table 16.1. Staffing Mississippi Forest archaeology.

Year	Delta	Bienville	Chicka-sawhay	DeSoto	Holly Springs	Homochitto	Tombig-bee
1987	Brookes						
1988	Brookes						
1989	Brookes						
1990	Brookes						
1991	Brookes		Reams	Reams			
1992	Brookes		Higgins	Reams		Fant	Peacock
1993	Brookes	Higgins	Higgins	Reams	Peacock	Fant	Peacock
1994	Brookes	Bryan	Higgins	Reams	Peacock	Fant	Peacock
1995	Brookes	Bryan	Higgins	Reams	Fant	Reams/Dukes	Peacock
1996	Brookes	McClung	Higgins	Reams	Fant	Dukes	Peacock/McClung
1997	Brookes	McClung	Higgins	Reams	Fant	Dukes	Peacock
1998	Brookes	McClung	Higgins	Reams	Fant	Dukes/Kelso	Peacock/Mitchell
1999	Brookes	McClung	Higgins	Reams	Fant	Dukes/Kelso	Peacock/Mitchell
2000	Brookes	Davies	Schleidt	Reams	Fant	Dukes	Kelso
2001	Brookes		Schleidt	Reams	Fant	Dukes/Kelso	McClung
2002	Brookes		Schleidt	Reams		Dukes/Ascher	McClung
2003	Brookes	McClung	Schleidt	Reams		Dukes/Ascher	Bruce
2004	Brookes	McClung	Schleidt	Reams	McAnally	Ascher	Bruce
2005	Brookes	McClung	James	Reams	McAnally	Gagné	Bruce
2006	Brookes	McClung	James	Reams	Ryerse	Gagné	Triplett
2007	Brookes	McClung	James	Reams	Ryerse	Gagné	Triplett
2008	Brookes	McClung	James	Reams	Triplett	Gagné	Triplett
2009	Brookes	McClung	James	Reams	Triplett	Gagné	Triplett
2010	Brookes	McClung	James	Reams	Triplett	Gagné	Triplett
2011	Brookes		James	Reams		Gagné	
Univ Rel				USM/USA	UM		MSU
MAA Chapter	Jackson			Black Creek			Tombigbee

that he knew so well): David Fant (Holly Springs), Evan Peacock (Tombigbee), Robert Reams (DeSoto), and Joel Dukes (Homochitto). In 1997 the full team had filled out at six, and four members of the team (Fant, Peacock, Dukes, and Terry McClung) were made permanent. It had taken 10 years, but the Mississippi forests were covered in a pattern that echoed the distributed locational pattern of the AAS. Between 1997 and 2011 there would be times when one or another of the forests would not be staffed, but the core group of Fant,

McClung, Dukes, and Reams held steady until Dukes left in 2003 and Fant in 2005. By 2004, however, other replacements were made, so that in 2005 four new archaeologists were on the Mississippi forests. Two of them remained in 2011, while two others were replaced (see Table 16.1). This process was not without difficulties of funding and availability of qualified archaeologists and support staff, but the longitudinal list is interesting to observe because in it we see the success of the first generational transition and the persistence of the established structure: it had been clearly established that there was enough statutory work to be done, that in the face of weather disaster archaeologists could make valuable contributions to the activities of forest care, and that with the expansion of university alliances and PIT projects, the work of the archaeologists could also build considerable goodwill for the USDA Forest Service at minimal cost.

Enhancing the Archaeology Arena in Mississippi

The establishment of a distributed team of archaeologists for the forests is only part of the story, though it is fundamental. But to understand how it *worked*, it is necessary to understand the context. At the same time that the forests in Mississippi were becoming better and better served by archaeology, the archaeologists themselves, encouraged and supported by Brookes, were participating broadly in Mississippi and regional archaeological activities, activities that further rooted them in the region and promoted their careers while making forest archaeology in Mississippi increasingly visible. An attempt at an overall view of the context of forest archaeology, inclusive of many more elements than can be explained here, is shown in Table 16.2.

A first important constituency was the avocational community, and the focus here must be on the MAA, with which Brookes had already established an active and supporting role well before 1987. The forest archaeologists all reached out to—and substantively supported—local MAA chapters by attending meetings, giving talks, and encouraging participation in excavations that chapters had been wanting for years: the beginning of PIT projects in Mississippi in 1993 helped with that. Where there was no MAA chapter, they worked to start, support, or revive one: Robert Reams served as Black Creek chapter president; when Brookes moved to Jackson, he acted to revive the Jackson chapter himself; Terry McClung served as MAA president. Further outreach to the MAA included support (and frequently program organization) for Mississippi Archaeology Week in the late 1990s, which grew into Mississippi Archaeology Month beginning in 2002. In connection with both, the USDA Forest Service supported and partnered with MAA to create an archaeology booth at the state fair, to be joined by MDAH somewhat later. In return this

Table 16.2. Actants in Mississippi Forest Service archaeology.

Collective human actors	Relevant practices in USFS arena
USDoA/USFS	Archaeological
USDoI/NPS	Survey/Hunting
USDoD/Army/CoE	Excavation
MDAH	Classifications
MSDoT	
MSP&W	Equipment
MARIS	Tools, Vehicles
Cottanlandia Museum	Instrumentation
Mississippi State Historical Museum	Theories, Practices
UM	Forest management
MSU/Cobb Institute	
USM	Care (pine beetle, fire)
JSU	Environmental management
Millsaps	Harvest
Delta State	Heritage
Alcorn	Public use
Community colleges	Discourses involving forest archaeologists
Archaeological Conservancy	
Sierra Club	Mississippi State Site File
Lower Delta Partnership	GIS mapping of sites
MAA	MAA Newsletter
MS Heritage Trust	*Mississippi Archaeology*
SAA	*Southeastern Archaeology*
SEAC	*American Antiquity*
MidSouth AC	*Louisiana Archaeology*
MAPA	*Alabama Archaeology*
Individual Human Actors	MDAH *Archaeological Reports*
	Gray literature reports to regulators
Professional archaeologists	Brochures
Academic	Posters
Organizational	Websites (MAA, USFS/PIT, GDBA, MAPA)
Contract	Events
Government Regulators	
Professional forest practitioners	MS Archaeology Week/Month
Foresters	State Fair booth
Timber markers/heritage resource technicians	MS Archaeology Expo
Avocationals	MAA meetings
Archaeological	USFS publications
Reenactor groups	USFS citation to Brookes
	Laws
Subjects	Federal: NEPA, NARFA, NAGPRA, etc.
Native Americans	State: MDAH, grave desecration, etc.
African Americans	
European settler descendants	

work with avocationals assisted forest archaeologists in many ways as well as meeting the USDA Forest Service's interest in public outreach and putting the forests to use as recreational venues.

Much of this activity was reported steadily in the *MAA Newsletter*, especially after the regular USDA Forest Service column "Central Midden" was started in 1996 (*MAA Newsletter* 1996[3]). This column served to legitimate the new initiatives that Brookes was establishing and to introduce the new forest archaeologists to the avocational community more broadly. Although the forest archaeologists prepared individual reports, the whole column was regularly put together by one or another of them: Melissa Higgins during the early years and Terry McClung more recently. Through the years this column frequently dominated the content of the *Newsletter* and eventually encouraged similar though not so regular contributions from MDoT, MDAH, and Camp Shelby (Mississippi National Guard). The regular preparation of reports also assisted with the creation of identity and community for the forest archaeologists themselves, as well as providing opportunities for young archaeologists to begin to publish their findings and to formalize their outreach to the MAA membership.

Outreach of a more ambitious kind was also encouraged by Brookes, as he and forest archaeologist partners helped organize not only MAA meetings, but Mid-South Archaeological Conference and Southeastern Archaeological Conference meetings as well. These organizational efforts helped to support the regional knowledge-sharing infrastructure for the Forest Archaeologists' larger community of practice, while at the same time reporting the new scholarly work on the forests to a broader professional audience. On the academic side, Brookes had also looked to establish relationships that connected USDA Forest Service archaeologists with the academic community by beginning partnerships with the three largest Mississippi universities early, in 1992, and then took advantage of special USDA Forest Service programs to involve anthropology departments and their students directly with forest archaeology work through internships and eventually jobs. In 1997 Mississippi was home to the only National Forest in the Southeast to receive foreign student volunteers in a program that lasted several years. An internship program for American graduate students led to multiple Master's theses (see Table 16.3) as well as solid practical learning about day-to-day archaeology on the forests, survey as well as excavation. Andrew Triplett, working on the Tombigbee forest, described an active community of practice using reflection-in-action when in 2008 he observed a mosaic of theses developed by such students on the Tombigbee: "Perhaps the greatest benefit is the endless number of thesis topics that present themselves as we come across sites and then discuss as we trudge our way through the woods. There are several present and past

Table 16.3. Theses written based on work on USFS in Mississippi sites or on artifacts from them.

University	Student	Year	Thesis title
USM	Mark F. DeLeon	1981	A Study of the Environment and Prehistoric Occupation in the Black Creek Basin of the Piney Woods of South Mississippi
USM	John Blitz	1984	An Archaeological Study of the Mississippi Choctaw Indians**
UM	David Fant	1996	Early Woodland Sites on the Holly Springs National Forest, Archaeological Survey from 1992–1995, and the Testing of Site 22 MR 539 and 22 BE 585
USM	Grace F. Keith	1997	A Technological Analysis of Ceramics from the Leaf River Drainage, Southeast Mississippi*
USM	Scot Keith	1998	Settlement and Lithic Organization from the Paleoindian through Late Woodland at the Sandhill Site (22-Wa-676), Southeast Mississippi
USM	Michael C. Dunn	1999	An Analysis of Lithic Artifacts from the Swamp Child Site (22FO666): An Investigation into Site Function and Adaptive Strategies
USM	Rita D. Fields	2001	Settlement Organization, Site Variability, and the Organization of Technology in the Pine Hills: An Intersite Study of the Oo-Oo-Lation Site (22GN668) and Tanya's Knoll (22WA642)
UM	Michelle Renee McAnally	2002	A Land Use History of the Holly Springs National Forest
USM	Kelly C. McClave	2004	A Little Turn-of-the-Century Town in the Piney Woods: An Ethnohistorical Examination of Howison Mississippi
MSU	Jason Lee Parrish	2006	An Archaeological Investigation of Four Woodland-Period Sites in the North Central Hills Physiographic Region of Mississippi: 22CH653, 22WI536, 22WI588, and 22WI679
MSU	Andrew Mickens Triplett	2008	A Study of the Chronological Placement of Selected Mississippian-Period Occupations within the Ackerman Unit of the Tombigbee National Forest
MSU	Keith Allen Baca	2008	Elemental Analysis of Marksville-Style Prehistoric Ceramics from Mississippi and Alabama*
MSU	Weston Bacon-Schulte	2008	The Selection for Sedentary Settlement Patterns in East-Central Mississippi*
USM	Michael P. Fedoroff	2009	Earth-Oven Technology in the Mississippi Pine Hills: An Experimental Approach to Archaeological Investigations and Method Development*
MSU	Jessica P. Gisler	2014	Intensification as a Survival Strategy on the Tombigbee National Forest (prospectus on file; thesis in progress)

* Data taken from USFS excavations.
**Data from contract work performed for USFS.

students that have worked on the Tombigbee who have been able to use these impromptu brainstorming sessions to develop ideas for their thesis" (Triplett 2008b:6). At least three students would become forest archaeologists, while others entered CRM, government archaeology, and academic careers. Forest archaeologists published their work in *Mississippi Archaeology* as time went on, but their work also appeared in the journals of neighboring states and in the regional *Southeastern Archaeology*. And excavation projects on the forests, exploring sites found during routine survey, made excellent field schools for university archaeology programs, thereby expanding the archaeological information coming out of the forests and making the forests into venues that attracted academic archaeologists for their own research and teaching.

At the same time, Brookes began building a government and NGO network of support for archaeology as he took the USDA Forest Service into a variety of partnerships with other federal agencies—the CoE, National Park Service (NPS), and Department of Defense (DoD)—and with the state—MDAH and MDoT. Nongovernmental organizations with common interests also became partners. In 1992 Brookes became a founding member of the Mississippi Heritage Trust and began promoting the work of the Archaeological Conservancy in Mississippi, whose Mississippi field officer Jessica Crawford eventually became regional director for the Conservancy as a whole in 2006. Brookes recruited the interest of the Sierra Club through some of the earliest Delta mound tours he led; and together with the Lower Delta Partnership, a group of individuals, government agencies, and NGOs, he developed his work on the Delta forest into a set of archaeological tours referring to Teddy Roosevelt's experience in the Delta that became part of the town of Rolling Fork's "Great Delta Bear Affair" celebration in 2002. Finally, he drew on the funding possibilities for public programs from the Mississippi Humanities Council to bring well-known speakers to archaeological events and to bring in the public as well. Evidence of all this can be seen in the list of sponsors on posters for Mississippi Archaeology Month, of which the Humanities Council was a supporter from the beginning. Finally, Brookes was also able, backed by the cadre of six forest archaeologists and alliances with university, CRM, and other federal archaeologists, to help broker archaeological ethics and standards through the Mississippi Association of Professional Archaeologists.

Growing an Embedded Activity Set to Make New Knowledge

I haven't even begun to say anything about the archaeology that has been carried out on Sam Brookes's watch, because so many of the papers gathered in this volume have addressed it. But I am interested in working through a few cases in which he was able to take advantage of the synergy of building a work situation where archaeology became naturalized as a USDA Forest Service activity in order to develop new ways of doing archaeology and new ways of observing archaeologically.

First, he established a principle of repeated surveys in one place after land use likely to expose new surfaces. In 1997 both Joel Dukes and Sam Brookes talked about the effects of this repetition on previous views of site depth and distribution on the forests (Dukes 1997; Brookes 1997; Dukes 1997). It is not surprising that Brookes took to the next level his experience of repeated fieldwalking after agricultural plowing as a boy and his geographically rooted work doing county surveys with John Connaway in the Delta for MDAH. But the next level was possible because the routine work of survey on the forests was tied to the routine timber harvesting that characterizes the southern pine forests. This fact led to partnerships with USDA Forest Service timber managers and their knowledge of what was to be found where archaeologists had not previously looked, because forest lands had been presumed less favorable for human settlement than for hunting. This experience was naturalized into the archaeological enterprise when a cadre of Timber Markers was recruited to work for four years as Heritage Technicians with the forest archaeologists (Schleidt 2005:7). And the agreements with the Army Reserve that covered compliance regarding heritage sites on forest lands used regularly for tank maneuver training practice included repeated surveys that brought the same kind of results as those made after the disturbances of annual plowing elsewhere, particularly in discovery of stratified sites—again, where nobody expected them.

Second, the Passport In Time projects and the university field schools bringing projects to the forests facilitated excavation of sites found in timber and environmental compliance surveys. These excavations in turn permitted the recovery of new information as a service to the public and in some cases to the bioscience of forest ecology, especially in connection with the newly discovered xeric sites in the Piney Woods of south Mississippi. Because the public could be involved, more extended projects were undertaken and another row of site names, referring in shorthand to an unsuspected chronological and typological variety of sites, entered the Mississippi archaeology lexicon: Swamp Child (22FO666), Gopher Farm (22WA676), Achin Head (22FR665), Dantzler (22HR652), Deathly Silent (22FO826), Stinking Water (22WI516), Tanya's Knoll (22WA642), and Wade's Tesoro (22WA1053)—not by any means to name them all.

Many more aspects of Brookes's work are emergent from the *MAA Newsletter* dataset. During Brookes's career, the USDA Forest Service has, for one thing, made a huge shift into technology to manage and mine archaeological data, and the forest archaeologists, Heritage Technicians, and student interns have translated that data into working order through databases and GIS systems: this has laid the groundwork for much more systematic archaeological management on the forests. Watching the patterns of work and the people and the shifts of staff and assignments as reflected in the *Newsletter* reports, I had other questions that cannot be answered here but are further suggestive of the importance of the Brookes example: how strong were the relationships across the cadre of forest archaeologists? There were certainly periodic organized face-to-face meetings, but how were they reinforced by the annual meetings of the MAA, MAPA, SEAC, Mid-South, and MAM? Perhaps more importantly, how united were they as a community of archaeological practice, given that forest work is characteristic of what they all encounter? Was it only the institutional constraints that they shared, or was there something more?

Perhaps a deeper question is: what does it mean to be a Forest Archaeologist, and does that difference contribute something to archaeology as a *whole* that hasn't existed before in Mississippi? In 2002, Brookes wrote,

> I read with pride the Central Midden in the last issue. The district archaeologists, student interns, and heritage technicians are ... doing outstanding work. A few years ago the National Forest lands were considered cultural backwaters with no significant sites located on them. The work done by all the aforementioned folks has changed that forever. We have great sites on the Forest, ranging from mounds to stratified deposits to the fascinating xeric sites of the Piney Woods [Brookes 2002a].

Having read the same reports and especially having considered the temporal process of creating a "forest archaeology," it seems to me that it is impossible to ignore the fact that of necessity, both in carrying out their own archaeological tasks and in taking on at times of need the duty to assist with controlled burns, pest control, and the aftermath of weather-created disasters, the forest archaeologists have also come to join a larger and different community of practice, to learn and share the tasks of forest care with a range of other professionals working for the Service. In this way Forest Archaeologists—and Heritage Technicians who assisted them, themselves having begun their work with the Forest Service in carrying out primarily forestry-related tasks—emerged as *participants with commitments in more than one community*. Perhaps central to the creation of a forest archaeology has been actually putting archaeologists *on* the forest, sending them not only after endangered archaeological sites, but also after pine beetles and tornado damage and even to manage and fight fires, setting them to *learning the forest* by working side by side with forestry professionals. Thus this community of practice evolved into something more, an epistemic community creating a set of archaeologists who were prepared to see the new kinds of sites and their new ways of manifesting so that now there can *be* a "forest archaeology" in Mississippi.

Finally, I would like to say something about the impact of this work and this brokering for archaeology in Mississippi in the larger sense. There is no contesting that more and better archaeology is now being done in Mississippi and by many people, in and out of the forest. But the USDA Forest Service's control of very large tracts of land in the state (which offered lots of work to do and no bar to access apart from statutory requirements), plus the fact that its archaeologists were not competing for academic rewards, and finally the fact that the work was embedded in a value-adding activity from almost any public point of view—all this meant that archaeology on the forests constituted a win-win for everyone involved in it, and Brookes made it possible for that to happen, thus making the USDA Forest Service program a catalyst for the noticeable growth of archaeology all across Mississippi as no other institution had been before. Mississippi archaeology has come together in this way at least partly because Brookes always instinctively knew that at the core of the job is the need to institutionalize a community of practice embedded in the broader arena of the multiple stakeholders in Mississippi archaeology, and that part of that real work is to keep the social as well as the intellectual reward coming, to make sure it remains to some extent a joy. When you build a community like that, everybody learns and everybody wins.

Appendix

Citation for USDA Forest Service National Heritage Award

EXCELLENCE IN THE HERITAGE PROGRAM
NATIONAL AWARD

"A land without ruins is a land without memories."
From *Heritage—It's About Time*! A National Strategy

This award recognizes *overall excellence in the Heritage Program* in the three areas of the National Heritage Strategy. Nominees have exceeded expectations in protecting cultural resources through public outreach, resource stewardship, and providing an historical context for natural resources management.

The nominee must be a FS employee. A joint jury consisting of representatives from the FS, the Advisory Council on Historic Preservation (ACHP) and the National Trust for Historic Preservation (NTHP) will select a national winner from regional nominees. *The winner will automatically be nominated for the NTHP/ACHP joint award for Federal Partnerships in Historic Preservation and for an NTHP Honor Award.*

State: Mississippi

Region: Southern

FS Unit: National Forests in Mississippi

Awardee(s): (Please list by name and FS unit *as you want it to appear on the award*.)

Samuel Brookes, Forest Archaeologist, National Forests in Mississippi

Please address one or more of the criteria (bulleted items) in *all three* Heritage Strategy categories, stewardship, public service, and context for natural resource management.

Contribution to Stewardship
Did the nominee
- contribute to protecting our most significant sites?
- increase our stewardship capabilities through use of improved technologies?
- strengthen our relationship with American Indian tribes?

Appendix

Public Service
Did the nominee
- develop new approaches for bringing heritage experiences to the public?
- strengthen links with conservation education and interpretive services?
- involve and help local communities?

Context for Natural Resource Management
Did the nominee
- use archaeological data to contribute to sound natural resource management decisions?
- strengthen cooperation between heritage and ecosystem management?
- strengthen links with Heritage Research?

In December of 2011, the Southern Region of the USFS will be saying goodbye to Sam Brookes, one of our giants in the Heritage Program, as he enters retirement. Sam has served as the Forest Archaeologist / Heritage Program Leader for the National Forests in Mississippi (NFs in MS) since the beginning of his Forest Service career in the late 1980s. In 1991, Sam was successful in making a strong case to his Forest's leadership that additional professional staff was needed to manage the workload and locate and protect the Forest's most significant cultural resource sites. Over the years, Sam carefully fostered several newbie archaeologists fresh out of graduate school, turning them into strong field-going Forest Service archaeologists and researchers. Some of these archaeologists have gone on to become highly respected university professors, archaeologists for other federal agencies, forest archaeologists, and even one of our Regional Heritage Program Leaders.

Sam loves sharing his passion for archaeology with the public. Over the years he has donated thousands of hours of his own time to do thousands of public presentations. Sam is a favorite and regular speaker for the Mississippi Humanities Council Speakers Bureau, the annual "The Delta: Everything Southern" conference, Mississippi Archaeology Month, and leads his famous tour of Indian mounds in the Mississippi Delta every October for the Great Delta Bear Affair (GDBA). Sam helped forge a strong partnership agreement between the Delta National Forest (NFs in MS) and GDBA organizers. He is a founding member of the Mississippi Heritage Trust. Sam is a member and past president of the Mississippi Archaeological Association (MAA), an organization of professional archaeologists and lay people actively involved with archaeology and archaeological preservation, uniting in a common effort to understand the prehistory and history of Mississippi and the surrounding region. Sam actively connected the Forest Service to this organization early in his career, and the Forest Service and Passport in Time are featured links on MAA's website. The NFs in MS have had a regular column in the MAA newsletter for almost twenty years. Sam developed a Forest Service partnership with Mississippi's Lower Delta Partnership to help develop the Mississippi Mound Trail, modeled on the highly successful Mississippi Blues Trail. Sam is a strong supporter of Passport in Time, and the NFs in MS have been regular participants for nearly 20 years, hosting hundreds of PIT volunteers.

Sam's personal research interests lie in the lithic technologies and environmental conditions of the Middle Archaic period in Mississippi, particularly the Hypsithermal. His research has contributed to the NFs in MS Forest Plan revision efforts in its discussion of climate change and potential unexpected impacts that current changing climate systems could induce on the local environment. In the early 1990s, Sam supported District efforts to partner with local universities to develop Challenge Cost Share agreements for undergraduate and graduate students to work as archaeology interns for the Forest Service. These partnerships strengthened and closely connected the research efforts being conducted by these universities and their students and faculty members with the cultural resources on National Forest Lands. Given that some of the Ranger Districts were located in areas of the state that had seen very little archaeological research in the past, these partnerships have helped to flesh out and even re-write our understanding of the prehistory and early history of Mississippi. Much of this research has been disseminated to the public and to the professional community in published papers, books, Master's theses, and presentations at professional conferences.

Though not a native to Mississippi, Sam has truly adopted it as his home. He has spent his entire career celebrating the rich and sometimes eccentric prehistory, history, culture, food, music, and people of Mississippi with joy, warmth, grace, and an enviable ease. Sam is highly regarded and loved in the state by professional and avocational archaeologists and fans of archaeology and history, and as a result, the U.S.D.A. Forest Service is held up as the state's model for cultural resource management and public engagement.[1]

Notes

1. Used with permission of the USDA Forest Service.

Bibliography

Adkins, Howard G.
   1979   The Historical Geography of Extinct Towns in Mississippi. In *A Sense of Place: Mississippi*, edited by Peggy W. Prenshaw and Jesse O. McKee. University Press of Mississippi, Jackson, Mississippi.

Aldenderfer, Mark S., and Carolyn A. Hale-Pierce
   1984   The Small-Scale Archaeological Survey Revisited. *American Archeology* 4:4–5.

Aldenderfer, Mark S., and Frank J. Schieppati
   1984   To Be or Not to Be: The Small-Scale Archaeological Survey and Archaeological Research. *American Archeology* 4:49–53.

Ammerman, Albert J.
   1981   Surveys and Archaeological Research. *Annual Review of Anthropology* 10:63–88.

Anderson, David G.
   1994   *The Savannah River Chiefdoms: Political Change in the Late Prehistoric Southeast.* University of Alabama Press, Tuscaloosa, Alabama.
   1996   Approaches to Modeling Regional Settlement in the Archaic Period in the Southeast. In *Archaeology of the Mid-Holocene Southeast*, edited by Kenneth E. Sassaman and David G. Anderson, pp. 157–176. University Press of Florida, Tallahassee, Florida.
   2001   Climate and Culture Change in Prehistoric and Early Historic Eastern North America. *Archaeology of Eastern North America* 29:143–186.
   2004   Archaic Mounds and the Archaeology of Southeastern Tribal Societies. In *Signs of Power: The Rise of Cultural Complexity in the Southeast*, edited by Jon L. Gibson and Philip J. Carr, pp. 270–299. University of Alabama Press, Tuscaloosa, Alabama.

Anderson, David G., and Kenneth E. Sassaman (editors)
   1996   *The Archaeology of the Mid-Holocene Southeast.* University Press of Florida, Gainesville, Florida.

Anderson, David G., and Robert C. Mainfort, Jr.
   2002   An Introduction to Woodland Archaeology in the Southeast. In *The Woodland Southeast*, edited by David G. Anderson and Robert C. Mainfort, Jr., pp. 1–19. University of Alabama Press, Tuscaloosa, Alabama.

Anderson, David G., and Steven D. Smith
   2003   *Archaeology, History, and Predictive Modeling: Research at Fort Polk, 1972–2002.* University of Alabama Press, Tuscaloosa, Alabama.

Andrefsky, William
   1994   Raw-Material Availability and the Organization of Technology. *American Antiquity* 59:21–34.

Bibliography

Anzalone, Ronald D.
- 1987 Archaeological Conservation as Process and Product: A Federal Perspective. In *Perspectives on Archaeological Resources Management in the "Great Plains,"* edited by Alan J. Osborn and Robert C. Hassler, pp. 91–107. I & O Publishing Company, Omaha, Nebraska.

Aranyosi, E. F.
- 1999 Wasteful Advertising and Variance Reduction: Darwinian Models for the Significance of Nonutilitarian Architecture. *Journal of Anthropological Archaeology* 18:356–375.

Aslan, Andres, and Whitney J. Autin
- 1999 Evolution of the Holocene Mississippi River Floodplain, Ferriday, Louisiana: Insights in the Origin of Fine-Grained Floodplains. *Journal of Sedimentary Research* 69:800–815.

Atkinson, James R.
- 1974 Test Excavations at the Vaughn Mound Site. Appendix A in *Archaeological survey and test excavations in the upper-central Tombigbee River Valley: Aliceville-Columbus lock and dam and impoundment areas, Alabama and Mississippi,* by Marc D. Rucker, pp. 115–158. Report submitted to the National Park Service by the Department of Anthropology, Mississippi State University, Starkville, Mississippi.
- 1986 The Location of the Nineteenth-Century Choctaw Village of Wholkey in Chickasaw County, Mississippi. *Mississippi Archaeology* 21(1):70–72.
- 1987 Historic Chickasaw Material Culture: A More Comprehensive Identification. *Mississippi Archaeology* 22(2):32–62.

Austin, Robert J., Kathleen S. Hoffman, and George R. Ballo (editors)
- 2002 *Thinking About Significance: Papers and Proceedings, Florida Archaeological Council, Inc., Professional Development Workshop, St. Augustine, Florida.* Special Publication 1, Florida Archaeological Council, Inc., Riverview, Florida.

Baca, Keith A.
- 1992 National Register of Historic Places nomination form for the West Mound (22CA502). On file at the National Park Service, US Department of the Interior, Washington, D.C. Copy on file at the Historic Preservation Division of the Mississippi Department of Archives and History, Jackson, Mississippi.
- 1993 Test Excavations at a Pre-Mississippian Platform Mound in the North-Central Hills of Mississippi. Paper presented at the 14th Mid-South Archaeological Conference, Memphis, Tennessee.
- 2008 Elemental Analysis of Marksville-Style Prehistoric Ceramics from Mississippi and Alabama. Unpublished Master's thesis, Department of Sociology, Anthropology, and Social Work, Mississippi State University, Starkville.

Bacon-Schulte, Weston
- 2008 The Selection for Sedentary Settlement Patterns in East-Central Mississippi. Unpublished Master's thesis, Department of Sociology, Anthropology, and Social Work, Mississippi State University, Starkville.

Bailey, Lewis
- 2002 Interview. January 28, 2002.

Bibliography

Barber, Michael B.
- 1981 Cultural Resource Management on the National Forests in Virginia. *Contract Abstracts and CRM Archaeology* 2:22–24.
- 2001 Small Sites on the Appalachian Mountain Slopes: Changes in Altitudes, Changes in Attitudes. *Journal of Middle Atlantic Archaeology* 17:85–94.

Bar-Yosef, Ofer, and Steven L. Kuhn
- 1999 The Big Deal about Blades: Laminar Technologies and Human Evolution. *American Anthropologist* 101:322–338.

Baumler, Mark F., and C. E. Downum
- 1989 Between Micro and Macro: A Study in the Interpretation of Small-Sized Lithic Debitage. In *Experiments in Lithic Technology*, edited by Daniel S. Amick and Raymond P. Mauldin, pp. 101–116. BAR International Series 528, British Archaeological Reports, Oxford, U.K.

Beasley, Virgil R.
- 1998 Feasting and Mound Construction at the Mound 4, Block 1 Locale, the Anna Site (22AD500), Adams County, Mississippi. Unpublished Master's thesis, Department of Anthropology, University of Alabama, Tuscaloosa, Alabama.
- 2007 Feasting on the Bluffs: Anna Site Excavations in the Natchez Bluffs of Mississippi. In *Plaquemine Archaeology*, edited by Mark A. Rees and Patrick C. Livingood, pp. 108–144. University of Alabama Press, Tuscaloosa, Alabama.

Bense, Judith A. (editor)
- 1983 *Archaeological Investigations in the Upper Tombigbee Valley, Mississippi: Phase I.* Report submitted to the US Army Corps of Engineers, Mobile District, Mobile, Alabama. Report of Investigations No. 3. University of West Florida, Pensacola, Florida.
- 1987 *The Midden Mound Project: Final Report.* Report of Investigations No. 6, Office of Cultural and Archaeological Research, University of West Florida, Pensacola, Florida.

Binford, Lewis R.
- 1962 Archaeology as Anthropology. *American Antiquity* 28:217–225.
- 1979 Organization and the Formation Processes: Looking at Curated Technologies. *Journal of Anthropological Research* 35:255–273.

Binford, Sally R., and Lewis R. Binford (editors)
- 1968 *New Perspectives in Archaeology.* Aldine Publishing, Chicago, Illinois.

Blitz, John H.
- 1984 *A Cultural Resources Survey in the Tombigbee National Forest, Mississippi.* USDA Forest Service, Jackson.
- 1985 *An Archaeological Study of the Mississippi Choctaw Indians.* Archaeological Report 16, Mississippi Department of Archives and History, Jackson, Mississippi.
- 1988 Adoption of the Bow in Prehistoric North America. *North American Archaeologist* 9:123–145.
- 1993a Big Pots for Big Shots: Feasting and Storage in a Mississippian Community. *American Antiquity* 58:80–96.
- 1993b Locust Beads and Archaic Mounds. *Mississippi Archaeology* 28(1):20–43.

Bibliography

Blitz, John H., and C. Baxter Mann
    2000   *Fisherfolk, Farmers and Frenchmen: Archaeological Explorations on the Mississippi Gulf Coast*. Archaeological Report 30, Mississippi Department of Archives and History, Jackson, Mississippi.

Bohannon, Charles F.
    1972   *Excavations at the Pharr Mounds, Prentiss and Itawamba Counties, Mississippi and Excavations at the Bear Creek Site, Tishimingo County, Mississippi*. United States Department of the Interior, National Park Service, Washington, D.C.

Boudreaux, Edmond A., III, and Hunter B. Johnson
    2000   Test Excavations at the Florence Mound: A Middle Woodland Platform Mound in Northern Alabama. *Journal of Alabama Archaeology* 46:87–130.

Bozeman, Tandy
    1982   *Moundville Phase Communities in the Black Warrior River Valley, Alabama*. Ph.D. dissertation, University of California, Santa Barbara. University Microfilms, Ann Arbor, Michigan.

Bradley, Bruce A.
    1975   Lithic Reduction Sequences: A Glossary and Discussion. In *Lithic Technology: Making and Using Stone Tools*, edited by Earl Herbert Swanson, pp. 5–13. Aldine Publishing, Chicago, Illinois.

Brain, Jeffrey P.
    1978   Late Prehistoric Settlement Patterning in the Yazoo Basin and Natchez Bluffs Regions of the Lower Mississippi Valley. In *Mississippian Settlement Patterns*, edited by Bruce D. Smith, pp. 331–368. Academic Press, New York.
    1979   *Tunica Treasure*. Papers of the Peabody Museum of Archaeology and Ethnology, Harvard University, Vol. 71, Cambridge, Massachusetts.
    1988   *Tunica Archaeology*. Papers of the Peabody Museum of Archaeology and Ethnology, Harvard University, Vol. 78, Cambridge, Massachusetts.

Brain, Jeffrey P., Alan Toth, and Antonio Rodriguez-Buckingham
    1974   Ethnohistoric Archaeology and the DeSoto Entrada into the Lower Mississippi Valley. In *The Conference on Historic Site Archaeology Papers 1972*, Vol. 7, edited by Stanley South, pp. 232–289. The Institute of Archeology and Anthropology, University of South Carolina, Columbia, South Carolina.

Brain, Jeffrey P., and Stephen Williams
    1971   Archaeological Survey in Southwest Mississippi. *Mississippi Archaeological Association Newsletter* 6(3):6–12.

Brandon, James C., and Charles H. McNutt
    1995   The "Sardis" Cormorant Cord Impressed Vessel. *Mississippi Archaeology* 30(2):1–20.

Briuer, Frederick L., and Samuel O. Brookes
    1991   Site Preservation in Mississippi: Report of the MAA Committee. *Mississippi Archaeology* 26(1):56–66.

Brookes, Samuel O.
    1969   Excavation at 22-CO-572. *Newsletter of the Mississippi Archaeological Association* 4:9.
    1974a   Two Issaquena Sites. *Mississippi Archaeology* 9(6):7–9.

1974b An Unusual Point from Monroe County. *Mississippi Archaeological Association Newsletter* 9(4):4.

1974c Projectile Points from the North Delta. *Mississippi Archaeology* 9(7):2-6.

1974d Kirk-like Points. *Mississippi Archaeology* 9(7):7-8.

1975a Test Excavation at the Lawson Site. *Mississippi Archaeology* 10(4):3-6.

1975b The Cedar Creek # 1 Site: A Mississippian Period Site in Lowndes County, Mississippi. *Mississippi Archaeology* 10(7):21-23.

1975c More Kirk-like Points. *Mississippi Archaeology* 10(1):11.

1976a *The Grand Gulf Mound (22-CB-522): Salvage Excavation at an Early Marksville Burial Mound.* Archaeological Report 1, Mississippi Department of Archives and History, Jackson, Mississippi.

1976b Morrow Mountain Points. *Mississippi Archaeology* 11(1):12.

1976c A Greenbriar Point from the Mississippi Delta. *Mississippi Archaeology* 11(2):3-4.

1978 Preliminary Observations at the Hester Site, Mississippi. *The American Archaeologist* 3:2.

1979 *The Hester Site: An Early Archaic Site in Monroe County, Mississippi, I. A Preliminary Report.* Archaeological Report 5, Mississippi Department of Archives and History, Jackson, Mississippi.

1980a The Prairie Phase in the Upper Sunflower Region. Unpublished Master's thesis, University of Mississippi, Department of Sociology and Anthropology, Oxford, Mississippi.

1980b Survey Report of the Hutchins Ridge Site, Adams County. *Mississippi Archaeology* 15(2):42-47.

1980c The Prairie Phase: Late Marksville in the Upper Sunflower Region. *Mississippi Archaeology* 15(2):42-47.

1981 Everyman's Guide to Arrowheads, Part I. *Mississippi Archaeology* 16(2):22-31.

1982a Everyman's Guide to Projectile Points, Part II. *Mississippi Archaeology* 17(1):9-14.

1982b Everyman's Guide to Projectile Points, Part III. *Mississippi Archaeology* 17(2):6-12.

1983a Everyman's Guide to Projectile Points, Part IV. *Mississippi Archaeology* 18(1):45-46.

1983b Everyman's Guide to Projectile Points, Part V. *Mississippi Archaeology* 18(2):2-3.

1984 Everyman's Guide to Projectile Points, Part VI. *Mississippi Archaeology* 19(2):46-47.

1985 The Kirk Point That Ate the Eastern United States. *Mississippi Archaeology* 20(2):24-30.

1988 Foreword to *Early Marksville Phases in the Lower Mississippi Valley: A Study of Culture Contact Dynamics*, by Edwin Alan Toth, pp. ix-xiv. Archaeological Report 21, Mississippi Department of Archives and History, Jackson, Mississippi.

1989 Know Your Mississippi Archaeologists: Sam Brookes: Forest Service. *Mississippi Archaeological Association Newsletter* NL-5:2-3.

1997 Aspects of the Middle Archaic: The Atassa. In *Results of Recent Archaeological Investigations in the Greater Mid-South: Proceedings of the 17th Mid-South Archaeological Conference, June 29-30, 1996*, edited by Charles H. McNutt, pp. 55-70. The University of Memphis, Anthropological Research Center, Occasional Papers 18, Memphis, Tennessee.

1997 Central Midden. *Mississippi Archaeological Association Newsletter* NL-4:8-11.

1999a Review of I. Randolph Daniel, Jr., *Hardaway Revisited: Early Archaic Settlement in the Southeast*. *Mississippi Archaeology* 34(1):109-112.

1999b Prehistoric Exchange in Mississippi, 10,000 B.C.–A.D. 1600. In *Raw Materials and Exchange in the Midsouth*, edited by Evan Peacock and Samuel O. Brookes, pp. 86–95. Archaeological Report 29, Mississippi Department of Archives and History, Jackson, Mississippi.

2000 Archaeology from Memory: Lyon's Bluff, 1968. *Mississippi Archaeology* 35(1):15–22.

2001 Clarence Bloomfield Moore: Some New Perspectives. In *Historical Perspectives on Midsouth Archaeology*, edited by Martha A. Rolingson, pp. 51–58. Arkansas Archeological Survey, Research Series 58, Fayetteville, Arkansas.

2002a The Central Midden. *Mississippi Archaeological Association Newsletter* NL-1:4.

2002b The Herring Cache: A Middle Archaic Find in Mississippi. Paper presented at the 59th Annual Meeting of the Southeastern Archaeological Conference, Biloxi, Mississippi.

2004 Cultural Complexity in the Middle Archaic of Mississippi. In *Signs of Power: The Rise of Cultural Complexity in the Southeast*, edited by Jon L. Gibson and Philip J. Carr, pp. 97–113. University of Alabama Press, Tuscaloosa, Alabama.

2007 Typology: Some Thoughts on Scottsbluff, Hardin and Lost Lake Points, 7100–5500 BC. *Mississippi Archaeological Association Newsletter* 42(4):4–7.

2010 A Butterfly Moth Motif in the Middle Archaic. Paper presented at the Mid-South Archaeological Conference, Memphis, Tennessee.

Brookes, Samuel O. (editor)

1977 The Owl Creek Site. *Mississippi Archaeology* 12(2–3):3–29. Reprinted in 1985 in *Anthology of Mississippi Archaeology*, edited by Patricia K. Galloway, pp. 225–245. Mississippi Department of Archives and History, Jackson, Mississippi.

Brookes, Samuel O., and Byron Inmon

1973 *Archaeological Survey of Claiborne County, Mississippi*. Archaeological Survey Report 3, Mississippi Department of Archives and History, Jackson, Mississippi.

Brookes, Samuel O., and Cheryl Taylor

1986 Tchula Period Ceramics in the Upper Sunflower Region. In *The Tchula Period in the Mid-South and Lower Mississippi Valley*, edited by David H. Dye and Ronald C. Brister, pp. 23–37. Archaeological Report 17, Mississippi Department of Archives and History, Jackson, Mississippi.

Brookes, Samuel O., and John M. Connaway

1975 Morrow Mountain Projectile Points. *Mississippi Archaeology* 10(10):5–8.

Brookes, Samuel O., Bruce J. Gray, Byron Inmon, and Angela Rodrigue

1974 Greenbriar Projectile Points: A Discussion of Form and Function. *Mississippi Archaeology* 9(8):6–9.

Brookes, Samuel O., and Samuel O. McGahey

1974 Discovery of an Early Site in Northeast Mississippi. *Mississippi Archaeological Association Newsletter* 9(1):2–7.

Brookes, Samuel O., and Thomas D. Potts

1981 The Bobo Site. *Mississippi Archaeology* 16(1):2–24.

Brose, David S.

1988 Seeing the Mid-South from the Southeast: Second Century Stasis and Status. In *Middle Woodland Settlement and Ceremonialism in the Mid-South and Lower Mississippi*

Valley, edited by Robert C. Mainfort, Jr., pp. 147–157. Archaeological Report 22, Mississippi Department of Archives and History, Jackson, Mississippi.

Brown, Calvin S.

    1926   *Archeology of Mississippi*. Mississippi Geological Survey, University, Mississippi. Reprinted with an Introduction by Janet Ford in 1992 by the University Press of Mississippi, Jackson, Mississippi.

Brown, Ian W.

    Early 18th Century French-Indian Culture Contact in the Yazoo Bluffs Region of the Lower Mississippi Valley. Unpublished Ph.D. dissertation, Department of Anthropology, Brown University, Providence, Rhode Island.

    1983   Historic Aboriginal Pottery from the Yazoo Bluffs Region, Mississippi. In *Southeastern Archaeological Conference Bulletin 21*, edited by William H. Marquardt, pp. 1–17. University of Florida, Gainesville, Florida.

    1985   Plaquemine Architectural Patterns in the Natchez Bluffs and Surrounding Regions of the Lower Mississippi Valley. *Midcontinental Journal of Archaeology* 10:250–305.

    1994   Recent Trends in the Archaeology of the Southeastern United States. *Journal of Archaeological Research* 2:45–111.

    1998   Benjamin L. C. Wailes and the Archaeology of Mississippi. *Mississippi Archaeology* 33:157–191.

    2004   Sun Plates, Human Effigy Pots and Mississippian Relationships. Paper presented at the 69th Annual Meeting of the Society for American Archaeology, Montreal, Canada.

    2007   Plaquemine Culture in the Natchez Bluffs Region of Mississippi. In *Plaquemine Archaeology*, edited by Mark A. Rees and Patrick C. Livingood, pp. 145–160. University of Alabama Press, Tuscaloosa, Alabama.

    2008   Culture Contact along the I-69 Corridor: Protohistoric and Historic Use of the Northern Yazoo Basin, Mississippi. In *Time's River: Archaeological Syntheses from the Lower Mississippi River Valley*, edited by Janet Rafferty and Evan Peacock, pp. 357–394. University of Alabama Press, Tuscaloosa, Alabama.

    2011   The Anna Site (22AD500) Great Ravine, Adams County, Mississippi: Analysis of the Prospere Collection. Manuscript on file, Gulf Coast Survey Archives, Alabama Museum of Natural History, University of Alabama, Tuscaloosa.

Brown, Ian W. (editor)

    1997   Excavations at the Anna Site (22AD500), Adams County, Mississippi: A Preliminary Report. Manuscript on file, Gulf Coast Survey, Alabama Museum of Natural History, University of Alabama, Tuscaloosa.

Brown, James A.

    1986   Food for Thought: Where Has Subsistence Analysis Gotten Us? In *Foraging, Collecting and Harvesting: Archaic Period Subsistence and Settlement in the Eastern Woodlands*, edited by Sarah W. Neusius, pp. 315–330. Occasional Paper No. 6, Center for Archaeological Investigations, Southern Illinois University at Carbondale, Carbondale, Illinois.

Brown, James A., and Robert K. Vierra

    1983   What Happened in the Middle Archaic? Introduction to an Ecological Approach to Koster Site Archaeology. In *Archaic Hunters and Gatherers in the American Midwest*, edited by James L. Phillips and James A. Brown, pp. 165–195. Academic Press, New York.

Brown, Richard L.
- 2003 Paleoenvironment and Biogeography of the Mississippi Black Belt. In *Blackland Prairies of the Gulf Coastal Plain: Nature, Culture and Sustainability*, edited by Evan Peacock and Timothy Schauwecker, pp. 11–26. University of Alabama Press, Tuscaloosa, Alabama.

Broyles, Bettye J., Robert M. Thorne, and Harry P. Owens
- 1982 *A Cultural Resources Reconnaissance of the Four Corps Owned Lakes in Mississippi: Grenada Lake, Enid Lake, Sardis Lake, and Arkabutla Lake*. Final Report submitted to the US Army Corps of Engineers, Vicksburg District, by the Center for Archaeological Research, University of Mississippi, Oxford, Mississippi.

Buchner, C. Andrew
- 1996 Mound A Excavations at the West Mounds Site, Tunica County, Mississippi. In *Mounds, Embankments, and Ceremonialism in the Midsouth*, edited by Robert C. Mainfort, Jr., and Richard Walling, pp. 78–86. Research Series 46, Arkansas Archeological Survey, Fayetteville, Arkansas.

Cain, Daniel
- 2012 Revisiting Lithic Scatters: A CRM Perspective. *Southeastern Archaeology* 31:207–220.

Cambron, James W., and David C. Hulse
- 1975 *Handbook of Alabama Archaeology: Part 1 Point Types*. Alabama Archaeological Society, Huntsville, Alabama.

Camilli, Eileen L.
- 1988 Interpreting Long-Term Land-Use Patterns from Archaeological Landscapes. *American Archeology* 7:57–66.

Carleton, Kenneth H.
- 1999 Nanih Waiya (22WI500): An Historical and Archaeological Overview. *Mississippi Archaeology* 34:125–155.

Carr, Philip J.
- 1994 The Organization of Technology: Impact and Potential. In *The Organization of North American Prehistoric Chipped Stone Tool Technologies*, edited by Philip J. Carr, pp. 1–8. International Monographs in Prehistory, Ann Arbor, Michigan.

Carr, Philip J., and Andrew P. Bradbury
- 2011 Learning from Lithics: A Perspective on the Foundation and Future of the Organization of Technology. In Special Issue: Reduction Sequence, Chaîne Opératoire, and Other Methods: The Epistemologies of Different Approaches to Lithic Analysis, edited by Gilbert B. Tostevin. *PaleoAnthropology* 305–319.

Carr, Philip J., Andrew P. Bradbury, and Sarah E. Price
- 2012 Lithic Studies in the Southeast: Retrospective and Future Potential. In *Contemporary Lithic Analysis in the Southeast: Problems, Solutions, and Interpretations*, edited by Philip J. Carr, Andrew P. Bradbury, and Sarah E. Price, pp. 1–12. University of Alabama Press, Tuscaloosa, Alabama.

Cegielski, Wendy, and Brad R. Lieb
- 2011 Hina' Falaa "The Long Path," A GIS-Based Analysis of Chickasaw Settlement in Northeast Mississippi: 1650–1840. *Native South* 4:24–54.

Bibliography

Childress, Mitchell R., Guy G. Weaver, and Mary E. Starr
    1999   Lake Cormorant Chronology and Cultural Context. In *Archaeological Investigations at Three Sites near Arlington, State Route 385 (Paul Barrett Parkway), Shelby County, Tennessee: Archaeological Testing at 40SY525 and 40SY526 and Archaeological Testing and Data Recovery at 40SY527*, by Guy G. Weaver, Mitchell R. Childress, C. Andrew Buchner, and Mary E. Starr, pp. 140–153. Publications in Archaeology 4, Environmental Planning Office, Tennessee Department of Transportation, Nashville, Tennessee.

Civilian Conservation Corps
    1934   *Memories of District G, Civilian Conservation Corps, 1934*. Park-Harper Company, Little Rock, Arkansas.
    1936   *Annual of District G for 1936, Fourth Corps Area*. Direct Advertising Company, Baton Rouge, Louisiana.

Claassen, Cheryl
    1996   A Consideration of the Social Organization of the Shell Mound Archaic. In *Archaeology of the Mid-Holocene Southeast*, edited by Kenneth E. Sassaman and David G. Anderson, pp. 516–555. University Press of Florida, Gainesville, Florida.

Clark, John E.
    1995   Craft Specialization as an Archaeological Category. *Research in Economic Anthropology* 16:267–294.

Clark, John E., and William J. Parry
    1990   Craft Specialization and Cultural Complexity. *Research in Economic Anthropology* 12:289–346.

Clarke, Adele
    2005   *Situational Analysis: Grounded Theory After the Postmodern Turn*. Sage, Thousand Oaks, California.

Cobb, Charles R.
    2000   *From Quarry to Cornfield: The Political Economy of Mississippian Hoe Production*. University of Alabama Press, Tuscaloosa, Alabama.

Collins, Michael B.
    1975   Lithic Technology as a Means of Processual Inference. In *Lithic Technology: Making and Using Stone Tools*, edited by Earl Herbert Swanson, pp. 15–34. Aldine Publishing, Chicago, Illinois.

Conarro, Ray M.
    1977   *The Beginning: Recollections and Comments by Ray M. Conarro*. USDA Forest Service, Jackson, Mississippi.

Connaway, John M.
    1977   *The Denton Site: A Middle Archaic Occupation in the Northern Yazoo Basin, Mississippi*. Archaeological Report 4, Mississippi Department of Archives and History, Jackson, Mississippi.
    1981   The Keenan Bead Cache, Lawrence County, Mississippi. *Louisiana Archaeology* 8:57–71.
    1982   *Archaeological Investigations in Mississippi, 1969–1977*. Archaeological Report 6, Mississippi Department of Archives and History, Jackson, Mississippi.
    1987   The Irby Beads. *Mississippi Archaeology* 22(2):32–45.

Connaway, John M., and Samuel O. Brookes
- 1983   The Dam Site (22-AD-734). *Mississippi Archaeology* 18(2):41–48.

Connaway, John M., and Samuel O. McGahey
- 1971   *Archaeological Excavation at the Boyd Site, Tunica County, Mississippi*. Technical Report 1, Mississippi Department of Archives and History, Jackson, Mississippi.

Connaway, John M., Samuel O. McGahey, and Clarence H. Webb
- 1977   *Teoc Creek, a Poverty Point Site in Carroll County, Mississippi*. Archaeological Report 3, Mississippi Department of Archives and History, Jackson, Mississippi.

Cook, Terry
- 2011   Documenting Society and Institutions: The Influence of Helen Willa Samuels. In *Controlling the Past: Documenting Society and Institutions*, edited by Terry Cook, pp. 1–28. Society of American Archivists, Chicago, Illinois.

Costin, Cathy Lynne
- 1991   Craft Specialization: Issues in Defining, Documenting, and Explaining the Organization of Production. *Archaeological Method and Theory*, Vol. 3, edited by Michael B. Schiffer, pp. 1–45. Springer, New York.

Cotter, John L.
- 1950   The Miller Pottery Types in Review. *Southern Indian Studies* 2(1):20–29.
- 1951   Stratigraphic and Area Tests at the Emerald and Anna Mound Sites. *American Antiquity* 17:18–32.

Cotter, John L., and John M. Corbett
- 1951   *Archeology of the Bynum Mounds, Mississippi*. Archeological Research Series 1, National Park Service, US Department of the Interior, Washington, D.C.

Crawford, Jessica F.
- 2003   Archaic Effigy Beads: A New Look at Some Old Beads. Unpublished Master's thesis. Department of Sociology and Anthropology, University of Mississippi, Oxford, Mississippi.

Creasman, Steven D., Andrew P. Bradbury, and Jonathan P. Kerr
- 2000   The Archaeological Potential of Small Sites. In *Current Archaeological Research in Kentucky: Volume 6*, edited by David Pollack and Kristen Gremillion, pp. 25–46. Kentucky Heritage Council, Frankfort, Kentucky.

Crystal Camp Chatter [CCC Camp F-8, Richton, Mississippi]
- 1934   Forestry Service. 17 November:5. Richton, Mississippi. Available on microfiche from The Center for Research Libraries, University of Chicago, Chicago, Illinois.

Curren, Cailup
- 1982   Middle and Late Archaic Period Utilization of Tallahatta Quartzite in Southwestern Alabama. In *Archaeology in Southwest Alabama: A Collection of Papers*, edited by Cailup Curren, pp. 31–41. Alabama Tombigbee Regional Commission, Camden, Alabama.

Dancey, William S.
- 1988   Archaeological Survey in Central Ohio: The 1970s. *American Archeology* 7:13–17.

DeBloois, Evan I., and Kent A. Schneider
- 1989   Cultural Resource Management in the U.S.D.A. Forest Service. In *Archaeological Heritage Management in the Modern World*, edited by Henry Cleere, pp. 227–231. Unwin Hyman, London, U.K.

Bibliography

DeJarnette, David L., and Steve B. Wimberly
- 1941   *The Bessemer Site*. Geological Survey of Alabama, Museum Paper 17, Tuscaloosa, Alabama.

Delcourt, Paul A., and Hazel R. Delcourt
- 1979   Late Pleistocene and Holocene Distributional History of the Deciduous Forest in the Southeastern United States. *Veroffentilichungen des Geobotanischen Institutes er ETH, Stiftung Rubel* 68:79–107.
- 2004   *Prehistoric Native Americans and Ecological Change: Human Ecosystems in Eastern North America Since the Pleistocene*. Cambridge University Press, Cambridge, U.K.

Downs, Lauren E.
- 2004   Plaquemine Culture Structures in the Natchez Bluffs: Architectural Grammar at the Mound 3 Summit Locale, the Anna Site, Adams County, Mississippi. Unpublished Master's thesis, Department of Anthropology, University of Alabama, Tuscaloosa, Alabama.

Dukes, Joel
- 1997   Central Midden. *Mississippi Archaeological Association Newsletter*, NL-1:6–7.

Dunnell, Robert C.
- 1970   Seriation Method and Its Evaluation. *American Antiquity* 35:305–319.
- 1971   *Systematics in Prehistory*. Free Press, New York. Reprinted in 2002 by Blackburn Press, Caldwell, New Jersey.
- 1980   Evolutionary Theory and Archaeology. In *Advances in Archaeological Method and Theory*, Vol. 3, edited by Michael B. Schiffer, pp. 35–99. Academic Press, New York.
- 1982   Science, Social Science, and Common Sense: The Agonizing Dilemma of Modern Archaeology. *Journal of Anthropological Research* 38:1–25.
- 1984   The Ethics of Archaeological Significance Decisions. In *Ethics and Values in Archaeology*, edited by Ernestene L. Green, pp. 62–74. Free Press, New York.
- 1988   The Concept of Progress in Cultural Evolution. In *Evolutionary Progress*, edited by Matthew H. Nitecki, pp. 169–194. University of Chicago Press, Chicago, Illinois.
- 1989   Aspects of the Application of Evolutionary Theory in Archaeology. In *Archaeological Thought in America*, edited by C. C. Lamberg-Karlovsky, pp. 35–49. Cambridge University Press, New York.
- 2008a   Archaeology in the Lower Mississippi Valley. In *Time's River: Archaeological Syntheses from the Lower Mississippi River Valley*, edited by Janet Rafferty and Evan Peacock, pp. 16–44. University of Alabama Press, Tuscaloosa, Alabama.
- 2008b   Archaeological Things: Languages of Observation. In *Time's River: Archaeological Syntheses in the Lower Mississippi River Valley*, edited by Janet Rafferty and Evan Peacock, 45–68. University of Alabama Press, Tuscaloosa, Alabama.

Dunnell, Robert C., and William S. Dancey
- 1978   Assessments of Significance of Cultural Resource Management Plans. *American Society for Conservation Archaeology Newsletter* 5(5):2–7.
- 1983   The Siteless Survey: A Regional Scale Data Collection Strategy. In *Advances in Archaeological Method and Theory*, Vol. 6, edited by Michael B. Schiffer, pp. 267–287. Academic Press, New York.

Dunnell, Robert C., and Julie K. Stein
- 1989   Theoretical Issues in the Interpretation of Microartifacts. *Geoarchaeology: An International Journal* 4:31–42.

Dye, David H.
    1996   Initial Riverine Adaptation in the Midsouth: An Examination of Three Middle Holocene Shell Middens. In *Of Caves and Shell Mounds*, edited by Kenneth Charles Carstens and Patty Jo Watson, pp. 140–158. University of Alabama Press, Tuscaloosa, Alabama.
Dye, David H., and C. Andrew Buchner
    1988   Preliminary Archaeological Investigations of the West Mounds, 22-Tu-520: Tunica County, Mississippi. *Mississippi Archaeology* 23(2):64–75.
Ebert, James I.
    1988   Modeling Human Systems and "Predicting" the Archeological Record: The Unavoidable Relationship of Theory and Method. *American Archeology* 7:3–8.
Edgeworth, Matt (editor)
    2006   *Ethnographies of Archaeological Practice: Cultural Encounters, Material Transformations*. AltaMira Press, Lanham, Maryland.
Emerson, Thomas E., Dale L. McElrath, and Andrew C. Fortier (editors)
    2009   *Archaic Societies: Diversity and Complexity across the Midcontinent*. State University of New York Press, Albany, New York.
Ensor, H. Blaine
    1981   *Classification and Synthesis of the Gainesville Lake Area Lithic Materials: Chronology, Technology and Use*. Report of Investigations 13, Office of Archaeological Research, University of Alabama, Tuscaloosa, Alabama.
Ermentrout, Robert A.
    1982   *Forgotten Men: The Civilian Conservation Corps*. Exposition Press, Smithtown, New York.
Evans, David H.
    1976   Transcription of "The Carrier Line," by Sid Hemphill. Liner notes, Folk Music of the United States, Mississippi Collection 936, OCLC# 4447604, Library of Congress Recording Laboratory, Washington, D.C.
Fant, David
    1994   *A Cultural Resource Survey for the Exchange of Land Within Compartment Five of the Holly Springs National Forest*. USDA Forest Service Report submitted to the Mississippi Department of Archives and History, Jackson, Mississippi.
    1996a   Early Woodland Sites on the Holly Springs National Forest: Archaeological Survey from 1992 to 1995 and Testing of Sites 22MR539 and 22BE585. Unpublished Master's thesis, Department of Sociology and Anthropology, University of Mississippi, Oxford, Mississippi.
    1996b   *Heritage Resource Survey within Compartment 32 of the Holly Springs National Forest, Marshall County, Mississippi*. USDA Forest Service report submitted to the Mississippi Department of Archives and History, Jackson, Mississippi.
    1996c   The Testing of Site 22BE588, an Early Woodland Upland Site Within the Holly Springs National Forest, Benton County, Mississippi. Partial draft manuscript faxed to Evan Peacock on May 5, 1997. On file, Cobb Institute of Archaeology, Mississippi State University, Starkville, Mississippi.

Feathers, James K.
- 2006 Explaining Shell-Tempered Pottery in Prehistoric Eastern North America. *Journal of Archaeological Method and Theory* 13:89–133.
- 2009 Problems of Ceramic Chronology in the Southeast: Does Shell-Tempered Pottery Appear Earlier Than We Think? *American Antiquity* 74:113–142.

Fields, Rita D.
- 2002 Site Function, Mobility Strategies, and the Organization of Technology in the Pine Hills: A View from Tanya's Knoll (22WA642). *Mississippi Archaeology* 37:45–80.

Fisher, Charles
- 1980 Significance Evaluation of Low Density Surface Sites: Another View. *Journal of Field Archaeology* 7:498–499.

Fladmark, Kurt R.
- 1982 Microdebitage Analysis: Initial Considerations. *Journal of Archaeological Science* 9:205–220.

Ford, James A.
- 1936 *Analysis of Indian Village Site Collections from Louisiana and Mississippi*. Anthropological Study No. 2, Department of Conservation, Louisiana Geological Survey, New Orleans, Louisiana.
- 1954 The Type Concept Revisited. *American Anthropologist* 56:42–54.

Ford, James A., and Gordon R. Willey
- 1940 *Crooks Site, a Marksville Period Burial Mound in LaSalle Parish, Louisiana*. Anthropological Study 3, Department of Conservation, Louisiana Geological Survey, New Orleans, Louisiana.
- 1941 An Interpretation of the Prehistory of the Eastern United States. *American Anthropologist* 43:325–363.

Ford, Janet
- 1977 Seasonal Occupation and Utilization of the Yocona River Valley: The Slaughter Site (22-La-513), a Test Case. Unpublished Ph.D. dissertation, Tulane University, New Orleans, Louisiana.
- 1980 Alas, Poor Womack! *Mississippi Archaeology* 15(2):26–32.
- 1981 Time and Temper in the North Central Hills of Mississippi. *Journal of Alabama Archaeology* 27:57–71.
- 1988a An Examination of the Twin Lakes Phase. In *Middle Woodland Settlement and Ceremonialism in the Mid-South and Lower Mississippi Valley*, edited by Robert C. Mainfort, Jr., pp. 61–67. Archaeological Report 22, Mississippi Department of Archives and History, Jackson, Mississippi.
- 1988b Alexander Mound Ceremonialism? *Southeastern Archaeology* 7:49–52.
- 1989 Time and Temper Meet Trend and Tradition. *Mississippi Archaeology* 24(1):1–16.
- 1990 The Tchula Connection: Early Woodland Culture and Burial Mounds in North Mississippi. *Southeastern Archaeology* 9:103–115.
- 1996 Preliminary Impressions from the Batesville Mound Group. *Mississippi Archaeology* 31(1):56–67.

Franklin, Jay D., Maureen A. Hays, Sarah C. Sherwood, and Lucinda M. Langston
    2012   An Integrated Approach: Lithic Analyses and Site Function, Eagle Drink Bluff Shelter, Upper Cumberland Plateau, Tennessee. In *Contemporary Lithic Analysis in the Southeast: Problems, Solutions, and Interpretations*, edited by Philip J. Carr, Andrew P. Bradbury, and Sarah E. Price, pp. 128–145. University of Alabama Press, Tuscaloosa, Alabama.

Frison, George C., and Zola Van Norman
    1993   Carved Steatite and Sandstone Tubes: Pipes for Smoking or Shaman's Paraphernalia. *Plains Anthropologist* 38:163–176.

Fuller, Richard S.
    2003   Out of the Moundville Shadow: The Origin and Evolution of Pensacola Culture. In *Bottle Creek, A Pensacola Culture Site in South Alabama*, edited by Ian W. Brown, pp. 27–62. University of Alabama Press, Tuscaloosa, Alabama.

Fuller, Richard S., and Ian W. Brown
    1998   *The Mound Island Project: An Archaeological Survey in the Mobile-Tensaw Delta*. Bulletin of the Alabama Museum of Natural History 19, University of Alabama, Tuscaloosa, Alabama.

Fuller, Richard S., and Noel R. Stowe
    1982   A Proposed Typology for Late Shell Tempered Ceramics in the Mobile Bay/Mobile-Tensaw Delta Region. In *Archaeology in Southwestern Alabama: A Collection of Papers*, edited by Cailup Curren, pp. 45–93. Alabama Tombigbee Regional Commission, Camden, Alabama.

Fulton, R. B.
    1898   Pre-Historic Jasper Ornaments in Mississippi. *Mississippi Historical Society Publications* 2:91–95.

Futato, Eugene M.
    1975   *Archaeological Investigation in the Little Bear Creek Reservoir*. Research Series 1, Office of Archaeological Research, University of Alabama, Tuscaloosa, Alabama.
    1989   *An Archaeological Overview of the Tombigbee River Basin, Alabama and Mississippi*. Report of Investigations 59, Division of Archaeology, Alabama State Museum of Natural History, University of Alabama, Tuscaloosa, Alabama.
    1999   Lithic Raw Materials and Settlement Patterns in the Western Middle Tennessee Valley Uplands. In *Raw Materials and Exchange in the Mid-South: Proceedings of the 16th Annual Mid-South Archaeological Conference, Jackson, Mississippi—June 3 and 4, 1995*, edited by Evan Peacock and Samuel O. Brookes, pp. 44–56. Archaeological Report 29, Mississippi Department of Archives and History, Jackson, Mississippi.

Gagliano, Sherwood
    1967   *Occupation Sequence at Avery Island*. Coastal Studies Series 22, Louisiana State University Studies, Louisiana State University Press, Baton Rouge.

Galaty, Michael L.
    2008   Ceramic Petrography and the Classification of Mississippi's Archaeological Pottery by Fabric: A GIS Approach. In *Time's River: Archaeological Syntheses from the Lower Mississippi River Valley*, edited by Janet Rafferty and Evan Peacock, pp. 243–273. University of Alabama Press, Tuscaloosa, Alabama.

Ganopolski, Andrey, Claudia Kubatzki, Martin Claussen, Victor Brovkin, and Vladimir Petoukhov
    1998   The Influence of Vegetation-Atmosphere-Ocean Interaction on Climate During the Mid-Holocene. *Science* 280:1916–1919.

Garland, Elizabeth Baldwin
    1992   *The Obion Site: An Early Mississippian Center in Western Tennessee*. Report of Investigations 7, Cobb Institute of Archaeology, Mississippi State University, Starkville, Mississippi.

Gates, Gerald R.
    2004   A Thematic Evaluation of Small Prehistoric Foraging and Logistical Locations on a Portion of the Modoc Plateau of Northeastern California. *Proceedings of the Society for California Archaeology* 18:70–75.

Geier, Clarence R.
    1981   Comments on Developments in the State of Archaeology in Central Western Virginia. *Contract Abstracts and CRM Archeology* 2:25–28.

Gell, Alfred
    1992   The Technology of Enchantment and the Enchantment of Technology. In *Anthropology, Art, and Aesthetics*, edited by Jeremy Coote and Anthony Shelton, pp. 40–63. Clarendon Press, Oxford, U.K.

Gibson, Jon L.
    2001   *The Ancient Mounds of Poverty Point: Place of Rings*. University Press of Florida, Gainesville, Florida.

Gibson, Jon L., and Philip J. Carr (editors)
    2004   *Signs of Power: The Rise of Cultural Complexity in the Southeast*. University of Alabama Press, Tuscaloosa, Alabama.

Giliberti, Joseph A.
    1995   San Patrice and Related Early Tool Assemblage from the Beaumont Gravel Pit Site (22PE504): A Late Paleoindian Site in South Mississippi. Unpublished Master's thesis, Department of Anthropology, University of Southern Mississippi, Hattiesburg, Mississippi.

Gisler, Jessica
    2014   Intensification as a Survival Strategy on the Tombigbee National Forest. Unpublished Master's thesis prospectus on file, Department of Anthropology & Middle Eastern Cultures, Mississippi State University, Starkville, Mississippi.

Gremillion, Kristen J.
    2002   The Development and Dispersal of Agricultural Systems in the Woodland Period Southeast. In *The Woodland Southeast*, edited by David G. Anderson and Robert C. Mainfort, Jr., pp. 483–501. University of Alabama Press, Tuscaloosa, Alabama.

Griffin, James B.
    1952   Culture Periods in Eastern United States Archaeology. In *Archaeology of Eastern United States*, edited by James B. Griffin, pp. 352–364. University of Chicago Press, Chicago, Illinois.
    1986   The Tchula Period in the Mississippi Valley. In *The Tchula Period in the Mid-South and Lower Mississippi Valley*, edited by David H. Dye and Ronald C. Brister, pp. 40–42.

Archaeological Report 17, Mississippi Department of Archives and History, Jackson, Mississippi.

Haag, William G.
- 1952 *Archaeological Survey of the Grenada Reservoir in Mississippi*. Report prepared for the National Park Service. Copy on file, Mississippi Department of Archives and History, Jackson, Mississippi.

Hadley, Alison M.
- 2003 Beads, Bifaces, and Blade Cores from the Middle Archaic. Unpublished Senior Honors thesis, University of South Alabama, Mobile, Alabama.

Hadley, Alison M., and Philip J. Carr
- 2010 The Organization of Lithic Technology and Role of Lithic Specialists During the Archaic. Paper presented at the 67th Annual Meeting of the Southeastern Archaeological Conference, Lexington, Kentucky.

Hajic, Edwin Robert
- 1981 Geology and Paleopedology of the Koster Archaeological Site, Greene County, Illinois. Unpublished Master's thesis, Department of Geology, University of Iowa, Iowa City, Iowa.

Hamilton, T. M.
- 1979 Gunflints. In *Tunica Treasure*, edited by Jeffrey P. Brain, pp. 210–211. Papers of the Peabody Museum of Archaeology and Ethnology, Harvard University, Vol. 71, Cambridge, Massachusetts.

Harris, Marvin
- 1968 *The Rise of Anthropological Theory*. Thomas Y. Crowell Company, New York.

Hart, John P.
- 1999 Maize Agriculture Evolution in the Eastern Woodlands of North America: A Darwinian Perspective. *Journal of Archaeological Method and Theory* 6:137–180.

Hattiesburg American
- 1933 Local Lumber Company Gets Large Order. 25 October:1. Hattiesburg, Mississippi.

Hayden, Brian
- 1998 Practical and Prestige Technologies: The Evolution of Material Systems. *Journal of Archaeological Method and Theory* 5:1–55.

Hays, Christopher T., James B. Stoltman, and Richard A. Weinstein
- 2011 From Missouri to Mississippi to Florida: More Research on the Distribution of Poverty Point Objects. Paper presented at the 68th Annual Meeting of the Southeastern Archaeological Conference, Jacksonville, Florida.

Hays, Christopher T., James B. Stoltman, Robert H. Tykot, and Richard A. Weinstein
- 2010 Investigating the Exchange of Poverty Point Objects and Pottery in the Poverty Point Culture Using X-Ray Fluorescence and Petrographic Thin Sectioning. Paper presented at the 75th Annual Meeting of the Society for American Archaeology, St. Louis, Missouri.

Hays, Christopher T., Richard A. Weinstein, and James B. Stoltman
- 2010 Poverty Point Objects and Baked-Clay Objects in the Southeast: A Consideration of Function, History, and Meaning. Paper presented at the 67th Annual Meeting of the Southeastern Archaeological Conference, Lexington, Kentucky.

Heinrich, Paul
   1988   Preliminary Petrographic Study of Some Sedimentary Quartzites from South Western Alabama. In *Cultural Resources Testing on the Mobile Bay Pipeline Project, Choctaw, Washington and Mobile Counties, Alabama*, Vol. 1, by New World Research, Inc., pp. A-1-A-6. Report of Investigations No. 167, New World Research, Inc., Mary Esther, Florida.

The Herald [CCC Camp F-8, Richton, Mississippi]
   1936   News. 19 December:4. Richton, Mississippi.

Hill, Mary C.
   1981   Analysis, Synthesis, and Interpretation of the Skeletal Material Excavated for the Gainesville Section of the Tennessee-Tombigbee Waterway. In *Biocultural Studies in the Gainesville Lake Area*, by Gloria M. Caddell, Anne Woodrick, and Mary C. Hill, pp. 211–334. Report of Investigations 14, Office of Archaeological Research, University of Alabama, Tuscaloosa, Alabama.

Hodder, Ian
   2003   *Archaeology Beyond Dialogue*. University of Utah Press, Salt Lake City, Utah.

Hodge, Fredrick Webb (editor)
   1907   *Handbook of American Indians North of Mexico*. Bulletin 30, Part I, Bureau of American Ethnology, Washington, D.C.

Hogue, S. Homes
   2007   Mississippian and Protohistoric/Early Contact Diet and Health: Biological and Cultural Continuity and Change in Oktibbeha County, Mississippi. *Southeastern Archaeology* 26:246–268.

Hogue, S. Homes, and Evan Peacock
   1995   Environmental and Osteological Analysis at the South Farm Site (22OK534), a Mississippian Farmstead in Oktibbeha County, Mississippi. *Southeastern Archaeology* 14:31–45.

Holland, Judith, and Ana Gordon
   1984   The Architecture of Andrew Johnson in North Mississippi. National Register of Historic Places Nomination form on file with Mississippi Department of Archives and History, Jackson, Mississippi.

Holland-Lilly, Mimi
   1996   Batesville Mounds: Recent Investigations at a Middle Woodland Site. *Mississippi Archaeology* 31(1):40–55.

Holloway, Marguerite
   2004   Passport In Time. *Scientific American* 290:100–102.

Hopkins, John L.
   1990   *The National Forest of Mississippi: A Cultural Resources Survey*. Report submitted to USDA Forest Service, Supervisor's Office. Copies available from USDA Forest Service, Jackson, Mississippi.

Howe, Tony
   2003   "Mississippi Logging Railroad List." http://www.loggingrailroads.com/ms.htm (accessed March 7, 2011).

Hull, Kathleen L.
   1987   Identification of Cultural Site Formation Processes Through Microdebitage Analysis. *American Antiquity* 52:772–783.

Bibliography

Jackson, H. Edwin, Bryan S. Haley, and Rita D. McCarty
    2006   An Evaluation of the Effectiveness of Remote Sensing in the Pine Hills Region of Mississippi. *Mississippi Archaeology* 41:137–165.

Jackson, H. Edwin, Melissa L. Higgins, and Robert E. Reams
    2002   Woodland Cultural and Chronological Trends on the Southern Gulf Coastal Plain: Recent Research in the Pine Hills of Southeastern Mississippi. In *The Woodland Southeast*, edited by David G. Anderson and Robert C. Mainfort, Jr., pp. 228–248. University of Alabama Press, Tuscaloosa, Alabama.

Jeffries, Richard W.
    1994   The Swift Creek Site and Woodland Platform Mounds in the Southeastern United States. In *Ocmulgee Archaeology, 1936–1986*, edited by David J. Hally, pp. 71–83. University of Georgia Press, Athens, Georgia.
    1996   The Emergence of Long-Distance Exchange Networks in the Southeastern United States. In *Archaeology of the Mid-Holocene Southeast*, edited by Kenneth E. Sassaman and David G. Anderson, pp. 222–234. University Press of Florida, Gainesville, Florida.

Jenkins, Ned J.
    1981   *Gainesville Lake Area Ceramic Description and Chronology.* Volume 2 of *Archaeological Investigations in the Gainesville Lake Area of the Tennessee-Tombigbee Waterway.* Report of Investigations 12, Office of Archaeological Research, University of Alabama, Tuscaloosa, Alabama.

Jenkins, Ned J., and Richard A. Krause
    1986   *The Tombigbee Watershed in Southeastern Prehistory.* University of Alabama Press, Tuscaloosa, Alabama.

Jennings, Jesse D.
    1940   Archeological Report on Anna Mound Group, Anna, Mississippi. Manuscript on file, National Park Service, Southeast Regional Office, Tallahassee.
    1941   Chickasaw and Earlier Indian Cultures of Northeast Mississippi. *Journal of Mississippi History* 3:155–226.
    1944   The Archaeological Survey of the Natchez Trace. *American Antiquity* 4:408–414.
    1952   Prehistory of the Lower Mississippi Valley. In *Archaeology of Eastern United States*, edited by James B. Griffin, pp. 256–271. University of Chicago Press, Chicago, Illinois.

Jennings, Jesse D. (editor)
    1947   Nutt's Trip to the Chickasaw Country. *Journal of Mississippi History* 9:34–61.

Jeter, Marvin M., Jerome C. Rose, G. Ishmael Williams, Jr., and Anna M. Harmon
    1989   *Archeology and Bioarcheology of the Lower Mississippi Valley and Trans-Mississippi South in Arkansas and Louisiana.* Research Series No. 37, Arkansas Archeological Survey, Fayetteville, Arkansas.

Johnson, Glen
    1969   Excavation of the McCarter Mound. *Newsletter of the Mississippi Archaeological Association* 4(1):56.

Johnson, Jay K.
    1979   Archaic Biface Manufacture Production Failures: A Chronicle of the Misbegotten. *Lithic Technology* 8(2):25–35.

1981   *Lithic Procurement and Utilization Trajectories: Analysis of Yellow Creek Nuclear Power Plant Site, Tishomingo County, Mississippi*, Vols. 1 & 2. Report submitted to the Tennessee Valley Authority by the Center for Archaeological Research, University of Mississippi, Oxford, Mississippi. Tennessee Valley Authority Publication in Anthropology 28.

1984   Prehistoric Settlement in the Upper Yocona Drainage, North-Central Mississippi. *Mississippi Archaeology* 19(2):13–23.

1988   Woodland Settlement in Northeast Mississippi: The Miller Tradition. In *Middle Woodland Settlement and Ceremonialism in the Mid-South and Lower Mississippi Valley*, edited by Robert C. Mainfort, Jr., pp. 49–59. Archaeological Report 22, Mississippi Department of Archives and History, Jackson, Mississippi.

1996   The Nature and Timing of the Late Prehistoric Settlement of the Black Prairie in Northeast Mississippi; A Reply to Hogue, Peacock, and Rafferty. *Southeastern Archaeology* 15:244–249.

1997   Stone Tools, Politics, and the Eighteenth-Century Chickasaw in Northeast Mississippi. *American Antiquity* 62:215–230.

2000a Beads, Microdrills, Bifaces, and Blades from Watson Brake. *Southeastern Archaeology* 19:95–104.

2000b The Chickasaw. In *Indians of the Greater Southeast: Historical Archaeology and Ethnohistory*, edited by Bonnie G. McEwan, pp. 85–121. University Press of Florida, Gainesville, Florida.

2001   *Cultural Resource Studies in Nine Watersheds, Demonstration Erosion Control Project, Yazoo Basin, Mississippi*. Report submitted to the US Army Corps of Engineers, Vicksburg District by the Center for Archaeological Research, University of Mississippi, Oxford, Mississippi.

2004   Lithic Artifacts. In *The Chickasaw: Economics, Politics, and Social Organization in the Early 18th Century*, by Jay K. Johnson, John W. O'Hear, Robbie Ethridge, Brad Lieb, Susan L. Scott, H. Edwin Jackson, Keith Jacobi, and Donna Courtney Rausch, pp. 3.1–3.27. Report submitted to the National Endowment for the Humanities, Washington, D.C.

2009   *Cultural Resources Monitoring of the Proposed Toyota Wastewater Pipeline, Lee County, Mississippi*. Report Submitted to the Mississippi Department of Archives and History, Jackson, Mississippi.

Johnson, Jay K., and James R. Atkinson

1987   New Data on the Thelma Mound Group in Northeast Mississippi. In *The Emergent Mississippian*, edited by Richard A. Marshall, pp. 63–79. Occasional Papers 87-01, Cobb Institute of Archaeology, Mississippi State University, Starkville, Mississippi.

Johnson, Jay K., and Bryan S. Haley

2006   The View from the Periphery: The Excavation of a Chickasaw Hamlet in Western Lee County. Paper presented at the 63rd Annual Meeting of the Southeastern Archaeological Conference, Little Rock, Arkansas.

Johnson, Jay K., and Fair Hays

1995   Shifting Patterns of Long Distance Contact During the Middle Woodland Period in the Northern Yazoo Basin, Mississippi. In *Native American Interactions: Multiscalar*

Analyses and Interpretations in the Eastern Woodlands, edited by Michael S. Nassaney and Kenneth E. Sassaman, pp. 100–121. University of Tennessee Press, Knoxville, Tennessee.

Johnson, Jay K., and Edward R. Henry
    2011   Excavations at the South Thomas Street Site, 22Le1002: A Small Woodland and Chickasaw Occupation in the Coonewah Creek Drainage Lee County, Mississippi. Report submitted to Wildlife Technical, Vicksburg, Mississippi.

Johnson, Jay K., and John T. Sparks
    1986   Protohistoric Settlement Patterns in Northeast Mississippi. In *The Protohistoric Period in the Mid-South*, edited by David H. Dye and Ronald C. Brister, pp. 64–87. Archaeological Report 18, Mississippi Department of Archives and History, Jackson, Mississippi.

Johnson, Jay K., and Samuel O. Brookes
    1988   Rocks from the Northeast: Archaic Exchange in Mississippi. *Mississippi Archaeology* 23(2):53–63.
    1989   Benton Points, Turkey Tails, and Cache Blades: Middle Archaic Exchange in the Southeast. *Southeastern Archaeology* 8:134–145.

Johnson, Jay K., Gena M. Aleo, Rodney T. Stuart, and John Sullivan
    2002   *The 1996 Excavations at the Batesville Mounds: A Woodland Period Platform Mound Complex in Northwest Mississippi*. Archaeological Report 32, Mississippi Department of Archives and History, Jackson, Mississippi.

Johnson, Jay K., John W. O'Hear, Robbie Ethridge, Brad R. Lieb, Susan L. Scott, and H. Edwin Jackson
    2008   Measuring Chickasaw Adaptation on the Western Frontier of the Colonial South: A Correlation of Ethnohistoric and Archaeological Data. *Southeastern Archaeology* 27:1–30.

Johnson, Jay K., John W. O'Hear, Robbie Ethridge, Brad R. Lieb, Susan L. Scott, H. Edwin Jackson, Keith Jacobi, and Donna Courtney Rausch
    2004   *The Chickasaw: Economics, Politics, and Social Organization in the Early 18th Century*. Report submitted to the National Endowment for the Humanities, Washington, D.C.

Johnson, Jay K., Susan L. Scott, James R. Atkinson, and Andrea B. Shea
    1994   Late Prehistoric/Protohistoric Settlement and Subsistence on the Black Prairie: Buffalo Hunting in Mississippi. *North American Archaeologist* 15:167–179.

Jolly, Fletcher
    1971   Poverty Point Zoomorphic Beads from the Pickwick Basin in NW Alabama. *Journal of Alabama Archaeology* 17:134–139.

Jones, Reca B.
    1983   Archaeological Investigations in the Ouachita River Valley, Bayou Bartholomew to Riverton, Louisiana. *Louisiana Archaeology* 10:103–169.

Keith, Scot
    1998   OCR Dating of Prehistoric Features at the Sandhill Site (22-Wa-676), Southeast Mississippi. *Mississippi Archaeology* 33:77–114.

Kennedy, Jason Alan
    2011   Disturbance and Its Effects on Archaeological Significance and Integrity. Unpublished Master's thesis, Department of Anthropology & Middle Eastern Cultures, Mississippi State University, Starkville, Mississippi.

Kidder, Tristram R.
    2002   Woodland Period Archaeology of the Lower Mississippi Valley. In *The Woodland Southeast*, edited by David G. Anderson and Robert C. Mainfort, Jr., pp. 66–90. University of Alabama Press, Tuscaloosa, Alabama.
    2006   Climate Change and the Archaic to Woodland Transition (3000–2500 cal. B.P.) in the Mississippi River Basin. *American Antiquity* 71:195–231.

Kidder, Tristram R., and Kenneth E. Sassaman
    2009   The View from the Southeast. In *Archaic Societies: Diversity and Complexity Across the Midcontinent*, edited by Thomas E. Emerson, Dale L. McElrath, and Andrew C. Fortier, pp. 667–694. State University of New York Press, Albany, New York.

King, James E.
    1981   Late Quaternary Vegetational History of Illinois. *Ecological Monographs* 51:43–62.

Kintigh, Keith W.
    1988   The Effectiveness of Subsurface Testing: A Simulation Approach. *American Antiquity* 53:686–707.

Kistler, Logan
    2011   Report on Macrobotanical Analysis of Flotation Samples from 22LE1002 and 22LE678, Lee County, Mississippi. Appendix A in *Excavations at the South Thomas Street Site, 22Le1002: A Small Woodland and Chickasaw Occupation in the Coonewah Creek Drainage Lee County, Mississippi*, by Jay K. Johnson and Edward R. Henry. Report submitted to Wildlife Technical, Vicksburg, Mississippi.

Klippel, Walter E.
    1969   The Hearnes Site: A Multi-Component Occupation Site and Cemetery in the Cairo Lowland Region of Southeast Missouri. *Missouri Archaeologist* 31:1–20.

Knight, Vernon James, Jr.
    1990   *Excavation of the Truncated Mound at the Walling Site: Middle Woodland Culture and Copena in the Tennessee Valley*. Report of Investigations 56, University of Alabama Division of Archaeology, Tuscaloosa, Alabama.
    2001   Feasting and the Emergence of Platform Mound Ceremonialism in Eastern North America. In *Feasts: Archaeological and Ethnographic Perspectives on Food, Politics, and Power*, edited by Michael Dietler and Brian Hayden, pp. 311–333. Smithsonian Institution Press, Washington, D.C.
    2004   Characterizing Elite Midden Deposits at Moundville. *American Antiquity* 69:304–321.

Knight, Vernon James, Jr., and Vincas P. Steponaitis
    1998   A New History of Moundville. In *Archaeology of the Moundville Chiefdom*, edited by Vernon James Knight, Jr., and Vincas P. Steponaitis, pp. 1–25. Smithsonian Institution Press, Washington, D.C.

Knorr-Cetina, Karin

    1999   *Epistemic Cultures: How the Sciences Make Knowledge.* Harvard University Press, Cambridge, Massachusetts.

Koehler, Thomas H.

    1966   *Archaeological Excavation of the Womack Mound (22-Ya-1).* Mississippi Archaeological Association Bulletin 1, Jackson, Mississippi.

Krakker, J., M. Shott, and P. Welch

    1983   Design and Evaluation of Shovel-Test Sampling in Regional Archaeological Survey. *Journal of Field Archaeology* 10:469–480.

Kuchler, August W.

    1964   *Potential Natural Vegetation of the Coterminous United States.* Special Publication 36, American Geographical Society, New York.

Kwas, Mary L., and Robert C. Mainfort, Jr.

    1986   The Johnston Site: Precursor to Pinson Mounds? *Tennessee Anthropologist* 11(1):29–41.

Kyle, John W.

    1913   Reconstruction in Panola County. *Publications of the Mississippi Historical Society* 13.

Landrum, James

    2002   Interview. April 12, 2002.

Lane, Henry C., and William A. Cole

    1963   *Soil Survey of Claiborne County Mississippi.* US Department of Agriculture, Washington, D.C.

Larralde, Signa

    1988   The Timeless Survey: Problems in Defining Component Assemblages. *American Archeology* 7:8–12.

Laurel Leader Call (LLC) [Laurel, Mississippi]

    1933a   Lumber Order for Gilchrist-Fordney Mill. 30 September:1. Laurel, Mississippi.

    1933b   Forest Camp Located for This County. 10 October:1. Laurel, Mississippi.

    1933c   Over Thousand Go to Camps in South Mississippi. 27 October:1. Laurel, Mississippi.

    1934   Chickasawhay Forest Tower Is Dedicated. 22 October:1, 3. Laurel, Mississippi.

    1938a   U.S. Forest Service Fire Organization Helps Fight Fires in Homes Over Area. 4 January:5. Laurel, Mississippi.

    1938b   Chickasawhay Places Second in Fire Tests. 7 January:3. Laurel, Mississippi.

    1938c   New August and Richton Losing Camps. 10 March:3. Laurel, Mississippi.

Lave, Jean, and Etienne Wenger

    1991   *Situated Learning: Legitimate Peripheral Participation.* Cambridge University Press, Cambridge, Massachusetts.

Lees, William B., and Vergil E. Noble

    1990   Other Questions That Count: Introductory Comments on Assessing Significance in Historical Archaeology. *Historical Archaeology* 24(2):10–13.

Leib, Brad Raymond

    2004   Chickasaw Pottery. In *The Chickasaw: Economics, Politics, and Social Organization in the Early 18th Century,* by Jay K. Johnson, John W. O'Hear, Robbie Ethridge, Brad R.

Lieb, Susan L. Scott, H. Edwin Jackson, Keith Jacobi, and Donna Courtney Rausch, pp. 2.1–2.45. Report submitted to the National Endowment for the Humanities, Washington, D.C.

Lenihan, Daniel J., Toni L. Carrell, Stephen Fosberg, Larry Murphy, Sandra L. Rayl, and John A. Ware

    1981   *The Final Report of the National Reservoir Inundation Study, Volumes 1 and 2.* National Park Service, Southwest Cultural Resources Center, Santa Fe, New Mexico.

Leonard, Robert D., and George T. Jones

    1987   Elements of an Inclusive Evolutionary Model for Archaeology. *Journal of Anthropological Archaeology* 6:199–219.

Lewis, Thomas M. N., and Madeline Kneburg Lewis

    1961   *Eva: An Archaic Site.* University of Tennessee Press, Knoxville, Tennessee.

Lightfoot, Kent G.

    1986   Regional Surveys in the Eastern United States: The Strengths and Weaknesses of Implementing Subsurface Testing Programs. *American Antiquity* 51:484–504.

    1989   A Defense of Shovel-Test Sampling: A Reply to Shott. *American Antiquity* 54:413–416.

Lindauer, Owen, and John H. Blitz

    1997   Higher Ground: The Archaeology of North American Platform Mounds. *Journal of Archaeological Research* 5:169–207.

Lipe, William D.

    1974   A Conservation Model for American Archaeology. *The Kiva* 39:213–245.

Lipo, Carl P.

    2001   *Science, Style and the Study of Community Structure: An Example from the Central Mississippi River Valley.* BAR International Series 918, British Archaeological Reports, Oxford, U.K.

Lipo, Carl P., Mark E. Madsen, Robert C. Dunnell, and Tim Hunt

    1997   Population Structure, Cultural Transmission, and Frequency Seriation. *Journal of Anthropological Archaeology* 6:301–333.

Lloyd, Janet R., Judith A. Bense, and Jesse L. Davis, Jr.

    1983   Tallahatta Quartzite Quarries in the Escambia River Drainage. *Journal of Alabama Archaeology* 29:125–142.

Lomax, Alan

    1993   *The Land Where the Blues Began.* New Press, New York.

Lorenz, Karl G.

    1990   Archaeological Survey and Testing within a Five-Kilometer Radius of the Old Hoover Platform Mound in the Big Black River Valley. *Mississippi Archaeology* 25(1):1–42.

    1996   Small-Scale Mississippian Community Organization in the Big Black River Valley of Mississippi. *Southeastern Archaeology* 15:145–171.

Lovis, William A., Jr.

    1976   Quarter Sections and Forests: An Example of Probability Sampling in the Northeastern Woodlands. *American Antiquity* 41:364–372.

Lowe, Epraim N.

    1911   *Soils of Mississippi*. Mississippi State Geological Survey Bulletin 8.

Lusk, Tracy Wallace

    1956   *Benton County Geology*. Bulletin 80, Mississippi State Geological Survey, University, Mississippi.

Lyman, R. Lee, and Michael J. O'Brien

    2003   Measuring and Explaining Artifact Variation with Clade-Diversity. In *Style, Function, Transmission*, edited by Michael J. O'Brien and R. Lee Lyman, pp. 265–294. University of Utah Press, Salt Lake City, Utah.

Lynch, B. Mark

    1980   Site Artifact Density and the Effectiveness of Shovel Probes. *Current Anthropology* 21:516–517.

    1981   More on Shovel Probes. *Current Anthropology* 22:438.

Lynott, Mark J.

    1980   The Dynamics of Significance: An Example from Central Texas. *American Antiquity* 45:117–120.

Madsen, Mark E.

    1992   Lithic Manufacturing at British Camp: Evidence from Size Distributions and Microartifacts. In *Deciphering a Shell Midden*, edited by Julie K. Stein, pp. 193–210. Academic Press, Orlando, Florida.

Madsen, Mark, Carl Lipo, and Michael Cannon

    1999   Fitness and Reproductive Trade-Offs in Uncertain Environments: Explaining the Evolution of Cultural Elaboration. *Journal of Anthropological Archaeology* 18:251–281.

Mainfort, Robert C., Jr.

    1986a   *Pinson Mounds: A Middle Woodland Ceremonial Center*. Research Series 7, Division of Archaeology, Tennessee Department of Conservation, Nashville, Tennessee.

    1986b   Tchula/Miller I: A Perspective from Pinson Mounds. In *The Tchula Period in the Mid-South and Lower Mississippi Valley*, edited by David H. Dye and Ronald C. Brister, pp. 52–62. Archaeological Report 17, Mississippi Department of Archives and History, Jackson, Mississippi.

    1988   Pinson Mounds: Internal Chronology and External Relationships. In *Middle Woodland Settlement and Ceremonialism in the Mid-South and Lower Mississippi Valley*, edited by Robert C. Mainfort, Jr., 132–146. Archaeological Report 22, Mississippi Department of Archives and History, Jackson, Mississippi.

    1994   *Archaeological Investigations in the Obion River Drainage: The West Tennessee Tributaries Project*. Research Series 10, Division of Archaeology, Tennessee Department of Environment and Conservation, Nashville, Tennessee.

    1996   Pinson Mounds and the Middle Woodland Period in the Midsouth and Lower Mississippi Valley. In *A View from the Core: A Synthesis of Ohio Hopewell Archaeology*, edited by Paul J. Pacheco, pp. 370–391. Ohio Archaeological Council, Columbus, Ohio.

    1997   Putative Poverty Point Phases in Western Tennessee: A Reappraisal. *Tennessee Anthropologist* 22(1):72–91.

    2013a   Pinson Mounds and Its Setting. In *Pinson Mounds: Middle Woodland Ceremonialism in the Midsouth*, by Robert C. Mainfort, Jr., pp. 3–18. University of Arkansas Press, Fayetteville, Arkansas.

2013b *Pinson Mounds: Middle Woodland Ceremonialism in the Midsouth.* University of Arkansas Press, Fayetteville, Arkansas.

Mainfort, Robert C., Jr., and J. Shawn Chapman

1994 West Tennessee Ceramic Typology, Part I: Tchula and Middle Woodland Periods. *Tennessee Anthropologist* 19:148–179.

Mainfort, Robert C., Jr., and Charles H. McNutt

2004 Calibrated Radiocarbon Chronology for Pinson Mounds and Middle Woodland in the Midsouth. *Southeastern Archaeology* 23:12–24.

Mainfort, Robert C., Jr., and Richard Walling

1992 1989 Excavations at Pinson Mounds: Ozier Mound. *Midcontinental Journal of Archaeology* 17:112–136.

Mainfort, Robert C., Jr., and Richard Walling (editors)

1996 *Mounds, Embankments, and Ceremonialism in the Midsouth.* Research Series 46, Arkansas Archeological Survey, Fayetteville, Arkansas.

Mandelbaum, David G.

1940 The Plains Cree. *Anthropological Papers of the American Museum of Natural History.* Vol. 37, Part II, pp. 155–308.

Marshall, Richard A.

1984 Three Paleo-Indian Projectile Points from East-Central Mississippi. *Mississippi Archaeology* 19(1):60–72.

Maudsley, James R.

1998 What's Your TQ (Tallahatta Quartzite) IQ? *Central States Archaeological Journal* 45:166–170.

McAnally, Michelle Renee

2002 A Land Use History of the Holly Springs National Forest. Unpublished Master's thesis, Department of Sociology and Anthropology, University of Mississippi, Oxford, Mississippi.

McCarty, Rita D.

2011 Exploring Lithic Raw Material Use Patterns in South Mississippi. Paper presented at the 68th Annual Meeting of the Southeastern Archaeological Conference, Jacksonville, Florida.

McClung, Terry L.

2001 Archaeological Investigations at a 20th Century African American Farmstead on Tombigbee National Forest, Winston County, Mississippi. USDA Forest Service report submitted to the Mississippi Department of Archives and History, Jackson, Mississippi.

2003 Preliminary Findings Concerning the Distribution and Procurement of Archaic Period Stone Beads throughout Mississippi. Paper presented at the annual meeting of the Mississippi Archaeological Association, Hattiesburg, Mississippi.

McCrocklin, Claude

1992 The Sarah Frances Kennedy Bead, A Zoomorphic Locust Bead Find in Northwest Louisiana. *Central States Archaeological Journal* 39:162–163.

McGahey, Samuel O.

1971 *Archaeological Survey in the Tombigbee River Drainage Area, May–June 1970.* Mississippi Archaeological Survey Preliminary Report 2, Mississippi Department of Archives and History, Jackson, Mississippi.

1999   Use and Avoidance of Kosciusko Quartzite in Prehsistoric Mississippi. In *Raw Materials and Exchange in the Mid-South: Proceedings of the 16th Annual Mid-South Archaeological Conference, Jackson, Mississippi, June 3–4, 1995*, edited by Evan Peacock and Samuel O. Brookes, pp. 1–11. Archaeological Report 29, Mississippi Department of Archives and History, Jackson, Mississippi.

2000   *Mississippi Projectile Point Guide.* Archaeological Report 31, Mississippi Department of Archives and History, Jackson, Mississippi.

2005   Prehistoric Stone Bead Manufacture: The Loosa Yokena Site, Warren County, Mississippi. *Mississippi Archaeology* 40:3–29.

McGahey, Samuel O., David T. Dockery III, and Stephen L. Ingram

1992   Indian Artifacts of Tallahatta Quartzite from Tallahatta Creek Site 22-LD-645, East-Central Mississippi. *Mississippi Geology* 13(3):37–43.

McGimsey, Charles R., III

1972   *Public Archeology.* Seminar Press, New York.

McGimsey, Charles R., III, and Hester A. Davis (editors)

1977   *The Management of Archeological Resources: The Airlie House Report.* Special Publication of the Society for American Archaeology. Washington, D.C.

McGimsey, Charles R., III, and Jossette van der Koogh

2001   *Louisiana's Archaeological Radiometric Database.* Special Publication No. 3, Louisiana Archaeological Society, Baton Rouge, Louisiana.

McManamon, Francis P.

1984   Discovering Sites Unseen. In *Advances in Archaeological Method and Theory*, Vol. 7, edited by Michael B. Schiffer, pp. 223–292. Academic Press, New York.

McMullen, J. W., J. S. Huddleston, Charles Bowen, and R. E. Davis

1965   *Soil Survey of Calhoun County, Mississippi.* US Department of Agriculture, US Government Printing Office, Washington, D.C.

Means, Bernard K.

1999   Sites on the Margins Are Not Marginal Archaeology: Small, Upland Sites in the Vicinity of Meyersdale, Pennsylvania. *North American Archaeologist* 20:135–161.

Meeks, Scott C.

1999   The "Function" of Stone Tools in Prehistoric Exchange Systems: A Look at Benton Interaction in the Mid-South. In *Raw Materials and Exchange in the Mid-South: Proceedings of the Mid-South Archaeological Conference, Jackson, Mississippi, June 3–4, 1995*, edited by Evan Peacock and Samuel O. Brookes, pp. 29–43. Archaeological Report 29, Mississippi Department of Archives and History, Jackson, Mississippi.

Meiszner, Woody C.

1981   CRM Archeology: Federal Variations. *Contract Abstracts and CRM Archeology* 3:44–48.

Metcalf, Duncan, and Kathleen M. Heath

1990   Microrefuse and Site Structure: The Hearths and Floors of the Heartbreak Hotel. *American Antiquity* 55:781–796.

Mickelson, Andrew, and Eric Goddard

2011   The Ames Site (40FY7), a Very Unobtrusive Mississippian Settlement Located in Southwestern Tennessee. *Tennessee Archaeology* 5:157–172.

Milanich, Jerald T., Ann S. Cordell, Vernon J. Knight, Jr., Timothy A. Kohler, and Brenda J. Sigler-Lavelle
    1984   *McKeithan Weeden Island: The Culture of Northern Florida, A.D. 200–900*. Academic Press, Orlando, Florida.

Milner, George R.
    1998   *The Cahokia Chiefdom: The Archaeology of a Mississippian Society*. Smithsonian Institution Press, Washington, D.C.

Mistovich, Tim
    1988   Early Mississippian in the Black Warrior Valley: The Pace of Transition. *Southeastern Archaeology* 7:21–38.
    1995   Toward an Explanation of Variation in Moundville Phase Households in the Black Warrior Valley, Alabama. In *Mississippian Communities and Households*, edited by J. Daniel Rogers and Bruce D. Smith, pp. 156–180. University of Alabama Press, Tuscaloosa, Alabama.

Moore, Alexander (editor)
    1988   *Nairne's Muskhogean Journals: The 1708 Expedition to the Mississippi River*. University Press of Mississippi, Jackson, Mississippi.

Moore, Charles E.
    1999   The Occurrence of Zoomorphic and Other Stone Beads. *Central States Archaeological Journal* 46:20–22.

Moorehead, Warren K.
    1932   Explorations near Natchez, Mississippi. In *Etowah Papers*, edited by Warren K. Moorehead, pp. 158–165. Yale University Press, New Haven, Connecticut.

Morgan, David
    1997   *The Mississippi De Soto Trail Mapping Project*. Archaeological Report 26, Mississippi Department of Archives and History, Jackson, Mississippi.

Morphy, Howard
    1989   From Dull to Brilliant: The Aesthetics of Spiritual Power Among the Yolngu. *Man* 24:21–40.

Morse, Dan F.
    1986   McCarty (3-Po-467): A Tchula Period Site near Marked Tree, Arkansas. In *The Tchula Period in the Mid-South and Lower Mississippi Valley*, edited by David H. Dye and Ronald C. Brister, pp. 70–92. Archaeological Report 17, Mississippi Department of Archives and History, Jackson, Mississippi.

Morse, Dan F., and Phyllis A. Morse
    1983   *Archaeology of the Central Mississippi Valley*. Academic Press, New York.

Mueller, J. W. (editor)
    1975   *Sampling in Archaeology*. University of Arizona Press, Tucson, Arizona.

Nance, Jack D., and Bruce F. Ball
    1986   No Surprises? The Reliability and Validity of Test Pit Sampling. *American Antiquity* 51:457–483.

Nance, Jack D., and Bruce F. Ball
    1989   A Shot in the Dark: Shott's Comments on Nance and Ball. *American Antiquity* 54:405–412.

Bibliography

Neiman, Fraser
    1997   Conspicuous Consumption as Wasteful Advertising: A Darwinian Perspective on Spatial Patterns in Classic Maya Terminal Monument Dates. In *Rediscovering Darwin: Evolutionary Theory and Archeological Explanation*, edited by C. Michael Barton and Geoffrey A. Clark, pp. 267–290. Archeological Papers of the American Anthropological Association 7, American Anthropological Association, Arlington, Virginia.

Neitzel, Robert S.
    1965   *Archeology of the Fatherland Site: The Grand Village of the Natchez.* Anthropological Papers Vol. 51, Pt. 1, American Museum of Natural History, New York.

Nelson, Margaret C.
    1991   The Study of Technological Organization. In *Archaeological Method and Theory*, Vol. 3, edited by Michael B. Schiffer. University of Arizona Press, Tucson, Arizona.

Neusius, Sarah W.
    1986   Generalized and Specialized Resource Utilization During the Archaic Period: Implications of the Koster Site Faunal Record. In *Foraging, Collecting and Harvesting: Archaic Period Subsistence and Settlement in the Eastern Woodlands*, edited by Sarah W. Neusius, pp. 117–143. Occasional Paper No. 6, Center for Archaeological Investigations, Southern Illinois University at Carbondale, Carbondale, Illinois.

Nicholson, B. A.
    1983   A Comparative Evaluation of Four Sampling Techniques and of the Reliability of Microdebitage as a Cultural Indicator in Regional Surveys. *Plains Anthropologist* 28:273–281.

O'Brien, Michael J., and R. Lee Lyman
    2000   *Applying Evolutionary Archaeology: A Systematic Approach.* Kluwer Academic/Plenum Publishers, New York.

O'Brien, Michael J., Robert E. Warren, and Dennis E. Lewarch (editors)
    1982   *The Cannon Reservoir Human Ecology Project: An Archaeological Study of Cultural Adaptations in the Southern Prairie Peninsula.* Academic Press, New York.

O'Hear, John W., and Elizabeth A. Ryba
    1998   The Immokakina'fa' Site: Introduction and Overview of the Excavations. Paper presented at the 55th Annual Meeting of the Southeastern Archaeological Conference, Greenville, South Carolina.

Odell, George H.
    1996   *Stone Tools: Theoretical Insights into Human Prehistory.* Plenum Press, New York.

Olive, Wilds W., and Warren I. Finch
    1969   *Stratigraphic and Mineralogical Relations and Ceramic Properties of Clay Deposits of Eocene Age in the Jackson Purchase Region, Kentucky, and in Adjacent Parts of Tennessee.* Bulletin No. 1282, US Geological Survey, Washington, D.C.

Orlikowski, Wanda J.
    1996   Improvising Organizational Transformation Over Time: A Situated Change Perspective. *Information Systems Research* 7(1):63–92.

Osborn, Alan J., and Robert C. Hassler (editors)
    1987   *Perspectives on Archaeological Resources Management in the "Great Plains."* I & O Publishing Company, Omaha, Nebraska.

Overstreet, Robert M., and Howard Peake
>   1981   *The Official Overstreet Identification and Price Guide to Indian Arrowheads*, 2nd edition. The House of Collectibles, New York.

Parrish, Jason Lee
>   2006   An Archaeological Investigation of Four Woodland-Period Sites in the North Central Hills Physiographic Region of Mississippi: 22CH653, 22WI536, 22WI588, and 22WI670. Unpublished Master's thesis, Department of Sociology, Anthropology, and Social Work, Mississippi State University, Starkville.

Parrish, Jason Lee, and Evan Peacock
>   2006   Delineating Prehistoric Occupations in the North Central Hills Physiographic Province of Mississippi. *Mississippi Archaeology* 41:107–136.

Peacock, Evan
>   1988   Benton Settlement Patterns in North-Central Mississippi. *Mississippi Archaeology* 23(1):12–33.
>   1989   Microdebitage from Cached Pitted Stones. *Mississippi Archaeology* 24(2):17–27.
>   1992a *Archaeological Survey in the Bagley Creek Bottom, Compartment 84, Holly Springs National Forest, Lafayette County, Mississippi.* USDA Forest Service report submitted to the Mississippi Department of Archives and History, Jackson, Mississippi.
>   1992b *A Cultural Resources Survey of Timber Stands 17 and 19, Compartment 49, Tombigbee National Forest, Winston County, Mississippi.* USDA Forest Service report submitted to the Mississippi Department of Archives and History, Jackson, Mississippi.
>   1993   *A Cultural Resources Survey of Selected Timber Stands in Compartment 43, Holly Springs National Forest, Benton and Marshall Counties, Mississippi.* USDA Forest Service report submitted to the Mississippi Department of Archives and History, Jackson, Mississippi.
>   1994   Twenty-Five Years of Cultural Resource Management on the National Forests of Mississippi. *Mississippi Archaeology* 29:72–81.
>   1995a Subaqueous Site Deflation beneath Choctaw Lake, Tombigbee National Forest, Mississippi. *Journal of Alabama Archaeology* 41:37–54.
>   1995b *A Final Report on Ice-Storm Damaged Timber Tracts on the Holly Springs and Tombigbee National Forests, Yalobusha and Chickasaw Counties, Mississippi.* USDA Forest Service report submitted to the Mississippi Department of Archives and History, Jackson, Mississippi.
>   1996a Some Comments on Significance and Federal Archaeology. In *Cultural Resource Significance Evaluation: Proceedings of a US Army Corps of Engineers Workshop*, October 3–4, 1994, Vicksburg, Mississippi, edited by Frederick L. Bruier. IWR Report 96-EL-3, 42–47. US Army Corps of Engineers, Waterways Experiment Station, Vicksburg, Mississippi.
>   1996b Archaeological Site Survey in Wooded Environments: A Field Study from the Tombigbee National Forest, North-Central Mississippi. *North American Archaeologist* 17:61–79.
>   1996c Tchula Period Sites on the Holly Springs National Forest, North-Central Mississippi. In *Proceedings of the 14th Annual Mid-South Archaeological Conference*, edited by

Richard Walling, Camille Wharey, and Camille Stanley, pp. 13–23. Panamerican Consultants, Inc., Special Publications 1, Tuscaloosa, Alabama.

    1997   Woodland Ceramic Affiliations and Settlement Pattern Change in the North Central Hills of Mississippi. *Midcontinental Journal of Archaeology* 22:237–261.

    1998   *A Heritage Resources Survey in Compartments 74, 75, 76 and 77, Ackerman Unit, Tombigbee National Forest, Choctaw and Winston Counties, Mississippi*. USDA Forest Service report submitted to the Mississippi Department of Archives and History, Jackson, Mississippi.

    1999   *Cultural Resources Survey in Compartment 56 of the Ackerman Unit, Tombigbee National Forest*. USDA Forest Service submitted to the Mississippi Department of Archives and History, Jackson, Mississippi.

    2002   Shellfish Use during the Woodland Period in the Middle South. In *The Woodland Southeast*, edited by David G. Anderson and Robert C. Mainfort, Jr., pp. 444–460. University of Alabama Press, Tuscaloosa, Alabama.

    2003   Excavations at Stinking Water (22WI515/516), a Prehistoric Habitation Site in the North Central Hills Physiographic Province of Mississippi. *Mississippi Archaeology* 38(1) (whole issue).

    2004   Using Macro- and Micro-artifacts to Investigate the Function and Duration of Short-term Prehistoric Sites: An Example from North Mississippi. *Mississippi Archaeology* 39:3–24.

    2005   *Mississippi Archaeology Q & A*. University Press of Mississippi, Jackson, Mississippi.

    2008   Paleoenvironmental Modeling in the Central and Lower Mississippi River Valley: Past and Future Approaches. In *Time's River: Archaeological Syntheses from the Lower Mississippi River Valley*, edited by Janet Rafferty and Evan Peacock, pp. 69–98. University of Alabama Press, Tuscaloosa, Alabama.

Peacock, Evan, and Samuel O. Brookes (editors)

    1999   *Raw Materials and Exchange in the Mid-South: Proceedings of the 16th Annual Mid-South Archaeological Conference*. Archaeological Report 29, Mississippi Department of Archives and History, Jackson, Mississippi.

Peacock, Evan, and Barrett Burnworth

    2010   What Are We Saving? A Nationwide Review of Phase I Survey Reports. Paper presented at the 75th Annual Meeting of the Society for American Archaeology, St. Louis, Missouri.

Peacock, Evan, Phillip J. Carr, Sarah E. Price, John Underwood, William T. Kingery, and Michael Lilly

    2010   Confirmation of an Archaic-Period Mound in Southwest Mississippi. *Southeastern Archaeology* 29:355–369.

Peacock, Evan, Stephen Michael Davis, and Timothy M. Ryan

    2008   Microdebitage Analysis at a Prehistoric Site in Grenada County, Mississippi. *Mississippi Archaeology* 43:49–66.

Peacock, Evan, and David W. Fant

    2002   Biomantle Formation and Artifact Translocation in Upland Sandy Soils: An Example from the Holly Springs National Forest, North-Central Mississippi, U.S.A. *Geoarchaeology: An International Journal* 17:91–114.

Bibliography

Peacock, Evan, James K. Feathers, Jeffrey Alvey, and Keith Baca
  2008 Space, Time and Form at the Pinnix Site (22GR795): A "Lithic Scatter" in the North Central Hills of Mississippi. *Mississippi Archaeology* 43:67–106.

Peacock, Evan, Paul F. Jacobs, and Christopher Holland
  2003 *Stinking Water: Public Excavations on the Tombigbee National Forest, Mississippi*. CD accompanying *Mississippi Archaeology* 38(1).

Peacock, Evan, and Cliff Jenkins
  2010 The Distribution and Research Value of Archaeological Mussel Shell: An Overview from Mississippi. *Midcontinental Journal of Archaeology* 35:91–116.

Peacock, Evan, and Katy M. Manning
  2008 Analysis of Chert and Sandstone at the Pinnix Site (22GR795), Grenada County, Mississippi. *Mississippi Archaeology* 43:1–33.

Peacock, Evan, and Alanna J. Patrick
  1997 Site Survey and Land Records Research: A Comparison of Two Methods for Locating and Characterizing Historic Period Sites on the Tombigbee National Forest, Mississippi. *Mississippi Archaeology* 32:1–26.

Peacock, Evan, and Janet Rafferty
  1996 Settlement Pattern Continuity and Change in the Mississippi Black Prairie: A Response to Johnson. *Southeastern Archaeology* 15:249–253.
  2001 Change in Woodland Settlement in the Upper Tallahatchie River Valley, Mississippi. Paper presented at the 66th Annual Meeting of the Society for American Archaeology, New Orleans, Louisiana.
  2005 1999 Test Excavations at Owl Creek Mounds (22CS502), Chickasaw County, Mississippi. *Mississippi Archaeology* 40:31–45.
  2007 Cultural Resource Management Guidelines and Practice in the United States. In *Quality Management in Archaeology*, edited by Willem Willems and Monique van den Dries, pp. 113–134. Oxbow Books, Oxford, U.K.
  2013 The Bet-Hedging Model as an Explanatory Framework for the Evolution of Mound Building in the Southeastern United States. In *Beyond Barrows: Current Research on the Structuration and Perception of the Prehistoric Landscape through Monuments*, edited by David R. Fontijn, Arjan Louwen, and Karsten Wentink, pp. 253–278. Sidestone Press, Leiden, Netherlands.

Peacock, Evan, John Rodgers, Kevin Bruce, and Jessica Gray
  2008 Assessing the Pre-modern Tree Cover of the Ackerman Unit, Tombigbee National Forest, North Central Hills, MS, Using GLO Survey Notes and Archaeological Data. *Southeastern Naturalist* 7:245–266.

Peacock, Evan, and Jennifer Seltzer
  2008 A Comparison of Multiple Proxy Data Sets for Paleoenvironmental Conditions as Derived from Freshwater Bivalve (Unionid) Shell. *Journal of Archaeological Science* 35:2557–2565.

Peebles, Christopher S., and Susan M. Kus
  1977 Some Archaeological Correlates of Ranked Societies. *American Antiquity* 42:421–448.

Perino, Gregory
    1985   *Selected Preforms, Points, and Knives of the North American Indian*. Published by the author, Idabel, Oklahoma.

Phillips, Philip
    1970   *Archaeological Survey in the Lower Yazoo Basin, Mississippi, 1949–1955*. Papers of the Peabody Museum of American Archaeology and Ethnology 60, Parts 1 and 2. Harvard University, Cambridge, Massachusetts.

Phillips, Philip, James A. Ford, and James B. Griffin
    1951   *Archaeological Survey in the Lower Yazoo Basin, Mississipi, 1949–1955*, Parts 1 and 2. Papers of the Peabody Museum of Archaeology and Ethnology, Harvard University, Vol. 25, Cambridge, Massachusetts. Reprinted in 2003 by the University of Alabama Press, Tuscaloosa, Alabama.

Pielou, E. C.
    1991   *After the Ice Age: The Return of Life to Glaciated North America*. University of Chicago Press, Chicago, Illinois.

Pietak, Lynn Marie, and Jeffrey L. Holland
    2002   Excavations at the Colclough Farmstead: Exploring Rural Life in Nineteenth- and Twentieth-Century Northeastern Mississippi. *Mississippi Archaeology* 37:159–206.

Pietak, Lynn Marie, Jeffrey L. Holland, and Tasha Benyshek
    1999   *Exploring the Colclough Farmstead: Rural Life in Nineteenth and Early Twentieth Century Oktibbeha County, Mississippi*. Report submitted to the Mississippi Department of Transportation, Jackson, Mississippi, by TRC Garrow Associates, Inc., Atlanta, Georgia.

Pine Tree Newspaper [CCC Camp F-4, Laurel, Mississippi]
    1935a   Beautification Program Big Success. 7 September:1. Richton, Mississippi. Available on microfiche from The Center for Research Libraries, University of Chicago, Chicago, Illinois.
    1935b   Forestry News. 16 November:2. Richton, Mississippi. Available on microfiche from The Center for Research Libraries, University of Chicago, Chicago, Illinois.
    1937   A Letter from the Project Superintendent. Richton, Mississippi. Available on microfiche from The Center for Research Libraries, University of Chicago, Chicago, Illinois.

Plog, Fred
    1984   The McKinley Mine and the Predictive Model, Limited Survey Approach: The Archeology of Red Herrings. *American Archeology* 4:89–95.

Plog, Stephen, Fred Plog, and Walter Wait
    1978   Decision Making in Modern Surveys. In *Advances in Archaeological Method and Theory*, Vol. 1, edited by Michael B. Schiffer, pp. 383–421. Academic Press, New York.

Pluckhahn, Thomas J.
    1996   Joseph Caldwell's Summerour Mound (9FO16) and Woodland Platform Mounds in the Southeastern United States. *Southeastern Archaeology* 15:191–210.
    2003   *Kolomoki: Settlement, Ceremony, and Status in the Deep South, A.D. 350 to 750*. University of Alabama Press, Tuscaloosa, Alabama.

Power, Susan C.
    1999   Archaic Effigy Beads in the Native American Southeast. *Ornament* 23(2):54–57.

Prentice, Guy
    2000   *Ancient Indian Architecture of the Lower Mississippi Delta Region.* Southeast Archaeological Center, National Park Service, Tallahassee, Florida.
Price, Sarah E.
    2012   Omnipresent? We Don't Recover the Half of It! In *Contemporary Lithic Analysis in the Southeast: Problems, Solutions, and Interpretations,* edited by Philip J. Carr, Andrew P. Bradbury, and Sarah E. Price, pp. 13–27. University of Alabama Press, Tuscaloosa, Alabama.
Price, T. Douglas, and James A. Brown
    1985   *Prehistoric Hunter-Gatherers: The Emergence of Cultural Complexity.* Academic Press, New York.
Proper, Judith G.
    1988   The Program: Managing Cultural Resources in the Southwestern Region. In *Tools to Manage the Past: Research Priorities for Cultural Resources Management in the Southwest,* edited by Joseph A. Tainter and R. H. Hamre, pp. 7–11. US Department of Agriculture, Forest Service, Rocky Mountain Forest and Range Experiment Station, General Technical Report RM-164, Fort Collins, Colorado.
Quimby, George I., Jr.
    1942   The Natchezan Culture Type. *American Antiquity* 7:255–275.
Raab, L. Mark
    1981   Getting First Things First: Taming the Mitigation Monster. *Contract Abstracts and CRM Archaeology* 2:7–9.
Rafferty, Janet
    1980   Surface Collections and Settlement Patterns in the Central Tombigbee Valley. *Southeastern Archaeological Conference Bulletin* 22:90–94.
    1983   A New Map of the Ingomar Mounds Site, 22-Un-500. *Mississippi Archaeology* 18(2):18–30.
    1985a The Archaeological Record on Sedentariness: Recognition, Development, and Implications. In *Advances in Archaeological Method and Theory,* Vol. 8, edited by Michael B. Schiffer, pp. 113–156. Academic Press, New York.
    1985b A Seriation of Historic Period Aboriginal Pottery from Northeast Mississippi. *Journal of Alabama Archaeology* 41:180–207.
    1986   A Critique of the Type-Variety System as Used in Ceramic Analysis. *Mississippi Archaeology* 21(2):40–50.
    1987   The Ingomar Mounds Site: Internal Structure and Chronology. *Midcontinental Journal of Archaeology* 12:147–174.
    1990   Test Excavations at Ingomar Mounds, Mississippi. *Southeastern Archaeology* 9:93–102.
    1994   Gradual or Step-Wise Change: The Development of Sedentary Settlement Patterns in Northeast Mississippi. *American Antiquity* 59:405–425.
    1995   *Owl Creek Mounds: Test Excavations at a Vacant Mississippian Mound Center.* Report of Investigations 7, Cobb Institute of Archaeology, Mississippi State University, Starkville, Mississippi.

1996   Continuity in Woodland and Mississippian Settlement Patterning in Northeast Mississippi. *Southeastern Archaeology* 15:230–243.

2001   Determining Duration at Prehistoric Sites: Short-Term Sedentary Settlement at Josey Farm, NE Mississippi. *Journal of Field Archaeology* 28:347–366.

2002   Woodland Period Settlement Patterning in the Northern Gulf Coastal Plain of Alabama, Mississippi, and Tennessee. In *The Woodland Southeast*, edited by David G. Anderson and Robert C. Mainfort, Jr., pp. 204–227. University of Alabama Press, Tuscaloosa, Alabama.

2003   Prehistoric Settlement Patterning on the Mississippi Black Prairie. In *Blackland Prairies of the Gulf Coastal Plain: Nature, Culture, and Sustainability*, edited by Evan Peacock and Timothy Schauwecker, pp. 167–193. University of Alabama Press, Tuscaloosa, Alabama.

2008   Settlement Patterns, Occupations, and Field Methods. In *Time's River: Archaeological Syntheses from the Lower Mississippi River Valley*, edited by Janet Rafferty and Evan Peacock, pp. 99–124. University of Alabama Press, Tuscaloosa, Alabama.

Rafferty, Janet E., B. Lea Baker, and Jack D. Elliott, Jr.

1980   *Archaeological Investigations at the East Aberdeen Site (22Mo819)*. Report submitted to the US Army Corps of Engineers, Mobile District, by the Department of Anthropology, Mississippi State University, Starkville, Mississippi.

Rafferty, Janet, and Evan Peacock

2008   The Spread of Shell Tempering in the Mississippi Black Prairie. *Southeastern Archaeology* 27:253–264.

Rafferty, Janet, and Evan Peacock

2008a   Introduction: Reconsidering the Archaeology of the Lower Mississippi River Valley. In *Time's River: Archaeological Syntheses from the Lower Mississippi River Valley*, edited by Janet Rafferty and Evan Peacock, pp. 1–7. University of Alabama Press, Tuscaloosa, Alabama.

Rainville, Lynn

2000   Microdebris Analysis in Early Bronze Age Mesopotamian Households. *Antiquity* 74:291–291.

Rau, Charles

1878   The Stock-in-Trade of an Aboriginal Lapidary (Mississippi). *Smithsonian Institution Annual Report for 1877*, Washington, D.C.

Rausch, Donna Courtney

2004   Glass Trade Beads. In *The Chickasaw: Economics, Politics, and Social Organization in the Early 18th Century*, by Jay K. Johnson, John W. O'Hear, Robbie Ethridge, Brad R. Lieb, Susan L. Scott, H. Edwin Jackson, Keith Jacobi, and Donna Courtney Rausch, pp. 5.1–5.62. Report submitted to the National Endowment for the Humanities, Washington, D.C.

Reams, Robert E.

1995   A Red Flag Predictive Model for the Black Creek and Biloxi Ranger Districts, DeSoto National Forest. Unpublished Master's thesis, Department of Anthropology, Wake Forest University, Winston-Salem, North Carolina.

Reimer, P. J., M. G. L. Baillie, E. Bard, A. Bayliss, J. W. Beck, C. J. H. Bertrand, P. G. Blackwell, C. E. Buck, G. S. Burr, K. B. Cutler, P. E. Damon, R. L. Edwards, R. G. Fairbanks, M. Friedrich, T. P. Guilderson, A. G. Hogg, K. A. Hughen, B. Kromer, F. G. McCormac, S. W. Manning, C. B. Ramsey, R. W. Reimer, S. Remmele, J. R. Southon, M. Stuiver, S. Talamo, F. W. Taylor, J. van der Plicht, and C. E. Weyhenmeyer

    2004   IntCal04 Terrestrial Radiocarbon Age Calibration, 26-0 ka BP. *Radiocarbon* 46:1029–1058.

Reith, Christina B. (editor)

    2008   *Current Approaches to the Analysis and Interpretation of Small Lithic Sites in the Northeast.* New York State Museum, Albany, New York.

Richton Dispatch

    1933   Government to Construct CCC Camps. 20 October:2. (Richton, Mississippi).

Rolingson, Martha A.

    1990   The Toltec Mounds Site, A Ceremonial Center in the Arkansas River Lowland. In *The Mississippian Emergence*, edited by Bruce D. Smith, pp. 27–49. Smithsonian Institution Press, Washington, D.C.

Rolingson, Martha Ann, and Marvin D. Jeter

    1986   An Assessment of Archaeological Data for the Tchula Period in Southeastern Arkansas. In *The Tchula Period in the Mid-South and Lower Mississippi Valley*, edited by David H. Dye and Ronald C. Brister, pp. 93–101. Archaeological Report 17, Mississippi Department of Archives and History, Jackson, Mississippi.

Rosen, Arlene Miller

    1989   Ancient Town and City Sites: A View from the Microscope. *American Antiquity* 54:564–578.

    1993   Microartifacts as a Reflection of Cultural Factors in Site Formation. In *Formation Processes in Archaeological Context*, edited by Paul Goldberg, David T. Nash, and Michael D. Petraglia, pp. 141–148. *Monographs in World Prehistory* 17. Prehistory Press, Madison, Wisconsin.

Roskams, Steve

    2001   *Excavation.* Cambridge Manuals in Archaeology. Cambridge University Press, Cambridge, U.K.

Russo, Michael

    1994   A Brief Introduction to the Study of Archaic Mounds in the Southeast. *Southeastern Archaeology* 13:89–93.

Saatkamp, Andrew, C. Andrew Buchner, and Jay Gray (editors)

    2000   *An Intensive Phase I Cultural Resources Survey of 6,535 Acres within Portions of Training Areas Sixmile Creek 1, 2, & 3, and Slagle 7, 8, 9, 10 & 11 on Fort Polk Military Reservation, Vernon Parish, Louisiana.* Report submitted to the US Department of Defense by Panamerican Consultants, Inc., Memphis, Tennessee.

Salmond, John A.

    1967   *The Civilian Conservation Corps, 1933–1942: A New Deal Case Study.* Duke University Press, Durham, North Carolina.

Sandweiss, Daniel H., Kirk A. Maasch, and David G. Anderson
    1999   Transitions in the Mid-Holocene. *Science* 283:499–500.

Sassaman, Kenneth E.
    1996   Technological Innovations in Economic and Social Contexts. In *Archaeology of the Mid-Holocene Southeast*, edited by Kenneth E. Sassaman and David G. Anderson, pp. 57–74. University Press of Florida, Gainesville, Florida.
    2010   *The Eastern Archaic, Historicized*. AltaMira Press, Lanham, Maryland.

Saucier, Roger T.
    1994   *Geomorphology and Quaternary Geologic History of the Lower Mississippi Valley*. US Army Corps of Engineers, Waterways Experiment Station, Vicksburg, Mississippi.

Saunders, Joe W.
    2004   Are We Fixing to Make the Same Mistake Again? In *Signs of Power: The Rise of Cultural Complexity in the Southeast*, edited by Jon L. Gibson and Philip J. Carr, pp. 146–161. University of Alabama Press, Tuscaloosa, Alabama.

Saunders, Joe W., E. Thurman Allen, Dennis LeBatt, Reca Jones, and David Griffing
    2001   An Assessment of the Antiquity of the Lower Jackson Mound. *Southeastern Archaeology* 20:67–77.

Saunders, Joe W., E. Thurman Allen, and Roger T. Saucier
    1994   Four Archaic? Mound Complexes in Northeast Louisiana. *Southeastern Archaeology* 13:134–153.

Saunders, Joe W., Reca Jones, Kathryn Moorehead, and Brian Davis
    1998   "Watson Brake Objects," an Unusual Artifact Type from Northeast Louisiana. *Southeastern Archaeology* 17:72–79.

Saunders, Joe W., Rolfe D. Mandel, C. Garth Sampson, Charles M. Allen, E. Thurman Allen, Daniel A. Bush, James K. Feathers, Kristin J. Gremillion, C. T. Hallmark, H. Edwin Jackson, Reca Jones, Roger T. Saucier, Gary L. Stringer, and Malcolm F. Vidrine
    2005   Watson Brake: A Middle Archaic Mound Complex in Northeast Louisiana. *American Antiquity* 70:631–668.

Saunders, Rebecca
    1994   The Case for Archaic Period Mounds in Southeastern Louisiana. *Southeastern Archaeology* 13:118–134.

Scarry, C. Margaret
    1993   Agricultural Risk and the Development of the Moundville Chiefdom. In *Foraging and Farming in the Eastern Woodlands*, edited by C. Margaret Scarry, pp. 151–181. University Press of Florida, Gainesville, Florida.

Schambach, Frank F.
    1998   *Pre-Caddoan Cultures in the Trans-Mississippi South: A Beginning Sequence*. Research Series 53, Arkansas Archeological Survey, Fayetteville, Arkansas.
    2005   Gulf Coast Shell and the Poverty Point Interaction Sphere. In *The William G. (Bill) Haag Honorary Symposium, March 7–9, 2002, Lousiana State University, Baton Rouge*, edited by Paul Farnsworth, Charles H. McNutt, and Stephen Williams, pp. 42–54. Occasional Paper No. 26, Anthropological Research Center, The University of Memphis, Memphis, Tennessee.

Schambach, Frank F., and Ann M. Early
- 1982 Southwest Arkansas. In *A State Plan for the Conservation of Archeological Resources in Arkansas*, edited by Hester A. Davis, pp. SW1-SW149. Research Series 21, Arkansas Archeological Survey, Fayetteville, Arkansas.

Schambach, Frank F., and Leslie Newell
- 1990 *Crossroads of the Past: 12,000 Years of Indian Life in Arkansas*. Popular Series No. 2. Arkansas Archeological Survey, Fayetteville, Arkansas.

Scheitlin, Thomas E., John W. Clauser, Jr., and Michael T. Southern
- 1979 U.S. 221 Survey Data Analysis, Results, and Recommendations. In *North Carolina State Wide Archaeological Survey: An Introduction and Application to Three Highway Projects in Hertford, Wilkes, and Ashe Counties*, edited by Thomas E. Scheitlin, Mark A. Mathis, Jerry L. Cross, Thomas H. Hargrove, John W. Clauser, Jr., Michael T. Southern, Dolores A. Hall, Linda H. Pinkerton, Dale W. Reavis, and Thomas D. Burke, pp. 207–218. North Carolina Archeological Council Publication 11, Raleigh, North Carolina.

Schiffer, Michael B.
- 1972 The Archaeological Context and Systemic Context. *American Antiquity* 37:156–165.

Schiffer, Michael B., Alan P. Sullivan, and Timothy C. Klinger
- 1978 The Design of Archaeological Surveys. *World Archaeology* 10:1–28.

Schleidt, Maria
- 2005 Central Midden. *Mississippi Archaeological Association Newsletter* NL-1.

Schoeninger, Margaret J., Lisa Sattenspiel, and Mark R. Schurr
- 2000 Transitions at Moundville: A Question of Collapse. In *Bioarchaeological Studies of Life in the Age of Agriculture: A View from the Southeast*, edited by Patricia M. Lambert, pp. 63–77. University of Alabama Press, Tuscaloosa, Alabama.

Schoeninger, Margaret J., and Mark R. Schurr
- 1998 Human Subsistence at Moundville: The Stable-Isotope Data. In *Archaeology of the Moundville Chiefdom*, edited by Vernon James Knight, Jr., and Vincas P. Steponaitis, pp. 120–132. Smithsonian Institution Press, Washington, D.C.

Schön, Donald
- 1983 *The Reflective Practitioner: How Professionals Think in Action*. Basic Books, New York.

Schuldenrein, Joseph
- 1996 Geoarchaeology and the Mid-Holocene Landscape History of the Greater Southeast. In *Archaeology of the Mid-Holocene Southeast*, edited by Kenneth E. Sassaman and David G. Anderson, pp. 3–27. University Press of Florida, Gainesville, Florida.

Schurr, Mark R., and Margaret J. Schoeninger
- 1995 Associations between Agriculture Intensification and Social Complexity: An Example from the Prehistoric Ohio Valley. *Journal of Anthropological Archaeology* 14:315–339.

Scott, Kate M.
- 1888 *History of Jefferson County*. D. Mason & Co., Syracuse, New York.

Sease, E. C., R. L. Flowers, W. C. Mangrum, and R. K. Moore
- 1970 *Soil Survey of Shelby County, Tennessee*. US Department of Agriculture, Washington, D.C.

Seifurt, Christopher L., Randel Tom Cox, Steven L. Forman, Tom L. Foti, Thad A. Wasklewicz, and Andrew T. McColgan
    2009   Relict Nebkhas (Pimple Mounds) Record Prolonged Late Holocene Drought in the Forested Region of South-Central United States. *Quaternary Research* 71:329–339.

Sellet, Frederic, Dennis Stanford, and Pegi Jodry
    2010   "Ceci n'est pas une pipe?" A Possible Paleoindian Pipe from the Lindenmeier Site. Poster presented at the 75th Annual Meeting of the Society for American Archaeology, St. Louis, Missouri.

Sheets, Payson D.
    1975   Behavioral Analysis and the Structure of a Prehistoric Industry. *Current Anthropology* 16:369–391.

Sherwood, Sarah C.
    2001   Microartifacts. In *Earth Sciences and Archaeology*, edited by Paul Goldberg, Vance T. Holliday, and C. Reid Ferring, pp. 327–350. Kluwer Academic/Plenum Publishers, New York.

Sherwood, Sarah C., Jan F. Simek, and Richard R. Polhemus
    1995   Artifact Size and Spatial Process: Macro- and Microartifacts in a Mississippian House. *Geoarchaeology: An International Journal* 10:429–455.

Shott, Michael J.
    1985   Shovel-Test Sampling as a Site Discovery Technique: A Case Study from Michigan. *Journal of Field Archaeology* 12:457–468.
    1989   Shovel-Test Sampling in Archaeological Survey: Comments on Nance and Ball, and Lightfoot. *American Antiquity* 54:396–404.

Shuler, Kristina A., Shannon C. Hodge, Marie Elaine Danforth, J. Lynn Funkhouser, Christina Stantis, Danielle N. Cook, and Peng Zeng
    2012   In the Shadow of Moundville: A Bioarchaeological View of the Transition to Agriculture in the Central Tombigbee Valley of Alabama and Mississippi. *Journal of Anthropological Archaeology* 31:586–603.

Silver, James W.
    1957a   Paul Bunyan Comes to Mississippi. *Journal of Mississippi History* 19:93–119.
    1957b   The Hardwood Producers Come of Age. *Journal of Southern History* 23:427–453.
    1984   *Running Scared: Silver in Mississippi*. University Press of Mississippi, Jackson, Mississippi.

Sims, Douglas C., and John M. Connaway
    2000   Updated Chronometric Database for Mississippi. *Mississippi Archaeology* 35:208–269.

Skates, John R.
    2001   German Prisoners of War in Mississippi, 1943–1946. *Mississippi History Now*. Electronic document, http://mshistory.k12.ms.us/featurs/feature 20/germanprisonersofwar.html (accessed September 14, 2003).

Smith, Bruce D.
    1978   Variation in Mississippian Settlement Patterns. In *Mississippian Settlement Patterns*, edited by Bruce D. Smith, pp. 479–503. Academic Press, New York.

1986 The Archaeology of the Southeastern United States from Dalton to de Soto (10,500 B.P.–500 B.P.). In *Advances in World Archaeology*, Vol. 5, edited by Fred Wendorf and Angela E. Close, pp. 1–91. Academic Press, Orlando, Florida.

1990 Research on the Origins of Mississippian Chiefdoms in Eastern North America. In *The Mississippian Emergence*, edited by Bruce D. Smith, pp. 1–8. Smithsonian Institution Press, Washington, D.C.

Smith, Gerald P.

1972 The Late Archaic Through Early Woodland Periods in West Tennessee. Paper presented at the 28th Annual Meeting of the Southeastern Archaeological Conference, Morgantown, West Virginia.

1979 Archaeological Surveys in the Obion-Forked Deer and Reelfoot-Indian Creek Drainages: 1966 through Early 1975. Occasional Papers 9, Anthropological Research Center, Memphis State University, Memphis, Tennessee.

1996 The Mississippi River Drainage of Western Tennessee. In *Prehistory of the Central Mississippi River Valley*, edited by Charles H. McNutt, pp. 97–118. University of Alabama Press, Tuscaloosa, Alabama.

1998 Notes on Terminal Archaic/Poverty Point Culture and Its Transition into Woodland in Western Tennessee. *Tennessee Anthropologist* 23(1–2):29–35.

Smith, Gerald P., and Charles H. McNutt

1990 Poverty Point in Tennessee. *Louisiana Archaeology* 17:37–55.

Smith, Howard L.

1983 Research Designs in Cultural Resource Management: Future Trends and Potential Pitfalls. *Contract Abstracts and CRM Archeology* 3:116–118.

Smith, Marvin T., and Mark Williams

1994 Mississippian Mound Refuse Disposal Patterns and Implications for Archaeological Research. *Southeastern Archaeology* 13:27–35.

Snow, Dean R.

1980 *The Archaeology of New England*. Academic Press, New York.

Sparks, John T.

1987 Prehistoric Settlement Patterns in Clay County, Mississippi. Archaeological Report 20, Mississippi Department of Archives and History, Jackson, Mississippi.

Spielmann, Katherine A.

2002 Feasting, Craft Specialization, and the Ritual Mode of Production in Small-Scale Societies. *American Anthropologist* 104:195–207.

Stallings, Richard

1989 Factors in Interpreting the Prehistoric Use of the *Citronelle Gravels* in Mississippi. *Mississippi Archaeology* 24(1):35–58.

Star, Susan Leigh, and Karen Ruhleder

1996 Steps Toward an Ecology of Infrastructure: Design and Access for Large Information Spaces. *Information Systems Research* 7(1):111–134.

Starr, Mary Evelyn

2002a *Cultural Resource Survey of Approximately 140 acres in Covington County, Mississippi*. Report submitted to Wildlife Technical Services by Archaeology Mississippi, Inc., Jackson, Mississippi.

2002b   *Phase II Investigations at Mish.* Report submitted to Wildlife Technical Services by Archaeology Mississippi, Inc., Jackson, Mississippi.

2003   *Cultural Resources Survey of Approximately 700 Acres, O'Keefe Wildlife Management Area, formerly the village of Chancy and State Penal Farm Camp B, Quitman County, Mississippi.* Report submitted to Adam Tullos and Robbie Kiihnl, Mississippi Department of Wildlife, Parks and Fisheries, Jackson, Mississippi.

2013   http://www.deltaarchaeology.us/stoneware.htm (accessed January 9, 2013).

Stein, Julie K.

2005   Environment of the Green River Sites. In *Archaeology of the Middle Green River Region, Kentucky,* edited by William H. Marquardt and Patty Jo Watson, pp. 19–39. Monograph No. 5, Institute of Archaeological and Paleontological Studies, Florida Museum of Natural History, Gainesville, Florida.

Stein, Julie K., and Patricia A. Teltser

1989   Size Distribution of Artifact Classes: Combining Macro- and Micro-Fractions. *Geoarchaeology: An International Journal* 4:1–30.

Stephenson, Lloyd W., and Watson H. Monroe

1940   *The Upper Cretaceous Deposits: A Report on the Stratigraphy and Paleontology of the Upper Cretaceous Beds in Mississippi.* Mississippi State Geological Survey Bulletin 40.

Steponaitis, Vincas P.

1983   *Ceramics, Chronology, and Community Patterns: An Archaeological Study at Moundville.* Academic Press, New York.

Steponaitis, Vincas P., Stephen Williams, R. P. Stephen Davis, Jr., Ian W. Brown, Tristram R. Kidder, and Melissa Salvanish (editors)

2002   *LMS Archives Online.* http://rla.unc.edu/archives/lms1/ (accessed November 1, 2011).

Stewart-Abernathy, Leslie C.

1999   From Famous Forts to Forgotten Farmsteads: Historical Archaeology in the Mid-South. In *Arkansas Archaeology: Papers in Honor of Dan and Phyllis Morse,* edited by Robert C. Mainfort, Jr., and Marvin D. Jeter, pp. 225–244. University of Arkansas Press, Fayetteville, Arkansas.

Stoltman, James B.

1989   A Quantitative Approach to the Petrographic Analysis of Ceramic Thin Sections. *American Antiquity* 54:147–160.

1991   Ceramic Petrography as a Technique for Documenting Cultural Interaction: An Example from the Upper Mississippi Valley. *American Antiquity* 56:103–120.

Stone, Glenn Davis

1981   On Artifact Density and Shovel Probes. *Current Anthropology* 22:182–183.

Strauss, Anselm

1982   Interorganizational Negotiation. *Urban Life* 11(3):350–367.

Strauss, Anselm, Shizuko Fagerhaugh, Barbara Suczek, and Carolyn Wiener

1997   Articulation Work. Chapter 7 of *Social Organization of Medical Work,* pp. 151–190. Transaction Publishers, New Brunswick, New Jersey.

Stubbs, John D.

1982   A Preliminary Classification of Chickasaw Pottery. *Mississippi Archaeology* 17:57–59.

1983 A Report Presenting the Results of Archaeological Survey in Lee County, Mississippi, June 1981 to June 1983. Manuscript on file, Mississippi Department of Archives and History, Jackson, Mississippi.

Stuiver, Minze, and Paula J. Reimer
1993 Extended 14C Database and Revised CALIB Radiocarbon Calibration Program. *Radiocarbon* 35:215–230.

Styles, Bonnie W.
1986 Aquatic Exploitation in the Lower Illinois River Valley: The Role of Paleoecological Change. In *Foraging, Collecting and Harvesting: Archaic Period Subsistence and Settlement in the Eastern Woodlands*, edited by Sarah W. Neusius, pp. 145–174. Occasional Paper No. 6, Center for Archaeological Investigations, Southern Illinois University at Carbondale, Carbondale, Illinois.

Styles, Thomas
1984 Holocene and Late Pleistocene Geology of Napoleon Hollow Archaeological Site in Lower Illinois River Valley. Unpublished Master's thesis, Department of Geology, University of Illinois, Urbana, Illinois.

Suhm, Dee A., and Edward B. Jelks (editors)
1962 *Handbook of Texas Archeology: Type Descriptions*. The Texas Archeological Society Special Publication 1 and The Texas Memorial Museum Bulletin 4. Austin, Texas.

Sullivan, Alan P., III (editor)
1998 *Surface Archaeology*. University of New Mexico Press, Albuquerque, New Mexico.

Tainter, Joseph A.
1979 The Mountainair Lithic Scatters: Settlement Patterns and Significance Evaluation of Low Density Surface Sites. *Journal of Field Archaeology* 6:463–469.
1987 The Politics of Regional Research in Conservation Archaeology. *American Archaeology* 6:217–227.

Tainter, Joseph A., and R. H. Hamre (editors)
1988 *Tools to Manage the Past: Research Priorities for Cultural Resources Management in the Southwest*. USDA Forest Service, Rocky Mountain Forest and Range Experiment Station, General Technical Report RM-164, Fort Collins, Colorado.

Tally, Marvin
2003 Interview. September 15, 2003.

Thomas, Cyrus
1894 *Report on the Mound Explorations of the Bureau of Ethnology*. Twelfth Annual Report of the Bureau of American Ethnology, 1890–1891, US Government Printing Office, Washington, D.C. Reprinted in 1985 by the Smithsonian Institution Press, Washington, D.C.

Thomas, David Hurst
1986 *Refiguring Anthropology: First Principles of Probability and Statistics*. Waveland Press, Prospect Heights, Illinois.

Thomas, Prentice M., and L. Janice Campbell (editors)
2005 *Investigations in the New Madrid Floodway: Data Recovery at 23MI20, the Burkett Site, Mississippi County, Missouri, Volume 1: Final Report*. Report submitted to the US Army Corps of Engineers, Memphis District, by Prentice Thomas and Associates, Report of Investigations No. 500, New World Research, Inc., Fort Walton Beach, Florida.

Thomas, Prentice M., L. Janice Campbell, and James R. Morehead
  2004 The Burkett Site (23MI20): Implications for Cultural Complexity and Origins. In *Signs of Power: The Rise of Cultural Complexity in the Southeast*, edited by Jon L. Gibson and Phillip J. Carr, pp. 114–128. University of Alabama Press, Tuscaloosa, Alabama.

Thorne, Robert M.
  1981 *Archaeological Data Recovery and Preservation of Hurricane Mound (22-La-516), Lafayette County, Mississippi*. Report submitted to the US Army Corps of Engineers, Vicksburg District, Vicksburg, Mississippi, by the Center for Archaeological Research, University of Mississippi, Oxford, Mississippi.

Titterington, P. F.
  1938 Correspondence for Identification. *American Antiquity* 3:354–355.

Toth, Alan, and Samuel O. Brookes
  1977 The Martin #1 Site (22-TU-533), Tunica County, 1976. *Mississippi Archaeology* 12(1):8–13.

Trigger, Bruce G.
  1990 Monumental Architecture: A Thermodynamic Explanation of Symbolic Behaviour. *World Archaeology* 22:119–131.

Trinkley, Michael
  1994 *Analysis of a Corn Sample from the Owl Creek Mound, 22CS502, Chickasaw County, Mississippi*. Chicora Research Series 155, Chicora Foundation, Inc., Columbia, South Carolina.

Triplett, Andrew Mickens
  2008a A Study of the Chronological Placement of Selected Mississippian-Period Occupations within the Ackerman Unit of the Tombigbee National Forest. Unpublished Master's thesis, Department of Sociology, Anthropology, and Social Work, Mississippi State University, Starkville, Mississippi.
  2008b Central Midden. *Mississippi Archaeological Association Newsletter* NL-1.

USDA Forest Service
  1976 *Highlights in the History of Forest Conservation*. US Department of Agriculture, Forest Service, History Unit. AIB-83. Washington, D.C.
  1988 *The South's Fourth Forest: Alternatives for the Future*. US Department of Agriculture, Washington, D.C.
  1997 *Establishment and Modification of National Forest Boundaries and National Grasslands: A Chronological Record—1891–1996*. US Department of Agriculture, Forest Service, Lands Staff. FS-612. Washington, D.C.

Underwood, John R.
  1998 Chickasaw Material Culture and the European Deerskin Trade: An Analysis of Two Eighteenth Century Chickasaw Sites in Northeast Mississippi. Unpublished MA thesis, The College of William and Mary, Williamsburg, Virginia.
  2009 Trip Report—Inadvertent Discovery on SR 6. Report on file, Mississippi Department of Transportation, Jackson, Mississippi.

Vance, Elizabeth D.
  1986 *Microdebitage Analysis in Activity Analysis: An Application*. Northwest Anthropological Research Notes 20:179–189.

Bibliography

Venegas, Miguel
- 1759 *A Natural and Civil History of California*, Vol. 1. James Rivington and James Fletcher, London, England.

Wait, Walter K.
- 1993 Alternative Approaches to the Analysis of Low-Density Artifact Scatters. In *The Star Lake Archaeological Project*, edited by Walter K. Wait and Ben A. Nelson, pp. 59–94. Southern Illinois University Press, Carbondale, Illinois.

Walling, Richard, Lawrence Alexander, Jamie C. Brandon, and Shawn Chapman
- 1995 *Phase II Archaeological Testing, Site 40SY540, SR385 (Paul Barrett Parkway), Shelby County, Tennessee.* Report submitted to Parsons De Leuw by Panamerican Consultants, Inc., Tuscaloosa, Alabama.

Walling, Richard, Robert C. Mainfort, Jr., and James Atkinson
- 1991 Radiocarbon Dates for the Bynum, Pharr, and Miller Sites, Northeast Mississippi. *Southeastern Archaeology* 10:54–62.

Walthall, John A., and Steve B. Wimberly
- 1978 Mississippian Chronology in the Black Warrior Valley: Radiocarbon Dates from Bessemer and Moundville. *Journal of Alabama Archaeology* 24:118–124.

Warhop, Jennifer R.
- 2005 Investigations of a Unique Structure at the Anna Site (22AD500), Mississippi. Unpublished Master's thesis, Department of Anthropology, University of Alabama, Tuscaloosa, Alabama.

Watts, William A., Eric C. Grimm, and T. C. Hussey
- 1996 Mid-Holocene Forest History of Florida and the Coastal Plain of Georgia and South Carolina. In *Archaeology of the Mid-Holocene Southeast*, edited by Kenneth E. Sassaman and David G. Anderson, pp. 28–38. University Press of Florida, Gainesville, Florida.

Wayne County News
- 1933a Reforestation Camp to Locate in This Territory. 7 September:1. Waynesboro, Mississippi.
- 1933b Will Make Haste on Reforestry Project. 14 September:1. Waynesboro, Mississippi.
- 1942 Abandon CCC Camp in This County. 28 May:1. Waynesboro, Mississippi.

Weaver, Elizabeth C.
- 1963 Technological Analysis of Prehistoric Lower Mississippi Ceramic Material: A Preliminary Report. *American Antiquity* 29:49–56.

Weaver, Guy G., C. Andrew Buchner, and Mary E. Starr
- 1999 Results of Testing and Data Recovery at the Fulmer Site (40SY527). In *Archaeological Investigations at Three Sites near Arlington, State Route 385 (Paul Barrett Parkway), Shelby County, Tennessee: Archaeological Testing at 40SY525 and 40SY526 and Archaeological Testing and Data Recovery at 40SY527*, by Guy G. Weaver, Mitchell R. Childress, C. Andrew Buchner, and Mary E. Starr, pp. 85–139. Publications in Archaeology 4, Environmental Planning Office, Tennessee Department of Transportation, Nashville, Tennessee.

Weaver, Guy G., and Mitchell R. Childress
- 1999 Conclusions and Recommendations. In *Archaeological Investigations at Three Sites near Arlington, State Route 385 (Paul Barrett Parkway), Shelby County, Tennessee:*

Archaeological Testing at 40SY525 and 40SY526 and Archaeological Testing and Data Recovery at 40SY527, by Guy G. Weaver, Mitchell R. Childress, C. Andrew Buchner, and Mary E. Starr, pp. 180–182. Publications in Archaeology 4, Environmental Planning Office, Tennessee Department of Transportation, Nashville, Tennessee.

Weaver, Guy G., Mitchell R. Childress, C. Andrew Buchner, and Mary E. Starr
    1999   *Archaeological Investigations at Three Sites near Arlington, State Route 385 (Paul Barrett Parkway), Shelby County, Tennessee: Archaeological Testing at 40SY525 and 40SY526 and Archaeological Testing and Data Recovery at 40SY527*. Publications in Archaeology 4, Environmental Planning Office, Tennessee Department of Transportation, Nashville, Tennessee.

Webb, Clarence H.
    1968   Extent and Content of Poverty Point Culture. *American Antiquity* 33:297–331.
    1971a   Another Zoomorphic Locust Stone Bead from Lafayette County. *Arkansas Archeologist* 12(2):39–40.
    1971b   Archaic and Poverty Point Zoomorphic Locust Beads. *American Antiquity* 36:105–114.
    1981   *Stone Points and Tools of Northwestern Louisiana*. Special Publication of the Louisiana Archaeological Society, No. 1, Baton Rouge, Louisiana.
    1982   *The Poverty Point Culture*. 2nd revised edition. *Geoscience and Man*, Vol. 17. School of Geoscience, Louisiana State University, Baton Rouge, Louisiana.
    2000   *Stone Points and Tools of Northwestern Louisiana*. Franklin Press, Baton Rouge. Originally printed 1981 as a Special Publication of the Louisiana Archaeological Society, Baton Rouge, Louisiana.

Webb, Clarence H., James A. Ford, and Sherwood M. Gagliano
    1969   Poverty Point Culture and the American Formative. 2 vols. Unpublished manuscript and correspondence between authors on file, Coastal Environments, Inc., Baton Rouge, Louisiana.

Weinstein, Richard A.
    1991   The Tchula Period in the Lower Mississippi Valley and Adjacent Coastal Zone: A Brief Summary. *Louisiana Archaeology* 18:153–187.
    2005   A Review of the *Archaeological Survey in the Lower Mississippi Alluvial Valley*, with an Update of Subsequent Archaeological Research at PF&G's Mississippi Sites. *Mississippi Archaeology* 40:141–239.

Welch, Paul D.
    1990   Mississippian Emergence in West-Central Alabama. In *The Mississipian Emergence*, edited by Bruce D. Smith, pp. 197–225. Smithsonian Institution Press, Washington, D.C.
    1991   *Moundville's Economy*. University of Alabama Press, Tuscaloosa, Alabama.
    1994   The Occupational History of the Bessemer Site. *Southeastern Archaeology* 13:1–26.
    1998   Middle Woodland and Mississippian Occupations of the Savannah Site in Tennessee. *Southeastern Archaeology* 17:79–91.
    2006   Interpreting Anomalous Rural Mississippian Settlements: Leadership from Below. In *Leadership and Polity in Mississippian Society*, edited by Brian M. Butler and Paul D. Welch, pp. 214–235. Occasional Paper 33, Center for Archaeological Investigations, Southern Illinois University, Carbondale, Illinois.

Bibliography

West, Terry L.
    1992   *Centennial Mini-histories of the Forest Service*. US Department of Agriculture, Forest Service, History Unit. FS-518. Washington, D.C.

Wheat, Joe Ben
    1979   The Jurgens Site. *Plains Anthropologist* 24(84), Part 2:1–153.

White, Nancy Marie
    1999   Hester A. Davis: A Legend in Public Archaeology. In *Grit-Tempered: Early Women Archaeologists in the Southeastern United States*, edited by Nancy Marie White, Lynne P. Sullivan, and Rochelle A. Marrinan, pp. 206–229. University Press of Florida, Gainesville, Florida.

Widmer, Randolph J.
    2004   Explaining the Sociopolitical Complexity in the Foraging Adaptations of the Southeastern United States: The Roles of Demography, Kinship, and Ecology in Sociocultural Evolution. In *Signs of Power: The Rise of Cultural Complexity in the Southeast*, edited by Jon L. Gibson and Philip J. Carr, pp. 234–253. University of Alabama Press, Tuscaloosa, Alabama.

Wiener, Carolyn L.
    1991   Arenas and Careers: The Complex Interweaving of Personal and Organizational Destiny. In *Social Organization and Social Process: Essays in Honor of Anselm Strauss*, edited by David R. Maines, pp. 175–188. Aldine de Gruyter, New York.

Wilkins, James Christopher
    2004   The Tchula Period in the Natchez Bluffs: The Grace MacNeil Site and the Homochitto Phase. Unpublished Master's thesis, Department of Anthropology, University of Alabama, Tuscaloosa, Alabama.

Willey, Gordon R., and Philip Phillips
    1958   *Method and Theory in American Archaeology*. University of Chicago Press, Chicago, Illinois.

Williams, Ray
    1968   *Southeast Missouri Land Leveling Salvage Archaeology: 1967*. Report submitted to the National Park Service, Omaha, Nebraska, by the Archaeological Research Division, Department of Anthropology, University of Missouri, Columbia, Missouri.

Williams, Stephen
    1991   Poverty Point North and Some Thoughts on Origins. In *The Poverty Point Culture: Local Manifestations, Subsistence Practices, and Trade Networks*, edited by Kathleen M. Byrd, pp. 95–101. *Geoscience and Man*, Vol. 29. Department of Geography and Anthropology, Louisiana State University, Baton Rouge, Louisiana.
    2002   LMS Archives Online: An Introduction. http://rla.unc.edu/Archives/LMS1/LMS_intro.html (accessed August 18, 2012).

Williams, Stephen, and Jeffrey P. Brain
    1983   *Excavations at the Lake George Site, Yazoo County, Mississippi, 1958–1960*. Papers of the Peabody Museum of Archaeology and Ethnology Vol. 74. Harvard University, Cambridge, Massachusetts.

Wilson, Moira A., Margaret A. Carter, Christopher Hall, William D. Hoff, Ceren Ince, Shaun D. Savage, Bernard McKay, and Ian M. Betts

2009 Dating Fired-Clay Ceramics Using Long-Term Power Law Rehydroxylation Kinetics. *Proceedings of the Royal Society A: Mathematical, Physical, and Engineering Sciences* 465(2108):2407–2415.

Winston, E. T.

1931 *Story of Pontotoc.* Pontotoc Progress Print, Pontotoc, Mississippi.

Wobst, H. Martin

1983 We Can't See the Forest for the Trees: Sampling and the Shape of Archaeological Distributions. In *Archaeological Hammers and Theories,* edited by James A. Moore and Arthur S. Keene, pp. 37–85. Academic Press, New York.

Contributors

Keith A. Baca, Mississippi State University
Jeffrey P. Brain, Peabody Essex Museum
Samuel O. Brookes III, USDA Forest Service (retired)
Ian W. Brown, University of Alabama
Philip J. Carr, University of South Alabama
Jessica Crawford, Archaeological Conservancy
Patricia Galloway, University of Texas at Austin
Alison M. Hadley, University of Kansas
Christopher T. Hays, University of Wisconsin-Washington County
Edward R. Henry, Washington University in St. Louis
Cliff Jenkins, Natural Resources Conservation Service
Jay K. Johnson, University of Mississippi
Evan Peacock, Mississippi State University
Janet Rafferty, Mississippi State University
Maria Schleidt, USDA Forest Service
Mary Evelyn Starr, Archaeological Consultant
James B. Stoltman, University of Wisconsin-Madison
Andrew M. Triplett, USDA Forest Service
Melissa H. Twaroski, USDA Forest Service
Richard A. Weinstein, Coastal Environments, Inc.

Index

Page numbers in **bold** indicate an illustration.

22BE544 site, 122–29, 131–44; ceramic vessels, 132–33, 134–35; lithics, 136–40, 137
22BE588 site, 120, 122–23, 125, 129–33, 136–37, 140–44; ceramic vessels, 130–32; lithics, 133, 136

Achin Head site (22FR665), 334
Ackerman, Mississippi, 15
Adams County, Mississippi, 216
Aden site (22IS509), 31
African American sites, 20
Agriculture, maize, 19, 213
Alabama Museum of Natural History, 218
Alvey, Jeffrey, 164
Ames mound site, 215
Ancient Indian Architecture project, 29, 30
Ancient Mounds Heritage Area, Louisiana, 23
Anna site (22AD500), 216–39; Great Ravine as eroded pits, 219–20; Stowers collection, 218
Apple Street site (22JA530), 101
Archaeological Conservancy, 23, 333
Archaeological education: field schools, 21, 76, 173, 333; internships, 331
Archaeological Resources Preservation Act, 327
Archaeological sites: 22BE554, 120; 22BE585, 121, 123; 22CA514, 159; 22CH515, 16; 22CH536, 15; 22CS828, 14; 22LA692, 15; 22LA702, 21; 22LE504 (MLe18), 258, 260, 264, 265; 22LE524 (MLe14), 258, 260, 264, 265; 22LE678, 262, 263, 264; 22LE907, 259, 260, 264, 265; 22LI504, 52; 22MR539, 121; 22PA592, 63; 22WI536, 17; 40DY42, 104, 106; 40FY36, 106, 109; 40GB42, 106, 109; 40OB54, 106; 40SY56, 104, 106, 109; 40TP37, 106
Archaic period, 3, 15–16; Early Archaic, 15, 43, 47, 49, 63, 72; Middle Archaic, 15–16, 43, 45, 47–51, 53, 60–65, 67, 69–71, 76, 81, 83, 86–89, 95, 97; Late Archaic, 15, 16, 52, 53, 57, 61, 67, 102
Arkansas Archeological Society, 325
Arkansas Archeological Survey, 325, 326
Articulation work, 322
Atkinson, James, 191, 215
Audubon Society, 23
Avery Island Conference, xii

Baca, Keith, 22, 215
Banana Bayou site, 51
Barnett, James, 325
Batesville Mounds (22PA500), 17, 158, 161
Beasley, Duke, 218
Beaumont site, 49
Benson, Carl, 273
Benton County, Mississippi, 119
Benton phase, 49, 62
Bessemer Mounds site, Alabama, 189–215; dating, 195; habitation extent, 207–8; layout and use, 198, 201; occupation, 205–6
Big Town site (22LE505, MLe90), 258–60, 265
Bison, evidence for hunting, 46
Black Prairie, 166, 169, 244
Black Warrior River, 189
Bossier Parish, Louisiana, 62
Boudreaux, Tony, 218
Bradbury, Andrew, 98

Index

Brain, Jeffrey P., 325
Brookes, Samuel O.: career, xi–xii, 3–6, 10–11, 21–23, 57–59, 164–65, 319–36; field methods, 119; publications, 4; scholarship, 55–70, 71–98
Brown, Ian, 325
Bryan, Robert, 215
Burgess, Catherine and Phillip, 116
Burkett site (23MI20), 101–2, 104
Bynum Mounds (22CS503, MCs16), 259–60

Calhoun County, Mississippi, 146
Camp Shelby, Mississippi, 48
Carrier, Cassius M., 292; C. M. Carrier & Son Corporation charter, 293–94; Carrier Lumber & Mfg. Co., 299; R. M. Carrier dissolves business, 306–8
Carroll County, Mississippi, 30
Central Mississippi Valley, 43, 120
Ceramics
  Anna site, Prospere Collection, 220–39, **222–23**; Addis Plain, 224; Addis Plain, *var. Great Ravine*, 224; Addis Plain, *var. Greenville*, 234; Addis Plain, *var. Ratcliffe*, 224; Addis Plain, *var. unspecified*, 230; Addis Plain ware, 232; Anna Engraved, 225; Anna Incised, 225; Anna Interior Engraved, 225; Avenue Polychrome, 225, 236; Avoyelles Punctated, *var. Dupree*, 224; Barton Incised, *var. Arcola*, 227; Barton Incised, *var. Barton*, 227; Barton Incised, *var. Portland*, 238; Bell Plain ware, 227, 232, 233, 234, 238; Coleman Incised, *var. Bass*, 228; Coleman Incised, *var. Coleman*, 228; Coles Creek Incised, *var. Hardy*, 228; Coles Creek Incised, *var. unspecified*, 224; Cowhide Stamped, 231; Cracker Road Incised, 237, 238; D'Olive Engraved, 225; D'Olive Incised, 225; D'Olive Incised, *var. D'Olive*, 234; Fatherland Incised, *var. Fatherland*, 237; Fatherland Incised, *var. Pine Ridge*, 237; Fatherland Incised, *var. Stanton*, 237; Fatherland Incised, *var. unspecified*, 237; Grace Brushed, *var. Grace*, 230; Grace Brushed, *var. Grand Gulf*, 230; L'Eau Noire Incised, *var. Anna*, 225; L'Eau Noire Incised, *var. L'Eau Noire*, 233, 234; Leland Incised, *var. Blanchard*, 234; Leland Incised, *var. Ferris*, 225, 235; Leland Incised, *var. Foster*, 235; Leland Incised, *var. Leflore*, 235; Leland Incised, *var. Leland*, 235; Leland Incised, *var. Russell*, 235; Maddox Engraved, *var. Emerald*, 236; Maddox Engraved, *var. Silver City*, 236; Marksville Stamped, *var. Manny*, 220; Matthews Incised, 231; Mazique Incised, *var. Kings Point*, 224; Mazique Incised, *var. Manchac*, 228, 229, 233; Mississippi Plain ware, 227; Mound Place Incised, *var. Chickasawba*, 233; Mound Place Incised, *var. McMillan*, 233; Mound Place Incised, *var. Waltons Camp*, 233; Moundville Incised, 231, 232; Moundville Incised, *var. Douglas*, 232, 233; Moundville Incised, *var. Moundville*, 232, 233; Nodena Red and White, *var. Nodena*, 225, 236; Parkin Punctated, *var. Hollandale*, 225; Plaquemine Brushed, *var. Plaquemine*, 228, 229; Pouncey Pinched, *var. Patosi*, 225; Tammany Punctated, *var. Duckroost*, 220; Winterville Incised, *var. Winterville*, 225
"pot-drops," 18
South Thomas Street site, 247–49, **249**; Baldwin Plain ware (heavily sand tempered), 248, 249; Furrs Cord-marked, 248; Oktibbeha Plain ware (fine shell temper, polished), 248; Saltillo Fabric Impressed, 248, 249; Wilson Brushed, 249; Wilson Plain ware (coarse fossil shell temper), 248
temper, 18, 170, 172, 211, 248

Index

Woodland-period, 17; Baytown Plain, 158; Cormorant Cord Impressed, 119; Crowder, 123; Furrs Cord Marked, 157, 159; Mulberry Creek Cord-marked, 158; Saltillo Fabric Marked, 157, 159; Tishomingo Cord-marked, 149, 157, 158; Tishomingo Plain, 149, 157, 158; Twin Lakes Punctated, 119; Withers Fabric Marked [Impressed], 119, 122, 159

Chambers, Moreau B. C., 191

Cherokee Indians, 60

Chewalla Lake Mound (22MR502), 121

Chickasaw County, Mississippi, 19

Chickasaw Indians, 243–65; settlement patterns in Mississippi, 261

Chickasaw Nation, 243, 245–46

C. H. Nash Museum, Chucalissa, 107, 116

Choctaw County, Mississippi, 16

Choctaw Lake, 14, 15

Chorley, John, 282–87; dealer in land, 285–86

Civilian Conservation Corps (CCC) in Mississippi, 266–80; camp life, 274–76; Chickasawhay Ranger District camps, closure of F-4 and F-24, 277–78; construction of camps F-4, F-8, and F-24, 272, 277; De Soto National Forest, 270; firefighting and lookout, 273–74; governance by US Army Fourth Corps, 270; land purchase, 269–70; lookout tower construction, 274; reuse of F-8, 278–80; staffing with enrollees, 273, 276; tree-planting, 273; Wausau Work Center, 274–75; work center design, 269

Claiborne County, Mississippi, 3, 71, 75

Claiborne site, 52, 60, 101

Clay County, Mississippi, 3

Climate change, 169

Colclough Farmstead, 20

Coles Creek period, 224

Columella beads, 211

Community of practice, 320–21, 324, 335

Connaway, John, 325, 334

Coonewah Creek, 243

Copena tradition, 162

Cornaline d'Aleppo trade beads, 257, 259, 260, 261

Craft specialization, 53, 71–72, 75, 82–85, 94–97

Crawford, Jessica, 333

Cultural Resource Management, 3–4, 9, 10, 13, 22

Curry site (22OK578), 189

Dantzler site (22HR652), 334

Davies, Chris, 215

Davis, Hester, 325–26

Deathly Silent site (22FO826), 334

DeLeon, Mark, 327

Delta State University, 31

Demographics, 86, 88, 167, 214

Denton site (22QU522), 16, 50–51, 57, 59, 61–63, 69; bead making, 61, 80, 83–85; radiocarbon dates, 64

Dexter, A. K., 273

Dockery, David, 140

Duck Lake site (22IS522), 31

Dukes, Joel, 328, 329, 334

East Baton Rouge Parish, Louisiana, 57

Elliot, Jack, 325

Emerald site (22AD504), 218

Epistemic community, 322, 336

Epps, Louisiana, 57

Ethnography of archaeological practice, 320

European ceramics, 19

Evans, David H., 291

Eva site, 49

Evolutionary archaeology: bet-hedging, 212–15; component definition, 12–13; costly signaling, 91, 210–11; frequency seriation, 185–87; occupation definition and delineation, 13, 170, 202–3

Exchange networks, 49, 52–53, 65, 68–69, 89, 99, 101, 256

Fairview Landing site (22YZ561), 28

Fant, David, 120, 122, 123–45, 164, 328

Field methods, 10; auger testing, 151; "kick tests," 11; repeated surveys, 334; shovel tests, 11, 16, 76, 119, 123, 125, 170; stratigraphic excavation, 170; surface collection, 170; topographic mapping, 14
Florence Mound (1LU10), 162
Ford, James A., 191, 324
Forrest, John, 98
Fort St. Pierre, 237
Frank, Smokye Joe, 219, 239
Frenchman's Bend Mounds (16OU259), 82
Frequency seriation, 14
Fuller, Richard S., 218
Fulmer site (40SY527), 120, 123, 133, 141–43
Fulton Cache (22LI500), 55, 57–58, 68; bead style, 61

General Land Office surveys, 15, 20
Gibson, Jon, 239
Gilcrease Museum, 55, 57
Godwin site (22WI613), 15, 16
Gopher Farm site (22WA676), 334
Grand Gulf Mound, 3
Grand Village of the Natchez Indians, 325
Grant Mounds, 52
Great Delta Bear Affair, 23, 333
Great Plains, 45
Grenada Reservoir, 149
Griffin, James B., 324
Gulf Coast, 58, 99, 110
Gulf Formational period, 17

Hamill Springs site, 21
Hancock County, Mississippi, 60
Hancock County Historical Society, 116
Harris Creek site (8VO24), 99
Harrison, Kim, 145
Harvard University, 324
Haynes Bluff (22WR501), 257
Hearns site (23MI7), 102
Heat treatment of lithics, 88–89
Heitzman Bead, 60
Hemphill, Sid, "Carrier Line" song, 289–91
Henry, Eddie, 246

Hester site, 3
Higgins, Melissa, 6, 331
Hilburn, Andy, 98
Historic Jefferson College, 325
Historic period, 19–20; cemeteries, 21; industrial sites, 21; railroads, 294–302
Hiwassee Island Red on Buff ceramics, 211
Hodder, Ian, 320
Holly Springs National Forest, 11, 14–18, 21, 119–45; unreported sites, 121
Holmes County, Mississippi, 30, 39
Humphreys County, Mississippi, 30, 39
Hunter, Donald, 116
Hurricane Landing site (22LA516), 161
Hutchins, William T., 55
Hypertrophic (ideotechnic, prestige) artifacts, 91
Hypsithermal (Altithermal, Climatic Optimum) climatic period, 43–54, 69, 86–87; climatic shift in flora, 44–45; faunal migration, 45; forest fires, 43; stream siltation, 46, 48, 50–51; weather variability, 87

Illinois River, 45
Infrastructure, 321
Ingomar site (22UN500), 160–62, 164
Inundation effects on sites, 14–15
Invisible work, 319
Irby bead, 63
Issaquena County, Mississippi, 30
Itawamba County, Mississippi, 62

Jackson, Ed, 22
Jacobs, Paul, 145
Jaketown site (22HU505), 52, 104, 111
James Creek, 75, 87
Jefferson Davis County, Mississippi, 55, 72, 92
Jefferson Peace Medal, 259–60
Jenkins, Cliff, 164
John Forrest site (22CB623), 71–97
Johnny Ford site (3LA5), 61
Johnson, Andrew, architect, 299
Johnson, Greg, 6

Index

Johnson, Hunter, 218
Johnson, Jay, 22
Johnston site (40MD3), 162
Jones, Steve, 123

Keenan, J. T. R., 55
Keenan Cache, 55, 57–58, 72, 77, 80–81, 83–84, 88, 90, 92–93
Kosciusko quartzite quarry site (22YA822), 21
Koster site, 46

Lafayette County, Arkansas, 55
Lafayette County, Mississippi, 15
Lake Bistineau, Louisiana, 62
Lake George site (22YZ557), 27, 29, 225
Lapidary industry, 57, 64, 72, 75; bead manufacture, production trajectory, 80–84, 92–93; bead use and meaning, 92–93; bow drill, 82–83; lathe, 82–83; perforated discoidals, 84; pump drill, 92; tool manufacture, 90
Leaf River, 49
Lee, Oscar, 55
Lee County, Mississippi, 243
Leflore County, Mississippi, 30
Leland Mounds (Avondale Mounds, 22WS501), 27
Lemley, Harry J. Bead, 55, 57
Lincoln County, Mississippi, 52
Lithics and lapidary industry materials: Arkansas novaculite, 49–50; Burlington chert, 50; chert, heat-treated, 60; Chickasaw gray chert, 250–54, 261; Citronelle Gravel, 46–47, 49, 79, 87, 89, 92, 156; Fort Payne chert, 15, 48–49, 53, 87–88; French flint, 254; greenstone, 76, 80; jasper, 57, 64, 89; Kosciusko Quartzite, 47; limonite, 48; quartzitic claystone, 140; sandstone quartzite, 48; slate, green-banded, 60; Tallahatta Quartzite, 47–49, 53, 87, 140; trachyte, 60, 63, 80; Tuscaloosa Gravel, 49, 156, 250–51, 261; wood, petrified, 141

Lithic and lapidary types: Ackerman Cumberland fluted point, 15; atlatl weight, ground stone, 76; bannerstone, shuttle-type, 16; bead, chipped stone, 78–79, 88–89; bead, ground stone, 80, 88–89; bead, tubular, 60–62, 64, 72; bead, zoomorphic effigy, 52, 57–64, 66–69, 72, 83–84, 89; Benton knife, 48; Benton point, 16, 49–50, 63; Big Sandy point, 15; blade cores, 77–78, 86, 89–90; blade removals, 78; Bolen point, 47; Castroville point, 49; Cobbs triangular knife, 46; Cody knife, 46; Cypress Creek point, 49, 63; Dallas point, 252; Dalton point, xii, 15; Decatur point, 142; Denton point, 63–64; end scraper, 16, 53; Eva/Morrow Mountain point, 63; Evans point, 64; Flint Creek point, 156; gun spalls, 250, 254–55, 264; Hardin point, 46; Johnson point, 50; Kirk Corner-notched point, 47; Lost Lake point, 47; Madison point, 159, 252; microdrills, 52, 78, 80–83, 86, 89–90; Opossum Bayou point, 63–64; oversized biface, 62–63, 72; pendant, ground stone, 67, 72; Pickwick point, 49; Pine Tree point, 47; plummet, ground stone, 76; Quad point, 15; Scottsbluff point, 46; Sinner point, 62; Sykes-White Springs bifaces, 76; thumbnail scraper, 50, 250, 252–53, 261; Turkey Tail point, 49; Vaughn point, 48
Little Ice Age, 53
Little Tallahatchie River, 17
Livingood, Patrick, 218
Loess Hills, 160
Logging equipment, 283
Lolley, Terry, 215
Longstreet site (22QU523), 64
Loosahatchie River, 143
Loosa Yokena (22WR691), 69, 72, 77–81, 84, 86–90, 92–93, 95

Index

Louisiana, Cody complex in, 46; Archaic mounds in, 51
Louisiana Division of Archaeology, 116
Louisiana Division of State Parks, 116
Louisiana State University, 191
Lower Delta Mound Inventory, 23–40
Lower Delta Mound Trail, 23
Lower Delta Partnership, 23, 333
Lower Jackson Mound (16WC10), 64
Lower Mississippi [Alluvial] Valley, 17–18, 72, 94, 99, 120, 324
Lower Mississippi Delta, 23, 26, 29
Lower Mississippi Survey, 31, 216, 324–26; Archives, 30
Lowndes County, Mississippi, 3
Lubbub Creek site, 189
Lyon's Bluff site, 189

Magee Mounds site (22SH501), 27
Mangum Mound site, 23
Marshall, Richard, 191
Marshall County, Mississippi, 119, 121
Mathus, James, 312
Mattics, Sarah, 98
McCarty site (3PO467), 101
McClung, Terry, 328–29, 331
McGahey, Sam, 325
McGimsey, Charles, 325–26
Meadowbrook site (22LE912), 259
Microartifact analysis, 14
Micro-wear analysis, 90
Midden Mound Project, 48, 51
Mid-South Archaeological Conference, 4, 147, 331
Miller Mound site, 189
Mississippian period, 18–19, 102, 169; Early (Moundville I), 192–95
Mississippi Archaeological Association, 4, 20, 23, 121, 324, 329
Mississippi Archaeological Association Newsletter, 323, 331, 334
Mississippi Archaeology, 4, 20, 332
Mississippi Archaeology Week/Month, 21, 329, 333

Mississippi Association of Professional Archaeologists, 4, 324, 333
Mississippi Department of Archives and History, 3, 12, 23, 33, 49, 57, 76, 116, 119, 150, 191, 243, 283, 321, 324, 325–26, 329, 333; archaeological site files, 26, 29, 30, 159; Clarksdale Survey Office, 58, 325–26
Mississippi Department of Environmental Quality, 140
Mississippi Department of Transportation, 23, 324, 331, 333
Mississippi Department of Wildlife, Parks and Fisheries, 295
Mississippi Heritage Trust, 333
Mississippi Humanities Council, 4, 333
Mississippi Landmark, 164
Mississippi National Guard, 331
Mississippi River, 30, 75, 216
Mississippi State University, 21, 173, 191, 324, 326
Monroe County, Mississippi, 3, 60
Monte Sano Mound site (16EBR17), 57, 61–62, 64–65, 69
Mont Helena site (22SH505), 28
Mosquitoville, logging camp, 283
Mounds, 120; Archaic, 51–52, 72, 83; inventory in Lower Mississippi Delta, 23–40; Woodland conical, 18, 121; Woodland platform, 146
Moundville site (1TU500), 189
Mussels, evidence for harvesting, 51

Nairne, Thomas, 243, 265
Nanih Waiya site (22WI500), 161
Napoleon Hollow site, 46
Natchez phase, 237
Natchez Trace Parkway, 75, 191, 218, 244, 258
National Environmental Policy Act (NEPA), 323, 327
National Forests
    Clarke-McNary Act (1924), 266
    expansion east of Mississippi, 267
    Federal Forest Reserve Act, 266

history of system, 266–67
in Mississippi, 119, 320; Forest Archaeologists team development, 327–29; MoA with Mississippi Native American tribes, 327; Purchase Units, 1930–1935, 267; shift to digital technology, 335
sites of archaeological work, 10
Weeks Law (1911), 266
National Historic Landmarks, 27, 216
National Historic Preservation Act, 10, 327
National Park Service, 218, 333
National Register of Historic Places, 27, 147, 150, 299
Native American Graves Protection and Repatriation Act, 323, 327
Natural Resources Conservation Service, 23; Wetlands Reserve Program, 28
Neitzel, Stuart, 191
Norman site (22QU518), 111
North Central Hills, 18, 19, 146, 157, 160, 167; abandonment of, 169
Noxubee River, 17, 167, 169
Noxubee Wildlife Refuge, 20
Nutt, Rush, 191

Obion mound site, 215
O'Bryan Ridge phase, 102, 115
Oktibbeha County, Mississippi, 20, 60
Old Hoover Place site (22HO502), 161
Organization of technology model, 71–97; craft specialization, 75, 85–86; elements of, 74; experimental archaeology, 96–97; lacking ideology, 71, 96; Lewis Binford, 73; Margaret Nelson, analysis model, 73–74; Michael Schiffer, life cycle model, 73; socioeconomic strategy, 85, 94; technological strategy, 85, 93–94; tool design, 91
Owl Creek Mounds site (22CS502), 19, 21, 189–215; dating, 192–95; habitation extent, 206–7; layout and use, 196–201; occupation, 202–4; peripheral mound site, 190

Paleo-Indian period, 3, 15–16
Panola County, Mississippi, 17
Parrott, John, 282–87, 312
Pascagoula, Mississippi, 52
Passport in Time (PIT) program, 20, 323, 327, 329, 334
Peabody Museum, 58
Peacock, Evan, 98, 164, 328
Pensacola culture, 225, 233, 234
Phase definition, 12–13
Pickwick Basin site, 61
Phifer, Newnoon, 123
Phillips, Philip, 225, 239, 324–25
Pimple mounds, causes, 44
Pinson Mounds site (40MD1), 160–62, 164
Plaquemine culture, 218, 235
Plum Creek site (16OU89), 83
Pollen (palynological) analysis, 43, 45
Pontotoc, Union, Lee Development Authority, 245
Population growth, 17
Poverty Point Objects, 72, 99–115; analysis methods, 101–2, 106; distribution in Mississippi, Missouri, Tennessee, 99–114; morphological types, 102, 112, 114–15
Poverty Point site (16WC5), 57, 64, 67, 81–82, 99; exchange system, 115; lapidary industry, 57, 61, 99; mound building, 51, 71; shell beads, 52
Prospere, Robert, Collection from Anna Great Ravine, 219–39
Protohistoric period, 169, 225
Pritchard, John, 312
Public archaeology, 3, 20–21

Quaternary geology, 43
Quitman County, Mississippi, 16, 282

Radiocarbon dating, 141, 154–55, 192–93, 195
Rafferty, Janet, 22, 164
Reams, Robert, 328, 329
Reflective practice, 321
Ridge Plain ware, 248

Roosevelt, Franklin Delano, 266, 267, 270
Roosevelt, Theodore, 333

Savannah site (40HR29), 162
Scales Effigy Pendant, 60
Schön, Donald, 321
Sedentariness, 17, 94, 167
Seger, Joe, 145
Seltzer, Jennifer, 141
Seriation, 17, 185–87, 247–48
Settlement patterns, 19, 20, 53, 65, 121, 166–67, 169, 244
Seven Mile Island site (1LU11), 61, 69
Sharkey County, Mississippi, 27, 30
Shell, manufacture of beads and gorgets, 52
Shellmound Archaic period, 51
Shutispear Creek, 147
Sierra Club, 23, 333
Sinner site (16BO1), 61
Site recording methods, 29, 30; LiDAR imagery, 31, 33, 38, 40; Satellite imagery, 31
Situated learning, 320
Skinner, Steven, 312
Sky Lake Mound (22HU521), 28
Slate Springs Mound (22CA502; West Mound), 146–64; 22CA552, 22CA553 artifact clusters, 150, 156; possible hearth, 153; single platform mound, 146; white clay layer, 152–53
Sledge, Mississippi, 283
Smithsonian Institution, 55, 192
Social complexity, 65–66, 72
Social worlds and arenas, 321
South Carolina, 45
Southeastern Archaeological Conference, xi, 4, 6, 23, 331
Southeastern Archaeology, 333
South Thomas Street site (22LE1002), 243–65; burial, 245–46; ceramics, 247–49, 261; Chickasaw settlement history, 261–65; European trade beads analysis, 255–60, 261; features, 245; field methods, 245–47; lithics, 249–55;

occupations, 245; skin trade, toolkit evidence, 255, 260
Spencer, Dewitt, 164
Stanton, John, 123
Star, Susan Leigh, 321
Starnes, James, 140
Starr, Ned, 312
Starr, Raynor, 312
Stephens, Doug, 6
Steponaitis, Vincas, 325
Stelly site (16SL1), 69
Stewart, Caitlin, 145
Stinking Water site (22WI515/516), 17, 20, 169, 334
Stoneware pottery kiln site (22WI692), 21
Stowers, Mrs. Luther, 218
Strauss, Anselm, 321
Sunflower County, Mississippi, 30
Swamp Child site (22FO666), 334
Swan Lake site (22WS518), 28
Swindle Bead, 60

Tallahatchie River, 144
Tanya's Knoll site (22WA642), 334
Taylor, Eloise Winston, 283
Tennessee River shell middens, 61
Tennessee-Tombigbee Waterway, 48
Tennessee Valley Authority, 243, 245
Teoc Creek site (22CR504), 101, 111
Thelma Mounds site (22CS501), 161, 189–215; dating, 195; habitation extent, 207; layout and use, 197–98, 201; occupation, 204
Tippah County, Mississippi, 119
Toltec Mounds site, 214
Tombigbee National Forest, 11, 13, 16–17, 119; 22CH515, 172, 173–76; 22CH814, 172, 176–78; 22WI666, 172; 22WI865, 172, 178–85; Ackerman Unit, 11, 14–21, 157, 167; Trace Unit, 14, 17, 19, 190
Tombigbee River, 45, 48, 51–52, 166–67, 189, 250
Tombigbee–Yazoo divide, 160–61

Index

Trice site, 51
Triplett, Andrew, 331
Trudeau site (16WF25; "Tunica Treasure"), 256

Underwood, John, 215, 245
University of Alabama Gulf Coast Survey Archives, 220
University of Michigan, 218
University of Mississippi, 3, 149, 324, 326
University of Missouri, 3; Museum of Anthropology, 116
University of North Carolina–Chapel Hill, 218
University of South Alabama, 76
University of Southern Mississippi, 76, 116, 324
University of Wisconsin Department of Anthropology and Sociology, 116
University of Wisconsin–Washington County Foundation, 116
US Army, 321, 333
US Army Corps of Engineers, 3, 324, 326, 333
USDA Forest Service, xi, 3, 4, 6, 10, 20, 22, 23, 119, 190–91, 319, 321, 324, 326, 331, 336
USDA soil maps, 20
Use-wear analysis, 97
US Fish and Wildlife Service, 23
US Geological survey maps, 31, 33

Vaughn Mound (22LO538), 45, 51–52
Vicksburg, Mississippi, 69

Wade's Tesoro site (22WA1053), 334
Wailes, Benjamin L. C., 218
Walling Mound site, 162
Walnut site (22IT539), 62, 63, 65, 69
Warren County, Mississippi, 30, 39
Washington County, Mississippi, 30
Watson Brake site (16OU175), 51, 72, 77–79, 82–83, 86–87, 89–90, 92–93, 95
Weems site (23MI25), 101–2, 104
West, Mickey, 151, 164

West, Mrs. Ruble, 164
West, Ruble, 149, 151
Wilkinson County, Mississippi, 3
Williams, Stephen, 324
Winston County, Mississippi, 21
Winterville site (22WS500), 30
Woodland period, 16–18, 119
    Early Woodland, 18, 61, 106, 109, 123; Lake Cormorant Culture, 120; Tchula period, 18, 119, 120, 133, 158, 220
    Middle Woodland, 13, 17, 18, 21, 109, 261; Baytown period, 162–63, 220; Marksville period, 163; Miller I–III sequence, 13, 157, 195, 213, 248
    Late Woodland, 13, 19, 159, 192–95

Yalobusha River, 147, 149
Yalobusha Unit, Holly Springs National Forest, 21, 119
Yazoo Basin, 18, 30, 38, 49, 50, 57, 108, 110, 120
Yazoo County, Mississippi, 30, 39
Yazoo-Mississippi Delta
    logging, 282–311; Delta and Pine Land Company, 292; Delta Development Corporation, 292; hardwood for cooperage, 284, 286; lumber business management, 284; reforestation by USDA Conservation Reserve Program, 311; trams and dummy lines, 289
    railroads: Batesville Southwestern, 292; Louisville, New Orleans, and Texas, 287; Mississippi & Tennessee, 287; Mississippi Central, 287; Sardis & Delta Railroad ("Carrier Line"), 289–302; Yazoo & Mississippi Valley (YMV), 284
Yazoo River, 31

www.ingramcontent.com/pod-product-compliance
Lightning Source LLC
Chambersburg PA
CBHW070257240426

43661CB00057B/2579

www.ingramcontent.com/pod-product-compliance
Lightning Source LLC
Chambersburg PA
CBHW070257240426
43661CB00057B/2579

www.ingramcontent.com/pod-product-compliance
Lightning Source LLC
Chambersburg PA
CBHW072022240426
43667CB00044B/2207

"In *The One Story*, John Simpson makes a sustained case for the thesis that Christian faith and life is rooted in the single story of creation and redemption—and that God's self-limitation is the unifying theme of that odd story. With perceptive exegesis of biblical narratives and discerning engagement with theologians across church history, Simpson argues that kenosis is the keystone to the structure of Christian theology. This intriguing book deserves, and rewards, careful reading."

—Darrin W. Snyder Belousek, author of *Atonement, Justice, and Peace: The Message of the Cross and the Mission of the Church*

"In his book *The One Story*, author John Simpson invites readers to a 'bottoms-up,' story-based, upside-down, table-turning understanding of God defined by the biblical word *kenosis*, or self-emptying. Simpson's argument for a kenotic understanding of God undergirding all of Scripture is story-based, even as it attempts to persuade the reader of its explanatory power for understanding Trinity, creation, sin, discipleship, and redemption. His narrative approach to reading Scripture allows for an expansive flexible interpretative method for understanding complex, even mutually exclusive insights, when constructing one's theology. Metaphor and story replace more rigid, traditional, and dogmatic disciplinary reading strategies. Yet, it remains deeply resonant with the best of Christian understandings of the nonviolent, benevolent God revealed in Jesus of Nazareth.

Simpson rightly places great confidence in the capacity of story to provide an understanding of the unity of God. By extension such a narrative arc supports the ancient biblical Shema, 'Hear O Israel, the Lord Our God is One.' He writes in such an accessible manner as to be a must-read for pastors, teachers, church leaders and others. While Simpson argues against having to read the footnotes if that in anyway detract from the overall narrative flow of his storytelling, I did not take his advice. For me, the footnotes were some of the most delightful parts of the book.

As a fellow Mennonite/Anabaptist Christian with the author, this is a book for which I have waited a long time, one that challenges standard approaches to theology from creation to the grave and beyond, in the Bible and out. One does not have to agree with all of his attempts to establish the unity of God as he sees it to appreciate his framing his interpretation of reality from the point of view of Jesus of Nazareth, as the protagonist of a literary story, a possible human-based projection, of who

God might be. Simpson's book is a voice from the ashes of Christian martyrdom and the margins of those early Anabaptists of the 16th century. Such a vision of God's kenotic unity that the author envisions may help us celebrate, if not reconcile, differences of the past that have too often led to escalating violence and murderous exclusion within Christ's body, the Church, and the world."

 —JAMES E. BRENNEMAN, president, Berkeley School of Theology, professor of Hebrew Bible, and ordained Mennonite minister